HOW TO BE A DIRT-SMART BUYER OF COUNTRY PROPERTY

Volume I

Curtis Seltzer

Copyright © 2014 by Curtis Seltzer

All rights reserved. No part of this book shall be reproduced or transmitted in any form or by any means, electronic, mechanical, magnetic, photographic including photocopying, recording or by any information storage and retrieval system, without prior written permission of the publisher. No patent liability is assumed with respect to the use of the information contained herein. Although every precaution has been taken in the preparation of this book, the publisher and author assume no responsibility for errors or omissions. Neither is any liability assumed for damages resulting from the use of the information contained herein.

The author is not a lawyer, logger, accountant, truck mechanic, real-estate broker, ditch-digger, tax consultant, wildlife biologist, agricultural economist, architect, forester, tractor salesperson, surveyor, minerals geologist, builder, Internet wiz, soils scientist, house inspector, marital-arts consultant, civil engineer, financial planner, cesspool guru or literary critic. Therefore, the views he expresses herein on these matters and all others should be taken by readers as opinions rather than professional advice. Neither the publisher nor author can assume responsibility or liability for how any individual reader applies the author's opinions.

Printed in the United States of America

Printed on Recycled Paper

Published September 2014

To Molly, a wonderful daughter and a good writer

ACKNOWLEDGMENTS

I've needed help and was fortunate to have gotten it.

Clif Rexrode, Appalachian Forestry Services of Waynesboro, Virginia, has been a boots-on-the-ground consulting forester for 30 years. His knowledge of forestry issues and his willingness to share it with me were invaluable. I cannot thank him adequately. I hope that I, at least, amused him with my questions as I wasted his time looking at one high-graded tract after another. He's been a true friend over the years.

Tom Arbogast, who heads the tax practice at Schnader Harrison Segal & Lewis, LLP in Pittsburgh, is both a lawyer and a CPA. His generous offer to review what I wrote on tax issues was a brilliant beacon in what always looks to me like impenetrable, unfathomable darkness.

Susan McCray, my CPA in Staunton, Virginia, reviewed drafts of Chapters 6 and 24, both dealing with tax issues. She saved me from myself many times. She prevented me from reaping in final form what I had sown in draft.

Les LaPrade, Jr., of McDowell, Virginia, rescued me from my computer ignorance. With patience and good humor, he reformatted the entire manuscript, taking out my "hard returns" line by line and justifying my right margins. Since I'm just a typewriter guy transplanted to a keyboard, I feel that Bill Gates treated me and all other old manuals pretty shabbily by ensnaring us in this hand-work booby trap. Les has a more sensible attitude toward computers than I have. He wants to understand why they do things: I just want them not to hurt me. I could not have submitted this manuscript without Les and his wife, Laura, who showed him a thing or two when he needed to be shown a thing or two.

Tom Atkeson, a retired engineer in Monterey, Virginia, drew several drawings that required a clear and steady hand, not my scritch-scratch penmanship. And even though Tom's hand is not as clear and steady as it was when he was at VMI and in Vietnam, it's still clear and steady enough to get the job done.

All errors of fact and misjudgments are mine.

I've picked up land knowledge over the years from many individuals, including Harrison Elkins, David R. Underhill, Portia and Tom Weiskel, Mike and Joy Brenneman, Charlie Taylor, Jim Loesel, Gibby Crummett, Harry Haney, Robert Barrett, Stephen W. Dorris, Sam Vansickle, M.C. Davis, Pete Johnson, Tim Linstrom, Joe Leininger, John Crites, Julia Elbon, Darrell V. McGraw, Robert W. Tufts, Robert Guerrant, Angela Blythe, John Alexander Williams, Nancy Debevoise, Thomas Taylor, John Lindsey, Mark Yanoski, Carey Dowd, Stephen J. Small, Willie Anderson, Barbara E. Smith, Helen Steele, Ann Swartz, Robert Payne, John David, Beverly Medgaus Jones and Melissa Ann Dowd.

I've also learned from Billy Shepherd, Alan Gourley, Mike McEver, Dan Girouard, Dave Mayo, Murray Gibson, Jim Woltz, Chris Bland, Huel Wheeler and Daniel McKittrick.

The first book I read about investing in real estate was formative—George Bockl, <u>How to Use Leverage to Make Money in Local Real Estate</u> (Englewood Cliffs, NJ: Prentice-Hall, 1965). I bought it for $1 at our library's annual book auction. It led to my first purchase of land—400 acres—with no money in the deal.

I have used masculine pronouns for lack of a gender-neutral alternative. I found using he to refer to a seller or buyer was less offensive to my ear than using she or the brain-jarring, they. My ear, of course, is now 61 years old; younger ears may find the old-fashioned masculine objectionable. For what it's worth, whenever I wrote he and him, my thoughts included she and her.

My mother, Rena C. Seltzer, helped me buy my first piece of land, and the estate of my father, Robert Seltzer, helped buy our farm. My aunt, Lucy Katz, helps me keep their memories.

My wife, Melissa Ann Dowd, didn't ask, didn't tell and didn't wonder out loud why I never seemed to be finished writing.

TABLE OF CONTENTS

Volume 1

Introduction..i

Chapter 1:   Three Writers Show How Not to Do It..1

Chapter 2:   What Am I Looking for and Why Am I Looking for It 14
                Know Thyself
                Make a Revocable List
                Types of Properties

Chapter 3:   Farmland and Farm Dirt 31
                Dirt
                Farms and Money
                Subsidies
                Rent with an Option to Operate
                Farm Leases and Crop Genetics

Chapter 4:   First-Time Farmers 54
                Conventional Farming

Chapter 5:   Non-Conventional Farming 61
                Organics

Chapter 6:   Farming The Tax Code, Sowing and Reaping..71
                Business and Hobbies
                Basis
                Severable Assets
                Estate Taxes

Chapter 7:   Manure Belongs on Your Boots, Not in Your Rap..97
                "Is there anybody left to walk that muddy mile?"
                Buying and Selling to Your Friends and Neighbors

Start New Things Slowly; Make Small Mistakes

Chapter 8: Farm Equipment: Stuff is Us 108
Tractors: New and Used

Chapter 9: Undeveloped Property for Hunting...125
Hunting Hunting Land

Chapter 10: Infrastructure-Land, Property and Site...134
Infrastructure Packages
Property and Site Infrastructure
Infrastructure Costs
Property and Site Infrastructure Check List
Flip, Flippers and Flipping

Chapter 11: Second Homes: Developers and Developments..157
Building a Second Home Out Here
Buying a Second Home in a Full-Package Development
Building a Home with a General Contractor
Your Contract with Your Contractor
Architects, Contractors and You
Owner-Built Second Homes

Chapter 12: Country Houses and the Second Home...179
Wrecks
Keepers
House Inspection Check List Choices

Chapter 13: Environmental Issues...201
Overview
Common Problems, Broadly Construed
Common Issues
Water Hazards

Chapter 14: Resources-Minerals and Water..238
    Discrete Assets
    Minerals
    Water as a Financial Resource

Chapter 15: Matchmaking...265
    Finding
    Real-Estate Brokers: The Seller's Agent
    Alternatives: Buyer's Broker
    Disclosures, Puffing and Fraud
    Auction Buying
    Been-heres and Come-heres

Chapter 16: Negotiating..292
    Communication Channels
    Non-Price Issues
    Price
    Horse-trading
    Mushy Bottoms and Hard Frameworks

Chapter 17: Property Location-Surveys and Such..322
    Location Surveys 101
    Surveys 102

VOLUME 2

Chapter 18: Thinking about Woodland...1
    Overview
    Forest Planning

Chapter 19: One Patch of Woods...10
    Getting Oriented Toward Timber
    Woods Work

Chapter 20:   Thinking about Timber……………………………………………………………27
              Landowner's Objectives for Woodland
              Consulting Foresters
              Self-Help

Chapter 21:   Scoping Timber Value……………………………………………………………..53
              Vocabulary
              Timbering the Jones Farm

Chapter 22:   Beware The Seller's Cruise……………………………………………………...74
              There's No Bogus Like Show Bogus Tricks

Chapter 23:   Selling Timber, Tools of the Trade……………………………………………..94
              FSBO-A Bad Idea
              Consultant-managed Sale-Sample Consultant Contract
              Timber-sale Contract

Chapter 24:   Timber Taxation…………………………………………………………………..124
              Set Up
              Basis and Income
              Conservation Easements and Taxes
              State and Local Timber Taxes

Chapter 25:   Country Lawyers and Country Real-Estate Law…………………………….149
              Finding a County Lawyer
              The Legal Frameworki
              Helping Hands: Buyer-Broker, Finder, Land Consultant

Chapter 26:   Common Messes………………………………………………………………...166
              Buyers Want 100 Percent of Everything
              Legal Descriptions
              Acreage Discrepancies
              Acreage Verification Contingencies
              The Special Case of Leases

Chapter 27: Tricks of the Seller's Trade: Legal, Not Legal and Otherwise............................187

Chapter 28: Bargaining Cultures and Resolving Property Disputes......................................208

Chapter 29: Writing a Purchase-Offer Contract: Strategies and Tactics................................216
    Make the Most of Your Contract Offer Information
    Contingencies
    All-Cash Offer With No Financing Contingency
    Seller Contingency
    Equitable Title
    Longer Rather Than Shorter Escrow
    Warranties to Survive the Contract
    Security Deposits: Their Uses
    Deposits: Size Should Not Matter
    Time 1: Time is Not of the Essence
    Time 2: First Response
    Negotiating Within the Contract
    A Non-Deal Deal: Seller's Remorse
    Lease-Purchase Option
    Buy a Lawsuit

Chapter 30: Some Ideas Organized as a Purchase-Offer Contract...252

Chapter 31: Thinking about Dirt Money..266
    Research and Futures Analysis
    How About a Trial Rental?
    Country Money is Different From City Money

Chapter 32: Borrowing Money..284
    System Overview
    Costs of Borrowing
    Interest Rates
    Pitching and Hitting
    Appraisals and Borrowing
    Mortgage Interest Deductibility

Chapter 33:   Sources of Dirt-Smart Money 332
               13 Places to Start

Chapter 34:   A Final Plea 367

Chapter 35:   Afterword 369

MONEY-BACK GUARANTEE 370

INTRODUCTION

Tired of living where it's hot and flat? Want to find a cool spot in the mountains?

Need to escape the city on weekends?

Ready to bail out permanently on the close-in "burbs"?

Looking to retire to an old farmhouse with a front porch and big shade trees?

You are not alone.

We are now a nation of 300 million, up from 200 million in 1967. Population growth increases demand for property, and income growth, particularly in the urban/suburban upper middle classes, makes feasible the purchase of land and second homes in the country. In almost every rural county, farms and undeveloped land are being divided and sold to both the 75 million of us who are Boomers and to those coming after us. Although data are lacking, my guess is that urban and suburban buyers are now purchasing annually about three million parcels of country property—broadly defined. These include farmettes, ranchettes, hunting lots, farms, second homes, timberland, investment properties, waterfront properties and lots in developed and semi-developed projects. This rising demand trend, coming from urban and suburban buyers like the readers of this book, has pushed up the price of all types of rural land for the last 20 years. Country property has proved to be an excellent investment for most buyers. If global warming does indeed raise the level of coastal waters over the next century, displaced individuals and shrewd investors will be buying higher and safer ground. They will look to the countryside, taking advantage of technologies that allow them to make a living away from their city offices. If you're reading this paragraph, you've probably already come to the same conclusions.

Thousands of us buy rural property each year. Some are looking for a weekend getaway; others to relocate full-time. Some want undeveloped, or **raw**, land. Others feel more comfortable in a planned community with **infrastructure**—roads and utilities—in place. Some want a cabin at the end of a long dirt road; others want a plantation house with hot and cold running servants or a solar-powered passive-aggressive statement of environmental correctness. As America's population grows and metropolitan areas become increasingly hectic and congested, more and more of us will be looking for a place in the country.

In most of America, country property has been a wonderful investment and is appreciating at a more or less strong and healthy clip. The average acre of farmland was valued at $1,900 in 2005, up from about $600 in 1987. That reflected a 15 percent rise in value in 2005, on top of a 21 percent increase in 2004. Pasture land now averages about $1,000 per acre, while cropland is now valued, on the average, at almost $2,400 per acre. The sharpest increases are found nearest urban areas. Timberland—with and without timber that can be sold immediately—and undeveloped recreational land are appreciating at similar rates (Jilian Mincer, "Tilling a Farmland Investment," <u>Wall Street Journal</u>, September 9-10, 2006.). Appreciation is being driven by large institutions, wealthy individuals and people like you and me. People want land because it can generate income, build wealth and is fun to have. These are good reasons to become a dirt-smart buyer of country property.

When I bought my first rural property in 1971, I lacked even a clue about how to think about the questions that such a purchase inevitably involves. I liked the idea of woods, on a hill with a view and a site for a pond. I found a spot near Wendell Depot, Massachusetts, about a 30-minute, back-roads drive north of Amherst. The woods, it turned out, had just been timbered, which I understood more abstractly than practically. The view appeared only from the crest of a snubbed off, north-facing ridge that was sort of accessible with a 4WD Bronco for a few months each year and during Sahara-type droughts. The site for a pond turned out to be a bottomless bog, which we now call **wetlands** and value for its habitat. The deed, I discovered after purchase, never specified the number of acres. I thought we bought 100, but wiser heads put the number at 60. We owned an undeveloped right of way that swamped through the Mekong Delta before it stalled in the Central Highlands.

Over the next 15 years, we bought a small parcel that brought frontage on a state-maintained road and also contained a usable access drive into the original 60-acre island. Through little effort, the land appreciated in value ten-fold owing to its proximity to a thriving college town. It was like having a high-interest passbook savings account that doubled as a sixth-grader's hide out. At 26, with wars raging abroad and at home, I was far more interested in finding a placid hole than in projecting my annualized return on investment. Nonetheless, the possibilities of rapid appreciation of rural land were not lost, even on me. Necessity forced me to learn a little about boundaries, roads, utilities, water and timber. But, in hindsight, I didn't learn very much. The next property I bought had a farmhouse that piped its sewage behind the barn, into the creek—a fact I discovered after taking possession.

I didn't start teaching myself how to buy country property until my fourth purchase. This 400+ acres was an investment, so I approached it as a research project. Researching property is a process called, **scoping**. I began my scoping with three **investment questions**: how can I buy it without any money; can the property pay most of its own mortgage servicing through rental; and, finally, if I need to sell it after a few years, am I reasonably confident that I can make a profit? In addition to these investment questions, I developed and then scoped a series of **property questions** that bore directly on the appropriate purchase price, risks, uncertainties and the value of saleable assets, such as merchantable timber and an old farmhouse. One question led to another, and I soon discovered that I had cobbled together a methodological approach that was adaptable in general terms to other rural properties, notwithstanding differences in size, purpose, location and type. I bought the 400 acres without any money and used the pasture rent to carry about half the mortgage costs. I had taken the first step to becoming **dirt smart**.

I discovered that I liked doing dirt research. I looked into other properties for my own account. The work was practical and, unlike academic research, did not drag on endlessly. It satisfied whatever interest I ever had in doing investigative reporting, which reporters tellingly refer to as, digging. Each property presented its own combination of assets, liabilities, knowns, unknowns and unknowns that I didn't know I didn't know. If I dug deeply, I would uncover any embedded deal-breakers. I started by writing long memos analyzing each purchase. (Writing is a bad habit that I'm hoping will solve itself as I age.) The memo format forced me to think through both a **buying plan** and a **profit plan**. Investors need both. The buying plan is akin to a plan for winning a war; the profit plan is what you do once you've won.

I used these research skills in the purchase of other properties, and then began to work as a **land consultant** for investors who were interested in buying large tracts of farmland and timberland. Part of the experience of buying country land is learning how to do it knowledgeably, a process I call **becoming dirt-smart**. There's always a trial-and-error element to learning a new skill, but learning how to buy country property is a process that need not involve supplying yourself with a lifetime of ironic stories for cocktail conversations. I wrote this book to show you how to be dirt-smart about buying country property. Consider it a piggy-back ride on me. I also wrote it to make some money.

Land buying starts with dirt. Look, first, at how the land lays—its **topography**. Which directions do its slopes face? How steep are they? If the land is flat, will it drain quickly or hold water because the subsurface contains a lot of clay? The surface vegetation and the feel of the dirt in your hand will give you an initial reading. Topographically interesting land is usually more interesting to spend time on, but it's also more expensive to work with and much harder to work against.

Look, second, at your **soils**. Different soils have different characteristics and capabilities, which will determine what you can do with your property at a reasonable cost. Your first stop in **scoping property** is to pick up a copy of the county's Soil Survey at the local U.S.Department of Agriculture office. In this book, you will find maps showing soil types throughout the county as well as the virtues and liabilities of each type. County-level aerial maps and soil-survey information are available for some states and counties on the Internet at http://soils.usda.gov/survey.

Look, third, at the **location of your dirt**. Will it be hard to get to in bad weather? Is it subject to flooding, earthquakes, mudslides, windstorms, fires and prevailing weather? If you have shoreline, is the land low (bad) or high (good)? Is the shoreline eroding? Is the land facing in the right compass direction for your plans?

Finally, look at your **dirt in terms of proximity to local goods and bads**—hospital, fire station, public water and sewerage, rescue squad, floodplain, job opportunities, distance from your current residence, post office, bank, supermarket and objectionable facilities, however you care to define them.

Most buyers from the city and suburbs, including me, focus first and almost exclusively, on the country house, whether existing or planned. This comes at the expense of paying attention to the dirt on which the house stands and which surrounds it. We do this, I think, because all of us have a passing familiarity with houses. So we evaluate country property in terms of what we know rather than what we don't. There's nothing wrong with thinking about "house in the country." Just remember that this thought contains two elements: house + country. Don't fall into self-induced house hypnosis. You'll find that dirt acquires more prominence in your country life over time.

I've come to think of buying rural property in terms of analogies.

Finding country property is like finding a mate. The more you look, the more possibilities turn up. Each is different. Some candidates will be warm and inviting; others can make your head pound. Love at first sight happens, but that kind of love may not survive the practicalities of living and working together. While love may conquer all, the more it has to conquer, the harder it's going to be to both stay in love and stick it out. You can't sign a prenuptial agreement with land, which exempts you from paying future costs if things don't work out. So you have to look for a good fit on many levels, not just sex. This book is written to help buyers learn to keep their heads and use them too. The object, of course, is to find a property that you like better over time, a property that fits you financially and emotionally, a property where love has to conquer as little as possible.

This book shows you how to find and buy such a property.

Here is a second analogy.

Most people judge books by their covers, even though we know we're supposed to be smarter than that. The publishing industry spends a great deal of effort and money in cover design because we're not. Standing in a bookstore, how else can we judge a book if not by its cover? If you judged this book by its cover, the worst that can happen is that you've bought an over-priced doorstop. If, however, you buy rural property on the basis of a once-over glance at its cover, you may find yourself selling over-priced doorstops to a village of tent dwellers.

As with any other large purchase, large mistakes can be made on country real estate. The most common are **under-scoping, overpaying and "poor fitting"**. The first can lead to unexpected, burdensome, aggravating and expensive surprises that affect your use, enjoyment and pocketbook. The second makes it harder for a buyer to carry the property, sell it and make a profit. Under-scoping leads to overpaying. "Poor fitting" refers to a buyer finding his property ill-suited to his evolving needs. This often results from an initial purchase of too much house and too little land, or land that is all one type, such as nothing but open, flat ground or all steeply sloped wooded land facing north. It's difficult for a new country buyer to anticipate what he might want to do with property five or ten years in the future. Consequently, I would advise such a buyer to buy more land and less house if a choice has to be made between the two, and buy a property that contains more rather than fewer types of soils and land—pasture, field, wooded, flat, hilly and bottom.

First-impression buying puts at risk not only thousands of your dollars but the hard work and love you will inevitably invest in your purchase. To prevent first-impression buying, you must learn to read the cover of a property enough to know whether it merits scoping effort. This initial process, called **screening,** requires that a buyer have a pretty firm idea of both what he seeks and what he doesn't want. Screening is a first-cut selection process that involves knowing how to **screen out properties** that have unfixable negatives or expensive problems (such as a pre-Revolution house whose historically correct reconstruction will cost no less than two launches of the space shuttle) and **screen in** those properties that can be cleaned up with reasonable investments of time, effort and money. Screening uses the same questions and research techniques found in scoping. The difference between them lies in the depth and breadth of the investigation. Neither process is long in absolute terms—screening should take minutes, scoping several days or weeks, at most. The more you look at properties analytically using the methods I describe, the faster and more confident you will become at making both screening and scoping decisions.

Screening is the same process of preliminary research as that which an investigative reporter does when he gets wind of a story. The tip is checked enough to decide whether to pursue it or forget it. Screening—and later, scoping—is rational and analytical. It is not a matter of "falling in love." A property, like a good investigative story, has to stand on its merits during both processes. Otherwise, it should be rejected.

First-cut screening is the opposite in principle and practice to first-impression buying. First-cut screening is not a decision to buy; it's a decision to investigate further. It's based on the more or less systematic acquisition of enough knowledge to decide between stopping and going further.

You can screen property quickly if you know the questions to ask and the level of information you need to make a decision. I am now usually able to screen investment properties in or out with a five- to ten-minute phone call to the owner or his real-estate agent. I bring to that conversation a general idea of current land values in the area and learn the seller's asking price. If this is your first time in an area, you can get a quick-and-dirty notion of market land values by subtracting ten to 20 percent from asking prices found in real-estate listings. Subtract another five percent if the seller is marketing with a real-estate agent whose commission will range between six and ten percent. (A rural-land **appraisal** determines the **fair market value [FMV]** of the property being sold by comparing it with three or four recent sales of comparable properties—called, **comps**—in the area, after adjusting for differences.) My shake-and-bake method gives a buyer enough sense of fair market value to get started.

My first investment screen is **price per acre ($/A)**. I eliminate property priced way above what I think its FMV is. I screen in property priced at, close to and below market. With property priced *some* above what I think its FMV is, I might pull it in for further study if it has some feature that makes it especially valuable or I think the seller's price is soft. Just keep in mind that you cannot count on selling land that you bought above market for an above-market price in the near future.

My next screens focus on size, location, improvements, current use and ratio of wooded land to open. Looking at property for investment rather than a personal residence, I avoid listings that are house-heavy and land-short. A $700,000 house standing on one country acre must be resold as a unit; profit in such a deal usually comes only from long-term appreciation. I screen in properties that are a mix of assets, some of which can be turned into cash quickly and easily. I also screen in properties that generate annual cash from production or rental that will cover at least 30 percent of an expected mortgage payment. I usually screen out properties where the minerals won't convey with the surface, where the timber has been reserved by the seller for his future benefit, where some regulatory condition devalues the property (such as a tobacco farm that has lost its tobacco subsidy, or land that can't be divided because of zoning restrictions), where a conservation easement is in place that limits profit potential, or where some property-specific factor hampers my plan for the property. The latter might include dirt that is unsuitable for septic systems, lack of sufficient sight distance on a state-maintained road that eliminates a proposed entrance, lack of legal or feasible access, road-building costs that are prohibitive, the presence of a protected species or its habitat, and the presence of expensive-to-settle boundary disputes. One or two unacceptable facts are usually enough for me to scratch a candidate.

Buyers who are less interested in rural property for its investment potential and more interested in its second-home or recreational values will develop a set of screens that are more personal. Total price, rather than price per acre, may be the money screen such a buyer uses. FMV may be a less important screen than a buyer requirement that cannot be added on later, such as a particular view or specific location. A second-home buyer may want to screen in properties with obvious, even hideously expensive, problems if it has unique virtues and the buyer's pocketbook matches his remedial plans. Many property-related problems can be fixed by throwing money at them. But some are impervious even to cash. If your dream farm is located next to an airport, you cannot buy your way free from over-flight noise. You cannot create a ridge-top view from a flat Iowa cornfield. You can, however, build a lake if you want one and replant large trees if you want shade.

Visiting and scoping property takes time, so it is productive to eliminate non-promising properties by phone or on the basis of a package of materials the seller sends to you. Screening is not kicking tires. You are a legitimate buyer, not an endless looker.

Screening is the first step in doing dirt-smart scoping, which is your deep research into a

promising property you've screened in. You might screen out 25 properties to find one worth a visit, visit five before you scope one, and scope three before you buy. There are no formulas to determine the amount of effort you need to put into screening and scoping before buying. Scoping is a process with a purpose; it is not a game played for the benefits of playing. Take comfort, however, in knowing that each scoping goes faster with experience. You don't need to own a property for 20 years before you know it well enough to buy it. A buyer will never acquire an equivalent level of intimacy when scoping a potential purchase. What you need to make a dirt-smart purchase is knowledge, not intimacy. This book will show you how to learn enough to know whether to buy and at what price.

The information in this book will save you money and make you money.

Inexperienced land buyers have two fears: paying too much and looking foolish. Fears like these can be self-protective when they are converted into rational analysis. That's what screening and scoping do. Fear can be made useful, but, left on its own, it can lead to paralysis or impulsive decisions. Buying rural land is not risky as long as you do your research. A buyer strips risk from a land purchase by acquiring specific information. You now have in your hand the way to get what you need to know.

If you don't like reading advice, put this book down now. This is a how-to book. Its purpose is to provide information on which the reader can base his own actions for his own benefit. The advice given is based on actual successes and disasters, including my own. I wrote this book, wishing that I had had one like it during the last 35 years.

CHAPTER 1: THREE WRITERS SHOW HOW NOT TO DO IT

Without being too didactic about it, my position is that there is a more-or-less right way to buy any rural property and several more or less not-so-right ways. If you approach buying more rationally and analytically than not, you will in most cases be more satisfied with your purchase. If you allow yourself to be emotionally stampeded into a purchase, or stampede yourself into one, you lower your odds for good results. A property that you fall in love with at first sight should not be exempt from rational analysis and the identification of lurking problems. I offer three illustrations of self-induced emotional stampeding.

Michael Korda, editor-in-chief of Simon & Schuster and prominent author, wrote Country Matters: The Pleasures and Tribulations of Moving from a Big City to an Old Country Farmhouse (New York: HarperCollins, 2001). His story is a self-deprecating celebration of his adventures with a house built in 1785 that he and his wife, Margaret, purchased on 20 acres in Dutchess County, New York in 1980. In a sequel, Horse People: Scenes from the Riding Life (New York: HarperCollins, 2003), he notes that their country house came with "...numerous problems.., literally enough to fill a book..," Country Matters. (Horse People, p. 347.)

The Kordas met while riding in Manhattan's Central Park. One snaffle led to another, and soon they were looking for a second home in the country where they might spend time with their horses. Margaret discovers their country place and shows it to her husband on a day, he writes, that

> could hardly have been less promising. Sheets of rain poured down...[with] heavy fog.... The house, when we got to it, was hard to see, being surrounded by huge old maple trees looming out of the fog. There was so much water that it was erupting out of the culverts [tops of the downspouts] like Old Faithful and cascading over the sides of the gutters. I glimpsed two barns, which looked as if they might need a bit of work...some run-down outbuildings. ...the path to the house was made of huge stones...which were lethally slippery with rain and moss. (Country Matters, pp. 10-11.)

The house had wide-plank floors, old windows, four fireplaces and hand-made hinges—in Korda's word, "character." "Less than an hour after we got there we had shaken hands on a deal," he writes.

In less than an hour, in a rain storm and without looking at the farm's land, the Kordas agreed to buy a country place for $250,000 (1980 dollars). Neither seems to have looked at the fields where horses would graze, fences built and water lines buried six feet deep. The land initially seems to have represented nothing more than distance between the charming house and the neighbors, charming and otherwise. When they later decided to use their land, the Kordas discovered that in the country, dirt counts. The fields were rocky and covered in scrub growth, both of which were costly and difficult to overcome.

He wrote, "...we did not...know it at the time, [that] no amount of hard work or money was going to turn *these* acres into the kind of grassy, rolling fields dotted with galloping foals and mares that appear in television commercials for banks and insurance companies every year about the time of the Kentucky Derby." (Horse People, p. 182.) As you read Dirt-Smart, you will learn how to acquire this very information in advance.

It was no secret in 1980 that "Dutchess County is just close enough to New England to qualify as rock country—plowing, even raking, merely brings up the next layer of loose rocks, and the soil is spread thinly over layers of solid rock." (*Id.*) It had not been a secret for more than 300 years. Not looking and not knowing are proven ways of ending up not happy. Had the Kordas done a little dirt research, they might have reoriented their property prospecting to an area better suited to a horse operation. Had the Kordas followed one all-purpose country buyer's gnome—**buy good dirt that can support multiple uses**—they would have saved themselves thousands of dollars in quarreling with rocks and whacking "scrubbish."

Korda applied only one faculty in buying country property—his heart. Am I instantly and hopelessly in love with this place no matter what? If so, let me give you my money. This method—to continue an analogy—is no different than a fellow marrying a woman only moments after glimpsing her once across a dark and crowded disco. The romantics and odds-makers among my readers will say, even some marriages of that sort work out. True, some do. It helps when the thunderstruck buyer has sufficient money to make a hasty and ill-matched union workable enough. Country Matters is the story of the consequences and costs of buying rural property using only your heart.

How exactly does one go about buying land in this fashion? Korda never left the charming house during his visit. He never walked his road frontage. Had he done so, he would have discovered that it was used as a community trash dump.

He never even realized where he was and where he wasn't. He tells his readers that the house with character was located on "the 'wrong' side of the Taconic [State Parkway]." He had inadvertently purchased west of the Taconic. His friends were east of the Parkway, where "excess scarcely even raises eyebrows," with showpiece barns made of "...rare paneled woods, crystal chandeliers [and] tack rooms that look as if Ralph Lauren had designed them." (Horse People, p. 164.) I will assume that my readers know how to read a common road map.

Korda did not look very hard at what he was buying and does not appear to have understood the implications of what he did see. Before submitting his purchase-offer contract, he never walked his boundaries or viewed prospective neighbors. One turned out to be a trailer-bound commune. Another was a "huge family with many snarling dogs and no-neck teenage children living in the middle of a kind of mini wrecking yard of worn-out snowmobiles and pickup trucks in a ramshackle house from which the toilet emptied onto the lawn without the benefit of a septic system." One neighbor "...had a son who, when he wasn't in and out of one of the many local psychiatric institutions, sometimes rode across our property bareback on a farm horse, grinning maniacally." (Horse People, p. 164.) If I can read between his lines, the Kordas never became tight as ticks with any of these souls. Neighbors who are genuine nuisances will spoil the best view or the most character-laden house so it's best to check out who shares your property line before making an offer.

The outbuildings at a distance looked to Korda as if they could use a nail here and a shingle there. If only farms were so accommodating. Outbuildings that look run down from a distance through the scrim of a monsoon will look worse on a sunny day up close. Wood buildings are usually old and have often had little maintenance. Foundations and roofs tend to go first. It is impossible to evaluate such needs without inspecting them, inside out. Big, old, swaggy barns smell richly of old hay and departed livestock. They creak pleasingly. Their amazing mortise-and-tenon framing will appeal to anyone who appreciates simple solutions to complex problems. They can be expensive to repair. Older barns are often not well suited to contemporary needs. A barn hayloft, for example, that was originally designed to store loose hay or 50-pound "square" bales stacked to the rafters, can rarely be adapted to hold an equivalent volume of modern 800-pound "round" bales.

A neglected barn may indicate that the farm's land is too poor to make a go of the type of farming the barn was supposed to support. Farmers invested in the building and upkeep of their barns because of their central importance to the economic viability of their farm enterprise. A barn in structural trouble signals extended neglect, which may or may not be localized to the building. The Kordas lucked out twice.

First, the barn was sound enough to be rehabbed and reconfigured to their horse needs, and, second, they found someone to do a good job for them.

When Korda did see a red flag, he seemed to note it as an observed idiosyncrasy—"culverts [sic] erupting like Old Faithful..," cascading over the gutters. A roof-and-drainage system that creates cataracts over its gutters is always a bad sign. It's likely to mean water-damaged walls and water-rotted sills. Systems that don't work properly may be charming when they belong to someone else, but not when they're yours.

Did it not occur to the Kordas that the lethally slick flagstone path leading to the house would soon be endangering their lives?

Would anyone buy a used car this way? No matter how much you loved its paint job and hood ornament, would you not crank the engine? Would you not sit in the driver's seat and work the controls? Would you not take it for a test drive? How many of us buy property with less consumer research than we would routinely apply to a 1980 Chevy showing 500,000 odometer miles whose owner claims it "runs like new"? The fewer of us, the better, I believe.

The only thing Korda did right on his first visit—and that inadvertently—was to arrive on a butt-ugly day. If a property's promise shines through the rain, you'll like the place even better when it's nice. Bad weather also gives you an opportunity to see how the property handles weather-related stress. Does the roof leak? Is the basement wet? Does water "pond up" in a low spot? Does the septic system backup when the ground is saturated? Is the entry road unusable in wet or icy conditions? In drought, does the spring, well, creek or stock pond dry up?

What Korda did wrong was that he failed to prepare himself for buying a house and land in the country. He didn't learn how to look at property; how to evaluate the dirt, outbuildings and house; how to read the property's subtle signals as well as its big red flags waving through the rain. Former UCLA basketball coach, John Wooten, put this situation into the aphorism: He who fails to prepare, prepares to fail. That's observed wisdom, trite though it is.

The predictable result was Korda's annual Brinks delivery of cash to local folks to do, maintain, rebuild and adapt.

<u>Country Matters</u> reads as if Korda spent the next two decades hiring every blue collar on his side of the Taconic to do something for him or his farm. From time to time, he employs a cook, housekeeper, garden person, barn lady, barn-lady helper, fix-everything man and non-resident excavation person who "adopts" the Kordas, along with practitioners of every trade and craft related to house maintenance, horses and vehicles. These people—"...the loyal, hardworking peasantry"—were essential to this area's horsey pseudo-feudalism in which the gentry were now more dependent on the "help" than the other way around. (<u>Horse People</u>, p. 171.)

Korda manages in these circumstances, because he says that he was "...pretty good at writing checks, a basic skill without which nothing gets done, though it seldom gets much in the way of attention or praise." (*Ibid.*, p. 166.)

Check writing is, indeed, one way of getting stuff done around the farm. (Another way is to hope the chore will go away if it's ignored long enough.)

You don't need to be Harry Homeowner to manage a second home in the country. You don't need to be skilled, strong or handy—though all three are useful country attributes. But you should be willing to prepare yourself to do a few basic things—light a pilot, drain water pipes, replace a fuse, flip a breaker, remove creosote from a chimney by tossing in a few tablespoons of creosote remover every couple of weeks, shut off the water into the house, make a fire in a woodstove and clean a filter. If you refuse to learn these most basic tasks of house mechanics, you will be completely dependent on local folks. Some will help you for free now and then because you're so pitiful or because you make such good copy down at the feed store. Most, however, you will have to pay—and should pay—to do the simplest and easiest bit of work regardless of your local comedic news value.

While local labor prospered from frequent visits to the Kordas' open vault, other locals appeared unbeckoned. Immediately upon taking possession, Korda more or less allowed himself to be bullied and guilt-tripped into allowing organized snowmobilers, pheasant hunters and the local fox hunt, among others, to have free run of his place in return for keeping off the unorganized riff-raff. Then, he feels put upon by his own posses, and, finally, bounces the fox hunters.

I reluctantly offer this bit of hard counsel: **the only way to keep folks off your land is to say no to everyone right from the start**. This will spare you accidents involving gun-shot pets, livestock stuck with arrows, strangers doing both familiar and unfamiliar things under your nose as well as fleets of ATVs, pick-up trucks, dirt bikes and snowmobiles disturbing you in their seasons. If you say yes to every request at the start of your ownership as Korda did, you will be overrun as he was. After some years of just saying no, you can make exceptions.

Had Korda done even minimal scoping, he would have had a ballpark notion of what his "going-in" fix-up expenses were going to be. Then, he might have used these cost estimates to help himself in negotiating a purchase price that took them into account. Instead, Korda negotiated as if he were buying a "cream puff"—a property that's turnkey perfect. This amounts to blindfolding yourself just prior to jumping off your own gangplank.

Despite my pokes at Korda's ways, I really have no objection to spending money on country property. Doing so, is, in fact, one of life's pleasures. It's fun to plan and execute improvements to property that you appreciate and enjoy. It satisfies something in us that goes back to both childhood and caves. It gives us an opportunity to mark our passage in a way that's different from making a profit or writing a book. Decisions about scale and style of how country property will be changed during your ownership are up to you. My concern is to protect a buyer from having to spend money to solve a problem that comes as a post-purchase surprise.

It's one thing to be inexperienced and not savvy about buying country property; that's nothing to be ashamed of and is, presumably, why you bought this book. It is, however, quite another, to be either intentionally blasé about basic self-protective consumer behavior or so incredibly wealthy that ignoring one's own self interest is no more than one of life's petty details.

Whether you're Bill Gates or Humble Pie, no good reason exists to buy rural property without scoping it first. I'm not arguing against buying an old country house with character. Rather, I'm arguing that any such purchase be made after you unemotionally and analytically add your initial purchase cost to those you estimate you will incur in required fix up. The total gives you a reasonably accurate idea of what your country place will cost. With the Korda place, almost every one of the basic house systems—roof, gutters, siding, fireplaces, wiring, plumbing, windows, heating, septic and water—had to be substantially repaired or totally replaced. A competent house inspector should have flagged every one of these problems—and perhaps the inspector Korda hired did. The cumulative weight of across-the-board repairs such as these is large in terms of time, emotional energy, inconvenience and money. If the seller is not asked to discount his asking price or make some repairs, the full weight of remedy, or lack of remedy, falls on the new owner. Even if you are fortunate enough to be able to say, "This is what I want. Money is neither object nor subject," you should consider your non-dollar costs—time, inconvenience and emotional energy—that will be involved for every improvement you plan and implement.

The Kordas bought without choosing to get an idea of what lay in store because the house's character trumped all. Certain properties are immediately pleasing, because of their overall effect. Character is quality construction and design that carries its age well. Be careful to distinguish between genuine character and imitation. Faux character is achieved through fake beams and windows with plastic pane inserts, and modern components made to look like old materials, such as flooring, cabinets and hardware. Be forewarned: true house character costs a lot upfront and is also expensive to maintain. Such places sing to us the way vintage steam locomotives do, with their bells and smells and chugga-chuggas. They too burn cash by the ton. Imagine shoveling your dollars into a roaring furnace. Still, if you want character, you have to buy it at a price that the market determines.

Often, buyers with limited cash to spend on a country second home face the choice between buying a cash-burning charmer and a less charming but cheaper and more practical alternative. One way of making that decision is to determine whether genuine character—wide-plank floors, hand-made hinges, hand-hewn ceiling beams, leaded glass—can be worked into the cheaper alternative without creating a composite freak. There are limits to your ability to add true character. You can't turn a 1950s bungalow into a four-story *ante-bellum* mansion by tacking up a couple of oversized white columns. Still, the buyer faced with such a choice should evaluate the possibilities of blending character piecemeal into the more plebian alternative. That approach is likely to prove more feasible than having to redo the basic systems in a house built more than 100 years ago. For instance, hand-made hinges—both old and new—are readily available if you think your doors need them and could wear them without shouting: "Look at my hinges!" Any reputable finish carpenter can hang them so that they squeak and stick.

Korda's place is what I call a "**look farm**," a spot in the country owned by someone who wants a country place that produces, not food or fiber, but the right look for themselves and their guests. People buy rural property for many, varied reasons. Some I endorse, others I don't. Look farms don't bother me. I want our farm to look the way I want it to look, which, I suppose, in its slightly run-down way reflects my own slightly run-down ways. If you want to own a look farm, you'll have to decide whether you're better off buying as much of the right look as you can afford at the outset or adding it as you go along. I added.

The Kordas had three audiences in mind for their look farm: their neighbors, their guests and themselves. They raised a couple of pet pigs to show to their weekend guests. The Kordas thought the pigs also proved to their neighbors that they were "not just another city couple with aspirations to play at being gentry with more money than is good for them, and not your typical city-bred weekenders…." It's not clear whether the neighbors were convinced; I wasn't.

To achieve the right look for their guests and themselves, the Kordas resculpt their front yard to imitate an English manor lawn. Here we find a situation where the Kordas are trying to prove to their down-at-their-heels neighbors that they were not gentry by raising a couple of Wilburs while trying to prove to their friends through strategically placed boxwoods and rocks of the right sort that they were.

Finally, there is the question of we-are-what-we-drive farm look. To that end, Korda buys a red Porsche 942, Ferrari 308 GTS, Honda 600 Nighthawk, Harley-Davidson Fat Boy, three tractors, two ATVs, two horse trailers, Chevy Blazer and one "seriously big" Ford pick-up truck. "If there is one thing I do enjoy doing," he writes, "it is buying motor vehicles of any kind." (Horse People, p. 206.)

Remember my analogy about finding land and finding a mate. Korda chose a property based solely on an intense emotional reaction to the look and feel of the house. The analytical skills he uses as an editor were never brought to bear. He was charmed by the house's character, but, practically speaking, this place got his nose open like a 16-year-old boy about to lose his virginity in the backseat.

The Kordas bought on impulse. There's no sensible reason to buy country property this way. If you fear that you will lose the property if you don't act quickly, you can submit a purchase contract with **results-acceptable-to-the-buyer contingencies** that will give you time to scope and allow you to back out of the deal without penalty. Impulse buying is not the same as **moving quickly**, which is what dirt-smart buyers do when their scoping indicates a good deal.

I urge readers to read Country Matters, though I would have re-titled it, Country Natters. Or Country Dirt Matters.

Michael Korda is not alone in his views. A cottage industry—a small industry working out of very large cottages—has emerged from writers who produce travelogues about their encampments in the American countryside, often within a two-hour drive of Times Square.

Laura Shaine Cunningham has written an honest and moving autobiography, A Place in the Country (New York: Riverhead Books, 2000). This is the second installment of her memoirs, which began with Sleeping Arrangements (New York: Knopf: 1989), the story of not knowing her father, her mother's early death and a make-shift upbringing involving two bachelor uncles who subsisted largely on popcorn and tuna croquettes, hot and cold. Orphaned at eight, she subsequently made it to large country estates, first at Tuxedo Park, and then to the Frederick Law Olmstead-designed Willowby Park in the Catskills. Her home there came complete with a genuine English Lord and Lady. She has lived there for more than 20 years.

Cunningham is a writer whose work I admire. I also admire her perseverance in the face of a tragic childhood, then divorce and cancer. Still, her normative observations to would-be country buyers are dumb beyond belief:

> The love of city people for the country is a mad love; it feeds on impulse and pays no attention to fact. We, the buyers of country places, don't really want to know too much about them before we take possession. We don't want our joy deflated by such details as *E. coli* counts, carpenter ants, and logging rights-of-way. Often, in the heat of purchase, we don't even want to know the actual location of the country house or how long it will really take to get there from the city. We never dwell on the nasty mathematics of cost or hear the 'mort' in 'mortgage.' We want that house, that plot of land, and we are as unstoppable as the blade of city grass that cracks through concrete.... (Place, pp. *iii-iv.*)

Perhaps only gifted writers like Michael Korda and Laura Cunningham are afflicted with this way of buying country property.

Following her own advice, Cunningham was smote by a 20-room place in Willowby Park on her first date. It was called, The Inn. She and her then husband did nothing to research the property once under what she calls a "trance of desire." (*Ibid.*, p. 112.) She writes: "There were, of course, flaws [in the house], but I saw these defects only as endearing traits. The bathrooms seemed weird, added in 1840.... At the front of the house, there were twin toilets that looked as if they had been sliced in half: I had to ease in sideways to view them." (*Ibid.*, p. 113.) If you feel yourself coming down with a trance of desire, or a trance of anything else, go home and get a good sleep. Don't look at property when you are buying under the influence.

This is where Cunningham's intoxication led her:

- Every year she is expected to pay her share of the upkeep for the Olmstead-designed gravel drive, "which is so expensive to maintain for cars. Every spring, the lord sets down costly gravel; every winter, the snowplow shovels it up." (*Ibid.*, p. *xvi.*). The road fees surprised her.

- "It's always beautiful to be here on the farm; it isn't often easy. ...even as I write, my hands stiffen from the cold, and I hear the roar of my generator, hooked up this dawn, at the start of one of the frequent power failures that afflict my dream place." (*Ibid.*, p. *xvii.*) "Am I deluded in insisting this lifestyle of medieval inconvenience has some charm?" (*Ibid.*, *xviii.*)

- A diagonal boundary line along the property's front puzzled her when the lord first pointed it out: "I wondered why the line was cut in such an odd way, but I was afraid to appear critical, and so didn't say anything. Seventeen years would pass before I knew the reason for that diagonal cut. [It had to do with the lord wanting ownership of a line of sight.] By then [with a new neighbor], the property line would be of crucial interest to me, and I would spend thousands in legal fees to determine my right to prevent a threat from the 'other side.' [The threat came from followers of the late Swami Vivikenanda who wanted to build a shrine trail near the common property line.] But, of course, I knew nothing of the future on this spring day, and I chose not to give the triangular design of my front lawn any further thought." (*Ibid.*, pp. 116-117.)

- At the time of purchase, she and her husband had been vaguely aware that there had been British renters [of the rear portion of their house, The Innlet] on weekends, but "...we'd been told that they had returned to England. In any case, according to our deed, their lease would be up in ninety days—then they would be gone forever. But without telling us, the outgoing tenant had sublet The Innlet to this new couple, who were now demanding that we turn on the hot water so that they could shower. And so my dream of privacy ended, and my true role of homeowner, that of custodian, began." (*Ibid.*, p. 118.)

    Within days, the original British tenants 'in the back' returned and took up residence in The Innlet. "They arrived with two children, two hairy dachsunds, and a parrot that spoke with an English accent. They had lots of friends on or around the estate, and when I arrived for my next weekend, I saw them playing tennis on 'my' court, while eleven guests (I counted them) lounged on the Adirondack furniture and drank gin." (*Ibid.*, p. 128.)

    The lord, not the Cunninghams, collected the rent from the tenants who were charged "'for wear on the sheets.'" (*Ibid.*, p. 142.)

- Cunningham, like Korda, had not bothered to check out her neighbors prior to purchase.

    "As I watched in horror [on her first owner's night], I also became aware of a strange glow in the sky. The sun had set, but a blood-red aura appeared across the fields, emanating from a site half a mile away. I knew that there was a commuter college somewhere over there, known as 'UCK' or 'Ugly College' officially, Ulster County Community College, and as the evening descended, the school's system of anticrime lights flared into phosphorescence [*sic*]. Atmospheric conditions stained the light red, and the college glowed like a Martian heliport. ...not only that, I was soon to discover, UCK was not silent. UCK would emit what Lord Hodgson called 'noxious noises,' rock concerts, football rallies." (*Ibid.*, pp. 118-119.)

- With respect to maintenance expenses:

"On our first morning in residence, we woke to several surprises. The workmen began to arrive, an invading army of pickup trucks and vans. While the sugar maples that lined the [graveled entrance] Avenue looked lush and healthy, [Arthur] Woodcock [their new tree man said:] 'They all have crotch or butt rot.' ...the projected medical bill—ten thousand dollars to treat their distress and chain their sick limbs together." (*Ibid.*, p. 122.)

Had the Cunninghams spent a few hours using their urban intellects in property scoping, they could have identified most of the elements of medieval misery that would later torment them. In some cases, they could have prevented their plagues; at the very least, they could have priced the cost of surgical repair into their purchase negotiations.

Country property need not be a source of existential agony and a self-imposed scheme for redistributing your wealth. You can buy a place here at an affordable price and enjoy it too! Here are some ways the Cunninghams could have improved their purchase.

When the lord told the Cunninghams that they would be expected to pay their share of the maintenance, all they had to do was ask to see what those expenses had been in the past and what the lord projected them to be over the next year or two. That would have eliminated the surprise of a first-day $10,000 tree bill. If the lord failed to volunteer this information, nothing prevented the Cunninghams from asking: Who pays for upkeep, repairs and snow removal on the entrance Avenue and other common areas? If the Cunninghams' deed and other purchase documents failed to provide for sharing of such expenses and they had no knowledge of a cost-sharing obligation at the time of purchase, they had a strong legal position for refusing to pay. Cost-sharing on common facilities is typically written into one or more of the purchase documents. The lord of a manor may have had a medieval right to impose such "taxes" on his peasants, but that is one feudal misery that the Cunninghams should have resisted.

Buyers can always include language in their purchase-offer contracts that states: Seller shall disclose any condition, situation or defect in the property that would adversely affect Buyer's possession, use and enjoyment, or lead to unanticipated expenses by Buyer arising from the failure of Seller to disclose such defects.

The boundary issue that Ms. Cunningham faced when her new neighbor wanted to erect the Swami's shrine trail near their common line could have been addressed 18 years earlier by arranging a mutual no-development, set-back easement on both sides of their common boundary. Such an easement would bind both property owners and their successors to keep that strip open. The easement would not have prevented the Swami's followers from meditating next to Cunningham's boundary line, but it might have stopped them from erecting shrines.

The Cunninghams have no one but themselves to blame for not reading the lord's rental lease with the tenants in the house they just purchased. The terms of this lease, like many others, lasts for its specified term regardless of any change in ownership. Apartment-dwelling New Yorkers know that the length of their leases is not affected by the sale of their buildings. Could the Cunninghams have thought that rent-paying tenants would evaporate for their convenience?

Similarly, how much sympathy should a reader muster for the Cunninghams' failure to notice UCK's presence even though they knew that it was just a half-mile away. A quick drive around Willowby Park would have revealed their neighbors, UCKy and otherwise. Buyers need to be alert to both the obvious and not-so-obvious annoyances that turn up on neighboring property. College students—their noise and their lighting—surely fall into the category of probable annoyances. Were both Cunninghams blinded by a trance of desire? Or was it a coma of deliberate witlessness?

And lest you think I am picking on New Yorkers, I offer a third example of a writer throwing urban brains to the rural winds. Jeanne Marie Laskas, a then-Pittsburgher, offers <u>Fifty Acres and a Poodle: A Story of Love, Livestock, and Finding Myself on a Farm</u> (New York: Bantam Books, 2000). Her sequel, <u>The Exact Same Moon: Fifty Acres and a Family</u> (New York: Bantam Books, 2003), recounts her adventures on a Virginia farm where she and Alex, her husband, moved following their first farm and farm book.

Laskas and Alex—self-described "country-wannabes"—found a house that sat on a hilly tract about a 50-minute drive south of Pittsburgh. She falls in love with the house at first sight because it is a "house with an identity crisis... something like a chalet stuck onto a trailer. ...this house needs me." (<u>Fifty Acres</u>, p. 34.) She is describing a large one-room artist studio recently appended to an older conventional residence. She is also smitten with a view from a hilltop and the fact that the property comes with free gas associated with an on-site gas well. On their first visit, she sees a pond, "...blooming with lilies *a la* Monet. We see a barn, a crooked old thing, baking in the sun *a la* Wyeth." (*Ibid.*, p. 32.) She sees the look of the place, not what it can and cannot do, not how it does and does not function, not what work it will and will not demand of its owners.

Though she walked through its fields, she failed to see that the "farm" is covered in multiflora rose, a fast-spreading, nearly indestructible shrub that must be bulldozed out of the ground in the winter at $50 per hour. A neighbor enlightens Laskas. She says to Alex, her then fiancé: "'We are stupid.' And this multiflora is a symbol of our stupidity. We bought fifty acres of thorns. Thorns we can't get rid of. Thorny weeds that attract both wild animals and bloodthirsty hunters." (*Ibid.*, p. 93.)

She also doesn't see that the Wyeth barn needs to be rebuilt or that the "farm," as it stood, was not a farm in an operational sense because it was incapable of supporting anything more than a couple of dogs and cats. This is seeing without comprehension.

Not knowing the difference between grass and hay or what a bushhog is, she and Alex keep "processing" the decision to buy the farm.

'We don't know the first thing about farming,' he said last night at City Grill, a South Side restaurant with excellent grilled shrimp. 'True,' I said. Then I said, 'How hard can it be?' (*Ibid.*, p. 39.).

No real farming occurs on Laskas's "farm," which in no way diminishes the experience of living on what she calls a "farm." Farming is very hard—physically, intellectually and financially. But living in the country on land that is not farmable is no harder than maintaining a suburban house. It can, however, be different.

In considering an offer, she and Alex reflect on the question of purchase money.

'Where in the hell are we going to get the money?' he said. 'Well, I don't know,' I said. We are, neither of us, moneybags. We are normal working stiffs. But hey, we have good credit ratings. And we both have some investments we can cash in. Not only that, but we both have equity in our houses. We'll pool our resources, make it work. Whatever. I mean, if I have learned anything about money in my thirty-seven years of living, it is to ignore it. It just scares you. Never, ever add numbers up. It just makes the numbers bigger and scarier. '...okay,' he said. 'So where are we going to get the money?' 'I have no idea.' Then I changed the subject. Because, well, that's another way of dealing with money. (*Ibid.*, pp. 40-41.)

If, as it seems, Laskas is recommending this method of farm purchase, I recommend that you pay no attention to her. Alex, at least, has enough sense to make an offer 25 percent below the seller's asking price. Still, it also seems, this "method" of costing out a purchase worked for her. They even had money left to buy a $13,000 tractor, found for them by a helpful neighbor.

Laskas comes to realize that doing farming is what she calls three-dimensional while wanting a place in the country is two-dimensional.

> Alex and I have been talking a lot about what to do with fifty acres. How, for instance, do you mow fifty acres? We learned that you mow fifty acres with the brush hog, which turns out to be the low flat thing that you attach to the back of the tractor. It's the mower attachment. [Not exactly. The bushhog is a device that's suitable for rough-cutting weeds and high grass. A separate mower attachment is available to keep large areas cut as grass. And a different type of attachment—a sickle-bar mower—is used to cut hay for baling.] See, now, I never knew tractors even *had* attachments. I mean, I never really thought about it. To me, a farm tractor is a thing you see in the distance when you are on the [Pennsylvania] Turnpike going somewhere, and it is out there on those fields doing very important farm things. That the farm tractor is made up of parts—attachments and levers and hydraulic-powered thises and thats—was not in my consciousness. Why should it have been in my consciousness? This is one example of a much larger principle I am dealing with, ever since we closed on the farm. Because, fifty acres. [*sic*] Fifty acres in a place called Scenery Hill. Fifty acres of gorgeous scenery. Scenery. We bought scenery. We bought a postcard. We bought green hills and a pond blooming with lilies *a la* Monet. We bought a creaky old barn leaning in the wind *a la* Wyeth. We bought the most beautiful picture we could possibly find. We bought 2-D. Not 3-D. It did not enter my consciousness that the three-dimensional version of this thing was included with the package. Because how could it be in my consciousness? When would it have had the opportunity to get in? Chaos never announces itself, never advertises. Who would buy chaos? (*Ibid.*, p. 68.)

That's a fair self-analysis. I started out the same way, seeing the two-dimensional postcard and not the three-dimensional reality. <u>Dirt-Smart</u> should help to prepare its readers for anticipating three-dimensional country life on the property of their choice.

A book of a different color is Mark Phillips's, <u>My Father's Cabin</u> (Guilford, CT: The Lyons Press, 2001), which describes the need of a welder in an old coal-fired power plant to buy a weekend escape in the Allegheny Mountains near Buffalo, New York. There's nothing impulsive about Jim Phillips's dream to free himself from his job, its dusts and fumes. He plans for years, as he works overtime to save the purchase price dollar by dollar. As the weekend searches progress, the screens he uses—price, size, water source, hunting potential, mix of open and woods—are refined. When he locks onto the right 42 acres, he buys quickly—$100 per acre in the late 1960s. The ice-cold spring turned the deal: "You can plant trees," he writes, "but you can't plant water." He pays immediately for the construction of the spring-fed trout pond. (Another property was rejected, because of a weak spring.) His primitive cabin—no electricity, no indoor plumbing—takes five years, time squeezed from a heavy workload and completed with the help of his son, Mark, and his father. When Jim Phillips dies young of prostate cancer, Mark inherits the cabin and upgrades it for year-round use. His book is about the importance of land to his father and later to him.

One lesson from <u>My Father's Cabin</u> is that you don't need to be rich to buy rural land. A buyer can substitute planning, work and clear objectives for cash. You will need some money and some cash flow, but you can adapt your needs and wants to fit your savings and your projected income.

A second lesson is to start "improving" the property slowly. Jim Phillips starts with a trout pond, not a house. Had the pond been made by damming a creek, it would probably have been washed out;

spring-fed ponds are more permanent than ponds in waterways. The cabin takes shape weekend by weekend. Lack of money and lack of time set the pace, which, in turn, allows the Phillipses to fit the construction project to their finances and the land.

A third lesson is to start small and add incrementally rather than in Maoist giant leaps. Small steps taken slowly usually mean small mistakes that are not that hard to correct. Large steps taken quickly can mean the opposite.

Finally, ask around. Jim Phillips came to his 42 acres by asking the owner of a general store if he knew of any FSBO land in the immediate area. The owner didn't, but one of the store's bench sitters suggested that he talk to a local who had "...been saying for years he's gonna break up the farm and sell. ...worth a try, Brown is." (Cabin, p. 120.) The jury hanging around Cookie's store were not keen on another fellow from Buffalo buying land in their neighborhood, but Jim Phillips apparently looked okay enough for one of them to feed him a lead. It's important for outside buyers to look and act okay enough.

Maybe I'm missing a subtle point that Korda, Cunningham and Laskas are making. Is it possible that certain city buyers want to be country fools, because they think that's part of the move-to-the-country experience? Is there urban status to having a country place fall down around your ears the day you move in? Do writers feel they deserve to endure these miseries for reasons of class or culture? Do they feel that the money they pay for unanticipated repairs is penance for having money in the first place? Are only writers so afflicted? I hope so.

I confess to being blind to cachet of this sort. I can't see how my interests are advanced by being deliberately obtuse about buying land, or anything else. Making a large purchase is hard enough when you're trying to be smart about it. If you find a logic in reading Consumer Reports before buying a $20,000 car, you'll see the same logic in reading Dirt-Smart before buying a $200,000 farm. If, on the other hand, you want to rely on the kindness of sellers, stop reading now.

The lesson from the Kordas and Cunningham is that large, old country houses with plenty of curb appeal can be made to function through large and regular cash transfusions. Such places will always be burdensome second homes since something or other will always be breaking down unless you are prepared to replace every system. This is not an argument for the bomb-proof brick rambler. It is, instead, an argument for country romance leavened with one eye on your wallet and the other on your tolerance for living the next decade in the anarchy of serial remodelings.

My point is simple: there's no need to be miserable in a country second home, despite Cunningham's endorsement. Nor is there a need to spend hundreds of thousands of dollars unnecessarily. The only reason for doing so is to acquire first-hand material for another book of this genre, Why I Paid $500,000 for a Pint of Wild Blueberries and a Family of Mice in My Country Bedroom.

Here are a few basic ideas that these three good writers should have kept in mind when searching for country property:

1. Ask questions.

Do your research, so that you can ask sensible, informed questions. Don't be snotty or nerdy in this. You're not trying to show how smart you are. You are trying to learn what you don't know, as well as what you don't know you don't know.

2. If something looks funny, figure it out before you submit a purchase offer.

If you stumble upon a non-working toilet, do not assume that it will be fixed on its own before you close. (I'm speaking both about toilets and metaphorically.)

If the house furnace looks like it heated a Roman bath in the days of Caesar, determine the cost of replacement. If you don't see ductwork, you will have to install it if you want whole-house air-conditioning. This can be a real mess on old houses with solid walls. If the electricity in the barn doesn't work, ask why?

If the pond is dry in July, ask about it. If you see a creek, ask how often it floods and how extensive the flooding has been. If you find a sump pump in the house basement, find out why water is entering. A rule of thumb applicable everywhere is this: basements should be dry.

3. If you can't see how something works, ask about it.

Ask where all solid and liquid house wastes go. If you are told they go into a septic system, get a copy of the permit to find out its capacity and design. Ask how the seller maintained the system? Were the solids in the settling tank emptied regularly; if so, check with the company that did the cleaning. Don't be surprised if grey water (from the laundry and kitchen sink) does not go to the same place as black water (toilet water). Country houses may pipe grey water into a hole or creek rather than a septic system. Your new country house may be grandfathered, but, if it isn't, you might be expected to build a modern septic system that takes both waste streams—an expense that can total anywhere from $3,000 to $30,000 or more.

If there's a motor in the sale, ask to see it operate and find out who has repaired it; check the repair record. Run all motors, including the furnace, AC, water pump, ventilating fans, freezer, washer/dryer, refrigerator, sewage pumps and everything used for agricultural work.

If the seller says the walls are insulated, take off the faceplate of electrical receptacles and look. As an alternative, ask your house inspector to check for insulation.

Examine the roof if you can. Look for signs of deterioration. Use a mirror to look up a chimney: you should see sky past the damper. Cheap cosmetic compacts work fine. If there's a crawlspace, crawl into it with a flashlight. Look for deterioration in the foundation, sills and floor joists. Look for evidence that critters are chewing on your wiring. Look for leaks in water and waste lines.

4. Talk to your neighbors before you buy.

Ask them about themselves, and then the target property. Does it have a history of flooding? Do its springs go dry? Ask about fences. How is fence ownership apportioned? Are there any boundary disputes or grievances? Do any neighbors feel they have a claim to own anything or use anything on the property you're about to buy? Look around for activities that could disturb your use and enjoyment of your new property. Barking dogs are obvious, as are shooting ranges, extra-bright outdoor lights, teenagers with jacked-up trucks, poultry houses, hog farms, manure lagoons and close-by fields that are fertilized with green (fresh) manure. Less obvious are lots where bawling, just-weaned calves are kept for a week, barrels and pits for weekly trash fires upwind of you, and individuals with alcohol or drug problems. More often than not, a helpful neighbor will take newcomers under his wing to protect them from the worst errors they might otherwise make. See if you can establish this protectorate status with at least one neighbor from the start by doing what you can to extend your own genuine friendship.

5. Get expert advice when you don't know something.

You may need a surveyor to check boundaries, forester to determine the value of the timber, lawyer to advise you on a title problem or zoning issue, insurance agent to give you a quote for a farm policy, civil engineer to give you a rough cost for a new septic system or bridge, architect, landscape planner, agriculturalist, well-driller, excavator and house contractor.

When you're out on a pretty fall Sunday afternoon with the sun warm and the sky clear, and you happen upon a rural place that jellies your knees, STOP! Take a deep breath. Say nothing. Keep your pen in your pocket along with your wallet. If you happen to be with a real-estate agent, mumble something like, "Very nice, but it sure is a long drive from home." This indicates cautious interest, which at this point is all you want to indicate both to the agent and to yourself. "Let's take a better look here before we go to the next place." A little caginess should be part of your property-hunting kit.

This book will show you how to take that better look. With the information you assemble from your scoping, you can submit a written offer within a week or two. The point of resisting impulse is not delay for its own sake or the building of your character through self-denial.

The point of scoping is to couple speed with security. **Scoping is, in other words, the vehicle that allows you to move fast by stripping risk out of the purchase.** Don't dawdle. Good deals on good properties don't last long.

Buyers must learn to use their eyes and brains to make **dirt-smart decisions**. Some individuals may be born with this talent, but anyone can learn how to do it. I know people who have a knack for buying property and others who find a dollar wherever they turn. I'm not one of either kind. When I've made money in real estate, it was directly related to thorough scoping, which, in turn, led to buying at the right price. The one time I lost, it was directly related to inadequate scoping. If you're looking for country property for your personal use and enjoyment, you may want to pay more for the right place than an appraisal says it's worth. If you're looking at an investment, the dirt-smart decision is always to buy at a price that guarantees a future profit. You must let the facts lead you to that decision. Your job as a dirt-smart buyer is not to rig your analysis to confirm what you want. Don't argue yourself into a deal. If your head and your pencil tell you to walk, don't let your heart buy it. Your decision is the product of work that you will do after your first look. Be prepared to work. Your scoping—the information gathering and analysis and evaluation—begins the moment you say to yourself, "I like this place."

CHAPTER 2: WHAT AM I LOOKING FOR AND WHY AM I LOOKING FOR IT

Few of us *need* a second home in the country or a patch of woods, though many of us want one or the other. Wants are often perceived as compelling as needs. Fulfilling a need is pedestrian, an obligation done because it's required. Satisfying a want, on the other hand, makes us feel good, successful and in control.

The first thing, then, is to interrogate yourself, Want or Need? There's nothing immoral about wanting country property just because you want it. My only caution is to make sure that you can afford this want over the life of your country mortgage without impinging on some future need. This chapter discusses how to think about your wants and needs in country property before you ever answer an ad or call a realtor.

My opinions are the product of my own experience, the limits of which I acknowledge and to which I alert each reader. I have not purchased property in most of our 50 states, though I've looked at and/or scoped land in more than 20. I have, for example, never had to understand western water rights as a practical matter, value a tract in Humboldt County, California where the big Coastal timber grows, or size up a cattle-and-corn operation along the North Skunk in Jasper County, Iowa. On the other hand, I've been asked to scope investment properties ranging from a couple of hundred acres to more than one million. I was once asked to screen—not scope—600,000 acres in Ontario in one afternoon. I was able to learn enough to advise my client to pass it up. Anyone can learn enough to avoid bad properties and buy good ones.

What I am sure of is that buying land is always local. A generic understanding of how to scope and buy property—which is what you get in this book—will always help as long as you adapt the generic to the particular, to the local. **Scoping is tract-specific** because each property has its own set of virtues, drawbacks and uncertainties, all of which are set in a context of state law, local zoning rules, market conditions and the personalities of the owner, neighbors, brokers, lawyers and lenders. Scoping, as a process, can be applied broadly whatever the specifics. I think my own experiences with sellers reflect common practices. Still, certain things I write or beliefs I pass on may not apply to your target tract, because of local conditions with which I have no experience.

The point I have held to in writing this book is not to tell you to buy a certain type of rural property but to show you how to approach buying any such property in a way that maximizes your chance for success and minimizes your chance for unpleasant surprises.

Dirt-Smart is a how-to manual on buying country property. Since my manual is based in part on my own errors and successes during the past 35 years, keep in mind that many ways exist to perform a particular task. My how-to approach may be different than yours or that of another author. When you find something that I've written doesn't square with your own experience, test both hard. I am not fool-proof. I will be pleased if my effort to help you become knowledgeable gives you the tools to turn up my errors and any you might make before you make them.

KNOW THYSELF

Most Americans who live in cities or suburbs can live full, satisfying lives without buying a country home or undeveloped rural land. I say this without any empirical proof, but I'm pretty sure it's true. Or at least true enough for most everyone.

Consider for the moment an urban buyer who comes to the decision one morning that he **needs** a place in the country. Perhaps you are such a buyer.

To me, a need is non-negotiable. Food, water, shelter—or the means to get them—those are needs. Affection and companionship could be added to the list without much of a quarrel. Looking for and buying a country place is usually not a need. It is usually a choice that is discretionary rather than coerced—a want.

A search for recreational land or a second home should never be conducted under the same pressure to find "something" that a buyer often feels with a job transfer. Buyers feeling desperate to find their place should bench themselves for a bit since desperation leads to decisions that can be bad and are usually costly. Buyers who are able to shift their thinking from needing to buy a country place to wanting to buy one make life easier for themselves.

If you find that you've been looking for the **one right place** without success, you have chosen to search for a lone needle in a field of haystacks. You may argue that every field of haystacks probably contains at least one needle. This may be true in your profession. It is always true in argument.

Since this is a book about country property, I feel obliged to reveal that farmers no longer make haystacks. The metaphor loses its lyrical punch when updated to "like finding a needle in a round bale." I've never found a needle in any hay, stacked or baled, through I have found snakes, nails, rusty horseshoes, pieces of balers and nests of bees.

The search for the one right place leads most often to ceaseless searching. As frustration builds, it can also lead to either the dreaded impulse purchase or buying a place because you're fed up with looking.

Few places will strike you as practically perfect in every way. But many spots can be made perfect enough with vision and money. Michael Korda demonstrated that **thrown money** can solve most country problems. I don't recommend his approach, because it may involve the hideous expenses of turning a sow's ear into a silk purse. (I also have no experience in actually implementing his approach, but I would certainly like to be able to try it some day.) Start with something closer to a silk purse and you spare yourself headaches and expense. Screen in properties that can be made into what you want within a sensible time-and-money budget. Don't screen in a place that has one or more absolutely unfixable feature that you hate. Don't screen out a place that has a few things that you dislike if they can be fixed within reasonable limits.

A viciously rational individual can calculate the costs and benefits of buying a country place and arrive at a startling though sensible conclusion: most of what people like to do on second properties in the country can be done without owning second properties in the country. What might these things be? Hunting and fishing. Hiking. Riding. Camping. Driving motorized vehicles (4WD vehicles, ATVs, snowmobiles, motorcycles) through the woods. Wildlife watching. Nature communing. Vacationing on a lake. Spending the summer in a beach house. Skiing at a resort. Puttering. Relaxing. Staying on working farms. Activities like these do not require owning any property.

Most of these recreational activities are available on state or federal lands that can be visited by the day or week. Public land provides variety, challenge, relaxation, wilderness, near wilderness and fully developed, multi-dimensioned recreation. State parks rent cabins—rustic to modern—at reasonable prices in all manner of rural settings. Fully equipped cabins are available within a few hours drive of most Americans that offer various packages of developed recreation—boating, swimming, horseback riding, nature education, restaurants and so on. And if you don't like public facilities, you can rent every type of rural property that interests you from private owners, in whatever form and setting pleases you. Vacations—working or not—are available on real farms. No farmer turns down volunteer labor, no matter how unskilled and klutzy. Dude ranches have made a living for more than century by providing pseudo-cowboy experiences. It's not hard to find any of these opportunities.

It's not the same, you say. I know. You're right. You can't invest your labor and your heart into a public campground.

It's emotional investment, not money, that drives much of the second-property market in rural areas. Despite the fact that most Americans now live in cities or suburbs, many of us feel a need for land of our own where we can sink roots. This is particularly powerful, I think, if your principal urban home is an apartment, townhouse development, planned community or suburban house. Each of those housing choices is efficient and practical, but also thoroughly regulated and tightly scripted. Having once lived in Washington, D.C., both in an apartment and my own house, I know the feeling of being penned up and incomplete. I wanted out, but I also needed to be in to make a living. Finding a permanent place in the country that would always be "home" regardless of the vagaries of career was how my thinking took shape. I was looking for a second home in the country, a sanctuary, an axis around which I would spin, a place to plant fruit trees, have a barn, rattle around in an old truck on warm fall afternoons, sleep in a hammock and sow wildflowers. Familiar?

I bailed out on Washington more than 20 years ago. My new wife and I moved to a 73-acre grazing farm in a mountain county with 2,500 people, perhaps the least populated county east of the Mississippi River. I argued that I "could continue to make a living off Washington from almost five hours away." Wrong. I argued that "we can always make a living from the farm." Wrong. I argued that we can "make a clean break, without going through the second home stage and without knowing how we'll make a living out there." Wrong. Our decision to buy and move was more impulse and less planned than I realized at the time. Owing to that, it has taken years of financial struggle to adapt ourselves to making a living in a beautiful place that has no need for my doctorate in international relations and her masters in public-sector labor relations. We discovered that small-scale cattle farming, no matter how efficient, never produced much net income even in the occasional good year. We ended up making her into a dirt lawyer and me into the writer of this book among other things.

Since you are reading this book, I will presume that similar thoughts are now floating in your mental ether. I offer this caution: certain city people should not think seriously about developing their "inner hick." There is no hard-and-fast set of characteristics that define those who will be better off staying on the urban side of the line, but here are some that I have seen that cause the most problems with new owners of country property:

1. Cash-strapped. Don't stretch your wallet to buy a country want. Wait until your fortunes improve and your cash pile is higher. Selling a country place can take time and cost money; don't assume that you can dump your second place quickly if you are unexpectedly RIFed and find yourself carrying two mortgages while unemployed.

2. Handy. If you're not at least below-average handy, you can either try to learn to be or pay others to fill in. If both options are unappealing, rural housing is not a good fit. Entropy is a fact of every second home's life. Everything breaks, wears out or needs to be replaced. If you are one of those few individuals who literally can't hammer a nail, stick with apartments that have friendly and competent supers. Even bare land will ask you to do something that involves having your brain instruct your hands to do something, like use a chainsaw, dig a trench, fix a fence or nail up a "posted" sign.

Rural property sooner or later entails internal combustion engines (ICEs)—a 4WD pick-up truck, tractor, gas-powered electric generator and chainsaw are a common quartet. If you know nothing about ICEs and can think of nothing so unpleasant as to learn a few basic remedies and preventives, don't buy rural land or a farm. ICEs are just the tip of the country berg—there can be hand tools, pumps, compressed air, diesels, hydraulics, vacuums, electrical gizmos, gravity-feeds and a whole bunch of other stuff that will cause you angst.

3. Discomfort. If your idea of permanent nirvana is a frisky game of tennis followed by ten hours of serious spa stewing, don't exchange netter's togs for bib overalls. Rural property always involves work. Sometimes the work is demanded at inconvenient hours and when you need to be in two places at once. Sometimes, rural property demands that you anticipate a problem and solve it before it becomes a disaster. If you want to enjoy a rural experience but don't really want to invest effort in the furtherance of your own enjoyment, visiting, not owning, a country place is for you.

4. Fear. If you do not like being around people who are not like you, if you fear the unknown, if you will not investigate a strange odor and if you will consciously ignore a weird sound coming from the basement, you now have four good reasons to rethink owning country land.

5. Exposure. If you detest the idea of your new neighbors knowing a lot about you, think again about buying a place in the country. There is no privacy here. Whether or not you are doing one thing or another, sooner or later someone is likely to tell someone else that you are. Gossip is common, since we mainly have each other as grist for our mental mills. Your words, manners and style will be noted. If you drive a new Mercedes convertible down a country road, you will inevitably get it stuck and have to ask a yup-and-nope guy with a tractor to pull you out. He may strike you as taciturn, even slow, but be aware that his powers of social observation are acute. So think twice before acting like even more of an idiot. He's the guy with common country sense, not you.

MAKE A REVOCABLE LIST

Before you start looking at the newspaper ads or riding the back roads on pleasant Sunday afternoons, make a **Revocable List** of those things you think you're looking for in rural land.

I stress the revocable quality of this list. Your ideas will and should change as you acquire knowledge of what's available, and more importantly, as you refine your needs, wants and the sense of your own capabilities. The last of these—your new capabilities—is important to track. A country place is likely to ask you to do things you haven't done before—hang a 14-foot-long farm gate, drive a tractor, build a bridge or inject antibiotics into the eyelid of a steer with pinkeye. Everyone does something for the first time. I learned from scratch how to do each of these tasks and many others. If you have no experience with a task, take little bites, one at a time. Be patient with yourself. You probably won't get something new right on the first try. Don't start a 10,000-square-foot dream house as your first hammer-and-saw project since making a broom holder in seventh-grade woodshop. The Revocable List should change as you find your needs and wants changing.

A buyer will use a Revocable List <u>after</u> he's screened in a property over the phone or through material sent to him. The completed List should give the buyer enough information to decide whether the property appears to meet enough of his criteria to justify the next bit of time and money that initial scoping requires.

I've provided the start of a generic Revocable List. This should be taken as a way to get you moving on developing your own List. I've set up four categories for you to work with: **Needs, Wants, Don't Wants and Possibilities.** I've further sub-categorized Needs and Wants into things you need or want now, that is, immediately; things you need or want within five years; and things you project you will need or want after your first five years of owning the property.

The more cash you have to spend, the more of your needs and wants you should be able to satisfy upfront. The choice the cash-heavy buyer may face is between a more expensive property that requires little additional work and one where a great deal of time and a hard-to-forecast amount of cash is needed to obtain the same result. There's no always-right formula for deciding between these choices. If you value convenience more than money, buy the ready-to-go place. If, on the other hand, interest rates are high and you think your future cash flow will increase, take the cheaper alternative and put up with the sawdust. Every buyer should calculate his upfront purchase costs together with those improvements projected in the foreseeable future to avoid buying more than he can afford. When doing this calculation, add in at least 25 percent more than your projected improvement costs, and one-third if you're feeling skittish about the accuracy of your projections. If you follow Laskas's advice and ignore money, you may find yourself cash squeezed and land poor. It makes no sense to buy land whose debt and expenses keep you cashless. Thomas Jefferson resolved being chronically land poor by dying.

I would begin filling in your Revocable List with your Don't Wants. You might have a clearer vision of the negatives you want to avoid than the positives you believe you either need or desire. Your Don't Wants might be a house next to a busy highway; or property adjoining a commercial dairy or hog farm; or house near airport; or all flat acreage; or house in floodplain; or property more than 100 miles from current residence. When you start filling in Needs and Wants, be very specific about items about which you feel strongly. These intensely felt considerations are not likely to change during your search. Each √ check represents the intensity of your feelings. Don't limit yourself to physical attributes of property. Include financial considerations, community infrastructure (church of your choice; condition of roads; proximity of fire department, rescue squad, medical clinic and so on), appreciation potential and tax-benefit opportunities.

You will undoubtedly have needs and wants that you can articulate generally but not with specificity. For example, you might write a Need as "pretty spot." That's fine, since many combinations of different physical components can add up to a "pretty spot," and its determination is always in the eye of the beholder. As you look at property, continue to turn generalities into specific, articulated wants and needs.

The danger in using generalities instead of specifics can be illustrated by the Need for privacy. Let's say you find a house in the middle of a 40-acre square. That puts you less than one-half mile from each of your four neighbors. Let's assume that the house is surrounded by deciduous trees along with an occasional pine. Is that privacy? It depends on your neighbors. If the adjoining property is uninhabited, it's privacy until a new second home is built on the adjoining property. Then you won't have privacy from unwanted sights (in the winter), sounds and smells, owing to changed circumstances beyond your control. If gunshots bother you, you'll need a far greater distance between you and the shooter. Privacy cannot be perfectly achieved, even with thousands of acres. Airplanes fly over; neighbors abut; trespassers come on. It will be helpful if you can break down "Privacy" into more articulated concerns, such as out-of-sound of neighbors and barking dogs (current and projected), no regular odor invasions, out-of-sight of neighbors, house is isolated from passing headlights, house cannot be seen from public road in all seasons. This set of criteria, I should add, would screen in a property on which you heard gun shots and smelled seasonal farm odors. Over the years, I've settled for operational privacy where intrusions are known, predictable and tolerable.

As you work through the Revocable List, you will soon get a feel for your **Hard Needs, Wants and Don't Wants** as against your **Soft Needs, Wants and Don't Wants**. The Hard items are those that you can articulate with unambiguous clarity and fervor; your Softs are less clear or less intensely held, but present and now accounted for. Hards are those that you do not want to negotiate with yourself; softs are those that can be compromised, adapted, fixed, ignored, sold or tolerated to a degree that you determine.

You can further indicate the intensity of your current feeling about each item by using a three-check system. One √ check indicates your preference; two √√ checks indicate high priority; and three √√√ checks indicate absolute requirement.

Like any other research, the search for property benefits from organization. Your first file folder is labeled Revocable Lists. Keep it stocked with blanks, as well as each dated iteration you do. As you become more knowledgeable, you should revise your Revocable List, even though the changes are slight. Anticipate both the wholesale revision and a lot of fine-tuning. Don't box yourself into a never-buy-anything corner by loading your List with impossibly specific requirements, such as access road built to state specifications or four sugar maples in front yard, each at least 75 feet tall. When listing your Needs-Now, exercise care that you don't overload this category, which will be the hardest to satisfy. Use the List's different time horizons to build flexibility into your plan while spreading costs over future years.

Possibles give you the chance to be flexible with the combinations of actual assets and liabilities you find in the field. For example, you might have listed that you Need Now not more than 100 acres, but have fallen for a farm of 250 acres with the perfect house. The Possible here that can make this work is for you to consider buying the larger farm and selling 150 surplus acres immediately after your purchase. As you look at properties, increase your ability to create Possibles in them. An orphan tract, down the road and removed from the main tract you like, is a saleable asset rather than a liability. A falling down barn may have significant old-lumber salvage value. An ugly, 100-foot-long, two-story turkey house can be converted into a convenient and efficient barn for feeding 60 steer calves through the winter. An old outbuilding might be remodeled into a homeoffice.

One question that can drive where you place Needs and Wants is whether you plan to live in a country house full-time or use it as a second home. How you answer that question in turn depends on how you tolerate make-shift conditions. Some buyers assume that a second home in the country will be—even should be—primitive, or at least, subject to old-fashioned quirkiness. Other buyers can live with a full-time construction project in their permanent residence, but want their country place to be a sanctuary of simplicity and reliability.

My experience is that all houses require maintenance; older houses require more than newer ones; and second homes that are not visited often tend to suffer problems that escalate or build on each other. A small roof leak, for example, in your permanent residence will be immediately obvious and simple to repair. The same leak in a second home can rot out a ceiling, floor and even cause an electrical fire before you discover it. With second homes that stand uninhabited for weeks, even months, at a time, you need to list as Needs items related to the dependability of various house systems, heat and water in particular. Second homes should be easy to open when you roll in late on Friday night and easy to close down. Water systems should have a single drain at their lowest point. Radiators should have an antifreeze solution in them, not water. Heating systems should have reliable thermostats with programmable timers, if possible. It's far more pleasant to pull into a warm house on a cold night rather than one where you have to start a fire while hauling in groceries and turning on crawl-space water systems. These types of considerations can be thought of as Wants rather than Needs, because they usually can be added after purchase. But don't assume too much. If there's no water in your rustic cabin at 4,000 feet elevation, it may be related to a lack of feasible water and not the lifestyle preferences of the current owner.

Here is a starting list of things to consider:

Generic Revocable List

| Needs | Wants | Don't | Possibles | Unknowns/Uncertainties |

	Now	<5 Yr.	5 Yr.>	Now	<5 Yr.	5Yr.>	Wants

Acreage
    <10
    10-25
    25-100
    100 +

2WD access
    All year
    Good weather only

4WD access
    All year
    Good weather only

Open Land (__%)

Woods (__%)

Special Facilities
    Horse layout
    Crop land
    Ag. buildings
    Garage
    Kennel

House
- New
- Modern
- Old
- Needs work
- Systems dependability
- View from
- Tree shade
- Garden spot
- Home orchard
- Approved septic
- Well/spring/public water

Amenities
- Rental unit
- Home office
- Pool
- Other assets
- Wetlands
- Year-round stream/river
- Pond/lake
- Land suitable for hunting

Features
- Minimum elevation
- Soil type
- Water quality/quantity
- School district
- Proximity to
  - certain church
  - airport
  - town
  - doctor
  - hospital

Security
- Police
- Fire protection
- Break-in potential if used for weekends
- Medical providers
- Rescue services

Money
> Property asking price,
> less than $_____
> Anticipated closing costs,
> less than $_____
> Interest rate, __% or lower
> Monthly payment, $_____
> or less
> Seller financing
> Income from property
> Timber worth ___% of
> total purchase price

Legal
> General Warranty Deed
> No boundary disputes
> Acceptable easements
> Minerals convey
> Right to water (if appropriate)
> No reservations of interest

When you get your Revocable List completed, consider screening in properties for additional thought but not full scoping that have at least, say, 80, percent of your checked Needs, 50± percent of your checked Wants and at least 95± percent of your Don't Wants. If you reject every property that does not satisfy 100 percent of your Needs and Don't Wants, you'll exclude some that you may be able to work with. Be willing to consider properties that can have your Needs met within five years. You're looking for a package, a property that fits you as a whole. It makes no sense, to me at least, to exclude an otherwise terrific property because it doesn't have one of your Needs Now, such as a mature home orchard. Put up with purchased fruit and plant your own trees, which will bear within five years.

Your Revocable List is one important defense against the **hot-flush buying** of Korda, Cunningham and Laskas. The listing process forces you to evaluate property analytically rather than emotionally. At the same time, it doesn't force you into a numerical straitjacket in which you buy only when 92 percent of your immediate needs are met.

You should, of course, use the List to help you make decisions about which properties deserve to be scoped and at what level of seriousness. It's unlikely that you will be able to complete a Revocable List on your first visit. But you may be able to learn enough to screen the property in or out for scoping.

When you make a note under Unknowns/Uncertainties, make sure to clear it up. Nothing feels dumber than getting burned by an Unknown you identified and then ignored. Staple whatever free-hand notes on the property you've made to your Revocable List. Throw no note out, ever.

Your Revocable List file is one of the first that you start in your **Search Kit**. I've found it easiest to organize a Search Kit by county. The Search Kit is a collection of documents, information, maps, plans and notes that profile the county's land and resources. In each Kit, a buyer should include notes on properties he's screened in and out, along with any Revocable Lists and scoping results on individual target properties.

The Kit's **county-specific** documents include:

Soil Survey, from the local USDA's Natural Resources Conservation Service or USDA Farm Service Agency

Road Map showing all roads, available from state highway department in each county. A buyer should "drive the county" to determine which sections he likes more than others. That familiarity will focus the search and provide the buyer with knowledge of local resources and landmarks.

Topographical map, state topographical maps are available in book form from DeLorme, P.O. Box 298, Yarmouth, Maine, 04096; 207-846-7000; www.delorme.com. These 11" x 16" books are available in bookstores. Their maps are scaled at 1 to 150,000, or 1" equals 2.37 miles. This provides sufficient detail to get you started. Maps with greater detail are available from the U.S. Geological Service (USGS) and are generally available at book stores and local surveyors. At nominal cost, a surveyor will print out a 1"-to-300' topographical map that shows waterways, woods, elevations and roads. Using the deed's description of the property, he can draw the boundaries on the map.

Local weekly and daily newspaper, subscribe to both; clip relevant articles

Telephone books for relevant communities in and around county

Zoning Ordinance, relevant portions, including division and subdivision. The ordinance book may be purchased at the county's zoning office. The Zoning Ordinance will set forth what can and can't be done in each type of land classification, e.g., residential, agricultural, conservation etc.

Real-Estate Guide, this is the monthly publication put out by local real-estate brokers that includes all current listings. Local papers also carry listings. Most real-estate agencies now have websites where additional information is provided.

County Economic Development Plan, which shows areas where residential and industrial growth are planned.

Local ordinances and regulations, such as an ordinance prohibiting the installation of wood-burning fireplaces; or one that regulates outdoor lighting; or one that requires a minimum number of square feet for new construction; or one that imposes limits on non-agricultural uses of agricultural property, etc.

Property tax information. Counties and other jurisdictions calculate property tax based on the assessed value of the land and a tax rate, e.g., so many cents of tax due per each $100 of assessed value. These formulas differ from place to place. You can find these formulas for each type of land in the office of the county tax assessor. Determine whether the county has adopted **land-use valuation**, which is a tax break for agricultural land. **Greenbelt** status is a conservation-oriented tax break that seeks to keep undeveloped land undeveloped. An owner who changes such a status is usually expected to pay **rollback taxes**.

Other types of public information, such as maps showing floodplains, maps of federal and state lands, county-level geological information related to subsurface minerals (oil and gas, coal, stone, etc.), rules pertaining to any areas designated historic districts, plans for any public lands near your target property, hunting regulations and seasons.

Comparables, is information that you gather on current asking prices and current selling prices for properties that fit your search profile. You want to get a sense for how much land of each type (timberland, open farmland, pasture) is selling for in various size ranges, expressed in **dollars per acre ($/A)**.

Information on current asking prices will come from a brokerage-published Real-Estate Guide, newspaper ads, bulletin ads, **For Sale By Owner (FSBO)** information, websites and word of mouth.

Information on current selling prices is available in the county courthouse where deeds are recorded and/or tax records kept. Sale records—deeds, mortgages—will often provide the selling price, show the transaction tax on the sale from which you can calculate the selling price, or provide information on the financing of the sale from which you can infer a likely selling price.

The next step in your Search Kit is to set up a Resources file that will include the names, addresses, phone numbers, fax numbers, websites and e-mail addresses of individuals and service providers that you are likely to need, including:

Lawyers with real-estate expertise

Accountants, who are experienced in handling farm and timberland taxation issues

Lenders—banks, mortgage companies, federal sources (Farm Service Agency/Farm Credit Administration), credit unions

Surveyors, licensed in the state where the property is

Consulting foresters, names are available from the Association of Consulting Foresters (ACF) and state forestry agencies

Certified soils engineers, who may be needed to locate soil on the property where a septic system can be installed

Physical Engineer (PE), if the property requires a constructed septic system, which is installed where the dirt is unsuitable for a conventional system

Testing laboratories, where you can send samples of water and materials for analysis. The county's extension agent will be able to tell you where to send soil samples.

Title insurance companies, if you want or need title insurance

Farm-related businesses, such as local stockyard where farm livestock is sold, farm supply stores, fence-builders

Insurance agencies, to provide a Farmowner's Policy

Utility companies

Excavation contractors for road building, foundations, septic systems

Architects

Building contractors for new construction

Carpenters/remodelers, and other tradesmen (plumbers, electricians, roofers, painters)

Home inspectors, to evaluate existing residences prior to purchase

Building supply/hardware companies

Well drillers

Consultants: environmental (testing for hazardous materials, wetlands, endangered species); historic preservation; farm-business evaluation; appraiser; mortgage broker; landscape architect, etc.

Government Offices

<u>**Local**</u>
Sanitarian or Health Department
Zoning Office
Building Inspector
Planning Office
County Clerk, where deed books are kept
County Assessor, where tax information and tax maps are kept
Water and conservation districts

<u>**State**</u>
Local office of state forestry department
Local office of state fish and wildlife department
Local office of state environmental protection agency
    Surface-water division (streams, lakes, coasts)
    Underground-water division
    Solid-waste disposal division
Local office of state highway/road department
State Office of Natural Heritage Resources, the state agency that is responsible for the management of state-listed endangered, threatened and sensitive species.
County extension agent, an employee of a state university that offers agricultural graduate programs

Federal
U.S. Army Corps of Engineers
Federal Emergency Management Agency (FEMA), if your property is in a floodplain
Regional office of U.S. Environmental Protection Agency (USEPA),
Regional office of U.S .Fish and Wildlife Service, if you suspect the presence of a **federally listed endangered, threatened or sensitive (ETS) species**. Ask if any portion of the target property is included in a **habitat-management plan**; this designation severely limits what an owner can do with his property.
District office of National Forest or National Park, if you share a boundary
Other federal offices that may be relevant in a particular area, such as Bureau of Land management or the Office of Surface Mining

I'll explain in other parts of this book how these resources are useful to you in scoping property. You won't need to contact all these information sources on every property. But the more scoping you do, the more likely you will need such services. Whenever you have special needs, such as for specialized medical care or a particular type of school, you will need to narrow your property search to areas that are convenient driving distance to those facilities. Long drives, particularly long daily drives, become increasingly less palatable as you get older.

The last item in your Search Kit is a **separate file for each target property that you scope**. Properties that you've visited but not thought worthy of scoping can be gathered and clipped together. These are your **non-starters**, which provide useful pricing information, even though you were not interested in a purchase. You can group your non-starters into a separate file.

Every property that you scope should be organized into a **Scoping File**. Each property-specific Scoping File will contain these types of materials:

Maps and other location documents
Road map showing general location of property
Topographic map (s) of property with boundaries
Tax map
Survey of target property if available. May also need surveys of adjoining properties.
Aerial photograph, available from local USDA office
Photographs
Google Earth map

Deed of current owner. May also need earlier deeds if boundary **calls** (compass directions and linear measurements) are incorporated in current deed by reference to earlier deeds.

Other documents of record, such as access easements, conservation easements (which limit what the owner can do with the land), liens, mortgage documents, leases, contracts, water rights and agreements, utility rights of way, etc. that affect the property. ("**Of record**" means that the document is publicly recorded, i.e., on file, in the office—county or city—where such documents are kept. The time and day of entry is logged on the document. "**Recording**" a deed, easement or other legal document refers to this process.)

Property tax information—current assessment value and property tax for land, improvements and minerals on target property are available in one or more county offices, usually in an annual **Land Book**, Tax Roll or a computer-accessible database.

Permits running with the property—approved septic permits; building permits, variances and conditional uses permits; mining permits; water permits, etc.

Timber cruise—if the property has timber with substantial present (**merchantable**) value, you should hire a consulting forester to work up a cruise that estimates timber volumes and dollar values. In many cases, a forester will be able to estimate merchantable timber value with a simple **walk-through** rather than the more elaborate and expensive cruise.

Current income produced by property—property-based business (e.g., farm), hunting leases, rent, mineral royalties, agricultural subsidies, conservation-practice payments.

Information on improvements—house inspection report; notes or cost estimates you've received from contractors; sketch of house floor plan; your notes on house and outbuildings.

Notes on seller—the more information you have on the seller—his motivation for selling, financial resources, personality, plans for the money received from the sale, willingness to self-finance—the better you will be at negotiating with him

Notes on Problems, Unknowns and Uncertainties—jot down whatever you're not sure about. Put a big star next to things that are problems that will require your money or time.

Names and Contact Information for all adjoining neighbors.

Kitchen Sink—include scraps and tidbits of information that might possibly come in handy, such as the name and number of a fellow who knows old apples and might do some grafting for you; names of neighbors and their out-of-town children; livestock prices; current rental rates for pasture; delivered hay prices; and your likes and dislikes about different areas in the county.

The last package of materials that you should take on your property visits is a **Personal Kit**, which, for starters, might include:

Hard-back clipboard with note pad

Pen (water-proof pens eventually prove their worth)

Compass

Sunglasses, hat, bug dope, water-proof matches, long-sleeve shirt and long pants

Hiking-type shoes or boots. (Do not appear in Gucci heels; this goes for women too.) If you're looking at land, anticipate getting your boots muddy and wet; if you're looking at a farm, don't wrinkle your nose at manure.

Unobtrusive camera

Decent flashlight (something more than a pen-type but less than a deer spotter. You'll use it in attics, crawlspaces and far corners.)

Duct tape (If you're going on land where ticks, chiggers and the like crawl up legs, you'll need to seal your cuffs tight with tape.)

Snake boots or leggings if you will be walking on their turf

Emergency car stuff kept in car—spare and jack, tire-inflation aerosol, tow strap or chain

Light-weight rain parka

Small backpack

Cell phone (it may work)

Hiking stick—helps with balance; good for whacking brush out of your path, probing impenetrable brush for snakes and flicking branches off trails

Water-filled bottle; hard candy or chocolate, fruit or trail mix

Think of your Search Kit as a pyramiding process. You start by building a very wide and solid base of information on which each higher and increasingly focused level of information and analysis rests. The point of the pyramid is the purchase of one of the properties that you've scoped. Properties that you've screened out or rejected after scoping to one degree or another are the surplus building materials that all pyramid builders end up with.

Let me summarize the organization of your Search Kit:

Generic Revocable List (blanks)

County Documents File

Resources File

Property-specific Scoping File

Completed Revocable List

Other materials

Non-starter File

Personal Kit

Two questions that buyers typically ask of themselves are: Will I ever find the right place? and How long will it take? Both questions are understandable. Both also depend on what the buyer means by "the *right* place."

It's hard but not impossible to find the one needle in a field of haystacks. It's easier and a lot more practical to find a place that is mostly right. Whatever gap you find between perfect and mostly right ought to be either closeable over time or of not much significance. You want to set your sights high, but not impossibly high; you want to settle pretty close to what you want. The saddest buyers I see are those who spend years looking for the one spot that is absolutely perfect. I'm not of that school; life goes by too quickly.

I advise buyers to settle for a place whose aesthetics feel right, a place that can be adapted to their goals and one that can be bought within the buyer's budget. The last point must be balanced with the first two. It is important for buyers to come to a property search with a definite and disciplined idea of the amount they can spend—in upfront cash, monthly mortgage payment, carrying costs (local taxes and fees, insurance, utilities) and immediate repairs following purchase. Buyers need not spend up to their **budget cap** to achieve their objectives, nor should they consider only properties they consider "deals" because they are less than their budget cap. If a property exceeds the buyer's budget, I would not buy, except in circumstances where some marginal asset of the property can be quickly sold and the buyer's purchase exposure brought back in line with his financial capability. "Stretch" is a concept that should apply to minds and Spandex, not to dirt-smart land purchasing.

The length of a search depends largely on the buyer's capabilities and pickiness. Industriousness shortens the length of a buyer's search. Putting together a Search Kit saves time. As you become increasingly familiar with a target county, you will be able to screen out properties that appear to have promise with your own first-hand knowledge. You can also shorten your search by adapting your wants and needs to the local property supply. Don't, for example, insist on finding a Swiss chalet in south Florida or an adobe ranch in Franconia, New Hampshire.

Macro-economic forces, such as interest rates, can affect when you search. Since most hunts for country property involve discretionary spending, it makes superficial sense to search only when interest rates are low. Low rates help buyers by reducing the cost of financing a purchase over time. The longer the term of a mortgage, the more interest the borrower pays on a given amount of money. Borrowing $100,000 at 6 percent for 10 years involves a monthly payment of principal and interest of $1,110.21, or 120 payments totaling $133,225.20, of which $33,225.20 is interest. Borrowing the same for 30 years involves a monthly payment of $599.56, or $215,841.60 in all, of which $115,841.60 is interest. Borrowing $100,000 at 10 percent for 30 years involves a monthly payment of principal and interest of $877.58, or 360 payments totaling $315,928.80, of which $215,928.80 is interest. The lesson is obvious: borrow at the lowest interest rate possible and pay off the debt as soon as you can. Buyers help themselves by amortizing a loan over a long period of time—which brings down their monthly payment—but accelerating the pay back of principal to minimize total interest paid. You can follow this tactic only when your mortgage document allows for early payment of principal without penalty.

Be aware, however, that low interest rates can work against buyers to the extent they heat up the real-estate market. More buyers appear, and asking prices can rise as mortgage money becomes cheaper. On the other hand, high interest rates can hammer asking prices, and persuade desperate sellers to self-finance purchases at below-market rates. Seller financing can be used as a bridge to a low-interest-rate environment in the future. Sellers in a high-interest-rate environment are pressured to deal with any buyer who looks half serious; with lower interest rates, you risk becoming a supernumerary buyer in a cast of dozens. Every buyer knows that it's to his advantage to be the only game in the seller's town. If a seller is trying to move his property when interest rates are high, the buyer should investigate the seller's motivations. Chances are he needs to sell quickly, which is leverage for the buyer.

Assuming a buyer is comfortable with the available interest rate, he should be able to find a suitable rural property within 18 months, and often much sooner.

The exception to that seat-of-my-pants generalization is the buyer who wants a property that is idiosyncratic in his target county. Examples of such idiosyncrasy are the buyer who demands a 4,000-acre wooded tract in a county that is mostly open farmland divided into parcels of fewer than 500 acres, or the buyer who needs a private air strip in a mountainous county where flat land does not occur naturally. Such properties are hard to find in the target counties of these buyers, but not elsewhere. The good news for a buyer is that out-of-the-ordinary properties can be even harder to sell than they are to find. Buyers will probably do best by looking for a type of property in a county where many such properties of that type occur.

If you're looking to buy a needle, don't look for it in a haystack; look in a pin cushion. Shape your expectations—Needs, Wants and Don't Wants—to the types of properties that are available where you are looking. Within those types, there will be enough variety to suit most buyers.

Renting can be used to test-drive a farm property for possible purchase.

You might consider a **rent-with-the-option-to-buy approach (lease-purchase option [LPO])**, for a target property that you can't quite afford at the present time. In this format, you rent the target farm/land for a fixed period, say one to three years. You agree on the future purchase price and terms as part of the deal. If you decide this farm is not for you, you can walk away from the property at the end of the rental period. An LPO usually requires that you agree to pay the full rental value for the full term. In this case, your contract should allow you to sub-lease the property and/or buy your way out of agreement for a specified sum. Some LPOs are negotiated in a way that allows a portion of rent paid to be credited against purchase price. You might also find it advantageous to agree, for example, to pay $700 per month rent for three years for a farm that both parties agree should rent for no more than $500 per month in return for a $400 deduction (not $200) in purchase price for each month of rent you pay during the term.

If an LPO seems to you to be more of a commitment that you're ready to make, consider renting a house in a small rural town from which you can scope properties on weekends. And if that seems to be a stretch, share the rent with another couple with whom you alternate country weekends.

TYPES OF PROPERTIES.

A place in the country means different things to different readers of this book. In the next section of chapters, I'll organize this discussion of property types in the following way:

Farmland
Undeveloped (Raw) Land
    For Hunting
    For Second Home
    For Investment
Developed Land for Second Home
    Full-package Developments
    Half-package Developments
The Flip
Land with Existing House
Owner-built House in the Country

CHAPTER 3: FARMLAND AND FARM DIRT

Dozens of types of farmland can be found in the United States. They range from western deserts and dairy pastures in Wisconsin to Iowa cornfields and trout ponds in New York's Adirondack Mountains; from row crops like soybeans, cotton, wheat and tobacco to orchards, vineyards and Christmas trees; from intensive, industrial-type poultry and hog operations to hardscrabble mountain plots where Old MacDonald would feel right at home. Operating farms range from hundreds of thousands of acres to just a handful.

Farmland begins with dirt. The type of dirt and its qualities have determined what's been done in the past and what you can do with it in the future.

Louis Agassiz, the famed Harvard naturalist, would give his students a fish and expect them to figure out its evolutionary history from sustained, concentrated observation. Superficial student analyses were met with Agassiz's instruction: "Look at your fish!"

Land buyers: Look at your dirt!

Farm buyers: Look at your dirt harder!

You are looking at its **topography**, as well as what it's best suited to do, what it's not well-suited to do, what it might be adapted to and how it should be cared for. Some dirt has been so neglected or abused that a fortune is needed to reclaim it.

Your first task when looking at land, including farmland, is to get oriented in several senses.

First, take out your compass and determine how the land lies in terms of directions. Estimate how much of the total acreage faces each way. Certain crops, such as native grass and hardwood timber, grow more vigorously on north-facing slopes, which are cooler and wetter than south-facing slopes.

Second, classify the land into rough topographic categories—essentially flat (wooded and open), rolling, steep slope, river bottom, swamp/wetlands, frontage on a public road and so on. Use the topographic map you've sagely brought with you to match what you see on the map with what you see on the ground. Locate boundaries to the extent you can, using the **topo**, a survey if one is available, a tax map (where a survey is lacking) and the **legal description** of the property's boundaries found in the deedwork. (Subsequent chapters explain how to do all of these things.) Note any problems, such as eroded hillsides and gullies, floodplains, overhead power lines crossing the property, bare spots, reclaimed strip-mine acreage, landslide area, wetlands/bogs/swamps, atypically dry areas, evidence of fire damage in the woods, garbage dumps, among others.

Third, determine which way the weather usually comes from. On a house, paint will peel first and worst on the side that takes the brunt of prevailing wind and rain. Trees lean away from strong winds. Other things being equal, you probably want to orient new buildings with their long sides in line with prevailing weather.

Your first eyeball survey will give you an idea of how the farm is internally distributed among **land types**: crop land (relatively flat and fertile), grazing areas (ranging from planted pasture to arid land to steep mountainsides), hay fields (planted crops, such as alfalfa, to native grasses), woodland (usually at the back of the farm) and agriculturally non-productive areas (gullies, wetlands, rocky areas, steep slopes, etc.) The same eyeball survey will tell you how the seller has worked with the dirt on each section of the farm. Look for the logic and balance in what you see. The seller might be grazing three acres for every acre in hayfield and every acre in corn. If he's running a self-sufficient farm with few purchased inputs, his land allocation may tell you that he can produce enough grass, hay and corn to feed the number of cattle he's carrying each year. You will see crops or crop residues on crop land. Livestock and their droppings indicate active pasture—or possibly a new breach in the seller's fence. Hayfields can be waist-high grass prior to cutting, uniformly short grass just after cutting, somewhere in between, or livestock pasture after haying is completed. Fenced land is used for pasture and hay; cropland, too, may be fenced. The seller, or his agent, can give you the acreage breakdown for each current use. Most farmland is also tracked by use categories by the local Farm Service Agency (FSA) office of the U. S. Department of Agriculture (USDA). Farmland that is no longer being farmed will have grown up in brush, weeds and trees—the mixture of which depends on how long ago farming was abandoned.

As you walk through the farm, look at the dirt in each area. What's growing on it? Vegetation will tell you a lot about the dirt quality under your feet. Good dirt, with sufficient natural precipitation or irrigation, grows healthy plants owing to its fertility, chemical composition, drainage and other factors. Bad dirt generally tends to grow good things poorly, but thistles, teasels and other weeds do just fine. If you are clueless about which plants indicate good dirt and which the opposite, talk to the **county extension agent** or a local farmer about the local species that indicate one or the other. A field guide to wildflowers, like <u>The Audubon Society Field Guide to North American Wildflowers</u>, Eastern and Western editions, will describe preferred habitats. Plants growing on bad dirt (for agricultural purposes) will be described as being found on waste areas, barrens, roadsides, damp open ground and the like. If you are unsure about a plant in the field, take a specimen home and check it against a field guide from the local library or <u>www.enature.com</u>, where you click on native plant guide and then click on wildflowers, grasses, grass-like plants or shrubs.

What type of dirt is under your feet? Sandy? Clayey? Rocky? Shaley? Is the topsoil thin or deep? How far below the surface is rock or hard pan—the seller will know. Get down on your knees and look at it carefully. Is it hard packed, cracked and dry? Gummy and wet? What color is it? Dig down about 12 inches. Does it look rich, with grass roots, worms and life in it? Does it smell rich? Pick up a handful in each field. Compress it. Does it ball up into a spongy wad? Or does it crumble for lack of moisture and tilth? Better dirt has a deeper color, ranging from black to red, than poorer dirts, though color alone won't tell you all that you need to know. Poor dirt will grow vegetation that's adapted to what it provides, and that vegetation can support livestock as long as many acres are available for each animal. It may take 20 or 30 acres to graze a steer in parts of the arid West compared with one acre in fertile Mississippi. What you will learn from your dirt will depend, in part, on when you visit during the year and recent local weather so adjust your opinion for those factors. Don't count on grabbing a handful of dirt from a frozen field in the middle of January: a winter visit will rely on farm records and the local <u>Soil Survey</u> for information on dirt qualities. County <u>Soil Survey</u>s are discussed below.

Start learning about the properties of soil, and how soil quality can be maintained and improved. Visit the National Sustainable Agricultural Information Service's website at: <u>http://attra.ncat.org</u>. Click on to soils management, which provides information on soil testing; manure, compost and green manure (tilling a cover crop into the ground); pasture soils; soil and water quality; and links to other sites. This website also covers other aspects of sustainable (organic) agriculture. This information is worth reading whether or not you see yourself producing organic farm products. ATTRA is the acronym for Appropriate Technology Transfer for Rural Areas. The USDA funds numerous programs to improve and protect agricultural and rural soil. Access these through <u>http://www.nrcs.usda.gov/programs</u>.

The single handiest dirt book is the target county's **Soil Survey**, available through the local office of the USDA's Farm Service Agency (FSA). It shows the soil type on every acre in your county. The <u>Survey</u> locates each type of soil on **soil maps**, which are aerial photographs with the soil-type boundaries drawn on. Your target property may have a dozen or more soils. The Survey explains what each soil type is both suited and unsuited for in terms of agriculture (crops, pasture, hay), tree production, recreational uses such as hunting and wildlife habitat, construction purposes (dirt has to be sufficiently stable and firm to support the weight of a house) and waste disposal using a conventional septic-tank system. The tests used to determine whether dirt will support a conventional septic system are often called "**perc tests**," pronounced, perk, which assess a soil's absorption capacity by timing how long it takes water to drain from a hole. **Dirt-color analysis** is also used for this purpose. Many types of dirt won't pass a septic-system test, and some soils won't support house construction. If you are looking at a county whose soil has not been surveyed, talk to the local FSA official or a USDA soils specialist in the closest county where a survey has been completed. The chances are very good that you will get a reasonably accurate read on your farm's dirt based on the same types of topography and dirt found in a nearby county survey. You can find out about soil surveys, county-by-county, by accessing the USDA's Natural Resources Conservation Service's (NRCS) website at: http://soils.usda.gov/survey/printed_surveys/. Additional information on soil surveying is available from NRCS's National Cartography and Geospatial Center (NCGC) in Fort Worth, Texas. **Soil tests**, where you sample the dirt in each field and send it off for lab analysis, are described below. The NRCS now has soil-survey maps online at http://soils.usda.gov/survey.

I would reject property that had unsuitable dirt—soils that are lacking in fundamentals (workability, sufficient top soil, organic matter, productivity, "percablity," etc.)—for the type of use I had in mind. I would not reject property with bad dirt if my only "uses" for acreage were to look at it and keep distance between me and my neighbors. If you want land area for these reasons alone, consider buying bad dirt cheap. I would be inclined to reject property whose dirt is limited to one or two types, each of which is seriously unbalanced in terms of acidity or are disproportionately clay, sand or rock. You can balance and build soils, but it takes time and money. In my area, I've come to appreciate the difference between soils based on limestone and those based on shale. The latter are less productive for crops and trees, difficult to perc and tend to have problems with water quality. You cannot escape the characteristics of your dirt in your country property if you intend to make any use of the dirt. For that reason, I tend to screen out property with unsuitable dirt, look skeptically at property with uniformly bad dirt and celebrate property with a variety of soils, most of which are pretty good. I look for farmland dirt that can support multiple uses with reasonable efficiency.

Farms that have pastured cattle and sheep should be screened for overgrazing and eroded land. In my mountainous area, steep hillsides were cleared for pasture. Grass, however, can't absorb rainwater on a slope as well as forest. Some of these slopes have lost all their topsoil as a result. Overgrazed slopes tend toward landslides under heavy rain. When the soil on these hillsides reaches the limit of its capacity to absorb water, the rain will slide off them in sheets. Flooding results. If you see bare dirt and weeds, pastures are overgrazed. Thin soil and erosion are other signs of too many animals spending too much time on that pasture. Overgrazing and the environmental impacts that follow are common patterns on western ranches. Overgrazed pasture can be brought back by grazing fewer head or installing a rotational grazing system. You may need to fence livestock out of some areas. You may need to plant soil-building and water-holding vegetation in other spots. Remediation requires work and money.

As you drive and walk over a prospective property, look for trouble spots in the ground. Every farm is likely to have a couple of soft places where the tractor gets stuck every spring. These spots can be caused by a seasonal spring or a layer of impermeable subsurface clay that keeps the topsoil saturated with water. There are two places on my farm that are too slick in wet conditions for me to drive uphill in my 2WD tractor; there's a steep spot at a gate where it's impossible to stop coming downhill on wet grass without sliding. My wife refers to my learning efforts in these areas as "Mr. Toad's Wild Rides." Ask the seller to tell you where his land's little quirks lie. While on the subject of vehicles, ask the seller which hillsides are too steep for sideways driving. (You can drive safely straight up or down a slope whose steepness would cause a rollover in a truck or tractor if you were to try to drive across it.) Don't test yourself on steep slopes: rollovers kill.

Ask how the seller manages his land and works with its assets and trouble spots. What is each field used for? Where does he stop plowing because of wet ground? Is there a hidden rock in a hayfield that has to be skirted? Are there sinkholes to avoid? Which hillside meadows are too steep for hay-making? Which fields require what inputs of manure, chemical fertilizer, lime, weed control and pesticides for the use he made of each one? Ask the seller to rank his fields in terms of their best use, production and **productivity**. The latter—a measure of input efficiency in terms of output, not gross production—will be expressed as a ratio, such as pounds/bushels/bales/tons produced per acre, or number of acres required to carry one grazing animal for either a year or the spring-to-fall season. (Grazing ratios may be expressed in terms of a cow-calf unit or animal unit, so make sure that you understand the local definitions of "unit" as well as their equivalencies, that is, one unit equals so many steers each weighing so many pounds. A cow-calf unit might weigh 1,200 pounds together at spring turn out, so, roughly speaking, three 400-pound steers would equal one cow-calf unit. Keep in mind that as animals put on weight, they will be consuming more grass.) Ask the usual date when cattle can be turned out on spring grass. Are there any hot spots in the pastures where concentrated clover or alfalfa might cause bloat in newly turned out livestock? Find out the usual dates of the last spring frost and first autumn frost, because, together, they determine planting and harvesting schedules.

The farm and land will provide the buyer with climate clues. Snow fences indicate a pattern of deep drifts. Windmills indicate regular winds. Trees broken in their main stems usually indicate strong wind or ice storms. A cistern indicates the need to store water. You can find out current county-level climate information from the local **weather station**, which collects primary data on precipitation, temperature, wind speed, etc. The County's local chamber of commerce should have basic information regarding annual rainfall and temperature ranges. Most counties have several weather stations. You can identify the whereabouts of these stations in each county at http://lwf.ncdc.noaa.gov/oa/climate/stationlocator.html. Extensive data from each station can be purchased through this website.

Dirt needs moisture to grow vegetation. Is the farm located in an area where rainfall is sufficient and regular to grow crops without irrigation? I suggest looking at the target county's **annual precipitation map**. An example of such a map for Napa County, California can be viewed at http://www.ca.nrcs.usda.gov/mlrao2/napa/figure1.html. Rainfall and other weather conditions can vary significantly within a county owing to elevation, topography and other factors. Buyers are interested in the **micro-climate** of their target property, one clue to which is found on the annual precipitation map. The seller and his neighbors are first-hand sources of information on the farm's micro-climate. Don't ask the seller about his farm's micro-climate. Ask how many times during the last ten years his crops have been affected by drought. Or how many times he's had to sell calves early due to lack of grass growth, which is another way of measuring rainfall. Frame this question so that it is sensibly answered, not laughed at.

Do you see evidence of irrigation systems? Irrigation is usually accomplished by watering the surface either through long tubes mounted on large wheels or center-pivot sprays. Drip systems use buried water lines and porous tubing. All irrigation systems involve both upfront costs for equipment and continuing costs. The latter may include the cost of purchasing water, which is often sold as dollars per acre foot (43,650 square feet by 12 inches deep, or 43,650 cubic feet). Irrigation is not environmentally neutral. Continued draw downs can dry up a river, or a body of water as large as the 24,500-square-mile Aral Sea or your local **aquifer**, which is your subterranean strata of water-bearing rock. Aquifer depletion is a factor to weigh in purchasing land in the American Southwest, parts of California and in the southern Great Plains. (Lester R. Brown, "Dry, With a Chance of a Grain Shortage," <u>Washington Post</u>, December 14, 2003.) Where irrigated water is applied, it can deposit salts and minerals on the land. These can build up over time. If you are looking at an irrigated farm, I would advise retaining a local agricultural consultant to help you understand its requirements and implications.

As you walk the farm's dirt, notice ponds, springs and creeks, particularly in late summer. It is very important to learn whether ponds, creeks and springs go dry—never, rarely or routinely. I know of houses in my end of our county that are without household water when their springs dry up during droughts. This has happened several times during the last two decades. If the farm's water supply weakens during drought, how does the farm make it through? Does water have to be trucked in? How was agricultural production affected in the past?

If your target farm is east of the Mississippi River, you should generally have sufficient precipitation to grow area-appropriate crops. Even so, certain areas tend to summer drought if they lie just east of a line of mountains that catches rain as weather moves from west to east. Our farm lies east of the Allegheny Front, a line of 4,000-foot-high ridges running southwest to northeast. On our side of the Front, you find lots of Dry Creeks, Dry Forks, Dry Branches and Dry Runs. Such places were named for that important characteristic. Inasmuch as precipitation is always iffy, some farms in Southeast states have installed irrigation systems to guarantee a steady supply of water to their crops, even though irrigation may not be needed in most years. Drought can ruin a crop and shorten a livestock grazing season—both of which cost farmers money. Protracted drought that lasts for several years or more can lead to farm bankruptcy. The further west you are beyond the central Midwest corn belt, the more precipitation, underground water and irrigation determine your agricultural choices. In dry areas, you need to get detailed information from the seller and others about where the farm's water comes from, how much is needed, its quality, how it is accessed, its reliability in dry years, restrictions and constraints on its use and its cost. You must make sure that you have a legal right to the quantity of water the farm needs as part of your purchase.

The wildcard in scoping local climates is the impact of changes in global climate patterns, particularly temperature. Local trends over the last ten or 15 years may be more of a predictor of trends over the next ten to 15 years than averages derived from a 50- or 75-year sample. If you're buying property in an area that's borne drought for the last five or six years, I would make a call to a university-based or federal climatologist to discuss temperature and precipitation forecasts.

I've been discussing some of the elementary considerations of buying farmland. My reason for doing so is that much of the rural land that I've seen for sale during the last three decades was once, or is currently, being farmed in one way or another. Much of the wooded land that is now being sold in the East was once cleared for pasture or crops. Abandoned farmland continues to have potential for certain agricultural purposes, but the buyer should recognize the risks and limits of "re-agriculturalizing" land dismissed as uneconomical. Small pieces of such farms might be reworked as modern commercial agriculture under intensive management for high-profit, niche crops. Buying a 200-acre mountain farm with 25 acres of good bottomland might be a good *farming* buy if your idea is to convert the bottom to trout ponds and a large patch of specialty garlic. Such a place will not work economically as a traditional farm raising traditional crops in the traditional way; the market has already made that judgment. So don't count on making a profit from running cattle on its overgrown or overgrazed pastures, or planting corn on hillsides so steep that the seller's grandfather had to prop up each growing stalk with a rock. In such a case, the buyer is only interested in the dirt qualities of the 25 acres for a new use—trout ponds and garlic. The remaining 175 acres could be evaluated for timber production, recreation and woodland aesthetics—another new use. Old farms that are no longer economical cannot be made economical doing old farming the old way with new ownership. When you find a seller who has reached the end of this particular rope, you might find a very good deal. But don't take up where he left off.

It is also common for non-farm buyers to find grazing farms and dairy farms beyond the suburbs being marketed to them more as second homes and less as agricultural businesses. The 42 acres that Jim Phillips bought in the late 1960s were part of a working dairy farm whose owner was old and tired and ready to parcel out his land to fund his retirement. Such places obviously have dirt that is suitable for pasture, hay, row crops and woodland. What is equally obvious—to their sellers, at least—is that this dirt is far more valuable as second homes than as the type of working farms their sellers operated. Where dirt becomes economically marginal for one purpose, it may find a new and higher value with another purpose. The existing farm with such dirt is not competitive and provides a modest income, at best. The owner is finally forced to make a cold business choice between continuing to struggle for $20,000 a year as a farmer on one hand and the sale of his farm and its capital stock for 25 times that on the other. From the buyer's perspective, however, you should not pay a developer's price for this farm if your intent is to keep it in agriculture. You need to find a farm whose price is not inflated by a new or "higher" use.

The point here is that a buyer should evaluate the agricultural qualities of the dirt on farms of this sort in terms of both their current agricultural use and the buyer's projected use, agricultural and otherwise. Once that is done, the buyer should evaluate the value of this target for his projected use. The buyer wants to reach a price with the seller based on its value to the buyer, not on the seller's notions about the land's highest and best use. The buyer can sometimes turn this difference in market values to his advantage by bargaining with the seller on the basis of the land's value in its current use, which is likely to be lower than its highest-value use (i.e., second-home property sold to the likes of Mr. Korda), and lower than its value for the buyer's new use.

FARMS AND MONEY

I will assume that most readers are not interested in buying working farms as the first step to becoming full-time working farmers. This assumption, if true, shows good sense on your part. Still, many readers will be intrigued with this idea, and many more will like the idea of having a working farm as a second home. I offer these observations.

Working farms run by full-time working farmers who make a respectable living are a subset of American farm operations that novices have a very small chance of joining upon the acquisition of such places. It is very hard for real farmers to make a respectable living, particularly those working on comparatively small acreages and those producing basic commodity crops, like grain and beef cattle. On farms of fewer than 200 acres in the mid-Atlantic and New England states, it is next to impossible both to make a living and retire a farm's mortgage from full-time conventional commodity production. The value of these farms often lies not in what they can produce but in where they sit. Thus, the seller wants the buyer to pay a premium for location.

Family farms that are financially successful generally involve large acreages (much of which may be leased), huge investments in capital stock and manageable debt. The individuals who in my experience survive at conventional farming have been farm-raised, trained in agriculture, operate on a sufficiently large scale and are blessed with a cash cushion to ride out the inevitable bad years. I have not come across a successful farmer who started from scratch, borrowing for land and equipment. Most full-time farmers made their learning-curve mistakes on someone else's nickel (often their parents') or squeaked past their errors when times were more forgiving. Many got their start from their parents: it's a lot easier to make a living from a farm "when it was give to ya" free and clear of a mortgage. They have survived by figuring out farm-specific resilience strategies, including what to do and how to do it when most everything goes wrong at the same time. Many also seem to have made shrewd acquisitions of land and timber over the years, the equally shrewd sales of which have provided income subject to a favorable capital-gains rate. Farming's ever-present danger is debt. When farm debt—mortgage, equipment and operating expenses—exceeds farm income, its servicing can consume farm profit, cash reserves, other assets and non-farm income. The farmer ends up living to pay down his debt.

Making a living from full-time, conventional farming is so experience-dependent, capital-intensive, complicated, weather-dependent and risky that any reader who contemplates a career change would be well-advised to begin burning $100 bills in preparation. Better yet, burn your money after working a 12-hour day, half of which was spent pleading with a banker not to call a note, and the other half shoveling manure as self-imposed penance for wanting to produce food or fiber.

I should add that I've run into several examples of inexperienced newcomers who succeed after buying working farms. All of these exceptions involve individuals who have a lot of money from some non-farm source that is used to buy and then subsidize large farms. I have not seen these farms work out as businesses. I have seen them work as long-term investments when land appreciation creates profit taxed at the capital-gains rate or otherwise discounted through sophisticated tax strategies. The individuals who do this type of farming have a lot of fun being farmers.

The other group of non-farm buyers interested in farms are those who like the idea of farming and are free of the burden of having to support themselves through that type of work. These folks buy modest places, not the large showpieces. Some relocate to the farm, particularly if they have early retirement. They find a job off the farm or make one up to generate the cash they need. I've seen one member of a couple continue city-based employment on a four-day work week while the spouse lives full-time on the farm. These non-farm farmers started with a money cushion—either cash in a pile or cash flow—that muddles them through their farming errors and spells of rural underemployment. Trust funds, savings, inheritance, non-farm employment and pension benefits are the most common cushions I've seen. It is foolhardy to move to a working farm if you do not have either cash in a pile or cash flow—and preferably both—from non-farm work or investments. Buyers of this sort need to be confident about the long-term sustainability of their cushion. Financial circumstances change, and not necessarily for the better.

Most American farmers don't make a living from farming. The USDA reported that in 1993, the most recent year for which survey data were available, the average farm operator household income was just over $40,000, of which only 12 percent came from farm income. (See www.usda.gov/news/pubs/factbook/003e.pdf.) The rest came from wages and salaries (46 percent), off-farm business income (17 percent), other off-farm income (18 percent) and interest and dividends (7 percent). Of the slightly more than 2.03 million farm operator households that year, almost 152,000 reported a negative income, averaging $28,526. Forty-five percent of all farm households earned less than $25,000, and all of these households earned most of their income off the farm. Households reporting income of between $50,000 and $249,999 that year, derived an average of $14,590 in farm income and $26,718 in off-farm income. Only when income exceeded $250,000 did farm operator households average more income from farming than from off-farm sources. USDA projections for 2003 forecasted average farm operator household income at $68,900, with only $5,250—7.6 percent—from farming. (See http://www.ers.usda.gov/publications/agoutlook/aotables/oct2003/aotab31.xls.)

Rather than non-farm income supplementing farm income, it appears to me that most farmers, except for the very wealthiest, are supplementing their non-farm income with farm income. Why, then have a working farm? For most farm households, the farm generates a little spending income and a lot of depreciation, deductions, tax breaks, credits, subsidies, cost sharing, loss and income taxed at the capital-gains rate from the sale of land and timber. This pattern can be a wonderful fit for a buyer in the highest tax brackets with most of his cash flow in salary and taxed as current income. Such a buyer is helped by the deductions, depreciation and losses that farms generate. Renting out your farm keeps most of these benefits in your pocket, though you get more tax goodies if you operate the farm yourself. Chapter 6 discusses farm-taxation issues.

The relationship between farm income, farm size and federal policies, particularly crop subsidies, was the subject of a series of articles in the <u>Washington Post</u> at the end of 2006 (See www.washingtonpost.com/harvestingcash). Large farms—with revenue of more than $250,000 per year—produce almost 60 percent of all agricultural production but account for only seven percent of farms.

These large farms get more than 54 percent of federal subsidies—and their share is increasing. The average farm size has doubled to 441 acres during the last decade, but the sector employs fewer farmers. Subsidies have encouraged these trends. (Gilbert M. Gaul, Sarah Cohen and Dan Morgan, "Federal Subsidies Turn Farms into Big Business," <u>Washington Post</u>, December 21, 2006.)

To those few readers who are sitting in a city office still thinking about earning a living from farming. I urge you to invest your time and money in self-education before buying. Take a degree—or at least college-level courses—in the agricultural specialty of your choice before you put dollar one into that type of farm. Apprentice yourself to a farmer you want to emulate during your next summer vacation. Approach your move-to-a-farm idea as a long-term business plan, not a lifestyle choice. Being broke, or farm-poor, is not a fun-filled lifestyle. It's fine to aspire to produce healthful, organic produce in a way that allows you to live on a healthful, organic farm. But doing so can lead to bankruptcy if you lack a non-farm source of cash or a feasible business plan along with the management skills and experience to make the plan work over time. Making a subsistence income year after year in the service of higher values wears thin. Test your plan. Send various drafts to extension professors for comments. Talk it out with real farmers who are doing similar ventures. Make your mistakes on paper, not on the ground. Don't be shy about adding 25 percent to your most inflated cost calculations to represent the unexpected that almost always breaks against the novice. Force your farm to make a profit on an unforgiving sheet of paper before you ever try it in a merciless field.

When we bought our farm in 1983, I confidently told my trusting wife that "we could always make a living off the farm if the economy went into the tank." This was one of those opinions that I routinely express based on nothing more than the rumored fact that one male ancestor clad in animal skins got lucky one morning and spotted a mammoth just as it was having a fatal heart attack outside his cave. This ancestor then boasted to his spouse that rational thinking and analytical planning lay behind his successful hunt. All future opinions, he informed her, would be similarly based, and, therefore, not to be questioned. Using reason and analysis, he then left her the job of butchering 8,000 pounds of fresh mammoth before it spoiled. I've often wondered where my pre-purchase wisdom about "living off the farm" came from. At first, I blamed a book whose cover I may have glimpsed. Now I blame my ancestral crock in which such opinions still occasionally ferment.

About six months after purchase, I received a nice little analysis from Virginia Tech in response to my sending along our farm's particulars. The crunched numbers showed I couldn't hope to break even on running 35 spring stocker steers as had always been done in the past. Loss was programmed. What did they know, I said. I invested in a **rotational grazing system**, which allowed me to double the number of animals and add each pound of gain as cost-efficiently as possible. The farm now produces about 75 percent more pounds per year than it did before I installed this system. But after ten years of trying every which way to make money from our small grazing farm in a pretty place, I gave up and began renting it for seasonal pasture. There's no risk in renting as long as the cash is paid upfront. The annual income—$3,000—turned out to be about what I would net from running the steers myself, with no risk and less work.

Producing basic product is the hardest and riskiest end of the agricultural business. The risk-taking, investment and work of basic production supports layer upon layer of businesses above it. Market forces have divided producers of agricultural commodities into two groups: 1) full-time producers who have achieved a level of efficiency, scale and capital to farm at a profit, and 2) part-time (marginal) producers who don't have to be efficient because they consider their farm income as a supplement to non-farm earnings. Producers whose operations fall between these groups don't last. A novice farmer reading these words should consider joining the second group, not the first.

While it's easy to enter farming, it's not easy to make it pay. If you want to try conventional production farming because you want to be outside, work with your hands, produce something of value and live in a clean environment, look for some other occupational vehicle. These are fine goals and farming meets them. But those goals get submerged in farming by the inherent, depleting hassles of operating a farm as a business—debt management, unpredictable weather, low prices, increasing input costs and genuine catastrophes. No prospective farm buyer, especially one who has not done much farming, should ever enter a barnyard romancing the seller's dirt. If you insist on thinking about farming as a livelihood, approach it as capitalism at its least forgiving...and you will be in the right frame of mind. The odds are that you will find yourself an entrepreneur who feels like a 19th Century "immiserated" industrial worker whom Marx predicted would rebel against the hopeless degradation free-market capitalism imposed. Perhaps the farm revolution will be led by an individual who comes into farming from outside the system and soon asks: Why does anyone put up with this?

In the fall and winter of 2003, a bit of luck fell to the one million American farmers—about half of the total—who run either beef cattle or dairy cattle. Together, cattle are America's single largest agricultural sector in terms of gross revenue. The prices paid for feedlot-ready cattle spiked due to a combination of unforeseen events—principally, a U.S. embargo on Canadian beef imports after one cow had been confirmed with bovine spongiform encephalopathy (BSE, or mad-cow disease) and the popularity of high-protein, low-carbohydrate, weight-loss diets that encourage the consumption of beef. Beef producers had been squeezed for more than two decades by oversupply, softening demand and stagnant prices. Suddenly, cattle farmers were getting $100 more per head sold than ever before. Normally, they might net $25-$50 per head. Blaine Harden, a Washington Post reporter, talked with ranchers in Montana:

> Ranchers here have taken out larger-than-normal operating loans in recent years, owing to the drought, smaller herds and depressed beef prices. 'We are trying to make up for losses we suffered for five straight years,' said Rick Kuntz, 53, who raises cattle on 20,000 acres south of Dillon [Montana]. During that period, drought and lack of range grass forced him to cut his herd by more than 30 percent, to 450 head from 690. He said he has had to borrow more and more money just to keep the ranch operating. At the same time, he said, he has not been able to spare any cash for mending fences, painting his barns or buying new equipment. His 30-year-old tractors and haying machines, he said, are held together with 'spit and chewing gum.' The hurt, though, seems to be ending. (Blaine Harden, "Protein Diet Craze, Thin Supply of Cattle Fatten Ranchers' Wallets," Washington Post, December 22, 2003.)

The market, it seemed, had finally thrown cattle farmers a life line. And then, a few days later, an old "downer" (non-ambulatory) cow from Canada that had presumably been fed feed containing infected cattle tissue was found in Washington state and diagnosed with BSE. Fifty countries banned U.S. beef imports within a month, affecting about 10 percent, or 2.6 billion pounds, of total U.S. beef production. (Scott Kilman, "Farm Economy Seems to Absorb Impact of First Mad-Cow Case," Wall Street Journal, January 21, 2004.) Cattle prices plunged 20 percent, and then recovered about half. To the extent that export is slowed in the future, U.S. farmers will be producing more beef than the domestic market wants. This will reduce cattle prices paid to farmers. Since much range and cattle pasture are not well-suited for alternative uses, this production capacity is likely to hang on. "Cattle keep the fields mowed" is an oft-expressed opinion by farmers who know they net little from "running some beeves" every year. The long-term, structural impact on U.S. cattle farmers from changes in beef imports and exports is hard to predict. The temporary life line may have looped itself into a noose. Good times for American cattle producers had lasted about three months. In July, 2005, beef imports from Canada resumed, whether or not Canadian beef represents a BSE threat. U.S. beef packers expect lower cattle prices, hence more demand for their finished product. Cattle farmers are expecting to be paid these lower prices as supply increases.

And in March, 2006, another cow—this one in Alabama—was diagnosed with BSE. Cattle producers sought comfort in that all three U.S. cows found carrying the disease were likely infected prior to August, 1997 when both the U.S. and Canada more or less prohibited their feed industries from using rendered cattle remains that are contaminated with BSE. USDA announced that it would reduce BSE testing, which had screened 650,000 brain samples since June 2004. (Scott Kilman and Janet Adamy, "Mad-Cow Diagnosis is Confirmed," Wall Street Journal, March 14, 2006.)

The BSE episode is the tip of an iceberg of questions about the safety of beef. The high-protein diets that I've seen don't address such safety issues. Consumers of conventional beef have no way of knowing what their hamburger ate, how it was medicated and what growth hormones, if any, were implanted.

The World Health Organization (WHO) recommended in 2003 that all nations ban the routine use of low-levels of antibiotics as growth stimulators. (Marc Kaufman, "WHO Urges End to Use of Antibiotics for Animal Growth," Washington Post, August 13, 2003.) About one-half of animal antibiotic use worldwide goes for growth stimulation, not treatment of disease. WHO, and others, are concerned that such levels of antibiotic use are leading to resistant bacteria, which some scientists believe are decreasing the effectiveness of antibiotics in humans. Resistant bacteria can get into meat products in the slaughtering process; they also get into the environment from farm runoff. (Margaret Webb Pressler, "9 Steps to Safer Beef: Much of What Advocates Propose, Cattlemen and Government Oppose," Washington Post, January 18, 2004.) Denmark imposed a ban on growth-oriented antibiotics in 1998, and McDonald's told its suppliers to cut back. Apart from antibiotics, animal products are still used in animal feeds. Cattle blood is processed into a milk substitute for calves, and cattle byproducts are fed to chickens and hogs.

As of October, 2005, it was still permitted to feed cattle poultry litter (protein-rich manure, urine and whatever else is cleaned from a poultry house); I did this for several years in the late 1980s. In January, 2004, the federal Food and Drug Administration proposed to end the practice of including high-risk meat and bone meal derived from cattle in animal feed, prohibit using mammalian and avian meat and bone meal in ruminant feed, and stop using materials from disabled and dead cattle in animal feed. The FDA's proposed rules would not end feeding litter to cattle. In slaughterhouses, Federal inspectors do not inspect each carcass, and testing for pathogens like the deadly *E coli* Q157:H7 is inadequate.

My feeling is that the American beef and meat industries would do far better in the long run to embrace product safety fully rather than reluctantly and piecemeal. Each scare—mad-cow, *E-coli* deaths from contaminated hamburger, the January 2004 recall of Giordano ready-to-eat deli meats due to *Listeria monoctyogene* contamination, hormone implants, resistant bacteria—softens demand and price, making it harder for farmers to make a living from raising cattle. (Food recalls can be accessed at the USDA's Food Safety and Inspection Service's website: http://www.fsis.usda.gov; click on Food Recalls and Alerts. Most meat and poultry recalls involve contamination that occurs at the processing plants, but mad-cow and concerns over hormones and resistant bacteria would need to be regulated on the farm.) If you are looking to buy a small cattle farm, the bottom line is something like this: count on cattle to keep your pasture cropped, your farm qualified for IRS farm treatment and a source of Christmas money

What the mad-cow episode blurs is the fundamental problem in agricultural commodity production, beef and otherwise, namely **chronic overcapacity**. Too much production capacity leads to overproduction and low producer prices. America has the capacity—land and other resources—to increase the supply of most row crops by 25 percent in a year or two with no increase in productivity. Meat and milk products would take additional time. In a real pinch, some crops might be increased by 50 to 100 percent by planting marginal land, crop shifting and other strategies. The marginal capacity—land, capital, labor—for each crop is not cost-efficient and is normally used for activities that make more financial sense. But this capacity can be swung from one use to another when the cold winds of January bring the scent of higher fall prices. The relative ease of having farmers of most kinds being able to increase output quickly undercuts producer prices permanently. Farmers are selling many commodity crops and products at roughly the same prices today as 20 years ago, despite inflation. Oligopolistic processors encourage overcapacity and excess supply, because they profit from cheap farm commodities. Many farmers find themselves in a permanent economic squeeze manufactured by the constricting triangle of excess capacity, oversupply and weak prices.

The other factor that is now contributing to excess capacity is the increasing flow of agricultural imports into the United States from cheaper foreign producers. Cheap imports discourage marginal domestic producers who might move their land into familiar harbors, such as corn and soybeans, thus contributing to their oversupply. The North American Free Trade Agreement and other similar arrangements have encouraged U.S. consumption of foreign agricultural products—winter tomatoes from Mexico, farm-raised salmon from Chile, garlic and apples from China, for example—whose cheapness is based on cheap labor and inadequate safety and environmental regulations. (Gannett News Service, "Farmers eye trade deals with both fear, optimism," January 27, 2004.) Those American agricultural sectors such as corn, soybeans and wheat where labor is not a significant cost factor in production will probably benefit from "free trade" of this type. Where labor is significant, American producers will not be able to export and may lose much of their domestic market. If these trends develop in this way, American agriculture will be further divided between crops that can be kept price competitive through increasing productivity based on technology and highly articulated specialty crops that serve particular domestic and foreign niches. A farm buyer should approach labor-dependent farm operations with much caution.

Farming works best these days for farmers who don't need to extract a living from their farming. At the macro level, these farmers bolster their sector's overcapacity. Their supply contributes to low prices for their product. But at the individual's level, voluntary marginal farming is perfectly sensible, particularly for absentee owners and those who are not farming to make a living. My advice, then, is to think of marginal farming as a secondary vehicle for getting you into a second-home farm. Marginal farming will not pay for your farmstead. The primary vehicle for purchasing a farm must be cash from some other source. Assume that farm production will never pay for the farm's purchase—until you sell it.

The books by Jeanne Marie Laskas and Michael Korda illustrate the absolute necessity of financing and subsidizing marginal farms externally. The more marginal the farm, the more this rule applies. With both Laskas and Korda, it appears to me that their "farms" never produced a dollar in net farm income, and possibly not many more in gross farm income. These farms are farms in the sense that work is done there and money is spent on agriculture, broadly, very broadly, defined. Such places are farms for life pleasure and, perhaps, the IRS. "Farming" the tax code and federal agricultural-support programs has become as important a farm skill as driving a tractor in a straight line. Like it or not. For better or worse.

SUBSIDIES

While trying to work a farm for a profit is a chancy proposition, buying a working farm is not as long as it is not expected to pay for itself. Working farms bought for second homes usually require that they continue to be operated as farms of some type, even if not the type that was being worked when they were bought. Otherwise, they revert to weeds and woods. Continuation in one form or another also makes sense in terms of the owner getting a farm discount on local property taxes as well as numerous federal tax breaks.

Apart from tax benefits, readers should know that the federal government continues to subsidize certain farm products and farm (conservation-enhancing) practices. USDA subsidies amounted to about $12.2 billion in 2002, $8.8 billion of which went for commodity subsidies, about $2 billion for conservation practices and the rest for disaster relief. (See http://www.ewg.org/farm/regionsummary.php?fips=00000.) Most subsidy money goes to the very largest corporate farm operations. The top ten percent of the 2.8

million individuals and companies that received subsidies in 2002 took in 65 percent of the $12.2 billion total. (See http://www.ewg.org/farm/findings.php.) Crops with the largest subsidies are corn, wheat, soybeans, cotton and rice. Annual subsidy to an individual farmer is supposed to be capped at $360,000, but there are loopholes that allow higher payments.

You can identify individual subsidy recipients by city, county or zip code since 1995 through the Environmental Working Group (EWG) Farm Subsidy Database 2.0 (http://www.ewg.org/farm/). This site allows you to track the recent "**subsidy history**" for any target farm property you're scoping. It provides the dollar amount of subsidy for each year, divided into three categories—commodity, conservation and disaster. Ownership information and farm location are also provided. Absentee farmowners receiving subsidies for their farm operations are found everywhere. You will find subsidized farmowners in Beverly Hills, California like Mary Ann Mobley as well as in Washington, D.C. and New York City. Most subsidy money goes to corporate farmers and trusts, because they own the largest farms and produce the most of whatever crop is receiving the subsidy. Nonetheless, small farmers are equally eligible and receive payments according to their output. If you operate or rent your new farm, you are eligible for whatever commodity subsidies may apply. The farm is also eligible for conservation programs.

Some readers may want to immerse themselves in the vat of ethical quandaries commodity programs stir. Most Americans don't get paid to not produce the product of their job. Most Americans don't have a price guarantee for the work product they produce. Subsidies maintain the overhang of excess capacity and oversupply. The EWG subsidy data show the lopsidedness of American subsidies in practice: the biggest producers, who need help the least, get most of the subsidy; the struggling small farmer gets a pittance, which helps to keep him in a game that he can't win. Subsidies help maintain marginal farmers—the politically mythic small, family farmer—whose continued presence legitimizes continued payments to the largest producers.

To the extent that our subsidized crops compete in foreign markets, "rich" American farmers as a group are making a living at the expense of poor Third World farmers who generally can produce whatever cheaper because their standard of living is so low and labor, including themselves, is paid a few dollars a day. (Most developed countries retain subsidies of one sort or another for at least some of their farm products, which is a chronic and contentious "globalization" issue.) Eliminate commodity subsidies and production shifts to the lowest-cost producers. American production will be squeezed out of foreign markets. If the American market is open to cheaper foreign crops (themselves, often aided by their governments), American farm products will lose domestic market share as well. This has happened to textiles, shoes, steel, cars, electronics, shipbuilding and even some services. If it keeps happening, sector by sector, some Third World living standards will rise marginally as living standards for large numbers of ordinary Americans decline. Eliminate agricultural subsidies and many marginal producers—small, inefficient (even family) farmers—will be forced to either produce something that earns them a profit in the marketplace or turn their land to some other activity. None of these paths are lined with rose petals. (The social and political consequences of nation-state agricultural policies have been apparent since the 1600s, if not earlier. The consequences of how Europe and America organized the production of quinine, sugar, tea, cotton, coca and the potato are discussed in Henry Hobhouse, Seeds of Change: *Six* Plants *That* Transformed Mankind [UK: Macmillan, 1999].)

Every American farmer has a right to avail himself of crop subsidies in the same way that every taxpayer has a right to avail himself of every tax break. As a buyer, you need to factor subsidies into your scoping as have thousands of absentee farmowners who receive their checks at home in America's cities and suburbs. You should also perform some rudimentary risk analysis to determine the probability of your target-farm's crop subsidy continuing in the future at existing levels. National policy has backed out subsidy to some products, such as tobacco, through buyouts. If you are the type who tries to align his behavior with ethical standards that involve national economic policy and global justice, you probably want to think through accepting crop subsidies. I don't think such a person would have any problem accepting federal subsidy for conservation practices or disaster assistance.

My own preference is to not get hooked on subsidized crops, more for reasons of economics than ethics, though the latter clinches it for me. I think the political and economic undertow of our increasing debt is pulling against crop subsidies over time. A marginal farm counting on a subsidy payment to squeak by is a vulnerable investment. A farm whose equipment and buildings are customized to produce one or two subsidized crops may not be readily adaptable to other crops. If corn, for example, were to have its subsidy withdrawn tomorrow, some marginal producers with thousands of dollars of specialized corn-only equipment and storage facilities would exit the market. If you're planning to grow tomatoes on former corn land, you will have to remodel the farm's infrastructure and obtain different harvesting equipment. A new buyer needs to consider both current and alternative uses of a farm's resources. In terms of subsidies, a buyer must determine whether non-subsidized production of the previously subsidized crop still suits his overall financial needs; it very well may. If you are a buyer who is basically looking for the tax benefits from a farm investment coupled with long-term appreciation of the land, the prospect of losing a crop subsidy payment may not deter a purchase. Less farm income, in other words, might mean more farm loss available to offset non-farm income. If, however, you are looking to buy a farm that you plan to farm, concentrate on land with facilities that allow you to produce different crops each year and make substitutions from year to year without a whole lot of additional investment. Farmers these days need to be nimble, flexible and adaptable.

On the day I was proofreading this chapter, I took a break when the <u>Wall Street Journal</u> arrived. On the front page I read the top-right headline: "In Fight Against Farm Subsidies, Even Farmers Are Joining Forces." Here are relevant excerpts regarding the record $23 billion paid to farmers in 2005:

> A movement to uproot crop subsidies, which have been worth nearly 600 billion to U.S. farmers over the decades, is gaining ground in some unlikely places—including down on the farm.
>
> [A Republican running for Iowa's state agriculture secretary]…told a room full of farmers recently that federal payments spur overproduction, which depresses prices for poor growers overseas.
>
> …any significant change in the payment formula would rock the farm economy. Federal money could shift between regions, possibly at the expense of Southern farmers who are subsidized to such a degree currently that no new system would likely maintain their level of payments. The price of land, which is tied to the income it generates, would likely fall, denting farmers' biggest source of wealth and collateral.
>
> …the gluts spurred by production-based subsidies are a key reason the U.S. enjoys some of the world's lowest food prices.
>
> …nor do subsidies do much for rural economic development. Most rural people are no longer engaged in farming and two-thirds of those who farm are growing nonsubsidized crops such as fruits and vegetables.

The Bush Administration, which pushed through a huge five-year $150 billion farm bill in 2002, criticized farm subsidies in 2006 inasmuch as they "'hurt countries that could benefit from exporting these commodities to the United States,'" in the words of the White House Council of Economic Advisers, "Economic Report of the President" of February, 2006. (Scott Kilman and Roger Thurow, "In Fight Against Farm Subsidies, Even Farmers Are Joining Foes," <u>Wall Street Journal</u>, March 14, 2006.)

I anticipate some cherry-picking-type reforms of the farm-subsidy framework in the near future. One likely change would be to lower the annual subsidy cap from $360,000 per individual per year to

$250,000 while continuing obscure loopholes. Or a buy-out program might be set up for one or more particular crops, similar to the one crafted for tobacco. But it would not surprise me to see farm bills continue to pump increasing amounts of money into agriculture, if not as crop subsidies, then as tax credits and price guarantees for production of biomass feedstocks used as petroleum substitutes. Given that every state has an agricultural sector and two U.S. senators, I'd anticipate continued payments to agriculture with some continuing reconfiguration of how the money is spent to show "reform of the subsidy system."

RENT WITH AN OPTION TO OPERATE

The least risky and most sensible way of making a transition from an urban non-farm person to the owner of a farm operation is to **rent out the farm soon after purchase.**

Farming is not simple in practice, and often not in theory. While it may look easy enough to have 50 head of calm cattle munching your grass for six months, the novice cattle farmer will be expected to be able to apply a world of skills including knowing how and where to buy cattle, selecting medications and applying them properly, identifying illnesses as they arise, knowing how to fix old fence and build new fence, disposing of those animals who "up and die" and choosing a marketing strategy. All such tasks are not beyond your abilities if you read the literature, ask questions and watch your neighbors. "Running" several dozen cattle is easy farming compared with other types of farming that depend even more on judgment and experience.

As a first step in getting your feet dirty, I recommend renting your newly purchased farm to a local farmer who is patient with having you around and is willing to answer your questions. Keep notes on what your tenant does, how he does it, when he does it, and then ask why he did it the way he did. He may be out of date and out of step with the latest advice from the ag school experts. Still, old fashion has a lot to teach you about the tricks of your ground and what has worked in the past, whether or not it is now state of the art. I learned about thrift in farming when I saw my neighbor, then in his late 60s, bend down in the heat of the afternoon to gather small clumps of hay that the baler had missed and place them in the next windrow. Maybe it amounted to a half a bale altogether, of the 300 we made that day. This was my hay that he was saving for my cattle.

Consider renting out your newly purchased farm for two or three years before trying to run the farm as a business on your own. I write as one who did not follow this advice, and spent many hours in self-taught crash courses involving the injection of antibiotics into the eyelids of sick cattle as well as trying to herd blind steers through open gates. Calling this on-the-job training a "crash course" is apt since my 700-pound ingrates spent a good deal of our moments together mashing me into the boards of my barn like demented hockey players.

The seller can recommend likely renters. You can also advertise in the local paper. One or more neighbors will probably approach you about renting your place. You need to step carefully with the choice of tenant. The neighbor who offers you the most money may or may not be the best match for your land. You may want to take a little less rent from a farmer who sees you less as a rich dope and more as a kind of farm-literacy project.

Some potential tenants may be controversial among your neighbors who will be acutely attuned to the "business" alliances you make—or seem to make—during your first year or two. You may not know the implications of what will appear to you to be a simple choice to rent your land for a year to Neighbor Y rather than Neighbor X. Your neighbors know that Neighbor Y comes with a history of crooked dealing, which your decision has accepted, if not endorsed. (You, of course, are blissfully unaware of Neighbor Y's baggage. He was the first farmer to approach you, so you took the first money because it was easiest.) If Neighbor Y rents your place out from under Neighbor X who's rented it for the last three years, rest assured that most of X's family will never be friendly since you are now aligned with the hated Y. If you know no one in your new community, ask your lawyer and the seller for guidance. Be aware, of course, that each of these individuals has his own relations with both the Xs and the Ys. If you ask these questions often enough—To whom, should I rent and why? To whom, should I not rent and why? Who will be miffed if I rent to this individual and why? Am I making a good renter choice if I choose this person?—you're likely to pick up the dimensions of the local alliance networks. Ignorance of these networks will not serve as a defense. Your neighbors—Xs, Ys and Zs—will read more into your choice of renter than you mean to invest. Try your best to make an informed choice.

If you rent your land, you will be entering your new country neighborhood with a second financial step, the first being what you paid for your new farm. The details of your purchase are likely to become common knowledge as will be the seller's opinion of how you comported yourself in the negotiations with him. The selling price is often available from the deed documents recorded in the county at the time of purchase or in the tax records. Assume, for this discussion, that you have overpaid for your farm in the eyes of your new neighbors (but not in your eyes and not objectively in terms of comparable properties). Your rental candidates will assume that since you overpaid for your farm, you will accept something less than fair market rental value for your land. If these potential renters pay fair market rental, they may fear they will be seen as fools by the boys down at the Home-Cooked, Slow-Speed Interface Grille who scrutinize such matters.

A new owner can approach this rental problem in one of two ways. First, you can use **neutral third-party authority** to establish a fair rental rate. Your "neutral" authorities might be drawn from the local banker, county extension agent, real-estate brokers, stockyard owner, grain merchants, buyers of your farm product, Farm Bureau representatives, the local lawyer who handled your purchase and the local CPA who will advise you on farm taxes. Ask such folks what the going rate is for your type of land, even for your particular farm. Use that information to establish a fair rental value. Then use the generic "they say" to inform your prospective tenant of what you expect: "They [local, objective authorities] say my farm should rent for $X per acre. I've checked around on this number, and there's a consensus." You should plead in your own ignorance on this subject and rely solely on the impartial, uninterested and never named authorities you've consulted. If really pressed by the renter on this point, say something like, I've talked to several farmers, bankers, lawyers and CPAs in the county. This method should get you pretty close to a fair rental number, if not dead on. Don't inflate the consensus number; that type of behavior will backfire. If the seller rented the farm a year or two before you bought it, use that number as your own.

The second method relies on the same research from local authorities, but you use it to **market your farm rental outside your neighborhood**. You might offend all your new neighbors if you choose to not rent your land locally, but you will probably spare yourself making long-term neighbor enemies if you stiff everyone a little, equally. (At least, you can't be accused of playing favorites.) The exception to this small-offense-to-everyone tactic is the case where a neighbor has rented your land for a number of years and has come to depend on it, psychologically and/or financially. Make your best effort to continue with this person. If he's been paying less-than-market rental, it's fair for you to show him your consensus per-acre rental number, which he can meet or not at his choice. If you back him out of a long-standing arrangement or if he backs himself out because he's unwilling to pay market value, assume that relations between the two of you (and his alliance network) will be stiff for at least a decade or two. Make sure to consider the non-dollar benefits from continuing a below-market rental with a neighbor. You can agree to continue the discounted rental if he's willing to help you in other ways. If, on the other hand, the negotiations descend to a point where he's threatening you with one thing or another if you don't do what he wants, don't start with him. Extortion feeds on itself.

Non-local rental works best when the property has not previously been rented to a neighbor. It buys you a couple of years to learn the folks in your new neighborhood and how each relates to you and you to them. Once you have a sense of the **alliance networks** in your neighborhood, you can choose to join or stay out. These networks are often based on family connections (and disconnections), church, club memberships, work relationships and assorted historic squabbles, loyalties and sleights that will never be forgotten or forgiven. It will take you years to discover all the layers, ties and crossed circuits within and among these networks. Do not be surprised to find 60-year-old grievances recounted as if they are current. Do not be surprised if you are held partially responsible for a dispute that happened 50 years earlier where your predecessor in title did something that offended a neighboring family. If a fence line you now own was built on your neighbor's property three owners back, you will be partially blamed for that transgression—and you should fix it the next time new fence is built. The trick is not to step too deeply into too many of these holes; give yourself time to learn where they are and how deep each is.

You can find a non-local renter by advertising in both local and non-local papers. Non-local farmers read your local paper for just this reason. The ad should be placed at least two months before the renter will need the property, and certain types of farming will require their farmers to plan as much as a year in advance. The advance time is needed to integrate the new rental property into the farmer's other lands, figure out schedules, labor and financing. Some farmland is easier to rent to non-local farmers than others. Grazing land is readily rented, both locally and non-locally, since cattle and sheep are easily transported and can be bought at spring sales for six-month, spring-to-fall grazing leases. Rental may become more difficult when large pieces of equipment have to be trucked from a distance. There are farmers who are set up to manage equipment rotation, but they may want a discounted rental price owing to their additional logistical expense.

If, incidentally, no local farmer expresses an interest in renting the farmable portion of your new property, it's reasonable to assume that they know something that you didn't and don't—at least, until you're able to prove otherwise. I would not attribute the absence of local renters to shyness. Had the Laskases tried to rent their 50 acres of thorns, local cattle farmers would have probably passed it up, even at a discount. Fences would have had to have been repaired. Dense multiflora rose will scratch the eyes of cattle, increasing the likelihood of pinkeye. Renters do not want to "get up" their livestock through pasture clogged with blackberry brambles and thorn groves. The hassle of making use of that type of pasture would discourage most renters. The same hilly acreage, reasonably clean and clear, should find a ready pasture market.

Inasmuch as this is your second "public" piece of local business, treat everyone involved with respect and care, especially those who propose terms to you that are so nonsensically one-sided that you want to laugh. Try to pick a tenant who you feel will take some responsibility for your land and who comes across as a rational problem-solver. Avoid the candidates who tend to personalize business relationships, those who talk about how they got the better of someone in some past deal, the man who tells you how the world of "them" is arrayed against him, the man who can see only his way to accomplish any particular task, and the man who sees every transaction as a zero-sum game and is uncomfortable with the idea of win-win. Look for someone you can count on to live up to the terms of your agreement. Look for someone with a history of successful farm rentals in your area. If you have doubts about an individual, ask for and then check several local references.

Rent payment is a matter of how much but also of when. Many farmers borrow to get their crop in during the early spring and repay after the fall harvest. They will want to pay their rent at the end of the season when they have money, not in the spring when they may have to borrow it. If you agree to an end-of-the-season payment you risk not getting paid the full rental owing to any of a dozen bad breaks that befell your tenant—none of which are your fault. You will certainly lose the use of or interest on money paid at the beginning of the lease. I recommend against end-of-season rental payments because the renter has nothing to lose by trying to reduce the rent when it's due. If he chooses to short you $500 or $1,000 because of drought, low prices or any other reason, it may not be worth suing for full payment. **I recommend getting all farm rental money upfront in a lump sum**. In most situations, you will not have to discount the rental sum for full payment at the start of the tenancy. If you agree to a two-step payment schedule—half at the beginning of the lease, half at the end—make sure that the second payment occurs before the renter has left with his equipment, livestock and harvest.

Rent is usually paid in cash. Part of the rental can be worked out as in-kind labor, materials or equipment. Keep in mind that you will have to treat in-kind rental "income" no differently than you treat cash for tax purposes.

I advise inexperienced farmowners against renting their property on the basis of a division of anticipated crop income unless they made their fortune by consistently beating the house in Las Vegas. This is generally referred to as "**shares**," whereby the landlord (you) and the tenant divide either the gross income or the net income according to percentages agreed to at the time the rental agreement is negotiated. While a shares format may entice you with penciled-in upsides, the reality of farming may teach you the many downsides of playing in this crapshoot. Apart from the risks from natural phenomena—rain, drought, flood, lightning, disease, pests, hail, freezes, etc.—you are vulnerable to dishonest dealing by your tenant in the sale of his crop. Never do shares with someone who knows more than you know about what he's doing unless you have solid reasons to trust him. A shares format can work for an inexperienced, absentee farmowner, but it requires a thoroughly conscientious and ethical tenant. Such folks exist. I've run into them, but I've also run into their lesser relations.

You, a landlord now in the literal sense, should have a **written lease** with your tenant that spells out the terms of your arrangement. You will want to believe that a handshake will do. It probably will in the sense that you will allow your land to be used and your tenant will pay you the agreed-on amount, according to the payment schedule. What a handshake leaves out are all the details of a contract concerning the allocation of liability, things you want to prohibit, how disagreements or contract breaches are to be resolved and so on. While oral business contracts are binding on both parties (oral "contracts" are not binding when they involve the sale of real estate with a few exceptions), oral terms are easily forgotten or misconstrued whether or not a disagreement has arisen. It's easy enough for written contracts to have different interpretations. Oral agreements are difficult to enforce if only because it's so hard for the disputing parties to agree on what they had agreed. Before you (or your lawyer) write a farm lease, talk to your tenant at length about the terms that will be mutually acceptable. Work out as much as possible orally and then commit those understandings to paper. Don't blindside your new tenant with a full-dress lawyer's contract whose liability exclusions, waivers and except-thats are designed to flummox the U.S. Supreme Court.

While your new neighbors will stamp you as an incorrigible urban intellectual for insisting on a written farm lease, the alternatives are worse and can lead to more troublesome disputes than any you might foment in negotiating a written contract. "Paper people" like me tend to trust paper more than people while "non-paper people" tend to distrust both paper and paper people. If you are a college-educated paper person—i.e., someone who makes a middle-class living manipulating words and numbers—who is renting to a farmer unlike yourself, you should be prepared to overlay your written contract with a full discussion of what you think the written language means. In other words, get your contract down and understood, both in writing and face to face. You are not doing this because your tenant is dumb; he is far smarter than you are about renting your land. You are doing this because you are getting into a business and legal relationship that is both familiar and unfamiliar to both you and your tenant. It's important for you to explain yourself, eye to eye, because your tenant will understand a lease for your farm from the dirt up while you will understand it from the words down. The **oral overlay** will benefit both parties by clarifying intentions in light of on-the-ground reality. As landlord, you have to work with the tenant "within the four corners of the lease," and working with the tenant demands frank discussion before problems emerge. When you find your tenant objecting to something you've proposed in writing, work it out then and there. Leaving ambiguity or disagreement hovering in the background buys nothing but trouble in some future foreground. Finally, don't surprise your tenant with a new "demand" after you've reached an agreement. Make sure to live up to your obligations. Act toward your tenant as you want him to act toward you, so to speak. If the tenant is a neighbor, a lease provides you with another channel to introduce yourself to your new community. Hissy-fits over pennies may be your preferred negotiating tactic in the urban jungle, but don't use it with your new country neighbor.

Farm/land leases will vary with the type of land and type of farming operation. Local lawyers will be experienced with rental terms appropriate for your new farm. State agricultural universities, which you can access directly or through the **county extension agent**, will usually have model contracts for different types of agricultural operations. Agricultural and forestry faculty at land-grant universities who are associated with the state's **Cooperative Extension Service** make themselves available to the public by phone, letter and e-mail as well as through seminars. Many extension publications are available on the Internet. They should be available on each state's extension service's website, e.g., Virginia's is www.ext.vt.edu/pubs with "vt" standing for Virginia Tech. Virginia's site links to other states. These publications provide an introduction to their subjects, but vary greatly in their depth and detail. Many agricultural counties have extension offices with one or more agents. Some extension agents specialize in one or more crops of local interest. Sample leases and other agricultural documents of a legal nature are available from the extension service in many states. I would review any generic legal document from any source with my local counsel. If you are working with organic agriculture, environmental practices and non-conventional ideas, you will have to dig deeper for lease language than the extension service's forms. You can work up this language yourself and have your lawyer review it. You can also contact advocacy organizations, such as your state's association of organic farmers, for help in drafting specific language.

The minimum components of your lease agreement are:

- **parties** to the agreement. (Is the tenant an individual or a corporation? Who is bound by the agreement?)

- **mailing address, phone and fax numbers of both parties**

- **duration** of the lease

- **description of the land** that is subject to the lease

- **description of land and facilities** that are outside the lease or exceptions to it. (specify land and/or buildings reserved by the landlord for his exclusive use; or woodlands to be used for grazing but not for harvesting timber)

- **definition of what is being rented** (all land and all agricultural buildings and facilities; all land, but just some facilities; water rights; federal subsidy payments or crop allotments; capital equipment; livestock)

- **post-lease**; what happens if tenant's livestock, crop or equipment are still on the land after the lease expires. (grace period; penalty for late removal?)

- **rental payment schedule**

- **storage rights**, if any, in landlord's barns, silos, buildings

- **allocation of maintenance responsibilities** between landlord and tenant for rented buildings, facilities, fences, etc. (Have some idea of what normal wear and tear means. Who fixes fence holes? Who chases fugitive cattle?)

- **practices permitted and prohibited** (Spell out which agricultural practices you will permit/prohibit under the lease. Specify, if necessary, where each practice will occur. If you are renting grazing rights, specify the type of animals you want pastured. Steers, for example, are less trouble than cows and heifers who attract fence-wrecking bulls. Spayed heifers are usually ignored. Steers are also easier to manage than a bull running with a herd of cows and calves. Stallions are far more trouble than geldings, which are stallions lite.)

- **specify place/entrance of tenant access**

- **times of tenant access** (If you don't want to see your tenant early, late or on certain days, put those conditions in the lease with an except-in-emergency clause.)

- **limits/reservations on tenant's use of non-farmland** (Tenancy does/does not convey hunting rights, for example. If you do not specifically exclude hunting, fishing and firewood harvesting, you may find your tenant doing all three on your land.)

- **use of agricultural chemicals** (If you are renting land to be farmed organically, you should get in touch with your state organic-agriculture association and one or more national organizations to determine the specific practices allowed and prohibited. If you are not organic but want to impose some constraints on the tenant's chemical use, you will have to become knowledgeable about the chemicals, their applications, duration and environmental consequences. Conventional tenants will want as few constraints on their farming practices as possible, whether or not you can "prove" that less chemical application will produce greater profit. The lease should state that tenant shall dispose of chemicals, chemical residues and their containers in accordance with applicable state and federal regulations. If disposal will take place on your land, you will need to spell out exactly where and under what conditions. Landlord should be released from liability in the event that tenant's chemical use produces environmental harm or violates regulations.)

- **how will sick livestock be cared for**; who will do what and when. (Tenant should be expected to treat/medicate livestock in timely manner to prevent spread of illness in his own herd and to neighboring farms. Your cattle-raising neighbors will not like a herd of cattle oozing with contagious infection next to their healthy cattle.)

- **how will dead livestock be handled;** who will dispose of them, where and when. There may be a local ordinance requiring burial or incineration. Otherwise, the carcass needs to be dragged to a spot where its natural decomposition will not offend you or your neighbors.

- **landlord is not responsible for accidents** on his premises involving tenant, his laborers, family or bystanders arising from tenant use of landlord's land.

- **landlord usually inserts lack of liability** for tenant losses due to theft, vandalism and accident. (If the landlord is negligent, however, tenant may be able to win a suit against him. If, for example, the landlord left a bucket of antifreeze in a field where tenant's cattle could drink it, landlord would probably be responsible for any loss. Open gates are a not uncommon source of dispute. If the landlord left a gate open that should have been closed and the tenant's prized stallion wandered into the road and died after being hit by a truck, the landlord may be liable for damages to both tenant and truck driver.)

- **landlord waiver of liability for loss arising from natural conditions**. (Landlord bears no responsibility or financial liability for natural conditions such as, but not limited to, drought, snow, rain, hail, windstorm, insects, disease, flood and lightning that may adversely affect the tenant's farming efforts and property.)

- **landlord retains right of entry** to leased property; right to repair leased facilities; to use and enjoy these premises in any way that doesn't interfere with tenant's business.

- **who is responsible for injury/accident involving tenant's livestock escaping from landlord's farm**. (This will depend on who is responsible for fence maintenance and also state law regarding livestock in the road and on property other than the landlord's.)

- **landlord bears no liability for tenant's crop and farming practices adversely affecting neighbor's property and livestock.** (Tenant should be held responsible for damage done by his practices to landlord's neighbors. If tenant's pesticide application poisons neighbor's livestock, it's the tenant not the landlord who should make things right with the neighbor.)

- **how is the tenant expected to leave the land** at the end of the lease. (How are crop areas to be left? If tenant is expected to plant a cover crop for the winter, the particulars should be spelled out.)

- **how are disputes to be resolved**

- **tenant may sublet** only with advance written permission of landlord

- **specify the state** whose laws are to govern the lease when two states are involved

- **premises will be subject to lease** even if landlord sells or transfer ownership

- **provide emergency (backup) phone numbers for both parties**

- **when does the lease come into effect** (Usually it's the date of second party's signature or a date specified in the contract itself.)

- **what happens if the lease is breached or in default** (What happens to rent already paid? What obligation does landlord have to minimize his income loss?)

- **who pays the property taxes on the farm** (It should be the landlord.)

- **tenant is expected to comply with all applicable local, state and federal laws** and engage in no illegal activity

- **no partnership or joint venture is created** by the lease. Neither party has the authority to obligate the other without written consent.

- **tenant's leasehold is subject to, subordinate to and inferior to any lien or encumbrance placed on premises by landlord**.

- **indemnification of landlord** for claims arising from tenant's negligence.

- **if either party fails to perform** once the lease comes into effect, the other has full claim to all damages incurred.

- **notarized signature is/is not required** for contract to become effective.

I've presented these contract components in a general form because farm/land leases are drawn up and interpreted in light of the laws of each state. I'd advise against using a sample lease that you find in a book of legal forms. Such forms can get you started thinking about issues to address, but generic lease language needs to be adapted and customized to your particular farm. It's worth paying a local lawyer to draw up your first land lease. You can then modify the lease in succeeding years on your own if you feel confident in doing so.

FARM LEASES AND CROP GENETICS

If you're leasing your land to a tenant who wants to use **genetically modified (GM) seed,** you, as the owner/landlord, have another set of issues to consider. Genetically engineered crops are grown in the U.S. on about 100 million acres compared with less than one million acres in organic crops. (The U.S. has about one billion acres of all types of farmland.) About 35 percent of our corn and 55 percent of our soybeans are grown from GM seed. The majority of U.S. crop acreage is planted in crops that are not genetically modified as I write this, but the GM fraction has been growing as a share of the whole. (Environmental Working Group, www.ewg.org, June, 2000; Justin Gillis, "Debate Grows Over Biotech Food," Washington Post, November 30, 2003.) All food crops have been genetically changed over the centuries to enhance their size, taste, nutritional value, color, quantity and other attributes. The genetic modifications that are now at issue in the GM crops are those that arise from the insertion of genes from other species to achieve either specific characteristics or new "behaviors" in the host species.

Some GM seed contains a gene that causes each plant cell to produce its own pesticide, often *Bacillus thuringiensis (Bt)*, a bacterium that controls budworms, caterpillars, beetles, the European corn borer and moths. Organic farmers use *Bt* as a spray on an as-needed basis, as do landowners protecting trees against gypsy moth. GM seed with a *Bt*-gene will lead to *Bt*-resistant pests if it is used exclusively, just as herbicides create their own survivor weeds. Another practice is to engineer into a crop plant the ability to survive the application of an herbicide like Roundup. This makes weed control simpler and possibly cheaper. If your conventional-farming tenant does not use GM corn, he will use more chemicals to bring in his crop. If he does plant GM corn, he will use fewer chemicals, but may suffer a price discount depending on the market for his crop.

If GM corn is planted fence line to fence line for a number of years, you can expect to see resistant pests. This is bad farming practice. Your lease with your tenant should require planting of conventional (non-GM) corn on at least 20 percent of your corn acreage to prevent resistance. Twenty percent is the U.S. Environmental Protection Agency's standard, but the Agency has survey evidence that at least one-third of farmers violated that standard in 2000. (Washington Post, "EPA Calls Biotech Corn No Threat," October 17, 2001.) The 20-percent requirement provides "habitat" for a sufficient number of non-resistant corn borers, for example, to reproduce with resistant borers so that resistance is minimized in succeeding generations. Corn-raising tenants can also vary their planting practices by using new GM seed (if it's available), or non-GM seed with pesticides, or crop rotation (growing a non-corn crop that is unaffected by the resistant corn pests who may disappear for lack of food). *Bt* corn appears to have no significant effect on monarch butterflies. National Academy of Sciences' researchers estimated that at most "...500 in a million caterpillar larvae would die from eating corn pollen deposited on the milkweed," which is their food. (Id.) GM corn, canola and other crops have accidentally mixed with conventional plantings through cross-pollination, a situation likely to upset neighbors and lead to disputes.

A majority of food products available in the U.S. market contain GM commodities; most products of this type are not available in Europe. (Gillis, "Debate.") A particular GM corn—StarLink—has not been approved for human consumption at the time of this writing owing to questions about its theoretical potential to cause allergic reactions. Approved GM corn does not appear to have been linked to such reactions after a decade of consumption. Hundreds of recalls occurred when StarLink corn became mixed with non-StarLink corn and found its way into food products that carried no warning of possible allergic reactions. An EPA panel reported in July, 2001 that since its investigation was not able to rule out the possibility of allergic reactions, the ban on even trace amounts of StarLink in human food should be continued. The Agency's green light given to *Bt* corn in October, 2001 did not extend to StarLink.

Genetic engineering is also working with insects (pests like the pink bollworm that ruin cotton, honeybees and silkworms, among others) to modify their DNA either to control the pest or increase the ability of good insects to resist disease. The dangers, critics point out, lie in creating resistant pests or accidental crossbreedings that weaken good insects. (Marc Kaufman, "A Glowing Achievement or a Can of Worms? Proposed Field Test of Gene-Altered Pest Worries Some," Washington Post, April 25, 2001.) Critics are also concerned with "gene flow," the transfer of modified traits to non-GM-modified species with unpredictable results for that species, other species and the wider ecosystem. Much of the battle is currently being fought over whether GM crops and insects will perform exactly as predicted and whether the process of altering one or two genes out of 50,000 is exempt from the "law" of unintended consequences.

New farmowners should keep in mind that modern agriculture has depended for years on crossbreeding and genetic manipulation to encourage or discourage one or more traits in both animals and plants. Our food supply, including what we call organic agriculture, does not use species as they existed before Columbus. (Kaufman, "Alter Genes, Risk an Ecosystem?" Washington Post, June 4, 2001.) The choice that faces the conventional farmer is between choosing a GM-modified stock that holds the promise of greater yields and more disease protection (less chemical use) but carries the prospect of unknown environmental consequences and possible price discount on one hand and sticking with established products with familiar upsides and downsides.

I would advise every new farmowner to go slowly and cautiously. Don't be the first to allow a tenant to use a GM product; approach genetic engineering the way you might evaluate buying a new but promising brand of automobile from a country relatively new to the market. Give GM products enough time for field reports to generate more reliability data and analysis. It seems at this time that the problems that may appear with GM crops are less those associated with the consumption of the end food products and more those that can appear on the farms where they are grown.

Ask the farm seller whether any GM seed was used in the past and then talk to your tenant about his preferences. The tenant will like GM seed because it's a cheaper input than the normal non-GM seed plus pesticides, and he doesn't have to apply as much pesticide—an awful job. On the other hand, his GM crop may have a limited market and a price discount owing to the controversy now swirling around GM seed. The tenant may offer to pay more rent if he can use a GM seed. As the property owner, you have to weigh both short-term and long-term ecological and financial considerations. There is no easy or obvious answer to this situation. You can try to have your tenant rotate crops if that's an option, so that the same crop is not planted in the same field year after year. This is good practice on its own, and staggers pesticide and GM use. Perhaps you can work in a livestock component and a hay crop into your multi-year, rotational land-use plan with the tenant. If your tenant is likely to rent for no more than a year or two, assume he will try to get as much crop/livestock gain as he can without much concern for your land's long-term condition. This may have unacceptable consequences for your land or your long-term plans, and if it does, you have to establish the ground rules in the first lease. If you object to both pesticides and GM seed, your choices narrow to using the land for livestock (which has its own set of environmental and ethical issues), planted grass/hay or doing nothing.

An organic tenant is not likely to be found for conventionally farmed land, except, possibly, on a lease that runs substantially longer than five years. I have not heard of any examples of organic farmers renting conventional land. If you can find one, expect that he will pay below-market rental since your land is worth little until he brings it into compliance with organic standards. That process demands a lot of work on his part and at least three years.

CHAPTER 4: FIRST-TIME FARMERS

Some readers will disregard all of the sound advice I've offered about the pitfalls of buying a farm and farming it themselves. I, myself, dumb and innocent, fell into this very curriculum for acquiring the sound advice I now offer. Once again, I advise that you seriously consider renting out your newly acquired farm for a year or two while you get your feet dirty observing. (The object of your observation is not your feet getting dirty.)

Before you start thinking about farming your new farm, you need to perform an existential and practical self-analysis of what exactly you have just purchased. Many readers will have purchased what real-estate brokers call, "**pleasure farms**," which are long on providing an opportunity to play farmer and short on being able to support a family doing farming. The Laskas's thorn patch with the pretty view and the Kordas' scrub with its nice house are **non-farm farms of the pleasure type**. Often such places were once active farmsteads. Their current agricultural value is usually minimal owing to a lack of maintenance, outdated infrastructure or a scale problem (usually that the farm is too small to produce its traditional product efficiently and at a reasonable profit).

There's nothing wrong—and many things right—with buying a non-farm farm for pleasure. You will, however, run into considerable expense and aggravation in trying to resuscitate it as a profit-making operation, which it might have once been. A pleasure farm is intended to be fun whether it's a second home or a full-time residence. You can have fun bringing back some barnyard attributes to such a place—a cluck-cluck here and a moo-moo there. You can acquire stuff that goes with farming—noisy, dangerous stuff like chainsaws, tractors and ATVs. I know of pleasure farms that revolve around the raising of token numbers of sheep, cattle, buffalo, horses, dogs and semi-exotic livestock such as llamas and Asian pigs. These operations are mainly about lifestyle and don't support themselves as farms. If they qualify as a farm for IRS purposes, so much the better for their owners. You can view an intriguing effort to raise alpacas in a way that qualifies as a farm-business within IRS guidelines at www.alpacas.com. This site shows how to incorporate tax planning into a small farm operation based on breeding niche livestock.

It is possible to take a pleasure farm and convert it to a different agricultural purpose. **Farm conversions** can work if the new farmer has thoroughly scoped the idea and understands its requirements and risks. For instance, you might buy 100 acres of grown-up cattle pasture but only intensively farm five acres of high-profit lavender that you package and sell over the Internet. You might then plant trees on the remainder with the help of federal and state programs. To be successful, you would have to have developed a business plan for the growing, drying, packaging, marketing, financing and distribution of lavender. The tree-planting component of this farm might be divided between fast-growing pines and slow-growing hardwoods. The pines can be thinned about halfway through their scheduled growth cycle and completely harvested when they get to 20 to 30 years old. If you had replanted in pine at the end of the first cycle, you would have taken four pine cuts over 60 years and would then be close to harvesting the hardwoods.

If you are intending to purchase a **full-time working farm** as an absentee owner who is available part-time for farm work, you might consider a small operation that is less than 300 acres and within a couple of hours drive of your principal residence. It's possible that you could carry this off if you had extremely reliable local help who didn't need much management from you. Your help is likely to know far more than you about what you are trying to do and when and how you are supposed to do it. Pay this person fairly and treat him well, because your operation needs his skill and time. A neighbor might be willing to do this work for you, but don't expect him and his family to work for free. Managing a farm for you is likely to be a principal source of your manager's income. Farm size always increases the number of things to do as well as their cost. The further you are from the farm, the harder it will be to be a hands-on manager. Small places can be run from a distance with part-time local help, but at some point size and distance will lead you to hire a full-time manager.

CONVENTIONAL FARMING

Most full-time, commercially viable farm operations are capital intensive and use chemical inputs. I'll call these **conventional farms** in contrast to **organic farms**, discussed below. Conventional farms will come with barns, machine sheds, storage facilities (like silos and grain tanks) and require expensive and often highly specialized equipment. You can obtain background information on different types of conventional farming by reading the literature that is available through your library and on the Internet.

Land-grant universities in each state conduct research and produce publications on every aspect of conventional farming—production, inputs, financing, marketing, disease/pest control, equipment, design of buildings and facilities, handling of agricultural chemicals and so on. These "extension" universities have faculty specialists in the state's principal agricultural products (crops, livestock, fish, timber) whose job is to teach, publish and educate the state's farmers. I have had positive experiences with such faculty over the years; they were accessible, knowledgeable and patient. The county extension agent can get you started on informational materials, which are available for free or at low cost, and provide university contacts. If you are thinking about doing something out of the ordinary—say, grow organic cotton and raise tropical birds on Alaska's North Slope—you will have to go beyond the extension service, which is oriented to the conventional and ordinary. Extension services in other states may be able to help.

Each conventional crop and type of livestock has at least one trade or producers' organization (e.g., National Cattlemen's Beef Association) that should be able to link you to sources of information. Since conventional farming has both a local/state aspect (weather, site-specific conditions, local markets and costs) and a national/international aspect (interest rates, international demand, trade restrictions, national supply-and-demand factors, transportation costs, prices and federal policies), you have to check into both in evaluating how they intersect on the specific farm operation you have in mind. A directory of the major trade/producers' organizations can be found at www.reeusda.gov/agsysapp/farmorgs.htm.

The voice of production-oriented, conventional agriculture is the American Farm Bureau Federation (www.fb.com). The Farm Bureau and its state affiliates provide lobbying, information, links, education, market news, insurance and other membership benefits. It lobbies for government policies that help agriculture directly and indirectly. It favors subsidies, tax breaks, more farm exports and less regulation. It is broadly supported in the farming community for its conservative political positions. www.FarmPage.com provides additional information on conventional agriculture. http://directory.google.com/Top/Science/Agriculture/Publications/Journals displays agricultural journals.

Conventional agriculture is intimately wrapped up with a wide variety of federal assistance and credit programs, national and international marketing efforts, environmental and safety regulations, research and tax policies. Each product sector is organized to promote its interests, and umbrella organizations represent agriculture as a single industry. A farm buyer needs to become aware of the specific benefits (crop subsidies, research, technical help) that are available for the products his farm produces as well as the general benefits that are available to farm operators (tax breaks, financing, loans, cost-share programs and assorted assistance such as payments through the Agricultural Market Transition Act [AMTA] and Loan Deficiency Payments [LDPs]). The scope of federal agricultural policy can be best gleaned by scrolling through the **Farm Security and Rural Investment Act of 2002 (PL 107-171)**, the most recent omnibus farm legislation. (See http://www.fsa.usda.gov/dam/BUD/PL107-171.pdf.) The farm bill was renamed the "Farm Security Act" after September 11, 2001 and signed on May 13, 2002. The extension agent in the target county and the local CPA you plan to use for farm taxes can get you up to speed quickly on USDA programs that match your needs. It is also useful to note that federal money runs parallel with federal farm regulation on matters of air and water pollution, food safety and issues of land use.

Agricultural benefit programs through the USDA are numerous, and a number of them involve huge sums. In addition to crop subsidies, the Federal Money Retriever (http://www.fedmoney.com/grants/f0000000.htm) groups current USDA programs into seven categories: resource conservation and development; production and operation; marketing; stabilization and conservation service; forestry; research and development; and technical assistance and information. Programs are often found in more than one category. Individual farmers (new and old alike) would be interested in farm-operating loans ($2.90 billion); loan-interest assistance ($903 million in loans); livestock assistance ($189 million in grants); crop-disaster programs ($1.299 billion in grants); emergency loans ($572 million); crop insurance ($3.31 billion in grants); commodity loans and Loan Deficiency Payments ($661 million in loans and grants); production-flexibility payments for contract commodities ($5.01 billion); farmownership loans ($1.15 billion); temporary assistance for needy farmers ($19.08 billion); and forest-incentives program ($10.5 million).

USDA through its county-level **Farm Service Agency** (FSA) offices provides these loan and loan-guarantee programs to individual farmers to purchase farmland and finance production. These functions were formerly performed by the USDA's Farmers Home Administration (FMHA). Borrowers must meet a set of eligibility criteria, one of which is that they are unable to obtain private commercial credit. Most of the loan programs provide favorable amortization schedules and below-market interest rates. Federal credit, however, is "supervised credit." Borrowers can expect FSA planning and oversight. These USDA farmownership and production programs are separate from the farm loans that are available through the **Federal Land Bank**, an independent, non-USDA agency that is a borrower-owned lender. The USDA programs may be limited to farmers at risk, that is, loans the Federal Land Bank and other commercial lenders would turn down. When the farmer is no longer at risk, FSA expects the borrower to refinance with a commercial lender. General information on these programs can be obtained from the local FSA office, which will provide Fact Sheets and a pamphlet, "Producer's Guide to FSA Loan Programs." Specific information on FSA loans can be had from the USDA FSA Loan-Making Division, 1400 Independence Ave., S.W., STOP 0522, Washington, D.C., 20250-0522; 202-720-1632; and at www.fsa.usda.gov. Novice farmers may not find the USDA loan programs available to them if their financial profile is strong. Some programs require the borrower to have three years of farm-operation experience as a precondition, but the three years need not be immediately prior to applying for the FSA loan. Federal Land Bank financing is open to novice farmers for the purchase and equipping of farms.

In addition to the loan and loan-guarantee programs, USDA's FSA administers other programs that seek to stabilize farm income, encourage farmers to conserve water and land resources, and provide assistance in the event of disasters. The county FSA offices provide information on these programs, which are available to farmers regardless of their financial strength. The 1996 farm bill recast some of the price-support programs by establishing "**production flexibility contract payments**," a set of seven annual fixed-but-declining payments that were independent of commodity prices and production. A one-time sign up was held in 1996. The program was supposed to liquidate itself in 2002.

The 2002 Farm Security Act, above, extended these crop-support payments, but renamed them, **direct payments**. In addition to the seven 1996 crops—wheat, corn, grain sorghum, barley, oats, upland cotton and rice—that were renewed, Washington added soybeans, other oilseeds and peanuts to the crop-subsidy list. The payment is limited to $40,000 per person, per crop year. A farmer need not plant the crop for which he is receiving a payment. If the farm is not currently enrolled, you will probably have to wait until the next sign-up period. A farm buyer should check with the local FSA office to determine whether the farm he's interested in buying is signed up and the scope of the payments it has received. Additional information on this program can be found at http://www.ers.usda.gov/Features/farmbill/analysis/DirectPayments2002act.htm. Federal deficits are putting pressure on Washington to reduce crop-support programs.

FSA offers **commodity loans** for wheat, rice, corn, grain sorghum, barley, oats, oilseeds, tobacco, peanuts, cotton and sugar where the expected crop is the borrower's collateral. Certain dairy products will be purchased directly to support the farmer's price of milk. If you need more information about these programs (as well as the disaster assistance and conservation enhancement) than the local FSA office provides, contact the USDA's FSA Public Affairs Office in Washington at the address above, STOP 0506; 202-720-5237.

The first-time farmer should look particularly at the various **conservation programs** that provide money in several forms—payments, cost shares and rents. These funds help farmers who agree to stop producing on highly erodible land (HEL) and other sensitive areas, or agree to develop water for livestock, invest in fencing for rotational grazing systems, implement nutrient (manure) management systems and so on. Such practices help the farmer's land and benefit the public as well.

The **Environmental Quality Incentives Program (EQIP)**, for example, provides technical and financial assistance to farmers/ranchers in complying with state and federal environmental laws, including those related to HEL and wetlands. EQIP requires that the landowner apply a conservation plan for a period of five to ten years. The plan involves various conservation-enhancing practices, many of which bring a 75 percent cost-share from the government. EQIP, like other farm programs, uses a "concentrated" sign-up period, often in the spring. Your chances of getting funded are better if you apply during the relevant window of opportunity. The **Conservation Reserve Program (CRP)** provides money to farmers for practices that promote conservation of soil resources. The **Conservation Reserve Enhancement Program (CREP)** provides "enhanced" (more) funds for "enhanced" CRP-type practices, including removal of certain lands from agricultural use. The USDA paid farmers about $2 billion in 2006 to leave fallow about 37 million acres of marginal farmland. (Bill Tomson, "U.S. Sees High Retention Rate of Idled Farmland," Wall Street Journal, November 20, 2006.) The local FSA office is the point of landowner contact, but each conservation plan is drawn up by the local agent of the **Natural Resources Conservation Service (NRCS)** with the landowner. The proposed plan is then reviewed and judged by the local **soil conservation district** and the FSA's county committee

Farmers have the benefit of federally subsidized, cheap crop-insurance programs to protect against risks. Various plans are available for different crops in different states, including alfalfa, almonds, apples, apricots, avocados, barley, beans, blueberries, cabbage, canola, carambola trees, cherries, chili peppers, citrus, clams, corn, cotton, cranberries, cucumbers, figs, flax, forage, grain sorghum, grapefruit, grapes, table grapes, lemons, lemon trees, lime trees, macadamia nuts/trees, mandarins, mango trees, millet, mint, mustard, fresh nectarines, nursery, oats, onions, oranges, peaches, peanuts, pears, peas, pecans, peppers, plums, popcorn, potatoes, prunes, raisins, rangeland, raspberry/blackberry, rice, cultivated wild rice, rye, safflower, soybeans, stonefruit, strawberries, sugar beets, sugar cane, sunflowers, sweet potatoes, tangelos, tobacco, tomatoes, walnuts, wheat and winter squash. The six basic programs insure against natural hazards, low prices and low yields. The insurance is written through private companies; premiums are the same regardless of the provider. An overview of these offerings is available from **National Crop Insurance Services (NCIS)**, 7201 West 129th Street, Suite 200, Overland Park, Kansas, 66213; 913-685-2767; http://www.ag~risk.org.

Along with federal benefits and assistance come the systems of overview, direction, constraints, costs and regulations that are imposed on particular crops as well as farm operations generally. During the last 80 years, farming has moved from being essentially unregulated to an increasingly regulated industry. These programs/regulations affect production, environmental protection, marketing, processing, financing, workplace safety and health, labor standards, taxation, land use, R&D and disaster relief. The scope and depth of agricultural regulation is likely to increase in the future. The most probable areas of increased farm regulation are air and water quality, food safety and aesthetics.

The last-named in my opinion is increasingly invoked as more non-farmers move to the country and are offended by some of what they find. (These folks drive the "offending" farmers nuts. It's useful for the newcomer to draw a distinction between the normal sights, smells and noises of normal farm operations in that area and those associated with large dairy farms and **concentrated animal feeding operations [CAFOs]**—cattle feedlots and confined operations for hogs and poultry.)

Agriculture can expect increased environmental regulation, because it is the pollution-generating sector that has been least regulated relatively speaking. I expect that such regulations will be applied to smaller and smaller farms over time. The USEPA, for example, proposed new water-protection regulations for agriculture since an estimated 50 percent of "**nonpoint source**" pollution in surface water comes from agricultural runoff of nutrients (such as nitrogen), agricultural chemicals, manure and sediment. (A point-source of pollution is a discharge pipe into a river; nonpoint sources, like runoff, are general in nature.) **Agricultural runoff** has been linked to about 60 percent of all river pollution. (Small Flows Quarterly, "EPA Proposes New Controls To Reduce Water Pollution from Large Livestock Operations," Spring, 2001, Vol. 2, Number 2.) The point sources—municipal and industrial waste pipes—were the principal targets of the early regulatory rounds insofar as they were readily identified and measured. The next set of water regulations was targeted at the 39,000 CAFOs, each of which is, by definition, an operation feeding 1,000 or more cattle or equivalent "animal units." CAFOs are large—often huge—industrial-type production operations; readers of this book are not likely to be buying one of them. The EPA proposed in 2001 to define a CAFO in such a way as to include smaller operations and require Clean Water Act permits for more than the estimated 2,500 CAFOs operating with permits in 2000. The next level of regulation will undoubtedly involve farm operations that are smaller than CAFOs.

Buyers of operating farms should expect to work within a tighter regulatory framework in the future. Sooner or later, even small farmers will be swept into more and more of it. My guess is that most farms will eventually be expected to fence livestock out of surface waters (ponds, creeks, rivers) and use troughs instead; leave vegetative buffer strips between fields and waterways; abandon erosive practices on steep pasture; implement a nutrient (manure) management plan covering all animal wastes, whether deposited naturally or mechanically; further limit the use of chemicals; keep records related to livestock purchase and sale, livestock medication, seed used, production and crop practices; and follow certain soil-conservation practices that heretofore have been voluntary, such as crop rotation, contour strip planting and no-till/low-till planting methods. Each new requirement will probably be accompanied by a cost-share program that will ease the burden of the initial investment. "Homeland security" may be used to justify the scrutiny. If you hate the idea of civil servants involving themselves in what you do, farming will become an ever less comfortable sandbox.

The best way to scratch-start your education is to contact local federal agricultural offices—USDA Farm Service Agency, USDA Natural Resources Conservation Service and the cooperative extension agent in the county where your target farm is located. Ask for both general and crop-specific information about how their programs have been applied to the target farm in the past and which programs could be applicable in the future. You can then sift through the information to find what's relevant to your goals and situation. Every agricultural sector has its own trade group, and that is your next contact. Each group has a detailed understanding of how the crop-specific and general agricultural-benefit programs apply to its sector. These sources will also provide some information on regulatory constraints, enough to start getting you acclimated.

Environmental regulations involve state and federal environmental-protection agencies, wildlife agencies, natural-heritage agencies, soil-conservation agencies, U.S. Army Corps of Engineers, state forestry departments and local offices (planning commission, zoning board, etc.). Other regulatory constraints materialize if you intend to process agricultural products, either on your farm or at a separate location. You may, in that case, become involved with compliance regulations involving records, reports, inspections and enforcement actions with the Food and Drug Administration, USDA inspectorates and occupational safety and health agencies. If you employ farm labor—full-time, part-time, seasonal or migrant—another set of public agencies appear in your life. Certain benefit programs (money) are available only if you agree to come under certain regulatory programs.

One of the first portals for information about environmental requirements affecting farming is the USEPA's **National Agriculture Compliance Assistance Center** (901 North 5th Street, Kansas City, Kansas, 66101; 1-888-663-2155; http://es.epa.gov/oeca/ag/). The Center provides advice and publications on a wide range of topics, including air and climate, animals, compliance, drinking water and wells, emergency planning and response, fertilizers, facilities, health and safety, heating and cooling, land use, pesticides, surface groundwater, tanks, toxics, vehicles, waste and risk management. The Center's advice covers the ten federal laws USEPA enforces that affect agriculture: Clean Air Act (CAA); Clean Water Act (CWA); Coastal Zone Management Act (CZMA); Comprehensive Environmental Response; Compensation and Liability Act (CERCLA) and Superfund; Emergency Planning and Community Right-To-Know Act (EPCRA); Federal Insecticide, Fungicide and Rodenticide Act (FIFRA); Oil Pollution Act (OPA); Resource Conservation and Recovery Act (RCRA); Safe Drinking Water Act (SDWA); and Toxic Substances Control Act (TSCA). There are other environmental regulations that apply to agriculture as well. The Center is also able to provide county-level environmental maps on its Website.

Most new farmowners are likely to be "**small farmers**" in one sense or another—acreage, production, net revenue, amount of time devoted to farming, portion of farmer's net income derived from farming, etc. No matter how the term is defined, small farms have an outsized political voice if only because they represent the vast majority of farm operations and farm-based voters. There are, in other words, more small farmers than large farmers though the latter are much more central to agricultural production. USDA programs benefit large farm operations disproportionately, because federal crop subsidies and other assistance are linked to the scale of production or the scale of need. USDA also offers assistance to small farms specifically in the form of publications, counsel and money in various forms. The USDA site includes links to more than 150 small-farm websites. (http://www.reeusda.gov/agsys/smallfarm/guide/webs.htm#VIRTUAL.)

Agriculture speaks with many voices politically, sometimes in unison when faced with a common threat, sometimes against each other on the basis of region, product or size. Two voices singing discordantly at times amid the Farm Bureau's chorus on behalf of conventional agriculture are the **National Farmers Union (NFU)** and **National Farmers Organization (NFO)**. The NFU's constituency is mainly agricultural cooperatives and small farmers, two groups that do not necessarily and always share the same financial and political interests. (See http://www.nfu.org.) NFO is a producer-owned marketing organization that applies principles of collective bargaining to agricultural production. It finds buyers for its members' products and also offers a price-hedging service. (NFO, 2505 Elwood Dr., Ames, Iowa, 50010-2000; 515-292-2000; 515-292-7106 FAX; e-mail: NFO@info.org; website: http://www.nfo.org.)

Conventional farming is the first step in a stairway of conventionally organized food and fiber production and consumption. Most sectors of conventional agriculture are set up primarily to work with large producers. The little guys can sell in these markets, but, as individual producers, they have no leverage on price and other matters. The smaller you are in the production of a plentiful commodity like beef or corn, the harder you will find it to make a living selling your product into the conventional markets. It follows that the number of small farmers making a living at it has declined steadily. My guess is that most of these withdrawals were farmers who produced conventional crops in the conventional way and sold them through conventional channels into conventional markets. While the farmers themselves were forced out, their land—at least, the best of it—probably stayed in production. Investors, large (local) farmers and large agri-businesses have probably taken ownership or control. Most of our food is now produced by corporate farms, not Old MacDonald and his horizontally integrated, diversified barnyard.

My county may be an instructive example of larger patterns in farm communities. We are overwhelmingly rural and agricultural—cattle and sheep. Yet, I can't buy locally grown beef or lamb in any local grocery. Our one small slaughterhouse closed in the late 1980s, owing to the high cost of regulatory compliance. Our store-based food supply is far inferior to that available in any suburban supermarket, and we eat less well and less healthily. We have a dozen or so poultry growers in the county, but all of their output is dedicated to vertically integrated processors who supply the chicks. We have one farm-based shop that sells some local food products and a couple of farmers who sell lambs to individuals that they then arrange to have slaughtered. We have one company that produces trout which it sells to individuals at their facility, though most of their product is shipped out. Locally produced maple syrup is available locally. A farmer's market was started several years ago to encourage small-scale production of agricultural goods and local consumption. An effort is underway to determine the feasibility of starting a slaughterhouse. With modest exceptions, my county is as dependent on the national corporate food chain as the most urban neighborhood.

In many agricultural sectors, a small number of buyers/processors structure the market and price for a large number of producers. More and more production—hogs and poultry are familiar examples—is vertically integrated so that the farmer becomes a contract producer who is paid a fixed rate per pound of gain. The contracts that establish these arrangements require the producer to build facilities and accept the price the buyer/processor chooses to pay. The latter may terminate the contract, leaving the farmer holding the bag of debt. This arrangement echoes the "furnish-and-shares" format that was the heart of Southern tenant farming. Tenants did not fare very well under that system.

One view of how modern farmer-to-consumer agriculture works is found in Eric Schlosser's, <u>Fast Food Nation: The Dark Side of the All-American Meal</u> (Boston: Houghton Mifflin Company, 2001). He discusses how the enormous business of fast food has changed the business of producing food, tracing the processor-led restructuring of how we produce potatoes (for French fries), beef and chicken. My experience confirms Schlosser's analysis, which is that it's next to impossible to make a living producing conventional farm commodities on a small scale for sale in the established markets. You can try, as many do, for which you will be rewarded at tax time. Avoid buying the producing farms that are the bottom of the integrated corporate ladder; you will be indentured to your debt and the self-interested decisions of your processor. Don't think you can hustle the system because you're smarter; smarter counts, but your kind of smarter doesn't count for as much as you think down on your conventional farm.

CHAPTER 5: NON-CONVENTIONAL FARMING

ORGANICS

Organic farming is less a subset of conventional commercial agriculture than a different worldview of ideas and practices that are expressed in lifestyle and often business. While conventional agriculture, as I've been using the term, has borrowed a few practices from the organic-farming community, the transfer has not been great. Organic farming must be carried out in accordance with very specific and rigorous dos and don'ts farm-wide. Organic products must meet rigid standards that establish how the item is and is not to be produced. A certification process, periodic inspections and controls enforce these standards. Farm products that carry the word "organic" should only apply to items that have been grown on farms that embrace the totality of this way of doing things.

Organic standards and practices are a matter of continuing discussion. The USDA operates the National Organic Program (NOP) through its Agricultural Marketing Service, which has developed standards and practices for the organic farming industry (www.ams.usda/nop/). Although these continue to be a work in progress, it's reasonably safe to assume that a food product that carries an **organic certification label** is about as unadulterated as a general consumer can expect. Words like "natural," "free-range," "chemical-free," "hormone-free," "pure," "veggie," "meatless" and "farm-fresh" can mean almost anything as well as not much of anything. Such products probably fall short of official organic standards, though they may be nutritious and perfectly safe to eat. The "USDA organic" label means that at least 95 percent of a product is farmed without chemicals, hormones, pesticides or environmentally harmful methods. "Natural" now means no artificial ingredients or food coloring; it does not mean "organic" (Kylene Kiang, Cox News Service, "Is the Organic Food Label Being Corrupted?," <u>Richmond Times-Dispatch</u>, September 10, 2006).

I have backed into a discussion about organic farming by way of talking about its products. Operating a certified organic farm involves having your facilities and practices inspected and approved. Organic farming associations and **certifiers** are organized state-by-state, regionally and nationally. Since the term "organic" has become a vernacular term that is often used to describe a wide assortment of farm practices and products, it's best to define "organic" as those farms and products that are certified by an appropriate association of organic producers. Certification separates those who are organic farmers from those who are not.

As a new farmowner, you may be taken with the idea of growing organic crops and livestock. Your definition of what you mean by organic may not be the same as the relevant certifying agency. You may want to consider working up to certified-farm status over a period of years. You can incorporate some "organic" ideas immediately, in whole or part. You can, for example, decide to not implant cattle with hormonal growth stimulators and confine your wormer to organic-approved products. You can also use techniques for raising crops that require fewer chemicals to control weeds and pests. The only thing wrong with being sort-of organic is that you can't sell your product in the premium-priced organic market. The markets for conventional agriculture either don't value your efforts or actively discount your products for various reasons, often appearance. A one-step-at-a-time transition is a conservative way of trying on organic farming to see whether it fits you and your farm. It may not. I couldn't make it work on my farm, because I couldn't find a reliable supply of organic calves or a reliable market for the finished cattle. While the farmer gets a higher price for organic farm products, he bears more risks and does more work for the money. If you're comparing operating your farm conventionally as against organic, compare your projected net income, labor requirement and risk under both scenarios.

Several national organizations provide services and information about organic agriculture. The

Organic Crop Improvement Association (OCIA, 1101 Y St., Suite B, Lincoln, Nebraska 68508-1172; 402-477-2323; 477-4325 FAX; e-mail: info@ocia.org; www.ocia.org) is the source on certification and standards. The **Organic Farmers Marketing Association** (OFMA, POB 2407, Fairfield, IA 52556; 515-472-3272; e-mail: erorganic@aol.com; ripplebrook@aol.com; www.iquest/net/ofma/) provides marketing information, news updates, prices, land-for-sale ads and links. Research information is available from the **Organic Farming Research Foundation** (OFRF, POB 440, Santa Cruz, California 95061; 831-426-6606; 831-426-6670 FAX; e-mail: research@ofrf.org; www.ofrf.org. OFRF has published a National Directory of Certifiers and a summary, "State of the States," of the organic farming research at America's 67 public land-grant agricultural schools. The research found that of the 886,000 research acres at these schools, not surprisingly only 151 acres were certified organic. The Rodale Institute is a long-standing source of information on organic gardening and farming (Rodale Institute, 611 Siegfriedale Rd., Kutztown, Pennsylvania, 19530; 1-800-832-6285; 610-683-1400; 610-683-8548 FAX; 610-683-6009 bookstore; e-mail: info@rodaleinst.org; e-mail: ribooks@fast.net; www.rodaleinst.org. A good starting point for information links is www.ibibio.org/farming-connection/links/organic.htm. A useful overview is Nicolas Lampkin's, Organic Farming (UK: Farming Press Books, 1992; distributed in North America by Diamond Farm Enterprises, Box 537, Alexandria Bay, New York, 13607.).

Sustainable agriculture is a fuzzier label than certified organic. It is a set of farm-level practices that share certain approaches and objectives with organic agriculture. It differs in that it is not a process judged by a certifying agency and product standards. A lot of farmers can feel comfortable in describing their operations as implementing sustainable agriculture principles, though they would never qualify as organic. A comprehensive list of organizations involved in sustainable agriculture is available on the Internet from **Appropriate Technology Transfer for Rural Areas** (ATTRA, POB 3657, Fayetteville, Arkansas, 72702; 1-800-346-9140; 501-442-9842 FAX; www.attra.org/attra-rl/susaorg.html.) The ATTRA list includes national and state organizations and sources of published information. A second hub site is the Factory Farm Project, sponsored by the Global Resources Action Center for the Environment (GRACE) at The Johns Hopkins University, through David Brubaker, 410-502-7577; 410-502-7579 FAX; www.factoryfarm.org.

Agricultural books—both conventional and organic—are available through the large Internet booksellers like www.amazon.com and www.barnesandnoble.com and specialty sites, such as www.books@agribook.com. (See Fertile Ground Books, 3912 Vale Ave., Oakland, California, 94619; 530-297-7879; 530-298-2060 FAX.)

If you are looking to buy an operating organic farm, the seller should be able to show you its certification papers and production records. Do not buy an "organic farm" without certification papers from the organization whose standards and practices you intend to follow. Do not take the seller's word that his farm is "organic" without confirming its certification history. The seller's notion of "organic farming" may or may not fit the organizational definitions with which you are intending to comply. If, for example, certain chemicals have been applied to the farm within the last several years prior to its sale to you, it will take you several years of non-chemical farming before even being eligible to apply for organic certification. Ask to see annual production records, showing all inputs, control measures, yields, buyers of products and correspondence with the certifying agency. (This, of course, is in addition to the normal farm financials and tax schedules that you want to examine.) If the seller says he is organic, but he's selling to a conventional market, be suspicious. He may be sort-of organic, but not rigorously so and certified. He's also not getting market value for his harder-to-raise product. The buyer should also check with the farm's certifying organization to make sure the target farm is in full compliance. Ask for inspection reports and records of violations or complaints. Talk to the certifier.

If you think you are buying an organic farm and intend to farm organically and market as a certified organic operation, you should write an **organic contingency clause** into your purchase contract on the order of:

> **Buyer's offer is contingent on obtaining full satisfaction that Seller's farm is currently a certified organic operation according to the rules established by the _____.**
>
> **Buyer's offer is further contingent on satisfying himself that the farm is currently in full compliance with organic farming standards and practices set forth by the _____.**
>
> **Seller warrants that the farm has been certified organic according to the standards of the organization (s) referred to above and has been in full compliance with those standards for at least _____ consecutive years, beginning in _____.**
>
> **Buyer may void this contract without penalty if he is unable to obtain information and results acceptable to him**

Organic sellers will not object to such a contingency clause because they know that the financial viability and market value of their farm depends on their certification and being in continuing compliance. Organic certification is worth a premium to an organic buyer who values that certification and wishes to continue the organic status of the property. Organic certification is not worth a premium to a buyer who is uninterested in organic status.

Buyers should exercise much caution and apply a great deal of research effort before buying a conventional farm with the idea of taking it organic. The process of conversion can take five years of exclusive organic practice before organic certification eligibility is reached. Conventional farming equipment that comes with the farm may need to be supplemented. Storage facilities will need to be cleaned in certain ways. The first years of converting from conventional to organic methods will be the riskiest and toughest. Organic soil takes time to build.

A buyer considering conversion should hire a consultant, if only another farmer in the area who is doing successfully what you want to do, to develop a **conversion plan**. If the buyer is truly dirt-smart, he will get a preliminary conversion plan in his hands before submitting a purchase offer to the seller. The plan should address the feasibility of conversion; the types of transition products, markets and prices envisioned; needed inputs; suggested measures for soil and water development; strategies for controlling weeds, disease and pests; livestock medication plans; timing issues, required investments; expected yields; expected gross revenues; expected net profit; risk analysis; and financing sources. You may find on the last of these points that conventional lenders may be a reluctant to lend for a non-conventional operation. A conversion plan should also include a human-capital component. How do you propose to get smart enough fast enough to prevent you and your organic butt ending up in bankruptcy? If you are going to need farm help, where are you going to get it; who's going to train and manage it; what regulations will apply to your farm; and what is the projected cost of the labor you will need?

Plan on planning. Organic farming is not like military battle where The Plan is changed as soon as first contact is made with the enemy. Your plan should include contingency tactics for possible adverse events, such as infestations and disease. Develop your plan through reading, going to conferences, talking to organic farmers who are raising your intended crops and retaining a consultant if necessary. Your plan should include a **time line**, which is a schedule that indicates when things—planting, weeding, thinning, application of control measures, harvesting—need to be done. Where possible, start the conversion slowly to minimize disaster and maintain cash flow. Plan for changes based on feedback and experimentation. The conversion process will take at least five years if you're starting with conventional dirt. Soil needs at least that long to clear out years of chemical inputs and be rebuilt with organic inputs. Anticipate trial and error in figuring out the best way to control pests and disease in the micro-environment of your fields.

Yields may never be as high as before conversion, but input costs could be lower and product prices (when sold to organic outlets) should be higher. You can consider phasing in organic farming by starting with livestock as a source of both cash and manure, assuming you can find a suitable market.

Part of your marketing plan should be to determine the feasibility of **direct marketing to consumers**, a strategy that should generate higher returns than selling organic commodities to an organic processor or wholesaler. The more you can process the organic products you raise, the more money you should net. Farm-based marketing works best when your farm is within a reasonably convenient drive of a city or town. Proximity to college towns and communities devoted to second-home recreation and retirement would be ideal. The more distant your farm is to its consumer markets, the harder you will find it to build a local customer base. You can, alternatively, develop an order-and-delivery operation to overcome distance, but it will require a lot more management and expense on your end. You can also market over the Internet after complying with state and federal regulations and inspections.

If you are looking to convert a conventional farm to organic, seek out land that maximizes your chance of success and has capabilities that lend themselves to your goal. That should be self-evident, but I've seen heads bloodied against the wall of unsuitable ground. Avoid trying to rescue "reclaimed" strip mines, eroded lands, shale banks and arid, overgrazed areas unless you are both a missionary about organic techniques...and wealthy. "Conventional" farms differ among themselves in the intensity of their conventionality. The less invested in conventional agriculture the farm has been, the easier it's likely to be to make the switch. A farm that's been abandoned may be a better choice for conversion than one that's actively producing through conventional methods, assuming the soils are what you're looking for.

It's hard, labor-intensive, sustained work to bring a conventional farm into organic compliance. I would look for a conventional farm that has some of the makings for a conversion rather than fight the problems of converting a hard-shell heathen. Many farms have scaled back on chemicals, and some have adopted soil-saving and soil-building methods. I would look for a place that meets as many of the following basic criteria as possible:

- sufficient, regular rainfall appropriate to your purpose

- fields that have been treated with as few (type) and as little (quantity) chemicals for at least a couple of years

- land that is not subject to second-hand chemical exposure from neighbors or upstream farms

- appropriate soils for your purpose (find out the pH, mineral and other needs of your target crops)

- sufficient topsoil—dirt depth for your target crop (thin soils will require the addition of a lot of organic material, which takes money, labor and time)

- local sources and costs of *acceptable* inputs (manures, lime, hay, mulch, wood chips, crop wastes, leaves, compost, etc; the inputs have to meet organic standards)

- land capable of being grazed intensively on a rotating basis, which, with additional fencing, adds lot of manure to fields and pasture (the livestock need to have been medicated and fed in an acceptable way); sufficient water sources to allow rotational grazing in paddocks

- acceptable perimeter fencing to get started

- weather-tight storage (facilities will have to be cleaned and brought up to organic standards)

- community of organic farmers ("organic neighbors" will be the source of practical wisdom and sources of information about where to get acceptable inputs locally)

If you are looking at a farm that grazes livestock, you should investigate the practice of **intensive rotational grazing**. The idea of rotational grazing is to graze a small paddock intensively for a couple of days then shift the entire herd into the next paddock with fresh pasture for another couple of days, and so on. The number of paddocks, number of animals and the size of the paddocks should be designed to allow sufficient grass growth in the first paddock by the time the last paddock has been grazed. The grazing cycle will depend on your farm's location and the time of year. The cycle is shortest when grass growth is fastest. Rotational grazing allows the farmer to produce more pounds of gain per acre (though each animal may not gain as much as it would have with a lower stocking ratio of animals per acre), use his grass as efficiently as possible, improve the pastures by forcing the stock to eat the less palatable vegetation and increase soil fertility through higher rates of manure deposit. Since livestock is being changed into fresh grass every few days, internal parasites are less of a problem. Using cattle in a rotational grazing system will load manure onto a field five or six times each grazing season without compacting the soil or having the grass eaten down to the dirt. Five years of rotational grazing on conventional fields will go a long way toward preparing them for organic crops.

Rotational grazing requires investment in fencing and water. Large fields need to be cross-fenced, permanently or with portable electric wire, into paddocks of two to ten acres each. Water needs to be available to, if not in, each paddock. Design of such a system can use a hub model whereby the hub is the water source surrounded by a number of paddocks. Any corridor and area around a water source will be subject to heavy livestock traffic. This can lead to compaction and erosion. I've used rotational grazing for 20 years and am completely sold. I run almost one head of cattle (one head = one animal) per acre, which is twice the stocking ratio of comparable farms as well as this farm prior to installing the rotational system. I get almost the same gain per head as when the farm was carrying half the number of cattle. Federal conservation cost-share money is available to help with the costs of installing fencing and water systems.

Much material has been written on rotational grazing, especially during the last 20 years. Three books helped me: Andre Voisin, <u>Grass Productivity</u>; Bill Murphy, <u>Green Pastures on Your Side of the Fence</u>; and Allan Nation, <u>Grass Farmers</u>. Nation edits <u>The Stockman Grass Farmer</u>, a magazine devoted to providing farmers with information about efficient and profitable grazing methods (SGF, 282 Commerce Park Drive, Ridgeland, Mississippi, 39157; 1-800-748-9808; 601-853-1861; 601-853-8087 FAX; e-mail: sgf@stockmangrassfarmer.com; www.stockmangrassfarmer.com). SGF sells books, videos and holds conferences. See also: www.grassfarmer.com.

A farm buyer should have a **soils test** and, where appropriate, a **forage test** done on the target property's fields and pastures whether or not he is interested in organic farming. These tests should be done as part of your pre-purchase scoping. Both tests are available through state cooperative extension services for a modest cost; the county extension agent can provide sampling information. Proper sampling procedures are critical for each test. The test kits come with instructions; containers are usually plastic or paper bags, not metal. An organic farm is likely to require more extensive soils testing.

A soils test will indicate the sample's **pH**, which is the symbol for the logarithm of the reciprocal of hydrogen-ion concentration in gram atoms per liter of solution. pH, standing for the "potential of hydrogen," expresses the level of acidity or alkalinity on a scale of 0-14, where 7 is neutral, less than 7 is increasing acidity and more than 7 is increasing alkalinity. The pH scale is logarithmic, such that each numerical step away from 7 represents a multiple increase in the level of intensity. A pH of 4.3 is, for example, ten times more acidic than a pH of 5.3 while 3.3 is 100 times more acidic than 5.3. Farmers may call acidic soils "sour" and alkaline soils "sweet." Pasture should have a pH of at least 5.8, with closer to 7 being better. Each plant (grass, legume, tree and crop) does best in a specific pH range, which can be adjusted by adding lime and other inputs. Be careful with the kind of lime you apply to lower acidity. Most lime is high in magnesium, which is generally okay, but not always. Some lime—burnt or "hydrated"—helps for a season because it releases quickly, but must be reapplied. pH also indicates acidity in surface waters, notably trout streams. A stream with high acidity, i.e., low pH, stops being trout habitat. Acidic precipitation, caused by emissions from power plants and other sources, has been linked to forest decline in Germany's Black Forest, the northern Appalachians and other areas. The soils test will also indicate the sample's levels of Nitrogen (N), Phosphorus (P), Potassium (K), Calcium (Ca), Magnesium (Mg); and trace elements such as Zinc (Z), Manganese (Mn), Copper (Cu), Iron (Fe) and Boron (B). The **forage sample** analyzes hay and other livestock feeds, indicating levels of protein, energy, phosphorus, calcium, potassium and magnesium.

"Alternative" farmers criticize the conventional soils tests because they recommend conventional remedies, usually more N, P or K, from conventional, chemical-fertilizer suppliers. Application of such fertilizer year after year can leave the land burned out and ill-suited for growing much of anything without its annual fertilizer goosing. The soil tests available through your state's land-grant university's extension service will not recommend more carbon, organic material, manure or compost because those materials are not in the conventional box (though manure and compost, of course, have been in farmers' boxes for thousands of years).

A conventional soils test will tell you what your soils have and what they need, but it will not explain the alternatives available for adding needed elements. If your soils test reveals that every field in the target property lacks a lot of many elements, you will need to get a feel for the cost and amount of time needed to build the dirt up to what you want. Every input will cost you money, time and labor, and organic inputs may involve even more investment, take longer and cost more. The best strategy is to work with the land's existing constituents as much as possible rather than trying to grow crops in land badly suited for them.

If you find yourself attracted to organic, alternative farming, hire a soils consultant from the alternative farming community to test your soils, evaluate your farm's capabilities and needs and recommend a long-term soils-building plan. Farming begins with dirt, so things you do to build the dirt give you more farming flexibility. Organic farmers build their soils by applying manure (naturally through rotational grazing or mechanically), planting organic cover crops and turning them into the ground, alternating crops to supply soil nutrients and "dressing" fields with compost and other organic materials, such as wood chips (exclude artificially colored mulch and chemically treated woods), spoiled hay, saw dust and other products. Naturally occurring sources of fertilizer encourage soil bacteria and earthworms. Though I do not operate an organic farm, I once built **worm bordellos** in each of my pasture paddocks. I stocked them with hundreds of purchased guests who I hoped would engage in a lot of carrying on. Worms aerate soil, and their castings (manure) enrich it.

Building farm soil organically is a basic building-block subject in its own right, and the interested reader might look at Allan Savory with Jody Butterfield, Holistic Management: A New Framework for Decision-Making (Washington, D.C.: Island Press, 1999); Andre Voisin, Grass Productivity (Washington, D.C.: Island Press, 1988); and Joel Salatin, You Can Farm: The Entrepreneur's Guide to Start and Succeed in a Farming Enterprise (Swoope, Virginia: Polyface, Inc., 1998, especially pages 233-324. Available from author at Rt 1, Box 281, Swoope, Virginia, 24479; 540-885-3590.). See also The Savory Center, 1010 Tijeras NW, Albuquerque, NM 87102; 505-842-5252; 505-843-7900 FAX; http://www.holisticmanagement.org.

If you are planning to farm your target property, you should include a **soils-test contingency in your purchase offer** when pH and other constituents are critical factors for operational success. Here is one version of such a contingency:

> **Buyer at his expense shall be permitted to take soil samples from the property's fields and pastures and have them analyzed at his expense. The sampling and analysis shall be completed within ___ days of the date on which this Contract takes effect.**
>
> **Buyer may terminate this offer without penalty and with the full return of his deposit if the test results are unsatisfactory for his intended purposes.**

This is an unusual contingency, and it should only be used when a specific soil constituent (s) is essential to your plan and remediation would be costly. The buyer should know prior to submitting his offer the acceptable range of soil-test results for his intended agricultural uses. I recommend, however, against putting this range into the contingency language. Soil-test results can vary according to the places in a particular field where the samples are dug. A seller could easily perform his own soil test simultaneously with the buyer's. If the seller's results fall within the range and the buyer's don't, the dispute could end up in court. Soil-test results should not be a deal-killer if you plan to use the farm as it has been used in the past. Results are likely to show that the soils need additional inputs, but that should be expected.

This contingency is intended to protect you against extremes—too little of something and too much of something else—in terms of your intended use. If, for example, your pH results show high acidity and your planned use requires a pH of no less than 7, you will be fighting your dirt every year. I would summarily reject a farm whose dirt is obviously unsuited to my agricultural plans. While chemical and organic fertilizers are available to correct soil deficiencies, it's always better to start with dirt that is close to what you want. A **long-term soils-building plan** should be part of your farm planning. You will adopt certain practices (and reject others), grow certain crops (and not others) and add certain inputs (but not others) in accord with your long-term goals for soil building. A soils-consultant's expertise is a wise investment.

One other farm-related issue a buyer should investigate is the **occupational safety and health aspects of the type of farming** he plans to do. Conventional farmers are routinely exposed to toxic materials on their skin and through their inhalation of dusts, fumes, bacteria and other substances. Farmers are in and around manures, soiled bedding, waste litter, disease-carrying domestic livestock and dead animals. Lifting causes back problems as anyone who has pitched 300 hay bales on an August afternoon can attest. Repetitive-motion injuries are not uncommon on farms. Farm equipment—particularly tractors, PTOs, augers, conveyors, and other machines that handle and process raw materials—is dangerous. Children are especially vulnerable to farm accidents.

Farming is dangerous work. I know of two young farmers whose hands were mangled in harvesting equipment. I know of three farmers who killed themselves in tractor accidents. I have had my tractor pop out of gear when going downhill with a loaded hay wagon behind. I have had my tractor's front end rear up like the Lone Ranger's "Silver" when a log I was skidding caught on an unseen stump that held the tractor in place as its spinning back wheels lifted its front.

Farm-related occupational health and safety is not liberal hand-wringing. The National Institute of Occupational Safety and Health (NIOSH) has eight agricultural centers in the United States, each of which provides information and counsel on agricultural health and safety issues. NIOSH is headquartered in the Hubert H. Humphrey Building, 200 Independence Ave., S.W., Washington, D.C., 20201; 1-800-356-4674; e-mail: pubstaft@cdc.gov.

I have used my region's center, New York Center for Agricultural Medicine & Health, 1 Atwell Road, Cooperstown, New York, 13326; 1-800-343-7527; e-mail: nycamh@lakenet.org; www.nycamh.com. My question was whether broiler (poultry) litter, which is mixed with corn and fed to beef cattle as part of a winter feeding program, posed any health hazard to me when I was exposed to its voluminous dust. Litter is the cheap bedding-type material—usually sawdust or peanut hulls in my area—that is spread on the floor of a poultry house. When the grown-out birds are removed, the litter contains feces, urine, spilled food, residues from medications and whatever the poultry shed during their confinement. Litter is high in protein and cheap, which explains its use as cattle food. The poultry grower cleans out the litter and piles it in a covered shed where it generates enough heat to kill bacteria. The resulting material is a nitrogen-rich field fertilizer, and certain types are fed to cattle. The Center did a literature search whose results prompted me to begin wearing an $800 full-face, self-contained respirator. The next year, I stopped feeding litter altogether. While litter has many advantages as a cattle feed, the Virginia Tech professors who were advocating its use had not done sufficient research in my opinion on the health hazards to farmers handling this material or to consumers eating this beef.

In January, 2004, the US Food and Drug Administration seemed to ban farmers from using poultry litter in cattle feed. FDA's concern was that feed given to poultry contained beef products that could contain tissues where BSE (mad-cow disease) is found. Spilled chicken feed went into the litter and then was fed back to beef cattle. Poultry litter as cattle feed certainly fit the conventional farming mode. Whether it is safe for the farmer to handle and its beef safe for human consumption is a matter of debate. My first-hand experience with the dusty, ammonia-smelling stuff for three years—feeding eight wheelbarrows a day for about 150 days each winter—was enough to raise doubts. As of October, 2005, poultry litter as cattle feed was still allowed. Surely, we can do better than feed shit and sawdust to animals we eat.

The photograph below shows a 1950s-style two-story poultry house that I converted to a cattle-feeding facility in the mid-1980s. The grain-tank on the left holds corn that is carried through an auger into the top of the building and unloaded through tubes into swinging trays on the ground floor. The trays are chained to the floor joists above them. The top floor can store square bales of hay as well as about 30 tons of grain at each end. The hay is fed through drop holes along the back wall into a long rack, capable of handling 60 head. The plywood doors on the front wall open outward; grain can be put into reinforced storage rooms at each end with a front-end loader or wheel-mounted auger. These buildings are readily converted to other agricultural purposes, but they cannot be converted to organic agriculture without a lot of cleaning and resurfacing with 1/4"-thick plywood.

PHOTOGRAPH 5-1

An Unphotogenic Barn

If you are intending to have animals on your new farm, you should invest in the latest edition of <u>The Merck Veterinary Manual: A Handbook of Diagnosis, Therapy, and Disease Prevention and Control for the Veterinarian</u> (Rahway, New Jersey: Merck & Co.). The <u>Manual</u> is comprehensive, covering all diseases of pets, livestock and exotica. It offers conventional drug therapies for conventional farming.

Organic farmers use certain naturally occurring substances to prevent livestock disease. Their emphasis is on minimizing illness through clean farm-management practices, like rotational grazing and no large-scale confinement of animals. Since true organic programs prohibit antibiotics in the product, organic livestock growers have to invest in prevention through management. Organic standards do not rule out all vaccines and all "drugs." The certifying organization is the source of what is currently permitted and prohibited. **Herbal remedies** are favored. Homeopathic treatments may also be permitted. **Homeopathy** treats disease and symptoms with highly diluted solutions of active ingredients (possibly a poison) and bacteria of the disease that is being prevented. Homeopathy, unlike vaccines, does not produce antibodies; its intent is to raise the resistance level of the whole animal. **Probiotics** is a bacterial treatment that stimulates an animal's gut flora and "outcompetes" harmful bacteria. If you are operating a certified organic farm, you will be expected to make sure that your medications, wormers, feed and mineral salt are approved under the group's rules.

Different farmers hold different beliefs about medicating animals. Some do only the most rudimentary preventive vaccinations and worming. Most, if not all, feed mineral salt to livestock. Opinion differs about clipping, filing teeth, dehorning, debeaking, castrating, spaying, using growth hormones, docking tails, delousing and a dozen other practices of that type. Some farmers invest in rigorous proactive regimens of what they believe are cost-effective, profit-enhancing medications to control worms, parasites, flies, pinkeye, disease and the like. They believe that each dollar invested pays for itself at the very least. Concerns about resistant bacteria and pests are rarely part of this common dollar-and-cents calculation. If many animals show symptoms of illness, you will need to treat them to avoid a disaster regardless of your preferences. If one animal has something that is not infectious, you will need to weigh the cost of paying for a vet visit against the risk of doing nothing or playing vet your self. Sometimes, the cost of care is more than the value of the animal. Do not be surprised if a neighbor advises you to let a sick animal go without treating it; I've both taken and given that advice. Each case presents its own choices about dollars and ethics. Animals that look and act really sick generally are, and a vet is unlikely to be much help by that time. I have medicated a sick calf because I thought it was the right thing to do, only to prolong its sick life for a week or two. Although each sick calf is its own call, I'm more inclined now to allow a calf without much chance to die. (Recall, if you will, its ultimate fate is the slaughterhouse.) Each of you who raise animals for profit will have to make such decisions.

Many farmers accept the loss of an ordinary animal rather than spend the money on a vet call. Most will do what they can themselves, though a few I know are from the swim-or-sink school. Farmers do not see farm animals raised for market as pets; they see them as economic objects with certain subjective attributes. Farm kids who hand-raise lambs and calves for 4-H livestock auctions learn early that farms raise livestock to make money, not friends. Do not expect that your barnyard will have Charlotte spinning "Some Pig" to save Wilbur's life and your conscience.

CHAPTER 6: FARMING THE TAX CODE, SOWING AND REAPING

Buyers of country property need to inform themselves of the **tax benefits and tax consequences** of owning a working farm, rural second home or unimproved rural property before making an offer. Each of these types of land involves a different set of tax implications. The more you think about buying properties like these **as an investment or business**, the more opportunities you will have to take advantage of federal programs and state and federal tax benefits. Federal tax law is found in the U.S. Code, Title 26, online at www.law.cornell.edu/uscode/html/uscode26. The Internal Revenue Code (IRC) should be read together with Revenue Rulings, case law, IRS letters of opinion and instructional booklets. Farm-tax policy is summarized in **IRS Publication 225, Farmer's Tax Guide**, at www.irs.gov; or 1-800-829-1040 or 1-800-829-3676. Another site with farm-tax information is www.irs.gov/business/small/farmers/index.html.

Real-estate investment has much to recommend it. It lends itself to **leveraged buying**, where a small amount of cash can start the acquisition of a much larger asset. While markets fluctuate and track interest rates, property generally **appreciates in value** over time. As the owner pays off the property, he builds **equity**—cash value—in it. Interest on investment and business real estate is generally deductible dollar for dollar from the taxpayer's gross income, but exceptions exist. If the real estate has buildings and other improvements used to produce income or in a business, their cost can be **depreciated**—a tax benefit that is not available to alternative investments such as stocks, bonds and CDs. Depreciation amortizes the cost of an asset like a barn or a tractor over a certain number of years, allowing the taxpayer to reduce his taxable income during that time. (See IRC, Sections 167 and 168.) Any depreciation allowed or allowable to the taxpayer over the years is subject to **recapture** in the year of the asset's sale. That portion of the depreciation recaptured is taxed at the taxpayer's ordinary-income rate, with exception for residential or nonresidential property.

There are other advantages. If real estate is held for more than a year, any taxable gain on its sale qualifies for the **capital-gains rate**, which in most cases should be lower than the taxpayer's rate on ordinary income. Income taxed as a capital gain would be at 15 percent compared with a rate of more than 30 percent on ordinary income for higher-income taxpayers. If the real estate is held in a self-directed Roth IRA, the taxpayer can have the trustee sell the asset in his retirement tax free. If the taxpayer does not need to capture immediate profit when he sells his real estate, he can do a tax-deferred **1031 exchange for another like-kind real-estate asset** by which he sells his business property and acquires a new one without receiving either income or profit from the sale. Since the 1031 taxpayer has realized no taxable gain through the exchange, he owes no tax at the time the exchange is made. (See Chapter 33 for more on 1031 exchanges.)

In my opinion, real estate is far easier for a layperson to research and understand than any publicly traded stock. To that extent, the investor who does his homework on real estate buys into a less risky investment than the investor who must depend on the financial statements corporations release about themselves. Most real estate is not illiquid, though it may not sell quickly at the price you want. It also carries several kinds of loss potential: you can lose real estate to your lender if you fail to make payments on your mortgage debt; you can suffer a loss to the property from natural events; and you can lose money when you are forced to sell in a down market. Investing in rural real estate shares these benefits and risks. It also involves other financial benefits that I discuss in later chapters. And, of course, you can enjoy country property for itself.

A **farm business** combines real-estate qualities, such as long-term appreciation in land value, with business treatment from a tax perspective. If you are living on a farm that is a business operated for profit, you should qualify for farm treatment. This will allow you to either deduct ordinary and necessary expenses from gross income in the year you incurred them or amortize them as a capital expense over several years. A farm loss can be used against off-farm income, subject to certain limitations. Farm tax benefits are fewer if you do not materially participate in the farm business, or if the farm you own is not operated as a profit-oriented business, or if you rent the farm rather than operate it yourself. The ability of a taxpayer to use farm loss against ordinary income from other sources is limited by IRC Section 469, **passive activity losses** and credits (referred to as PAL) and Section 465, deductions limited to amount at risk (referred to as **at-risk rules**).

From a tax perspective, I would advise buyers to look for rural property that can be operated as and qualify as a **farm business** rather than either recreational land or a for-personal-use-only second home. Even if you do nothing but rent your farm acreage to your neighbor, you will be eligible to deduct some farm-related expenses and get other benefits. Similarly, I would advise a buyer to buy woodland and build a cabin rather than a five-acre country home in a development. The woodland can be managed for timber production—a legitimate business. I would also advise buyers to favor property with an existing home, because it can be a source of rental income and a variety of tax benefits, the extent of which depends on how much the taxpayer occupies the house for personal use. A second home also gives the taxpayer the opportunity to live in it as a principal residence for two years and gain the benefit of excluding as much as $250,000 (single taxpayer) to $500,000 (married taxpayers, filing jointly) of taxable gain (net profit) upon its sale.

From a tax perspective, the optimum investment would be a working farm, with a habitable farm house, with usable outbuildings, with some equipment thrown into the deal, with some immediately **severable assets** (such as, unneeded land that could be quickly sold), with a tenant house that could be sold or rented, with crop land that is currently receiving some production subsidy, with some land that is eligible for a conservation easement, and, finally, with as much land containing **merchantable timber** (trees with immediate sale value) as a buyer can find. These qualities have an income or a tax benefit, or both, depending on how the taxpayer uses each one.

From a tax perspective, I would not buy a property that carries a **conservation easement,** because a prior owner has captured the associated state and federal tax benefits, leaving me with the restrictions in perpetuity. Lacking one or more rights in the property, most of these tracts will always appreciate at a discounted rate, possibly sharply discounted. Adjoining properties, however, may appreciate at an inflated rate, now that they will always be next to land that's not developed or never timbered. I often look for land that is suitable for a conservation easement because of these benefits in circumstances where the land with the easement will continue to appreciate at near-market rates. (Conservation easements are discussed in Chapter 33.)

I would advise against buying land that has been recently clearcut unless you get it very cheap, want it for hunting or plan to put it in a self-directed IRA. It will appreciate, but it will take at least seven to ten years for the logging detritus to disappear and another ten for the 20-year-old trees to gain "treely" presence and shade out the dense new-growth underbrush in the areas opened to the sun by logging. Clearcuts can be good buys for hunters whose game prefers thick brush and young growth, and who are looking to sell at some point in the long-term future.

When looking for farms—and rural land generally—look for property containing **merchantable timber**—standing trees the landowner can sell immediately. Income from the timber sale held soon after closing can be used to buy the property. If you sell the timber for an amount less than or equal to its value at the time you purchased the property, no taxable gain is realized and you will pay no tax on that sale. The timber sale will reduce your **basis** in the overall property, thus increasing your likely taxable gain when the property as a whole is sold. Timber sales and taxation are discussed in Chapters 21-24. Farms often come with woodland at the back of the property where merchantable timber may or may not exist.

I prefer to buy property that is conveyed in **fee simple**, that is, with all mineral rights running with the surface rights. If you own your mineral rights, you can lease them to a mineral developer. Mineral leasing produces rental income and, if minerals are produced, royalty income. Royalty owners can deduct a portion of their annual payment for **depletion**. State taxes on minerals and royalties can also be deducted. As an alternative, mineral owners may be able to get tax benefits from placing a conservation easement on their minerals by forgoing development. A farm whose mineral rights are severed may find a new gas well operating 200 feet from its front porch.

I look for a farm that has a couple of **immediately severable assets**—a second house, land across or down the road that can be divided into second-home lots, merchantable timber—that could be sold without substantially affecting my interest in and enjoyment of the core property. Cash from the sale of severable assets can be used to pay down acquisition debt or for any other purpose. I discuss the **purchase strategy using severable assets** in Chapter 33.

Taxpayers report farm income and expenses on either **Schedule F, Profit or Loss from Farming** (if the seller himself is actively farming) or **Form 4835** where the taxpayer receives crop or livestock shares, but no cash. **Schedule E** is used by a taxpayer who receives income from the rental of his farm. **Schedule F** is used for a farm business and permits the taxpayer to charge all farm expenses against farm income. A taxpayer who is renting his farm is allowed to charge only those farm-related expenses that are necessary to the rental of the farm. Do not claim a farm business using a Schedule C or combine farm profit and expenses into one of your other farm-based businesses, such as consulting, antiques or B&B. **IRS Publication 225, Farmer's Tax Guide** is your starting point for understanding this subject.

Farms are eligible for a wide range of public price supports, cost-share programs, emergency relief and the like—all of which have tax implications.

Genuine farm-business operations are eligible to take farm-related losses against current income from other sources, such as wages and salaries. (This is why taxpayers with high incomes want to own farms.) The most loss benefit can be claimed by a taxpayer who is a "**material participant**" in the farm business, which requires under Section 469 PAL rules that he, for example, spend more than 500 hours doing farm-business work during the tax year. Other options to qualify as a material participant might include taxpayer's participation in the activity substantially constituted all material participation in the tax year; participation exceeded 100 hours and no other individual participated more; aggregate participation in all of the significant participation activities exceeded 100 hours; material participation has occurred in the activity for any five of the preceding ten tax years; and taken as a whole, the taxpayer's participation was done on a regular, continuous and substantial basis for at least 100 hours during the tax year while no other individual participated more and a paid manager was not employed. The at-risk rules in Section 465 limit the amount of loss the taxpayer can claim from farming to the amount of money the taxpayer has at risk in the farm operation. Despite these restrictions, farm-business loss can help many taxpayers.

Capital improvements (farm buildings, bridges, big fencing projects, etc.) and equipment purchases used in farming (tractor, ATV, pick-up truck, hydraulic log splitter, trailer, etc.) are **depreciated**, which allows the taxpayer to write off a portion of each asset's beginning cost (called, "**basis**") every year for a certain number of years according to one of several IRS depreciation formulas. Expenses related to ordinary and necessary farm supplies, fuels, feed, labor, professional fees, insurance, animal medications and other farm-related costs can be charged against current farm income. Interest on the farm's mortgage and loans for farm equipment, livestock, improvements and crops is deductible. Certain capital expenditures may be deducted rather than depreciated when they are **Section 1245 (a) (3) assets** that are acquired for use in an active business. This is called **Section 179 property**, and a qualifying taxpayer may deduct up to $108,000 in 2006 worth of tangible, depreciable property that is "acquired by purchase for use in the active conduct of a trade or business." If you buy a farm that you then rent out, you are not actively engaged in farming, so the 179 tax break is not available. Section 179 property can include breeding stock, pick-up trucks and certain SUVs (the vehicle must have a loaded gross vehicle weight exceeding 6,000 pounds; a $25,000 expensing cap applies)—as long as they are used in a trade or business. If you buy a big vehicle for $20,000 and use it 80 percent for business, you can deduct $16,000 from your gross income in the year of purchase. You can get the same deduction if you borrow the money to buy the vehicle. A taxable-income limitation on Section 179 deduction expensing exists as well.

A taxpayer can set up a **home office** in his new farm as long as it meets the IRS criteria set forth in **Publication 587, Business Use of Your Home and Section 280A**. The home office must be the taxpayer's principal place of business, and it must be used regularly and exclusively for business purposes. The home office, of course, cannot be in the taxpayer's second home, because that residence is not the taxpayer's principal residence. If you move to your farm, look into setting up a home office. A taxpayer who owns an operating farm with a farmhouse on it should not have a problem qualifying that portion of the farmhouse used exclusively for running the farm business as a business expense. This arrangement is not a home office; it is the farm business's business office. A taxpayer with a farm-business business office of this type should not file a home-office form, unless he operates another type of business from it.

Part of your pre-offer scoping of any target farm is obtaining the advice of a farm-savvy, tax-preparing CPA. He can review the farm's financial performance and assets from the perspectives of both income and tax benefits. The time to think through a farm's tax strategy and ownership structure is prior to purchase; I go a step further, think it through before submitting a purchase offer. Planning in advance of purchase will make post-purchase accounting and tax preparation easier and more productive. I recommend the buyer hire a CPA in the target county who prepares a fair number of local farm returns. He will have a good sense about the financial performance of similar farms. He's also likely to have been involved in IRS audits of local farmers. Your local CPA can coordinate his advice with your regular tax preparer to give you a blended opinion as to how the new farm business will alter your tax situation. After purchase, you should consider having this CPA do the farm part of your return if your tax preparer is not experienced. Don't attempt to prepare a farm schedule on your own, particularly the first return where you have to allocate **basis** among different assets, select depreciation schedules and make decisions with future tax consequences.

CPA tax advice is even more important if a buyer is considering rural property that the IRS might consider a **hobby farm** or **tax shelter**. The buyer will be in a little stronger position if the seller operated the property as a farm business, but the IRS will make its determination on your operation, not your predecessor's. Farms, especially those that might look a little fishy to the IRS, should be set up as a business separate from the taxpayer's other income streams. To help establish your farm-business purpose, you can name the farm, set up a separate checking account for the farm alone and transact farm business in the farm's name. You should also write/assemble a set of business-planning documents, beginning with copies of key documents you collect during your pre-purchase scoping. The taxpayer should orient the farm around making a profit from its farming activities. Your accountant can help you think through the tax implications of different farmownership formats and different agricultural products.

You should have your CPA review the seller's farm records and IRS farm returns to help you in evaluating the income performance of the property. The seller has priced his farm as an income-producing business, not as a pretty place for a second home. Your CPA will help you project expected income and tax benefits if you continue running the farm as the seller has. He can also project estimates of future income, net profit, costs, deductions and depreciation for different farming scenarios you might have in mind. (The extension service in your target property's state may also be able to run farm-operation financial scenarios for you; the more conventional your scenario, the more likely that the extension service will have a forecasting program that fits.) Your CPA's estimated projections will fall into a fairly large ballpark inasmuch as each is subject to your management skill, macro-economic factors such as interest rates and commodity prices and risk factors like weather.

You can ask your CPA to work into his projections several **discount rates to account for your farm-business risk**, say 15, 30 and 50 percent. The resulting lower projections will give you a pretty good idea of your possible down sides. The more "alternative" your farm plan is, the greater your down-side risk in my opinion, particularly if you haven't done it before and you're doing it without mentors. You should understand that it's possible that you will produce less farm revenue than your most steeply discounted projection anticipated. The probability of disaster decreases in step with careful, knowledgeable planning and prudent implementation of your plan. Starting small keeps your beginning mistakes small. Your farm plan is not a roll of the dice or in for a dime in for a dollar. It's a conservative business plan, using conservative assumptions and conservative expectations.

Remember that non-farm income represents the majority of household income in most farm households. That's where you probably want to be. Successful farm-business households of this type lose money on paper for tax purposes. Unsuccessful ones lose cash out of pocket. As long as you see the farm as supplementing your non-farm income and providing some tax-sheltering loss and other tax benefits, the financial down side of your farm's business should fall into an acceptable range.

When a farm property meets IRS criteria for a farm business**, active farm losses can offset active income from non-farm sources.** That is why the eyes of big-city CPAs light up when one of their high-income clients says he's looking at farms. But be very careful about buying a farm mainly for its anticipated **tax-loss benefits.** If, for example, you want to find about $50,000 in farm loss to reduce your gross income by that amount, you will probably have to break even on the sale of the farm's output and pick up most of your loss from depreciation and the deduction for interest payments. Assume for illustration that you would need to purchase about $500,000 (or more) worth of farm to produce that $50,000 in paper loss each year while breaking even on cash. The subtraction of $50,000 from your gross income might save you $17,500 in annual tax. The annual principal-and-interest payment on borrowing $500,000 at 7 percent is $39,919 amortized over 30 years. Of that payment, about $400 is principal in the first year, leaving interest at about $39,519. (The interest portion of your annual mortgage payment slowly declines each year, making it slowly ever harder to find your $50,000 loss.) The remaining tax loss of $10,500 that you are seeking would be found in depreciation (a paper loss) and in farm-related expenses that exceed income (cash out of pocket). If your depreciation is $10,000, you are spending $40,000 in interest payment and cash expenses to save $17,500 in taxes at the 35 percent tax rate. All of that $40,000 is deductible. You are also using that money to buy the farm, which generates cash and is an asset that should appreciate while giving you pleasure and aesthetic value.

You might also be able to pick up some non-loss tax advantages through a conservation easement and tax credits for conservation practices. Various types of tax credits and exemptions are available in every state, ranging from a family-farm credit, to a homestead property-tax exemption and a beginning-farmer credit. State tax-credit information as of 2003 can be found at www.ctahr.hawaii.edu/awg/ workshops.asp. Federal credits are available for certain conservation actions and reforestation (a ten percent credit up to $10,000). A typical Iowa county—Mills—lists nine credits/exemptions available to farmers beyond a homestead tax credit, military tax exemption and family-farm credit, including forest reserve, fruit tree reservation, wetlands, native prairie, wildlife habitat, water-impoundment structures, pollution control, cattle facilities and historic property. (See www.millscoia.us/ assessor/ assessor2.html.) The county's assessor will have information on local property-tax breaks. The tax benefits of farmownership are substantial compared with other investments, but I would not take on a farm for that reason alone.

If you're mainly looking for farm-based tax-loss benefits, consider investing in a *large* farm with other similarly situated investors. The group can set up its own investment-ownership structure—e.g., as a limited liability company (LLC), tenants-in-common (TIC) or limited partnership—which then buys the farm and either hires farm management or works out a share-the-crop arrangement with the tenant. Investment advisers in farm areas know of properties for sale and will take care of the management for a fee. If you are a passive investor in the farm, you will get fewer tax-loss benefits compared with an active participant in the investment.

Another way of investing in farmland is to buy shares in a Real Estate Investment Trust (REIT) that concentrates in farm properties. Other REITS concentrate in timberland. (See www.nareit.com and www.inrealty.com. Real-estate books on agriculture can be found at the latter site by clicking on "timberland" and then clicking on "books.")

While farming continues to offer tax benefits of many kinds, investors should not look at farms primarily as a tax shelter, but as a multi-faceted investment that produces income, loss and long-term appreciation of the property. The tax-shelter aspects of farming are of less importance today than they were 20 years ago when marginal income tax rates were much higher and exclusions, deductions and credits more numerous. The passive-activity-loss rules begun then limited the ability of high-income taxpayers from sheltering this income through farm losses.

It's worth a quick look to see how farming has been affected by federal tax policy. The USDA's Economic Research Service found that federal income, estate and gift-tax policies together supported growth in very small and very large farms. As discussed above, a relatively large number of small farms tend to be unprofitable while the relatively few number of very large ones are. Federal tax policies also worked to inflate farmland value; concentrated farmland ownership with high-income taxpayers, both farmers and non-farmers; and encouraged increased supply and lower prices for some farm commodities, such as cattle. **Those taxpayers with substantial farm income—the top ten percent, in particular—had "significantly lower federal income tax burdens compared with all other taxpayers."** (See USDA, ERS, "Effects of Federal Tax Policy on Agriculture—Conclusions," May 1, 2001 at www.mindfully.org/Farm/Tax~Policy~Agriculture~USDA.htm.) My guess is that these taxpayers with high farm incomes were not considered passive participants in the farm enterprise, thus allowing them to offset non-farm income with farm losses.

Looking at these USDA conclusions from the perspective of advice to a prospective farm buyer, I draw three suggestions. First, the larger the farm operation, the larger the tax benefits of all types. Second, while farm operators of all sizes have access to tax benefits, the current set of policies mainly benefits those with the largest farm incomes. Third, federal tax policies taken as a whole over time have helped rich farmers stay rich while most of the rest get by with not much help from their friends in Washington.

BUSINESS AND HOBBIES

Properties that are operated as **farm businesses** offer the most opportunities for tax benefits as well as the federal subsidies discussed earlier. The IRS does not require that a farm business meet a certain acreage threshold, though more acreage would probably help the taxpayer make a stronger case that he's operating a farm business. An organic garden on just a few acres that sold its vegetables should qualify as a farm business consistent with a profit-making intent. So would a livestock breeding farm that contained no more than one registered stallion on five acres. Both farm businesses would generate income from the sale of products or service, and both are run to make money regardless of whether or not they net very much. The taxpayer's intentions and manner of operation are very important in persuading the IRS to accept a farm as a business operated to make a profit. The more conventional a farm looks on its return and the more conventional an operation looks in the field, the less likely the IRS will be to question the taxpayer's farm business. I base this opinion on the image of the slippery slope that constitutional lawyers are always invoking. In this case, if the IRS disallows a non-profitable conventional farm, it will have to apply its reasoning to all other similarly situated farms. That's the politically slippery slope—so it's best not to take the first step down it. Don't get cocky or greedy. The pleasant, farmy places that Laskas and Korda purchased would not qualify as farm businesses at the time of purchase in an IRS audit, because they don't appear to have been operated to make a profit if they were farmed at all. Korda's horse operation could qualify if it goes beyond a hobby. Showing a little net income each year is not enough to prove that you are trying to run a for-profit farm business.

The IRS is trying to catch—and weed out—high-income taxpayers who are **using their farming losses to shelter non-farm income** and are not genuinely trying to operate a farm business. The other type of farm-taxpayer that the IRS will disallow is the "**hobby farm**," discussed below. The IRS's distinction between qualified farm businesses on one hand and non-qualifying tax-shelters and hobby farms on the other can make a huge difference in your annual tax payment. As an active participant in a farm business, you can deduct expenses, count farm losses against non-farm income and depreciate farm assets, all of which reduce your tax payment. It may go without saying but I will anyway, **the dirt-smart buyer wants to operate a farm business that will qualify as such if the IRS chooses to perform an audit.** It follows that a dirt-smart buyer prefers to buy rural properties that lend themselves to operating as a farm business.

The IRS's official position in **Section 183 (Hobby Loss rule**) is that a farm business must earn a profit three years out of five (3/5 rule) to qualify as a farm for tax purposes and allow the taxpayer to deduct expenses above income in succeeding years. (Horse farms have to show profit in two of seven years.) If the IRS determines that the farm business failed to hit these profit goals, the taxpayer will be able to deduct expenses in the future up to, but not in excess of, income. (You can read the IRS's audit guidelines at www.dese.state.mo.us/divcareered/ ag_helpful_webblinks.htm; click on IRS Hobby Farm Audit Guidelines.) You want to be able to deduct expenses in excess of income, because that excess represents loss that you can deduct from non-farm income.

Cattle and horses are two of the most common farm activities. If you are thinking about them, read through IRC Section 183: Farm Hobby Losses with Cattle Operations and Horse Activities, 2001 at www.ors.gov/pub/irs-mssp/a1farms.pdf. This is the manual that the IRS instructs its auditors to use. It shows taxpayers what the auditors look for, such as gross farm income not exceeding deductions; LUQ items (large, unusual, or questionable deductions); taxpayers with other substantial income sources who are sustaining financial farm losses to offset other substantial income; and the presence of fancy buildings, barns and expensive fence.

While Section 183 sets forth the 3/5 profit rule, my experience and sense is that the IRS does not apply this rule either rigidly or rigorously in practice. Why? For one thing, profit from farming is such a manipulable number that it can be achieved, if necessary, simply by not counting expenses. Anecdotal evidence is that a lot of part-time farmers deliberately underreport expenses to make sure their Schedule Fs show a profit on paper.

More important, I think that the IRS recognizes that a large number of America's small and part-time farms are incapable of ever making a profit in any authentic sense. If the IRS were to apply its 3/5 rule scrupulously, Congress would be visited by waves of tax-clobbered, newly-disqualified farmers looking to reinstate the status quo *ante*.

The IRS acknowledges that the 3/5 rule is not the only criterion it uses to determine whether a farm is a genuine business. If an audited farmer/taxpayer does not meet the 3/5 rule, he then has the burden of showing that his farm activity is motivated by profit. The IRS has developed a set of nine criteria to apply in this situation:

1. Does the taxpayer operate the farm in a business-like manner?

2. Does the amount of time and effort the taxpayer spends on the farm business demonstrate that he intends to make a profit?

3. Does the taxpayer depend on farming income for his livelihood?

4. Are the taxpayer's losses due to circumstances beyond his control? Are the losses normal for the start-up phase of the taxpayer's farm business?

5. Has the taxpayer changed his methods of farm operations in an effort to improve profitability?

6. Do the taxpayer and his advisers have sufficient knowledge to implement the taxpayer's farm business successfully?

7. Has the taxpayer made a profit from farming of a similar type in the past?

8. Can the taxpayer document profit from farming in other years? How much profit was made in each of those years?

9. Can the taxpayer anticipate a profit in the future from the appreciation of his farm business's assets?

A first-time farmer can ask for a grace period from the 3/5 rule. A first-timer who does not have three years of profitable farming in his past can file a Form 5213, which postpones for five years any IRS eyeballing of his farm business. Before filing a 5213, consult with your CPA who can advise you as to whether your audit chances increase if you use it.

My opinion is that the IRS mainly looks for the farmer-taxpayer's effort and commitment toward making money, rather than successful results. But I also suspect it also depends on who you are financially. A couple with $10-per-hour, off-the-farm jobs is likely to have a part-time, cattle operation scrutinized less than a CEO with the identical farm profile. Ironically, the CEO may be able to substantiate his farm business on paper far better than the couple, owing to his CPA's counsel to make the farm look like a business and his own "paper skills." And if both these hunches are true, it would confirm my other notion that the IRS mainly looks for egregious examples of hobby farming and high-income tax sheltering. *Absentee farmowners, particularly those with high salaries and incomes, should expect a close inspection of their farm business.* Full-time farm residents should have a better starting point with the auditor than an absentee. But plenty of absentee farm operators have no trouble with the IRS just as plenty of full-time farm residents—like the Kordas—whose farms are mainly a lifestyle get disallowed. I do not know, of course, whether absentee farm operators are classifying themselves as active or passive participants. Full-time farmers will be given a presumption of operating a farm business, whether or not they show any profit, ever. Taxpayers with part-time farm operations, whether absentee or in residence, must show that the part-time farm business is aimed at and operated to make a profit. The expenses and losses the farming generates must have some reasonable relationship to revenues generated or expected in the future. A $400,000-a-year, big-city doctor should not expect to shelter his salary by purchasing a 20-acre weekend farmette on which he runs two potbelly pigs, one of which he sells for more than he paid. Doc will end up with an audit, back taxes and a lonely pig.

I cannot determine whether the IRS screens Schedule F returns for possible **hobby farms**, but if a taxpayer with a farm is one of the randomly selected audits his operation is likely to be scrutinized, as mine was. Your job will be to show (not tell) the IRS auditor that you are trying to make as much money from your farm as your farm is capable of making. Don't wax eloquent about either the spiritual side of your hideously expensive llama or the Zen of watching worms eat the apples on your three organic dwarf trees that you've called a working orchard. Talk about wanting to make money! If you have trouble doing this, have your CPA do as much of the talking as possible.

The presence of farm animals and farm equipment does not make a farm business. (See http://www.irs.ustreas.gov/pub/irs-mssp/alfarmls.pdf or IRS, "Farm Hobby Losses with Cattle Operations and Horse Activities.")

You cannot establish that you are a farm business by showing that you have a lot of farm-related expenses—all of which you deducted or depreciated—or by displaying a lot of manure on your boots—all of which you've left on when you met your auditor.

A hobby farm can use its expenses and deductions only against the income the hobby activity generates and only up to the amount of that income. A farm business, in contrast, can use its expenses, deductions and loss against non-farm income and these write offs can exceed the amount of farm-business income. The difference can amount to thousands of dollars each year in tax paid or tax saved.

If you think your operation might look like a hobby farm, make sure that you do all of the following: 1) consult a tax-and-farm savvy CPA in the set up phase; 2) write a five-year business plan with profit shown by at least the third or fourth year; 3) periodically adapt and amend your original business plan to show that the plan is a working part of your business and you are incorporating feedback lessons; 4) take some university and extension courses related to your farm plan; 5) buy appropriate books and subscribe to journals; 6) join the appropriate crop/livestock associations; 7) go to some agricultural meetings (the travel and other expenses are deductible); 8) track and record everything—your time, expenses, travel, planting and animal histories; 9) look like a business—name your farm, set up a farm-exclusive checking account, put up a farm website describing what you do, have a phone and/or fax/and or e-mail in the farm's name; 10) keep a set of farm books (not a shoebox with receipts); 11) set up your farm as an LLC or other appropriate legal structure (since land appreciates in value, the rule of thumb is to not put real estate into a corporation); and 12) try to show gross sales of at least $10,000 in farm products; the more gross you can sell, the less net, I think, you'll have to generate.

You want to be an **active farm-business operator**. An active farm operator is one who is sufficiently involved in the farm business to qualify as "active" for the IRS. A passive farm investor or operator is one who is insufficiently involved to qualify as an active participant. The reason that you want to be, and qualify as, an active operator is that you are then eligible to offset active income from non-farm sources with losses from the farm. Keeping a **time log**—date, time spent, purpose—can help substantiate your claim of active farm participation.

You want your Schedule F to raise as few flags as possible. The most common flag I've seen occurs when the new, high-income owner buys thousands of dollars of farm toys—tractors, ATVs, trucks, wagons, equipment and new barn—to support a dozen pet sheep and a wild burro that can't be ridden. Expenditures way out of proportion to farm revenue cast a very dark shadow on a farm business. Let me put this a different way: **a great big loss is a redder flag than real small income**.

The IRS has no problem with a taxpayer working full-time off the farm and operating a farm business after work as long as the **part-time farming** is intended to make a profit. This part-time farm is considered a genuine business whereas a full-time hobby farm is not. If you are audited, the IRS will judge whether your part-time farm is a farm business based on your records, your motives as indicated by what you say and show to the auditor and your farm's annual **profit-and-loss statements**. The more business-like your paperwork is, the easier it will be for the IRS to endorse your farm business.

Most farms in America are **small**, measured either in number of acres or net income. The IRS, in practice, does not seem to expect that small farms will ever achieve genuine, sustained profitability, despite its own *pro forma* requirement of profit three years out of five. If it did, it would have to disallow about half of all farm operator households—about one million altogether—who earned less than $25,000 in income, most of which was made off the farm. The Agency seems to judge a small farm only in terms of itself—Is it run for profit, with levels of investment, time, production and loss in some reasonable relationship to gross revenues? The IRS auditor I had understood that my part-time, cattle business would never show net income owing to legitimate farm-business expenses, such as mortgage interest; depreciation; loan interest for livestock and equipment; purchase of non-depreciable supplies; and chronically low selling prices at market time.

Apart from spending two days watching the auditor comb through three years of receipts—all of which I had combed through in advance of the audit—I had no problem establishing that I was operating our 73-acre farm residence as a part-time farm business, with a B&B business in two bedrooms and two baths, and a home office in another room. Expenses exceeded income for the farm and the B&B, but they were proportional and in line with other Schedule Fs and Schedule Cs for the same levels of business activity. My receipts were well organized. The errors found were mainly those in adding long columns of receipts; some were in my favor, others were not. I walked the auditor through the house showing the B&B rooms, the B&B license, brochure, advertising and labeled spots in the refrigerator and pantry where we kept B&B supplies separate from our own food. I also walked the auditor around the farm, showing her the profit-based rationale for installing a rotational-grazing system (lots of fencing and gates) and winter-feeding barn. It was obvious that I was trying to crank out every dollar from the farm that I could. Showing worked.

There are three common IRS-ethics situations that you should consider before getting into any of them.

First, farming presents opportunities to not report income. Farmers can sell manure, hay, seasonal grazing rights, water, supplies, livestock, equipment and labor without leaving a paper trail. Not reporting cash income reduces gross income, hence taxable gain, hence tax owed. If you get caught doing this, expect no mercy. It's a deliberate cheating strategy.

Second, farming also presents opportunities to inflate expenditures. No one will know whether you paid your neighbor $1,000 or $1,500 for some hay, except your neighbor. If you claim $500 of phony hay cost, it will save you at most $175 in tax. The auditor will probably not pick this up from your records if you forge a receipt. Maybe your neighbor will cover for you, if the auditor asks. But do you really want to be a tax cheat, a forger and at the mercy of your neighbor? I think not.

Third, some individuals whom you hire for farm work or from whom you buy something for the farm will ask to be paid in cash. You might infer that they want cash so that no paper trail will establish that they received income. Cash payments, it might be further inferred, may not be reported to the IRS by those who receive them. A cash payment is usually made without the payer—that is, you—obtaining a receipt. If these payments are for legitimate business or farm expenses keep some record of them and write them off. If an auditor asks why you have no receipt, simply say that you paid in cash. If the auditor wants further confirmation of the expense, try to get a receipt. Don't be surprised if that turns out to be harder to obtain than it should be. I would not advise shorting yourself on legitimate deductions for business expenses because the vendor wants cash. What he does with your cash payment and his 1040 is his affair, not yours.

BASIS

The IRS taxes **ordinary income**, such as wages and salaries, on a sliding scale that imposes higher rates on higher incomes. The highest rate on ordinary income for 2006 was 35 percent for single filers, married joint filers and heads of households earning $336,550 or more in taxable income. In descending order, the tax rates are 33 percent, 28 percent, 25 percent, 15 percent and ten percent. (www.bankrate.com/brm/itax/2005taxrates.asp) The IRS has a two-step sliding scale for most **long-term capital gains**, which is the net profit on the sale of capital assets held for more than one year. Depending on the taxpayer's income, the current scale for long-term capital gains is ten percent or 15 percent. (See discussion in Chapter 31.) Farming can provide income of both kinds. The tax-wise farmer in the high tax brackets wants as much of his income classified as capital gains as possible.

If capital assets are sold after one year of ownership, they qualify for the IRS's **long-term capital-gains rate**, which is commonly shortened to, the capital-gains rate. Sale of tangible or intangible business property is not technically a "capital asset" sale although the gain may be taxed as "capital gains." Rather, it's a gain or loss on the sale of a **Section 1231 asset**, which is property used in a trade or business. The gain on a 1231 asset is capital, but the loss is ordinary—the best of both worlds. The highest capital-gains rate is now 15 percent which is applied against the taxpayer's **taxable gain**, i.e., net gain on the sale of the capital asset. Only capital assets, such as land, property, buildings, rental units, big pieces of equipment, depreciated items, vehicles, timber and minerals, qualify for the capital-gains rate. Sale of livestock or crops will be taxed as ordinary income, even if you hold them for longer than one year. They are not considered capital assets.

To figure your taxable gain, you must first calculate what your **adjusted basis** is in the asset. **Basis** is an IRS term that refers to the dollars the taxpayer has "in" the asset. You need to understand basis and its adjustments, because **adjusted basis** is the number that is subtracted from net sale revenue to produce your **taxable gain**. Your tax obligation will be determined by multiplying your taxable gain by the appropriate tax rate. Some expenditures the taxpayer makes increase his basis, and other expenses have no affect because they are deducted against current income. Depreciation decreases a taxpayer's basis in the asset that he's depreciating. **Adjusted basis**, then is, the taxpayer's net basis left in the asset after all permissible additions and subtractions to his beginning basis—the original cost of acquisition—are made.

Adjusted Basis = Original purchase cost of the asset

+ Permissible expenses related to purchase
+ Capital improvements made to the asset
- Depreciation (if any)
- Previous sale of part of the asset (if any)

Adjusted basis starts with the taxpayer's **beginning basis**, that is, the cost of acquisition. Beginning basis in property will include the amount of money you pay to the seller, plus routine acquisition-related expenses—attorney fees, escrow fees, recording costs, broker or finder's fee, appraisal cost, survey cost, title search, title insurance, cost of acquiring outstanding leases, inspection fees and other miscellaneous expenses. Farmowners will do things over time that change their beginning basis, often significantly. All expenditures that prolong the capital asset's useful life or add to its value are added into its basis, dollar for dollar. Such expenditures include construction and/or reconstruction, other improvements, certain special assessments, casualty losses and demolition losses. The sale of a portion of an asset, such as selling timber from the land asset or selling a five-acre lot from a 100-acre farm, decreases basis in the root asset, in these examples, the land and the farm. With certain assets, such as minerals and timber, your CPA may set them up independently, each with its own basis that is adjusted over time.

It is the taxpayer's adjusted basis, not his beginning or original basis, that is used to figure taxable gain when the asset is sold. **Taxable gain** on the sale of a capital asset is figured this way:

Taxable Gain = Gross sales income to the taxpayer/seller
-Permissible expenses related to sale
-Adjusted Basis

Taxable gain is considered a **long-term capital gain** if the taxpayer holds a capital asset, such as land or a tractor, for more than one year from the date of purchase. Sold within one year of acquisition, the taxpayer will pay on the capital asset's taxable gain at his **ordinary income** rate. Most readers will probably fall into the higher tax brackets for ordinary income, which means you will benefit from treating income as capital gains and paying a 15 percent tax where possible. (Capital-gains are taxed at different rates depending on how long the asset is held, taxpayer income, the type of asset and what type of account it is held in. I'm using 15 percent as a short-hand, because it is the highest and most likely rate.) Other things being equal, owners will net more from an asset sale after taxes if their gain qualifies as a long-term capital gain**.** It follows that where a taxpayer has a choice between selling an asset for a profit within his first year of ownership or sometime after the 365th day, he'll choose the latter because of the lower tax hit.

A buyer should start thinking about basis with his CPA prior to purchasing a farm. Your tax-preparing CPA can allocate total purchase basis among various component assets—land, depreciable buildings and structures, timber, minerals, equipment and so on. Basis in the components cannot exceed the property's total acquisition basis. You will need to have the basis allocation and depreciation schedules set up, beginning in the tax year that you bought the farm. All future adjustments are made to the basis values assigned in this first-year allocation. If you're planning to sell a component asset soon after buying the farm, it may be in your interest to allocate as much basis to this asset as you can. Ask your CPA for his suggestions about basis allocation in light of your plan. He will know the minimum basis value that he must assign to each asset. If you have managed to find a farm with a lot of immediate timber value, assign as much basis to your timber as you can so that you pay as little tax as possible when you sell it a few weeks after closing.

SEVERABLE ASSETS

Think of a farm purchase as a bundle of assets—a farmhouse, crop land, pasture, farm buildings, equipment, timber, minerals, rights and so on. Every buyer will consider most of his farm's assets as **core assets**, things he doesn't want to part with. Other items he might consider as **severable assets**, something that can be sold without materially detracting from the core farm assets that he wants to keep together as a unit. The larger the farm, the more severable assets the new owner is likely to find.

Selling a **severable asset** after a year of ownership is a handy **buying tactic** for farm properties that contain such assets. When you are formulating your offer to the seller, you can factor into your calculations the anticipated sale of one or more such assets after a year. In negotiating with a farm seller, be open to buying severable assets—throw ins—that you can sell after a year with only a 15 percent capital-gains hit. It's often more advantageous to hold that asset for a year and pay 15 percent on your gain than to flip immediately after purchase and pay as much as 35 percent. If your ordinary rate is 15 percent, then, of course, you would do better to flip rather than hold. Taxpayers in the 25-to-35 percent brackets are probably better holding, but it depends on the individual circumstances. The capital-gains rate helps a taxpayer who has little basis in an asset and sells for a lot of taxable gain. The sale of a severable asset can help to pay down the cost of buying the core property.

To minimize your tax payment on the sale of a severable asset, you need to do two things.

First, **obtain an appraisal of the individual severable asset's value prior to purchasing the property**. This valuation will help you in negotiating with the seller, and it will also establish your **beginning cost basis** in each asset that you plan to sell. (An appraisal of the entire property will not, as a general rule, provide values for each asset that in combination make up the target property.) The asset's appraisal is a neutral, third-party's estimate of its FMV. This appraisal should satisfy the IRS as to the severable asset's market value at the time you bought the whole property. Insofar as you plan to sell the severable asset, **you want the appraisal of any severable asset to come in as high as possible**. This will keep your tax liability as low as possible to the extent that it increases its basis and thus decreases your taxable gain on its sale whenever that occurs. Don't be shy about explaining your strategy to the appraiser. You should share with him as much information and evidence as you have to support your high valuation. A high appraisal may also help you sell the asset for a higher price. While it's true that you want to establish as high a basis in your severable asset as you can, you don't want to put money into the asset for the sole purpose of increasing your basis if a buyer will not pay you a proportionately higher price to make your additional investment worth your while. The tax tail should not wag the profit dog. Still, the idea is that the higher your basis in the severable asset you sell, the lower your taxable gain; the lower your taxable gain because of high basis, the lower your tax hit on the sale of the asset.

The severable asset's basis may increase or decrease between the day you buy the whole property (and establish your beginning basis) and the day you sell the asset. Basis will be adjusted according to what you do with the asset. A business-related asset like a barn will be depreciated, which decreases its basis over its depreciation-recovery period. If you add three stalls and a water system to the barn, you will have increased your basis. Basis does not increase on its own like land appreciation. Once your CPA sets up a depreciation schedule, basis in an asset will decrease each year. If you're selling soon after purchase, your asset's basis is not likely to have changed much in normal circumstances. When you sell timber, your basis in the timber asset will decrease; where sale income equals or exceeds your basis, it will vanish.

The net effect of additions and subtractions is your **adjusted basis**—what you have in the asset at the time of sale. Adjusted basis is subtracted from net sale income to arrive at taxable gain on the asset's sale. You then apply the appropriate tax rate to your taxable gain to determine the amount of tax you pay on the sale. If you sell your severable asset for the amount of its adjusted basis, you have no taxable gain, hence you will pay no tax on that gain at that point. If you sell your asset for more than its adjusted basis, you will pay either at a capital-gains rate or your ordinary income rate depending on the timing of the sale. The selling of timber from land you continue to own will reduce your basis in your timber, which will have the effect of increasing your taxable gain when you sell the land itself. The tax consequence of the timber sale will in most cases be deferred until you sell the land on which the sold timber stood. If the timbered land is passed on as part of your estate, there may never be any tax liability at all to anyone, depending on the size of your estate and how much estate value federal tax policy allows to be free of estate tax in the year of your death.

With the quick sale of a severable asset, is it possible that you can show a loss? Let's say you buy 100 acres for a total of $100,000. Your pre-purchase timber cruise indicated fair market value of $50,000 for the merchantable timber. Your CPA allocated your basis in the property as $50,000 in land and $50,000 in merchantable timber. When you sold the timber a month after closing, you only received $40,000 from the highest bidder in a competitively bid sale. You can take a loss of $10,000 on that sale of your merchantable timber. Or you might want to reallocate your basis between land and timber so that timber has a starting basis of $40,000, which produces no taxable gain on your sale.

Second, **you may want to determine the most efficient ways to increase both the value and the tax benefits of the severable asset before you sell it**. This is not a simple exercise, and you will need a CPA's advice on the tax angles for your individual circumstances.

Consider the following example. You buy 150 acres, of which your core keeper asset is 130 acres with a farm house and farm buildings. At the far end of the property, there is a smaller residence that the seller rented out. You decide during your scoping that you want to sell the rental house and 20 acres. You pay $400,000 for the 150 acres, and your appraisal for the rental house is $50,000. Your CPA allocates your beginning basis in the entire property as follows:

Small rental house basis	$50,000
Residence basis	100,000
Farm buildings basis	25,000
Land, 150 acres @ $1,500/A basis	225,000
Total Original Basis	$400,000

(I'm simplifying your beginning basis by not adjusting for purchase expenses that increase your basis.) Let's further assume that you borrow the entire purchase price of $400,000. (I'm simplifying again, by not considering borrowing expenses, such as fees and points.)

Your plan is to sell the smaller house and 20 acres in which you have a beginning basis of $50,000 in the house and $30,000 in the land (20 acres x $1,500/A = $30,000), for a total beginning basis of $80,000 in the asset that you want to sell. If you do nothing to the property over your first year of ownership and then sell it for $80,000 against $80,000 in basis, there is no taxable gain in this deal. (I'm simplifying again by not reducing your basis in the rental house by one year's depreciation or paying the 25 percent tax on recaptured depreciation at the time of its sale.) This means you have $80,000 in your hand deferred of tax, and possibly free of it depending on other things that you do and don't do.

If you sell the smaller house and the land for $100,000 after one year of ownership, you will have a capital gain of $20,000. If you pay a capital-gains rate of 15 percent on your taxable gain, you will owe the IRS $3,000 (.15 x $20,000 = $3,000), for an after-tax net profit of $17,000. You will have made a $20,000 gross profit and a $17,000 after-tax net profit by repackaging the two assets—rental house and a little land—into one, then scheduling the sale for a year and a day after you bought the entire property.

Your strategy in buying the original property was a simple variation of "**buy all of it wholesale; sell some of it retail**." The twist in this example is that you divided the property into pieces and then combined two pieces to make a marketable sale property. Smaller acreages always fetch a higher per acre price than larger acreages of the same type. You might have made even more by packaging the rental house with five acres and then dividing the remaining 15 acres into three five-acre lots. Your strategy rested on having an FMV appraisal of the rental house in hand prior to your purchase. If the house appraisal was on the high side, that would lower your taxable gain. Allocation-of-basis decisions may be made by your CPA at the time of your purchase. Your CPA might help you by allocating more basis to the rental unit and proportionately less to the residence that you're keeping and putting into your estate. The CPA's allocation cannot be arbitrary or unreasonable, but within those guidelines, judgment can be exercised.

You can consider adding value to this house prior to its sale in two ways, each of which has different tax consequences.

First, you can make **maintenance-related repairs and upkeep** whose costs you write off against your income in the year they are incurred. "**Write off**" means subtract from gross income; a **deduction** is a write off. For tax purposes, consider this house a rental unit whether or not you rent it out during the year that you own it. Maintenance costs might include exterior and interior painting, fixing broken windows, replacing a broken toilet, refinishing a floor and patching a roof. Together, these maintenance costs amount to $10,000 and bring you an additional $10,000 in sales income above what the house would have brought without the repairs. (More often than not, cosmetic repairs of this type more than pay for themselves by working together to create an overall favorable impression of a property cared for and in good order.) You can also write off the $10,000 in repairs if you use the entire house during that year exclusively for some business purpose—such as a farm office; a storage facility for farm and business records, farm equipment and supplies; or a business library and conference area. If you are not using the house for business and are simply sprucing up an investment for sale, you can deduct maintenance expenses in the year you incur them. Money a taxpayer puts into maintenance repairs and upkeep—whether a rental unit or not—does not increase his basis in the asset.

Your sales price of $110,000 is now $30,000 more than your $80,000 beginning basis in the house and 20 acres. You've not put any money into a property improvement that would significantly increase the house's value or extend its life—that type of expenditure would increase your basis. After one year, that $30,000 is a long-term capital gain on which you pay 15 percent, or $4,500, in tax. (Had you sold the rental house and 20 acres within your first year of ownership, your taxable gain would have been taxed at your ordinary rate.) The $10,000 in maintenance repairs that you've made reduces your gross income in the ownership year by $10,000. At the 35 percent tax rate on ordinary income, this write off would save you $3,500 in income tax on your return filed for the year you incurred these costs. By waiting a year, you will pay $1,500 in capital-gains tax on the extra $10,000 in sales income. If you had flipped the property during your first ownership year for $10,000 more after the repairs, you would have saved $3,500 in tax against your gross income but paid $3,500 as tax at your ordinary rate on the extra taxable gain of $10,000. If you hold for more than a year, you get the $3,500 in deductions for the repair year and a tax hit of $1,500 on the $10,000 in taxable gain. Your total capital-gains tax is $4,500 (.15 x $30,000 taxable capital gain = $4,500). But you've saved $3,500 in overall tax payment in the first year by writing off the $10,000 in maintenance repairs against your gross income.

Your net tax situation looks like this:

Capital Gains Tax on $30,000	= $4,500	($110,000 income -$80,000 basis)
Tax savings from $10,000 write off	- 3,500	
Net Tax	$1,000 on sale of house and 20 acres	

While you make a tax payment of $1,500 on the additional $10,000 in capital-gains income you've made from the $10,000 in maintenance, it really only costs you $1,000 in tax when your total tax obligation is netted out over two years. If you did not actually rent out your rental house during the year you were off-and-on repairing it, you can still take deductions for maintenance and upkeep on Schedule E as long as it was available for rent during the year. Remember: maintenance repairs and upkeep are expensed against income in the year your incur them and do not increase your basis.

Second, you can add value to rental houses and business-related structures by making **capital improvements**. Improvements include room additions or replacement of a major system, such as plumbing, HVAC, roof or foundation. This type of expense is defined as one that extends the life of the asset or adds significant value to it. Unlike maintenance repairs and upkeep, the costs you incur for capital improvements must be **depreciated**, about which more below. The money that you invest in a capital improvement cannot be deducted in the year that you incur the cost, but it will be added to your basis, which helps you when you sell.

Let's say you add a second full bathroom to the small rental house that you want to sell. It costs $10,000, and you receive $10,000 more in house-sale income than you would have without it. The

$10,000 improvement boosts your starting basis in the property by $10,000. You sell the improved property for $110,000, but your basis has now increased to $90,000 instead of $80,000. So your taxable gain is $20,000 ($110,000 in sales income -$90,000 in adjusted basis = $20,000), on which you pay the 15 percent capital-gains rate, or $3,000.

In this example, you would be better off to add value through maintenance repairs than through a capital improvement, because you would pay only $1,000 in net tax over two years instead of $3,000 in capital-gains tax during your second ownership year. Talk over adding-value options with your CPA to determine which are the most tax efficient in light of your selling plans and individual circumstances.

As a general rule, maintenance-type repairs and cosmetic brightening will generate more sales revenue than they cost. If you can combine these deductible expenses with classifying the income as a capital gain, you should come out ahead in net-after-tax income compared with putting the same number of dollars into a capital improvement prior to sale. Capital improvements—roof replacements, rewiring, replumbing, bathrooms, swimming pools and kitchens—do not generally pay for themselves dollar for dollar, though the degree of discount varies from improvement to improvement. The worst situation—at least in a theoretical sense—is to make a capital improvement and then flip the rental house in your first ownership year, thus paying tax on your sale gain at your ordinary rate. These relationships change internally depending on your tax bracket. The carrying costs of mortgage interest and property taxes should also be factored into your calculations.

Let me continue with the idea of selling your new farm's small rental house in light of **depreciation**, which is a tax-accounting process that occurs on your returns whether or not it occurs in the condition of the house itself. The common occurrence, of course, is for an improvement like a rental house to depreciate in value on paper for tax purposes while appreciating in value on the ground.

The general depreciation rule set forth in **Section 167** is that a reasonable allowance for exhaustion, wear and tear, and obsolescence can be taken on property used in the taxpayer's trade or business, or property held for the production of income. The taxpayer's original cost—basis—in an income-producing property is recovered over time by taking a portion of it each year in the form of a depreciation deduction. Rental property, which is held for income production, is depreciated. The house and its new bathroom in this example can be depreciated even if it did not yield any rental income since rental-income production was your intention and the house was capable of being rented.

Depreciation reduces your gross income and lowers your tax liability each year that a portion of an asset's cost is deducted. Different types of assets have different depreciation schedules (recovery periods), ranging from three years for a race horse more than two years old at the time it's placed in service, to five years for a pick-up truck, to ten years for a single purpose agricultural structure to 27.5 years for residential rental property. Commercial property and commercial rental property are currently depreciated over 39 years. Buildings and improvements have much longer depreciation periods than equipment. Generally, a shorter depreciation schedule will be more tax-advantageous to most taxpayers, though the total amount the taxpayer can depreciate is determined by original basis. Basis in the property or asset is decreased each year in equal steps, according to whichever recovery period applies.

The IRS provides several depreciation formulas, each with its own rules. These and related information are found in Section 167 (a), Depreciation—General Rule; Section 168, Accelerated cost recovery system; and Section 179, Election to expense certain depreciable business assets. Revenue Ruling 69-229, 1969-1 CB 86 sets forth the principles that distinguish capital expenditures taken as depreciation from maintenance expenses deductible as ordinary and necessary business expenses.

When thinking about depreciating a new asset, you also need to consider the potential applicability of the **Section 179 deduction** when you acquire what are called **1245 (a)(3) assets** that are used in business. Qualifying business equipment bought and placed into service in 2006 could have up to $108,000 of the cost deducted in the purchase year, instead of depreciated over seven years. A taxpayer can choose to take a Section 179 deduction for the full cost of a qualifying asset, or depreciate the full cost, or take some of the cost as a deduction and the rest as depreciation. Qualifying 1245 property, new and used, must be tangible, depreciable under Section 168 and acquired by purchase for use in the active conduct of a trade or business. Office furniture, telephones, appliances, books, fax machines and farm-related equipment used for a farm business qualify. Business vehicles with a gross vehicle weight of more than three tons—like a big SUV or pick-up truck—can be deducted up to $25,000 if they are used at least 50 percent for business in the first year. Equipment used in a rental property would not qualify unless your business is operating rental properties. If you rent out your new farm, you cannot deduct the cost of your new tractor under Section 179, but you can depreciate it. The IRS would not consider a taxpayer who rents his farm actively engaged in a farm business so the newly purchased tractor would not fit within Section 179, but it would if you were actively operating a farm business. The maximum Section 179 deduction will be adjusted for inflation annually through 2009 when it falls to $25,000 in 2010. Financing has no effect on the 179 deduction. There are other limits on using Section 179 involving a cap on the cost of the property and setting the amount of the expensed property as no more than the total amount of taxable income derived from the active conduct of the trade or business. Current Section 179 terms may or may not be changed, so you need to check with your CPA in the year you are thinking of making such a purchase to determine what level of deduction, if any, is available.

Your personal residence cannot be depreciated and neither can land. Any property or asset that a taxpayer holds for personal use—vehicle, ATV, boat, shop equipment, computer—cannot be depreciated. You cannot depreciate a second home unless it qualifies as either a rental property or as a business property.

The IRS has four ways of categorizing second homes, which have different levels of tax benefits. All second homes qualify for deducting mortgage interest and property taxes. The four categories sort themselves by the amount of time the taxpayer spends in the second home.

Category 1: Fewer than 14 days of annual rental. The taxpayer can deduct mortgage interest, property taxes and uninsured casualty loss, but not insurance, maintenance and depreciation. The taxpayer does not need to report this rental income.

Category 2: Taxpayer uses second home either more than 14 days or ten percent of rental days, which are days rented over 14. The taxpayer can deduct mortgage interest, property taxes, uninsured casualty loss, loss expenses, operating expenses, insurance, maintenance, repairs and depreciation. When these expenses exceed rental income, the taxpayer cannot apply that excess loss to his other income. But he can suspend these losses and take them in the future. The taxpayer must take expenses in the order listed above.

Category 3: Taxpayer uses second home less than either 15 days or ten percent of rental days. In both cases, the taxpayer has no limit as to how much tax loss he can take against ordinary income, subject to the $25,000 passive-loss cap for taxpayers with adjusted gross income of $100,000 or less for 2005. This taxpayer, in other words, can take up to $25,000 of qualifying loss, including depreciation, against other income. Loss in excess of $25,000 is suspended and carried into the future. To take passive-activity loss from a second home rental, you must "**materially participate**" in managing it. Material participation requires at least a ten percent ownership interest, and the rental property cannot be part of a rental pool that others manage. There are other tests as well.

When a taxpayer materially participates on a regular, continuous and substantial basis, he can deduct losses in full from his trade or business. Both his losses and income are treated as nonpassive (active) and are deductible. A taxpayer who rents out his second home is considered to be engaged in a passive activity. If he "materially participates" in his passive activity, he can take losses. The IRS has seven tests to establish material participation, with the taxpayer having to meet only one of the seven. These are:

1. He participates in the activity for more than 500 hours during the tax year.

2. His participation amounts to all of the participation in the activity of all individuals—owners and non-owners—for the tax year.

3. He participates in the activity for more than 100 hours during the tax year, and he participates no less than any other person.

4. The activity is classified as a significant participation activity, which your CPA needs to explain to you.

5. He materially participated in the activity for any five of the immediately preceding ten tax years.

6. The activity is a personal service activity, and he materially participated for any three tax years preceding the tax year.

7. He participated in the activity on a regular, continuous and substantial basis during the tax year, for more than 100 hours. (See IRS Temporary Regulation, Section 1.469-5T.)

Category 4: Taxpayer doesn't use second home, except for a few days of repair time. Every expense is deductible as long as the property was either rented or available for rent. A reasonable amount of travel expenses to inspect or repair the property may also be deducted. (See Robert Bruss, "Real Estate Newsletter," February, 2006.)

The tax benefits of a second home by themselves would not justify the expense of acquiring one. Where, however, loss can be taken against ordinary income and the second home is appreciating on the ground, a second home is a helpful investment.

Loss has a different benefit for each tax bracket. A taxpayer in the 15 percent bracket pays $150 on every $1,000 in taxable income. If he has a $100 second home loss per $1,000 in taxable income, he reduces his taxable income to $900 and his tax is lowered by $15 ($900 x 15% = $135.) A taxpayer in the 35 percent bracket pays $350 per $1,000 in taxable income. A $100 second home loss for him reduces his taxable income to $900, on which he would pay $315 in tax ($900 x 35% = $315). He saves $35 in tax. For the same level of loss, the 35%-taxpayer saves more than twice as much as the 15-percent taxpayer. In both cases, taxpayers want their out-of-pocket, second-home expenses—mortgage interest, property tax, maintenance, insurance—covered by their rental income, and the tax loss to be generated by depreciation as much as possible.

Depreciation is complicated, and I would advise against trying to figure it out with no more than a high IQ and a Ph.D. in logic.

Depreciation of a capital asset is an obvious tax benefit that owners of farms, businesses and rental properties use. But depreciation comes with two costs of its own. First, depreciation of rental property, business property, equipment and improvements used in an income-producing operation (like a farm) lowers the taxpayer's basis in that asset, which in typical circumstances will increase the taxable gain at the time of its sale. Second, when you sell depreciated real estate, you will pay a 25 percent tax on the amount of money you depreciated. This is called the **depreciation recapture rate**. When figuring your total tax due on the sale of real property after one year, the 25 percent recapture tax is applied to the depreciated amount and paid at your ordinary-income rate; remaining tax liability is taxed at your appropriate capital-gains rate. Recapture can burn you. If you were to buy a country rental house for $100,000 when the market was high and sold it for $100,000 five years later when the market was soft, you would end up netting no income on the sale but owing the IRS several thousand dollars in recapture tax on the five years of depreciation you took.

Remember my example of the small residential rental house at the back of the farm? Instead of considering it a residential rental, you might want to think of it as a non-residential rental property that you intend to rent to a self-employed individual or business. This house might appeal to a writer, artist, contractor, craftsperson, consultant, telecommuter and so on. In this circumstance, you can take a **50 percent depreciation bonus** write off for certain types of improvements in your first year, subject to 1) the improvement is made or pursuant to a lease, 2) the portion of the building where the improvements are made is exclusively tenant occupied, and 3) the improvement must be placed in service more than three years after the building itself was put into service. Certain types of improvements do not qualify for the 50 percent depreciation bonus—enlarging the building, elevators, a structural component that benefits a common area and work on the building's internal structure. Qualifying improvements include electrical and plumbing systems, permanent lighting fixtures, heating and air-conditioning systems, security systems, and non-maintenance recarpeting, retiling and repainting. Non-real estate assets that qualify for the 50 percent first-year depreciation bonus include trucks, trailers, business furniture, business machines, computers and most software. You might find a situation where the numbers work in favor of having you rent the small house for three years, then redo it as a rental office for a lease-holding tenant, after which you sell it and 20 acres to the tenant. The maximum amount you can expense under the 50 percent bonus in the first year is $100,000. This 50 percent bonus was enacted in 2003. A property to qualify must have been acquired after May 5, 2003 and before January 1, 2005. It must have been placed in service before January 1, 2005. Like all other tax breaks, this one is subject to change.

Related to tax issues is how you take ownership of your newly purchased farm or farmland. You, your CPA and your lawyer should choose the **most advantageous ownership structure for your farm in light of at least seven generic needs: 1) estate planning, 2) minimize annual income tax, 3) minimize tax when you sell or otherwise dispose of the farm and its component assets, 4) privacy, 5) protection from creditors, 6) liability and 7) control of property**. I discuss ownership considerations in later chapters. This is an important decision, so make sure your CPA and lawyer have experience in evaluating alternative farmownership structures.

ESTATE TAXES

Most farm operations don't make much net profit, though they do keep money flowing through the farm economy. It's hard for small and mid-size operations to squeeze savings and capital out of their cash flow. Therefore, the common pattern is for farmers to build wealth through the long-term appreciation of their farm operations and land. Their heirs get most of the benefit. The less tax their estates pay, the higher the pass through.

Many farmers complained to their political representatives in the 1990s that the **federal estate tax** fell with particular harshness on them, owing to their common plight of being land wealthy and cash poor. They wanted the elimination of this so-called "**death tax**," referring to the federal estate tax that applied when the decedent's taxable estate exceeded the tax-exempt amount. Heirs—family farmers—said they were forced to sell the decedent's farm to pay this tax.

This was infrequently the case from what I can determine, though undoubtedly it occurred. Most estates paid no federal estate tax at all, because they either fell beneath the taxable estate cap (the exemption amount was $675,000 in 2001 with a top rate of 56 percent), or they were passed on tax-free to a surviving spouse, heirs and/or charity. Only two percent (48,000) of all U.S. estates paid any federal tax in 1998, and only 1,200 of those were made up primarily of farms and small businesses. (Jane Bryant Quinn, "Winners, Whiners and the Estate Tax," Washington Post, August 13, 2000.) A Congressional Budget Office study in 2005 found that estate returns filed by farmers and small business owners in 1999 and 2000 confirmed that only a small number of such estates were too cash poor to pay their tax. Only 1,659 farm estates had taxes due in 2000, and only 138 of those reported inadequate liquid assets to cover their liability. At the 2005 exemption of $1,500,000, only 300 farm estates would have owed any tax, and only 27 of that number would have been pinched. By 2009, when the exempt amount rises to $3,500,000, only 65 farm estates would owe taxes, of whom only 13 would be cash-strapped. (Washington Post, "Estate Tax Myths," July 24, 2005.) Overall, of the 2.3 million individuals who died in 2004, only 30,276 estate tax returns were filed; 3,500 estates were greater than $5 million—and they paid about two-thirds of all estate taxes. (Christopher Swann, "Estate tax repeal is on its last legs," Financial Times, June 13, 2006, quoting Joanne Johnson, wealth adviser at JP Morgan Private Bank.) Swann reported no evidence that family farms were being sold because of the "death tax."

While the tax rates on estates exceeding the exemption cap ranged from 37 to 55 percent in 1996, an IRS study found that the average tax on estates of $600,000 to $1 million in that year was only six percent. The higher rates fell on the very wealthy and/or those who did no estate planning. A federal estate tax return had to be filed only if the decedent's cumulative gifts and estate value exceeded the exemption amount. Thus under the old rules, 98 percent of estates never had to file a federal estate return. Under the old rules, every individual estate was entitled to a federal unified credit that amounted to an exemption of $675,000 on the decedent's taxable estate in 2001. **Taxable estate** represents the gross value of the estate, less allowable deductions. The taxable estate is always less than the gross estate.

Here is a summary of exclusion amounts and tax rates between 2001 and 2011.

New Tax Law, 2001

Individual

YEAR	Old Exclusion Amount	New Exclusion Amount	New Highest Marginal Rate Above Exclusion Amount
2001	$675,000	$ 675,000	55%
2002	700,000	1,000,000	50
2003	700,000	1,000,000	49
2004	850,000	1,500,000	48
2005	950,000	1,500,000	47
2006	1,000,000	2,000,000	46
2007	1,000,000	2,000,000	45
2008	1,000,000	2,000,000	45
2009	1,000,000	3,500,000	45
2010	1,000,000	Repealed (no cap)	Repealed
2011	675,000	675,000	55

The new rules under the 2001 tax-cut legislation provided for an annual increase in the exemption cap to $3,500,000 and a gradual reduction to a 45 percent top rate in 2009. Exemption means the estate is not required to pay any federal tax on taxable amounts less than the cap. In 2010, the exemption is repealed under the 2001 legislation, which means that wealthy individuals with strong family values should schedule their estates for that year. In 2011, the $675,000 exemption cap and top rate of 55 percent (the 2001 rules) are reimposed. It's difficult to imagine that this death lottery will not be modified before taking effect since it makes absolutely no sense. As I write in the summer of 2005, Congress is again debating whether to abolish the estate tax entirely, recast the truly nutty rules for 2010 and 2011, impose a flat 15 percent rate or increase the tax burden on the very richest estates. My bet is that only the largest estates—farm and otherwise—will pay federal tax in the future, which was the case even before the 2001 legislation was enacted.

Individuals whose estates are likely to be subject to the estate tax are usually smart enough to have their CPA and lawyer develop an estate plan that reduces their taxable estate so as to lower the anticipated tax bite. This involves transfers of wealth to others, charitable donations and gifts, along with different ways of structuring the ownership and control of assets. Many ways are available for individuals to give or transfer assets and income streams to family, beneficiaries or trusts to reduce their estates.

Many farmers—and others—avoid federal estate taxes by using the full tax-free exemption and then leaving everything above the cap to the surviving spouse, which is known as the **unlimited marital deduction**. A tax burden then falls on the spouse's estate when it exceeds the joint cap.

The current rules do contain a clinker for the tax conscious. Under the old rules, a beneficiary would inherit assets whose value was determined at the time of death. The gain in an asset's value, between its cost at time of purchase (beginning basis) and its value at time of death, was put into the taxable estate on which the estate tax was figured. The asset's value at time of death is called the **stepped-up basis**. The estate might pay a tax on the gain, but the beneficiary did not since he was being given the asset with the tax already figured against and paid by the estate. Once the beneficiary possessed the inherited asset, his gain over the succeeding years was figured against the stepped-up basis at the time of inheritance rather than the original cost paid by the decedent. Under the new law in 2010, the beneficiary receives the asset on a **carry-over basis,** which is the original basis not the stepped-up basis. There exists an "allocation" with carry-over basis whereby the carry-over basis is usually higher than the original basis. The 2001 law shifts the tax burden from the estate to the beneficiary. On assets that have greatly appreciated, this will produce significant tax hits even at a 15 percent capital-gains rate. Eliminating the "death tax" will mean that heirs will pay a capital-gains tax on inherited real estate—like farms and timberland, going back to the original basis in the property.

When the estate tax is repealed in 2010 under current law, many estates will end up paying more in taxes, not less. Allan Sloan wrote:

> under the 2009 rules, estates of up to $3.5 million ($7 million for a married couple) would be exempt from federal estate tax. The tax rate on assets above that level would be 45 percent. Inheritors would be able to step up the basis of $3.5 million (or $7 million) of inherited assets to their value the day they inherit them. Flash forward to 2010, when the estate tax is repealed. …heirs would be able to step up only $1.3 million in assets to their value on the day of death. …assets above $1.3 million would be valued for tax purposes at carry-over basis—their cost (for income-tax purposes) for the person who died. So any estate with $1.3 million to $3.5 million in assets ($2.6 million to $7 million for a married couple) is worse off under full repeal in 2010 than it would be in 2009. Inheritors in the $1.3 million-to-$3.5 million range would face higher taxes if they sold inherited assets than they would under the 2009 rules. …but if you're dealing with an estate of $3.5 billion, you'd be far better off inheriting in 2010. (Allan Sloan, "Doing a Big Favor for the 'Small Rich,'" <u>Newsweek</u>, June 19, 2006.)

A study by the Congressional Joint Committee on Taxation projected that 7,500 estates would pay the federal estate tax in 2009, none would pay in 2010 and 63,900 estates would be worse off in 2010 than in 2009. The wealthiest estates benefit from repeal; the least wealthy wealthy are hit harder; the vast majority of estates are unaffected. Most farmers who would be ensnared in an estate tax would be the small rich, not the big rich.

In June of 2006, the Senate rejected President Bush's effort to repeal the estate tax permanently. A few weeks later, House Republicans introduced legislation that would retain a reduced estate tax on the wealthiest estates and eliminate it for estates less than $5 million, beginning in 2010.

The tax rate for estates worth between $5 million and less than $25 million would be the capital-gains rate, now 15 percent, compared with 2006's 46% estate-tax rate. Estates above $25 million would be taxed at twice the capital-gains rate, a cut of 16 percent. (Brody Mullins, "House Republicans May Settle for a Muted Estate-Tax Reduction," <u>Wall Street Journal</u>, June 20, 2006.)

The 2001 law did not repeal the **gift tax**. The exemption amounts that continue to be in effect until 2010 **unify** the gift exemption and the estate exemption. You can get a tax benefit by gifting an asset but the value of that gift is added into your estate on which you may pay a tax if the estate's value exceeds the exemption amount. In 2010, the top gift tax rate will be reduced to 35 percent, the top individual rate. The gift tax will survive repeal of the estate tax, as I write.

Farmers, rather than sad-sack victims of jack-booted IRS thugs, were—and still are—better situated than most individuals to protect their assets from estate taxes. Much of a farmer's estate is tied up in land, improvements and equipment rather than easily valued and easily sold mutual funds and stocks. The executor need only open a book to determine the value of the decedent's three-year-old sedan, but the value of a barn, or a lot, or subsurface minerals, or a stand of timber are matters of judgment. On such farm items, the cash value can be typically discounted by as much as 50 percent. The degree of discount for a farmowner like you depends, of course, on the degree of anticipated scrutiny.

Another common discount tactic is to use **property-tax valuations** to assign a fair market value to the farm's land, structures and minerals. Despite periodic reappraisals, these assessed values frequently underestimate fair market value. Valuing with property-tax assessments can lower the value of most estates with a land asset, but it helps most those estates, like farms, whose assets are disproportionately concentrated in taxed property. It appears to me to be the case that rural property assessments always lag current fair market values. In this fashion, the estate of the land-rich, cash-poor farmowner from Blue Grass, Virginia is advantaged over the cash-rich, land-poor investment banker from Wall Street. This is one more reason why both bulls and bears like to buy and operate farms.

Farm estates can also benefit from inherent difficulties in placing a fair market value on **fractional ownership interests**. When, as is usually the case with large farms, the property ownership is organized either as a family corporation or a closely held entity (e.g., corporation, partnership, limited liability company, family limited liability corporation, limited partnership), the decedent's fractional share will usually be discounted owing to its lack of broad marketability and minority. The same discounting can occur when a farm is operated as a "non-organized" business (sole proprietorship without any additional legal structure). In this case, it is not fractional ownership that is hard to value, but the assets and profitability of the farm itself. Judgment, once again, can be applied to discount the estate's farm value.

The IRS does not have a fixed set of rules for valuing a business or a farm business. The Agency looks at certain "factors," including the nature of the business, its financial history, the economic outlook for the type of business, book value of stock, current financials, future earning capacity, dividend history, stock sales and comparables. If the heirs sell the farm soon after the decedent's death, the IRS will value the farm at the net sale price. If there is an agreement among the owners on a value for each interest prior to any death, that value could be presumed to represent fair market value since all the owners are both willing to buy and sell at that price.

The estates of farmers and woodland owners can also be discounted when the present value of the estate's merchantable timber is not determined through a consulting forester's **cruise**. A cruise is a sampling technique by which the forester estimates the volume of timber and projects its current dollar value. Timber that has immediate sale value is referred to as "**merchantable timber**." (Timber cruises and related issues are discussed in Chapters 18-24.) Without a current cruise, wooded land in an estate would usually be assigned a **default value**, typically the off-the-shelf, property-tax valuation for generic woodland in the county. Where the woodland has recently been timbered, the property-tax assessed value will overestimate fair market value of the acreage, since the tract will not produce another crop of trees for 20 to 80 years, depending on the land and the tree species. In that situation, the estate should hire a forester to cruise the recent cutover land to get an appraisal value that's more realistic, i.e., lower, than the property-tax valuation.

Consider the opposite situation. An estate finds itself with woodland that contains a substantial amount of merchantable timber. Here, the estate will want to use the property-tax valuation, which can easily be $1,000 to $1,500 per acre lower than the timberland's true fair market value. Estates containing a lot of merchantable timber can be worth two or even three times more than the property-tax value. Undervaluation of this type of asset benefits the estate at the expense of the tax collector. The estate, obviously, should not sell the timber, because that act would accurately establish its value. The better strategy is to convey the woodland to the heirs as is. The heirs should have a cruise done immediately to establish the value of the timber, which will be their **timber basis** for tax purposes. The heirs can then sell the timber with little, if any, taxable gain inasmuch as they are selling the timber for what the forester determined was its value at the time of their inheritance.

Charles Davenport, a tax specialist at the Rutgers School of Law and former assistant director for tax analysis in the Congressional Budget Office, argued that a farm couple under the old 2001 rules who planned properly could pass about $8 million in assets to the next generation free of federal estate taxation. That's $6,650,000 more than the $1,350,000 joint exemption in effect before the 2001 legislation. The first step in organizing a farm to achieve this end would have been to establish a **limited liability company (LLC)** in which the farmowner and his spouse each held 49 percent ownership. Each principal is considered a minority interest, and such interests are difficult to value given the lack of marketability. The residual two percent could be held in Professor Davenport's words by "almost anybody, including one of the street homeless if there is no other deserving person." (Charles Davenport, e-mail to Curtis Seltzer, May 17, 2001.) The farm interest is now a minority interest that passes to a trust when the first spouse dies. By passing the first estate to the trust, it is not aggregated with the estate of the surviving spouse. The joint farm asset worth $8 million is divided into two equal 49 percent shares, each of which is worth $3.92 million. Owing to the lack of marketability and other discount factors, each spouse's estate would be valued at a 50 percent discount, that is, $1.96 million apiece. From that sum, $750,000—the unified credit—is deducted from each estate. Where land is a large part of each estate, it is possible to get all of the $750,000, Professor Davenport says. Subtracting $750,000 from $1.96 million leaves $1.21 million, which was less than the unified credit and the small business deduction of Section 2057 together under the old rules. This farm-owning couple armed with an LLC, a trust and tax planning that set up the farm as a small business could have protected most if not all of $8 million in joint assets from estate tax. The higher exemption caps would under the new rules, presumably, allow an even larger farm estate to be free of an estate tax. The cost of setting up the LLC and the trust might be $2,000 to $3,000, depending on an area's hourly rates for lawyers and CPAs. Farm-owning estates that exceed the exemption would do well to consider structuring their assets in light of Professor Davenport's observations. Using limited liability companies and trusts provide other tax benefits, liability protection and privacy apart from estate considerations.

If your estate is likely to be $2 million or more, you should talk with your CPA about setting up a **family limited partnership (FLIP)**. Under a limited partnership, a general partner runs the enterprise though he may own as little as one percent of the partnership's assets. Parents set up the FLIP with themselves as both general and limited partners. Then they gift to their children their limited partnership interests, 99 percent of the partnership's assets, but retain the one percent of the assets that is owned by the general partner. The parents continue to control the partnership and its assets, but they have given their kids 99 percent of the ownership. Accordingly, 99 percent of the partnership's assets are now removed from the parents' estates. Appreciation of the partnership's assets is out of the parents' estates as well. There is also a discounting process of about 40 percent that applies to the gift of the limited partnership interests, because ownership of these interests does not bring control. Farms are just the type of asset that are put into FLIPs. (See Jeff Schnepper, "Protect your family with a partnership," http://moneycentral.msn.com/ content/ Taxes/ Taxshelters/P33545.asp; February 29, 2004.)

Lifetime gifts together with donations to charity are often used to whittle estates. As of 2006, an individual could give away as much as $12,000 a year to any person without incurring any taxation. The allowed annual gift exclusion is not counted against the unified credit and does not reduce the exemption cap. The 2001 tax act did **not** reduce or repeal federal gift taxes.

If the couple has set up a trust and transferred title to some or all of their farm assets into it **during their lifetimes**, estate sheltering becomes even more reliable and less dependent on Professor Davenport's 50 percent discount rate. **Lifetime asset transfer** is critical to keeping large estates, farms and others, under the cap. Spreading ownership of and income from your assets increases the family's spending income by reducing taxes. New taxpayers are created (who pay taxes at lower rates), and income is leveled, thus reducing the aggregate tax on the family. You can reduce the size of your estate without losing control of your assets or any of their benefits by creating one or more **trusts** to accept the transfer of your assets.

Trusts may be part of a comprehensive farmownership and farm-estate plan, depending on the amount and type of your assets. A **living trust** (which is different from a living will) is one way to hold real-estate title that avoids the delays and costs of probate. A **joint living trust** is a common choice that spouses make, which allows either to make decisions in the event of incapacity of the other without the expense of becoming a court-appointed guardian or conservator. Once created, you transfer assets and retitle them to the living trust which you can continue to control in your role as trustee. A co-trustee whom you name will assume control quickly and without complications in the event of your death or incapacity. A living trust can be **revocable**, that is, you can change or cancel it if you, the trustee, find it is not to your liking.

A living trust, standing alone, does not reduce an individual's estate taxes. For that reason, a second trust or other ownership structure (s) is needed whose purpose is to hold assets or pass them on with as few tax bites as possible. This can be done by placing assets in other types of trusts—**generation-skipping trust, charitable remainder trust, charitable lead trust, bypass trust and credit shelter trust, among others**—in conjunction with the living trust. You may also want to consider using life insurance to offset the bite of anticipated estate taxes and setting up a life insurance trust for further tax benefit.

Establishing the right farmownership structure and estate plan for a farm is not a do-it-yourself job over one weekend. Many ownership options exist, as do many estate-management structures. They intersect where estate-planning needs require certain ownership structures during your lifetime. The tax implications of various ownership structures and estate-plan components are both immediate and long-term. Trust laws differ from state to state, as do state inheritance and gift tax policies. Each state has its own set of rules for setting up corporations, partnerships and other entities. Whether or not you like lawyers and accountants, you should ask for their help in planning your farmownership, for both current tax benefits and as shelter for your estate.

The 2001 tax act does not free farmers and others from the need for tax and estate planning, especially since it's not certain whether the law will stand unchanged (which leaves the 2010 and 2011 crapshoots in place) or be modified. If your estate exceeds the rising exemption caps, I would advise you to have your CPA and estate lawyer work up a structure and a plan reasonably soon.

You can inform yourself of the general ideas involved in farmownership structures and estates through reviewing citations found at the **American Agricultural Law Association's** (AALA) website (http://www.aglaw-assn.org/biblio/), the section (#33) on Organizational Forms for Agriculture. Citations are provided on family farm corporations, S corporations, limited liability companies, partnerships and individual ownership. Experienced lawyers in farming communities should be knowledgeable about these ownership structures. AALA has more than 40 subject bibliographies relating to all aspects of farming. It's located at the Robert A. Leflar Law Center, University of Arkansas, Fayetteville, AR 72701; 501-575-7389; 501-575-5830 FAX; e-mail: bbabione@uark.edu. A selected bibliography on agricultural law in 2000 was published in the Spring, 2001, 54 Arkansas Law Review, by Sally J. Kelley *et al.* (earlier bibliographies go back to the mid-1980s). That document provides references on air quality, alternative agriculture, animal law, antitrust, aquaculture, bankruptcy, biotechnology, business organizations, commodity futures, cooperatives, credit and finance, endangered species and wildlife protection, energy, environmental issues, farm programs, food, food safety, forestry, general farm issues, intellectual property, international trade, invasive species, labeling, labor, land use, liability and insurance, marketing and sales, pesticides and herbicides, production contracts, property law, public lands, recreational use, soil conservation, taxation and estate planning, water quality, water rights and wetlands. All of the bibliographies are available through the **National Center for Agricultural Law** (NCAL) website at http://law.uark.edu/arklaw/aglaw (University of Arkansas, School of Law, Fayetteville, AR 72701; 501-7646; 501-575-5830 FAX; e-mail: awinfred@uark.edu).

The process of choosing from among these options and integrating your financial, legal and personal elements into a plan for current and estate purposes is too complicated and arcane for the layperson to do on his own. It's certainly too complicated and arcane for someone like me to offer advice. The interface between current ownership structures, tax minimization and estate planning is not a problem with a one-size-fits-all solution. Read a couple of background books so that you have a basic sense of what trusts do and how ownership structures can benefit both current and future tax obligations. Among those I found useful were: Martin M. Shenkman, The Complete Book of Trusts (New York: John Wiley & Sons, Inc., 1993, or most recent edition); Denis Clifford, Make Your Own Living Trust, 7th ed. (Berkeley: Nolo Press, 2005); and Kathleen Adams and Robert Brosterman, The Complete Estate Planning Guide (New York: New American Library, 1998, or most recent edition). Books on ownership entities are readily available. A local law school library will have vanilla forms along with detailed information that is given to lawyers at their Continuing Legal Education (CLE) seminars. Nothing, however, substitutes for competent CPA and legal assistance.

Two other considerations might be relevant in planning the best way to own land. If you have pre-college kids, you may want to think about how your ownership options affect each child's ability to qualify for financial aid if assistance might be required. Transfer of farm or landownership into your child's name or a trust with a child as the beneficiary may disqualify him from eligibility.

A second factor is providing for your own long-term elder care. If, for example, you are not likely to be able to self-finance such care and will need to rely on Medicaid to pay for nursing home costs, the current rules require that you spend almost 100 percent of your assets paying for your own care before you become eligible for the federal program. The Medicaid rules can be a huge bite out of your potential estate and can swallow all of it. This "tax" falls heaviest on the middle class whose members have some assets but not enough to finance long-term care. The poor qualify for Medicaid because they are poor and have few assets to spend down; the rich can afford to buy care on their own without liquidating their estates. To protect your assets, you have to structure or restructure their ownership in advance of when you would otherwise need to spend them down to finance your care. Consequently, it's best to think through the question of farmownership structure at the time of acquisition with a lawyer and an accountant in light of all your short-term and long-term needs.

As a rule, I would not hold ownership of either land or a farm operation in my name and my wife's name in light of the seven needs I outlined above and repeat below. If your estate is modest, however, ownership in your own name is certainly workable. I cannot recommend a one-type-fits-all ownership structure that can be applied to every individual situation. The optimum ownership structure for your land or farm is part of a plan you should have for meeting seven needs: 1) estate planning, 2) minimizing annual income tax; 3) minimizing taxes when selling farm/land; 4) privacy; 5) protection from creditors; 6) liability; and 7) control of property. While all property-owning taxpayers share these needs, each plan requires a custom fitting. There is no substitute for getting CPA and legal help.

CHAPTER 7: MANURE BELONGS ON YOUR BOOTS, NOT IN YOUR RAP

"IS THERE ANYBODY LEFT TO WALK THAT MUDDY MILE?"
Eric Andersen, "Plains of Nebrasky-O," Today is the Highway, Vanguard, 196?

Farms are getting bigger as their number steadily declines. Conventional agricultural production requires scale economies. High-cost farmers are being squeezed out, and the more profitable farm operations are picking up the best agricultural lands, hence the steady increase in average farm size. Farms that disappear may be converted into housing, commercial developments or non-farm second homes. The lesson in the size trend is that whether or not larger farms are more efficient than smaller ones, larger and fewer is the trend.

Small farms, consequently, are no longer valued as full-time farming operations because, with some exceptions, full-time farmers can't make a living from them. In my rural county, no one is able to make a living from operating livestock farms of less than 200 or even 300 acres. Where such small farms were family-supporting as late as the 1950s, today they are not. In some places, this has led to large farmers buying small farms as part of their own land-accretion process. In my area, small farms are generally owned either by natives who work full-time off the farm and operate the farm in their spare time or city folks using them as retirement residences or second homes. Most of the first group inherited their farm residences in one way or another. They are not farm buyers. The market for small farms comes almost entirely from the second group. A small farm in a place like mine can be a good investment for a buyer who understands the many hurdles in trying to make small farms pay their own way and is willing to allow long-term ownership make his profit through appreciation of property value.

The more conventional your agricultural operation, the more full-time farming is about managing debt and scrounging cash. Most farmers have to borrow. Farm debt consists of business-related loans that finance land, equipment and crops. Not infrequently, land is mortgaged to buy equipment and pay for improvements. Federal programs are a central player in the system of farm debt. This house of cards is sustained by the underlying appreciation in land value, which is the lender's security in the debt. Since farming yields relatively little net income for most farmowners, farmers have a hard time piling up cash over the years after servicing their debt. Consequently, they are always borrowing and repaying to keep the farm going.

Debt can slowly crush the life out of you as you eke out each month's payment. Live on the edge long enough, and inevitably you slide over. That's what foreclosure auctions are about: farmers going splat. As a rule, you will do best by keeping yourself off the hamster wheel of farm debt as much as possible. You do this by containing both your annual input costs and your investment in capital stock. Look for cheaper ways to do a job consistent with getting it done reasonably right. Invest labor (both mental and physical) instead of cash. Manage more rather than invest more. Follow the principle that's incorporated in the time-honored tactic of buying cheap stocker steers in the spring that might be upgraded for fall sale through care and good grass rather than the best quality at the highest price. Figure out your marketing strategy before you buy or plant: test it small at first, increasing your production in step with your feedback. Consider ways of achieving predictable cash flow at the sacrifice of upside potential. In other words: hedge don't gamble. Take satisfaction in making a little money, not in driving up your dirt road on a new, $50,000 tractor.

Farmers, historically, have tended to be **land poor**, that is, rich in land but poor in cash because farming and landownership consume so much of their income in debt service and operating costs. Virginia plantation owners, like Jefferson, were poster boys for this predicament which resulted from their continuing need to buy additional land to replace that which their farming practices wore out. Non-farmer buyers like you can become land poor just like everyone else if you don't have reliable non-farm income sufficient to cover the farm's mortgage (if necessary) and your expenses. Prudently run farms can contribute to a non-farmer's net worth and an estate protected from federal taxation. A farm can provide you with yearly tax benefits that help build wealth. It can provide income, even some net income. But farming is a risky venture at best. A non-farmer buyer can fold a farm into his asset base and lifestyle, but it must be planned properly and effected cautiously.

A first-time small farmer must choose between producing conventional commodity crops—many of which enjoy price supports—and less-conventional alternatives. The smaller your farm, the more a full-time farmer has to find his way within the less-conventional group. I would not try to make a living that includes a mortgage payment from a small farm that produces conventional crops. Your choice, I think, will come down to a few conventional alternatives that might work on small acreage (such as a specialty orchard, vineyard or niche crop) or a less-conventional alternative, (such as organic crops, pick-your-own fruit/berries, exotic livestock breeding, specialty products and farm-added-value products.) I don't think you can beat the conventional system if you're small; you must go around it.

All farming is hard, constant and dangerous work. Even hobby farming is like this, though there's less of it. You might begin your farm work by reading Bryan Jones's, The Farming Game (Lincoln, Nebraska: University of Nebraska Press, 1982; reprint 1995), which has the farm experience dead right, though some specifics are now out of date. You can obtain books and other information on all aspects of farming from these websites: www.onthefarmradio.com; www.reviewcentre.com; www.farmingbooksandvideos.com; www.streetSmartfarmer.com; www.freeplants.com; www.keepmedia.com; and www.draftresource.com.

You might also want to read Joel Salatin's, You Can Farm: The Entrepreneur's Guide to Start and $ucceed in a Farming Enterprise (Swoope, Virginia.: Polyface, Inc., 1998; available from Stockman Grass Farmer, 1-800-748-9808 and Acres USA, 1-800-355-5313; or Rt 1, Box 281, Swoope, Virginia, 24479; 540-885-3590). Salatin's book is written for the individual who wants to make a living from full-time livestock farming and who has little experience doing so. His approach is to fly under the radar of conventional agriculture, looking for labor-intensive but not capital-intensive, value-added, *organic* farm products that can be sold directly to consumers. The book touches on many sensible ideas and experience-based insights.

Like all missionaries, Salatin is selling a total package of beliefs, liturgy and practices. You need not buy the package to appreciate and apply particular bits of insight. His objective is to find a way to make his inherited farm provide a living for his family. He's quite right to avoid conventional agriculture, and stress thrift, direct marketing to nearby population centers, soil improvement, flexibility, diversity, pastured chickens ("free-range" is the menu-preferred adjective), rotational grazing, record-keeping and environmentally enhancing agriculture. The key to his success is having a farm located within a two-hour drive of several Virginia cities, which allows direct marketing of higher-priced organic beef, pork, chicken, turkey, rabbit and eggs to upper-middle-class consumers and regular deliveries to fancy local restaurants. Customers contract for the meat they want and are then assigned a pick-up day. His marketing pitch is based on raising organic livestock in the field and processing it on a small, even backyard, scale. For a look at the conventional alternative, visit www.factoryfarming.com. Salatin has been operating his farm for about 20 years. In itself, this is proof of success even though he does not provide the numbers that would allow a reader to judge the farm as a business. Salatin's farm business is undoubtedly helped by sales of his field-tested farm books and his other promotional activities.

Farms are great second homes, great places for kids and great ways to make connections of many kinds—to the past, to the land, to the future, to values that are often obscured. Our farm gives our lives a balance between doing and thinking that I had a hard time finding in a city. You can get that balance even on a weekend farm. But the key to balance is…balance. Do a little bit of farming, then maybe a little more. But keep it balanced—less than half—of your life.

BUYING AND SELLING TO YOUR FRIENDS AND NEIGHBORS

Farming is not a gentleman's business. As I think about that sentence, I realize that I can't come up with any example of a gentleman's business.

Let me start again. Farming is self-employment where your costs tend to rise faster than your revenues. If you're a small farm producing conventional products, you will often find yourself less in competition against fellow producers and more in the same slowly sinking boat with them. Price competition—that is, cutting your price to keep yourself afloat—often results in a quicker trip to the bottom. You will find moments when the price of your farm's product is set by supply-and-demand interactions that can be seen and are understandable, and moments when the price you receive makes little sense in light of what is visible and comprehensible. Buyers tend to be large and oligopolistic while producers tend to be small and many. You, the new farmer, will be one of the small and many.

You will find, as a farmer or rural landowner, that you will need to buy from and, occasionally sell into a local market. The cost of purchasing locally produced farm-related products, labor and services can be substantial, but each purchase is often in the $250 to $5,000 range. Purchased items and services might include excavation work, fence-building, custom farm work (haying, harvesting), materials (stone, fertilizer, manure, fencing, firewood), used equipment, livestock, hauling and labor, both skilled and unskilled. These purchases and your local sales can be freighted with community scrutiny, and you will do well to realize that your approach to buying and selling can be published on the front page of your community's oral newspaper.

Few experienced farmers—your supply-side competitors—will give you—a new farmer—much of a break because of your inexperience. Why should they? Some will try to take advantage of you before you smarten up. Others won't. A couple will help you out. Obviously, it's important for you to learn who is in each camp. It's also important to keep your opinions about who's who to yourself. You won't know enough yet to know who is related to whom, who can keep your confidence and who likes to stir up pots in which you are the one being boiled.

If a knowledgeable neighbor takes you under his wing, consider yourself blessed. This individual is a treasure. Don't expect, however, that he will provide Farming 101 on demand. His advice is not likely to be offered as: "You should do it this way." Advice came to me something like this: "A man could think about it this way if a man was going to think about this at all, which a man might not do because there's not enough time to do everything that needs doing and too much thinking is like driving your vehicle into thicker and thicker mud, which sooner or later, stops you dead...if a man was foolish enough to drive through a mud hole in the first place. But if a man had a mind to try something, a man might think about it this way." Listen for the "**local subjunctive**," since it's offered for your benefit. I was fortunate enough to have a couple of neighbors like this. They let me bloody my own nose with flawed cattle decisions that they knew were limited enough to teach me a lesson while preventing me from knocking myself out. They assumed that I would learn and profit from these mistakes. I appreciated their efforts to contain my exuberance...and losses.

Fellow local producers have no incentive, no reason, to help you learn their business. They don't benefit by you becoming smarter from their hard-won wisdom. You wouldn't open your Rollodex to the fellow who opened a business like yours down the street, so don't expect your neighbors to share their survival skills with you because you need them. Nonetheless, several will, mainly because they're decent people and know what it feels like to lose money. Try to ask as few questions as possible. It's better to learn through unobtrusive observation, which is the way a lot of farm kids pick up things. Limit your requests for free advice since the knowledge you seek was acquired at a cost. You should offer to pay for continuing advice just as you would pay a consultant. Neighbors should—but probably won't—take your money, but you've done the right thing by valuing their expertise. While their information has great value to you, it is not similarly valued by those of your neighbors who have it; they consider such information common knowledge.

You might handle this situation by hiring the neighbor whose advice you want to do some "real work" for you, and while you are working together introduce your questions. Since you are paying for his time at that moment, both of you should feel comfortable with the arrangement. When neighborly advice is given without compensation, provide something of value in return to keep things square. Make available your urban skills, advice and contacts as a kind of standing swap for farm wisdom. Any expertise you have in filling out forms, taxes, law, medical insurance, college applications, financial aid, estate planning, finding doctors and lawyers, understanding consumer protection, haggling with creditors, evaluating business plans, interpreting rules and regulations and finding information on the Internet can be worth something in a swap.

The farming efforts of newcomers are watched microscopically, and both innovations and mistakes are likely to be the subject of hours of café dissection. (Diners need fresh material, having already exhausted each other's mistakes—about which you will only learn later. Live somewhere long enough and you may be accorded visitor seating, from where you can offer your opinions about the latest newcomer who is doing strange things.) What you do with your new land—which has probably been the seller's for a while and is, in any case, somebody's homeplace—is a matter of public interest. Get used to it. Fresh paint, orderliness, mowed yard grass and tended fences will reflect well on you. Large changes and flashy remodelings will raise eyebrows. Be neighborly.

Farmers buy and sell certain things from one another—livestock, equipment, supplies and occasionally land. You will find that some farmer-sellers have a price for whatever it is they're selling and will not budge. These folks are easy to deal with: you either meet their price if you want it badly enough or don't. Most sellers, however, anticipate, even look forward to, a little horse-trading negotiation with buyers, particularly the likes of you. If you are an urban professional, some sellers, not all, will consider you smarter than they are about certain things, which gives them just a bit more reason to make you pay a little more than you should for things they know about and are selling. This seller's intention is not to gouge you, but to come out just a bit more up than he thinks he should be...at your expense. This is not about money. It's often about self-image as well as evening self-perceived class, educational and cultural differences that are never really evened. The seller's self-image is involved, and you will do well to understand this in advance. The meta-issue from his perspective is who he is sociologically and who you are sociologically. It may not make any difference to you whether you pay $48 for a metal gate at the store or $52 from your neighbor, just as long as you get the thing hung before dark. But you will do better in the long run to bargain a little over the $4 so that you can both win at $50...or even $51. You won't need the store down the road as much as you are likely to need something from that neighbor. You should consider the little bit extra he tacks on as a kind of political contribution that buys you access and goodwill. It's best, I think, to buy from this neighbor-seller a time or two, using your friendliest bazaar-style negotiating skills. Don't walk away from his gate over a couple of bucks. Down the road, you will find he'll start treating you the same as everyone else. More importantly, by bargaining and buying, you've entered into the local economy and presumably did good enough. More than good enough is not what you want.

You will undoubtedly run into at least one local seller who is willing to sell you whatever you are dumb enough to buy, regardless of how dangerous it is and whether or not it runs. (Any time a seller tells me that "it runs good," I'm wary.) You have two ways of protecting yourself in these situations. First, when you have no experience buying what you have decided that you want to buy, pay a knowledgeable individual to go with you. Busy the seller while your expert checks out the goods. He'll tell you whether or not to make an offer and what it should be. Don't lay off the buy/no-buy decision onto your helper, because that will cause bad blood between him and the seller. Take responsibility and ownership of a no-buy decision: "It's more than I can afford"; "It's not quite what I was looking for."

If you are buying on your own and you're not sure after a first inspection, walk away from it. Come back for a second look. Don't be rushed into a purchase. When the seller says that there's another buyer begging to buy it for twice the money you've offered, quietly suggest that he should consider making that deal. Your deal at close to your price is likely to be available a couple of days later. Be especially careful when buying farm equipment and livestock on your own. Greenhorn buyers bring out the worst in a few sellers.

A newcomer will inevitably pay too much for some country goods, but he makes up for it when hiring local labor, which is always priced below city and suburban rates for equivalent skills. Do not gloat over or take advantage of this situation. Pay a dollar or two more than the going hourly rate for certain jobs to get quality work. You will still get the job done for half what you would otherwise pay.

Most sellers will judge you by **how you horse-trade**. Horse-trading is not like finding a price on the stock exchange floor where sellers and buyers make instant deals. Horse-trading is much more like having sex between consenting adults. It should be done with self-deprecating humor, creativity, concern for the other person and reasonableness. Expect some veil dancing. Neither side should make take-it-or-leave-it offers. Everyone should feel good the morning after. If the seller's price is outrageous and he does not seem inclined to budge, it's best not to move into horse-trading with him because you will wind up with either a bad deal or no deal—and everyone frazzled by the experience. Horse-trading, in other words, is a process that you enter after you've scoped out enough of the seller to know that he is receptive to dickering. If the seller is a horse-trader, don't pay his first asking price. Slip into the process that he offers and be creative. Horse-trades are often swung by using "throw ins" that are not part of the original negotiation. You come out okay in horse-trading when you know the going price for what you are selling and what you are buying. Never horse-trade without knowing both numbers.

If you're trying to horse-trade on the price of land and get stuck, throw in something you think the buyer values more than you do: offer free hunting and fishing rights for a couple of years; or use of all or part of the property for agricultural purposes for a transition time; or hay-making rights; or free storage in the barn for a year; or some professional assistance or skill that the seller might need that you can offer. It's easier to trade horses when saddles, bridles and hoof picks are available to help make the swap. In return for the cash and "throw ins" you offer for land, you might ask the seller for return considerations, such as building fence with materials you provide or dipping out a stock pond with the backhoe he has, or including a functioning tractor in the farm purchase. Horse-trading should be done with an eye cocked to establishing a functional relationship in the future with the other person. You may find yourself relating to the seller in many ways over the coming years. And if not him, his parents, siblings, children or friends.

While most service vendors in your new farm community will treat you fairly and expect to be treated the same, you should not be surprised to find a few who use a **two-tier pricing system: a lower price for locals and a higher price for newcomers**. Advertised prices, of course, apply uniformly to everyone. But prices for local services—house painting, roofing, excavation, fencing and other trades—lend themselves to tiering. (Lest you are starting to think that newcomers are virtuous and locals are not, I can report that I've seen new farmowners bargain with needy locals like they were parting with their Uncle Scrooge's first dollar and then demand a discount when it came time to pay.)

If the two-tier vendor appears to be your only choice, then you may have to work with him though I would keep asking around. The best response is to walk away from any deal that turns you into a knowing patsy. If you discover after the deal has been struck that your vendor charges a different rate to others for the same service, you can choose to confront him or forget about it. Confrontation usually leads to the vendor's explanation that different jobs require different things, which explains different hourly rates. (See?) If you've agreed to his terms, you should pay the bill and learn from the experience. If you're dickering over terms, I'd forget about hiring the vendor whom you've just accused of cheating. If you go ahead with him, the work will not be done well.

The virtue in rising above this situation is that hard feelings can last forever in rural places, and grudges complicate life far beyond the dollars at stake in the initial dispute. It doesn't matter that you may be "right"; what matters in the long run is that you have asserted your rightness in a way that reveals the vendor to be less than honorable. In the normal course of urban life, you would not think twice about pitching a fit over two-tier pricing. In your new rural neighborhood, you will be judged over the accusation you make, not whether you are objectively right. And in the event of a dispute over money, you should know that the vendor's communications network is far more extensive than yours. It is his side of the dispute that will become common currency, not yours.

Having been in these situations, I believe it is best to continue to shop your work rather than confront the vendor in hope of trying to shame him into fairness. Where you are looking for a vendor in a not-very-competitive market, you may find it hard to locate an alternative. Try nonetheless, since it is better for your long-term relations with your new community to avoid this type of dispute than to prevail. Only in the most desperate circumstances should you pay the inflated non-local price. When I've done so, I've found that the vendor does a bad job despite the premium, or perhaps because of it. The element of mutual respect is at the center of all successful rural buy-sell deals. When the vendor forces you into the non-local price, he's forced you to lose respect in his eyes, which, in turn, enables him to do shoddy work because he thinks you won't know the difference, or don't care, or won't do anything about it. When you do stick up for yourself with a vendor like this, he will be affronted that you've questioned his ethics and work quality—both of which are likely to stink for you, regardless of his reputation with others.

I suggest invoking the Golden Rule in horse-trading. You can back into it by saying that you want to bargain with the other person the way you want him to bargain with you. Backing in is more acceptable than demanding adherence as your opening gambit. Make sure that you live up to your end of your offer.

In all dealings, it is critical for you to remember that you are interacting with an individual, not a sociological group. If a person treats you fairly or unfairly, it is that person—not his family, his neighbors or his community—that did so. It's easy to fall into a habit of thought that says everyone of such and such a group thinks this way and behaves that way. That habit is just plain wrong. The "other" group is just as varied as "your" group. Your new community is made up of individuals whose responses to you will be individual. If you start thinking in terms of them and us, you're destined to end up in that unfortunate place.

Price is the rural platform on which stand both respect and effort. When you negotiate a price that both sides regard as fair enough, then you have the standing to expect quality work. Don't be a fool just because you can afford to be, except where you will gain over the long term by accommodating the vendor's insecurities in the short term. On the other hand, don't feel that you need to show you're no city fool by squeezing pennies out of the vendor's wallet. While he needs your cash, he's gotten along without it until then. You are likely to need him more than he needs your dollars. Don't count on being able to bully a guy into a deal; bullying seldom works. I've seen rural vendors walk away from fair offers proposed by newcomers for no reason other than the source of the offer.

I've run into a few local guys who are so existentially angry over the influx of outsiders and their own inability to prosper that they try to skunk every non-local and newcomer they run into. Avoid these people; nothing is to be gained from dealing with them—win, lose or draw. You should also be aware that your behavior in these affairs will be judged locally by a different standard than locals judge themselves.

While you might see a price squabble with farmer Jones as a price squabble between you and farmer Jones, some of your new neighbors—fortunately, a minority—will see it as a fight between farmer Jones, who is one of them, and you, who is not. It will not matter to such folks that they too have squabbled with farmer Jones or that he is notorious for slippery behavior when it comes to money. Most of the time, your new neighbors will judge you on your own merits as you should judge them.

Newcomers should be aware of a **second-bite tactic that arises on fixed-price contracts.** Some vendors, not all, do not see a fixed-price agreement as involving a fixed price. They will want more money at the end of the job, because it took them longer to do the work. It's fair to both ask and pay if the vendor ran into problems that he could not have anticipated. It's also fair to refuse additional payment if you feel you're in a stick up. Don't pay a portion of the demand if you are *absolutely* convinced that the claim is groundless.

The main local **sell-buy relationship** you will have is with the purchaser of your farm products. Depending on the product, this buyer can be a multinational corporation, local cooperative, individual or the general public. When dealing with a "big" buyer, whether an institution or individual, the new farmer needs to remember that the buyer is not his friend. You should assume that most commodity buyers approach your deal as a zero-sum game in which every penny you make is a penny they lose. Don't expect them to help you out in a bad year when they can buy your product below your production cost. There's no sympathy for a novice in the agricultural marketplace.

If you are a conventional producer of a common commodity, you will soon learn that buyers of your product usually get the longer end of your stick. Such buyers are more liquid as a rule than individual sellers. They also have more precise information than you do about what your product will bring at the next step. If the buyer has a locked-in price for your product, you'll never know what it is. In contrast, you, the farm producer, are trying to determine your range of feasible selling prices using incomplete local data, your costs which you know all too well, hearsay, misinformation and macro-level price data at the state and national levels. Even when you, the small-guy producer, sell for a profit, it does not mean that the buyer has not won his little game with you. Since the buyer knows where the product is going and, usually, at what price, he knows in advance how much money he will make at each price for your product. As long as such a buyer has alternative sources of your product, he'll pay you as little as he can. You can do a little better when he needs your product to fill out a shipment. A farm producer almost always does best when several buyers are competing for his product.

Economics for small farmers boils down to a "**bottom analysis**," that is, net profit is what's left at the bottom of the producer's purse after he pays for everything off the top. When there's something left on the bottom, it's rarely because the farmer is a sharpie who got the better of the commodity buyer. It's usually the result of an increase in wholesale prices based on macro supply-and-demand factors.

Cattle are a common farm product and one which new farmers often try. In my part of Virginia, we have two usual ways of selling cattle. The first is to run your animals through a stockyard sale where they are weighed, graded and grouped for auction. The stockyard imposes predictable charges and certain risks. The farmer pays the stockyard a per-head fee for selling. If your cattle truck must wait three hours before unloading your steers before the sale, you can anticipate that each animal will lose five to ten pounds in the truck as additional **shrink** before it is weighed. Shrink is the loss of weight (feces and urine) in farm-to-sale transit; producers want to keep shrink as low as possible, while buyers benefit from more shrink. With 50 head in a truck and a six-pound-per-head shrink due to a jam at the dock, the farmer has "lost" 300 pounds, possibly $300, before he even gets his livestock into the auction ring. Moreover, the farmer has no control over which frame category the state graders assign each head of his stock. The difference between an 800-pound steer being classed as a "Medium-1" frame as against a "Number 3" can easily swing the selling price by $100. And, finally, the farmer's sales revenue will be directly affected by the number and motivation of the bidders. Most local stockyards are now connected by phone to distant feedlot buyers who are often the best money.

Some farmers avoid the stockyard's risks and fees in favor of dealing directly with independent cattle buyers who come to the farm, estimate the weight and quality of the stock in the field, and then offer a straight-through dollar-per-pound price for the scale weight. These buyers estimate scale weights of cattle herds every day. The good ones can project herd-wide average scale weight in the field to within ten pounds or less. These dealers will know before they step out of their fancy trucks what they can sell your cattle for and the cost of delivery. The buyer will generally offer you a penny-per-pound (or dollars per hundredweight) price that you think you might get at the stock market. You then figure that you'll save the stockyard's charges—as much as $10 per head—and avoid the risk of a truck jam, downgrading on frame size and poor bidder turnout. Then the buyer allows that he believes your cattle weigh a little more than you figure. You do the arithmetic in your head: cents per pound times more pounds than you thought, which puts more money in your pocket than the stockyard sale. So you make the deal. Lo and behold...when you get to the scales, you find your cattle weigh less than what the dealer believed and even less than what you thought they'd weigh. So you end up with a little less than you thought you'd get. On a trailer load of cattle—48,000 pounds—the $500 you lost on this deal is cash in your buyer's pocket. The safest method of working with these field buyers is to have at least three bid in a competition for your cattle.

Selling directly to a feedlot is likely to be more profitable, though it's difficult for a small seller to arrange. You will need to have a trailer load. A professional grader can be secured to field grade your stock. An identification system will be used to make sure the cattle bought are the cattle shipped. The seller will figure in a shrink factor.

Whether you will come out ahead at the stockyard or with the field buyer is always unknowable. In dealing with field buyers, I've done best—though not particularly well—by getting two or more bidding against each other and never accepting a price-per-pound offer when it is presented in the field. Give the field buyer a decision in a day or two after shopping your cattle to other buyers. It's useful to get a knowledgeable cattle person to look at your cattle before the buyers do, to give you an impartial idea of average field weight and the distribution of frames. Remember to subtract shrink from your average weight to account for hauling from field to scale.

If you're fooling with cattle as a novice, spend time at the stockyard in an effort to develop a cattleman's eye for judging weight and frame in the field. You should assume that a field buyer will play a couple of games with you to get your cattle for a price that he figures is a little lower than what he would pay at the auction. This keeps money in his pocket that could be in yours. The most common game I've seen involves the buyer inflating the field weight to induce the seller to accept a lower per-pound price. Another game manipulates a **price slide**, which is a device that should be used in field weighing to protect both buyer and seller equally.

A price slide starts with the price per pound that the buyer and seller have negotiated in the field based on an agreed average weight per head. If the average scale weight varies from the agreed field weight by five to ten pounds, the field price remains unchanged. If the average scale weight exceeds the no-change range, then the price per pound is reduced by a specified number of cents. If the average scale weight falls below the no-change range, the price per pound is increased by the same number of cents. A seller gets taken when the slide uses big changes in price per pound and the dealer forces an agreed field weight on the seller that he knows is higher than what the weight will be at the scale. This technique gives the dealer-buyer your herd at a much lower price per pound than is fair. Field buyers are much smarter than novice sellers about slides. A seller can protect himself against an unscrupulous buyer by having a professional grader provide him with an average field weight just prior to the buyer's visit. The seller must then subtract farm-to-scale shrink from the field weight. The net weight is what the seller will be paid for. If the seller accepts the buyer's weight estimate and the buyer's slide formula, he is opening himself to losing money on the deal.

If you are a person who will stew all winter over the loss of $500 in the selling of $40,000 worth of cattle in October, sell your cattle in the most conventional way open to you. Otherwise, you will turn into one of those individuals who nurse small grievances over lifetimes, which is not a good way to spend yours.

Increasingly, the end-buyers of agricultural products, such as poultry and hog processors, integrate vertically by turning individual farm producers into captive contractors who are paid for their captive production at a price the end-buyer sets. This is an updated version of sharecropping that rarely works to the benefit of the guy producing the crop. Farmers enter these contracts because they promise more or less predictable cash flow and the prospect of being able to make a living from farming. Sharecropping worked enough to last a long time, and contract farming works enough to last too.

Depending on your location and your product, farmers will have developed marketing venues and tactics that may or may not work for you. Certain agricultural sectors still use middlemen, such as an independent livestock sale, to bring sellers and buyers together in an auction. Livestock is often sold this way. Other crops—grains and milk—are sold through, or to, cooperatives. Cooperative commodity selling maximizes suppliers' market power. Some farms have the ability to time their sales by having on-farm storage. Some producers use financial tools to hedge their price exposure or sell on a forward contract at a fixed price. New owners of farms should consider ways to make their revenue predictable, though it means less up side. Many things can distort expected farm revenue every year. For the first-time farmer, I advise choosing ways of getting cash in hand rather than playing in future craps games. Many farmers I know do not try to improve their marketing. They sell the same way every year, because they have concluded that they can't beat the system. They're probably right about that.

START NEW THINGS SLOWLY; MAKE SMALL MISTAKES

As part of a pre-purchase farm plan, the dirt-smart buyer will have thought about a marketing plan for both the products the farm is producing and those it could produce. I urge caution on new uses. A new farmer with a new plan is at risk on both counts. Be careful about plunking a book model down in your new field, or assuming that you will make money because money looks like it can be made on paper.

When we first moved to Blue Grass in 1983, I had a notion to graze hogs instead of cattle on our pasture. Sometimes a great notion is best left alone. While our grass would have fattened hogs, everything else was wrong. All perimeter fences, including those of my neighbors, would have had to have been seriously upgraded or electrified. Concrete water troughs that fit cattle are too high for hogs. Stock-handling facilities would have had to have been rebuilt. The investment was too great to have made it pay. Further, I would have had to have found a reliable market for grass-finished hogs, or, alternatively, finish them myself with purchased grain. Finally, I couldn't find a steady supply of several hundred spring pigs ready for pasture. My pig idea was impractical on too many fronts. Our local county extension agent sagely told me as much. Twenty years later, however, a consumer market has emerged for this product. The farm's infrastructure, however, remains all wrong.

It is too easy for folks who are used to thinking analytically to design a theoretically better way of making money from a farm that they've never actually farmed. Puff pieces in agricultural magazines about the guy 400 miles away doing something that you think you can make work too are bait for people with too many degrees and a wide open mouth. Farming is at the mercy of forces beyond your control. Farmers must be gamblers, because they control so little of what affects them.

Most farmers, I think, assume that the mean will always occur; others try to protect themselves against the atypical through insurance, hedging, diversifying and adding redundancy to their operations. A person new to farming a new piece of land has no dirt-experience with managing the atypical. So a theoretical plan to change a farm's use assumes that the new owner knows the mean, as well as the range of variation. Such assumptions are fragile. The mean rarely occurs, though one can always be found in the longitudinal data on rainfall and temperature.

There is only one way to avoid the potentially disastrous consequences of your enthusiasm to create your own farm immediately. Don't do it. Be patient. **A new dirt-smart farmer learns his land before he starts substantially changing how it is used**. Land-learning is a huge step beyond the pre-purchase scoping that a buyer does. It takes several years—at least five, preferably more—for a novice to have sufficient experience to understand what his land can do, can't do and might do in specific circumstances. Your ability to produce an agricultural product is totally dependent on local factors—weather, water, soils, topography—and how each works with the others in a given year. You have to be on land over a sufficient period of time to see how various combinations occur and what their effect is on farm produce. There are few short cuts to time-tested, site-specific knowledge. While a piece of flat land may look to the inexperienced eye like any other piece of flat land, the farmer who preceded you will know that it has water-bearing clay soil six inches below the surface which makes it unsuitable for certain crops, particularly the Iranian elephant garlic that has captured your imagination. Change slowly.

Having said all of that, I don't mean to discourage you from thinking outside the conventional box when it comes to revising your farm's uses. You should be collecting research and new ideas, and keeping your ear tuned to *long-term* shifts in consumer tastes. Think about ways to add value to farm products and market them directly to retail consumers. Diversifying your product mix helps to insulate your cash flow from short-term events that often clobber conventional producers of one conventional commodity. Federal crop supports and insurance programs are intended to manage risk, though I think they encourage dependency and discourage innovation. Small, intensive production systems for specialty products can be explored, because they may be less subject to some of farming's risk factors. Rather than dedicate your new 20 acres to garlic consider building a couple of greenhouses to grow both garlic and salad greens all year long. The cautionary homily—"Don't put all your eggs in one basket."—came from farms where families knew first hand about both eggs and baskets.

It is critical to any new marketing plan to know where you can sell your new product and to understand that market's pricing and supply-and-demand balance. Don't become the tenth producer of organic spinach selling in a Saturday morning farmer's market in a town of 10,000—unless you have a trust fund. Don't start raising Kobe beef on a hardscrabble patch of glacial till in northern Maine because you've heard the Japanese pay a high price for it. You'll never be able to get a competitively priced product to Tokyo. Hearing something is not a marketing plan. Don't covet your 640 acres of cornfield to pick-your-own blueberries when the closest city is 200 miles away and the dirt couldn't grow a blueberry if Little Sal herself planted and watered each bush. Specialty products and direct marketing are excellent ways to make farming profitable, but the production has to fit the many features of your land, and you must be able to access a market that is ready and able to buy your products.

Many farm products are easier to produce than they are to sell at a profit. New farmers are often attracted to fads, exotic crops or livestock that are hot for a year or two. I've often seen new farmers fasten themselves to farm ideas that sacrifice trying to make money from their farm to promoting other values and aesthetics. While it may be neat to have five Polish longhorn steers on your farm, you cannot make any profit from this investment. (Steers, unlike bulls, cannot reproduce, and this breed, while now valued in Europe because it is outside the circle of beef animals that consumers fear carry mad cow disease, have no market in this country.) Resist investing heavily into crop-specific or livestock-specific infrastructure to take advantage of the latest agricultural tulip frenzy. You're likely to be too late to catch the really high prices, and you may find yourself with a locked-in and exclusionary infrastructure that can only produce a faddish product that is fading fast.

It's far better to build flexibility into your farm infrastructure, diversify your products and be able to sell into more than one market. You will always be in a good position if you keep improving your dirt. Unfortunately, failure is the mother of knowledge. Try not to be the farmer who fails gloriously so that others benefit.

CHAPTER 8: FARM EQUIPMENT: STUFF IS US

Farms are nice places to live and have as a second home. They provide opportunities to do simple, straight-forward labor. (Endless opportunities, I should add.) Such work provides a balance for people who spend most of their time in urban offices pushing paper, numbers and people. Real farm work is also hard, often boring, and ranges from highly skilled to endlessly unskilled. Most farmers could step into most Fortune 500 companies and do a passable job as the CEO because they are used to doing many tasks of many different kinds all at once and in sequence. Very few CEOs could switch places with one of these farmers and do anything except lose their shirts.

Farm work also provides opportunities to play in the dirt with big sandbox toys. Equipment and machinery is intended to enable an individual to accomplish more for a given amount of time and effort. Modern farmers, organic and conventional, need such tools to produce the quantities we require at a competitive cost. As farming systems were engineered to require less and less labor, more and more money had to be invested in the necessary "labor-saving" capital stock to maintain and increase output. Today, there is no escaping the need for large investments in equipment and machinery on large conventional farms.

For a new farmowner who is eyeing these unknown waters, I advise against doing a cannonball into the near bottomless pool of farm equipment. Buy equipment with the same careful research methods you've applied to buying land. Never buy anything without knowing its approximate value before negotiating, and the prices being asked by other sellers.

If your new place comes with no equipment, ask yourself whether you can do what you want without any equipment at all. Ask your neighbors whether it's possible to hire machinery work, such as fence-post driving, tractor work and baling. Felix Dennis, the British publisher, offers this sound advice on buying stuff: "If it flies, floats, or fornicates, always rent it. It's cheaper in the long run." (<u>How to Get Rich: The Distilled Wisdom of One of Britain's Wealthiest Self-made Entrepreneurs</u>, quoted in Stephan Stern, "Confessions of a Self-Made Multimillionaire," <u>Financial Times</u>, August 23, 2006.)

You may want to consider renting your agricultural land, rather than buying equipment and doing it yourself. Some products—cattle, sheep and hay—can be produced with the owner owning no equipment as long as hired machinery is available. When trucks and other equipment are needed, hire a neighbor to help out. It's relatively easy to hire most machinery work as needed, though you have to make sure that hired harvesting comes to your place at the right time. If you are cash short after purchasing your land, you will need to do without equipment, or hire what you need, or buy used or some combination of these choices.

When you have determined that you need to buy equipment, you face a number of decisions about each piece:

new or used

bigger or smaller (more power or less)

more complicated or less complicated

well-known brand or lesser known brand (often foreign made)

newer or older

more easy to use or less easy to use (newer tractors have hitch systems that are much easier to use than older tractors)

buy from dealer or buy from individual

more expensive or less expensive

more safe or less safe (older tractors and machinery have fewer safety features engineered into their design than newer models)

harder to service and maintain or easier to service and maintain

more fuel efficient or less fuel efficient

more comfortable to operate or less comfortable

If you see yourself as a part-time farmer or a weekend user of a farm second home, the only reason to load up on expensive new equipment is in the case where the tax benefits make sense in your circumstances. New equipment is hideously expensive. A basic small tractor runs $10,000 to $20,000 in 2006, and cost can easily rise to $20,000 to $30,000 or more with attachments and implements. If you're dollar conscious, I suggest going with multi-task/flexible equipment rather than one-task/specialized machinery, used rather than new, newer rather than older, simple rather than complicated, reliable rather than temperamental, common rather than exotic, smaller rather than larger, and functioning rather than beat to hell. You can upgrade your combination of equipment as you better understand your changing needs.

As a some-time farmer or non-resident landowner, you don't need to own the most efficient piece of equipment, nor do you have to perform any particular task with cutting-edge efficiency. Your goal is not to be as efficient as is technologically possible; your goal is to produce your product and do your land work at the mix of cost and efficiency that allows you to reap a reasonable—not maximum—return for your effort. For those who are farming full-time, you will learn that buying production efficiency at the expense of net income can ruin you. The last increments of productivity are expensive and often unnecessary.

To take a simplistic example: it will undoubtedly be more efficient to work a 50-acre field with a 100-horsepower tractor than one that only has 20. It will also take you less time. But if you only have one field to work, the smaller tractor will do the job at a fraction of the capital cost. A $50,000 tractor is "too much tractor" in terms of your bottom line for work that a $5,000 one can do, almost as well.

Full-time conventional farms have to be capital intensive, substituting mechanical energy for human labor wherever possible. Productive and cost-efficient agriculture now requires constant investment in new capital stock—newer and bigger machinery, different infrastructure and production systems; upgraded facilities, computer controls and so on. That is one reason why full-time farmers are so knowledgeable about **debt-management tactics**. Each full-time farmer will have evolved his own set of choices about buying equipment, new and used. If they're making a profit, they'll buy big and new; if not, it's finding used with low hours.

This chapter discusses **buying new and used tractors** as a way of walking through the broader topic of buying farming equipment. The information comes from my own seat-of-my-pants experience along with what I've culled from tractor-savvy friends, mechanics, articles and old-timers who've sat on steel seats for hour upon hour.

TRACTORS: NEW AND USED

I operated a 73-acre cattle farm without a tractor for five years. I put the money I could have spent on a tractor into building fence for a rotational grazing system. That investment allowed me to almost double my farm's carrying capacity, from about 30-35 head to about 65-70 head, depending on the size (weight) of the cattle I was grazing. I didn't need to own a tractor to do this type of farming. When I wanted to make hay, I worked out a shares deal with a neighbor.

When I did buy a tractor, I bought a '57 Ford with a front-end loader, bushhog, scoop and scraper blade for about $4,000. I could have bought new equipment for four times that sum, but it would have done no more work than the old stuff, though it would have been easier to operate and required less maintenance. I also could have bought newer used equipment, but the additional cost would not have yielded any increment in productivity that I needed. In other words, a 1977 tractor in the same horsepower (hp) class as the 1957 Ford would have done the same work in essentially the same way for at least twice the initial cost. My ability to raise cattle efficiently was not increased by having a tractor, either old or new. But a tractor is handy and makes many tasks easier, particularly lifting, loading, pulling, skidding logs, scraping, moving materials, building fence and mowing.

Some ten years after buying the farm, I bought a 1980 4WD Toyota pick-up truck with about 250,000 miles on the still-working odometer for $1,000. It's a "FARM USE" truck—unlicensed, uninspected and restricted. It's perfect for hauling materials around the farm, and its nimbleness is especially good for working in the woods. As much as I like having this vehicle, I did not need it to produce cattle, hay or timber. I could have made do with a $300 trailer behind my street pick-up truck and saved the $1,000. At the level of $1,000, gaining work and time efficiency at the expense of cost efficiency is not of great concern. At many multiples of $1,000, it is. You will observe that most farmers have something similar to my old beat-to-hell Toyota that they use for farm work. It saves wear and tear on their good vehicles.

To perform the same tractor and farm-truck work, I could have easily spent $40,000, rather than $5,000. If money were no object, maybe I should have done so. However, I've never found that money is never an object.

If you're cheap, or even a little thrifty, you'll start with a used tractor, probably a bit smaller than what you might like. Working with it will teach you which equipment upgrades you think are worth the additional investment. In my case, I'd like a slightly more powerful tractor with 4WD, more comfortable seat, better rollover-protection, an exhaust pipe that doesn't blow back in my face and an easier rear hitch. I could buy a better seat. The roll bar that I had fabricated is the best that I can get given the tractor's pre-safety frame and configuration. The exhaust now vents in front because the front-end loader I added required the removal of the down-and-under system. I cannot economically retrofit more hp, 4WD or an easier hitch. To get a better tractor package means buying a newer and more expensive tractor—a $10,000 to $20,000 shift. It's not worth that money for the 50 hours a year I use it.

The most obvious first step is to determine what you want your tractor to do and where. The work you need done will determine tractor size, attachments, implements and other features. The work you need done is what you have to do regularly or normally. It excludes jobs that you might need to have done every ten years. Such work is more economically done on a hired basis. If you try to size for every eventuality, you wind up with too much tractor at far too high a cost. The exception to this rule might be where you have to dig a 3,000-foot-long water line to your new farm house and the cost of the backhoe attachment would be less than the cost of hiring out the job.

The "topography" of your tractor work is a major screening factor. Smaller tractors are more maneuverable and have tighter turning radii than bigger ones. The tighter the radius, the handier your tractor. A lot of cleaning out barn stalls with a front-end loader will skew your decision toward nimbleness rather than horsepower. That type of work will also lead you to power steering. Tractors with a wider wheelbase are more stable than narrower models. On hilly terrain, I'd look for lower, wider models. Stumps, groundhog holes and 18"-deep gullies can roll a tractor if you hit them wrong. Don't be afraid to ask "stability" questions of the seller, particularly the degree of angle at which the model you're looking at will roll. If you will be doing a lot of inside-the-barn work, ask about emissions and emission controls. Breathing either gas or diesel exhaust (particulates in particular) for several hours at a time is not advised.

Despite my scrimp-and-save advice, there will be readers who want to buy a **big, new tractor**, whether or not it is needed. I will now stop berating these readers for wanting all things bright and shiny, as well as something they probably don't need. Here are some considerations for buying a new tractor.

You want to size a tractor to the work you want it to do. Size is mostly judged by **horsepower (hp)**. The heavier the stuff is that you want the tractor to pull and operate through its **power take-off (PTO)** and **hydraulics**, the more horsepower you need. PTO refers to an engageable, rotating shaft at the back of the tractor that can run both stationary and mobile attachments like grain elevators, generators, hay balers, bushhogs, winches and crop machinery. Look between the rear wheels for a splined shaft sticking out of the rear end of the engine—that's the PTO. A nearby lever engages it. It rotates at the speed of the tractor's motor. Both PTO and hydraulics are discussed below.

If you undersize a tractor for its work, you will use it up; if you oversize, you will be wasting your money, in both purchase and maintenance. A safe rule is to get sufficient power for all your foreseeable tasks with maybe a little extra for what you might need in the future. The previous farmowner—the seller—is an excellent source of information on tractor sizing for the farm work he did. And you may want to package your farm purchase with his equipment, assuming it checks out.

When sizing the tractor to the job, you also have to size the implements to the tractor and the work. An implement too big for its tractor will not do what you want it to do, and the undersized tractor will not last long trying to do it.

"The Little Engine That Could" might make a candy run over the mountain once or twice, but it would soon collapse from repeated efforts of that magnitude. You can ask your tractor to do more than it's sized for every so often, but that practice catches up with it eventually in blown thises and stripped thats.

Horsepower is a unit of power measurement. One hp was fixed by James Watt, the modern steam engine's inventor, as equal to doing 33,000 foot-pounds of work in one minute. (A "foot-pound" is the work done by the force of one pound moving through a one-foot distance in the direction of the force.) Since horses were the standard engines of work at the time Watt was tinkering, "horsepower" has been our way of rating engine power for more than 150 years. One hp is equal to 745.7 watts, named after James.

Tractors have different horsepower ratings at different points in their mechanical anatomy. **Gross engine horsepower, or indicated horsepower**, is the power the manufacturer estimates is produced at the cylinders. This is usually the type of horsepower that is used to rank tractors, even though it is a theoretical rather than an actual rating. It is theoretical, because as power is transmitted mechanically through shafts and gears, gross horsepower is lost. Some manufacturers publish a **net engine horsepower** rating, which is generally three or four "horses" lower than gross. You may also find tractor engines rated according to **kW**. (One kilowatt equals 1,000 watts; a watt measures the amount of energy the tractor's engine consumes at a certain speed.) The kW rating will be about 75 percent of the horsepower rating.

You will also find tractors rated according to **PTO horsepower or shaft horsepower**, which is the power available to do work at the PTO shaft when the tractor is stationary. PTO horsepower will be less—a lower number—than engine horsepower, somewhere between 85 to 90 percent of gross horsepower.

The third type of horsepower is **drawbar horsepower or effective horsepower**, which is the power available at the drawbar when the tractor is moving forward. The drawbar is a horizontal steel bar at the back of the tractor where implements and trailers/wagons are hooked on. Drawbars are discussed below. Drawbar horsepower represents the power that's left to pull or power equipment. There's roughly a ten to 15 percent horsepower loss between each rating step—gross, net and drawbar. Manufacturers' sales literature usually gives gross/indicated engine and PTO horsepower ratings. A 20 hp (gross) tractor will be underpowered when hooked to an implement that requires 20 hp at the drawbar.

You may also find reference to **brake horsepower**. This rating is the maximum horsepower available from an engine as measured by a dynamometer. A tractor engine's brake horsepower should exceed its expected normal operating load. An engine should not be run in excess of 80 percent of its brake horsepower—those red areas on the rpm (revolutions per minute) gauge where you want to be as little of the time as possible.

You will also hear some other "enginey" terms that you may or may not need to understand. **Displacement**, measured in cubic inches or "cubes," is the total volume of space that the engine's pistons move through on a single stroke. Bigger engines have more cubes. More displacement in a given engine size means that it won't work as hard to generate the same amount of horsepower and will operate at a slower engine speed, which is good for fuel consumption and service life. **Cylinders** are the spaces inside the engine's block in which the pistons move and where the fuel is combusted. Today's smaller tractors will have three cylinders and the bigger ones, four. **Lugging power** is the ability of an engine to continue to pull hard while the engine's rpms fall, which happens when the engine is under load. The more **torque** (the engine's ability to turn its central shaft under load), the more lugging power and overall power a tractor will have. **Engine speed** is measured in rpms; lower engine speeds are easier on the machine as well as on your ears. Other things being equal, a 25 hp tractor with a rated rpm of 2,600 will wear longer than the same horsepower tractor with a rated rpm of 2,800.

Smallish tractors were widely used after WWII, and the common ones are readily available in farming areas. Today, small tractors, called "**compacts**," are available in three gross horsepower classes: 1) 18 to 25 hp +/-; 2) 25-35 hp +/-; and 3) 35-45 hp +/-. A 25- to 35-hp (engine hp) tractor should be able to handle the work of most small farms with power to spare. While some compacts can be rigged for front-end loading, backhoe work, log skidding and other heavy-duty tasks, you will do better in the long run to hire a bigger machine and its skilled operator to do the occasional big, tricky or dangerous job. (Follow this advice and you may continue to have a long run.) New compacts are now priced between $10,000 and $25,000. Newsweek reported that Americans bought 900,000 garden tractors in 2005, and that hobby farmers, who make less than $500 annually from agricultural sales, made up 55% of these compact-tractor sales. (Karen Springen, "Let the Good Times Roll," Newsweek, March 13, 2006.) The next category of tractors are those in the 45-50 hp to 65-70 hp range. The largest tractors exceed 70 hp. A helpful article is Bryan Welch's "Discover Versatile Compact Tractors," Mother Earth News, April/May, 2006.

Here's a list of things you will probably get with a new tractor:

1.. Roll-Over Protection System (ROPS). Manufacturers began installing a ROPS (at the very least a rollbar) as a standard feature about 1985. Do not buy a new tractor without one. **A seatbelt must be used with a ROPS**, but if you are using an old tractor without a ROPS, do not use a seatbelt. Tractor rollovers (sideways) and flips (front end over backwards) are the most frequent cause of farm fatalities. Several U.S. manufacturers are encouraging their dealers to retrofit ROPS/seatbelts at cost—about $600, plus freight and labor—on older models. Make sure that your tractor with a ROPS will fit into the building where you will park it. Bigger tractors have cabs that include rollover protection. On old tractors, you may be able to get a local welder to fabricate a rollbar out 3" tubular steel that he bolts to the frame.

2. Earmuffs. Buy good-quality ear protection to protect your hearing. Noise reduction rating should be 25, or more. You may look like Michael Dukakis riding a tank, but you will be able to hear your kids ask for tuition when you are 50.

3. Four-Wheel Drive (4WD). It costs about $1,000 to $3,000 or more to add this feature. Take this option, and you will bless me at least twice a year. If you pay me no heed, buy a set of **wheel weights** for the back tires. You might also consider a set of chains. Buy the 4WD, and call it an investment in your safety—which it is.

4. Category 1, Three-Point Hitch. This rigging at the back of the tractor allows you to hook up and lift/lower common implements. Thus, you can lift a bushhog over a rock or raise a plow when you need to cross a road. Category 1 is the size that will work with most tractors under 50 hp. Your tractor hitch will need an adjustable **toplink** that has sockets at both ends; you hitch one to the tractor and the other to the implement. Toplinks are readily available at farm-supply and tractor stores. The other two "points" on the three-point hitch are sockets at the end of hydraulically operated **lift arms**, or rocker shafts**.** Each implement will have two cylindrical stubs that slip through these sockets. The stubs are secured with locking pins. Never substitute a chain for a toplink on an old tractor without a ROPS, because you risk having the implement swivel on the lift arms and come over on top of you. Old tractors may only have a pin hitch and a PTO. Lacking a hydraulic hitch, these tractors are limited to activities like pulling wagons and running a hay baler. Tractors made in the late 1950s and thereafter are almost always rigged for a hydraulic hitch. Avoid tractors that require brand-specific implements rather than Category 1's universality. Older models of Allis-Chalmers, Farmall and others used a **proprietary hitch**, which would only accept same-brand implements. The mid-50s Fords and Fergusons came with what became the standard Category 1 hitch. The 8N Fords from that era are still widely used because they are relatively cheap, reliable, parts friendly and can handle all the Category 1 implements. Category 0 ("ought") refers to a smaller hitch design; Category 2 refers to the larger hitch you find on 50 hp+ tractors.

5. Power Take-Off. Don't buy any tractor (new or old) without an independently engageable PTO, that is, a **live power take-off**. A live PTO allows you to operate stationary machinery at the rear of the tractor when the tractor is standing still and in neutral. You can run a hay and grain elevator, concrete mixer, electric generator, posthole auger, winch, arc welder, air compressor and pump from a stationary tractor with a live PTO. New tractors should have this. Make sure the exposed, six-spline shaft at the rear is protected by a **heavy metal shield** that is welded or bolted onto the tractor. The PTO shaft itself should be covered when not in use by a **protective plastic sleeve**. Never step on the bare PTO shaft, either at rest (which will wear down the splines) or when turning (which will wear you down quickly and badly). Keep yourself and your clothing clear of this spinning shaft.

6. Power Steering and Hydrostatic Transmission. Life is easier with both. Old tractors have neither. A tractor with a full front-end loader that does not have power steering is your upper-body work-out machine. Older tractors did not have synchronized transmissions, which means you, like me, have to come to a dead stop to shift into each gear. New tractors have synchronized transmissions and some have a hydrostatic transmission that allows you to slip from forward to reverse without coming to a dead stop and provides many speeds. If you have to do a lot of tight work, "backing and forthing"—shuttling material from one spot to another—the hydrostatic transmission at an extra $1,000 will be well-spent.

7. Hydraulics. Hydraulics refers to a tractor-mounted system that pumps fluid (oil) under pressure to operate attachments and implements, such as the front-end loader, three-point hitch, log-splitter and post-driver. Bigger tractors will have **live hydraulics** at the rear and possibly in the mid-section of the tractor (in addition to the loader controls) that allow you to operate an attachment like a post-driver from the ground. You need at least about 25 hp to operate these type of attachments. Live hydraulics is not a farm necessity, but it allows you to do more work with less effort. There's a cheap kind and a more expensive kind of hydraulic oil. You can use the cheap kind in the tractor's rear differential but not in the other hydraulic systems. Make sure you use the right kind of oil for each system. Better to use the expensive kind throughout. Try to keep dirt out of the system by cleaning/replacing breather filters and using clean funnels when adding hydraulic fluid. Do not put yourself under a raised loader or other attachment. If a hose were to choose that moment to blow out, you will learn that gravity pulling down heavy metal moves faster than you do. If you must be underneath, block up the load.

8. Friendly Ergonomics. Easy Mounting. You will be getting on and off your tractor a lot—to open and shut gates, hook and unhook stuff, fix stuff that you've just fixed, etc. Make sure that you can get on and off easily and safely. If you lose your footing getting off, what will your head hit? Also check for **visibility** in the front—a sloped front provides better visibility. Most new tractors and recent models have a sloped front. Favor a model where the **exhaust** is vented under or behind the driver's seat rather than in a stack sticking up in front of you—unless you get off on fumes. Exhaust smoke is unpleasant and bad for you, particularly in semi-enclosed spaces. The front stacks also tend to snag tree branches. The bigger tractors use the front stacks; many of the compacts vent behind. If the tractor has an enclosed cab, you can live with a front stack.

Check for **easy access** to dipsticks, liquid containers and grease fittings (which are little nipples that you attach your grease gun to and pump grease into; failure to grease your tractor results in large repair bills).

Check **hitch ease.** If you've never connected an implement to a three-point hitch or a PTO, do it on the dealer's lot. The design should let you attach stuff with as little lifting, leveraging, pushing and grunting as possible. If you start sweating on a fall day, look at other brands.

9. Front-End Loader. This is a hydraulically operated bucket at the front of the tractor that scoops, lifts and dumps. Bigger tractors have bigger buckets, higher lifts and more capacity. Very handy. Have your local machine shop or mechanic weld a couple of self-locking **grab hooks** onto the loader's frame (not the bucket itself) so you can pull and lift things with a chain. Some models have a quick coupling arrangement that allows you to install or uninstall the loader in a few minutes. These quick couples give you the opportunity to save fuel and tractor wear and tear by making it easy to take off the loader when you don't need it.

If an older tractor does not have a front-end loader, you may be able to find one that fits. I found a Dearborn loader in a cornfield that could be matched up with my old Ford. I discovered after the job was done that I could mount the tractor only by climbing into the seat from the rear. This meant navigating a jungle gym every time I got on and off. The

Dearborn's seller knew that I would lose the safety and ease of side mounting with this old design. I didn't know enough to ask, and he knew enough not to tell.

10. Forks. If the bucket on the front-end loader does not slip onto a set of forks, have your local welder add forks to the loader's frame. This will allow you to remove the bucket and use the forks. I use the forks far more than the bucket. Weld grab hooks onto the fork frame. Forks are far more useful than the one-prong **spikes** you can buy for round hay bales.

11. Stuff.

> **a. Drawbar**. This is a thick piece of steel with holes through it that attaches between the two lift arms of your three-point hitch when you are running without rear implements. It is the metal bar from which pulling power (hp) is measured. Make sure the cylindrical stubs of your drawbar match up with the size of your lift-arm sockets. You'll probably need some type of **stabilizer device**, which is one or two metal arms that keep the drawbar or implements from swaying back and forth as you drive. You hook wagons and other wheeled machinery to the drawbar with a thick metal pin.

> **b. Bushhog**. These are field/brush mowers used for rough cutting jobs, such as thistle whacking. The Category 1 models are four-to six-feet wide, and they're configured with one or more blades, or a bat-wing-style blade. New models have clutches to protect their joints and shafts when a rock or hidden stump stops the blade dead. They are usually powered off the rear PTO, though some have their own gas engines. **Bush Hog** is a brand of mower, though it has become the vernacular name. (See www.bushhog.com.) Get a **mounted model** that you can raise and lower using your three-point hitch, not a pull type.

> **c. Finish Mower**. Optional. If you have a big lawn, get one.

> **d. Adjustable Blade**. Allows you to scrape dirt, rock, gravel, manure and snow going forward or push it going backward. Get the heaviest blade your tractor can handle; the lighter ones bounce more than they grade. Make sure the blade is as wide as the outside distance between your rear wheels.

> **e. Trailer**. Get a single-axle, four-sided cart for hauling firewood, rocks, hay bales, gravel, heavy stuff, supplies, manure and kids. Saves wear and tear on your new $35,000 pick-up truck. Used trailer carts are always available. Unless you're suited to the task, don't try to make your own. Hook to the tractor's drawbar using a pin or ball hitch with safety chains.

> **f. Hay Wagon**. Optional. Four-wheeled, open-sided wagon with end rack. Handy for hay bales, both square and round. Also lumber and fence stakes. Get a couple of mechanical binders/tie-down ratchets to use with chains.

> **g. Manure-spreader**. Optional. If you have to clean out a barn (poultry, horses, cattle, etc.), the spreader allows you to haul the manure to a field where it then kicks it up and out as you drive forward. Operates from rear PTO or is ground-driven.

> **h.** If you did not get a front-end loader, consider buying a heavy-duty three-point **lifting boom** and a heavy-duty **three-point platform lift**. Both attach to the three-point hitch at the back of the tractor. The boom allows you to lift something heavy several feet in the air. The lift is a platform, either open-sided or boxed in. If you are intending to put a lot of weight on the rear end, get a set of **ballast weights** that

attach to the tractor's front end, otherwise your tractor will rear up and paw the air.

i. Posthole Auger. These work well in some soils, but are useless in others. For stony soils, you will need a **hydraulically operated post driver** that pounds the post/stake like a pile driver. Neighbors will have such drivers, and will know how to operate them safely. Posts, incidentally, are stouter than stakes. They are used in corners and for hanging gates. In my neighborhood, good posts are eight-feet long and at least 8" in diameter. Stakes are the same length, but split from logs. Yellow locust is the preferred wood. Unless you intend to spend a lot of time and money building fence, I'd advise against buying a post driver for your tractor. It's usually more economical to hire fence builders.

j. Plow and disc (harrow). A plow turns ground over as a first-step in planting row crops or a garden. A disc harrow breaks up dry clumps of dirt left after plowing. Harrows come in different sizes and need to be matched to the size of your tractor. A heavy-duty, walk-behind tiller can handle a garden of an acre or two. More than that, you should consider an appropriately sized plow and disc.

k. Low-boy trailer. What happens when your tractor breaks down? You have three choices: 1) field repair, using yourself, a skilled neighbor or a mechanic who makes house calls; 2) pay someone to haul the recalcitrant beast to a shop; or 3) haul it on a low-boy trailer that you hitch to a big-enough pick-up truck or SUV. Low boys are handy for other hauling chores. You will need to figure out how to get the dead tractor onto the low boy. Make sure the low boys's hitch matches the hitch arrangement on the pulling vehicle. Generally, buying a low-boy is an unnecessary expense; someone around you will have one for hire or rent.

l. Seat. You should fit comfortably. As you're sitting on it, turn and look behind you at an imaginary bushhog. You will be spending hours in a tractor seat looking behind you. Make sure the seat allows you to do this comfortably. Swivel seats are a great improvement. Old tractors have uncushioned steel seats bolted to a spring. The seat bottoms out hard when the tractor rolls over a bump. You always wanted to know why old farmers walk funny; this has to be one reason. It's why I walk funny.

12. Grease Gun. You'll need a grease gun whose nozzle head matches the ball-shaped fittings on your tractor and attachments. Use it. Put the cartridge into the gun with its opened end facing away from you unless you yourself are in need of lubrication.

13. Chains. Get at least two 3/8" x 14' log/tow chains with **grab hooks** on each end. This size chain gives you 2,600 pounds of capacity. Half-inch chain provides 4,500 pounds of capacity, but weighs 38 pounds vs. 19 pounds for the 3/8". High-test towing chain provides more capacity at roughly the same cost with just a little bit more weight. Do not put slip hooks at the end of these chains.

14. Diesel or Gasoline Engine? You will need to choose. A diesel engine is more expensive to buy and maintain, and can be cranky in the cold. It gives more power per unit of fuel input, and is simpler (no spark plugs). Gas engines are more familiar to first-timers. Some manufacturers, such as New Holland, use diesels exclusively in their compact tractors. New Holland's line of compacts is called, "Boomers," which says a lot about who's buying small, expensive farm equipment these days.

15. Rear Tires. Three kinds are available. The first type is referred to as R1, Agricultural or General. This tire is what you think of when you imagine a tractor tire. It has V-style grooves and is good in fields. Driving a lot on paved roads wears its tread. The second type is R 3, Turf or All-Weather. It has a flat tread that is designed to work on grass without tearing it up. It is used on lawns, but not fields, mud, woods or snow. The third type is R4, Industrial, which is intended for light industrial work. It's a variation on the R 1. Pavement won't wear R4 treads as fast as R1. The same tread designs are available for front tires on 4WDs. Have the dealer or a mechanic fill rear tires 50 to 75 percent full with the proper mixture of water and calcium chloride for better traction. This solution prevents freezing down to -60 degrees F. If you're buying a used tractor with worn rear tires, buy a new set. Otherwise, you will spend a lot of time spinning your back tires in place on mud and in snow.

16. Tricycle or Wide-Front Tire Configuration. Almost all new tractors are wide fronts. Stay away from the old tricycles because they are more "rolly" on slopes and don't bite into slick surfaces when turning. Consider a tricycle if you are only interested in row-crop agriculture on relatively flat land.

17. Hand tools and odds and ends.

   a. Come-a-long (power puller). Get a big one (four-ton) and a small one (one-ton).

   b. Heavy-duty jack. High-lift, upscale, bumper-jack model—7,000 pound capacity. Can also be used with a chain at either end as a winch in a pinch. You should also get a screw-type jack that raises the tractor from underneath.

   c. Tire-inflator. It works off the cigarette-lighter in your car. Front-tires of tractors pick up punctures from nails, fence staples and locust thorns. Unlike human beings, tractor tires pick up stuff more easily as they get older. You can now get an electric battery-charger and tire-inflator in one unit that you need to charge every so often.

   d. Drawbar hook, which is a grab hook for chains that pins through the drawbar, and a **drawbar clevis**, which is a u-shaped connector used to attach things that are being pulled.

   e. Miscellaneous. Screwdriver, locking pliers, electrical tape, tire gauge, extra **drawpins or hitchpins** that are used to connect pulled implements and extra **locking lynch pins** that are used to connect the three-point hitch. Your tractor should have a little toolbox for this kit. You'll also need hydraulic fluid, funnel, gear oil, engine oil, grease cartridges and shop towels.

   f. Fire-extinguisher—you won't laugh the one time you're out in drought-beset woods and an electrical short causes a fire. Attach the extinguisher to your tractor, using bungee cords.

18. Slow Sign. A red safety triangle should be fastened somewhere—on the ROPS or rear fender—facing traffic behind you.

19. Tractor Bunnies. Compact tractors are not designed to transport passengers. I will sleep better if I write that without qualification. Make your significant other and kids walk. Tractors are tools, not toys. While farm kids learn how to drive tractors and stick shifts when they're eight or nine, I would not let kids run farm vehicles until I had confidence in their maturity. Kids should not be driving 35 hp tractors—kids of any age.

And so inevitably we come to the subject of **used tractors**, a favorite topic in America's countryside. Tractors are worked hard on real farms. Little old ladies don't buy them to drive to church. (I know of only one little old lady who's bought a new tractor, and she's a retired lawyer. She drives to church in an SUV and used to drive sports cars.) "Used" usually means worked hard if it's been owned by a hard-working farmer.

I'd start thinking about a used tractor by finding out why the owner wants to sell it. Good reasons are: 1) he needs something bigger; and 2) he's leaving farming. You can get reasonably priced tractors in good condition in both situations. Buying from a tractor dealer can be a safer option, though you will pay more for the same tractor. Dealers take in trade used tractors that are in fair condition and better. They avoid the basket cases because there's not much profit on their resale and the buyer will soon be complaining and asking for free repairs. The basket cases are sold by FSBOs who can't do a trade in. Look for a dealer-owned used tractor with as few hours as possible, less than a 1,000 might be your target. Ask to test drive it at your farm for a week, with haulage at your expense. If the dealer refuses, ask for a 30-day money-back return agreement or, failing that, a 30-day parts-and-labor warranty. If the dealer refuses, give the tractor a hard workout on the lot, preferably on muddy ground going uphill and down.

There's no substitute for field testing a tractor. Driving around the dealer's paved and level lot in third gear is not a field test. Drive it through all of its gears, under load if possible. Hook it to a loaded hay wagon. Drag a log uphill. How much traction do your front wheels lose when skidding a log? Does the tractor slip out of gear under load? Is the steering tight? Does it feel tippy when you are traveling across a slope? Do you have pulling traction on mud, ice and slick ground? Can you brake coming down a hill with weight behind you? Drive with a loaded front-end bucket—how's your visibility ahead of you?; how hard is it to steer?

Farm liquidations often auction farm equipment, including tractors and farm trucks. If you can field-test these machines a day or two before the auction with a knowledgeable individual, you can buy with reasonable confidence. Simply hearing the engine run on auction day is not good enough. I've found that auctions often get above-market prices for tractors, but I've seen the opposite on occasion. Auctions are snapshots of a local market at a specific moment. As a rule, you will do best at equipment auctions when farm commodity prices are down and interest rates are high. But you can never know the hammer price in advance. Just keep in mind that auction tractors are bought "as is" with no guarantees and limited disclosures.

There are a lot of bad reasons to buy a tractor from a farmer FSBO, especially if this is your maiden tractor purchase. Most bad buying reasons involve a low "get-in" price, which is the first step into every quagmire, and a new paint job. Tractors, like every thing built and operated on a farm, are entropic. They start falling apart and wearing out from their first hour of use. Who better to know when a tractor's general entropy has passed the point of economic repair than its owner? Nonetheless, there are several recurring rationalizations that have run through my head on at least one occasion, including: 1) it's knocked to shit, but it's cheap; 2) it leaks oil, but...; 3) it smokes bad, but...; 4) it slips out of gear, but...; 5) it ain't got no power no more, but...; 6) the PTO slips out of engagement under load, but...; 8) it needs rings, seals, bearings, new electrics or "just a clutch," but.... Do you see the common noose in these lines of argument?

When you face a used tractor in a farmer's front yard, it will have been cleaned up. You will find yourself judging what you can't see by what you can. In these circumstances, you may be weighing a known—below-market price—against the unknowable future costs of repairing the tractor's interior woes. If you pick up one big reason not to buy, you probably should assume that a lot of little reasons are present though not obvious. Of course, "good deals" exist, which is why impulsive bargain hunters trick themselves into believing that their act of purchase inoculates the tractor from future distress.

If you ever hear a FSBO use any form of the word "rebuild" as in, "You might want to rebuild the binglebanger before you...," RUN HOME! Rebuild means a big, expensive job, which can approach a year at Harvard. Rebuilding the binglebanger may lead to rebuilding other parts that it is tied into or dependent on. The deeper into the engine the owner's whispered reference to rebuilding is directed, the faster you want to run home.

If you are new to tractors, you will discover that many farmers are intensely brand loyal and proselytizers to boot. It's helpful to get such an individual to go with you to evaluate a used model of *his* brand. He'll give you an honest opinion, as long as you agree that his brand, when hooked end to end, will pull every other brand all over the lot. But it may not be useful to have a brand-loyal man help you scope other brands, none of which, in his opinion, are worth anything by definition. It is, on the other hand, extremely helpful to have a general-practice farm mechanic or a brand-neutral farmer help you evaluate used tractors. Pay this person fairly—his normal hourly rate plus—for his consulting time, especially if he consents to go looking with you. If he hauls equipment, pay him to haul your beast home. Buy him a good breakfast and a big lunch.

The Yesterday's Tractors website (www.yesterdaystractors.com) posts a large number of useful articles dealing with the infirmities of older tractors. In "Buying your first tractor: Choosing the right one," the anonymous author assumes you are buying used. Here's his checklist in abbreviated form:

Does it start easily? Make sure that you try a cold start.
Does it run well when hot? Run it under drawbar/hydraulic load.
Do the brakes work well? Do they stop the tractor?
Does it smoke? (The author is referring to exhalation, not inhalation.)
Does it make clunking noises from inside the engine?
Is the oil foamy, filmy (with water) or so black and thick that you could cut it into brownies?
Is there engine head seepage?
Is the clutch good?
Does the electrical system charge?
Do the hydraulics and PTO work?
Are there cracks in the metal castings—engine, transmission housing, etc.?

Here are my additions to this check list: Be alert for engine roughness, dripping leaks (fuel, engine oil, hydraulic fluid, antifreeze, brake fluid), slow-moving hydraulics, electricals that don't work, six-volt battery rather than the preferred 12 volt, welds or metal patches on crankcase, blistered paint (fire!), evidence of roll-over damage, odd noises, fresh paint, new tires and fresh paint, gear slipping into neutral while under load, PTO slipping under load, hydraulics slipping (Lift a loaded bucket, turn the engine off. The bucket should stay up.), dreadful ergonomics, tires with little tread (rear tires are expensive), hard to shift gears, no grease in fittings, low liquid in differentials, outside parking (lots of rust) and, finally, not running.

Don't buy a **not-running tractor** at any price—especially a not-runner whose oil-filler cap has been lost thus allowing rain, dust and mice to get into the engine. A not-runner may be described as one of the "up boys"—**froze or locked**. This gang of two hangs out inside the tractor where a lack of lubrication, broken parts or rust prohibits the normal turning of shafts and gears. Nothing involving the up boys comes cheap. Cousins to the up boys are a couple of girls who never get asked to dance. They are always described as having a little something wrong with them—"Her ignition switch give out." or "Oh, she's just got her a blowed gasket." It stands to reason that a seller would make a minor repair to get a girl up and running before introducing her to a suitor. This no-runner is likely to have more wrong with her than a switch and a gasket. The lamest excuse for not running is a dead battery. If a seller is too lazy to charge a battery or get a new one, what greater evils has his poor character wrought? You don't want to buy this answer. In short, here is the best used-tractor advice I ever received: "If it don't run good, don't buy it."

I'd also be careful with buying a tractor that the seller claims "was running when I parked it." Every tractor was running before it wasn't, including the up boys. Sitting tractors can be either totally non-operational or victims of disinterest. In either case, **"sitters"** become homes for wasps and playgrounds for rodents who like to gnaw on electrical wire insulation. Gasoline left in a fuel tank and carburetor turns to a gunk that must be cleaned out before the engine will run. Moisture can build in an unused hydraulic system. Tires weaken when they stay in one position for a long time. Still, short-time sitters can be real bargains if the owner purchased a replacement and just never got around to selling the old one. Sooner or later, he'll want the parking spot in his shop or barn for something else. His wife may be on his back to "get rid of that old thing." When a seller is tired of looking at a tractor, that's a good time to see whether it's worth buying. And don't forget to dicker for some throw-ins—implements, grease gun, shop manual, PTO connector shaft (which has a universal joint at each end) and spare parts.

"Knocked to shit" is another type of tractor you should avoid. You know this fellow when you see him. He sort of runs, a kind of semi-functioning survivor of hard, long use and deferred maintenance. He looks like he just came out of fight. You'll find dents and welds, maybe even wire holding something in place. Certain farmers are cheap this way; I am sort of cheap this way. You want to leave to these farmers the spoils of their convictions. New paint is a frequent tip off that there's not much life left in this veteran.

Having said all of the above, I will also say that tractors carrying decades of age can be run another 20 years or more. The length of their future depends on what they've been used for, how many hours they carry, how well they've been kept up and how roughly or gently they've been handled. Tractors are designed to pull loads and run equipment. That work won't wear them out prematurely, but thousands of hours of that work inevitably will. What shortens a tractor's longevity is abuse—running it over stumps and rough ground, yanking rear loads out of jams, operating at high rpms, jamming gears, riding the clutch and failing to keep it oiled and lubed. Age alone is a factor, but not one that calls a third strike. Good deals can be found on old tractors whose owners no longer need them.

If a usable tractor from the 40s or 50s appears in your life, it may come with a rigid drawbar between its rear wheels and no three-point hitch system. You can either live within this limitation or consider a three-point retrofit. Kits are available to add a hydraulic hitch, and a skilled farm-implement mechanic may be able to fabricate one. (Before authorizing someone to jigger a hitch together, ask the jiggerer if he's performed this operation before and with what degree of success.) If your old tractor has no hydraulics, this will be a big-dollar retrofit. All things being equal, it's better to buy an old tractor with an operating Category 1 hitch rather than a cheaper old tractor that you plan to retrofit.

As a general rule, gasoline engines should be overhauled (big deal and costly) at 3,000 hours; diesels at 5,000 hours (bigger and costlier for same horsepower). Check the hours on the tractor; ask for rebuild records; don't be shy about this. Tractors built after the mid-1950s should have meters that record hours of full power on the engine. Ask how many rebuilds have been done? Talk to the mechanic if you can; he'll know the tractor as well as the owner. Ford 8Ns and 9Ns from the 1950s are common and may be in reasonable shape even without a functioning hour meter. Ask what the tractor has been used for. Don't buy a tractor that's been used for a lot of heavy logging: it's too rough a job for smaller farm tractors. Older, lighter tractors that have been fitted with a front-end loader will have front-end problems sooner or later if they have been used regularly for lifting heavy stuff (like wet manure) in tight spots that require a lot of turning. I'd recommend sticking with gas engines on older tractors, particularly if you're looking at one built before 1970.

I've included a photograph of my old Ford to illustrate a few points to keep in mind. The front-end bucket can be slipped off, leaving two forks for lifting logs, round bales and items that don't fit in the bucket such as woodstoves, water tanks and pianos. The forks are inserted from the rear into sleeves inside the bucket. The shop-made rollbar carries a warning sign and a fire extinguisher. The rear wheels on this 2WD tractor have new tires, which makes a huge difference in mud and in the woods. The wheels have been "turned inside out" to widen the rear wheel base and decrease roll-over risk. The three-point hitch is carrying a scraper blade, which can be turned so that it pushes material when the tractor's in reverse. The blade has been extended by about 12 inches on each side so that it is about as wide as the wheels, outside to outside. Heavier blades work better than lighter ones, though they're harder to wrestle on. The PTO shaft at the rear (under the hitch) is guarded by a metal shield. The two most objectionable features to this old rig are its front-mounted exhaust stack which inevitably forces me to share the engine's pollution, and, second, the necessity of climbing through the mess at the back to reach the seat. Small tractors of this vintage do not have 4WD, power-steering and rear hydraulics—all of which are handy.

PHOTOGRAPH 8-1

An Old-But-Still-Useful Tractor

It is possible that you are enough of a mechanic that you can do your own tractor repairs. If so, consider yourself one of Heaven's blessed. Working on a tractor is not like working on a 1967 VW bug. You'll need big wrenches and 1/2-inch drive sockets, and sooner or later a cutting torch and welder. Farm shops are heavy duty. Servicing a tractor is work that you will need to do, but working on one is not for the innocent.

If you are condemned, like me, to "lacking the aptitude," as my high school guidance counselor put it, find the nearest reliable tractor/farm equipment repair shop to your target property **before** you buy any farm that needs such machines. If the closest good mechanic likes to work on Fords, be disposed to buy a Ford. Don't assume that he will work on a foreign-made tractor, particularly one of the new entries. My experience is that local tractor mechanics like to do jobs they've done before on familiar brands. You want these mechanics to be your friends and welcome your business. Throw them nice big fat pitches, not screwballs. Ask the local mechanic what he thinks of the tractor you're about to buy.

Dealers charge labor rates that are almost always higher than rates charged by independent shops. Dealers may or may not work on brands other than their own. If the nearest tractor mechanic is a Kubota dealer, I'd look to buy a Kubota tractor, new or used. His rate will be higher, but convenience is worth money too.

My preferred mechanic would be an experienced independent, close by, who treats you and your tractor's woes with patience and humor. If he'll make house calls in desperate situations, you're set. When this wise man speaks, listen and obey.

Here are a few simple used-tractor tests.

A test for poor compression is to warm the engine and take off the oil filler cap. (This is where you put in motor oil; it is not the dipstick cylinder.) If oil or oily mist comes out, you have **blowby**, which indicates weak compression. If nothing oily comes out of the oil-fill tube, good.

On diesels, look for black jelly gunk coming out of where the engine block (bottom) and the engine head (top) meet. This fuel-and-oil mess will ooze out after the engine is warm and you turn it off. It means something is cracked inside.

On gas engines, look for antifreeze on the engine block. Start the engine and remove the radiator cap (remove slowly, using a mitt or towel to protect your hand). If you see air bubbles in the radiator liquid, there is a crack in the engine's block or head—both bad.

Smoke location and color are important. If smoke is coming off the engine as well as out of the stack or exhaust pipe, the tractor is leaking liquid and then burning it off. Could be a big repair. On gas engines, exhaust smoke should be white when you start and then clear. Blue smoke or black smoke indicates engine wear, usually a ring job, valve job, or both. If you find a lot of soot or oily mess at the end of the exhaust stack/pipe, oil is being burned—which is bad. On diesels though, black smoke is good when you're running with the throttle open; white smoke is a sign of burning oil.

Operate everything twice: once when cold (go on a miserable, rainy, freezing day); then when the engine's warmed.

Make sure the gauges, choke, levers, lights and hydraulics work. On older models, check the hand clutch and belt wheel.

On tractors with hand (gas) throttles, make sure the throttle handle engages fully and sticks in all positions. Throttle teeth tend to get rounded off in the most-used positions. If you find yourself with one hand having to hold the throttle in position and your other hand having to hold the gear shift in third, you have no hands left to steer. This can get hairy, especially when you're coming down a hill and you get a leg cramp.

Knock-out considerations. I would not buy a pre-1960 tractor for small farm needs if it had any one of the following shortcomings:

1. No live PTO.

2. No Category 1 three-point hitch.

3. No hydraulics capability.

4. Not running; froze up; locked up.

5. Loud internal clunking.

6. Smoking, indicating oil being burned or other liquids in wrong places.

7. Slipping of gears (transmission, PTO) under load.

8. Incapable of being retrofitted with ROPS.

9. An exotic brand or a model made by a now-defunct manufacturer. If you stick with familiar brands—Deere, Case, Ford, Massey Ferguson, IH—you'll be able to find parts and knowledgeable mechanics for the older machines. The more obscure American brands and foreign makes will be harder to service.

10. Too small to handle a front-end loader.

11. Anything that can be considered restorable as an antique.

12. Unless you like to do this work, leave the pre-1950s' stuff for the buffs. This includes everything with steel wheels.

Current prices for tractors are available in the most recent edition of Intertec's Used Tractor Price Guide (POB 12901, Overland Park, Kansas, 66212) or similar publications, available at any rural library and bank. Know your make (brand), model (year), model number, gas or diesel, number of engine cylinders, engine (indicated) horsepower, number of forward and reverse speeds and 4WD or 2WD. Increase value if it has a front-end loader, full hydraulics, good rear rubber and throw ins like a bushhog.

Parts is a subject in which you will become versed, well and otherwise. Before you buy an old tractor, check locally to see whether the nearest dealer can get parts for you. Sample his ability to get parts by asking if he can turn up a fuel filter, carburetor kit, clutch, rear differential, steering linkage, hydraulic seals and a radiator. Ask around to see how others with older tractors like the dealer's service. I try to avoid obscure brands for parts, though I might just be blindly prejudiced. Sometimes, you don't have a choice about where the part comes from and its price.

Check on the Internet for parts suppliers who handle your brand and model. Start with Yesterday's Tractors, www.ytmag.com, which posts shop manuals, recent used tractor values, links and specific information on Allis Chalmers, Case, Cockshutt, Farmall (IH), Ford, Ferguson, John Deere, Massey, Minneapolis-Moline, Oliver and others. The articles can be found at www.ytmag.com/articles/artint.htm. Use the Google search engine to look for brand-specific, tractor-parts suppliers, e.g., "antique Ford tractor parts." "Antique" sort of refers to pre-1970s models. You'll also find websites, newsletters and small magazines devoted to individual tractor brands. Common parts, for both old and new tractors, are available from Valu-Bilt, 3915 Delaware, POB 3330, Des Moines, Iowa, 50316; 1-888-828-3276; 1-800-433-1209 FAX. You can get buyer guides for different brands and shop manuals for the major brands from Valu-Bilt.

Once you have the tractor home, follow a few simple practices. Lubricate. Change the oil and various filters. Replace worn hydraulic hoses. Routine preventive maintenance on large and/or new tractors will save money over time. Other steps to take include storage out of the weather, periodic tune-ups, oil testing and not modifying the tractor's engine. (See Robert Grisso, "Five Strategies for Extending Machinery Life," Publication Number: 441-451, Virginia Cooperative Extension Service, January, 2002; www.ext.vt.edu/pubs/bse/442-451.html.) Run the tractor at least once every week or two, if only to keep the battery up. Pay attention to unfamiliar noises, wet spots and smoke. Do work slowly and gently; tractors are not dirt bikes. The more you ask your tractor to do what the tractor is not sized to do, the sooner you will be doing nothing at all.

Read up on tractors before you take your first look and test drive: "Compact Tractors: The Horseowner's Sports Car," Horse Journal, Vol. 8, Number 11, November 2001; Farm Journal editors, The Tractor Sourcebook 2002 from www.agweb.com/sig_home.asp?sigcat=farmjournal; Yesterday's Tractors at www.ytmag.com/articles/artint.htm; Chris Pratt, "Buying an Older Tractor," www.kountrylife.com/articles/art4.htm; Melody A. Snider, "Vintage Tractors: A guide to finding a used machine with years of work left in it," Country Journal, September/October, 1990. Get the appropriate owner's book and shop manual. Manuals and books on tractors/machinery, as well as other aspects of farm life, are available at www.diamondfarm.com; click on, general store, and then a specific category.

Tractors are not fun in the way sports cars are. They are useful, and, to that extent, provide satisfaction when they allow you to do a job properly. They've always served as markers of rural status and prosperity. You can buy one for $5,000 to $10,000 that will perform the same work as one costing two or three times that much. It will not be as shiny or as cool looking. If you buy a $30,000 tractor when a $5,000 tractor would do, your new neighbors will admire your tractor but maybe not you.

CHAPTER 9: UNDEVELOPED PROPERTY FOR HUNTING

Undeveloped property in the country is land on which there are no improvements, such as homes, barns and other structures, that carry an assessed value for tax purposes. Undeveloped land can be open or wooded, flat or hilly, dry or wet. When land is advertised as "undeveloped," it should mean that it contains no usable structures, no functioning utilities and no infrastructure to speak of. In practice, "undeveloped" land may contain functional improvements broadly construed such as a barely habitable house and a utility building or two.

When looking at undeveloped land, you should evaluate its possibilities for different levels of future development. Future potential directly affects the price you pay, whether or not you ever improve the property. Developing undeveloped property might mean anything from bulldozing a road to a cleared house site, to building a second home, to dividing 100 acres into 15-acre lots complete with paved roads, buried utilities and houses.

The value of undeveloped land is enhanced when utilities are either already installed or near *and* accessible. Not all nearby utilities are accessible. Neighbors may not be willing to agree to an easement, and the cost of bringing the service to where you want it may be high. It's easiest and usually cheapest to develop utilities on land where they have already been extended to the property. Land that contains **frontage** on a publicly maintained road usually has access to electricity. Frontage is valuable, because it gives property legal and physical access, except in cases where the latter is topographically impossible. If you have no plans to build a house or set up a mobile home, you need not look for undeveloped land with an eye toward a septic system, spring/well and electricity. But land that lends itself to the cheapest versions of these "utilities" has more uses down the road, should be easier to market and will bring a higher price than undeveloped land that lacks the possibility of development.

Undeveloped land is enhanced in economic value and usability to the degree that it is accessible, physically and legally, from a publicly maintained road. Though there are those with just the opposite opinion, I believe that undeveloped land benefits from **internal accessibility**, that is, a system of roads, creek crossings, culverts and trails that allow the owner to get around the property on most days of the year without getting his 4WD stuck. Hiking, horseback riding, fire protection, recreation and firewood-collection benefit from 12-foot-wide roads.

There are five main types of buyers for undeveloped land. Developers buy large tracts, divide them and then retail the resulting lots, which they may call **"farmettes"** in the East and **"ranchettes"** in the West. Second, individual buyers look for tracts of, say, 100 acres or less, for building a second home. The third type is an investor who tries to buy undeveloped land cheap and then sell it for an appreciated price in the future. Fourth, sawmills and timberland investors buy wooded tracts, mainly for their timber value. They may hold the tract or resell quickly after logging. These investors look for higher-and-better use (HBU) potential, which allows them to resell at a much higher price. Finally, there are buyers who are looking for a combination of open and wooded land for hunting. The second-home buyer tends to be the most willing to buy at the highest price per acre. Hunters are generally happy with larger tracts of cheap land as long as it provides habitat for the species they hunt.

HUNTING HUNTING LAND

If you're looking for a couple of hundred of acres of undeveloped woodland to use for hunting and fishing, you will save yourself the purchase cost if you can satisfy your needs on state lands and national forests, which provide game for the price of a license. The hitch is that you may find yourself sharing this space with others similarly inclined. That could be your best friend or a dozen obnoxious strangers. The closer your favorite public hunting or fishing spot is to a public road, the more likely it is that you will be sharing it just when you don't want to. Private ownership conveys the right to keep other hunters off. Privacy has a dollar value; people pay for it. And, assuming, that a particular tract produces only one ten-point buck a year, the hunter-owner wants to make sure that that buck comes within his gun's sights. For that reason, then, a hunter in my area will pay $1,000 per acre and more for scrub woods and old fields. This investment gets him into his woods on weekends—running a chainsaw, improving old logging roads, dozing out a couple of small ponds near his tree stands and putting in feed plots. What the hunter gets for his purchase is 1) the expectation that others won't hunt out his land when he's not there, and 2) steady appreciation in land value.

Serious hunters believe that having their own land is a *need*, not a want. The need is emotional and comes from their belief that hunting is a central axis in their lives and defines much of who they are. A cost-benefit analysis is misapplied to matters of identity and faith. If money, however, is an issue with you—in those moments when your field boots are drying and your wife is waving bills in your face—then allow me to present a few reasonable alternatives that can keep you hunting for a lot less than the cost of buying 100 acres.

Hunters can arrange a **hunting lease** with private landowners. The renter gets exclusive use of the land for a finite and reasonable amount of money. The renter does not bother with any of the hassles of ownership—taxes, insurance, fencing, insect infestations, flood repair and so on. The renter will need to arrange for accommodations during overnight visits. Some leases allow the renter to pitch a tent or set up a camper; others don't. You may be able to camp on nearby public land during hunting season. I've rented some of our property to hunters with good results all around.

The best version of a hunting lease is one that involves no money, that is, **free permission to hunt**. Farmers and absentee landowners are sometimes willing to give hunters permission to take fish and game from their land with no compensation. The landowner sees himself receiving benefit from reducing the number of wild creatures he considers nuisance "varmints," such as groundhog, rabbit, fox, coyote, skunk and deer. Certain game birds are hunted in harvested fields during the fall and have no value to a farmer's farming. As the deer population explodes, woodland owners who want to encourage tree regeneration may look kindly on hunters who reduce the whitetail population; I do.

Permission-hunters make arrangements in person with the landowner and often keep a connection for many years. If no money is paid for permission to hunt, the hunter should provide the landowner with something of value in return. The landowner may be interested in a portion of any edible game taken from his land. Or the hunter may bring the landowner a treat from his home town. Vermont hunters might give a gallon of maple syrup to a rancher in Idaho who lets them hunt fall birds. Or a hunter may swap some of his labor for permission. Lawyers, financial planners and auto dealers can offer advice or a discounted price in return for hunting privileges. Hunters discover permission tracts from their friends and from taking out ads in local papers. The key to a continuing relationship is for hunters to act responsibly. This means they agree to the landowner's ground rules about what and where to hunt, leaving gates open or closed exactly as found, cleaning up after themselves, shooting game (not cows, dogs, horses, hay balers and overalls hanging on a line) and paying for any accidental damage to same.

Landowners have some responsibility toward their hunter/tenants to notify them of concealed dangers (such as quicksand) and remove certain hazards (or provide warning where a hazard cannot be removed). Landowner liability increases if the landowner has done something willfully or grossly negligent that creates a hazard that results in injury. State law governs liability and responsibilities for both landowner and renter. Some states have a recreational-use statute that exempts landowners from the obligation to provide warnings or keep their property safe for individuals with permission to use the property for recreation. Where there is a fee- or rent-charging lease, however, the landowner may lose this protection. The hunting lease I provide for tenants places full liability on the tenant for property damage and injury that he either causes or sustains. If you lease hunting property as either a landlord or tenant, you should put the terms of the agreement in writing and have your local lawyer review it before signing.

Hunting leases are typically written to allow the lease holder access to the leased property for a calendar year. Different game species have different seasons. Wild turkey, for example, may be hunted in both the spring and fall in some states. Fall deer hunting may start with bow-and-arrow hunting, followed by black-powder hunting and then by a rifle season where bucks may be taken on any day but doe only on the last day. Game laws differ among the states, so the lease may have to be tailored to a particular state and even a particular county. Depending on the hunting schedules in a particular state, hunting leases may be expanded to allow non-hunting access during non-hunting times of the year. Woods-loving hikers or trail-riding horseback riders might share the cost of leasing land if it gives them access during non-hunting periods. Low-impact, off-season uses should present no problem to the landowner as long as he knows in advance who may appear in his woods. High-impact, off-season uses—four-wheeling, motorcycles, snowmobiles and the like—should never be done without advance permission from the landowner. If a renter's use produces road rutting and erosion the lease should require the tenant to repair the damage at the end of the use period.

The cost to lease hunting land depends on the type of land being rented, how often the hunters intend to be on it, the type of game that will be hunted, the degree of impact and other factors. Run-of-the-mill land might be rented for $5-$7 per acre/year, or more. Or the landlord may simply charge whatever his annual property tax is. Land for duck hunting and field birds is more expensive. Land and timber companies usually lease their land to hunters. Woods that have been recently timbered provide more game forage than mature woodland, so hunters will want to rent such land.

If a hunter persists in feeling the need to have his own hunting ground, he can consider buying into a **hunt club**. These are like-minded individuals who pool their money to buy a large tract. A club can also lease land in lieu of purchase. An individual may be able to buy a membership in an established club; otherwise, he will have to form a group from scratch and then look for land. Land-owning clubs can be organized as limited liability companies, corporations, partnerships, non-profits, trusts or other forms of joint ownership. Each type of ownership carries its own set of benefits, liabilities and tax consequences.

Buying a membership or a share in a hunt club is a commercial transaction that may put your future wallet in play for improvements to the club's land, facilities or future expansion. Where a club is governed either by majority rule or elected leaders, a member may be obligated for expenditures that he opposes.

As a member, you may also be entitled to a share in future revenue from the club's land. Club revenue can be generated from the development of minerals, the sale of timber or land. Clubs distribute current revenue to members or hold it in a club account for use in improving facilities and services, or a bit of both. It's important for a prospective member to have a clear idea of how the by-laws provide for future financial obligations, benefits, decision-making and leaving the club.

Your tax situation can also be affected by the structure of the club's organization. If you are buying an interest in the club's property and the club is set up as a business (anticipating revenues from timber sales and memberships), you will probably need to look at it as a business investment so that you obtain the appropriate tax benefits. A club membership, on the other hand, whereby you pay an entrance fee and dues is not an investment, though you may be able to consider it a business-related expense in some circumstances. Before buying into a hunt club, make sure that you understand the legal and financial implications of its organizational structure for your cash flow and tax obligations. If you're not sure how membership will affect your tax status, pay an accountant who does taxes (not all do) to review your finances and the club's structure.

Hunting clubs often buy back-country land that individuals interested in second homes reject because it's too rugged or too remote. Clubs are chiefly interested in good habitat for game species and sufficient size to provide good opportunities for all members. If you are thinking about forming a hunt club in anticipation of buying such land, you should plan for the estimated revenue the timber is likely to provide the next time it is cut and how your club members want that money handled. The kind of game the club focuses on will determine the kind of land it buys. Deer hunters, for example, value a mix of rough terrain with thickets, young woodlands, scattered openings/fields, and the tree species that provide fall mast and winter fodder. Views are unimportant, and electricity, telephone, soil productivity, timber quality and road frontage may be of less importance. Woods that have little timber value due to poor tree quality can produce abundant game forage. Hunters and hunt clubs can lower their acquisition expense by targeting land that has little value to second-home buyers who are seeking country aesthetics like big views and bold streams. Cost-conscious hunters should concentrate on finding tracts that combine the habitat of their game species with features repugnant to second-home buyers, such as remoteness, 4WD-only access, recent timbering, steep slopes, wetlands, lack of perimeter fencing and a seriously run-down house, which is good enough for hunters during deer season but not good enough to entertain the boss for a weekend. Hunting land should be cheaper than second-home land on a per-acre basis, unless it is also valued for timber resources or location.

In particular, hunters and hunt clubs should look for recently timbered tracts—**cutovers**—that should sell for a discounted price. A cutover discount should be twice applied: first, the seller has removed the timber's present value, and second, even in the best of circumstances, he has left the next owner a visual mess of tree tops that will last for at least five or six years. If the trees left standing are low-value species or worthless because of poor form, the buyer should add a third discount into his negotiations. A timber tract **high-graded** in this fashion impedes the regeneration of well-formed, high-value species on cutover land. It reduces the future value of the next timber cut.

From a hunter's perspective, cutover land provides better habitat for certain game species like deer and turkey than mature forest and pasture. Logging creates openings in the leaf canopy that allow sunlight to penetrate to the ground. This stimulates the growth of palatable vegetation and provides thick underbrush. Shade-loving vegetation is replaced by young, sun-loving plants such as tree sprouts, grass, high weeds and brambles. Logging also leaves **slash**, tree tops left on the ground after the logs are cut from the stem and taken to the mill. Slash provides cover for game and helps tree seedlings get established by protecting them from browsers. Slash is a big, ugly mess until it breaks down. Hardwood tops may have commercial value as pulp, chips or firewood, but loggers often find it not worth their time to work with it.

A **clearcut** removes all standing timber. Left in place are stumps and slash, which might be piled and burned. A **selective cut** removes some trees, usually determined by their diameter size and/or species. It leaves stumps, slash and standing timber. The more trees the seller has taken down in a selective cut, the worse the tract will look and the deeper the discount the hunter-buyer should propose. Both types of cutover may be called **raw land**, which is land lacking improvements, or **bare land**, which is land lacking both improvements and present timber value. Timbering turns raw land into bare land. When negotiating for cutover tracts, buyers should always refer to it as bare land to help lower the seller's sense of value. The value of bare land rests on its location, views, water resources, utilities, topography, subsurface minerals, access and other virtues. Cutover land is stripped bare when its owner wants to establish a tree plantation, which requires brush clearing and the application of herbicide to control unwanted vegetation. Woods with intermittent ten-to-20-acre clearcuts provide good habitat for many game species.

The concept of **bare-land value** does not refer necessarily to land that is physically bare. In my experience, rather, it refers to the fair market worth of cutover after the seller has removed or optioned whatever timber he could sell. Bare land, in other words, could have trees up to 14" in diameter and larger (where culls are left standing). Hunter-buyers should determine the current bare-land value of cutover land and use that number as the axis for their negotiations. Bare-land value on cutover tracts will increase over time as a result of timber regeneration and background appreciation. Typically, a hunter-buyer of a recent selectively cut tract should expect to pay about half the per-acre price the land would have brought with the timber in place. If the selective cut is severe, pay less than half. Clearcut land might be about one-third the price.

If the clearcut land has been replanted as a pine plantation, it will be valued at the cost of the replanting effort plus something for the dirt itself. Replanting cost—which involves preparing the site and planting the trees—varies with location, terrain, type of tree and its stocking density. Loblolly pine, a common fast-growing species, planted at 600 to 700 seedlings per acre might be valued in its first year at $600 to $700 per acre in many areas. An owner adds value to replanted pine by applying herbicide in a few years to suppress competition. Planted pine acreage is currently selling for between $1,000 and $3,500 per acre, depending on age and location. High prices are paid for tracts where the pine is ready to be cut. If the tract has residential development value (HBU), it will be priced above its timber value and above what a hunter should pay for hunting ground.

I have found in recent years a few selective cutovers priced at what I might offer for the land with all the timber in place. Their owners know the value of cutover to hunters and are pitching their property specifically to the cash-heavy urban hunter. These properties are located in areas where land is appreciating for reasons unrelated to hunting or timbering. In such cases, the buyer is usually paying for location. If the hunter-buyer's goal is simply to have a place to hunt, appreciating location is not a factor in his reasoning. Better to buy remote and cheap than near and dear. But if the hunter-buyer is looking at his purchase as an investment that offers hunting as a recreational benefit, a higher-priced cutover can work. Certainly within ten years, the cutover will look clean and have recaptured then-current, full market value.

A hunter will also value cutover tracts because they will have a network of 4WD-capable interior logging roads—called **skid roads**—that facilitate access throughout the property. These ten- to 12-foot-wide roads make it easy for hunters to get to their stands and then haul the field-dressed game out of the woods with a minimum of dragging and humping. Loggers bulldoze roads through the woods to allow them to pull out a half-dozen logs at a time using a large rubber-tired machine called a **skidder**, which usually has a dozer blade in front and a cable winch in the rear. A common plan is to have a main haulage way with spurs off to either side. On slopes, loggers may have the main road take most of the pitch, using switchbacks where necessary, with spur roads branching off along level contours. Skidders or dozers will drag a just-cut log from where it was felled to a place where it can be chained up with several others and dragged to the **landing**, or **deck**, for loading onto a truck. Landings are level spots of an acre or less near the entrance to the property. There, newly cut logs are sorted by species and quality, cut to length and then trucked to the log yard or sawmill. Some skid roads, left alone, are suitable for hiking or trail-riding on horseback, but they can be too steep for a tractor or too tightly curved for a truck. Still, the main skid-road network along with many spurs can usually be made truck capable with some dozer work.

Loggers want to build as little road as possible owing to the construction expense and the cost of applicable state reclamation standards. In some states, loggers are now expected to leave their logging roads with **waterbars** in place. Waterbars are dozed-out ditches that run diagonally across the road's width whose function is to funnel surface water off to the side where it is absorbed. They can be five feet wide and three feet deep. Waterbars minimize road erosion, but when they are too steep-sided or too deep they prevent subsequent vehicle use. In that event, the landowner has to rework them by hand or machine to make them passable. His purpose is not to fill them in. It is rather to keep an erosion-control channel in place, though in a broader, shallower form that allows traffic.

The logger should smooth a road disturbed by skidding or hauling before leaving. This is followed by seeding it with grass, which holds the dirt in place. The landowner will almost always need to tidy these post-logging roads by hand. Rocks and small tree branches need to be pitched aside and holes need to be filled. Some bulldozer work may be required to realign roads that are too steep or tightly switch-backed. Culverts and drainage ditches can be installed. While the hunter-buyer may object to redoing what the logger should have done, it is far cheaper to a new owner to upgrade existing roads—even ones left in poor condition—than to pay a dozer operator to cut new roads through a forest. A typical 50-acre hardwood tract that's just been logged and reclaimed might require a day or even two of bulldozer time to get the roads ready for vehicles, and then another couple of hours of hand work per ten acres to get them safe for travel by foot, hoof and tire.

With this level of effort, a hunter-buyer can improve most logging roads enough for near year-round 4WD use. Sufficiently deep snow or spring mud, of course, can bog a Hummer. If you use anything other than a 4WD vehicle on skid roads in the woods, expect to get stuck. Spruced-up skid roads are **not** suitable for year-round second-home access in wet and/or mountainous terrain. If you're looking to build a second home on a wooded tract that's been logged, you can start with a skid road but anticipate widening, ditching, regrading and adding culverts and stone/gravel if you're planning to bring in trucks loaded with cement, block and building materials. You may want to bury utility lines next to the roadbed when you're doing this work. Bridges are expensive and should be engineered to carry your heaviest load, plus 50 percent more for safety. Hauling base rock—about the size of a softball—and gravel to your road site can quickly involve a lot of money, because soft ground can eat up an enormous volume of rock. Where possible, work the road around wet spots rather than through them. Spots that are usually wet because of subsurface water may have to be dug out and filled in with rip-rap rock then topped with base rock and gravel. Water needs to be channeled out from under the road. Otherwise, the perma-mud will suspend rock and gravel like bits of sausage in gravy, and you've gained nothing for your expense.

As a hunter-buyer, you will save yourself time by asking the seller a few questions in your initial telephone conversation. First, you want to know the type of logging that's been completed—clearcut, selective cut or a combination of the two. The more cutting, the more open area and slash you will find. A hunter often prefers a combination of the two, which provides newly cleared areas within a selectively cut forest. If you are told it has been selectively cut, you need to pinpoint the date of the cutting and the selection criteria used to govern the timbering. The larger (wider) the diameter threshold, the more standing timber you will find when you arrive. A selective-cut threshold of 20" diameter and larger will leave much more timber in place than a 12"-diameter cut, that is, all the trees with diameters 12 inches and larger.

Timber size in the field is usually measured as **diameter at breast height (DBH**, which is taken at 4.5 feet above the ground.) Thus, a hardwood tract that was cut "18 and better" usually means that all the valuable 18" and larger DBH **hardwood sawtimber** was removed. You would find this cutover with stems smaller than 18" DBH, which is a stand with sizeable trees and future timber value within ten to 20 years. A heavier cut—using a smaller diameter threshold—usually benefits hunting because it creates more openings and edge in the remaining woods, but it lengthens the time needed for the remaining trees to add the diameter girth to make them merchantable.

The hunter also needs to ask whether all "18 and better" stems were taken, or just the high-value, hardwood sawtimber. If all stems—sawtimber and **culls**—were cut, the woods will be far more open than if the valuable sawtimber alone was cut. Culls are low-value species and trees that have no timber value for various reasons. Culls may have value as pulp, but not sawtimber. Hunting habitat will usually be better when both types of timber are cut. Dropping the culls also improves the woods in terms of future timber value, because the high-value trees left standing will have more access to nutrients and sunlight. From a hunting perspective alone, leaving the pulp logs in the slash will provide more wildlife forage and cover than if they're removed.

Be careful to pin down the seller's terminology. A seller telling you the timber was cut "18 and better" may be telling you either that the loggers took all sawtimber hardwood 18" and larger or all trees—hardwood and pulp—18" and larger. In addition, he may be saying either that all the trees were 18" and better **DBH** or 18" and better **at the stump**. In the latter case, the 18" diameter is measured at ground level, not 4.5 feet up the trunk. A stump cut of 18" and better can drop trees as small as 12" DBH, as long as the stump measures 18" across. The difference between 18" DBH and 18" at the stump will normally mean a huge difference in the number of trees cut and, accordingly, the number of trees left. The more timber removed, the deeper the price discount you should expect.

Hunter-buyers will also find timber tracts involving **planted pine**. Typically, these tracts are a mix of native hardwood that has been left along the water courses ("in the drains") for protection and even-age pine plantings. Where an entire stand of pine has been removed, hardwood and naturally occurring conifers will reestablish themselves. This provides food for wildlife, but not much cover until several years have passed. From an investment perspective, pine value comes in two "lifts": the first is a thinning cut that is taken at about 12 years, plus or minus, depending on local conditions; the second is the harvesting of the mature pine 12 to 15 years later. The cheapest price on pine-plantation land is just after a clearcut and before any replanting has occurred. Your next best price will be when the planted pine is less than ten years old, younger being cheaper. Pine land will be priced higher if hardwood growth has been suppressed by herbicides, which has the effect of increasing pine yield. Some pine is now being planted at 400+/-seedlings per acre with only a sawtimber cut planned.

Paper companies have been active sellers of this type of land since the 1990s. Typically, tracts of 20,000 to 100,000 acres or more will be divested to parties who then break them into smaller parcels of 5,000 to 20,000 acres which are then sold in 1,000- to 5,000-acre tracts that are then sold retail in lots of a 100 to 1,000 acres. At each step, the per-acre price is boosted by $50 to $200.

On mixed-species tracts, ask the seller what he thinks the most prevalent tree species is. This is usually framed in my neighborhood as, "What's it (run) heavy to?" You can then ask the seller for his opinion about the percentage distribution among species. If you're looking for deer habitat, you want the tract to run heavy to mast-bearing trees like oaks. These species allow deer to fatten in the fall, increasing their chances of surviving the winter and producing healthy offspring. You're also interested in young growth for winter feeding and a species like striped maple (moosewood) for browse. The County's <u>Soil Survey</u> provides soil maps with information ranking each soil's suitability for various wildlife habitats. Locate the seller's land on the soils maps and then refer to the table that sets forth habitat suitability. A hunter does not want to buy woodland whose standing trees won't provide good habitat for his preferred game. The question the hunter asks of cutover woods is: How productive is this cutover habitat for my game species?

The last information the hunter-buyer needs to find out in his first conversation with the seller concerns the tract's hunting history. The buyer needs to listen for what's not being said, as well as for what is. Most sellers of woodland will say, with varying degrees of honesty, "The hunting's great." Hunting for which game species? A deer hunter doesn't much care if the land is brimming with rabbits. How does the seller define "great"—by the number of trophy bucks or the number of deer taken each year? How hard has the land been hunted for the last five years? Are there too many deer for the land? Has he hunted the land himself recently? For what game? Does he get his legal limit each year? Is the land currently posted for hunting? (Yes is good; no could mean it's considered a public hunting ground.) Do neighbors and local residents hunt it? (Yes is bad; no is good.) Is it accessed by a locked gate? (Yes, means it has history as off-limits; no could mean anything.)

Do his relatives and buddies—R&Bs—also hunt the place? (If so, you may find the R&Bs showing up next hunting season. The seller, they will say, gave them permission to hunt before he sold to you, which is news to you. You can prevent this by including language in your purchase contract that requires disclosure of such an agreement.) If the buyer gets wind of R&Bs during negotiations, he must insist that the seller put the word out that the new owner will not grant hunting rights or recognize any claim to post-sale hunting rights. This might be accomplished by a newspaper ad. In years past, the seller may have given his R&Bs his personal permission to hunt. In the law, this is called a **license**, and it expires with the sale of the property. The buyer must be firm with both the seller and the R&Bs, otherwise the potential exists for continuing conflict during hunting season.

While cutover land can be a bargain for hunters, it can also work for thrifty non-hunters who are willing to live with unsightliness for a few years. A woodland buyer looking at cutover will find everything from land looking like it has just been bombed to land that has been roughed up but is essentially intact. Logging, no matter how careful, doesn't improve the immediate visual aesthetics of woodland. The day after a logging crew leaves, you can expect to find muddy skid roads, trees that have had their ground-level bark skinned off by logs being skidded out, trees with top branches broken by falling timber, slash everywhere and a general aftermath of recent mayhem. Don't be discouraged by slash. See it as an opportunity. It's easily gotten firewood. It rots pretty quickly and adds nutrients to the forest's soil. You don't want a spic-and-span forest floor free of debris if you're interested in healthy trees. In ten years, slash disappears completely in most environments on its own through Nature's recycling system.

I had a client who was selling about 500 acres in a very desirable, very pretty part of western Pennsylvania. The property had been a girl scout camp. My client had cut about 15,000 trees and put in about 15 gas wells. The camp—with all of its buildings, kitchens, pools and developed infrastructure—was untouched and in good repair. The timber sale and the gas development would almost pay for my client's purchase and then more over time. He was willing to let the surface go for a steeply discounted price, because he had no use for it. If a buyer could see seven or eight years out, he could acquire appreciating land and improvements at about 25 percent of their real value.

Bad logging jobs usually look worse than good ones. Bad logging is done as fast as possible, which generally maximizes the visual damage. These loggers drop trees with little concern for protecting those they're not taking. This leaves a lot of bashed up trees, leaning trees that will soon fall and widowmakers—broken branches hanging above the ground that fall without warning. A bad logging job looks ragged and messy. The skid roads are rutted, rocky and subject to erosion. You might find slash dropped across roads as a cheaper and faster alterative to waterbars. You might find tree tops in stream channels and straddling fence lines. The buyer needs to be able to distinguish between the roughed up look of a good logging job and the look of a bad logging job. A typical hardwood tract might take six to eight years for slash to rot to the point where it is no longer obtrusive. That process can be accelerated by wet conditions and some chainsaw work that lops the tops so that the wood lies closer to the ground. A bad logging job takes longer to heal. The battered trees are weakened and may never recover. Buyers should not equate immediate post-logging looks with future timber value, or roughed up aesthetics with environmental health. Cutover land can contain much future timber value and be environmentally healthy and productive as well. Hunters can make great buys on wooded tracts that have been severely cut and left a dreadful mess as long as they are willing to hold the land for at least 15 years. These opportunities allow the hunter to buy cheap and sell dear, after the land has healed.

My final point on aesthetics is that you can, as I have done, measurably improve a cutover's looks with a chainsaw, mattock, shovel and rock bar. Improvement does, however, take time and hand labor.

Slash decomposes fastest where as much of each tree top lies as close to the ground as possible. You hasten decomposition by lopping and bucking up the tops, cutting the branches from the main stems and cutting the stems into five- to ten-foot-long chunks. This allows both the top stem and the branches to settle. The combination of snow, rain, wildlife and bugs will get rid of the wood. After three to five years on the ground, most wood, with exceptions like yellow locust, gets punky and loses its value as firewood. By the third or fourth year, you will not see much of the slash in the summer as pioneer plants spring up in the open spaces. By the seventh or eighth year, most slash left to itself will be inoffensive. The best time to buy this type of land for an investor with a longer term horizon is immediately after logging when it looks its worst. Every year that passes improves cutover appearance and increases the land's value. A hunter should aim his buying at cutover and not clear its slash, except from roads.

If you want to accelerate slash decomposition, work a deal with a couple of local guys to take away all the slash firewood they want. In the best of circumstances, this work is hard and dangerous. It should not be attempted by inexperienced chainsaw users. If you wage this war yourself, wear protective chaps, gloves, steel-toed logger's boots, and helmet with hearing protection and a screen face mask. Cutting firewood out of tops is light on your cutover land, requiring nothing more than a pick-up truck and basic woods tools—chainsaw with extra blade and chains, splitting maul, logging chains, sledge hammer and a couple of wedges, peavey and a tie-pick. The last of these is an ax with its blade ground and sharpened to a point. It's used to pick up chunks of wood without bending. In addition to the aesthetic benefit of making your woods look better, the firewood boys will get your roads in shape for 4WD traffic. That means they'll help clear them of rocks and logging debris and remove anything that threatens their tires and exhaust systems. These folks are doing you a favor; don't charge them for the wood they remove and treat them well.

The first property I bought was a new cutover that was dirt cheap. I was too dumb-young to know how bad it looked or how bad a job the logger had done. But I did know that $5,000 for 60 acres 30 minutes from Amherst, Massachusetts wasn't likely to prove to be a risky investment in 1971.

Selectively cut hardwood tracts bought cheap will reward you financially in relation to the number of years you carry them. The longer you can hold a hardwood timber tract, the more value it produces. Depending on the individual characteristics of the site and the timbering job you've inherited, you should be able to take another selective cut 15 to 30 years down the road. And if you hunt the land every year—your main purpose, of course—you will have won three times.

CHAPTER 10: INFRASTRUCTURE—LAND, PROPERTY AND SITE

INFRASTRUCTURE PACKAGES

Many buyers are looking for second-home possibilities on undeveloped or semi-developed rural land. A second home can be anything from a mansion to a wilderness cabin. It is usually thought of as having a fixed foundation, but it may also be a mobile home or even a more-or-less permanently parked recreational vehicle. Mobile homes and RVs held by absentee owners are generally associated in my area with "hunt camps," places that are used a few weeks and a dozen or so weekends every year for hunting. Hunt camps, however, come in all sizes, ranging from a much-used trailer to a sumptuous lodge complete with servants. Hunters may or may not be concerned with a house site and house-related amenities.

The land buyers I discuss below are looking to have a second home on their land. This can take the form of buying a lot in a second-home development where the seller/developer is also the house builder, or land where the landowner needs to procure a **general contractor** to build the house, or a spot where the landowner wants to do the construction himself. The alternative is to buy land with an existing house. Each of these second-home options will involve you in the question of **infrastructure**—roads, utilities and so on—which is discussed in this chapter.

Second-home buyers in the country in my experience tend to be either folks in their 30s or 40s who are looking to build a weekend/summer place within a two- or three-hour drive of their principal residence or folks in their late 40s and 50s who are thinking about relocating in anticipation of retirement. The latter are looking for a low-stress rural environment where their pensions will stretch farther. In other areas, younger families with high incomes are in the second-home market. Individuals from each group differ in finances, time horizon and priorities, but they share the problems of evaluating an existing second-home house or building one from scratch.

Younger second-home buyers are looking for recreation and physical activity. Building their own house on unimproved land may become part of their lifestyle choices. Other buyers may be looking for a rural development of second homes, where they do nothing more strenuous than pick the model, write the checks and unlimber their woods and irons. These are the ends of the hands-on continuum, and they are very far apart.

Whether you buy rural land on your own or as part of a development, you should be concerned with both the level of existing infrastructure and the level that you might want in the future. As you age, the ease and convenience of your second-home infrastructure will become increasingly important to your ability to use your property.

Land infrastructure refers to roads, water, sewerage, utilities and the like that serve the land or development lot you're investigating. Land infrastructure is, around, near to or adjoining your target property.

Property infrastructure refers to these same components to the extent they are currently **on** your target property. While "on" is better than "planned" or "accessible," you may still not be able to get electricity, for example, from a pole at the front corner of a 200-acre property to its back boundary where you want to put a cabin. It may be physically impossible to build or bury a line to your spot, or the cost of doing so may be prohibitive. You will need to assess the feasibility and cost of putting in or upgrading property infrastructure according to your second-home plans.

Site infrastructure refers to the type and level of infrastructure you need and want **at** the spot where you are intending to build a house.

Most rural property has some degree of land infrastructure, though it may be no more than a primitive road. If you buy land that has been divided for resale or as a lot in a development, the level of property and site infrastructure will range from zero to fully developed, complete with amenities. Where you are intending to build a house, you will need to scope property and site infrastructure. Your beginning questions are: What kind of site infrastructure is feasible at my house site? and How much will each component of feasible infrastructure cost?

You may want no infrastructure of any type, because you intend to use your new land only for walk-in tenting. Even if you have no immediate plans for building a house, you should still consider the feasibility and cost of all three types of infrastructure. The easier and cheaper it is to put infrastructure in place, the more marketable your new property is and the more valuable it will be if you want to sell. I would avoid buying property that is deficient in infrastructure unless a wilderness-type use is what you and your heirs want. When a target property's infrastructure is deficient, I would use that projected expense to work down the seller's asking price. The cost of putting in infrastructure tracks inflation at the very least, and my guess is that it gets more expensive relative to other rural costs over time.

The first step a developer usually takes with a second-home project on a large, undeveloped tract is to propose a purchase contract with a contingency that makes the sale dependent on the developer securing whatever permits and zoning clearances he requires for division. This process can take a few months to several years, depending on the project's size, location and complexity; the site's topography and features such as wetlands, trout streams and endangered species; and the degree of administrative challenge and/or litigation. Sales should start once all regulatory hurdles are cleared, but sometimes lots are reserved or marketed before this happens on a contingent basis.

Permitting and project success is also directly affected by local opinion. Political opposition to building houses on farmland and woods can limit a project's size and design—and kill it in some cases. A buyer should be wary if he hears the project he's considering is bad-mouthed locally and has yet to be fully permitted. Such a buyer cannot be assured that the project's infrastructure will be developed and completed as the developer promises. One who buys a lot in a less than fully permitted project is assuming risk in return for no benefit. If you find yourself buying in advance, propose to the developer that he give you a discount for your willingness to buy early, which lends credibility and financial underpinning to his project. If the developer refuses, wait at least until he's fully permitted before buying. You can also propose **buying an option to buy a particular lot**, contingent on the developer getting all permits and/or putting in all infrastructure as promised. You are purchasing the right to buy the lot at a certain price at some future point; if you don't follow through with the purchase once the developer has satisfied your concerns, you lose your option money.

Permits and plans do not guarantee the project will be completed as presented. The risk of partial completion hovers over many developments; lack of cash being the most common problem. Projects done by large, well-capitalized developers with a track record are usually less risky than those done by local independents. But the buyer should check the record of any developer from whom he's considering buying a lot. Ask, in particular, whether the developer completed all the infrastructure that he promised.

The buyer who fears taking on the A-to-Z tasks in building a home on land with no infrastructure should look for a lot in developments that offer a **full package of infrastructure**—survey, all utilities (electricity, water, sewerage, phone, among others), surface-water drainage system and roads. (Sidewalks and street lights may or may not be part of the infrastructure a country second-home development needs.) Buyers benefit from fully developed lots, because they are purchasing property and site infrastructure at a group rate. The developer should be able to get this work done more cheaply by bundling it, scaling it efficiently and using competitively bid contracts or his own crew. The developer can pass along some of these savings to lot buyers. Of greater ultimate value, I think, is that you don't have to spend time and money finding, vetting and negotiating with infrastructure contractors; scheduling and sequencing their work; securing permits; getting materials to the site; and inspecting the finished job.

The alternative to a full-package development is one that offers a **partial package of infrastructure**. At the minimum, a developer will have clear title to the land, platted it into lots and put in enough of a road system to make each lot reasonably accessible to buyers like you. House construction may or may not be something the developer offers. The less infrastructure the developer has installed, the less likely it is that he will be building houses owing to the logistical hassles involved. The level of infrastructure in a partial package can be nothing more than a logging road into the property. Whatever property infrastructure the developer does not put in falls to the lot buyers either as individuals or as a group. If the buyers are of like mind and pocketbooks, they can organize and do the level of work they desire. When, however, buyers are dissimilar, making group decisions is difficult and often contentious. For that reason, I would avoid partial-package developments where the developer has punted property infrastructure decisions into both the future and the laps of lot buyers.

Partial packages offer cheaper lots than full packages. If the buyer is looking for 4WD-access, rough-and-tumble land, a development with nothing more than a dirt road can be a perfect fit. If, on the other hand, you and other lot buyers are likely to need more property infrastructure than the developer is putting in, then you must investigate feasibility and costs *with your new neighbors*. One reason why a developer may not offer a fuller property infrastructure could involve a cost that is prohibitive. If you don't find electricity service to each lot, for example, the explanation may lie in the upfront cost of installing it. Some steep, rocky or wet conditions can make certain typical infrastructure improvements too costly to be practical. When a lot buyer has infrastructure expectations that are higher than what he is purchasing, he is asking for future headaches.

A buyer approaching a partial-package development should keep in mind a few cautions about **surveys** the developer provides for both the lot you want to purchase and the tract from which it has been carved. (See Chapter 17 for a discussion of surveys.) Surveying costs can involve a considerable upfront cash outlay when the perimeter boundary is unmarked, in dispute, or requires the surveyor to dig out the "calls" (for metes and bounds) from the chain of title and possibly the chains of title in deeds of adjoining property owners. A developer looking to save dollars may not try to clear up boundary disputes before "lotting out" the tract. Some surveyors will not mark boundaries on the ground unless they are paid extra. The surveyor may or may not note a potential dispute on the survey he prepares. Even where nothing tricky is intended, ten surveyors may not come up with the same line owing to flaws, mistakes and typographical errors in the chain of title, though in most cases they will. A surveyor may or may not note on his survey that he suspects an adjoining neighbor may have a prescriptive easement over a developer's lot. Similarly, not all surveyors will indicate on their surveys where an existing fence line is not on the surveyed boundary line.

Buyers should be aware that even when they purchase a parcel of land with a current survey, that survey may not be accepted by adjoining neighbors who may have surveys or claims of their own. In a few cases, a new survey will create the very disputes the buyer hopes it has settled. A buyer should personally visit each adjoining neighbor outside the development before signing a purchase contract. Provide the neighbor with a copy of the developer's plat with your lot and the common line highlighted. Ask if he has any problem with the joint boundary as shown. The copy of the plat you provide will give the neighbor a chance to review it with his own surveyor. Your neighbors inside the development will be working off the new internal division lines, and there should be no dispute between you and them. If the developer offers lots in a division where the boundaries have not been recently surveyed, it is even more important for the buyer to check with the outside landowners adjoining his lot.

I ran into a situation in 2002 where a speculator had purchased an option to buy a 4,800-acre tract, 4,000 acres of which was wooded mountain land with various access problems and disputes. The remaining 800 acres was a 15-year-old clearcut and scrubby pasture. The tract had about 30 miles of perimeter boundary. A surveyor who was working for the option-holder said he estimated there were about 75 adjoining landowners, and most were going to have line disputes with any division the speculator/divider proposed based on the seller's 1908 survey. The surveyor estimated the cost of running a boundary survey around the 4,800 acres at about $125,000. The owner had shrewdly chosen not to do a survey; the less-shrewd speculator had optioned it without knowing that the 1908 survey boundaries were unreliable. The speculator's strategy was to divide the acreage into four or five chunks and sell them to hunting clubs with whatever boundary he had purchased. There's nothing illegal about this. It simply passes through to the next buyer a likely dispute and predictable expense. In my opinion, the shaky survey and boundary was a "defect" that a seller should disclose to a buyer. This seller had not disclosed it to the option-buyer who lost his option deposit when he failed to proceed with the deal. Had you bought a lot from the option-buyer in these circumstances, it's quite possible that you would have faced one or more lawsuits over boundaries and ended up with significantly less acreage than you had purchased.

Second-home developments often feature infrastructure and amenities (common community and recreation facilities) that may or may not be built at the moment you are asked to sign a purchase contract. In this situation, the buyer should assume the developer is well-intentioned and wants to build out everything shown in his plans. If you get the feeling that he is not well-intentioned, don't buy. The buyer should also assume that if you don't see things in place, they may not get there regardless of the developer's intentions and promises. The price of the lot you're buying should include the cost of building out all infrastructure and planned amenities. However, developers run out of money every so often, a situation that will cancel work promised. When a developer runs short of cash, individuals who have bought lots in the project may either abandon the developer's vision or complete it in full or in part. Where the buyers pool their resources to build a promised common facility, they will be paying twice for getting what was promised. When a group of buyers is left with a half-completed project, they will either spend time and money working out an acceptable solution or descend into feuding and paralysis. These experiences are not pleasant. When a buyer is looking to sign a purchase contract based mainly on plans and promises, he needs to coldly assess the probability that all the developer's promises will be fulfilled. Check the developer's track record—as reliable a guarantee as any. The buyer should grill—and I do mean **grill**—the developer and other knowledgeable locals on the project's finances (particularly sales and cash flow), break-even point (in terms of number of lots sold), scheduling for construction of common facilities and so on. If you feel you are standing on mush, jump away. Or put another way, if the meat smells bad, don't eat it.

Buyers should be especially careful when buying cheap land in the country that they've never seen. Why anyone would do this is beyond me, but it is not uncommon. My father bought two lots in a Florida development in the late 1950s, sight unseen. And he never found time to look before he died, more than 20 years later. They were barely developed and did not appreciate for 45 years. Many of these current "deals" involve antiquated subdivisions just like the one my father bought into that lack water, sewerage, paved roads and perhaps utilities. They might be sited on land that would now be considered unsuited for construction owing to slope, soil stability, floodplain and other factors. Some of these projects are marketed through companies headquartered in California, including National Recreational Properties, Inc. (NRPIPI), Land Disposition Company, Real Estate Disposal Corporation and LandAuction.com (aka NRLL). All are owned by Jeffrey Frieden and Robert Friedman in Orange County, California. Project names include, among others, Moon Valley Ranch (near Termo, California), California (Cal) Pines in Modoc County, Lehigh Acres (east of Fort Myers, Florida in Lee County), Palm Coast and Port Charlotte (both in Florida), Concho Lakeland (Apache County, Arizona), Hawaiian Ocean View Estates (Island of Hawaii), Shelter Cove (Humboldt County, California) and Deming Ranchettes (Luna County, New Mexico). These lots are sold "as is" and can be financed through the seller on installment contracts.

Some—marketed by Eric Estrada, the television actor—are pitched toward Spanish-speaking buyers. Never buy property sight unseen. (See Brian Melley, Associated Press, "Buyers beware: Many in California, Florida regret purchasing land in left for dead" and "For one couple, land looked good on paper, not in reality," Richmond Times-Dispatch, January 9, 2005.)

It is clearly much safer for you to buy into a fully completed project. The problem, of course, is that buyers coming in when the infrastructure is complete and most lots sold have only those lots available for purchase that all previous buyers have rejected. The last lots are not usually the most expensive or most desirable. More often, they are the least costly and have some factor discounting their appeal—an overhead power line, odd shape, poor site or uninspiring view. A smart buyer can make very good buys on these last lots, because the developer by that time has usually recovered his project costs and wants to move to the next deal. See if there's a way you can mitigate the offending feature by moving dirt, planting fast-growing trees or revising a house design. As an investment, the cheapest lot in a development may appreciate a bit faster than its pricier neighbors.

Second-home projects should be—but rarely are—marketed with all the project's infrastructure (however that is defined) complete and operational. Developers always begin marketing as soon as their plans are approved. Where the full infrastructure package is not complete, the buyer should insist on a specific itemization of infrastructure the developer promises to complete as part of the purchase contract he signs for his lot. The developer should not balk at giving you an itemized list of what's already in place and what he intends to do beyond what he has already done.

The next step is a bit harder: getting the developer to carry out the remainder of his infrastructure plan. When a project is slow to sell and the developer starts getting short on cash, promised infrastructure is the first place he'll look to cut costs. A lot-buyer's itemization should take the form of a promise in contract form that the missing elements will be completed. What happens, then, if the developer fails to complete the promised improvements? You can sue for performance. If the developer has assets, this might work. You can ask that the developer take on a performance bond for the value of the remaining work, though I would not count on this happening. You can also ask the developer to put a price on each infrastructure item in terms of your lot's share of the whole. He should be able to provide you with an average per-lot or per-acre infrastructure cost, because he has been projecting and refining these calculations since before the first spade of earth was turned. If the infrastructure does not get built, you will, at least, have a starting point for your claim for monetary damages against him. There may also be some tax benefits from this situation. I suggest bringing a real-estate lawyer in to help you think through the "what-if" scenarios.

Information on **land infrastructure** will be available from the agencies and companies that provide each service. You can find information on the road leading to the property from the state/county road department. You want to ask about road maintenance issues. Is the road plowed during the winter? Some properties are so remote or lacking in population that their roads receive little maintenance. What level of priority does the public road have for maintenance, such as snow clearance? Does the road have a flooding history? Does it need to be widened? Are accidents frequent? If so, where? Does the school bus serve road residents? If so, where would the closest stop to your property be? (School-bus service may be of no concern to you, but it does increase the value and marketability of your lot.) You will need to check with local utilities (electric, water, sewerage, telephone, cable TV, Internet, etc.) to determine the proximity of each service to the property and the cost of bringing it to your house site. And remember that you will need to obtain an easement (consent from the owner) to have your line cross another's property.

Your developer will have certain information on land infrastructure available on his property's **site plans**, which are used principally to set forth the infrastructure design for the property. Site plans are blue-print-type, technical drawings that show the location, specifications and design of all physical infrastructure on a developed property. The developer will probably have simplified drawings of the site plan, along with some dimensions and specifications, prepared as handouts. Ask to see the site plans, particularly as they affect the lot you're investigating. The site plans will include individual drawings for all planned excavations, roads, drainage of storm water and surface water, water pipes, sewerage, utilities, walkways, finished site grading and possibly landscaping. (Keep in mind that different second-home projects offer different levels of infrastructure.) You will be able to locate how and where each of the offered infrastructure components will service your particular lot. Make photocopies of the site plans that interest you and get a copy of the **specifications**, or **specs**, for each infrastructure component. These set forth the size, material and application of each component. If a civil or physical engineer (CE or PE) has drawn the plans, you should be reasonably confident that he has applied the standard formulas for sizing and materials. If you have doubts about the size of a culvert that will drain water from your lot, pay an engineer to review the plan. Roads, water and sewerage systems are expensive to rip out and do over, so you want to feel reasonably confident that the developer has not cut corners you can't see.

Installing and/or maintaining land infrastructure often involves coordinating and spending money with neighbors. Even where you own land outside a development, you can find yourself sharing an access road or a spring. Within a development, you will usually find that all lot owners will be expected to pay for infrastructure maintenance and upgrades. If you are philosophically opposed to such arrangements, make sure that your second home in the country is on land that is completely free of these obligations.

On a practical level, these sharing schemes range from well-functioning to disasters of various dimensions. The critical variable that I've seen is the degree of care, planning and thought that is invested in the documents the developer prepares for the **homeowners' association** he sets up that will take over the project's infrastructure management. A homeowners' association is a private neighborhood government whose board of directors is elected from among those who own a unit of property in the project. While homeowner associations are found mainly in metropolitan areas, an increasing number of the more than 50 million Americans who now live in projects whose house designs, aesthetics and governance are managed in this fashion are found in rural areas. (John Tierney, "The Mansion Wars," New York Times, November 15, 2005. A study by Amanda Agan and Alexander Tabarrok of George Mason University found that a home in the northern Virginia suburbs of Washington, D.C. that was in a private community with a homeowners' association sold for a five percent premium). About 275,000 community associations (homeowners' associations, condominiums and cooperatives) now exist in the United States.

Association documents are often long and complicated; sometimes, they are badly conceived and written clumsily. Nonetheless, you must understand them because they are the rules by which you must live as part of that community. Make sure you understand any house style and materials standards, provisions for pets, maintenance (what you're obligated to pay for; what your dues pay for), fees (both routine and special) and the governance system. An individual's buyer best protection against finding himself a neighbor to a stubborn fool is a rational, reasonable structure of decision-making that you've both agreed to at the time of purchase. Sharing the burdens of a common infrastructure requires everyone to be neighborly, especially when disagreements occur. If the developer tanks or has done a bad job in drafting the homeowners' association documents, you and the other owners will have to agree on many procedural and substantive issues involving taste, time and money. Agreeing on a method of how to agree is in itself a difficult boat to launch, particularly in a sea of hurt feelings and lost money. But where the documents are sound, a group of strangers can save their sinking ship.

The worst situation is when the developer drops out before completing the project and leaves a mess, both in the paperwork and on the ground. It is easy for me to write that folks in a nightmare should act rationally and reasonably. It is terribly hard to do. Nonetheless, reason and rational behavior should prevail sooner or later if only because no lot-owner has more power than any other. A problem-solving attitude will hopefully contain the anger that all feel. The goal should be to spread analytical reasonableness through the entire group.

Rural living rarely allows for the anonymity and isolation that you can find in a city or suburb. When you move to the country, you are forced to live with the culture and habits of mind of your immediate neighbors. These may not be to your liking, and yours may not be to theirs. A project with a homeowners' association provides a constitution of rules, procedures and structure for maintaining the development and handling neighborhood disagreements. It provides a common set of cultural and procedural assumptions that are intended to override personality quirks. Without an association, you're on your own with neighbors, the last resort of which is the local court to resolve country-type spats, such as fence fights and the nuisance of barking dogs. Court rulings may decide a dispute between neighbors without settling much of anything. Grudges can arise in other matters. In a developed project, you will inevitably find yourself solving common problems with your neighbors through channels that everyone understands. While forced neighborliness has its downside, the homeowners' association is a model that works, despite all the times it doesn't satisfy every individual.

The chances are greater, I think, for a country newcomer to discover neighbors who do not want to solve problems as he does when he buys outside of a development, especially one marketed toward a specific group of buyers who share cultural and income demographics. Do not assume that neighbors outside of a development will see a problem where you see one or engage in problem-solving in the manner you propose. It is unlikely that you will be able to organize them to solve your problem, which may be the way your neighbors have done things all their lives. They won't cooperate with your efforts to change them for your benefit—even for their own benefit. You are likely to build a problem-solving relationship if you can help to solve a problem that your neighbors have defined as a problem. As anywhere, you will run into individuals who go out of their way to be helpful and neighborly, as well as a few who go out of their way to be the opposite. In the country, you have to work with neighbors from time to time, and the format used for these interchanges is one of the more important choices you make when deciding between a second-home development with a homeowners' association and a stand-alone property. Whether or not you are in a development, you will be in a "neighbor process" with those on your boundaries. No matter how large your property, everyone has neighbors. Whether you're looking at property in a development or not, finding neighbors with whom you can work on common infrastructure issues is as important to your future happiness as any other consideration.

PROPERTY AND SITE INFRASTRUCTURE

For **roads**, you want to know their location in relation to your lot/land and house site. Important design elements are the width of the finished roadway (which is the portion that traffic normally uses), width of the gravel apron on each side, thickness of the rock base, composition of its substructure (type and thickness of various layers), whether geotechnic fabric was used as underlayment, and the type and thickness of surfacing material (gravel, concrete, asphalt, tar and chip). **Geotechnic fabric** is used under roads where the water table is high. It creates an impenetrable barrier between the subgrade beneath the road and the groundwater. The fabric prevents water from being "pumped" (i.e., drawn up) into the road's base rock by the traffic above. If pumping is not prevented, the road will eventually break up. The better the road—wider, thicker and surfaced—the more it has cost the developer, a cost he needs to pass on proportionally to each buyer. If you get the sense that he's put a lot of money into a rock base and below-ground drainage systems, it's reasonable to assume that he's tried to do a good job throughout. If site plans are not available, look for culverts, drainage ditches, hillside roads pitched slightly to the downhill side to encourage rapid runoff—all of which will give you an idea of whether the developer has tried to do a good job.

A project's road plan will show top-down and cross-section drawings of the road's design, along with dimensions and specs. Ask whether the project's roads are to be built to the **state's standards**. Ask which roads in particular will meet state standards. Then ask the state's local road department whether the state has agreed to incorporate the project's roads into the state system—which gives you a guarantee about the quality of the road and future maintenance. The more rural the second-home development, the less likely that its roads will be built to state standards. Perfectly usable roads can be built below these standards, depending on conditions and traffic loads. State-standard roads are not appropriate for undeveloped land that is "backup there"; they're too big, polished and expensive. Where a road system will not be built to state standards, make sure that you understand which standards will not be met—and then ask the state road engineer whether those shortfalls will have any practical significance. If the project's roads are to remain a private road system owned by the lot owners, they will have to pay for and manage its maintenance.

When you drive the public/private road to your lot or land, check for steepness, tight turns, floodplain, blind curves, narrow spots, hidden driveway entrances, improper pitch, washboarding (on dirt/gravel), clearance from trees and protruding rocks, turnarounds and adequate drainage. Imagine the property's road in bad weather. Do you anticipate problems? If a developer's road plan shows a 20-foot-wide, asphalt-surfaced roadway with a two-foot-wide gravel apron on each side and you find yourself driving on an 18-foot-wide gravel road with no aprons, you should presume that the developer is running out of money and/or has cut more corners than the two you've just discovered.

Public roads in the country range from paved to dirt. The further back you go, the narrower and rougher the roads will be. The least usable are a bit more than one-lane wide with wide outs and backup spots every so often. Dirt-and-gravel roads can be used year-round where they have a decent rock base, and are ditched, drained and periodically graded and graveled. But the fewer residents and vehicles on these roads, the less maintenance they get. I've driven over public country roads that were eroded, studded with rocks the size of gallon jugs and too narrow and steep for safe driving. The more inhospitable the road that services your property, the more *regular* inconvenience and expense you will have getting people, vehicles, material-loaded trucks, fire engines and rescue-squad ambulances in and out. Imagine the road to and on your property at night, then with snow and ice, then during a wet spring. Do not count on being able to persuade the local branch of the state road department to upgrade their road that you are now using. Assume that what is, is what will be, particularly if the county is poor or has a small population. Any road that you judge to be less than safe and usable in all conditions is just that. In some situations, local government may get a developer to upgrade a portion of a public road to accommodate traffic from his project. I've not seen this happen very often with out-of-the-way, second-home developments.

When you look at a development's **water plan**, your concerns are for quality, quantity, pressure and fire protection. Rural second-home developments usually have one of three types of water systems: 1) each lot owner installs his own system, usually a well; 2) centralized private system that serves houses in the project; or 3) a hook up to an existing public water system. If your lot is getting water from a central source, find out the details and the type of treatment it's subject to. Determine whether current users have experienced problems with **potability** (drinkability) or pressure. The developer's plan should show the project's water mainlines ("mains") configured in a loop, which keeps water moving through the system and prevents dead ends where bacteria can build. If yours is the house furthest from the source of water or highest in elevation, ask the developer to measure the water pressure in your presence. The comfortable range will be between 60 and 100 pounds per square inch (psi). Stepping down the pressure at your house with an in-line regulator is a far more desirable problem than insufficient pressure in the system. On level ground, you will need a minimum of 45 psi; on hills, a minimum of between 60 and 75 psi. Inadequate pressure will lead to, among other things, continuing frustration and the possibility of contamination.

In central-source water systems, the feeder water line to your house—called a **lateral**—from the main line should be no less than one inch wide (inside diameter), and 11/4" inside diameter is usually more reliable over time. Water-supply design details can be found in Ernest Brater and Horace King, Handbook of Hydraulics, 6th ed., (New York; McGraw-Hill, 1976).

A fire hydrant should be within 500 feet of your house if you're buying into a second-home development with that level of infrastructure. Homeowner insurance rates are higher for residences that are not close to a hydrant and higher still where no hydrant is available. Insurance companies look favorably on ponds close to rural houses not served by hydrants. If you have a pond on your property or close by, it is worth making sure that your local VFD pumper truck can get to it easily in bad weather. Another idea, assuming it's practical, is to bury a **standpipe** from the pond to a nearby all-weather road. The standpipe has a fitting that allows the pumper to connect at the road, a much more reliable procedure than getting to and away from a pond in ice and snow. The local VFD may help with the standpipe's cost, and make sure the pipe is sized correctly and the fittings match up. The standpipe's access fitting should be located to minimize the amount of vertical lift a pumper will have to provide.

Many rural second-home developments will not have their own water system or access to an existing public system. Each lot-owner then is expected to figure out a site-specific water solution—carry-in, cistern, spring, surface water (such as a pond or stream), dug well or drilled well. Talk to other lot-owners about what they know, or think they know, about water on your site. Talk to adjoining neighbors about their first-hand experience in drilling wells, particularly about cost, flow, depth, potability, contaminants and drilling contractors. Your neighbor will probably have had a water sample from his spring or well tested and should be willing to share the results. Ask about water sources during drought. Flow during drought will indicate the strength of the source at its most stressed condition. It's important to find out whether there's enough water underground to support the number of houses planned for the surface. Ask neighbors about sources of pollution that might affect the aquifer from which you both will tap. Determine whether a neighbor's septic system is likely to contaminate the water source that you want to use. The county sanitarian will be able to tell you the minimum required distance between septic field and well. In areas of porous rock, you may need to leave more distance than the minimum. Where karst topography underlies the surface, pollution can travel long distances through hollowed-out limestone.

In primitive situations you can use a gravity system to supply your house where the water source is higher than the tap; the higher the source, the more pressure up to a point. More common than a central water supply or gravity system in rural homes is to have a pump in or at the source (spring, well), or between the source and your tap. Pumps can be powered by electricity, gasoline, photovoltaic cells (solar energy), hand and the force of falling water itself. The latter is called a **hydraulic ram** and is used in circumstances where power is not available. (See www.pumpsandtanks.com; www.RamPumps.com; and www.theramcompany.com.) If you find flow or pressure is uncertain, you may want to install a reserve tank that holds a reservoir of water from which the house draws. A reserve tank is often used where supply is uncertain—and sized accordingly. In cold climates, you have to bury most water pipes below the frost line and put pumps in places that don't freeze. No one likes to dig up frozen pipes in frozen ground.

With municipal or project **sewerage systems**, your concern is that the pipes be sized sufficiently (have a wide enough diameter) to handle the expected load from your house and all the others on the line. Undersized pipes can lead to sewage backups in your house, a condition best avoided. An in-line butterfly-type valve at your house connection can prevent such backups. (When this valve is shut because of a backup on the mainline side, your own wastewater will backup after a few flushes.) The lateral sewer line from your house to the main sewer line should be no less than four inches in diameter, and the main line should be sized according to the maximum number of houses it will be servicing. I know it is obvious but I will write it anyway: your sewer pipe should run downhill from the lowest point in your household drain line. If your house is lower than the stub where your line connects to the main sewerage line, you will need to pump your sewage into the system. This is doable, but a sewage pump adds to your system a machine that will fail sooner or later. Gravity flow is what you want. The developer's sewerage plan will show the elevation of your house, the elevation of the sewer lines and the pitch from house to main. Lest it is not obvious, the plan should show the pitch of your lateral sewer line running downhill from your house; a level line will not work. If you run a water line and a sewer line in the same trench, the water line should be above, usually by a distance set by code. You might also ask to see any **as-built drawings** of the water and sewerage systems on your lot, which represent what's actually underground rather than what was envisaged.

Buyers should be cautious about buying undeveloped lots that lack either a municipal/package sewerage system in place or a septic (**percolation**, or "**perc**") permit. If you are considering an undeveloped lot that has neither a system nor a permit, consult the county official—the public health officer or the sanitarian—about the septic regulations that will apply to your house. Ask him whether other recent home builders on similar soils in that part of the county have been required to employ systems beyond the conventional septic tank and drainfield. You want a lot with soils that will "perc," that is, soils in place that will pass the sanitarian's percolation test and allow the use of a conventional gravity-flow septic tank and drainfield at a current installed cost of $3,500 to $5,000. Alternatives to a conventional septic system using sand or imported soil are three to four times as expensive and involve higher maintenance costs and requirements if they use pumps.

A buyer's interest is served when he finds a developer who has gone to the trouble and expense of obtaining a **septic permit** from the county for the specific lot or parcel the buyer wants. In many places, developers are required to get permits before being allowed to sell lots. That is not the case in my county, however. As percolation standards are made stricter, you may find even large lots—particularly mountain top and sloping lots—without a site that will be approved. Where there is a septic permit, read it carefully. Make sure the permit is specifically for your lot or land before signing a purchase contract! The permit will indicate the type of system the sanitarian has approved for a particular spot. It should also show the size of the system being permitted, often expressed in terms of the number of bedrooms. Make sure that your house floorplan conforms to the size of the system for which a permit has been granted. If you are planning a house that has more bedrooms than the developer's permit allows, you will not be allowed to build it without increasing the septic system's capacity. If you want to do something unusual with your system—such as hooking in a bathroom from another building, or running a B&B or home-based commercial enterprise, or use more water than might be normally expected—you will probably need to get additional approvals. Apart from permitting, if you overload a septic system with more liquid than it's designed to handle, it will fail.

On both lots and non-development land, I recommend that you put a **septic approval contingency in your purchase-offer contract.** This allows you to determine whether the parcel you are considering has an acceptable perc site near your house site. If an acceptable site can't be found, you will soon get an idea of the cost of installing an alternative system. Where there is an existing system, a septic contingency will allow you to have it examined to determine its condition. Where the results of your contingency inspections are not satisfactory, this contract language allows you to either back out of the contract or negotiate the issue with the seller. Having a perc test done usually involves about $500 to $1,500 in expenses, paid to: 1) the county for a fee, 2) a certified, buyer-hired soils engineer for locating possible septic-system sites, managing the test and reporting the results, and 3) a backhoe excavator for digging the test holes.

If the test indicates a conventional septic system will not be approved, the soils engineer can propose an alternative system, which is usually based on constructing a septic drainfield in good dirt placed on top of the bad dirt. The switch raises the cost to the lot buyer from, say, $4,000 for a conventional system to as much as $20,000 or more for the acceptable alternative. (Other systems, such as, digesters, composters and chemical toilets, may or may not comply with local requirements.)

A buyer faces other issues when a septic system is already installed on property he's interested in buying. The system should come with an approval or permit on file with the county health department that indicates its capacity, design, age and location on the property. An old system may be in need of repair or replacement.

Electricity and other utilities may or may not be part of your target property's infrastructure. Where electricity is not on the property you're buying, you may not be able to get conventional pole-strung power. Adjoining landowners may not be willing to work out an easement for you to cross their property. Or they may insist on burying the line where it crosses at additional expense.

Electricity and telephone lines are usually run on the same poles or in the same trench. If your house site is within 1,000 feet of an existing pole, your cost to run a new line is minimal and may be divided into 60 equal installment payments that you pay during your first five years of service. Each utility has its own way of calculating these costs and having you pay for them. The five things a buyer should be concerned about are: 1) the location of the nearest pole to his house site, 2) whether or not that pole is on the target property (if not, you have to obtain an easement), 3) the distance from the nearest available pole to the site, 4) the type of topography the line must cross and 5) the means the utility will use to suppress tree growth and underbrush under the line. Negotiating a utility easement with a neighbor can be easy or very sticky. He is not legally obligated to give you an easement, so you are asking for a favor. The two power companies with which I've worked have very reasonable cost-and-payment plans for distances of less than a couple of thousand feet; after that, the per-foot cost of a new line increases by a factor of five or more. Sites that cannot be economically served by conventional electricity are not uncommon.

A final thought about infrastructure is this: visit the property and your choices of house sites on a bad-weather day. Some developers and sellers may do just enough roadwork to get buyers to the site on a dry afternoon. If you can use the project's dirt road during and after a heavy rain, your confidence should build. If you see washouts and undersized culverts, you will live with these problems until you fix them. If you feel washboard as you drive in, it will be there until it's graded out. (Washboard is one of life's many problems that does not solve itself through deliberate indifference.) A wet or snowy day will also test your ability to access lots located on steep, winding roads. If your vehicle doesn't make it to your site when the road is wet or icy, plan on paying for roadwork, buying a more suitable vehicle, or both. If you are buying exposed ground or mountain land, ask about wind—frequency, velocity and prevailing direction. The higher your property is, the more you should think about wind as both a hazard and an energy source. You may be interested in leasing your land for large (400-foot-tall) wind turbines, and, if not, your neighbors may lease theirs. You may also need to consider a government "taking" of your wind site at fair market value through eminent domain for use by private wind-energy developers. Some land buyers object to wind-farm projects near their property; other's won't.

With each land-infrastructure component, you need to determine how close it is to your target property; its level of usability, reliability and safety; what is involved in gaining access to it from your property (easement, application, permit); and, finally, the work and cost involved in bringing each component to your property. And, then, you will need to go through the same set of questions when you want to bring each component to your house site. On large and remote properties, you may be able to get an infrastructure component to your property, but not to your first choice of house site. Where it is too costly or infeasible to hook into existing land infrastructure, you will then have to devise either a site-specific solution *that complies with local ordinances* or do without.

INFRASTRUCTURE COSTS

From your perspective, there's nothing necessarily wrong with buying a lot in a subdivision where the developer has put in little, if any, infrastructure. A lot of rural land is bought by **"flippers"** who purchase large, undeveloped parcels at a wholesale price, put in the least amount of infrastructure they can, divide and then sell the lots retail. With any division, you need to understand what infrastructure you're getting for your money, what it will cost to obtain whatever additions you want, and how decisions that involve all lot owners will be made.

If you—*and the other lot owners*—want no more infrastructure than what's in place at the time of purchase, then you've found the right spot. You will be buying land "as is, where is," and no more infrastructure will be forthcoming from the seller. Some dividers and developers can connect lot buyers with infrastructure contractors. The lot seller may have a commercial relationship with these contractors. You can ask other lot buyers about the practices of the recommended contractors. If there are troubles, you will undoubtedly hear about them. If you are the first purchaser in the development, you may be treated royally in hope that you will talk up the project to those who follow. Other things being equal, the developer and his contractors have more incentive to act decently with the first buyers than with the last.

Infrastructure costs vary from place to place and rise over time. The costs in the following example were representative in my area in the early 2000s. Assume that you are scoping 100 acres of undeveloped mountain woodland that has been carved out of a 1,000-acre tract. You've yet to offer a purchase contract to the seller. You're taking your first run at determining infrastructure costs. Your lot fronts a public road with electricity and telephone, but neither water nor sewer lines. The best house site on your 100 acres is about 500 feet in from the public road. An old logging road goes back that way. It crosses an intermittent creek and goes through a couple of wet spots. The site itself is a natural bench on a slope, which faces southeast. The seller's asking price is $2,000 per acre, for which you get the land and a survey of the lot's boundaries. Here is a quick-and-dirty cost estimate to get your infrastructure in place:

Road: $35,000

> Widen existing logging road to 12 feet along its length. Cut trees along the side as needed. Put in one turnaround about half way and widen in three spots to allow vehicle passing. Install two 16"-diameter, 16-foot-long culverts. Ditch uphill side where necessary. Grade road so that it sheds water to downhill side. Dig out two wet spots around culverts and fill in with rip-rap, stone and gravel as needed. Haul and emplace rock in four other spots. Install two or three 8"-diameter culverts. Widen entrance at public road, install rock and gate. Includes no finish surface material like gravel (with two exceptions) or asphalt. **$30,000**

> Creek is crossed using a low-water bridge consisting of three 20-foot-long, 24"-diameter steel culverts embedded in concrete. **$5,000**

Drilled water well @ $20 per foot, est. 250 feet: **$5,000**

> Includes pump and 2" line to the house from well. 100 foot-long trench, 36" deep. **$1,500**

Site preparation: **$3,000**

> Clear 1/2 acre (about 22,000 square feet) of trees and debris into burn pile. Level site; stockpile any usable top soil. Bring in needed rock and gravel for parking area. (Does not include foundation work or finish grading after construction is completed.)

Septic system: **$22,000**

> Soil won't pass perc test. Design and installation of **constructed sand filter**.

Includes cost of test, engineering and permit fees.

Utilities: $3,000, prorated over 60 months for above-ground service.

The total infrastructure costs in this example total **$69,500**.

The road costs assume a road that's capable of carrying a cement truck and other heavy vehicles related to house construction. The amount of work involved in clearing trees and the quantity of rock hauled to fill in the soft spots are cost variables driven by site-specific conditions. Graveling or asphalting the entire entrance road adds additional cost. Infrastructure costs are charged in several different ways—by the job, by the foot in the case of entrenching a water line or stringing above-ground electric service, by the ton for buying rock, by the hour for operating excavating machines (a mid-size bulldozer and operator now cost about $70-$100 p/h) and by the hour/day for labor.

At this point, the buyer should ask: What other properties are available for $269,500 that also suit my needs and wants? One answer might be a smaller lot with infrastructure in place. A second answer might be a smaller parcel with a usable house and basic infrastructure. A third answer might be to buy the 100 acres and use an RV or camper, both of which can be driven in and out in dry weather on a road that's less developed than one suited for heavy, house-building related trucks. A fourth answer might be a similar property, but with lower infrastructure costs.

A final possibility is to take higher-than-expected infrastructure cost estimates to the seller with a discounted offer for the land. Append the estimates to your contract. This shows that you're a seriously interested buyer and want to make a deal. Most developers who sell lots without much infrastructure want to sell out quickly. If you're one of the first buyers, you probably won't get much discount, because the seller doesn't want to set a precedent. If you're buying close to the end of the project, you may have some success. Don't inflate the estimates. The developer is likely to have as accurate an idea of these costs as you do, which is why he didn't do the infrastructure work himself. (Developers know that buyers like you balk at paying for infrastructure that they put in and you can't see.) You can make the point in your price negotiations that roughly equivalent properties—that are acceptable to you—are for sale nearby. FSBOs (For Sale By Owners) of semi-developed rural land may not add in to their asking price the value of a half-good interior road and electric service; they've taken both for granted for years. This attitude can allow you to buy more of what you want from a FSBO than the Flipper who expects you to do all the property infrastructure and site work. If nothing else, FSBO properties give you bargaining leverage with a developer.

You should also tell the developer that the bank you want to use is willing to lend only 80 percent of the land's selling price, which means that you will have to come up with both $40,000 in cash down payment and $69,500 to get the property ready for a house. Not a house, you emphasize, just ready for a house. Ask the seller to consider lowering the land price by the amount you think is beyond what was expected or what a reasonable person would consider reasonable. You could propose as well that the seller do part of the infrastructure work, or that you pay for the labor and fuel and he pays for the equipment time. You can get additional leverage in this negotiation by digging out the selling prices of other lots in this development and their infrastructure costs. In most cases, lots further from a public road will be cheaper per acre than lots with frontage, though I've seen just the opposite when the "far" lots had the best view. It's fair for you to ask for cost-sharing from the developer when unexpectedly high infrastructure costs appear, but you won't get anywhere with a developer who sold you an undeveloped lot or one "as is."

Each buyer has to assess whether the property's infrastructure meets his goals and his capability of getting this work done on his own. If, for example, you are 65 with a family history of heart attacks, I would not buy 100 acres of mountain land whose only infrastructure is a long, logging road to your planned full-time residence. If you try to build without putting in an all-weather road, you will precipitate another coronary. If you organize the infrastructure work through an assortment of specialized contractors, assume at least six stressful months of coordinating, haggling, redoing and inconvenience. If you think you can still drop trees and shovel dirt for eight hours straight the way you did one summer in high school, I hope you are not wrong.

If you try to make this 100 acres work by putting in the least amount of infrastructure you can live with, you will find yourself living with a hazard that regularly collapses when you most need it not to. I've had a marginal bridge that I hoped would suffice disappear during a thunder-storm flood, leaving an empty cement truck on the wrong side, at night, in the downpour; a loaded dump truck break a rear axle on a too-tight, sloped turn; and many episodes of sliding off, bogging down and hanging up. I now get the road right first. Heavy snow and other extreme conditions become harder to deal with as you age. Getting stuck on chancy roads shifts from an adventure in your 20s to an annoyance in your 40s to a nightmare in your late 60s. The easier a home in the country is to get to, maintain and live in, the longer you will be able to live there, despite the infirmities of age. I advise land buyers in their 50s and 60s to look for properties with owner-friendly infrastructure for this reason.

PROPERTY AND SITE INFRASTRUCTURE CHECK LIST

As you investigate the **land infrastructure** that services the target property, you will also be asking and answering questions related to the **property's infrastructure** (what's already in place and usable) and the **site infrastructure** needed where a house is planned. Again, you will be looking at road work, electricity, other utilities and options for water and sewerage.

The list below combines the principal property- and site-infrastructure issues within a broader analysis of the target property's attributes, both natural and man-made. The target property's physical features directly shape the type and cost of property and site infrastructure that can be installed. A buyer has to think about infrastructure in terms of terrain, distance, impediments and cost. As you walk through and come to be familiar with a target property, use the list below to assemble a picture of the land's suitability for your plans and the infrastructure they will require.

Property and Site Analysis for Infrastructure

A. Natural features

1. Compass orientation of land and specific house site

2. Land types—open/wooded; crop, pasture, hayfield, irrigated, range

3. Topography—elevation, slope, drainage patterns

4. Sheds—viewshed, windshed (look for tree sculpts), watershed, "odorshed"

5. House site—southern exposure, prevailing wind/weather, shade/sun

6. Surface water—floodplain, wetlands, creeks, springs, ponds

7. Walk the boundaries with a topographical map with boundaries drawn and/or survey and/or deed with boundary calls (compass directions and distance). Look for corners—metal stakes; described trees; three slash marks or ribbons; and marked lines—ribbons, paint, slashes; boundary fences/lines not coincident with surveyed boundaries; areas that possibly have overlapping claims; internal roads that appear to be in current use by others; check for boundary line congruence between deed calls/survey and ground reality; look for congruence of "Posted" signs with boundary lines

8. Walk/drive all drivable roads on property—they will lead somewhere, perhaps to a trash dump or spring

9. Neighbors—who joins the target property and what do they use their land for?

10. How much of the land is inaccessible by various types of vehicles?

11. Other factors, such as climate, rainfall, soil instability (landslides), ground instability (earthquake) and erosion

B. Soil analysis

1. Take copy of property's soil map (from <u>Soil Survey</u>) on your walk-around. Get a sense of where soils change and how soil change affects land use and capability; soil type can determine where you put a septic system and the type of house foundation you use

2. Take soil sample for analysis from crop fields

3. Observe vegetation—look for marker species that indicate dirt quality

C. Overview of woodland and timber

1. Get a sense for the extent of woodland, diameter size of timber and species distribution

2. Are woods accessible by usable roads?

3. How many trees need to be cut to clear a house site and gain road access to it?

4. Do you think there's enough merchantable timber to justify hiring a consulting forester to do a walk-through or cruise?

D. Land use

1. Rough percentage distribution among different land types/uses—such as woodland, pasture, cropland, wetlands, unusable land

2. Is property being sold with access to adjoining private or public lands? Is a state or federal land lease involved?

3. Does property have deeded use of adjoining property? If so, what for and what are the terms?

4. What percentage of property is unusable due to steepness, wetness, lack of water and so on? Draw these areas on your topographical map. Do these areas benefit the property in some way that is not connected to your intended uses, such as wildlife habitat, buffers from neighbors, or visibility screen from road?

5. Are there areas that have some obvious conservation/environmental value, such as wetlands, lakes, rare habitat, etc? You may want to determine whether the property in whole or part lends itself to a conservation easement.

6. Note land characteristics, such as stoniness, rock ledges, types of plants growing in different areas, eroded spots, floodplain—all of these characteristics will affect your infrastructure plans.

E. Access

1. Does your target property have physical and legal access?

2. Entrance road to property

Does your target property have frontage on public road or on developer's private road? Is its entrance road located on this frontage? If not, where is the entrance? Can the frontage be used to access your house site?

If property has frontage but no entrance road exists, is there 500 feet of sight in both directions on the public road from where you would put in a new entrance? Check with state road department to determine sight-clearance-distance requirements for new entrance roads.

If there is no frontage, how far is the target property from the nearest publicly-maintained or private four-season road?

Are there any physical features on the entrance road that might be a safety hazard—ford, steep drop off, eroding cliff, undrained wet spot, tree leaning steeply over road, turn that is too steep or tight, slippery surface?

Do you find evidence that others are using the target property's entrance road? Who and by what authority?

Is year-round use of this entrance road feasible as is? Can a fire truck get to the house site in winter? (Ask someone in the local VFD if you're not sure.)

Who is expected to maintain the entrance road?

3. Crossing others

If the entrance road to the target property crosses intervening land (public or private), what are the features of that entrance road? Length, width, condition, locked gates?

What is the legal basis for the target property using this entrance road? Does the property's seller have a deeded right of way or ingress/egress easement? If not, has the owner legally established an easement by prescription or necessity? Is the owner using the entrance road by permission of the property owner who is being crossed? (In that case, the permission can be withdrawn.) Is there a dispute about using this entrance road?

Is the entrance road that is being used the same as the one described in recorded documents? You may find that your legal entrance road is not the one that is being used, in which case the target property may have no legal right to use it.

Is the entrance road that is being used physically located where it is shown on the survey?

Who maintains your entrance road where it crosses another property? To what standard? Is the road currently in good shape? If not, determine with the seller who pays for which repairs.

F. Utility analysis

1. Electricity—closest pole to property; closest pole to house site

How far must an electric line be run to serve property/site? Cost and cost formula used by local power company? Feasibility/cost of running line underground versus above ground? Must service line cross others? If so, what are the prospects of getting easements?

Feasibility of alternative sources of electric power at house site—windmill, photovoltaic cells, low-head hydro, fossil-fuel-powered generator, other.

2. Sewerage system

Possible hook up to established central system. Cost.

Site for conventional septic system. Cost of non-conventional, alternative systems if conventional system won't comply with local requirements. Prospects for passing percolation test—check soil map in <u>Soil Survey</u> and with county sanitarian.

Site for non-conventional waste-disposal system. Feasibility, cost, maintenance issues, reliability. Does local ordinance permit this type of system? Can you find an excavator to install non-conventional system? Will it comply with local ordinance?

3. Water

Possible hook up to established central system

Natural sources close to house site—location of spring or creek

Well-drilling prospects. Cost.

Quality considerations—pollution potential; take water sample.

Quantity considerations—flow during drought

Fire-protection pond—possibility of building pond near house

Is water being purchased for irrigation or other uses? Source, cost, reliability, degree of target property's dependency.

4. Other utilities

Telephone, cable tv and other lines may be hung on same poles

Check reception for dish tv, cell phones, radio

Internet options

Possible hook up to established natural gas line. Some residences are entitled to free gas where a property has a gas well. Can a propane or fuel-oil truck make deliveries year-round?

G. Subsurface and Above-surface factors

1. Are subsurface minerals owned by the seller of the surface?

2. Evidence of past, present, or future mineral development?

3. Is property crossed by natural gas or oil pipeline, or overhead high-voltage power lines? Is there a pumping station or transformer on property? Pipelines and power lines will have recorded easements.

4. Is property/site adversely affected by nearby tower, wind turbine, structure or natural feature?

H. Constraints

1. Legal constraints on property and/or infrastructure

Restrictive covenants—are certain types/sizes of structures prohibited?

Conservation easement—limit on number, size or location of houses and structures; limit on timbering or grazing; limit on division.

Life estate—is property owner retaining a life estate in the occupation or use of some portion of the property?

Retained interest—is the owner retaining some interest or profit in the property?

Zoning restrictions

    Limits on uses of property

    Prohibitions on structures on property, e.g., towers, dishes

    Prohibition/restrictions on division

    Setback requirements

    Minimum house requirements, e.g., square foot requirement; fixed foundation

    Restrictions on height of structure

    Architectural style requirements

    Road construction standards

Regulatory/Environmental restrictions on property/infrastructure

    Wetlands

    Threatened, endangered or sensitive species, on state or federal lists.

    Floodplains

    Archeological resources on property

    Caves and karst geology

    Earthquake zone

    Hurricane hazard; storm-related flooding hazard

    Historic structures

    Restrictions on surface water access/use e.g., right to draw, right to fish

    Wildlife restrictions—no hunting rules

    Water quality—activities that affect surface waters, e.g., mining, point-sources of pollution in a high-quality stream

    Air quality—restrictions on certain activities, e.g., uses that create dust, sulfur oxides, nitrogen oxides, particulate

    Nuisance species on property that limit property uses, e.g., multiflora rose, coyotes (decimate sheep), Africanized bees, fire ants, termites, starlings and house pests (winter flies, ladybugs, termites, ants)

2. Physical constraints on infrastructure

Steepness

Soil not suited to buildings; can't find sewage-disposal site; soil won't hold pond; soil too rocky, etc.; insufficient nutrients

Access too narrow, too steep, to tightly cornered, too slippery etc.

Inadequate water quantity or quality

Land lays in the wrong direction, e.g., artists prefer light coming into their studios from the north

Too rainy, too cold, too dry to support plans

3. Encroachments that adversely affect use of property or its infrastructure

   Adverse possession (someone is occupying the target property without permission, which may or may not be legal)

   Adverse use (someone is using property/infrastructure without permission, which may or may not be legal)

   Common situations of adverse possession and adverse use involve fences that are not on the property line; the property's road being used by individuals without a right to do so; a neighbor tapping a spring on the target property; a neighbor's antenna mounted on the target property; unauthorized individuals hunting or otherwise recreating on the property without permission; a neighbor's building or structure on the target property;

I. Neighbors' uses affecting property or its infrastructure

   1. Pollution—air, water

   2. Noise—barking dogs, gunfire, equipment

   3. Smell—poultry, hogs, dairy cows, feedlot

   4. Bright night-time lighting

   5. Visual offense—junk cars, etc.

   6. Adjoining public land—trespass

These issues are discussed in detail in other sections of this book. Use this list during your walk-through as a way to organize your observations in terms of the property's current and needed infrastructure.

FLIP, FLIPPERS, FLIPPING

Flippers are land dividers rather than developers. They are interested in a quick turn-around profit on large undeveloped tracts that they divide with as little investment in infrastructure as possible. Flips are simple to understand: The Flipper buys 200 acres for $1,000,000, or $5,000 per acre, surveys it into 25-acre lots (farmettes), gets the division approved and then sells the lots for $10,000 per acre. A variation is to buy a timber tract, cut the timber or reserve it, and then go through the division-and-sale process. The timber variation demands that the Flipper project two paths to profit: a buy-divide-flip approach or the buy-divide-timber-flip approach where the timber harvest generates income but the land is discounted. The Flipper's form of capitalist enterprise is no different than that practiced on the Lower East Side in 1900: buy a yard of cloth for $1, divide and sell nine handkerchiefs from the pushcart for two bits each.

Since a considerable amount of rural property is being sold and resold in this manner, you should become familiar with the process and its pressure points. The Flipper must make his profit on the spread between buying something big wholesale and selling it fast in small pieces retail. Flippers add only the amount of work and value that is needed to effect the Flip. Flippers have a good eye for marketable property with features that lot buyers want—views, water frontage, a few decorative big trees. There's nothing wrong in buying from a Flipper. Just keep in mind that the property's lack of infrastructure will become the lot-buyers' collective problem once the Flip is sold out. I've also noticed that Flippers often price their lots above FMV for similar properties, which leaves room for negotiation. Some buyers like the Flipper's offerings because the lot is appealing and their hunt for property can stop. The buyer's work in "developing" the flipped property and lot, however, has just begun.

Flippers obtain property in different ways. Some buy land outright. Others buy a **purchase option** from the seller. This is a contract between the Flipper and the land seller that gives the Flipper the right to purchase the property at a certain price at a point in the future, typically three months to a year from when the option takes effect. The Flipper buys the option to purchase for one or two percent of the purchase price. This cash, often called **option money**, is forfeited to the seller if the Flipper fails to complete the purchase. A purchase option gives the Flipper the right to buy, but not the obligation to buy. If the Flipper does not exercise his option, he loses his option money but incurs no lawsuit or penalty. The Flipper uses his option time to market the property to buyers like you. He will divide the property on paper (and maybe on the ground too) and offer a sales contract to you that is contingent on completing his purchase with the seller. If he does not exercise his option, there is no sale to you. Any deposit you placed in escrow for this contingent sale should be returned to you; do not give a deposit directly to the Flipper. Flippers count on knowing the market price for their divided parcels.

The option's advantages to the Flipper are that he can bring a large property under control with very little cash in a way that gives him an opportunity to make a lot of money fast and without much work. But every option holder runs the risk of losing his option money if he is unable to flip the pieces. Options appeal to gamblers. A Flipper working an option wins when he sells the property without ever buying it. Option Flippers do not want to take title to the property since that would mean they have to come up with the full purchase price.

If you find yourself negotiating with a Flipper with or without an option, you may be able to work a very good deal depending on how far along in the selling process he is. The closer you are to the front end, the more resistance you will find to having him lower his asking price significantly. Flippers start their price at a level that allows them to make a concession so that the buyer thinks he did a good job negotiating. He'll cut an asking price meaningfully after he's paid for the property from previous sales and is marketing his profit. The last couple of lots in a Flip should be good buys, as long as they're not the dogs of the deal. You can do very well with an Option Flipper whose option time is running out. There's no risk to you in low-balling a Flipper: he knows this game better than you do.

You can also play chicken with a Flipper (who's flipping an entirety without dividing it) if you're convinced that you're his "best-money" buyer. If he doesn't meet your low-ball price, "sit with him in the waiting room." Watch for sweat. Time is working on him. He'll lose his option money if he doesn't make the deal with you. That's fine. It leaves you free to negotiate directly with the landowner once the Flipper slinks off. But games of chicken can lead to wrecks, yours included. The Flipper may turn up an acceptable buyer at the last minute. Or the seller may have an alternative to you in mind in the form of a **backup contract** once the Flipper loses his option.

This gaming of the Flipper raises questions of etiquette and ethics. Flippers with an option fear a buyer **backdooring** them in various ways, one of which is waiting them out. Another is for a buyer to approach the land seller directly while the option is still in effect. If the buyer offers the owner more than the option's purchase price, the owner has an incentive to "squirrel up" the Flipper's deal if he can. The buyer then wins the property at the Flipper's expense. I recommend against backdooring, because it diminishes the buyer. There's an honorable way to play these real-estate games, as well as other ways.

Here is an example of a real flip. The landowner advertised a 400-acre+/-property for $350,000. I looked at the property five days after the newspaper advertisement. A Flipper had already signed a deal with the owner to purchase, not option, for $300,000. The Flipper had a local surveyor divide the wooded property into three lots. The local zoning ordinance prohibited further division. One lot included a usable but bedraggled farmhouse that served as a hunt camp. The landowner had made several ten-acre clearcuts to provide better habitat for deer. About 50 percent of the land had been selectively timbered, and maybe ten percent had been clearcut. I estimated that a selective cut on the remaining timber would yield about

$75,000 to the new owner. The Flipper immediately sold the remaining timber for an unknown sum and advertised the three parcels without mentioning the timber had been sold. Here is an edited version of the ad that appeared about three months following the purchase:

COUNTRY HOME/LODGE

85 ACRES

$159,990

Old Country Home/Lodge on 85 ACRES adjoining the 14,000 ACRE STATE PUBLIC GAME AND FISHING LANDS in _____ County. This large 1935 Home is livable but needs tender love and care. It has water and electric heat, bathroom, four bedrooms, three fireplaces plus several small outbuildings. This 85 Acre Tract is bounded on the East Side by State Route ___ and has extensive frontage on the west side of the Game Lands. The house is situated on a manicured knoll with a rushing trout stream traversing the back yard and running most of the entire length of the property. There is a large meadow behind the house through which the stream runs, and there is a small garden on the south side. A few hundred feet south of the first meadow through a Sherwood Forest type setting there is another another larger, hidden meadow with a few old apple and pear trees. This wildflower meadow is loaded with game and fowl. There is yet another meadow further up the Valley. It is smaller, but even more protected, with unparalleled views of the Mountains in the distance and the Valley below. The balance of the property that leads up to_____ Mountain is level and wooded. The timber has been select cut, and there are numerous old trails and paths throughout this area from which you have fantastic views of the _____ Valley below. Adjoining this Tract are two other tracts of 160 Acres @ $129,990 and 147 @ $149,990.

Sounds interesting, doesn't it? A little scoping added useful information.

The "meadows" referred to were clearcuts whose stumps had been bulldozed off to one side. The resulting open space had been seeded for wildlife forage, though the dozing had skimmed off the topsoil cover and reduced the land's fertility. The ad makes no mention of any clearcuts.

The "livable house" was a two-story farmhouse that hadn't been lived in, save during hunting season, for many years. The "manicured knoll" was, in fact, quite lovely. It referred to the spot where grass was cut around the house.

The "old trails and paths" were old skid roads used by loggers to take out the timber, which the owner kept mowed to facilitate hunting.

The "select cut" referred to the timbering that had taken place in the past during the seller's ownership. No mention was made of the Flipper's timber reservation. The Flipper told me that he had sold the valuable sawtimber 14" DBH and larger when I asked him about it directly, but no cutting had yet to occur. Land buyers would see the property with all trees standing.

One other point. The Flipper's survey showed that he only had 392 acres to sell, not 400. The "+/-" covered him.

After seven months of trying to peddle a $300,000 property, less its merchantable timber, for almost $440,000, the Flipper hadn't flipped anything. So he "cut" his price to about $410,000: 1) 85 acres plus house, $159,990; 2) 159+ acres, $90,000; 3) 147 acres, $159,900. All the price reduction was taken out of the 159-acre tract of woods that had been "select cut," clearcut and was about to be cut again.

The property was worth $300,000 with the merchantable timber, maybe $225,000 with the timber sold. At the lowered price of $410,000, the Flipper was still looking to gross $185,000 if he could find three full-price buyers. The only value the Flipper had added was to have a surveyor run interior division lines (from which the correct total acreage was derived). Still, seven months into the Flip, ads were still summing the three parcels as 407 acres, despite the fact that they totaled only 391-392 acres.

The Flipper, I think, was having trouble selling land with the timber reserved. Land buyers knew enough to know that they would be left with a mess. He was also pricing the Flip at roughly $950 to $1,000 per acre, which was $200 to $300 above comparables for recent cutover land. The Flipper ran his ads in the big metropolitan Sunday papers, but not in the local weekly where local buyers would know the current value of this land.

One possible reason for the Flipper pricing the three lots above market would be to delay any resale for one year following acquisition so that the profit would be taxed as a long-term capital gain and not as current income. On a $100,000 gross profit, the difference at that time between the two tax rates would be $15,000 or more. The Flipper could afford to wait the year, because he had about $75,000 in hand from the timber sale.

The other reason this Flipper was waiting for his price had to do with the fact that the Flipper was actually two individuals, one of whom fronted the purchase price to the other at 20 percent interest. (The details of their arrangement were available in the courthouse records.) The lender was doing just fine getting 20 percent from his partner who had to hold out for a high price so that he made something too.

I felt they could have gotten close to $400,000 for the three parcels pretty quickly had they not sold the timber. Had I been flipping it, that's how I would have done it. Eventually, of course, everything sold, and each parcel is now worth about twice its purchase price. Rapid appreciation makes every one of these games a win-win.

I had the chance to watch another Flipper at close range. He bought a three-month option from a big paper company for $300,000 on about 40,000 acres of mountain woodland, some of which had been clearcut and planted in pine. The purchase price was $500 per acre (p/A), or $20 million. While valuable timber could be found here and there, I estimated that the timber was worth in the $250-$300 p/A range, straight through. But the timber value was concentrated rather than spread evenly across the tract. The Flipper was an older, country-boy-type who had wiggled through deals like this many times before. But he had mistakenly relied on the seller's outdated timber inventory to project the timber's market value. It didn't take him long to figure out that his option price was too high to flip to local buyers. His strategy from the first was to flip the entire property to another Flipper who would do the division and resale. He sold about 4,000 acres to adjoining landowners in "small" pieces for prices at and above $650 p/A. Then he sold 6,000 acres to an out-of-state Flipper who held an even more inflated idea of the timber's value. By this time, he had extended his option for another $300,000. With time and money running out, he dropped the asking price on the remaining 30,000 acres from $650 p/A to $535 p/A and found an entirety buyer—a former prominent Congressman—at the last minute for $525 p/A. And that buyer—a Flipper—has been trying to sell it for $1,000+ p/A without quick success. If I had a retail client in this game, I would have advised paying no more than $450 p/A for a large chunk of this 40,000 acres and no more than $550 p/A in small lifts. Other comparable property was available at those prices and less.

A buyer can benefit from understanding the Flipper's immediate circumstances. He's more likely to sell below his asking price if he's already paid for the deal from earlier sales. You can bargain better by determining the Flipper's purchase price for the root property and the selling prices he's received from prior sales. These prices can be found or calculated from deeds recorded in the Courthouse. You gain leverage by "knowing his numbers." Option contracts are not likely to be recorded. You'll have to put your ear to the local ground to listen for the Flipper's option price, his deadline and whether or not he can extend. It never hurts to ask the seller about the option price.

Buyers can assume that the Flipper is looking to make at least a 50 percent gross profit for his effort, and 100 percent is not unusual. When a tract has both good and bad sections, the Flipper may mark up the good sections proportionately more than the bad ones. The latter might be bought for not much more than what Flipper has in it. Bargain hunters may find a "bad" piece that perfectly fits their needs. If, for example, you're looking for hunting habitat, you should consider buying the "bad" lot with the recently clearcut areas; the more ugly slash, the better.

Flippers divide their property and sell the parts according to state law and local ordinance. Where those frameworks are lax, you will get less protection than where they are not. You should assume that a Flipper will disappear after the Flip. Any problem that emerges will be yours to fix. You should not rely on oral promises. Written statements bind real-estate transactions.

Rural residential developments, like any other business, have their share of people from whom you don't want to buy either the Brooklyn Bridge or a hillside lot that reminds the salesman of those "million-dollar cliff-hangers in California." Outright and intentional land frauds and swindles are harder to pull off today because of federal and state laws—and are, therefore, probably of less concern than they were before the era of regulation and consumer protection. Buyers still get taken, and it doesn't do you much good to have your developer jailed for mail fraud as you sit on Lot #31 on the top of a mountain with only a mile of goat trail to get you there.

One Flip that you want to avoid is the outright fraud. The clue here is that you, the buyer, find yourself negotiating with a "seller" who "has" a contract with the landowner that hasn't closed. In and of itself this is not a fraudulent situation. Most real-estate contracts allow the buyer to "assign" or sell his interest in it. The seller pumps the value of the property to you to make it appear that it's worth much more than the contract price, which he discloses. He can do this in several ways. The seller pays a compliant appraiser to provide an inflated value, or obtains a bogus cruise on the timber value (See Chapter 31), or links up with a pliant mortgage lender who agrees to lend you the inflated value. Your best protection is to scope the property thoroughly to determine its real market value. (A similar urban scam was described by Benny L. Kass, "Housing Counsel: Beware of Fraud in 'Flipping' Schemes," Washington Post, October 20, 2001. Kass, a lawyer, writes an excellent column on housing issues and will consider questions from readers; Benny L. Kass, Suite 1100, 1050 17th St., N.W., Washington, D.C., 20036.)

Some readers may be interested in learning how to flip property. Take a look at William Bronchick and Robert Dahlstrom, Flipping Properties (Chicago: Dearborn-Kaplan Publishing Co., 2001) and Bradley K. Haynes, How You Can Grow Rich Through Rural Land—Starting from Scratch (Front Royal, Virginia: Greatland Publishing Co., 1979). Mr. Haynes operates a real-estate brokerage in the north end of Virginia's Shenandoah Valley and runs ads in the Washington Post that offer a free report, "50 Ways to Buy Land With Little or No Money Down." He can be reached at B.K. Haynes Land Brokers, www.bkhaynes.com or e-mail: bkhaynes@shentel.net; Since the Haynes book was published, many rural counties have tightened their subdivision ordinances, making flipping harder, more expensive and more responsible than in the past.

CHAPTER 11: SECOND HOMES: DEVELOPERS AND DEVELOPMENTS

BUILDING A SECOND HOME OUT HERE

Whether you're building your own or buying a house off a developer's rack, it's worth doing background reading before you sit down with architects, excavators, contractors, developers or just the back of your own envelope. I've found these general books to be helpful: Alan and Denise Fields, Your New House: The Alert Consumer's Guide to Buying and Building a Quality Home, 3rd ed. (Boulder, CO: Windsor Peak Press, 1999); Myron E. Ferguson, Build It Right!: What to Look for in Your New Home (Salem, OR: Home User Press, 1997) and Better Houses, Better Living: What to Look for When Buying, Building or Remodeling (Salem, OR: Home User Press, 2004); Gary W. Eldred, The Complete Guide to Second Homes for Vacations, Retirement, and Investment (New York: John Wiley & Sons, Inc., 2000); Bob Johnson, Houses are Designed by Geniuses and Built by Gorillas: An Insider's Guide to Designing and Building a Home (Lenexa, KS: Addax Publishing, 1998); Dennis Wedlick with Philip Langdon, The Good Home: Interiors and Exteriors (New York: Hearst Books International, 2001); Janice Papolos, The Virgin Homeowner: The Essential Guide to Owning, Maintaining, and Servicing Your Home (New York: Penguin Books, 1999); and Katherine Salant, The Brand-New House Book (New York: Three Rivers Press-Random House, 2001). Robert J. Bruss, the knowledgeable and always helpful real-estate columnist. described the content of Salant's book as "superb" though its readability due to font choice and layout led him to write: "I have never encountered a book as hard to read as this one." Ferguson can be contacted at the Home User press, 1939 Woodhaven St., NW, Salem, OR, 97304; 503-391-8106, 1-800-530-5105, 503-375-2939 FAX; e-mail: info@betterhousebetterliving.com.

You will help yourself if you take the time to become familiar with the basic components of house construction. I recommend buying a comprehensive how-to book with a large index and glossary. The one I used in studying for my Virginia Class A residential-contractor's exam was John L. Feirer, Gilbert R. Hutchings and Mark D. Feirer, Carpentry and Building Construction, 5th ed. (Glencoe/McGraw Hill: New York, 1997), $59.95. Look for the most recent edition of this book or another of the same type and format. A simple and comprehensive discussion is found in Francis D.K. Ching and Cassandra Adams, Building Construction Illustrated, Third Edition (New York: John Wiley & Sons, 2001). Such volumes do not lobby for one type of house over others. Rather, they discuss the variety of *conventional* materials, practices (how stuff should go together) and design choices available to the trade. They provide common standards that should be applied, e.g., at a certain load, how much clear span can be designed for a floor with 2x8 joists spaced on 16" centers. Books like this are a handy generic reference when construction contractors start asking you to make decisions. The simpler the design and the more conventional the materials, the cheaper the square-foot construction cost—that's the rule of thumb that you will discover. Books devoted to specific building concerns—log cabins, passive-solar construction, stone work and so on—are available in bookstores, libraries and through the Internet. More exotic construction materials and practices will not be found in the conventional-building literature.

Reliable house-construction books and information are available from The Taunton Press and The Journal of Light Construction, 186 Allen Brook Lane, Williston, Vt., 05495; 802-879-3335. Fine Homebuilding (www.taunton.com; e-mail: fh@taunton.com) and The Journal of Light Construction (www.jlconline.com) are superb monthly magazines written for the trade that can be understood by semi-knowledgeable and half-handy prospective homeowners. (If you are not now semi-knowledgeable and are planning to build or have a house built for you, becoming semi-knowledgeable will pay for itself many times over.) While "book knowledge" has many limits, it's a very big first step toward being able to make sensible, cost-effective decisions in consultation with architects, excavators and contractors. Both magazines have been publishing for a number of years, and their back issues will have articles on specific subjects of interest. These collections are an amazingly rich source of trustworthy information, current as of the publication date. It is certainly possible for a non-knowledgeable urbanite to pay a contractor to build a second home in the country without ever asking a question, reading a book or learning the difference between a jamb and a joist. But when you are thinking of spending $100,000 or more in principal and (mainly) interest over the next 20 or 30 years, doesn't it make sense to spend $100 on books and magazines and $300 in fees for talking to an architect?

Certain residential-building practices and requirements will be set forth in the **local building code**. If you're hiring an architect or contractor, you won't have to know anything about these codes, unless the building inspector finds a problem. If you're being your own general contractor or doing the work yourself, you will need to know and follow the code requirements. If you violate the code, ignorance is not a defense.

Codes establish minimum practices governing residential design and construction, electrical work and plumbing. Until recently, no single national residential building code existed. In the late 1990s, the three regional code-writing organizations agreed on a single comprehensive code, 2000 International Residential Code (IRC), which provides standards for one- and two-family dwellings. The IRC also includes building standards for high-wind and high-seismic areas, as well as energy-efficiency standards. If you want a copy, contact the Building Officials and Code Administrators International, Inc. (BCOAI), 4051 W. Flossmoor Rd., Country Club Hills, Il., 60478; 708-799-2300; order from 1-800-214-4321, Ext. 777; www.bocai.org; e-mail: info@bocai.org. Request the most recent edition. The IRC is being adopted throughout the country, though localities choose which codes they want to use. If you do not want to become an instant expert on the IRC but want to have some idea of these standards, refer to the following books by Redwood Kardon from The Taunton Press: Code Check Electrical Revised Ed., 2nd ed.; A Field Guide to Wiring a Safe House; Code Check Plumbing; and Code Check Revised Ed., 3rd ed.: A Field Guide to Building a Safe Home. (The Taunton Press, publisher of Fine Homebuilding and building-related books is at 63 S. Main Street, POB 5506, Newtown, Ct. 06470; 1-800-283-7252.)

You may also hear reference to the National Electrical Code (NEC), or "The Code," which should be taken to mean whichever electrical code is used locally. Less technical books on electrical wiring and plumbing are available from Home Depot, Time-Life Books and Ortho. These are stocked at building-supply stores, online vendors, bookstores and libraries. If your house project is in a cold climate, you might also read Joseph Lstiburek's, Builder's Guide to Cold Climates from The Taunton Press. Make sure to use the most recent edition of codes and building books.

The local building inspector can tell you which code he applies. If the locality is not using the IRC, the inspector may be able to identify those sections of the local code that differ from the IRC and make recommendations for upgrades where he thinks they're a good idea. Nothing prevents an owner or his contractor from building "above" the code, for example, using stouter materials than the local code requires. Clear any upgrade with the local building inspector before you tell your contractor to do it. Make sure your architect, if you are using one, has designed to the local code. If you are using purchased house plans or developer plans, ask the local inspector to check them for code compliance before you build from them.

The local inspector can be counted on to know and enforce the local code, which may be customized to suit local conditions. Your house needs to comply with local standards. Areas prone to windstorms may—and should—require stouter roof designs. Earthquake areas have higher and different foundation standards. If you insist on building in a floodplain—some folks just have to have their fishing cabin a fly cast away from their trout stream—ask your architect, contractor and inspector what options you have, consistent with the local code, to protect your new house from the inevitable flooding. I have seen river-side houses perched on stout posts 14 feet above ground level. The code will provide the specifics on post height, dimensions and foundation.

Code inspections by the local building inspector are scheduled at different points in the construction process—typically before the footer is laid, when the foundation is complete, after the building is framed and when the electrical and plumbing are "roughed in" (that is, open for visual inspection). A code violation may imply a very small repair or thousands of dollars of new materials and rebuilding. Your contract with the developer and/or contractor should state that all work done on your behalf shall comply with local codes and that any instances of non-compliance will be corrected without additional expense to the owner (you). The local building inspector will only look for code violations; he will not inspect for things your architect and contractor have done that are impractical, stupid, wasteful and shoddy. If you have an architect working for you, he should keep an eye on your contractor. The architect's overview is limited to the times he visits the house, and some mistakes cannot be corrected once work proceeds beyond them. If you're not on the scene, you might hire a retired individual with some construction sense to visit the site every day as your representative. An arrangement of this sort is likely to keep down the number and size of mistakes and miscommunications. This **"clerk of the works"** should pay for himself in preventing costly errors.

Rural land buyers have four main ways of getting a house built: 1) buy into a second-home development where the developer also handles the building; 2) hire an independent, handle-everything **general contractor** who builds the house you want from plans you like either on a development's lot or on non-development land; 3) act as your own general contractor by hiring and coordinating other contractors to do the work; and 4) do the work yourself.

BUYING A SECOND HOME IN A FULL-PACKAGE DEVELOPMENT

Owners have several ready alternatives to buying undeveloped rural property and developing it on their own. You can find a **full-package second-home development** where everything—roads, utilities, house, community amenities—is in place or there for the buying. The advantage of a full-package deal is that you can see exactly what you're getting for your money, and you can talk to those who've already jumped in. Such developments usually come with a set of house-construction guidelines, such as minimum number of square feet, that every lot-owner follows. The full-package developer also handles house construction for each lot buyer, either acting as a general contractor or through an arrangement with one or more general contractors. The developer will usually set up a **homeowners' association** to manage the development after he's done.

Where a developer is also the contractor for the project's house construction, one or more models may be available for inspection. *Before signing a purchase contract for land and house*, ask the developer for a set of house plans and materials to review. Then hire an architect to check them. Buy two or three hours of his time, no more. Architects are trained to imagine two-dimensional drawings as they will be in three dimensions. They will know the standard formulas that house designs should incorporate, from the proper width of "elder" hallways to the height of counters. Ask him to scan the plan/materials for corner-cutting and point out both the good and bad features he sees. A common way for a developer or contractor to cut corners on a house is to skimp on the things you can't see. This can take the form of underinsulating (e.g., using insulation with a too-low R-factor; not insulating the ground floor; not installing whole-house insulation wrap); using plastic water pipe not copper; skimping on structural materials (e.g., using 1/2"-thick plywood as a roof underlayment rather than 5/8", or thicker; using 2x4 wall studs instead of 2x6s in climates where six inches of wall insulation is much better than four; not using treated lumber for sills); using cheap windows, doors, fixtures and cabinets, and so on. Stock second-home designs tend to provide as many square feet as possible and short the buyer on structural stoutness and quality materials.

Where the developer has built similar second homes in developments, ask owners for their opinions. A poorly constructed house will usually turn up problems soon after it has been occupied and certainly within five years. Ask the owners what they like and dislike about the design and materials, and what they'd change. Ask about roof problems and leaks around windows and doors; windows that don't work well; doors that have warped; cracks in masonry; plumbing problems; degradation of siding and interior surfaces; undersized heating and air-conditioning units; insufficient phone jacks and outlets; cheap appliances.

Take this information to the architect whom you have asked to suggest changes and upgrades in the developer's house plan. Remind the architect that you are looking for suggestions appropriate to the house the developer is planning to build. (If the architect tells you to bail out of this developer, do so.) The architect's review will cover the house plan's structural integrity, materials, design functionality (how well the design fits your needs) and quality. He can make *modest* floor-plan revisions to provide more efficient use of horizontal and vertical space. He can also propose more substantial revisions to fit your individual needs, subject to the developer's willingness to incorporate them. Make sure the architect understands the scope of what you're asking him to do; you are *not* asking him to redesign the entire house. If you find the architect you have chosen for this limited work is recommending wholesale changes with which you agree, you may want to walk away from the developer's project. The alternative would be to buy land outside a development, hire the architect and find a general contractor to build the house you want.

The architect's review is also a chance for you to evaluate the architect. You may want to reconsider the architect if you sense that his "vision" of your house is grander than or stylistically incompatible with yours. If you get stuck, hire a house carpenter or contractor to review the developer's plans. Not all carpenters and contractors can provide this kind of review. Some may be reluctant to act as an "outside" consultant, because they have business relationships with the developer. Regardless of the title or professional status of the individual you use, you're looking for a combination of hands-on experience and the intellectual ability to judge how systems will work together in practice on your site. The actual review-and-comment time should take no more than a couple of hours. The suggestions you get will pay for themselves many times over.

Despite my cautions, I believe that a second-home buyer gets substantial advantages from a full-package-infrastructure-plus-house development. First, most—but not all—of both the work and worries of house-building are done by those you hire. In the best of circumstances, you will still have to find the money to pay for things, make choices that involve taste and expense and do the final inspection and acceptance before making your last payment. (You might want to take your outside consultant on this last inspection.) Still, the thousands of decisions required of an individual building his own second home are not yours. You are also spared the hundreds of decisions required when you act as your own contractor. You cannot avoid several dozen decisions—most of which can be made over the phone and during a half-dozen, scheduled site visits. Buying a full package minimizes the stress and time you will spend getting your second home done. Convenience and simplicity have both psychic and monetary value.

Second, you will be choosing from developer-offered designs that have been conceived to be simple enough for run-of-the-mill crews and **subcontractors**, referred to as **subs**, to complete well enough. The crews building your developer house are not Old World craftsmen who lovingly hand plane each floor board and carve your likeness into your walnut fireplace mantle after hours and on their own nickel. They are for the most part adequate at what they do; and at least one—hopefully, the crew chief—can read a blueprint and has built your model before. The more times a crew has built a house design, the better job they are likely to do. They will have discovered design errors and made their mistakes on the earlier structures. As a later buyer, you will benefit from the crew's rise on the construction learning curve. The developer will offer house plans that he knows his crews are capable of building. Developer-contractors will offer you options on basic plans, but not the option of building anything you want. Since developers are in business to make money, the more you deviate from the package of options, the more uncertainty and time the developer will take on and the more it will cost you. Every customization and change order you make will involve extra cost, because each one inevitably requires extra work, time and risk of not getting it right.

Finally, if the house the developer builds fails to meet the terms of your contract or customary standards of workmanship, it will be far easier for you to get him to resolve the dispute—before your final payment—than it would be for you to chase down a general contractor and his subs. House building is sausage-making insofar as it turns raw land and thousands pieces of stuff into a functioning structure. It is hard, messy and, often, distasteful work. Houses built by developers must be put up quickly, efficiently and for a fixed price. Labor, a major cost component, is contained by using materials that can be put up fast, working off familiar designs and substituting cheap labor for skilled, expensive labor wherever possible. Mistakes are inevitable. Still, every developer depends for future sales on good word of mouth from buyers who have gone before. Both profit and customer satisfaction depend on making sausage simply, using the same basic recipe. This allows the developer to have confidence in his product, and he should stand behind it, making good whatever might turn up not quite right. An absentee owner will have a far harder time getting the average independent general contractor to right the same wrongs. It will be especially hard on one-of-a-kind houses and those with a lot of custom work. You will have little chance to resolve the dispute outside of court if you've given him his last payment.

When a house is built from scratch, you should expect to find some construction mistakes and defects. Before you accept your new house, you should inspect the house and fill out a **punch list** of items you think should be corrected. You might want to do this **walk-through** with your architect/consultant, home inspector, or even a friend with house-building experience. A completed house conceals most structural mistakes under exterior and interior finishes, siding, drywall, paneling and the like. You can catch these errors only if you or your **clerk of the works** is on the scene when they are still visible and correctable. Your final payment is contingent on the punch-list items being corrected. Most contractors guarantee their workmanship for one year. The head of one national real-estate engineering firm estimated that "…nationwide as many as 15 percent of new residences have serious defects.., the most common involve roofs and water intrusion in windows and doors." (John Handley, Chicago Tribune, "Welcome to Your Imperfect Dream Home," Washington Post, May 8, 2004, quoting Alan Mooney, president of Criterium Engineers of Portland, Maine.) Defects, Mooney said, are caused by house-building materials, weather and poor construction techniques. Cost-pinching builders can scrimp on nails, screws, caulking and vapor barriers—with major consequences. The temperature when concrete is poured and asphalt shingles are applied will affect job quality. Among other commonly observed defects are inadequate caulking, missing or unbolted anchor bolts that connect the foundation to the house frame, lack of flashing above windows and doors, unsealed seams on ductwork, nail and screw pops and foundation cracks. Lawsuits over construction defects now have put the cost of builder insurance at about $6,000 for the average new house. A lot of new houses will have a lot of little things not quite right. Your interest is in not buying a new second home with big things wrong.

If you are flexible about your house plans and schedule, consider buying the developer's model. You should expect a price discount in proportion to the amount of money you pay in advance of possession. If, for instance, the developer wants to use his model for one year and you are willing to give him cash a year in advance of his exit, you should be able to reduce the purchase price on the model considerably. He needs your cash more now (to pay his bills and debt service) than he will in a year, when the last sales revenue is profit. Be mindful of your tax consequences in working this tactic. Models tend to be loaded with options, built and maintained carefully, and located at the front of the project. They can be a great buy, as long as you're comfortable with a front-of-the-development location.

It's possible that you believe that you can save money by buying undeveloped land and hiring a contractor to build a house for you from plans you provide instead of buying into a full-package development. Possibly. Developers-contractors have salaried crews who must work efficiently if they are to retain their employment. They are able to purchase materials at the **contractor's price** where one is offered, usually two to ten percent below retail. They may be able to negotiate a quantity discount on top of the contractor's price. The contractor you hire on your own may or may not get the contractor's price, may or may not pass along any savings to you, and may or may not mark up materials to the point where you would have been ahead to buy materials retail. Developers should be skilled in using cost-estimator computer programs and should have **take offs** (price quotes that are good for fixed period of time, e.g., 90 days) from suppliers and prices from subs before they quote you. Certainly after building the first couple of project houses, the developer will know what his actual costs are and can price subsequent houses with some confidence.

If you are using a general contractor to build your house, he will get a contractor's discount on materials (where they are offered) and then mark up the cost of materials by ten percent or more to cover overhead and profit. Some contractors earn their markup by shopping around among suppliers for the lowest price. Others will simply buy all materials from a single supplier, making their lives easier but your bill higher. I once asked a general contractor working for me why he didn't get materials from the lowest-priced supplier, which I had researched for him, instead of using one supplier exclusively. He replied that his supplier would be "no more than ten percent higher on any item on my list than the cheapest guy." I pointed out to him that since he was getting a 20 percent mark up on materials he purchased, this could result in spending as much as $10,000 more on a $100,000 materials purchase, along with 60 percent more profit for him. (The math worked like this: $100,000 materials cost + 20 percent markup = $120,000 cost of materials to owner; $100,000 materials cost + 10 percent added for higher price = $110,000 + 20 percent markup = $132,000 cost of materials to owner; $12,000/$20,000 = 60 percent more profit on the materials mark up from a 10 percent higher price.) He agreed, but argued that there was a "convenience factor" that I should consider (his convenience, that was). This particular supplier, he added, always took back materials, he, the contractor, wrongly ordered or were wrongly sent. (Don't use a supplier who refuses returns.) With a fixed mark up over cost, neither the supplier nor my general contractor had any incentive or reason to hold down my cost of materials—and, of course, they didn't. With the project running over budget, I began ordering some supplies myself from low-cost suppliers and to save the contractor's mark up. He and I parted ways, though not soon enough in my opinion.

Shopping suppliers can save you five percent on a project's total cost. But you will spend a lot of time making comparisons and coordinating the delivery of stuff from different suppliers. I think the best way to handle this situation is to establish relations with no more than three multi-purpose building suppliers, buying from whichever offers the best price for the quality. You will have to purchase enough either to make a truck load or pick up materials yourself. You will learn from the take offs each of your suppliers prepares who is the cheapest on each type of material—framing lumber, windows, doors, blocks, hardware, drywall, paints, siding, roofing and so on. You will have to weigh price against other factors, such as whether you will need to store materials under cover or inside, and for how long. It's common to buy most materials from the overall low-cost supplier with specific items from others, as needed.

Some contractors will work out a sweetheart deal with a supplier, and others will treat you properly. It's fair for a general contractor to mark up materials cost when he is shopping for you, coordinating deliveries and hassling with returns. Doing these jobs well takes time and a good head for details. A conscientious contractor will save you money on materials and know which suppliers to avoid regardless of their prices. He'll also know when the low price reflects low quality. His time in managing materials will increase if he's building at a remote location where he has to drive a ways into town each time he finds he's short the proper nail.

I think the best way to handle this owner-contractor-supplier triangle is to have frank talks with your preferred contractor and various suppliers before you sign a construction contract. Your preferred contractor may want to work with one supplier more than others, and there may be good reasons to follow his advice. If you want to buy and manage materials yourself, make sure that your contractor understands this. Materials are usually about 50 percent of total new-house cost, so if you're taking this mark up away from a contractor, he needs to know this in advance and price his work accordingly. You should expect that a contractor will build in overhead and profit to whatever work he does on your project. Don't quibble over pennies, but, at the same time, be clear with each other over how you are being charged. Don't be rigid about insisting that the contractor always use the lowest-cost supplier, because other factors can weigh on this decision. A supplier who slips in low-quality, unusable materials is more trouble than the cost "savings" are worth. (I've seen roof framing stop dead when the last two rafters in the supplier's package contained defects that prevented them from being used safely.) Follow your contractor's advice when he gives you specific examples of a particular supplier delivering shoddy materials, or dumping a load out in the rain without covering it, or unloading in a way that damaged merchandise or consistently botching up orders.

Also make sure that either you or your contractor always pays suppliers in time to get any fast-payment discount offered. Suppliers will offer, as a rule, **10/1 Net 30** or **10/2 Net 30 discounts**, which mean that the purchaser can deduct either one or two percent from the bill if payment is received within ten days of the billing date, otherwise the full bill—the net—is due within 30 days of the billing date.

You can get a reasonably accurate idea of the cost of doing any piece of new house construction work by consulting **annual pricing guides** that are available in libraries and at major bookstores. (Remodeling work is harder to estimate, because conditions vary.) New construction work can be costed out in different ways: by the **square foot**; or as **unit cost** (one brick costs $1 x 5,000 bricks needed to build a wall; a unit might also be laying 100 linear feet of brick); or by the **item** (one free-standing fireplace with 24 feet of 12"-diameter insulated flue pipe costs $x.) R.S. Means Company, Inc., publishes Contractor's Pricing Guide: Residential Square Foot Costs, each year. (R.S. Means Company, Inc., 100 Construction Plaza, POB 800, Kingston, MA 02364-0800; 617 585-7880; 1-800-334-3509). This is an easily understood cost compendium of every new construction component and system that allows you to cost out a specific house in a specific geographic region in a given year. Much of the data is broken down so that you can find the cost of materials (which includes a ten percent mark up for profit) and cost of installation (labor plus contractor's overhead and profit) for everything from putting in a driveway to installing a skylight. Basic house types in economy, average and custom versions are costed out by the square foot along with the cost of common upgrades and modifications. The Means Company also publishes a cost guide for those who are thinking of remodeling: Repair and Remodeling Cost Data, annual edition. Another cost guideline that I've used is Marshall & Swift, Dodge Unit Cost Book, annual edition (Marshall & Swift [McGraw Hill], POB 26307, Los Angeles, CA 90026-0307; 213-683-9000; 1-800-526-2756).

These books will give you a reasonable estimate of average construction costs in your location. You should, of course, anticipate variation from these average estimates, depending on site-specific conditions, local labor costs and the always changing price of materials. If you're building a high-end second home, you should expect to pay a bit more per unit than if you're building a two-bedroom, one-bath ranch. Your budget for labor rates and profit will be larger, and your contractor will know that. These books cannot factor in site-specific variations from the norm—bad soils that require a more expensive foundation footer or a ledge that takes an extra-big backhoe to remove. As a rule, overall building costs are cheaper in the country than in urban areas, but not in the rural pockets of wealth like Aspen, Colorado or Jackson, Wyoming. Labor costs are usually cheaper in rural areas, but standard materials can be a bit more expensive. Locally produced materials—stone, native lumber for finish work—should be cheaper and, often better, than their nationally marketed counterparts.

If you are at the point where you have an architect-drawn house plan or a set of similarly detailed plans, take them to various building-supply companies near your site and ask them to prepare a **take off**. These companies can calculate your materials need from a set of detailed house plans. Better still, your plans may come with an itemized list of materials, quantities and specifications (including brands and model numbers; dimensions, wood species and special features, e.g., plywood with tongue-and-groove edge rather than the more common butt-edged type). A supplier's take off represents a quoted price to you of the materials listed on the company's response to your plans or list. Quoted prices are good for at least 30 days, with 90 days being common. When comparing take-off estimates, be alert to substitutions of what the supplier is able to provide with what your plans specify. Costs vary with the quality of materials used, and it's easy to become the low-bidder by substituting lower-quality materials for those that are speced. Suppliers will quote a take-off price to those owners buying materials for a general contractor in their employ or an owner-built project.

A developer-contractor will usually offer to build a house for you using a **fixed-price contract**. This will specify the work to be done (and imply what's not done) along with a schedule of payments. The developer will offer to build his house plan for you for a lump sum (fixed price). He may offer to finance the land, construction, or both. Contractors are usually paid in several lifts during construction, the last occurring after you've approved and accepted the house. You will not know either his cost of materials or labor. You can get a rough idea of his building costs by consulting the Means or Dodge estimating guides, described above. If you change the scope of work during construction, called a **change order**, you will negotiate its cost separately. The developer will incorporate into his fixed price all of his known costs, plus his estimate of unknown expenses, delays and risk—all of which may amount to as much as 30 percent above his hard projections of expenses and materials. He then may add in overhead if that factor has not been included in labor and materials. Finally, he'll add profit onto that number. This may sound like a formula for excessive charges, but keep in mind that his package must be priced competitively against all other new housing in the local market and to a lesser degree against the owner who acts as his own general contractor on land outside a development.

A developer-builder must price his houses competitively, because second homes are almost always discretionary purchases and buyers have alternatives. He must also keep to his quoted construction price unlike an independent contractor being paid on the basis of time and materials. Apart from cost certainty, the developer-builder offers an absentee owner convenience and security, which may seem like abstract and marginal benefits as you're reading this book but take on major significance when you're in the middle of construction 150 miles from where you live.

You will inevitably ask whether the same house can be built for less money working through your own general contractor on land outside a development or by doing some or all of the construction yourself. On paper, you will find yourself saving money. But you will rarely, if ever, be comparing one apple of a specific size, weight and quality to another with identical characteristics. Of course, you can save money if you do a lot of the work yourself—and have the time to spend doing it. You save money if you count your time and labor for free. That may or may not be a fair calculation, depending on your individual circumstances. I would count owner labor in for something, if only a fraction of current labor rates. You should assume that it will take you longer to do each task than the developer's work crew, particularly if you're working by yourself. Putting on a shingle roof might be estimated at six person days for a three-person crew; I'd increase the time by at least 50 percent to do it myself to account for a slower work pace, more care in doing the work and adding more nails than the crew would use. If you're older, count on taking more time to do a task than it would have taken you to do when you were not older. The solo builder is less efficient in performing a unit of this type of work, and he's also responsible for getting the materials to the site and humping them up the ladder. And if you're not an experienced builder, add in time for lack of familiarity with local vendors, forgetfulness, visitors and errors only an idiot like you and me would make. If you're taking time off from work in a manner that's forgoing a unit in your pay to not pay a dollar to a builder, you're probably netting a loss on a do-it-yourself. Don't forget to count in time that you spend fussing with house headaches by long-distance phone when you should be concentrating on your day job, as well as worry, stress and marital strain. There are, in other words, excellent reasons for an absentee buyer to build a second home through a full-package developer-builder when you can find one whose package meets all of your needs, most of your wants, a majority of your aesthetics and the available part of your pocketbook.

If you are inexperienced about house-building and wish to remain so, you should confine your search for a new second home in the country to full-package developments. You will still have to choose from among developments, and within a particular development you will have the ability to change the developer's house plans consistent with options he presents and the thickness of your wallet. The trouble with choosing among full-package developments is that you may not like the house designs or the prices. All things considered, the full-package second home is a safer and more reliable path than other new-construction options generally available to an absentee owner interested in a simple entry into country living. If, however, you hate faux 1890s farmhouses and places that look like someone stuck corks in their ears and shoved an air hose up their back door, you can jump in and look for non-development land and a general contractor, or limit your search to **improved land**, that is, country property with an existing house.

A typical **semi-developed project—a partial infrastructure package**—will offer a buyer sufficient infrastructure to allow him to place or build a dwelling of some sort on his new lot. (In rural second-home developments, a lot can be any size. Lots tend to be larger where the infrastructure investment is smaller.) Semi-developed infrastructure may be nothing more than interior dirt roads. The buyer must understand that he and other lot owners must add the remaining property infrastructure on their own or do without. Each buyer is then responsible for his own site infrastructure and house-building.

A common rural second-home development is one where the developer has purchased a large undeveloped tract and then divided it into lots in compliance with the local zoning ordinance. A developer might stop his capital investment at that point, proceeding directly to sell the newly surveyed parcels with nothing more than a marked-out road right of way. The developer might handle lot sales or run them through either a real-estate broker or an auction. This is The Flip described in Chapter 10; Flips do not offer a house-building package.

If you are looking to buy a house from a developer of any kind, never sign a purchase contract without first scoping the project, the lot and the house choices. Don't sign a purchase contract without having your local lawyer review it. Your lawyer should pick out your legal risks, but some risks will reveal themselves only through your own diligent scoping. Where a house is being purchased along with a lot, you may have a separate construction contract. Both standard developer-supplied contracts will favor the developer. Consider submitting your purchase offer for the land and house on a contract that you and your lawyer draft, using the standard contracts where they are fair to both sides. You are not required to use the developer's contract to buy his land or his house, though he's likely to resist using your version. If nothing else, your contract alternative will reveal those portions of the developer's contract(s) that he doesn't want to give up. That can give you a lot of information. If your lawyer tells you the developer's basic contract is acceptable from your point of view, then go with it and propose revised language where he recommends. I also recommend having your lawyer with you when you negotiate price for land/house and options with the developer or his sales personnel. This evens the sides, and gives you an excuse to leave the bargaining table for a private strategy caucus with your lawyer. If you feel inept or uncomfortable bargaining on your own behalf, have your lawyer take the lead.

The best-intentioned developers fail in whole or in part. Their failures can drag buyers into a protracted mess that costs money, time and emotional energy. These train wrecks occur when the developer runs out of money; train wrecks will change your journey. Less infrastructure and fewer amenities are installed. Another developer with a different plan might take over. The project design is changed, e.g., increasing the number of units or decreasing the size of unsold lots so as to have more to sell. House options may be narrowed; house prices are likely to be increased. The developer's investment in the project can be scaled back in many ways. Bankruptcy may be taken or the developer takes a one-way night flight to a beach near the Equator. Even where the developer sticks with a troubled project, a buyer can find that a problem condition is not disclosed or an oral promise is not kept (e.g., a promise that the State has agreed to take over ownership and maintenance of the project's roads when the State has made no such commitment). Financial shakiness can affect any development, no matter size or location. A big jump in interest rates over a couple of years can strangle the most well-planned development. Buyers must assume the responsibility for protecting themselves. It is impossible to eliminate all risks from buying in a development, but scoping and question-asking can minimize them.

The 1968 Federal Interstate Land Sales Full Disclosure Act covers projects of 25 or more undeveloped lots that are marketed through the mail or in interstate advertising. Various states have enacted laws regulating developments that are organized with homeowners' associations (also referred to as, "lot associations"). Make sure that the second-home developer gives you a copy of association regulations. In the absence of a homeowners' association, ask very detailed questions about how you and your fellow lot owners will manage infrastructure maintenance once the developer leaves.

You, as a development buyer, can also find some security in local building regulations. Counties may have ordinances that impose infrastructure and house standards that determine the number of houses on a particular project site and control the type and size of housing that can be built on its lots. House design may also come under the purview of a local county committee charged with reviewing the appearance and style of new housing. There's less regulatory framework in less-developed, second-home counties, and a great deal in highly developed areas. You should have confidence in a developer who has given the county a **performance bond** for the purpose of assuring completion of the project.

You, as a buyer, must do everything you can before buying into a development to assay the background risk of developer failure. Building contractors, as well, can fail unexpectedly. A useful exercise is to anticipate what you would do were the developer or the general contractor you've hired disappear the day after you sign your contract and hand over your check. You can't prevent the failure of others, but you can use your scoping and question-asking to measure the risk you will assume. Nothing beats direct questions from you to the developer prior to signing a contract: What happens if you run out of money before the project is completed? What happens if sales do not proceed as anticipated? What guarantee does he offer that he will build out all of his promises? What protection do you as a buyer have if he doesn't? What happens if he runs out of money with your house half built? If his answers smell off, don't hold your nose while signing the contract. Find another place.

Buying rural property can be one of your major life commitments. This is especially true when the property is a second home and carries with it ever more layers of family memories. "On Golden Pond" is not fictive in this regard. The second home can easily become a family's primary emotional residence. The process of acquiring such places becomes one of the family's foundation legends. Apart from the very sensible idea of spending your money wisely, it's far better to step into these places with positive feelings and a sense that you've managed the acquisition and construction well rather than stumbling in, feeling pummeled and ripped off. Bad start-up vibes reverberate for a long time, and, in my experience, never really go away. Good vibes are what we want. And good vibes will result from research, research, research and knowing increasingly what you want.

BUILDING A SECOND HOME WITH A GENERAL CONTRACTOR

A general contractor coordinates, arranges, schedules, secures, directs and carries out. He is responsible for getting each sub-task in the construction process done in the proper sequence, using either his own crew or subcontractors. The general contractor is responsible to you for the quality of any subcontracted work. General contractors will have house plans for you to select and should be willing to work from plans that you provide. Your plans can be purchased from a supplier or drawn by an architect. You hire a general contractor, but he is not your employee. You should do no building without a written contract with your general contractor.

When you pay others to build a second home, you spare yourself the physical labor of construction, but you will still bear certain responsibilities and associated stress of coordinating the process; finding, vetting and paying a contractor; and possibly getting property rezoned and various permits, obtaining certain materials and accepting finished work. If an architect is involved, he can help with these tasks, but he adds another level of owner coordination. Lest I sound that building a house in the country is a choice between worse and worst, it's obvious that it is a job that is done all the time by people just like you. Start this journey with cautious enthusiasm. Become knowledgeable about the implications of choices and realistic about the amounts of time, money and emotional energy that will be required. Talk to those who've gone down this road before. Do not expect a road without bumps, but you can expect a road without wrecks.

If you are unsure, inexperienced or in search of wise counsel about the multi-layered, quasi-existential experience of dealing with residential building contractors, take a look at the following: Duncan C. Stephens, The Unofficial Guide to Hiring Contractors (New York: Macmillan, 1999); Tom Philbin, How to Hire a Home Improvement Contractor Without Getting Chiseled, rev. ed., (New York: St. Martin's Griffin, 1996); and Alan and Denise Fields, Your New House: The Alert Consumer's Guide to Buying and Building a Quality Home, 2nd ed., (Boulder: Windsor Peak Press, 1996 [1-800-888-0385]). Tracy Kidder's classic, House, describes a wonderful architect, a dedicated general contractor and a talented construction crew. To hit three for three is, in my experience, improbable.

The absentee buyer must be prepared for a great deal of long-distance consultation and a number of site visits when he retains a local general contractor. Building a house requires many on-the-spot decisions that the owner will want to decide in consultation with his contractor. Cell phones and laptops with e-mail enable you to stay closely in touch. If you find a general contractor who seems reluctant to talk with you, keep looking. By "talk" I mean two things at the minimum: return your calls in a reasonable amount of time and genuinely communicate. I've had nothing but bad experiences with contractors who don't talk to their customers. For your part, don't be a pest and don't share your agonies. Be a professional customer even when you're a first-time amateur.

General contractors will build a "**turnkey**" house for you, but you should not assume that your involvement is limited to signing checks and turning the key in the finished product. Some general contractors handle everything from site work to landscaping, while others will expect the owner to arrange for certain permits, utilities and site work. You need to have a very clear understanding from the start with your contractor as to what "turnkey" includes and does not include. It's best to stay in regular touch with the contractor even when the house plans are detailed and he's built from them before. Every owner changes a plan. Any change you make in an off-the-shelf plan is likely to lead to other changes, about which you want to be consulted. Something as simple as the location of light switches is a decision that you should make, because you will be living with its consequences.

Each owner has to establish a functional relationship with his contractor. You have to be decisive when a decision is required. An owner who keeps changing his mind about a design will find his project costs skyrocketing. You have to be involved, but you should not be meddlesome, obsessive and constantly micro-managing. If you exceed the contractor's patience for this behavior, you may find yourself without a contractor.

It's hard work to find the right balance with someone you don't know very well, whose judgment you are forced to trust, who may see you as another rich and dumb outsider, and to whom you are paying a lot of money for something you may not know much about. If you get the feeling that a contractor will be hard for you to work with, get out before you get in. You don't want someone who is insecure, inflexible, dismissive, ill-humored, unreachable, too busy for you, stupid or dishonest. The process of an absentee owner working with a general contractor is fraught with opportunities for disagreement and misunderstanding even when personalities mesh. You need not find a friend in a contractor, but you do need to find someone who can work with you in a friendly, problem-solving manner for mutual benefit. You don't want a contractor who personalizes differences of opinions. If you don't feel comfortable talking with a general contractor in your first discussion or two, I'd look for someone with whom you have a better chemistry. But before you burn through every contractor in a four-state area, make sure you are coming across as patient, reasonable and rational. While you are obviously invested in the outcome of each problem as it arises, remember that your contractor is a large part of any solution.

The general contractor will handle getting all of the construction work done. Other things being equal, you will want him to manage all of the **pre-construction house infrastructure** as well. Site-grading, excavating, road building, hauling infrastructure materials, coordinating the installation of utilities, putting in a septic tank and well and doing the final grading—is a huge headache if you're trying to find and coordinate individual specialist contractors, especially from a distance. Infrastructure must be planned, coordinated, designed, secured and installed correctly prior to construction. Permits and inspections from the local building officer are required. Other permits involving a septic system, erosion control and water may be required. If an endangered species is in on your land, you may not be able to build anything at all if construction destroys needed habitat. Getting the site infrastructure in place usually involves surveying (set-backs may be involved; you will need to have elevations "shot" on sloping sites so that you know how deep to dig your foundation footer), obtaining permits (which may require elevations and other drawings), road work, electrical service, other utilities (gas, telephone, cable TV, internet service), site clearing and preparation, surface-water drainage, soil stability under the house foundation (a civil engineer tests the soil; you want soil that compacts and stays in place; if the soil doesn't pass the test you may want to move to a different site or cut out the bad dirt and replace it with rock and good dirt), potable (drinkable) water (tying in to an existing line or developing a source on site) and wastewater (sewerage) system.

Having your general contractor take responsibility for arranging all of this work is money wisely spent. I also think it usually works out best when your general contractor does the site infrastructure himself. The next best arrangement is for your general contractor to "sub out" the work that he doesn't do to specialists with whom he's worked before. The least preferable approach is for your general contractor to coordinate among contractors that you find for him to work with. Your general contractor should know which subs to pull into your project based on cost and competence. Any sub used should be expected to guarantee the quality of his work to the standards of his trade. Ask your general who he plans to have do the infrastructure work. Run those names through your growing network of local contacts. If you have chosen your general well, you should have confidence in his choices and his ability to coordinate and implement tasks in the proper sequence. This takes experience and communication skills. Keep in mind that all local building and ground-disturbance approvals must be secured prior to doing that type of work.

A general contractor hired to do your project, in whole or in part, should be state-licensed and approved to handle the dollar scale of your work. A **residential contractor's license** indicates that the individual has at some point complied with whatever requirements were then imposed for that particular type of license. In Virginia, residential building contractors can obtain one of three levels of licensure, "A," "B" or "C," which require different levels of experience and financial worth, and allow the holder to build projects of increasing value. Most of the Virginia contractors I've worked with were grandfathered into their licenses, because they were working as contractors when the licensure standards were established. Some "A" contractors who are allowed to build residences of any type and with no dollar ceiling could not in my opinion pass the written test that is now the sole gate controlling access to their trade. These older contractors are not comfortable with book-knowledge tests, but are perfectly capable of doing a good job in the field based on experience. The license categories are not awarded on the basis of demonstrated competence. Many licensure applicants now enroll in multi-day preparation classes to increase their chances of passing. The B and C contractors I've used have been more competent and honest than the As, who tend to be wealthier and better at the business side of contracting. The B and Cs have low overhead and work by themselves or with one or two others at most, always on small projects falling under the dollar ceiling of their license. If you were building an entire house in Virginia, you would probably have to work with an A, because he alone is allowed to build projects involving more than $70,000. Each state has its own licensing system with an oversight/regulatory board. The board can send you a list of contractors who have been disciplined over their business practices. You may be able to learn whether the contractor you are considering has complaints pending against him.

You, as an absentee buyer, will have to select a contractor and then work with him. Your choice should be based on feel (personal chemistry), intellectual compatibility and your interview findings with each contractor's recent customers. Get references, and check out the houses he's built. Try to fit your project to the contractor's usual construction profile. A contractor who builds nothing other than bungalows for $75,000 should not be hired to build a $600,000 architect-designed, three-story oval home with a conical roof. Ask other absentee owners about their level of comfort in working with him.

If you're feeling overwhelmed by the prospect of jumping into the unknown, consider ordering the Home Building Manual (www.HomeBuildingManual.com), which breaks down a building project into the tasks that you undertake with your contractor.

Conventional building contractors like to stick to conventional materials and designs. They are comfortable with basic frame construction using materials available from the local supplier, the "lumber yard." The farther your design and materials are from convention, the harder your road in finding a contractor to build it. In most rural areas—with some prominent exceptions—you will have a very difficult time finding a contractor willing to build a **green house with green materials**. Building green is a continuum of methods and materials that incorporate an environmental ethic. The materials continuum includes everything from rock construction to building with rammed earth, straw bales and timber that is certified as having been harvested in a certain way from forests managed in a certain way. (See www.greenhomebuilding.com for a one-stop overview and resource guide; also www.buildinggreen.com.) Two editors of Environmental Building News put out Green Building Products (Canada: New Society Publishers, 2005), which lists more than 1,400 green products. Alex Wilson, one of the editors, suggests that a new home have has its highest priorities energy-efficient windows, heavy insulation, high-efficiency furnace/air conditioning-system and materials that have low or no emissions of volatile organic chemicals (VOCs), such as formaldehyde in particleboard cabinets. Individuals sensitive to VOCs can find low-emission products at www.greenguard.org. Some areas in New England, Colorado, California and the like support green contractors; Blue Grass, Virginia does not. (Contact the U.S. Green Building Council, www.usgbc.org for a list of members who are architects, contractors and suppliers.) Where green construction has not taken root, you will probably have to build a green second home yourself.

Another type of home offered in rural areas is the **log house**, almost always built from a kit. Plans and discussions of log homes are available from the North American Log Homes Council, part of the National Home Builders Association, 1201 15th St., N.W., Washington, D.C., 20005; 1-800-365-5242; www.loghomes.org. The advantage of a kit home is that it will go up faster than a stick-built house—and probably with fewer hassles and mistakes. Kits won't be problem free, but they have been tested in the field before you buy yours. Some log kits have a construction crew option, which further reduces buyer risk. Before buying a particular kit, I would examine at least one in the field and talk with its owner. A kit buyer needs to be confident that the logs being used have been treated with preservatives to protect against insects and rot without affecting the health of the people who will live within its walls. Logs should not emit gasses. If the logs are untreated, carefully check the manufacturer's instructions regarding owner-applied sealants and other protections.

I once had a very small hand in building a log home from scratch, starting with cutting trees and encouraging a mule to drag logs to the site. It should have come as no surprise that this work is out of the 18th Century—hard and slow. The house was finished eventually, and the house finished the marriage. For every chink put in one, a chink fell out of the other.

Modular construction is a quick-house option that brings the efficiencies of assembly-line construction to housing. Modular housing is factory-built in units (modules) that are assembled on your site. (Panelized construction puts together factory-built walls on your site; pre-cut construction is another name for kits. Manufactured housing is now the official name for what had been called mobile homes.) An excellent collection of articles on modular housing is available from the National Association of Realtors, www.realtor.org/libweb.nsf/pages/fg321. See also www.modularhomeusa.com.

YOUR CONTRACT WITH YOUR CONTRACTOR

General contractors are in business to make money by building houses for the likes of you. If the general is experienced and familiar with your house plans, he should be willing to agree to a **fixed-price contract** for your house. His price will be based on his estimate of his costs, plus additional money to cover the inevitable unexpected events, plus a profit, which ranges between ten and 20 percent of the total. A fixed-price contract allows you to change plans during construction with attendant adjustments in cost. It's best to change as little as possible once you've started. You may want to include a provision that allows you to delete without penalty features, such as a deck, stand-alone garage or finish work (attic, basement) if your pile of construction money vanishes faster than expected. The more unusual and intricate your design, the harder it will be for a contractor to estimate his costs. He will have to bid high to cover his risk. While you want a fixed price to make your final cost predictable, you should expect to live up to that figure as well when your money tightens. A fixed price imposes obligations and discipline on both parties.

A residential contractor—often, himself and a crew of two or three—working for you with a set of plans that he's never used before will have a hard time costing out your project, particularly the labor. He will be able to get a firm materials cost from suppliers. But owing to the difficulty in estimating labor time, he will have to pad any fixed-price quote to cover himself. This can still lead to the uncomfortable experience of negotiating fixed-price contracts with contractors who then ask for additional money at the end of the job. (I've also had contractors live up to a fixed price even when it pinched them.) As a general rule, I think both sides should live up to the letter of the contract. Where performance has been good, I would add money where the contractor ran into a problem that he could not reasonably have been expected to foresee. I've also run into situations where the contractor's cultural perspective is that he sticks to a fixed price when it works for him and asks for more money when it doesn't. My best advice in dealing with contractors, particularly those you don't know, is to have a frank conversation before you sign a contract as to what you mean by fixed price. This discussion should be conducted after he has given you his fixed price, so that he doesn't immediately add 15 percent for his own comfort.

The other way to pay a contractor is to reimburse him on the basis of his **time and materials (TAM), plus profit**. The time cost will be calculated according to the hours each member of his crew works and their hourly rates. Where your general contractor uses subs, he will bill their cost to you, usually with some agreed mark up. It's fair for a general contractor to add overhead to his charges, but you need to determine whether his labor rates include overhead. If they do, he should not tack on overhead a second time. If his labor rates do not include overhead, he may add it as a percentage of his TAM costs. Profit can be added in different ways. It may be a fixed, agreed-in-advance number, or a percentage of total TAM cost, or a percentage of total TAM and overhead cost.

A TAM format does not give a contractor an incentive to work efficiently. The longer a TAM project takes, the more money the contractor makes. Many independent contractors prefer to work on a TAM basis because they are not skilled at estimating jobs and fear losing money on fixed-price contracts. TAM formats also encourage slow work and, for lack of a better term, "standing around"—which may involve more sitting than standing. It's fair for construction crews to take a couple of breaks and 30 minutes for lunch. These typically add up to about an hour a day. You need to agree in advance whether you will be paying for this time. A four-person crew on a 40-hour week will spend four hours a day, 20 hours total each week, on break. At $15 per hour, that's $300 a week, or $7,500 on a 26-week building job. It may be local practice for contractors to bill for break time, for which they may or may not pay their crews. My experience is that contractors bill for break time and will routinely bill you for 40-hour weeks, save where weather cancels work.

Since you are building a second home in a rural, possibly remote, small-population area, you should assume that you won't have a wide range of choice among local contractors. Most will bill and contract in the same way, whatever that is. Demand for building services will probably exceed supply. Weather may limit the building window. In these conditions, it's next to impossible to force TAM contractors to be efficient and competitive. You may find one contractor billing his labor at a lower rate than another, which can lead you to think that the whole job will cost less. His crew, however, may be less skilled and less efficient than those of his competitors. My experience is that it's best to find a general contractor whose crews are expected to work hard and efficiently, because that's the way the contractor is. You may pay higher labor rates, but you are likely to get faster and better work. The difference between hard-working, productive crews and their opposites is readily apparent to an experienced eye. Your architect consultant may be able to direct you to the best local contractor. The local lawyer you are working with may also be able to narrow your search. When you get references from each contractor you interview, ask them how they felt about the crew's effort and efficiency and the contractor's billing practices. I would try to avoid TAM contracts, particularly if you are an absentee owner. The fixed-price contract may "look" high, but it does force a contractor to work within its parameters, forgiving though they will be. Of course, you may have no choice in the matter where all local builders refuse to work on fixed-price contracts.

The worst experience I had with a contractor involved a deal where I paid him for time and materials plus 20 percent profit over the total cost. His overhead was built into his labor rates. This was an overly generous arrangement by local standards, but I had no choice in the matter—always a rotten position to be in. Predictably, vulnerability was exploited. The contractor would not agree to a written contract, or a time frame or a cost. I knew going in that this payment format provided no reason for the work to be done efficiently or costs controlled. The contractor did not like me, the design, the architect or the work. Being reasonable and generous with him did not produce reasonable work and efficiency. He refused to shop suppliers and buy materials for the lowest price. He insisted, instead, on buying everything from one supplier. I grew to suspect this arrangement. "Bad attitude" infected the work. The crew was packed with redundant labor when work on other houses was short. I once found him using six men to put up roof rafters—one cut, a second lifted the rafter to the second floor where four men installed it, two on either end. This is work that four men could have done. I never received an accurate bill; some were off by a few dollars, one was in error by $2,000, in his favor. I finally gave up and fired him, which he seemed to be expecting. In contrast, the excavation contractor on this job was a confident, competent individual whose tasks were difficult and required great skill. He was comfortable working on a fixed-price contract. His judgment was flawless, and his crew knew, without being told, how to incorporate effort and efficiency. I liked and trusted the excavation contractor from the time I first met him; I never had this feeling with the house contractor who lacked confidence in working with architects and me. This contractor might have done a better job had the work been more conventional, but I think the problem went deeper than that.

The lesson I drew from this mess will probably be applicable to your second home: **you have to feel comfortable with contractors to be able to work well with them**. This involves the ability to communicate, but more than that, it's the ability to solve problems without personalizing disagreements. It also involves the mutual feeling that fairness, honesty and reasonableness should be governing both parties. Most contractors with whom I've worked over 35 years produced work that was acceptable to good, and billed reasonably—and in each and every case they were individuals with whom I felt comfortable.

If you have reason to trust a contractor and trust his work habits and integrity, payment on an hourly basis or on TAM can work fairly for both sides. The more conventional your project is, the more TAM costs are predictable. Where construction is unconventional and/or involves a lot of custom work, hourly billing is a better payment format than a fixed price. In such circumstances, the contractor will have to set a very high price to cover time that he can't estimate very well. If you have to contract with a contractor you're not quite sure about in a locale where it would be difficult to find a replacement, I'd advise working very hard to get a fixed-price contract. If you agree to a TAM contract, you should insist that the general contractor be on the job every day. Lack of supervision creates too many opportunities for poor work and bad work habits.

On conventional construction, you can use a recent edition of a **cost-estimator book** and **supplier take offs** to project costs on which you can negotiate a fixed price. Or, you can hire a professional estimator or an architect to work up the numbers and help negotiate with the contractor. Your goal is fairness, not beating a contractor into the lowest price that he will accept. That tactic will backfire in poor quality and things not done that should be done. Every fixed-price contract will—and should—include some padding to cover what can't be projected with reasonable certainty. Your interest lies in containing padding, not eliminating it. Don't be self-righteous about paying five to ten percent over hard cost projections to cover the contractor's risk. Your concern over cost is legitimate, but it needs to be balanced with your concerns to employ a contractor who will work on schedule with acceptable quality, who does the things that make your house better without being told to, who makes an authentic effort to do a workman-like job and who you get along with. Your interest does not lie in haggling over padding, nor does it lie in being opened like a spigot.

ARCHITECTS, CONTRACTORS AND YOU

You don't need an architect to build many types of houses. Plans are readily available in magazines and on the Internet, e.g., www.natalieplans.com, www.homeplans.com, www.dreamhousessource.com, www.AreaPlans.com. and www.house-floor-plans.com, among others. One set of off-the-shelf plans costs between $150 to $500 or so, depending on the number of square feet and complexity. Make sure you are buying complete plans, including drawings for electrical, plumbing and heating/cooling systems, along with drawings of details where components fit together (doors, windows, counters, roofing, etc.). If the plan involves a large or complicated house, you might have an architect review it. And before you start, make sure your contractor is thoroughly comfortable with building from them. If he has questions or alternative ideas, you may want to get him together with an architect who can, if necessary, provide supplemental drawings.

Courses are also available for about $1,000 to help individuals learn the basics of house design and construction. (See www.yestermorrow.org and www.heartwoodschool.com.) Workshops are available on conventional construction techniques as well as alternative/green methods and materials. The Heartwood

School, for instance, specializes in timber-framing construction.

You can, of course, hire an architect to draw plans for a custom, one-of-a-kind house. With this in mind, you can approach an architect with ideas of your own in whatever form they might be—vague notions to drawings to scale. Alternatively, you can have a general discussion with the architect and then ask him to prepare some **rough concept drawings**. The more certain you are about particulars—one-floor or two, maximum cost, heating system, number of bedrooms, number of square feet, finished basement or attic, number of bathrooms, type of foundation, roofing material, style, etc.—the better the architect's first drawings will be. Your final cost will be determined, in part, by the degree of expense you want to incur for finished interiors and kitchen/bathroom fixtures. A 200-square-foot kitchen can be outfitted for $10,000 with standard appliances from Sears or $100,000 in restaurant-type appliances, coupled with expensive counters, cabinets, flooring and lighting.

Where your contractor will be working with an architect you've hired to draw plans and oversee the project, get them together as soon as possible to get a feel for their ability to work together. Often, a buyer acquires an architect and his drawings before he decides on a contractor. In that case, both you and the architect need to agree on the contractor. Another way is to search for an architect and a contractor who have worked compatibly before; the architect can point you in the right direction. You can also ask your architect to help you find a contractor where neither of you have any leads.

Contractors in rural areas may have little, if any, experience working with architects. They may be suspicious of architects and their plans, which promise to be harder than what they've built before. Some contractors can rise above these doubts and self-doubts; others cannot. You will probably find a tendency for architects and contractors to blame the other for screw ups. If this gets out of hand, it poisons the project. Neither can be a diva. They have to learn to function together.

While my next statement may strike you as dumb beyond the extraordinary, I state it anyway: **make sure the contractor you hire can read and understand the plans your architect draws**. I once had to have an architect make a balsa wood model of a roof system because my contractor could not figure out how it was supposed to go together from the drawings. Lack of understanding is not a contractor monopoly. I heard this architect say to this contractor, "Certain parts of these plans were not supposed to be taken literally." How else was the contractor to take them? I asked. Plans, unless otherwise noted, *are* to be taken literally rather than as suggested guidelines. Your contractor is your last line of defense against architect mistakes. If you find a contractor coming to you regularly with plan errors, you will need to ask the architect to review the drawings with a fresh, proofreader's eye.

The addition of an architect creates a triangle with you and the contractor. Both are working for you, but you may find yourself mediating between them. This triangle is shaped by personality as well as the contracts you sign with each. Architects have a standard, complicated contract they use with owners that is provided by the American Institute of Architects (AIA; 1-800-365-ARCH). This is not a client-friendly contract, and you need to adapt it to your circumstances. Make sure your architect's contract specifies how often or at what stages he will inspect the contractor's work; the level of responsibility he agrees to bear for any errors in design and construction; and how disputes will be settled. You must have all your wants and understandings clearly stated in writing with both contractor and architect soon after your first conversation with each. I urge you to communicate wants and understandings in writing, which forces you to be as clear as you can and notices those working for you about what you expect. Make sure to keep a file of all written correspondence and field notes. Don't let vagueness snowball into conflict. It is your responsibility for establishing the highest level of forthrightness in these discussions. Plow into the most uncomfortable topics as soon as they arise because they will become increasingly uncomfortable and harder to resolve the longer they are unaddressed.

There is another problem with plans that I should point out. When an architect revises a drawing, he will slip it into his roll of plans and assume that the contractor is now working off the revised drawing that he has given him. The architect assumes that the contractor has understood the revision and has started incorporating the changes immediately. Future revisions will be based on past revisions. This sounds simple enough. In the field, contractors want to work from one, never-to-be-changed, set of plans. They mark up plans, and it is often hard for them to work off both an original and one or more revisions. A roll of plans might start out with 15 blueprints and end up with 30 or more, owing to revisions and change orders. Try to get the original set as perfect as possible. One contractor I once used tended to ignore revisions, because they complicated his work.

I've backed into the subject of **architects** on the backs of contractors. My experience with architects has been mixed and, occasionally, lousy. But I don't think my experience is the rule because it's limited to academics who took fee work on the side. Having spent time in college and universities, I knew that professors live in odd environments that are insulated from the give and take of market economics. But I knew little about modern architecture design, particularly the pervasive intellectual grip of the hard, spareness tracing back to Wright and Johnson. I have seen glass-and-steel office buildings that look like Orwell's vision of political asylums as well ones that look like Dali on acid. That's not what I wanted. I wanted to build people-friendly cottages, reasonably priced and easy to maintain. I liked the architects I hired and connected with them on most levels, but I found myself stuck with their Wright-like, people-unfriendly designs that were only partially suited to my customers, people in their 50s and 60s. I had told them clearly and repeatedly what I wanted; they simply chose do it their way. I then discovered that I was being forced to sell against the design. Good things don't follow when you have to apologize for your product.

Architects should "ride for your brand," that is, they should help you think through what you want to do and then fit their design to your objectives. I'm not recommending that they abdicate giving you advice; obviously, they know more than you do about fitting all parts of a house together. I am recommending that any architect you hire not have a professional or style agenda other than helping you conceptualize and build the best place for your needs. This excludes "making statements within the profession" and "building his vision for you"—using your money. If you want a state-of-the-profession statement, turn a professor or architect loose. If you want a conventional look and feel, find plans in the house-plan books that are close to your objective. Show these plans to the architect and tell him what you like and what changes you think you want. Don't use the plan as a straitjacket; use it as a reference point. If you get the feeling that you are dumbing down his genius, by all means, dumb it down: it's your money, and you will be living in what your money builds.

There are three things you must state clearly when dealing with your architect. (By "clearly," I mean make them look into your eyes like a three year old so that you know they are focused on your words.)

First, be explicit in what you want and don't want. If you want big closets and many of them, don't settle for two broom closets. If you want to maximize usable floor space, don't let them use atriums that take away half of your second floor. If you want a house that's friendly to a 60 year old, don't accept a second floor and bathrooms the size of a laundry chute. Being explicit requires that you develop a basic knowledge and vocabulary of construction materials and designs. Books can give you this. You will also need to go through houses whose looks you like to determine whether you like the inside feel. Get a sense of what materials and floor space cost in your area. Take notes on your reading and observations. Consolidate your research into a **written memo**. Give this Memo #1 to all architects you interview. This will be the first of several written memos you will give to the architect you choose, copies of which you keep in a loose-leaf binder or file. Give them time to read your memo. If an architect talks down to you, get up and leave. If he's arguing you out of your thoughts, consider his arguments carefully. Valid ones are those pertaining to safety, feasibility, cost, practicality, zoning codes, historic-preservation guidelines, future marketability and the like. Others dealing with matters of taste, look, materials and design may be equally valid. Or there may simply be a conflict between what the architect likes to do and what you want.

Second, be clear about style. If you want a traditional look, don't go along with 24-foot-high walls of unwashable windows mounted in stainless steel. Give your architect pictures of houses and details that you like. Show features that suggest the style you want. If you like sharp angles and the "industrial" look that win design awards, don't okay drawings for the country cottage of the Seven Dwarfs. Size—floor space and volume—determine cost, but style decisions involving materials, quality standards and workmanship also drive cost. Stuff that's standard is cheaper than stuff that has to be ordered or custom-made. Materials that go together quickly and as a unit (like a 4x8 sheet of plywood) are cheaper than materials that do the same job but have to be applied board by board or by a skilled worker. Slate roofing is more expensive than rolled roofing; vinyl siding is cheaper than brick; brick is cheaper than natural stone (which takes more time because it has to be shaped and fitted); imported kitchen tile is more expensive than formica. If your architect finds your taste and preferred style beneath him, find a more compatible architect.

Third, tell the architect the exact total of what you want to spend, from buying the lot to the last seed of grass. Estimate with him the pre-construction costs—lot purchase (include cost of loan, legal, etc.), excavation and infrastructure (water, sewer, utilities, road-building) work and landscaping. He should have a computer program and books that provide accurate cost estimates for each task. If your non-construction, infrastructure costs come to 25 percent of your total budget, assign construction 65-70 percent of your budget and assume that the unassigned five to ten percent will be spent on things unforeseen.

Once you have determined the dollar figure for construction, say these words: **"I want you to design a completely finished house, including everything, that can be built on my lot for not a dollar more than $____. I understand that any change orders I approve during construction that involve additional materials and/or labor will cost extra."** I would go so far as to put the dollar number into the contract you sign with the architect, as in, "The parties agree that _____, architect, will design and provide other architectural services to _____, client, for the construction of a _____ square-foot-house on the client's lot to cost no more than $_____." If nothing else, a proposed sentence of this sort will focus the architect's attention on one of your objectives and remind him that you are serious about it. The process of construction tends in every aspect to go over budget. Your architect is both a cost cop and your proxy profligate. It's always more fun to upgrade materials or to design in more luxury than you can afford. If you have a finite number of dollars to spend, make sure that your architect designs below that figure, maybe by five percent. That gives you dollars to spend on upgrades and amenities. When your project goes over budget, you will be the one responsible for paying the difference.

Architects are skilled in imagining in three dimensions. Most of their clients don't have that ability. If you're like me, you will look at blueprints and see component views but not the true scale of the structure or how the components create interior space. Your architect should have a computer program that projects two-dimensional drawings in three dimensions. These **CADD (computer-aided architectural design) programs** allow you to "be" inside as well as see the finished design built to the blueprints. If your architect is not CADD-capable, have him arrange with a colleague a CADD display. You wouldn't buy a $30,000 car, or even a $5,000 car, without getting inside and seeing how it feels. Don't build a house without doing the same. I once used two prominent architects who insisted on drawing by hand and not using CADD technology. I liked the old paper-and-pencil approach until I discovered I was locked into building a house that created great volumes of vertical space at the expense of usable floor space. Had the design been put into a CADD, I might have been able to stop their visionary inefficiency before building it.

If you have a lot of money, patience and are building a "statement" second home, get an architect you like, review his work to make sure you're on the same beam (or planet) and be patient about choosing a contractor. You'll need one who is willing to put up with a demanding owner and his architect. If, on the other hand, you are comfortable with one of the hundreds of stock plans for second homes that are available, first pick a contractor who can build that house. Then, if necessary, bring in an architect for revisions. Many contractors are experienced enough to make their own drawings or even build a room or two without them. An off-the-shelf plan is a cheaper and safer way to build a second home, but a statement always has the last word, good or bad.

OWNER-BUILT SECOND HOME

Building a second home on your own demands that you become your own **general contractor, plus carpenter, materials gofer and anything else that you don't hire on a subcontract**. Among other things, you will arrange for everything—land purchase, site infrastructure, permits, house design, materials, finding/negotiating/supervising subs, scheduling work in proper sequence, inspections and compliance with local ordinance and code, securing the financing and paying the bills. Banging nails is the fun part of this job.

You will save the mark up and profit you would pay to a general contractor, but you will be spending your own time in his place. Every component of your project will take you longer to do than a general contractor unless you are almost a pro yourself. There are, of course, intangible satisfactions of doing a house yourself. Like writing, I've found it more fun to have built than to be building.

As your own general contractor, you will be responsible for buying materials and getting them to your site. Building supply houses will take your design or your list of materials and provide you with a time-limited quote, a take-off price. Some suppliers give owner-builders a **contractor's price**, and some don't. Some suppliers will give a contractor's price to an owner-builder routinely; others give the discount only if asked. You lose nothing by asking. You don't need a contractor's license when owner-building in the states with which I'm familiar.

When comparing take-off prices from suppliers, make sure that the suppliers are quoting prices for the items that you speced. They routinely substitute what they have or can easily get for anything in your materials list that they don't have and can't get easily. The more exotic the item you spec, the more likely it is that suppliers will throw in an off-the-shelf substitute. Suppliers in my experience do not work hard to get owner-builders what they want. Windows, doors, fixtures, hardware, cabinets, garage doors and roofing are items that are often substituted, varying by brand, quality and price. Substitutes may be as good as what you speced, but often are not. Lumber, for example, comes in different grades, which affect its strength and price. An architect or general contractor can give you some help in determining whether one brand or grade is equal to or better than another. It is often difficult to know whether a "utility-grade" 2x4 stud from Supplier A is the same as the "construction-grade" 2x4 from Supplier B and the "standard" from Supplier C. Your comparisons of price should take quality into consideration, which can only be determined by going to each supplier and examining the materials they are proposing to sell you. If you are building from an architect's plan, make sure that any substitution of the materials he speced is done with his approval. And remember to compare take-off prices from suppliers on a **delivered basis.** It is often more efficient to interview several suppliers before you work up your materials list; get their product literature; then develop your list based on what you know they have.

You can build the house yourself with whatever wives, children and friends you can conscript into the project's labor force. An **owner-built home** is an exercise in patience, character, skill and optimism. It stresses the builder, spouses and kids. It's hard, often frustrating, work. It requires time, money, knowledge, head skills, hand skills, friends, strength, perseverance and a tolerance for your own mistakes and amazing stupidity. It is a humbling experience; I speak with more first-hand knowledge than is necessary to make that statement. A sense of humor and irony is as useful as a level. Plan on doing some dumb thing (s) more than once, and you won't be disappointed. Errors in construction usually involve tearing something down or out, and doing it over. Foundation mistakes are particularly irksome. The killer owner-builts are the idiosyncratic designs that use unconventional materials and require inordinate amounts of hand work. Many of us can throw up a quick 1,200-square-foot ranch by ourselves; nobody can build the Taj Mahal single-handed, though some still try.

If you want to start thinking about an owner-built house on rural land, you should get in touch with the **Owner Builder Center**, 4777 Sunrise Blvd., Suite A, Fair Oaks, CA, 95628; www.ownerbuildercenter.com; e-mail: questions@ownerbuildercenter.com ; 1-800-233-4838; 916-961-2453. The Center provides classes, construction loans and answers to questions. A very good book is Myron F. Ferguson's, Build It Right! What to Look For in Your New Home, which can be ordered from the Home User Press, 1939 Woodhaven St., N.W., Salem, OR, 97304; www.userfriendlyhome.com; 1-800-530-5105; The Home User Press also sells a New Home Check List; the book and the list together are less than $25. Architect Dennis Wedlick designed the "Dream House" in 1995 for Life magazine. It is a flexible, 2,300-square-foot floor plan with ganged windows, lots of light and a dramatic roofline. You can view the model and floor plans at www.lifemag.com/Life/dreamhouse/wdlick/wedlick.html.

Lots of books have been written for non-professionals about how to build one type of house or another. But I've yet to find one that offers a story that fully recounts all of the things that actually go on. House, by Tracy Kidder, is wonderful reporting about the multi-level interactions over time among an architect, contractor and owner. First-person narratives of the same process are lacking. If I were to write a first-hand account of my owner-built efforts, the story would be that I was always hurt most by the things I didn't know I didn't know. This seems to be one of Life's Big Lessons, which responsible parents try to teach to their children—with mostly modest success. I was also done in by things I thought I knew and didn't, along with things that I thought I could fix later and couldn't.

The place to start thinking about owner-building is with a dispassionate assessment of your motivations, character, skills and tendency to become overwhelmed by a seemingly endless, overwhelming task. Saving money is often cited as the primary motivation for being your own builder. If you dollar-value your time at zero, you will "save" money in the sense of substituting your own time for purchased labor. You will save a contractor's mark up on purchased materials and his add-on profit. You will, of course, spend more of your time doing the work than it would take the contractor. The quality of the work may or may not be better. If you dollar-value your time spent building at or above the rate you pay purchased labor, you won't save money. If you're retired or between jobs, then building it yourself will save you money, though you might want to ask whether that's the best use of your time.

"Building your own space" is another common reason advanced for erecting your own house. I've used this one myself. It was very persuasive when I was 30. It has lost oomph over the years just the way I have. The virtue and romance of making your own space can be sustained through some houses, but in others I've seen where owner labor is substituted for expensive machine work, the project turns into a protracted, mind-numbing test of character. Solace can be found, at least abstractly, in knowing that all house-construction tasks are finite—none go on forever, though it can seem that way. As an owner-builder, you have to be prepared to live with the quality of your own work. If you're inclined to cut corners and say "good enough" short of good enough, you will find the space you've built is a permanent, unflattering mirror. Occasionally, building is fun, but most of the time it's hard work. A buyer needs to provide himself with an honest answer as to how much hard labor over how long a time does he want to do. This is apart from the question of how much you are physically able to do. If your main country objective is to relax, nap, read, eat and enjoy the sunsets, you want to avoid the pressure and effort of house-building. No second home is without the need for some owner maintenance, but installing screens is nothing compared to putting in a house footer by wheel-barrowing ten cubic yards of concrete up a hill. How do you really want to spend your time? If you don't want to spend hour upon hour doing mindless, repetitive tasks, you don't want to build a house from scratch. You will be much happier having resisted the romance of being an owner-builder than jumping in and failing badly.

You can also consider building a portion of your second home, depending on your time and skills. If you have no experience, I'd hire out foundation work. Rough framing, however, is something that a novice can do with a hammer, power saw, tape and level as long as he can read a blueprint. I would not advise an inexperienced individual to try finish carpentry, drywalling and certain roofing (metal, slate) with only book knowledge. A skilled person can contract out the rough work and then finish the interior as time permits. Inexperienced owners can do interior and exterior painting, decks and landscaping.

Apart from physical labor, owner-builders take on a highly charged, multi-dimensional emotional load when building a house on their own. Having undertaken several such projects on limited budgets, I offer the observation that they come to dominate your life and are hard on marriages, especially shaky ones. If you are trying to get a project done within budget and within an inflexible time window, you are asking for miseries.

Even if you enjoy all of that's involved in home construction, are good at it, have all the tools, can get extra hands when you need them, don't have competing demands on your time, have plenty of cash and don't mind dealing with pouting kids and grumbling spouses, yes, even when everything lines up, you will still spend a year or more of stressful physical and mental labor building your place by yourself. In places with six-month winters, a house-construction project can spread over two or three years. House construction that occurs only on weekends can stretch beyond that. For every 1,000 square feet of constructed space—from first free-hand drawing to last stroke of paint—I'd assume the need for 100 to 150 owner-built days invested in the project, counting everything, both onsite and off. If you're building single-handed or doing a lot of custom work, the time will lengthen. The same size house can be completed in much less time where an experienced crew is building to standard dimensions, e.g., a Habitat for Humanity home.

You can contain your effort and expense by building something small and simple, from which additions can be constructed. The virtue of something small and simple is that you can get it done reasonably well and within a reasonably short period of time. Owner-built second homes are often constructed in stages, starting with infrastructure and a core building. Bedrooms, studies, second floors, bathrooms, porches and decks are readily added as time and cash permit. It is also wiser to start educating yourself as house builder with a small and simple project. Your first house should not be an owner-conceived, no-blueprint, 13-sided structure that hangs over a cliff on cables of native weeds reinforced with silk from recycled pajamas. You want to start within your range of skill, cash, time and patience. If you build Monticello, you will never finish and end up broke just like Jefferson.

The best part of building a house is the advance dreaming, all of which stops when the backhoe dips out the first bucket of dirt for the footer… and bounces off granite 12 inches below the surface and 400 feet thick. If the dreaming and sketching weren't so much fun, I'm not sure any novice would want to build a house.

CHAPTER 12: COUNTRY HOUSES AND THE SECOND HOME

The easiest way to establish a second home in the country is to buy land with a house. Consider the merits of this approach before developer packages, contractors and owner-building. If you want a house in the country, buying an existing one gets you there faster and usually cheaper than other ways. Beware, however, of ending up with more house than you want and less land than you will ultimately need.

The advantages of buying a standing house are numerous.

First, you are spared the inconvenience and expense of installing the property and site infrastructure from scratch, though you may need to upgrade each. This factor is particularly important where the house is located in a remote area and at a distance from a public road and utilities. A road and an electric line that may have cost a few hundred dollars in 1940 might cost $50,000 today. The seller will not price in to his asking price $50,000 for the road and electric service. In this sense, the seller will discount the value of existing "background infrastructure assets," which benefits the buyer. Even where a seller gets an appraisal of his property as part of his marketing strategy, it's been my experience that appraisers do not value a dirt road, utilities, septic and well at their current replacement costs, which are the costs a buyer would pay to put them in. Appraisers, however, should and will lower their appraised value for any country house that doesn't have these background systems in place.

A buyer should have more confidence in infrastructure that a seller has installed for his own use and benefit than infrastructure quickly dropped in to make the property more marketable. You can *probably* assume that the seller did not short himself by using shoddy materials or by under-designing a system. Honesty, however, requires that I confess to having seen examples that belie this assumption. Most of these involved old systems where, for example, an undersized three-inch diameter pipe led from the house to the septic tank or a water line used too-small 3/4-inch pipe. I also once looked at an owner-built house that was constructed on a wooded slope with a parking area so small that it took me five minutes to turn my truck around. The owner apparently tired of digging rock from his cut into the bank. Left as it was, this parking strip would have been a daily nuisance. The best way to detect unforced errors of this sort is to test every system in the house/land you are scoping. An owner won't deliberately shoot himself in his infrastructure foot, but feet get shot through ignorance or penny-saved-pound-foolish choices.

Second, an existing house allows you to begin using your property immediately without additional investment. While it may not be the house of your dreams, it's probably functional enough to get started. It gives you a base from which to work, a place to store stuff. At the very least, you have a place to come to and get out of the rain once you're there.

Third, an existing house offers room for visitors who are valued for their company and labor. Scoff not.

WRECKS

These advantages apply to a "semi-functional house," and better. You will find houses in the country that don't rise to that standard. These are various versions of what is commonly known as, **A Wreck**. These structures appeal to men who want to resuscitate the dead after the autopsy has been completed. (I'm exaggerating a little, but not by much.) Prudence suggests that you don't invest your dreams, time and money in wrecks. Still, throw enough money at a building and you can make it work better than when it was new—because you are constructing a new, updated building in most respects.

Wrecks can be brought back with a lot of money, time, patience, determination and emotional energy. If the place is more of a wreck than you thought, it can leave you spent and regretting your good deed. Even when a buyer has both time and money, consider the **opportunity cost** of pitching a life into a bottom-to-top reclamation project. What will you forgo by spending your resources on a basket case? What will reclaiming the wreck cost you emotionally and personally? Ground-up projects tend to grind up people.

I have seen wrecks take three and four times as much time and money as the owners originally projected. I have seen them skewer marriages and stub off careers. The "right" basket case can turn into your very own gulag on which you slave and spend without respite. The romance of these projects wears off quickly even when you are not doing the actual work yourself. THE HOUSE turns into an endurance contest that tests your cash and character, one nail at a time. New houses and additions can be built fairly quickly. But extensive reclamation of old houses is always a long, surprise-filled trip into construction psychedelia where nothing much is square, plumb, level or consistently dimensioned.

Most buyers, even the incurable romantics with advanced degrees who look for land only on sunny Sunday afternoons, can recognize a real wreck when they see one. Recognition requires sharpening your analytical eyeballs and turning down your emotions. Look for signs that indicate more of a problem than the sign itself—a leak in a ceiling, green stuff growing on inside walls, spongy floor boards, funny smells, structural woodwork that crumbles at your touch, a bouquet of extension cords and multiple receptacles sprouting from a wall outlet, water stains around windows, amphibians mating in the basement wetlands, blackened structural beams, ceilings and doorways that are too short for you and a setting whose unfixable flaws you hate. When you are shown this fixer-downer, do not be swayed by a front-porch swing and a couple of hanging plants. You do not want to be fixed up with this one.

Home inspectors say that water in the wrong place is the most common threat to the integrity of a house. (See Judy Rose, Knight Ridder Newspapers, "Water, water everywhere: Inspectors list moisture as No. 1 house threat," Richmond Times-Dispatch, January 4, 2004.) This means water-saturated ground around a foundation because of improper grading; plugged gutters and overflowing downspouts; water penetrating roofs and exteriors through deteriorated flashing and caulking; and a faulty chimney cap. Old wiring and badly installed wiring are the second most common threat. Deteriorating heating systems with poor exhausts, old pipes, gas leaks around old appliances and inadequate ventilation in highly insulated homes are also on their list. In homes built before 1950, you're likely to find galvanized plumbing and sand-cast metal waste lines, both of which will be wearing out. Homes from the 50s have energy-efficiency issues, particularly steel-casement and single-pane windows. Homes from the 60s may still have aluminum wiring (banned in 1973), which can arc behind walls and cause a fire. (You can install an AFCI—arcing fault circuit interrupter—to detect arcing and shut down the system.) Homes from the 70s and 80s used cheaper lumber products and cheap windows; they were insulated but may not have been adequately ventilated. Composite sidings made of pressed wood were used in the 1990s and may now be rotting, particularly in damp climates. (Fiber-cement sidings are durable.) In my opinion, defects such as these that cannot be readily observed should be considered "latent" and, accordingly, disclosed to buyers. When you buy a property "as is," the seller is still expected to disclose the presence of such defects; the "as is" only gets him out of paying for their repair.

Any time a real-estate agent takes you to an advertised "fixer-upper" or "handyman special," you are being put on notice. Real-estate brokers don't advertise "Basket Case: only really big fools should buy this." Properties that are the true bargains—those that need cheap cosmetics and new doors on their kitchen cabinets—are often snapped up by agents themselves for resale. Further, country wrecks are likely to be worse than the city/suburban wrecks with which you may be familiar. The country version will, if nothing else, have less usable infrastructure. Its building quality can also be lower. Cheap materials might have been used, and the house may have been built by not-so-skilled owner-builders. One marker of material quality is windows. If they look and feel flimsy, if they don't work very well, you may reasonably assume the builder used low-end materials throughout. It's also the case that building codes, which set construction standards, came to rural counties late. This explains why the living-room floor of our 1916 farmhouse bounced like a trampoline when I jumped on it during my first visit. Soon after purchase, I slithered into a 16"-high crawl space littered with cat poop to prop up its joists, which were spaced on two-foot centers and had no bridging between them.

If your goal is to putter happily on the occasional sun-dappled weekend, avoid buying a wreck. Happy puttering is the last thing you will be doing. Wrecks require system replacement not puttering, upgrades and remodeling. It's the difference between an afternoon excursion on a friend's sailboat and doing a single-handed circumnavigation. Heartbreak wrecks are only for those who love doing—or paying for—this type of soup-to-nuts rebuilding—and maybe not even for them.

In my area, I've found two types of wrecks. The first and far more common is old farmhouses that sheltered cash-poor farmers poorly. They weren't much when they were new and have not improved with age. They are almost always found on marginal farmland. The two run together, of course, sorry ground, cheap housing. Tenant dwellings often fall in this category, though some tenancies are exceptionally well-built.

The second type of wreck is the idiosyncratic, owner-built house from the 60s and 70s when some of my generation "went back to the land," building south-facing structures that were abandoned after the divorce. I know of three of these, one of which I spent a year building, losing a marriage and a best friend in the process. These efforts have both the virtues and liabilities of being built by well-intentioned nincompoops. Even the well-built failures have, shall I say, off vibes, arising from both their failure to work out and the broader alienation that underpinned them. Most houses are built with hope and optimism, and all wrecks are sad. But the hippie wrecks seem the most forlorn.

A step above the wreck is the **marginal project**, a house that's been long neglected and which requires some structural rehabilitation and/or a lot of modernizing. You can start learning about how to evaluate these houses by reading Rex Cauldwell's, Inspecting a House, from the Taunton Press. The first level of decision is whether the place fits more comfortably in the wreck category or qualifies as a marginal project. If you have to totally replace four or more major systems—roof, foundation, exterior, plumbing, heating, window/doors, electrical, kitchen, all bathrooms—call it a wreck. In contrast, repairs like gutters, painting, floor refinishing and remodeling qualify a house as marginal. If you find a place where three major systems need to be fully replaced and everything else needs work, I'd consider it closer to a wreck than a project. To get into this amount of work, the house needs to have a lot of something else going for it.

If you think the place is a possible project, your next decision is whether its rehabilitation is financially, practically and emotionally doable. Use nothing other than gimlet-eyed analysis and the sharpest pencil you have. Do not make this decision with your heart; do not make it on the spur of the moment based on a "gut reaction"; do not make it on your first visit; do not make it on a cheerful day; do not make it while you are holding hands other than your own; do not make it while a real-estate agent is chirping out the charms of the old place ("Look at that native stone chimney!" cries the agent, turning your head with both of his hands. The chimney was built before fire-safe flue liners were available and, you might infer, that it's the cause of the charred remains through which you are stepping.) Do not make this decision without consulting at least one local contractor/carpenter who has been recommended by at least two or three knowledgeable people in the community, such as the county building inspector and the local lawyer you plan to use. A contractor/carpenter can give you a quick ballpark estimate of the time and cost required to do what needs to be done and the other things you want. Make sure to tell your contractor where you want to do specific activities. For instance, if you plan to put a four-person spa on an old farmhouse floor, you will need to reinforce the framing, redo the surface with impermeable materials, install an appropriate electrical receptacle, vent the moisture and figure out how to drain the thing without messing up your septic system.

You should also consider hiring a **consulting house inspector**. For a fee of several hundred dollars, an inspector will examine a house and provide you with a *written report of what he can see during the visit*. Inspectors are listed under "Home Inspection Service" in my Yellow Pages, or try the website of the American Society of Home Inspectors at www.ashi.com; National Association of Home Inspectors (www.nahi.org); and The National Association of Certified Home Inspectors (www.nachi.org). You may have to bring in an inspector from an adjoining county or work with a local contractor when your target property is located in a low-population area.

A house inspection is not a one-stop, fail-safe guarantee of anything. The inspector and his inspection report guarantees the buyer nothing. The inspector simply reports his observations and the results of whatever minor inspection-related tests he might perform, such as looking up a chimney flue with a mirror to check for creosote blockage. If something is concealed, the inspector may not pick it up. For instance, fire damage to floor joists and wall studs could be covered by new drywall and fresh paint. If the floor parts company with the wall two days after you move in, you can't sue. Inspectors may specifically exclude from their reports investigations for termites, indoor air quality, mold, water quality and radon gas among others. These may require specialists. You can get a mold inspection from a member of the National Association of Mold Professionals, www.moldpro.org. A professional inspection does not obviate the need for you to insert into your purchase-offer contract clear language requiring the seller to disclose all material defects in the house and property.

An inspector will report what he finds. Your question, however, is: What needs to be done to get this house to where I want it? This means you want two types of analysis: the inspector-type inventory of current conditions that will flag obvious things needing repair or replacement, and, second, a contractor/carpenter's estimate of the feasibility, time and cost of doing that work plus the work involved in whatever changes and upgrades you also want done. The first cost estimate will cover work that should probably be done before you move in, or soon thereafter. The second estimate is money that you can spend immediately, in the future or not at all. Both estimates can be helpful in negotiating price with the seller. A familiar example comes to mind. Old country houses often have old bathrooms, patched in decades earlier and never modernized. The fixtures still work, but even the seller will concede that they are ready for replacement. Move the cost of redoing the bathroom from your list of future upgrades to your list of immediately needed repairs—if only for the purpose of negotiations.

Pay for the contractor/carpenter to put together an itemized plan of work tasks with cost estimates for each one. To be safe, add another 25 to 50 percent to these preliminary estimates to take into account both what can't be anticipated and changes that you will undoubtedly want to make when you become aware of their availability.

If the house was well built but has been neglected and lacks modernity, it can be a project worth taking on **at the right purchase price**. You will determine the right price in light of the list of things that need to be done and their cost. If, on the other hand, the place was ill-conceived and badly put together when it was put up and has been subsequently "remuddled," then it becomes more of a wreck to avoid and less of a project to take on.

I can think of several project houses whose marginality I weighed with great seriousness. One was a two-story brick farmhouse from the 1760s that had been defaced with a new cathedral-style dining room (which had collapsed) about ten years earlier and further deformed by a second-floor apartment with outside stairs (also collapsed). Nothing could be salvaged from this mess save the original roof and walls. Somebody—me, in this case—would have to spend six months just pulling stuff down, ripping stuff out and hauling stuff away. After the collapsed "additions" had been subtracted, the advertised floor area would be cut by about half, leaving only the original two-story shell. The house came with a few acres, a very nice spot in an upscale farm suburb of a Shenandoah Valley town.

I figured it would take 18 months of my labor to bring this house back to family-habitable condition. I would be spending our savings during that time and not generating income. My wife, young daughter and I would have had to rent while I worked on the house or try camping inside the demolition and rebuilding. Neither choice was good. Having done some of this before, I knew this project would dominate my life across the board. The money—at least $75,000-$100,000 for demolition and rehab on top of the $80,000 purchase price—would yield a house with about 1,600 usable square feet. In that time and place, that amount of money could buy a whole lot more house than that, with no work at all. It took a few visits and some sober thinking, but it wasn't hard to affirm my first-impression conclusion that this old house was beyond my emotional and financial means.

A few years later, I evaluated another old farmhouse as part of a small land flip that I thought might work. This home sat in the middle of about 200 acres on the side of a mountain, at the end of a rocky, rutted farm road. It was frame construction with a familiar two-story, four-over-four floorplan. The virtue of the land and the farmhouse was its beautiful, long mountain views in an area known for pretty views. After drinking in the view, I nibbled around the wreck. I noted that water had been supplied by a now non-working hand pump bolted next to the sink and the pump was hooked to a collapsing cistern; the one non-functioning bathroom was located in an add-on shed next to the non-functioning kitchen; wiring dated from the 1930s; two unlined stone chimneys provided heat; a new roof was needed; the foundation had come apart at its seams; everything needed to be painted, repaired or replaced. It appeared that routine house maintenance had stopped about 50 years before—and those were only first impressions. Beyond that, all of the basics were wrong: the floorplan was impossible to reconfigure; ceilings were too low for Baby Boomers and their protein-pumped offspring; the entire stone foundation would have to be relaid (assuming someone could be found to do such work); the roof work would probably involve replacing roofboards and rafters. Like a ball of string, tug on any loose end and the whole thing would come undone. Most of the outbuildings were just a hair on either side of ramshackle, and several were dead center. Almost every section of fence that ran with this property needed replacement, not repair. I valued the house and the outbuildings at zero; none were in acceptable shape, and most needed to be demolished. Still, because I am sometimes given to being an idiot, I asked a carpenter friend to spend an hour with me looking it over. His dispassionate verdict was the same as mine: great spot, but don't try to bring the house back to what it never was.

I offered the seller $125,000 instead of the $200,000 they were asking because the "improvements" had so little worth, almost all of the site infrastructure had to be put in and the fencing alone was likely to be $10,000. I valued the house at zero, and I could not assume that anyone I might sell it to would value it more than I had. My plan was to divide the land into four or five parcels for immediate resale, so I offered what I thought the land alone was worth as an entirety. The owner, who knew the shape of his things better than I did, wanted $150,000. The $25,000 difference was the money I was budgeting for closing costs, carrying charges on the purchase, surveying, marketing, a little road work and one thing or another. I didn't want to pay the asking price, so I told the seller that I was not his best money. We both thought that the best buyer was someone who wanted to keep the 200 acres together and had a lot of discretionary cash for monkeying with the house. In effect, I was saying look for a buyer who hadn't read this book. Eventually, they found him, at full price no less. After the sale, I ran into the new owner and his wife; they were bubbly with the house project in front of them. I mentioned that I had looked at it and thought it would take a lot of work. "No," he said, "just some paint and a few things like that." Never correct a new owner who's made an obvious mistake that's not yet obvious to him: he'll blame you for what comes next. I wished him good luck. They painted and piddled and "did like that" for a year or so, then lost interest.

These stories are about two different "old" farmhouses, the first an 18th-Century place that probably had historic—but not certified historic—significance; the other a typical wood structure built in the late 19th Century. The first had been constructed stoutly and honestly, but had been degraded by cheap and inappropriate remodeling. It could have been restored, but was not worth the effort to me. The other could have been restored too with heroic effort. The degree of effort in both cases qualified them as wrecks in terms of my emotional and financial resources.

Wood-frame farmhouses built between 1865 and 1930 are fairly common throughout the countryside. They range from simple five- or six-room designs bordering on humble to big, rambly two- and three-story affairs. They usually have had at least one bathroom added. Their simple materials and architecture allow you to do a lot with them as long as their basic structure is sound. Wood framing allows motivated, semi-skilled Harry and Harriet Homeowners to do at least some of the work themselves. Wiring and plumbing must be done by—or at the very least checked by—professionals. Finish carpentry such as bookcases, molding and stairs are worth contracting out if you're not skilled. (Skilled is a lot more than being handy.)

One job that you should be careful in taking on is stripping old paint. The paint may contain lead, and the stripper chemicals can be harmful. If you need to strip more than one room or do a room that you suspect has lead paint, buy a professional quality full-face, filtered-air, breathing apparatus to protect from both fumes and dust. (Good-quality, industrial respirators are the opposite of a disposable paper dust mask. They are not cheap, but neither is being sick. The apparatus I've used for dust and chemical fumes is made by Racal Health & Safety [a division of 3M], 7305 Executive Way, Frederick, MD., 21701; 1-800-682-9500; www.3M.com/occsafety; e-mail: occsafety@mmm.com; 1-800-896-4223).

You should also be careful with older outside decks, stairs and playground equipment made from lumber treated with chromated copper arsenate (CCA). A phase out began in early 2002, which arose from lawsuits against retailers and manufacturers about health risks in situations where bare skin or food came in contact with this wood. Decks and other structures built before 2003 with treated lumber used the now-banned CCA product. Don't walk barefoot on this material, and don't put a sandwich on a CCA railing. The new treatment uses alkaline copper quaternary (ACQ) or copper boron azole (CBA), which make wood resistant to rot and termites. These materials too require care—dust masks and gloves when handling; hand washing when done; don't use them for mulch, burn them or put them where animals might chew them. They also require special new hardware that resists corrosion. Do not use aluminum flashing or old galvanized hardware with ACQ. If the new treated lumber is used with old hardware a new deck will collapse. The new lumber is more expensive than the CCA, and plastic/vinyl substitutes are twice the cost of treated wood. One country alternative might be locally available resistant woods, such as yellow locust or cedar, that a local mill can saw into lumber. Both old and new treated lumber are best sealed with solid stains; the other stains don't do much. Don't clean the old lumber with a deck wash or sand before sealing. (See www.ewg.org; Eric Pianin, "Use of Arsenic in Wood Products to End," Washington Post, February 13, 2002; Matthew Robb, "Deck Lumber, Hardware Present Risks," www.washingtonpost.com, May 1, 2004; Gene Austin, "Do-It-Yourself," Knight Ridder, Washington Post, May 15, 2004.)

KEEPERS

A big step above the marginal project is the **keeper**. This is the country house that can be restored and modernized without making it into an architectural clown, and at a sensible cost in terms of your budget and the final result. Older houses can be great buys when their structure is sound and they can be modernized without doing much structural work. You can update plumbing and electrical systems without changing the house's structure. You can usually add a fireplace onto an exterior wall without much change in existing structure, but you cannot add the same fireplace in the middle of the house without doing structural work at every level, from ground through roof. Older houses are sturdier than contemporary structures in some ways and flimsier in others. Finish flooring, for example, in old frame houses was usually at least 3/4-inch thick. (Flooring gets thinner with each sanding/refinishing cycle.) Today, new hardwood flooring may be as thin as $5/16^{th}$. New tongue-and-groove thickness ranges between 1/2-inch and $25/32^{nds}$. Thicker flooring is better than thinner. Old wall studs were often fully dimensioned 2x4s whereas modern studs are nominally 2x4s but are actually only 1 1/2 x 3 1/2. On the other hand, the fully dimensioned, oak floor joists in my WWI-era farmhouse are spaced too far apart (24 inches) and their clear spans are too long. (When looking at the seller's farmhouse, jump up and down in each room to see whether you spring like Tigger. Pay no attention to nasty looks; you are being careful, not rude. You generally have to do a lot of work to beef up floors and ceilings.) Old houses tend to be under-insulated and energy inefficient (leaky, single-pane windows; uncaulked doors, windows and other openings). Electrical and plumbing systems are undersized for modern needs. Kitchens may be large, but poorly laid out. (Ours has seven doors and about one-third the counter space we need.) Old farmhouse kitchens did not plan for refrigerators, freezers and dishwashers. Bathrooms tend to be small.

HOUSE INSPECTION CHECK LIST

To find a keeper, *take a slow walk* through the seller's house. Go by yourself or with a local contractor/carpenter. Don't do this with a real-estate agent or the seller; agents, in particular, like quick trips through old houses. Use a table like the following to organize your first look and a follow-up inspection.

TABLE 12-1: House Inspection: What to Look for

	System	Type	Condition	Comments

A. Site Infrastructure

    1. Access
    2. Driveway
    3. Turnaround/parking
    4. Drainage
    5. Landscaping
    6. View
    7. Compass orientation
    8. Shade, windiness
    9. Privacy
    10. Proximity of mailbox
    11. School pick up—distance to house
    12. Outbuildings
        a. Type
            1. Workshop
            2. Spring house
            3. Barn (s)
            4. Chicken/pig/wood
            5. Horse facilities
            6. Misc. storage
            7. Detached garage; single/double door
                a. Remote-control

  b. Virtues to look for
    1. Concrete floor
    2. Water outlet in barn/shop
    3. 220-volt outlets
    4. Shop
      a. Heat
      b. Lighting
      c. Ventilation
      d. Counters/shelves
13. Closest fire hydrant
14. Yards, front and back
  a. Condition
  b. Features
  c. Mowability
15. Trees around the house
  a. Shade providers
  b. Too close/gutter clogs
  c. Need to be trimmed

  d. Are the planted species of the type that break foundations and invade water/sewerage lines, e.g., willow, maples
16. Safety/ Security
  a. Lighting for safe night access
  b. Are pathways good for foot traffic?
  c. Condition of steps
17. Convenience
  a. Can big furniture be driven close to the house
  b. Is the most frequently used entrance other than the front door. (Old houses are often entered through the kitchen.)
18. Amenities—pool, garden, orchard

B. House Structure—exterior
1. Foundation
  a. Look for big cracks
  b. Look for missing mortar in brick and stone work
  c. Sagging corners/shifting
  d. Look for termite tunnels
  e. Look for rot in log sills and wood plates
  f. Ventilation
2. Roof
  a. Type and condition
3. Gutters/downspouts
4. Exterior wall materials
  a. Types and condition
5. Exterior Doors
  a. Quality/fit
  b. Screens
6. Windows
  a. Cracks/glazing
  b. Screens
  c. Insulation (double/triple glazing) or storm windows
  d. Caulk, where frame of window meets house siding
7. Steps or ground-level access
8. Chimney/flashing
9. Entrance weather protection
  a. Porches
    1. Front
    2. Back
  b. If no porch, is there some overhead covering?

        c. Does entrance face away from
 prevailing weather
           1. Front/back
  10. Deck
  11. Electrical outlets
  12. Water spigots/freeze protection
  13. Exterior access to basement/crawlspace
  14. Lighting—entrances
  15. Examine surfaces that face prevailing weather
      a. Which, if any, need repair or painting

C. Structure—interior
  1. Basement/crawlspace
      a. Height/access
      b. Finished/unfinished
      c. Evidence of termites or wood rot
      d. Wetness or evidence of past wetness
      e. Mold
      f. Insulation
  2 . Kitchen
      a. Size/layout
      b. Island
      c. Space for freezer (upright or chest)
      d. Dining area
      e. At least ten linear feet of counter top
      f. Wall cabinets—at least 12 feet for
 1,400 sf house
      g. Base cabinets—at least nine feet
 for 1,400 sf house
      h. Built-in dishwasher/portable
      i. Icemaker waterline hookup
      j. Disposer
      k. GFI outlets*
      l. Lighting
      m. Exhaust fan
      n. Flooring
  3. Utility room/area
      a. Washer
      b. Dryer
      c. Sink
      d. Cabinet/shelves
      e. Storage for vacuum
 cleaner/broom/supplies
      f. Space to work/iron
  4. Living area
      a. Windows
          1. Do they work/seal?
          2. Sufficient light/ventilation
      b. Compatibility with your furniture
      c. Usable wall space
      d. Bookcases

  e. Floor material
  f. Size—area/height
 5. Dining Room
  a. Size—area/height
 6. Front Entrance
  a. Adequate closet for outdoor wear
 7. Mud room/back entrance
  a. Space for winterwear/boots
 8. Bedrooms
  a. Number
  b. Area/height
  c. Groundfloor/upper floors
  d. Dedicated bathrooms/shared bath
  e. Closets
 9. Special areas
  a. Fitness
  b. Home office
   1. Computer/phone/fax capability
   2. Outlets/jacks
    a. Number; separate computer circuit
   3. Internet capability
 10. Closets
  a. Per bedroom/walk-in/size
  b. Linen closet—available?
  c. Junk closet—available?
 11. Attic
  a. Usable area (48"+ height)
  b. Access—permanent/pulldown/ease
  c. Ventilation/windows
  d. Finished/unfinished
 12. Bathrooms
  a. Number and location
  b. Features
  c. Fixtures—vanity/cabinet
  d. GFI

D. Mechanical Systems
 1. Electrical
  a. 200-amp breaker panel minimum
   1. Are heavy electricity users—e.g., baseboard heaters, dryer, spa, range, hot water heater—each on its own dedicated circuit?
  b. Signs of aluminum wiring? Aluminum is cheaper than copper and was used in the early 1960s, but has been banned for many years. Look in a switch or receptacle. Flickering lights and TV static are clues. Should be replaced. In very old houses, look for fabric-wrapped wiring and even wires run on insulated knobs. The fabric-insulation wire should be replaced eventually; the knob system immediately.
  c. Receptacles—modern wiring uses three-hole design; old two-holers require adapters and are less safe
   Old houses tend to be "under-receptacled"

d. Computer areas with dedicated circuit.
      Need phone jack in computer area.
      Whole-house surge protection can be added.
   e. Smoke alarms—wired or battery. Wired is better
   f. How often does power go out? Is there a need for emergency
      generator?
   g. Fixtures—how ghastly are they? Light fixtures
      can be very expensive.
   h. Timers and thermostats reduce electricity usage
   i. Ground-Fault Interrupters (GFIs) protect individuals from
      electrical shock. Should be in wet areas—baths, kitchen.
2. Phone—number of jacks/placement
   a. Internet provider/cost/reliability
3. TV—cable/dish/local reception
   a. Location of hookups inside
4. Heating/Ventilation/AC
   a. Source of heat
   b. Age/type/condition of furnace
   c. AC/windows
   d. Fireplace/woodstove
   e. Are space heaters used?
   d. Radiator/forced air/
      electric baseboard
   e. Insulation
      1. Location—groundfloor/wall/roof
      2. Type/estimated R value
   f. Location of heat source
      1. Accessibility
      2. Odors/leaks
   g. Estimated monthly cost
   h. Miscellaneous
      1. Heat pump
      2. Whole-house humidifier
      3. Air purifier
      4. Whole-house ventilation fan
      5. Heat recovery ventilator**
      6. Thermostats—number/placement
      7. Sited for passive solar benefit
   i. Fire-extinguishers in place?
   j. Energy efficiency of heating/cooling systems
5. Plumbing
   a. Bathrooms—number/features/GFIs
   b. Pressure when all faucets
      open/toilet flushing
   c. Hot water heater—energy/capacity
   d. Where does wastewater go?
   e. Source of water supply
   f. Adequate stack venting—do you smell
      sewage in bathrooms?
   g. Evidence of toilet backup
   h. Bathing

                1. Are shower stalls big enough?
                2. Grab bars
                3. Ventilation to outside—mechanical
        6. Security and Safety
            a. What level do you think you will need?
            b. Lights, locks and alarms
            c. Safety
                1. Stairs—treads, railings, steepness, construction, width
                2. Bathrooms—footing, heating, electrical
                3. Fire protection—chimney inspection;
                    nearest fire department

E. Environmental concerns in and around house
    1. Asbestos—pipe/furnace insulation, disintegrating
        floor tile, exterior siding/shingles; popcorn-type ceiling tiles
    2. Lead pipe in water supply lines; lead poisoning danger
    3. Urea formaldehyde foam insulation in walls
    4. Lead paint inside
    5. Radon gas in air; radon in water
    6. Carbon monoxide—unvented fuel-burning
        appliances; very tight houses
    7. Mold in basement or other areas—look for sump pump,
        damp smell, evidence of seepage in block work,
        basement should have a drain
    8. Infestations—ants, bugs, traps, bait, smell,
        corpses, little piles of fine sawdust, rotted wood,
        tunnels on outside walls, etc.

F. Overall impression
    1. Total square footage
    2. Room size
    3. Obvious repairs needed
        a. Leaks
        b. Breaks
        c. Peeling paint
        d. Roof
        e. Treatment for infestations
        f. Other
    4. Hard/expensive to retrofit missing pieces
        a. Masonry fireplace (woodstove is easy)
        b. Integrated garage (depends)
        c. Front entrance closet
        d. Whole-house AC/forced air heating
        e. Relocate stairs to second story
    5. Common can-do remodels
        a. Finish attic/basement
        b. Upgrade/add bathroom
        c. Convert bedroom to other function
        d. Add garage, particularly detached
        e. Modernize kitchen
        f. Replace windows

6. Things that you want to replace/do
   before moving in
   a. Kitchen remodel—$15,000 and up, and up
   b. Add bathroom—$5,000 and up
   c. Finish attic—$7,500 and up
   d. Rewire whole house—$5,000
   e. Replumb whole house—$7,500 and up
   f. New furnace—$5,000 and up
   g. Add deck—$2,500 and up
7. Maintenance level—general impression
   a. Compulsively neat and kept up
   b. Pretty good
   c. OK
   d. Not so good
   e. Everything's bad
   f. Acceptable—about the level you do at home
8. List anything that looks like
   a. Added on—e.g., room
   b. Recently repaired, upgraded, replaced or painted
      Determine whether this was done for
      marketing or functional improvement

*GFI, Ground Fault Interruptor, is a type of electrical receptacle that is typically installed in "wet" areas to reduce the chance of shock. It breaks the circuit when there is a short.

**Heat Recovery Ventilator is a device that removes dust and fumes from inside air while recovering most of its heat for reuse.

After working up this table, I found an even more comprehensive inspection check list in Robert Irwin, <u>Home Buyer's Checklist</u> (New York: McGraw-Hill, 2001). In his review, Robert J. Bruss of Tribune Media Services describes Irwin's book as "...the ultra-complete list of questions buyers should answer before purchasing a house." (<u>Richmond Times-Dispatch</u>, December 16, 2001, J3.)

Notice that almost everything on my list is substantive and structural. Stuff that is of little concern to a buyer are the cosmetics, which sellers routinely touch up to help market the property. If substance and structure are sound, don't worry about exterior details and the pile of junk farm equipment next to the barn. Where the house is structurally sound and can be readily adapted to your purposes, you, in fact, want to find a few easy-to-fix, obvious blemishes to use for leverage on price negotiations.

You can use this table format for screening properties, but its level of detail better fits a second-tour, take-your-time scoping. These types of questions at a general level, of course, help you to screen in a property that deserves a second, in-depth look. This format forces a buyer to look systematically and analytically at a house in all dimensions, both functional and aesthetic. Even more important, it forces you to *look slowly and deeply at the important stuff*. How many of us have bought a house based on a quickie visit or two? Have you noticed a seller or his agent marching steadily through the house, maintaining eye contact with you as much as possible. Why do you think that is?

It is important for you to **focus on individual house components**. Your brain is sabotaging this effort by running movies of the house and land as a whole and then packaging them with emotional previews of coming attractions. A disaggregating, analytical format forces you to identify what can be observed and then organize that information in a way that gives you useful evaluations. It flags items where a professional eye might be needed. A house inspector, specialist or contractor can fill in your blanks. Focusing on components is even more difficult when a real-estate agent is playing "Look at that vintage overhead light bulb!" just as you notice a hole in the floor. You don't need to be an expert on construction or a professional inspector to understand house components. But you will need to do reading in proportion to your existing knowledge. If you don't know some of the terms I've used in TABLE 12-1, buy a house construction book, such as the one I've recommended (Feirer, *et al*, Carpentry, latest edition, or Ching and Adams, Building Construction Illustrated, Third Edition). Terms are explained simply and illustrations show what makes up a component system and how these systems fit together. Understanding house basics is within everyone's ability. If you've lived in a house of your own, you will have a feel for how structures are built and what goes wrong.

Use the table format as an excuse to be microscopic. You are not observing the seller's house as you would admire a passing parade. You are there to use your wits. You need to be looking in a question-asking, data-gathering mode. This is business, not personal. Carry a hard-backed pad of paper for writing. Make drawings. Write out your specific questions so that you don't forget them. Note things that stick out, both good and bad. One trick that you can use with this format is to write your answers with a two-color (red/black) pen that can be switched back and forth. Use red for negatives and question marks; black for positives. Major stuff can be written in CAPS; minor stuff in lower-case letters. At the end of a tour, if you see a lot of capitalized words in red ink, you will know that you don't know a lot and/or a lot of costly work needs to be done. Take a camera with at least two rolls of 24 color exposures or the equivalent. At the house site, take a picture looking out from the structure North, East, South and West. Take at least one picture of every outbuilding, inside every room of the house, kitchen appliances, bathroom fixtures, furnace, problems and things you like. If you are thinking about upgrading or reworking some part of the seller's house, you can use one of the remodeling estimator guides, like the latest edition of Means, Repair and Remodeling Cost Data, to factor these expenditures into any purchase offer.

In most cases, the seller or his agent will accompany you through the house the first time you see it. That's fine. You're just trying to screen properties in or out on this walk-through. If you screen the property in as a possible candidate, then you need to schedule a second tour, which is when you unlimber your note pad and inventory table. Your second tour is often complicated by a house being lived in and the need for you to step over headless Barbies in the presence of the seller's family. You want to be cordial and respectful to those in attendance, but your uppermost thought is to visualize this house buck naked, and then use your x-ray vision to see its bones and organs. When you talk to the seller or the agent, concentrate on talking. Don't try to scope the house and schmooze at the same time.

One way of softening the intrusiveness of your inspection is to notify the seller in advance that you want a chance to look closely at the property on a second tour. Tell him that this will take a couple of hours, and you will try to be unobtrusive as you can. But make clear that you will be taking a long, serious look. The seller should be cooperative, since your level of effort shows him that you are not there to kick tires. If you hire a professional house inspector, the seller may want to be present during the inspection. You may not be able to avoid the seller walking around with the inspector, but you should insist that the agent not do the same. New York, in fact, prohibits agents from accompanying house inspectors.

Houses for sale can be thought of as a package of component systems and appliances. The systems are the exterior skin, roof, structure, heat, plumbing (water and waste), ventilation and so forth. Items sometimes thought to be **appliances** can be considered to be part of a system, as is the case with a garbage disposal (part of the plumbing system), electric baseboard heater (heating system) or roof fan (ventilation system). When such items are integrated permanently into a system, they are considered **fixtures**. As such, they always convey with the purchase, because they are thought to be permanently attached. Often, appliances that are not fixtures stand alone as is the case with a range, washer/dryer and refrigerator. Stand-alone appliances are the seller's **personal property**. The seller may or may not include items of personal property with the house he's selling. Some items, if not all, may be negotiable if you want them, such as a wood stove, shop tools, portable dishwasher, movable hot tub, window air conditioner and the like. Items/ appliances that are attached to the house or one of its systems by something more than a plug and/or detachable water hoses should convey with the property without elaboration, e.g., a garbage disposal, furnace-attached humidifier, smoke alarms (wired certainly, maybe battery), antenna, water pump and hot-water heater. Misunderstandings can crop up around items like mounted mirrors, blinds, curtain rods, curtains, adjustable screen inserts (but not screens that come with windows), TV dish, outside wood-burning furnace, porch swing and a roadside mail box. When you write a purchase offer, list every item that you expect to convey and might want. You can reduce your offer in step with those things from your list the buyer wants to exclude from the sale.

Each system, each component of each system and each appliance has an effective **life expectancy** during which investing in repair makes sense and after which a new unit is the more cost-effective choice. Most common appliances—dishwashers, clothes dryers, ranges, refrigerators, washing machines—cross the repair/replacement line at about seven years, according to Consumer Reports (Sandra Fleishman, "To Fix or Not to Fix," Los Angeles Times/Washington Post News Service, Richmond Times-Dispatch, February 10, 2002.). Furnaces and central air-conditioning units generally last 20 years or more, and new models are expensive. When valuing the seller's basic house systems and appliances, estimate their age to get a rough sense of when each will need to be replaced. Warranties should show the date of purchase. Appliances that are older than seven or eight years should be valued at zero, because they have crossed the repair/replacement line. If you do have an interest in buying the seller's personal property/appliances, you can fold your estimate of their value to you into your offer for the house, or make a separate offer. There are negotiating advantages and disadvantages to both approaches.

Do not take oral statements as facts or oral promises as legally binding. With real property (land, minerals, houses, etc.) sales, only written statements and written contracts are legally enforceable. (Certain states may have exceptions to this rule, but you will do best to act as if no exceptions exist.) You need to verify "facts" that the seller relates. If you're told the farmhouse has a septic system, ask to be shown where the tank and the drainfield are. You should find a cement lid over the tank itself, or at least a capped pipe where a clean-out hose can be inserted for emptying solids. If you are told that the county has approved the septic system for four bedrooms, you can make your purchase offer contingent on the seller providing a copy of the permit. Or, you can go to the health department in the county seat and ask to see the permit. If you are told the washing machine works just fine, run it through a cycle to see for yourself, preferably loaded with dirty jeans. All oral statements of facts must be confirmed, or put in the form of a written seller promise. A contingency that makes purchase dependent on the "house being in good repair with all systems and included personal property to be conveyed in good working order two days before closing" protects your interests. When your pre-closing walk-through turns up a problem, this contingency allows you to void your offer without penalty. This late in the game, however, it's more likely you'll work something out with the seller.

Sellers have developed many tactics for improving the cosmetics of a house. They want to draw your attention toward what looks pretty and away from what they don't want you to see. Since most buyers have been, or will be, sellers, you should become familiar with **seller house-selling tactics.** The basic strategy that sellers use is making the property *look* fresh, clean, flawless and ready to go. Removing trash, mowing grass, painting the front door, shampooing the carpet, tacking up a drooping gutter—are the type of low-cost, pre-sale investments that are intended to draw the buyer's eye away from those features of the house that cannot be readily seen. Sellers are counseled to focus their pre-sale spruce-up dollars on what's most visible. (See Steve Berges, 101 Cost-Effective Ways to Increase the Value of Your Home [Chicago, Ill.: Dearborn Trade Publishing, 2004]).

Sellers go beyond tying pretty ribbons around house exteriors. Other tricks include using wall mirrors to make small rooms appear larger; increasing wattage in certain light bulbs to "brighten" a room; using softer lights in the spot where the seller steers the buyer to negotiate; having a fire going in the fireplace to provide a "homey" feel; using odor-killing additives in humidifers to mask mildew, lingering tobacco smoke and other unpleasantness; decluttering closets so that they look one-third empty, hence big; taking one piece of furniture out of each room for the same optical effect; removing family pictures so that the buyer can imagine his family in the space; adding live plants to hide flaws and provide atmosphere; cleaning off kitchen counters to make the amount of counter space appear bigger; buying new slip covers to make the room look brighter; discarding shabby drapes; washing windows if they reveal a view, otherwise keeping them covered; sanding floors to make them appear larger; having freshly baked cookies (not boiled cabbage) wafting from the kitchen; setting fresh flowers out on the dining room table; placing candles in candlesticks to lure the buyer into imagining their soft, beneficial effects; and on and on. (Berges, 101 Cost-Effective Ways; and Nancy Dunnan, "Sell Your Home in 60 Days," MSN House & Home," July 15, 2004.) I've been given the gingerbread-in-the-oven version, and I can report that it worked before I knew I was eating my own lunch so to speak. The tactics don't work once you're clued in to them.

Selling a farmhouse presents additional tactical opportunities, such as throwing copper sulfate into the pond to clear up the algae (temporarily); hanging a hammock between a couple of shade trees; chaining a tire swing from a tree limb to invoke barefoot boys with cheeks of tan; installing a faux antique weather vain on the barn roof; purchasing a couple of no-good, paint-peeling chests for $25 from a neighbor (who's had mice and birds antiquing them for ten years out in his long abandoned chicken house) that the seller "throws in" to make the deal work for you (because you are pretty sure that you've seen these exact chests appraised for $10,000 each on the "Antiques Roadshow"). Dirt-smart buyers should know the difference between a sweetener that makes a pot and one that makes your teeth hurt.

Here are some recent books that either coach sellers on, or alert buyers to, seller tactics: Terry Eilers, How to Sell Your Home Fast for the Highest Price in Any Market (New York: Hyperion, 1997); Gary W. Eldred, The Complete Guide to Second Homes for Vacations, Retirement, and Investment (New York: John Wiley & Sons, Inc, 2000); Carolyn Janik, How to Sell Your Home in the '90s' With Less Stress and More Profit (New York: Penguin Books, 1991); Gregory D. Lerch, How to Sell Your Home When Homes Aren't Selling (White Hall, VA: Betterway Publications, 1991); and Eric Tyson and Ray Brown, Home Buying for Dummies (New York: Hungry Minds, Inc., 1996).

CHOICES

The vernacular farmhouse in good shape is usually priced in the middle of the spectrum of local housing choices. Style, size, condition and neighbors shift a specific property's asking price one way or the other. Manufactured housing (mobile homes) are usually among the least expensive options, along with small, older houses of fewer than 1,000 square feet. One-story houses from the 1940s-1960s and smallish, one-to two-story frame houses are found in the middle of the local price range. If you like their style, these houses can be good buys as long as they can be upgraded and enlarged to fit your needs. They tend to have small rooms and a chopped-up floorplan. But the rooms can be readily combined into larger living areas by taking down a non-load-bearing wall or two. The bottom half of the housing market tends to serve local buyers with local paychecks more than second-home buyers who are backed by inflated Big City incomes.

Certain second-home buyers are looking for what my wife calls, "**the big shack in the country**." She's referring to one of four kinds of big shacks: 1) *ante-bellum* "Taras" with white columns (the taller and thicker, the better); 2) "Englishy" brick/stone country houses that combine grandness with the feel of a cottage; 3) one-story ranch houses that sprawl like J.R.'s "Dallas" spread; and 4) pumped up, puffed out, over-fenestrated, exposed beamers with garage-sized closets that were built after 1970.

New big-shack owners tend to start making their places bigger and better right away. I urge a cooling-off period between the time you buy and the time you start to redo. Give yourself a chance to learn how the house works with your family in it. The Taras are the most difficult to remodel well, because their original materials are no longer used much, and craftsmen who can do period work are rare. These houses don't lend themselves readily to modern systems, such as forced-air heating and air conditioning; in-wall electrical wiring and plumbing; and insulation. They are hard to enlarge with stylistic integrity, because additions look like additions. The English country houses seem to appreciate with or without upgrades. Unlike the Taras, they were originally built with electricity, plumbing and central heating. Their structural framing allows modernization without tearing into floors, walls and ceilings. They can be added to without spoiling their style. The Dallas houses—basically bungalows on steroids—can be adapted and enlarged without damage to their architectural integrity since sprawl is their style. They're the easiest to upgrade/remodel because they have one-story floorplans and nothing tricky about their designs. The modern beamers are still in style, so you won't have trouble finding crews to work on them.

Each of these big-shack styles deserves consistency and maybe even fidelity from new owners wanting to make improvements. Remodeling should be in keeping with what is being retained. Otherwise, you end up with a **remuddle**.

The worst remuddling I've seen was a one-car garage made of T-111 (exterior plywood) stubbed out of an 1840s-era, three-story, white-columned Tara mansion. The owner boasted that he had been able to "game" the local zoning board into granting him a variance to house his sports car. He wanted an attached garage, so he attached one, by gum! Had his Tara grown a wart that size, it would have looked better.

The second worst remuddle I've come across involved a big, two-story country house in a pretty part of West Virginia that came with about 700 acres. The owner's children lived in three of the 15 rooms during the winter where I found them huddled next to a $150 woodstove. The exterior style and condition were good, and the setting was lovely, but the interior had been totally mish-mashed. The largest room on the first floor—what was once a grand dining hall—had been converted into a utility area where I found two elephant-sized, forced-air furnaces from the 1940s side by side, both non-functioning. Metal ducts sprouted from them and ran around the house's solid interior walls like a berserk hydra. Bathrooms had been clubbed into hallways and bedrooms, along with an elevator. Still, enough money and time could rescue this mess, because the basic structure was in good shape.

The older the house style, the more expensive faithful additions will be. Older houses require better trades people, costlier materials and more time. If you fall in love with a Tara, pick up one of the many coffee-table books on the history of Jefferson's Monticello, which looks better now than it did when he had it. Jefferson died broke. The causes were several but a main one was the ruinous expense of a 30-year, big-shack building/redoing project. It has taken years and millions of dollars to turn Jefferson's fantasy into what appears today to be an effortless reality where everything works (even without the slaves) while being stylistically honest and consistent. If a big shack is a stretch for your pocketbook, don't put yourself on that rack.

Second-home buyers often find nice big shacks being sold on postage stamps. The mansions have been severed from the land that originally supported them to pay debt or generate cash. You may find these houses surrounded by farmettes with modern homes. If you want a second home in the country without the country, a house-heavy/land-light package can work. I would, however, insist on getting at least ten acres. The long-term appreciation of a house like this depends as much on what happens around it as what the owner does with it.

Be careful when you are considering the odd duck on the local pond. They tend to not appreciate as fast as the rest of flock and are harder to sell. Conventional advice is to find the cheapest property in the most expensive neighborhood. In rural areas this type of buying advice is not that relevant, because the concept of neighborhood is a lot less defined in the country. The housing mix around any particular country house is likely to be a hodge-podge of ages, styles and values—the direct opposite of suburban neighborhoods which tend toward homogeneity. I would feel safe buying a country house that is one of a local type or one of a cluster. I would steer away from a one-of-a-kind unless it comes with enough land to make it a stand-alone property that is independent of, and shielded from, those surrounding it. You cannot change the look or the value of your neighbors' properties. The expensive country house is judged by the company it keeps. I know of two cases where owners of big shacks have been driven to distraction by the proximity of less sightly property—and eventually bought them to get rid of them.

Two common country houses are the **mobile home** and the **one-story rambler or bungalow**. Mobile homes have virtues and not-virtues, but their essential feature is that they can be moved. If you find a piece of land that you like, you can sell the mobile home that comes with it and start from scratch, using its well, septic system and utilities. The mobile home can also function as a base that you can use while building a new house. If the unit is in decent condition, you may want to consider donating it to a tax-exempt charitable organization for pass through to a family in need of housing. If you can't sell it or donate it, give it away. You can also offer the seller a contract for the land less the mobile home, which gives him an opportunity to sell it for more than what he valued it as a package with his land. Mobile homes are generally not what urban buyers are looking for when they envision their second home in the country. My advice, however, is not to reject land summarily because you don't like the mobile home that's on it. Resolving a mobile-home presence is much easier than you think.

Since WWII, the one-story ranch/rambler/bungalow design has become the country vernacular. One version of this style is the doublewide mobile home, which is often set atop a fixed block foundation (thus making it immobile). Doublewides provide more than 1,000 square feet relatively inexpensively and quickly. Newer models are designed to look stick-built. Ramblers and modulars are the preferred fixed-foundation options in my area. They range from small and cheap to large and not cheap. The ramblers are often owner-built or a Jim Walters-type, stick-built package. If the house comes with 50 acres or more and you don't like the house, consider buying the land without the house, or carving off one or two acres with the house for immediate resale. (When doing this, make to sure to retain an access right of way and utility easement if you need them for your own house site located deeper in the property.) With the right configuration of land and house, you will be able to recoup a substantial portion of the original purchase price. An alternative that I've also seen is for the new owner to build a new house elsewhere on the property and then convert the existing house into a rental unit, guest house or office.

Another option is to build or buy the two-story, faux farmhouses that look like the originals on the outside (and always have a covered porch) and contain modern, efficient floorplans. Faux farmhouse plans are widely available and not hard to build. If you're considering buying one that's been built, check the insulation, window and door quality and whether it has a mud-room entrance.

Second homes involving waterfront (beach, lake or river) location involve a special set of considerations. Many waterfront properties are in developments where the "ruralness" of the locale has been upgraded by project infrastructure. In these places, you can evaluate houses in much the same way you would suburban residences. Certain features will be different, such as a southern beach house's lack of central heating or insulation. Where tidal surges or flooding is a threat, you will need to establish that the house is outside or above the danger zone. Otherwise, anticipate water damage and knock down the seller's asking price. Such hazards increase your insurance rates, and, in some cases, may make it difficult for you to buy affordable homeowner insurance or prevent existing insurance from being cancelled. Ask to see the seller's insurance policy; if that doesn't work, ask for the name of his insurance agent, who should tell you approximately what the coverage is and its cost. More and more, water frontage is subject to local zoning and state/federal environmental regulations. Make sure you have a complete understanding of how these constraints will affect your plans. If you buy on the waterline, get flood insurance that will cover water damage from hurricanes and storm-caused water surges. Call the local building inspector and state environmental agency as first steps. Talk to neighboring landowners and folks active in the homeowners' associations. You will be unhappy if you buy a wonderful ocean-front house at half what you expected to pay and later discover that you are not allowed to protect your house from wave damage and beach erosion, both of which are coming at you with open jaws.

On developed waterfront property, you should be especially concerned about the density of development, current and future, which affects traffic, water quality and noise, among other quality-of-life factors. Check to see whether the developer is selling with covenants that restrict certain recreational uses on the water. Are there references in the seller's deed to local restrictions? If you like a lot of people and activity on your waterfront, you won't mind high-density development. But some types of water recreation may start to annoy, particularly noisy ones and those that you don't do yourself. Waterskiing, jet skis and loud motor boats grate on those who confine their water sports to sailing and paddling. Watercraft restrictions are common on lake property, especially small lakes. These can mean a horsepower limit on gasoline engines or no gasoline engines at all.

Two important considerations with waterfront housing are water and sewerage systems. Lakes are particularly susceptible to contamination and overloading from waterfront septic systems. I've rented summer property in New Hampshire on two lakes where every charming older house had its septic system near the water and every house drew its drinking water from the lake. One place prohibited putting toilet paper down the toilet. (I found this out only after I arrived.) The closer the house is to the water and the older it is, the more you should check out the septic/drinking water systems. It is not uncommon to find two pumps at work in these houses: one pumping sewage away from the house to a septic system, and a second pumping water to the house for domestic use. Empty water bottles on the back porch tell you that the tap water is not fit to drink.

A final factor to consider when thinking about buying a country house relates to **your likely use pattern**. If you expect to visit the place a half-dozen weekends a year and maybe a week in the summer, you can save money by purchasing a house smaller than you might otherwise want. I know this is abundantly obvious put that way, but I've watched many second-home buyers purchase much more house than they need. They tend to think of their second home in terms of their principal residence, and they don't want to downsize. Most folks don't need as much space in a second home, particularly one used sparingly, as they have in their full-time residence. Moreover, as kids move out, less space becomes increasingly appealing. A second-home buyer is often better off in the long run buying less house and more land if his finances force a choice. Self-denial, of course, applies only to those who need to budget dollars or are inveterately thrifty.

Existing country houses often present themselves to buyers who have evolving space needs as a choice between spending money upfront (for something newer or bigger) and spending time and money down the road (for additions and remodeling). If you are planning to use the country place as a second home until you can either move there full time or retire to it, the size-money question takes a different spin. You have to project your future space needs in light of future income. As a retiree or an empty-nester, your space needs are likely to be different than before. You may want to use the move to your country place as an excuse to cut back on the stuff you've accumulated. And it's probably cheaper to store the drag-along things in a rental unit than to buy a house large enough to function as your archives. Of course, the advantage of buying farms with barns and outbuildings is that you have even more space to fill. (Don't fill them with valuable furniture and papers.)

Average new-house size for retirees fluctuates year to year according to taste and fashion.

Recently, it's been in the 2,000- to 2,500-square-foot range. (This provides at least two or three bedrooms/study/work-out room/home office, two full bathrooms, good closets/storage, utility room and a kitchen-dining-living area.) My guess is that a couple who retires to a farm property can get along with 1,800 to 2,200 square feet, and additional space can be found in an outbuilding or rental storage unit. In 2006, you might assume typical new-house construction cost of at least $125 per square foot and new outbuilding construction cost at half that, or less. Buying an existing outbuilding for storage of durable items as part of a farm/second home is even cheaper.

If you are watching your dollars, you might want to buy a smaller second place and then add area if, and when, you need it as full-time residents. Finishing an attic or a stand-up basement is cheap space compared with building from scratch. Reworking a roof can also give you extra space for transients like children and grandchildren. Remodeling an outbuilding is another possible source of space as long as the building is worth the investment.

There's another time-money issue that relates to your anticipated use of the second home. Money buys convenience and reliability in a country place. A second home with a modern, whole-house, heating system is a welcome sight when you pull up at 11 pm on December 24th, braving a wind-chill factor of minus 5. Your cranky, sleepy family does not want to shiver for an hour while you start a fire in the woodstove. So the choice you face is spending $5,000-$10,000 for a heating system or having an impatient spouse, whiney kids and grimly cheerful guests pray that your last match ignites a frozen log. The same type of time-money dynamic plays out with water and sewerage systems, kitchens and driveways. Weaker and cheaper involves hassle and breakdown sooner or later. And the less frequent your visits to a second home, the more likely that problems materialize in weak, cheap systems. If you can't afford to go first class everywhere at once, you can add a few things that will make your comings and goings easier. For heating, install a few baseboard electric heaters that will warm a room quickly. For water, bring a couple of gallon jugs with you so that you don't have to crawl under the house first thing to get the pump working. Any water line or outlet that can be protected from freezing, should be. Install a spigot at the lowest point in the house's water system to allow you to drain all pipes with a few quick turns. Drain your system before you go home in the winter. Frozen water pipes are not how you want your ski weekend to begin. You can protect water traps (the U-shaped thing under your sink) by draining the system, then putting non-freeze windshield cleaner or non-toxic antifreeze in them.) Having lived in a country farmhouse for 23 years that I've had to shut down and open up periodically in below-freezing conditions, I would put scarce dollars first into reliable second-home systems at the expense of space if a choice had to be made.

If you're planning to retire to a country house, think through how you might want to adapt the structure to age-related needs. **Elder-friendly adaptations** can involve a lot of money or none at all, depending on what is being done. (For an overview/links, see www.infinitec.org; and www.design.ncsu.edu/cud/univ_design/princ_overview.htm for an explanation of "universal design" principles, which rethink housing so that it better fits everyone.) Elder-friendly changes may involve grade-level access, ground-floor bedroom, thermostat-controlled heating system, covered porch, lever-style handles rather than door knobs, dual hand rails on stairs, additional lighting (stairs, entrances), grab bars, slip-resistant floors (throw away throw rugs), wider doorways, ramps, and Personal Emergency Response System (PERS).

Buying a functioning country house as a second home makes the most sense to me for many buyers. The house has to be functioning at a level acceptable to you, which I hope now excludes wrecks and the more marginal projects. I would buy a setting (which I can't change) with a small house over a house I like better with a setting that doesn't suit. Small can always be enlarged; outdated can always be modernized, but the unchangeable will be with you always.

CHAPTER 13: ENVIRONMENTAL ISSUES

OVERVIEW

Buying rural property involves environmental issues in four basic ways.

First, how is the target property affected by environmental factors arising beyond the property's boundaries? These factors can be as global as long-range atmospheric transportation of acidic, fossil-fuel combustion products that are harming trees on the property and increasing the acidity in its lake, or as local as a neighbor dumping his dirty truck oil in the creek upstream.

Second, what adverse environmental impacts, if any, does the target property generate from its current uses? These impacts can be on the target property, as well as on adjoining properties.

Third, what environmental liabilities, if any, does the property contain? These can range from an insect infestation that limits the property's production of a particular crop to an abandoned underground mine that is leaking acid-enriched water.

Finally, what legal responsibilities and restrictions of an environmental nature come with the property? Restrictions can limit current uses and future plans.

The buyer must look at a target property with Superman's x-ray vision. To think about the land's environmental pluses and minuses, the buyer must look behind, through, under, around, above and into the property. It's easy to spot a 5,000-gallon, above-ground oil tank with a squirting leak. It is far more difficult to identify concealed problems unless you are looking for them and know what they are when you see them. It can be impossible to identify a federally listed endangered snail and its habitat, either of which can stop a second home from being built, unless you research the issue. Don't assume that you can dump clean sand in a bog or fill in that mosquito-breeding wet spot near the seller's house: you may be prosecuted for destroying wetlands.

The larger the tract, the more likely it is that buyers will discover one or more environmental issues in their pre-purchase scoping. But even small lots, located on ocean front or high-quality inland waters, can be affected. I advise asking the seller and his agent in your purchase offer to disclose *any* environmental condition of which they are aware that could affect your use and enjoyment of the property. You may also want to incorporate an environmental contingency in the contract that allows you to back out of the offer if you turn up any unacceptable environmental condition during, say, a 45-day study period.

On properties where you suspect an environmental issue—typically a restriction related to endangered species, wetlands, property adjoining water or water pollution—I recommend that you hire an **environmental consultant** to inspect the property and place a results-acceptable-to-the-buyer contingency in the contract. The consultant, who may be an engineer or a degree-holder in environmental studies, inspects the property for environmental problems just as a house inspector examines a building. The consultant should be broadly knowledgeable about environmental issues and be alert to a property's environmental values and benefits as well as its liabilities. Obviously, a lot of rural land can be—and is—purchased without an environmental inspection and without any resulting dire consequence. I simply submit the equally obvious response: state and federal restrictions on private property arising from environmental concerns are a fact of modern life, an increasingly prominent fact. Property-rights groups describe one horror story after another on their web sites about innocent individuals finding themselves ensnared over activities that appear to be harmless and minor.

A buyer cannot expect to become an overnight expert on the implications of environmental law for owners of rural land. But you should have a general overview of what these laws cover and a rudimentary checklist to go through. The U.S. Environmental Protection Agency (USEPA, or EPA) administers the following major laws that may be delegated to individual states for enforcement:

1. Clean Air Act (CAA)
2. Clean Water Act (CWA)
    a. Section 404 protects wetlands and designates permitting to the U.S. Army Corps of Engineers
3. Safe Drinking Water Act (SDWA)
4. Comprehensive Environmental Response, Compensation and Liability Act (CERCLA)
    a. Superfund Amendments and Reauthorization Act of l986 (SARA)
5. Resource Conservation and Recovery Act (RCRA)
6. Federal Insecticide, Fungicide and Rodenticide Act (FIFRA)
7. Toxic Substance Control Act (TSCA)
8. Marine Protection Research and Sanctuaries Act (MPRSA)
9. Uranium Mill Tailings Radiation Control Act (UMTRCA)
10. Hazardous Solid Waste Act (HSWA)
11. Endangered Species Act of 1973 (ESA)

Most of these acts regulate the pollution of air, land or water. Rural property can be the source of pollution or its victim, or both. Section 404, the Endangered Species Act and various coastal-preservation laws protect habitat and certain types of land from human activities that would harm them. This means that a landowner cannot use his in a way that has a detrimental effect on the habitat of a protected species. Good reasons exist for this restriction, but it also imposes costs and restraints on affected landowners.

COMMON ENVIRONMENTAL PROBLEMS, BROADLY CONSTRUED

Before discussing some of the land-buying concerns these federal laws raise, here are several unregulated "environmental" problems that are fairly common in the country.

Take **man-made light**, for example. If you look at rural property when most buyers do, you will be there during the day. Since you will be spending a good part of your time at your new country property in various degrees of darkness, it's sensible to know how things look from there at night. Sodium-vapor and other high-intensity lights on nearby properties can be intrusive and offensive. Remember how Laura Shaine Cunningham was shocked to discover that her country house was next door to a local community college whose anti-crime lights "glowed like a Martian heliport." (I'm not sure how an observant writer, even one besotted by big-shack ethers, could have missed a detail of this magnitude in broad daylight.) Look for neighboring (unlighted) light fixtures during your daytime visits. Big, modern-looking globes, often attached to barns and houses, are the ones that can disturb a neighbor. You will have no luck in asking their owners to turn off these monsters, which they've installed for security and safety, both valid concerns. You will lose a nuisance suit; the lights were there before you were. Even if they're installed after you join the neighborhood, you'll probably lose, because the lights are likely to be unexceptional and "in keeping" with community standards. Keep your eyes open, in addition for, blinking lights on nearby towers, tanks and silos. Another startling source of light is industrial-type poultry/hog housing. These long, one-story structures glow all night, and there might be five or six clustered together. If you can see a neighbor when trees have shed their leaves, **light pollution** may be a problem for you regardless of whether it bothers anyone else in the neighborhood.

Another type of annoyance is the practice of folks using your driveway entrance as a turnaround, particularly at night when their **vehicle lights** shine directly into your living room or bedroom. A turnaround habit can be long-standing, and you will be seen as a kill-joy crank if you object to that which has been visited on the previous owner. You should also determine whether the house catches headlights from the passing road. Houses situated at corners and curves are especially vulnerable.

Noise, constant or intermittent, can be a nagging bother. Teenage boys on big dirt bikes (motorcycles) are not the preferred peace-and-quiet neighbors. If you see a nearby neighbor with a big truck parked in his driveway, you should assume that you will hear its engine being cranked at five in the morning. If you don't like the sound of sirens, you don't want to buy close to a volunteer fire department. If you don't like the sound of bloodlust baying, avoid buying next to a kennel of hunting dogs. You can assume that you will hear gunshots in the country. Your neighbors—and maybe you too—will find it necessary every so often to shoot a rabid animal, snapping turtle or garden-ravishing groundhog. Some enthusiasts like to fire away at targets off their back porches. Gunfire noise can travel a fair distance, depending mainly on the gun's caliber (size). If gunfire bothers you, ask the seller and his neighbors whether this should be a concern, and don't buy next to a gun club or shooting range. You should expect to hear gunfire during hunting seasons, which vary from state to state and by game species. You may also want to avoid property situated near sawmills, wind-turbine farms (the towers are 400 feet high and impossible to ignore), oil or gas pumping stations, mines and quarries, dumpsters (green boxes) and small-engine repair shops.

Farms generate noise. Calves bawl for three or four days when they are weaned. When cattle are doctored, they protest loudly and often with justification. Sheep bleat. Donkeys bray. Roosters crow. And so on. Tractors and other types of equipment are noisy, but are generally not intrusive. If your property is next to a mechanized barn, you may hear the clank and rattle of a silo unloader and feed line. Farmers use all-terrain vehicles (ATVs) for farm-related tasks, such as herding cattle.

Normal farm noises are part of living in a farm community. Normal is usually defined as what is or what is typical, not what a newcomer would prefer. If you will find the routine of farm noise offensive, it's best not to buy around working farms. You don't have much of a right to tell a neighbor not to do what he was doing when you bought the property. The law of nuisance provides some protection against new noises and noises that exceed what a reasonable person might judge to be within the range of acceptability and typical by community standards, but local judges will be reluctant to tell farmers they can't farm—which is how the issue will be framed. States that adopted **right-to-farm legislation** will protect farmers in these circumstances.

You should anticipate **agricultural odors** in agricultural areas. If you're next to a dairy operation, you will smell fresh manure when the dairyman spreads it on his fields. A single dairy cow produces about 120 pounds of manure each day; a typical herd of 200 cows produces 8,760,000 pounds per year—all of which, in most cases, is used as field fertilizer. Farms gather liquid/slurry-type manure in open structures—concrete storage containers, earthen pits (lagoons or ponds)—and dry manure in sheds or piles. The closer you are to these gathering spots, the more you will notice the odor. When manure is applied to fields, the same rule of nose applies. Farm fields have manure/litter applied to them several times a year and smell bad for several days each time. Manuring pasture and crop land is a sensible agricultural practice that recycles nutrients, but you may want to avoid buying a property whose house lies close to such fields.

The no-buy rule should apply without exception to property within smelling range of **feedlots**. The stench of thousands of tons of cattle manure, especially when its wet, is unforgettable. (In dry weather, you get less odor but more dust.) Many Midwestern counties—where feedlots are common—have enacted zoning regulations to control odors. While property might be cheap downwind from a feedlot, it's not likely to prove to be a pleasing place to live. These odors don't stop on the weekend.

Factory farms are large operations that raise or handle livestock in concentrated areas, such as a feedlot or a building. Factory farms go by the official name, **Concentrated Animal Feeding Operations (CAFOs)**, and are now subject to EPA regulation through individual states. A buyer of land adjacent to a CAFO should assume that his nose will confront smells. EPA now requires that CAFOs obtain a pollutant-discharge permit and implement a nutrient-management plan by 2006 to protect surface waters. Nutrients, in this context, refers to manure's constituents—nitrogen, phosphorous and potassium; management refers to gathering, storage, handling and use of manure. EPA's CAFO regulations can be found at www.cfpub.epa.gov/npdes/afo/cafofinalrule.cfm.

Some folks are not bothered by farm odors, just as some folks are not bothered by the smell coming from plants that manufacture chemicals and paper. They are used to those smells and don't find them to be anything but routine. If, on the other hand, you have not been acclimated to CAFO odors, my advice is simple: Do Not Buy property near a CAFO or in an area where they exist. Certainly, the larger the farm or CAFO operation, the more potential for odor problems. But odor also depends on how it is stored and how manure is spread on fields. Certain types of applications—such as the injection technique where manure is inserted mechanically below the surface of the field and aerial spraying where the smelliest components of the manure are not the main part of the spray mixture—produce little odor. Composted manure also is inoffensive. Where fresh liquid/slurry manure or poultry litter is spread on fields, the odor is strong for several days.

A recent news story reported on a law suit in Nebraska where 11 residents living within two miles of a hog-raising CAFO won damages against Progressive Swine Technologies, because the stench forced them "…to stay inside and prevents them from eating food from their gardens or hanging clothes out to dry." A state Court of Appeals ordered the damages to be paid, and a trial court will determine their amount." (Kari Lydersen, "For Neighbors of Nebraska Farms The Days of Swine Aren't Rosy," Washington Post, June 20, 2004.) My impression is that it's next to impossible for a new resident to win smell-suits against farmers, and out of the ordinary to win against CAFOs.

I would ask whether any neighbors are planning on, or might be agreeable to, CAFOs or poultry houses, which tend to be located within a 90-minute truck drive of a processing plant. If you're driving down a pretty country highway and notice white feathers in the roadside weeds, you're in an area where large-scale poultry operations exist. The feathers originate with the fowl as they are being trucked to the processing plant. Local and national environmental and animal-rights organizations track these industries and can inform you of possible developments in your locale. (Start with the Environmental News Service, http://www.ens.lycos.com.) Trade associations and state cooperative extension services provide information from the producers' point of view. Urban/suburban buyers should distinguish between farm odors from small farms (which should be acceptable and accepted) and those of a CAFO, which are a different scale and intensity (and should be avoided).

CAFOs are to be shunned for another reason as well: high concentrations of nitrates and phosphorous from manure can easily contaminate both surface and underground water. The farmer's nutrient-management plan—which governs the storage, handling and distribution of manure—is supposed to prevent this.

You might also keep your eyes, ears and nose open for **sludge operations** near a target property. Municipal organic waste is treated and then transported to farms to be spread on fields as fertilizer. I like the idea in theory. Living next door to a farm that accepts sludge may be less likeable. It would depend on how it's managed.

Most, if not all states, have now adopted "**right-to-farm**" statutes that protect farmers from nuisance-type suits. These laws appeared in the 1980s for the most part as a result of successful suits that shut down some farms or forced their relocation. Owners of newly built suburbs in farming areas were winning complaints against farm operations about which the new buyers should reasonably have known.

The buyer can protect his interest by inserting into his purchase offer a requirement that the **seller disclose any condition around the property that constitutes an annoyance and might limit the buyer's use and enjoyment. Annoyance would include conditions such as noise, odor, excessively bright/strong lights and dust**. California now requires such disclosure. For more on neighbor law, check out www.nolo.com and search for FAQs on noise, boundaries, fences, trees, views, water damage, rural neighbors and the right to farm.

Roadside trash is a common irritation to urban buyers. Drive along many country roads and you will see aluminum cans, glass and plastic bottles, potato chip bags and styrofoam fast-food containers. You may run across a slope that has been used as a community dump before the days of scheduled trash pick up and dumpsters. Despite anti-littering laws, lifetime habits die hard, and, often, not at all. You may find the property you're investigating has a do-it-yourself dump, active or inactive. I once owned land along a remote road that someone insisted on using as a mortuary for his dead lambs every spring. In the fall, I would find butchered deer carcasses thrown over the fence. I had a couple of suspects in mind, but I never caught anyone in *flagrante delicto*. The gravel entrance to woods I own about one mile from my farmhouse attracts an evening parker every so often who leaves me a beer can or two for recycling and an occasional soiled diaper.

Roadside trash may upset country newcomers more than the trash they routinely see on urban streets and during their commutes to work. Newcomers, I think, expect things to be tidier in the country, because the country is prettier. But there's not much an individual can do to prevent littering, except clean it up and hope that others take note of a good example. (It's also therapeutic to grumble in self-righteous pique over every beer can.) Local families and community groups in Virginia adopt sections of road for regular clean up—and their effort shows amazing results.

It's easy for a newcomer to slip into a them-and-me perspective over littering which attributes a beer can thrown from a car to "their" culture (or lack thereof), "breeding" (or lack thereof) and ignorance. I urge you not to do go there, because it gets you stuck in unhelpful generalizations about your neighbors that are both unfair and inaccurate. "They" did not litter; one thoughtless jerk littered. If you or a group won't pick up the trash that bothers you, the best advice I can give is learn to live with it before it drives you crazy. Once a year, I walk my road frontage on trash patrol and feel virtuous afterward. (I've been unable to persuade anyone else in my family to share this virtue.) However, I would not move into a country place and on my first afternoon start picking up roadside trash. That's a statement about your neighborhood, even though it may not have been intended to be anything but a good deed.

With roadside dumps on your just-purchased property, erect several bold "No Dumping! Violators will be prosecuted" signs. This is fair notice that you don't want to be dumped on, despite local history and mores. A sign will usually be taken as a reasonable assertion of your property rights by most reasonable people. Violators, of course, will see you as an arrogant curmudgeon. Signs may be taken as an affront, which encourages more dumping just to show you. The best way of dealing with illegal dumping is to make a friend or two in the neighborhood, and then ask them to put the word out that you would really appreciate an end to the dumping.

Other types of **visual "pollution"** can mar a viewshed. A frequently complained about example is a sign or billboard that you see every time you enter or leave your driveway. Another is a sore-thumb house that doesn't fit into its setting or the neighborhood. It might be five times bigger than any other house in the county, or it might be the only hacienda in a school of Cape Cods. Wind turbines startle me by their out-of-scale size. A big water tank, a decrepit house, a fleet of junked cars on blocks—anything that snags your eye the first time you see it may or may not fade into the background if you have to see it everyday. Some things you will get used to, and other things are constant saddle burrs.

Country houses and barnyards attract **pests** of different kinds. Our farmhouse was infested with winter flies when we bought it, and has since become infested with the Asian lady beetle, which likes to winter in bright, sunny walls. Many houses in my county are similarly burdened. The flies emerge on warm days in cold seasons, buzz around the warm windows, then die in the cold night. (Unlike houseflies, they pay no attention to people, though they will get entangled in your hair, inadvertently.) The beetles eat aphids, which is good, but can stain stuff and cause allergic reactions in some individuals, which is bad. They smell, leave spots and bite. They are found in the South and Midwest, from the Gulf Coast to Canada. (The USDA released them in the 1980s to control aphids on pecan groves in Georgia and other places; the rest is history. Felicity Barringer, "Asian Cousin of Ladybug Is a Most Unwelcome Guest," New York Times, November 15, 2005.) Termites, carpenter ants and powder-post beetles can damage woodwork. Wasps often nest in a farmhouse attic or under an eave. Snapping turtles like farm ponds; snakes hang out under things; groundhogs burrow under buildings; rats and mice like barns, as do bats and some birds. Other critters you may face include skunks, raccoons, squirrels, deer, opossums, starlings, foxes, weasels, beaver, porcupines, feral cats and dogs, venomous spiders, coyotes, bears, mountain lions, javelinas and wolves. Alligators can be a dangerous nuisance.

Do not feed wildlife, including birds. (Other creatures, including bears, will raid your bird feeders.) A "fed bear is a dead bear" can be applied to other wild creatures, because they can't distinguish between when you want to feed them and when they want to eat the food they know you have. They become a pest to you and then to others. Sooner or later, a guy with a rifle gets fed up. Be neat and clean with food left for livestock and pets. Don't leave pet food on your porch at night unless you want to share. If you don't want a critter around, remove the habitat that lets him make a living there. Having shot or otherwise killed some of the aforementioned visitors, I can report that their descendants continue to journey through my habitat because it's theirs too. Passage is fine with me; residency is not. If wild creatures give you the willies, think again about buying a country place. They come with the territory. Country living will change your idea about the meaning of cohabitation.

The other category of pest is unwanted plants, insects, diseases and animals in the property's forest, fields and water. Often, these species are non-native, and, for that reason, have no local predators to control them. Trees have been greatly affected by invasive and non-native insects and diseases. Both hardwoods and pines are susceptible. Oaks, ash, maples, hemlock and pine, among others, are at risk. The best way to determine whether woods and valuable timber trees are being, or are likely to be, impacted, is to hire a consulting forester to walk through the target property's woodland before you submit an offer. He will be knowledgeable about prominent local pests. Don't assume that your target property is exempt. The county extension agent will be able to give you a first-cut opinion about the type of pests that affect local crops. Pests, broadly construed, can inflict serious economic damage to valuable trees and agricultural products.

Human visitors are not usually considered an environmental problem, but they are to the extent that unwanted ones negatively affect the use and enjoyment of your land. Properties bordering national forest land can be overrun during hunting season. Even where you clearly post your common boundary with a clearly marked national forest line, certain properties are routinely invaded by hunters and sometimes their packs of dogs. Hunters have the right to retrieve their dogs from posted land; if your land is properly posted they have no right to kill game on your land. The law of trespass is, shall I say, not always followed to the letter in the field. Ask the seller about this. He may be reluctant to reveal the extent of hunting-season trespass.

If your property borders a fishing stream, you can count on finding fishermen in your section of stream. Landowners normally hold **riparian rights** to waters in a river, stream, pond or lake flowing through or joining their property. If the waterway is considered **navigable**, the landowner owns land to the water's edge with the state owning the land under the water. Navigable waters are considered to be the same as public highways, allowing the public—that is, fishermen and boaters—to "travel" and use the navigable water without restriction. If the waterway is considered **unnavigable**, the landowner owns the land under the water to the centerline of the waterway. Landowners can prohibit fisherman access to unnavigable waterways, but not to navigable waterways. The legal definition of navigable can be broader than you think. Fishing access may also be controlled by special state provisions. A well-known trout stream near me, for instance, is off-limits to public fishing even though it is considered navigable because the original grant of lands from the English King specifically stated that the fish belonged to the holder of the grant, and by extension to all successors in title. The owner of a fishing right can give, rent or sell it to another. The **common of piscary** is a rarely used legal phrase that means the right to fish in waters belonging to another, which I once heard a trespassing lawyer in waders cite to a farmer in muck boots. The farmer said something like, "I don't give a damn about your piss, common or otherwise; get out of my fishing hole." When a buyer finds himself evaluating property with water running through it or adjoining it, he should determine whether it is considered navigable or unnavigable, because that fact will usually control what rights, if any, he has to restrict public access. This information can be obtained from the state's game and wildlife department, county sheriff or local game warden. The U.S. Army Corps of Engineers may also have to be consulted. Exceptions and unusual circumstances regarding fishing rights can be found in deeds and by asking state game and wildlife officials about local laws.

You may also find visitors checking out a well-known berry patch, fruit or nut tree, rock quarry, cave, picnic spot, spring, sand pit, bird's nest, mushroom spot, ginseng stand, snake den, swimming hole or dump on your newly purchased property. This is in addition to hunters, four-wheelers, motorcyclists and hikers who may also turn up. Yellow posted signs help spread the word that you do not want uninvited visitors, as do advertisements in the local paper. It should not take long for the word to get around the neighborhood that you do not welcome visitors unless they are invited or secure permission in advance.

Having said all that, I can report finding a birder's car parked in the middle of my woods driveway, not 15 feet from a No-Trespassing sign posted at eye level at the entrance with my name and address on it. I had left my gate open the evening before, and he pulled into my property rather than park on the roadside—something readily done and safe enough. I considered having him arrested. I considered having a sarcastic conversation about his level of literacy and eyesight. I considered scraping his SUV with my woods truck, which bears scrapes, dents and scratches with no ill will. I considered kicking his ass down the road. I was in high dudgeon over my violated property rights. But I knew I didn't have the right to harm his person or property. The cooler part of my head prevailed, so I simply growled at him to get his car out of my driveway. Other enforcement choices involve time and possibly money. Still, had he asked permission, he could have parked on the land and walked its trails all afternoon. Trespass often becomes a highly charged issue for country newcomers, especially when reasonable and rational efforts don't prevent recurrences.

My inclusion above of a swimming hole may seem petty to a reader sitting in his secure living room contemplating a wonderful life in the country. A recorded agreement to access another's swimming hole is rare. But your enjoyment of this swimming hole will diminish as soon as you discover that it has been used by at least seven generations of local kids as a matter of custom. Whether current kids have any legal right to use this hole is a matter of state law, and the answer is probably not. If you insist on ending or limiting their visits, you have fallen into a bad way to introduce yourself to the neighborhood. To learn about such water usages in advance, your purchase contract can ask the seller to **disclose any uses of the property and its resources that occur outside of a recorded easement.**

Laugh! Swimming holes have been the subject of disputes between new owners and "old" users in Crystal Springs, Florida; High Falls, New York; and Ben Lomond, California to name a few places. (Winnie Hu, "Locked Out," <u>Richmond Times-Dispatch</u>, July 29, 2001, p. A-2.) Landowners are subject to a lawsuit if an uninvited guest gets hurt in their hole, and they have not taken adequate precautions and erected adequate signs to prevent its use. The **doctrine of attractive nuisance** can pin liability on the landowner who did not do enough to prevent trespassers from using his swimming hole. If you are buying a swimming hole, check with a local lawyer to determine exactly what you need to do to satisfy your obligations under state law to keep out unwanted swimmers. On well-known swimming holes, you will need to do more than post a no-trespassing sign or put the word out. You may have to choose between becoming the new ogre for telling everyone to stay out or the community patsy by putting up with a dozen kids traipsing across your fields on hot afternoons. If you value privacy, become the ogre. If you let folks use your hole, you should carry liability insurance and have them sign a liability waiver. I'm serious.

Sooner or later, the new owner of rural land will have a run in with trespassers on his property. I quote below an extended account of one such incident in a part of West Virginia not far from where I live. It was written by non-resident-owner, Chris Bolgiano, in <u>The Appalachian Forest</u>:

…we arrived for a visit years ago. A new road greeted us, a narrow track up a vertical slope, with the forest floor churned into powder. Rain would soon turn it into a gully. We knew right off it was OHVs [Off-Highway Vehicles, or All-Terrain Vehicles (ATVs)]. We raced up the new road, cursing, yelling ideas back and forth about how to fell logs across the road and stud them with case-hardened nails. We felt righteous with ownership, passionate with protectiveness. The road continued up to the barbed wire fence that marked our boundary. The wire had been cut, and the track crossed our border to join an old path along the ridge. We had explored that path and then forgotten it, forgotten that our property was linked into a generations-old network of trails.

As I planned how to cunningly angle the nails, we heard the chugging of motors. A caravan of four OHVs came into view just below, moving toward us up the hill. Ralph [her husband] raised his arms and walked toward them down the middle of the new track, palms out, fingers spread, like an evangelist at a camp meeting. For a few seconds I thought that the vehicles might swerve clean around him and keep going. But they stopped. Ralph stood beside the first one while I walked up and straddled the front wheel, leaned into it, put one hand on the handlebars. I hadn't studied mountain manners all these years for nothing. There was going to be no doubt about who had rights here.

The lead vehicle was decked out like an Amish buggy: a square of thick black vinyl stretched over a pipe frame welded to the body of the OHV, with plastic windows zippered into the front and sides. Later we heard that the driver had black lung from a lifetime spent mining coal and couldn't tolerate wind in his face. From his creases and the texture of his skin, I guessed that he was in his sixties. His hair was still dark, and his eyes were the darkest, most solid brown I've ever seen. They were shaped like almonds, slightly tilted.

'I own this property,' Ralph began, 'and I'm just real surprised to find this road here.' His voice was calm and twangy with the mountain drawl we had picked up and slipped into years earlier, at first unconsciously, for protective coloration.

'We're just going to our hunting place to put this stuff out for the deer,' the man in the first OHV said. Near his feet, apples bulged, round and red through plastic mesh bags. 'It's legal,' he added quickly. 'Baiting's all legal except for bear.'

I had been looking for guns without even realizing it, scanning the rears of the OHVs and glancing at shoulders for rifles slung there as carelessly as sacks of apples. We almost always brought a gun with us when we camped here. Mainly we used it to answer when shots sounded too close for comfort—a rural dialogue to announce our presence. Now, I realized that this was one of the few times when we could expect not to see guns.

Hunters, accustoming their prey to being fed in certain places, were too easily accused of poaching if guns were in sight. It was a reassuring thought.

'Well, I don't know who put this road in, but it's eroding on that steep place there and I don't much like that,' Ralph said. 'And whoever put it in cut my fence.'

'We never cut no fence,' the man said. 'We started riding through here after we saw the road. I thought the preacher owned it yet. If I'd of knowed how to get in touch with you, I'd of asked you.'

Well, now, no one could demand more than that. Grateful to him for the face-saving he was offering, we eased a bit. 'He used to,' Ralph said, meaning the preacher. 'We bought it fifteen years ago, and this is the most people we've seen in all these years.' I was pleased that the man seemed surprised. I kept looking for a power fulcrum, a way to show that we weren't total strangers here, people from the city who didn't know spotlighting [hunting deer at night with high-powered lights, which cause the deer to freeze, making them easy targets] from a Sunday drive.

The three young men who were driving the other OHVs got off. We all stood around for some time, kicking our toes into clumps of grass and shielding our eyes from the sun as we talked in brief spurts between bouts of silence. The state did not provide a registration procedure for OHVs, they explained, and it was illegal to run unregistered vehicles on state roads. So they had to stay off-road or get a stiff fine. We walked around looking for a better place on our slope to put a road, but there wasn't any. In the meantime, three more OHVs and then two motorbikes drove up and stopped at a distance, waiting for the crowd to clear out. A regular wilderness road had developed across our place.

'Tell you what,' the man said. 'You give me and my boys permission to come through here to hunt, and we'll build you gates. We'll put one down below where we come on, and one up there where we go off. We'll do it and mail you the keys.'

It was an honorable solution, and without a doubt the best we could hope for under the circumstances. Ralph got out some paper and wrote Jesse Hoover's name down, followed by six sons. 'I knew you wasn't a hard kind of feller,' Jesse said, slapping his knee. Who could blame him for using the road, once he had noticed it? With locked gates, we could at least limit the damage to the forest. And by giving Jesse proprietary rights, we would make an ally and give him incentive to look out for our interests. Maybe this would prove to be the tie to the larger community we had been trying for years to make. Maybe it wasn't, as it seemed at first, the end of a dream, our outdated vision of serenity and isolation. We all shook hands, and a month later, two keys arrived in the mail. Jesse and his caravan pulled away, and Ralph walked down to the next group.

'I don't know who put this road in,' he began again, 'but it's tearing up...'

'You know Jesse Hoover?' one of the drivers interrupted him. 'He put it in.' (Chris Bolgiano, The Appalachian Forest: A Search for Roots and Renewal (Mechanicsburg, Pennsylvania: Stackpole Books, 1998, pp. 168-170.)

The result of this conversation is that the land's owners gave their oral permission to allow Mr. Hoover—an individual who had trespassed, destroyed their property (fence), eroded their ground, cut a road across their land that they did not want and lied to their faces—exclusive right to continue his activities in return for installing two gates to keep out his hunting rivals. This is not a face-saving or honorable solution. This was a shakedown. Ms. Bolgiano and her husband got nothing. While it is true that an absentee owner cannot keep determined intruders off his distant property, every owner should resist being maneuvered into accepting something that he feels is unacceptable. Don't start playing the patsy in an extortion racket; it will never end.

The choices an owner has concerning access are these: 1) let everyone in for approved purposes, 2) let some people in for approved purposes, and 3) let no one in for any purpose. If you choose the first option, you give away control of your property. You will be unhappy with the result. If you choose the second, you may make enemies of everyone you exclude. In the case of the Bolgianos, they thought they made the best of a trespass problem by authorizing its continuance. If you choose the third, your lack of exception will ruffle some feathers. At different times and in different places, I've tried all three, and now mainly use the third.

Enforcing a no-trespassing rule can be difficult for an absentee owner. I am, for example, half-owner of a West Virginia property that is about a 45-minute drive from my home. This is mountain woodland that we bought as a timber investment. We don't use it for hunting or recreation. Its few posted signs are not honored and a locked cable was cut during hunting season soon after I put it up. I deal with this trespass situation in the most reasonable fashion available to me in the circumstances: I neither think about it nor worry over it. While I would prefer that the land not be subject to trespass, we didn't care much about it. When I began to lease the property for hunting, I took out an ad in the local paper to notice readers that trespassing was prohibited. I also talked personally to a neighbor about the new arrangement. The word got around.

When an absentee owner *does* want to prevent trespass, he can take the following steps:

1. **Tack up posted signs**, according to state requirements.

2. **Place an ad in local paper before hunting season**. Property owned by _____ on _____ Road is posted. Trespassing is illegal, and trespassers will be prosecuted. We do not trespass on the land of others, and we expect others to respect our property rights.

3. **Talk to your neighbors**. Establish a rapport, or at least, give them your name, address and phone numbers. Put the word out that you do not want trespassing because.... Among other reasons, you may not want your land to be considered open access to the public; you do not want the **liability exposure** that can arise from visitors having accidents or injuries on your property; you do not want others using your land without permission because that unwanted usage over time can give rise to a legal right to use your property; you do not want your land to be degraded by individuals who do not share your environmental values; you don't want visitors if you have a second home and/or personal property on the land; you don't want visitors taking down trees for firewood; you do not want hunting, fishing or ATV use for whatever your reasons are; you do not want your property to be exposed to fire hazards from camping and cigarettes. If all else fails, say that you don't want your land to become a place of beer-drinking teenagers and all the trouble that entails.

4. **Erect a gate across your entrance**. Install a very heavy-duty chain lock. Give a key to your local volunteer fire department along with an annual donation.

5. **Talk to the local sheriff and game warden**. Tell them that you'd appreciate it if they kept an eye on your land and put the word out.

6. **Be prepared to prosecute trespassers**.

If I had discovered a road on my property and then an ATV convoy using it as the Bolgianos did, I would have told the intruders that I wanted no trespassing, that the road was an act of trespass and destruction of property and that I was fully prepared to prosecute trespassers and property destroyers. (I would have been in a stronger position had the property been posted before the encounter, which the Bolgianos' apparently wasn't.) I would also ask them for their names and addresses. Mr. Hoover, it should be remembered, could have easily found out who owned the Bolgianos' property by looking up the tract in the tax records at the county courthouse, something I would bet my farm he knew how to do. He was knowingly trespassing and then knowingly lying about what he had done. The last thing I would give him and his offspring is a license to do exactly what I didn't want done.

It is my experience that trespassers and hunters who trespass believe they have a right to do what they please with your land. They don't see how their use harms the owner. Most "locals" are not like this, and most hunters I know respect the rights of other property owners. Dealing with the exceptions can only be done by being firm, reasonable and consistent. In almost 30 years of living and owning property in the middle of Appalachia, I have never heard of a single incident of violence of any kind arising from a property owner asking a trespasser, hunter or birdwatcher to leave. I'm sure, however, such things have happened. Unarmed, I have asked groups of armed strangers to leave, and they have complied. The trick with armed men is to stay low-key and not get personal. Explain your reasons for posting; don't get self-righteous about the glories of private property and your civic virtuousness. Don't be surprised if a hunter claims that he did not see your signs. I once discovered a trespassing bird hunter in a friend's bog, aiming a loaded shotgun out of season, not more than 12 inches away from a posted sign at eye level. He said he never saw the sign. It's hard to prevent customary trespass, but you can make it clear through signage and ads—and mainly by word of mouth—that your land is not open. It will take several years for the word to spread. If you do not make this effort, you will find ATVs, hunters, birders and others visiting you whenever they like. You may live in fear of gunfire and will be deprived of the use and enjoyment of the property that you've purchased. The Bolgianos gave away their privacy because they were unable to say, "Please leave and do not come back."

COMMON ISSUES

Certain environmental situations can involve the property owner in regulatory and administrative law, which can be either federal or state, or both. Among the most commonly encountered are:

1. Wetlands
2. Floodplain
3. Endangered, Threatened and Sensitive (ETS) Species
4. Polychlorinated Biphenyls (PCBs)
5. Underground storage tanks (USTs)
6. Waste disposal on site/dumps
7. Animal waste
8. Oil/gas wells and coal mines
9. Asbestos
10. Wood smoke
11. Carbon monoxide
12. Radon
13. Chemical and hazardous exposures and wastes

14. Air-borne pollution

1. Wetlands are more or less permanently wet areas that fall within certain federal regulatory definitions, particularly Section 404 of the 1972 Clean Water Act as interpreted by the U.S. Army Corps of Engineers' regulations, the courts and the Act's 1977 Amendments. Wetlands are currently defined according to the Corps' 1987 Manual for Delineation of Wetlands, though this scheme is subject to continuing debate within the government and between the government and non-government interests, both private and public. Wetlands are coastal and inland areas between land and water. (See http://h2osparc.wq.ncsu.edu/info/wetlands.html.)

A wetland can be identified as land having groundwater (i.e., underground water) near to, at or over its surface for much of the year, or land that supports aquatic vegetation. Look for marshy, swampy, boggy areas and land with vegetation that indicates saturated soils, such as ironweed, Joe Pie weed and skunk cabbage, among others. These plants are "hydrophytes" and are found in "hydric" soils associated with wetlands. Bottom land and floodplains contain wetlands. Wetlands were historically places to be avoided or converted by drainage into usable property. Today, we know they provide important wildlife habitat and a reservoir-like function for gathering storm runoff for slower release. We now construct new wetlands for just such flood-mitigation purposes. Additional information can be obtained by logging on to http://wetlands.fws.gov, which leads to the U.S. Fish and Wildlife Service's National Wetlands Inventory Center.

A buyer may consider the presence of wetlands on a property either an asset or a liability, depending on what he wants to do. The general rule of regulatory thumb that now seems to be applied is that there should be no net loss of wetlands. If your plan is to alter a wetlands area by adding fill, drainage or other excavation, you will probably need to construct at least an equivalent wetlands area on your site or obtain an equivalent credit from a wetlands mitigation bank. Very small wetlands areas are exempt from these requirements. The Army Corps of Engineers administers the permitting, inspection and management of wetlands activity. The Corps' authority covers navigable waters, which have been defined to include any waters that have the capability of affecting interstate commerce. The commerce clause has been stretched to include headwaters where water flow is intermittent and often non-existent. A navigable waterway need not be navigable to be classified as navigable.

The US Supreme Court weakened the scope of wetlands protection in June, 2006 when a divided bench ruled that the Corps had exceeded its power under the Clean Water Act by defining almost any place that might have water as falling within the category of "waters of the United States." If a wetlands is not connected to water under Corps jurisdiction, it is not likely to be protected in the future, but the exact definition of how that is to be determined is likely to be settled case by case. The current Court is leaning toward narrowing wetlands protection, but a buyer should not count on any change until new interpretations are settled. (Jess Bravin, "Split Supreme Court Narrows Use of Wetlands Act," Wall Street Journal, June 20, 2006 and Patti Waldmeir, "Landowners baffled as court splits on wetlands protection," Financial Times, June 20, 2006, both referring to *Rapanos v. U.S.; Carabell v. U.S. Army Corps of Engineers*.).

On major wetlands-disturbing projects, including those involving federal land, the Corps must prepare an **Environmental Impact Statement (EIS)** that assesses the full range of environmental impacts projected to arise from the applicant's wetlands-changing proposal. (The draining of less than one acre may need only a Corps on-site inspection and go-ahead.) The applicant pays the cost of preparing an EIS, which can be enormously expensive as well as contentious, depending on the size of the project, location, type of wetlands and the projected impacts.

An urban buyer looking for a country property does *not* want to get entangled in the wetlands regulatory process. No second-home buyer wants to prepare an EIS or a lesser impact analysis, and go through that type of regulatory review. As long as you do nothing to change an existing wetlands, you should not be entangled in these regulations. Site your new house or barn on higher ground rather than in a floodplain or wet spot (that requires fill and/or underground drain pipes). If you have a farm plan for the target property, run it by the Corps' local office to determine in advance whether the farm has wetlands and, if so, whether your plan will change them. If the seller is currently grazing stock on wetlands, which is fairly common, a new owner can continue this practice or fence them out. Work around the wetlands, because they benefit the property's wildlife and drainage.

I once had to dry out less than two-thirds of an acre of wet land on which I was building houses. It was permanently wet because the uphill neighbor gathered the runoff from his uphill land and piped it onto mine. These pipes had been installed years before. My ground was an impermeable, water-bearing clay, which was why it was wet land. Much of my ground had to be cut out, the hole filled in with rip-rap-size rock and smaller rock; drainage pipes had to be laid under the rock, and fabric had to be installed in certain spots to help with channeling the new underground water system. It was a very expensive job, and I would never willingly enter this quicksand again. Had there been any other way to install the road, I would have taken it. The Corps official was quite helpful in not subjecting this wet land to wetlands review. A lot of wetlands was drained before protective legislation was enacted, and these pipes and ditches remain in various states of repair. Check with the Corps before purchasing any farm property with these systems in place. Determine what you will and will not be allowed to do without review and permit.

If you find yourself unavoidably having to develop wetlands acreage, you should first look to construct the same type of wetlands in a similar location on your property, using the same kind of dirt, vegetation and water. If that cannot be done, the Corps representative can put you in touch with a **wetlands mitigation bank**, which has constructed wetlands from which you can "withdraw" an equivalent parcel in various ways, including paying for it. Banks are operated by both public- and private-sector organizations. The property may also be eligible for a **conservation easement**, by which the owner donates the right to develop or use the wetlands in certain ways in return for tax benefits. Local land trusts or conservation groups accept the donation of such easements and hold them in perpetuity, unless the owner imposes a time limit. The higher the appraised value of the easement given away, the greater the tax benefit.

The presence of wetlands on a target property may not affect a buyer's plans at all. Once scoping finds wetlands, however, the buyer can use their presence to work down the seller's price, owing to the restrictions they impose on use. Wetlands lower asking price in my experience, except where they are integral to hunting. The seller may know something about wetlands on his property, but more likely than not he's simply cursed those "bad spots" and driven the tractor around them, hoping not to get stuck. Any wet area, whether official wetlands or not, should tip off a prospective buyer to the possibilities of a spring, seep or clay-rich soils that won't drain well. Wet soils are usually not suitable for road building, construction or septic fields. An excavator must remove them and then replace them with rock and good fill—all of which is expensive.

If you find yourself evaluating a target property that you suspect has a wetlands presence that is relevant to your plans, you can place a contingency in your offer that gives you enough time to have a Corps' representative visit the property and hire an environmental consultant.

> **Buyer's offer is contingent on obtaining a preliminary determination and assessment from the U.S. Army Corps of Engineers regarding any wetlands on said property, whose results shall be judged by Buyer to be acceptable or unacceptable for his purposes.**
>
> **Buyer shall have the right to investigate any wetlands on the property to determine their relevance to his future use and enjoyment. This may involve agents of**

Buyer taking soil samples, borings and other tests. Buyer will restore the land wherever it is disturbed by these activities.

Buyer shall complete this work within ___ days of this Contract taking effect. If Buyer determines the results of these investigations are unacceptable for his purposes, he may void his offer without penalty and all security deposits shall be returned to him in a timely manner.

A contingency also gives the buyer the opportunity to recast his offer at a lower price where his wetlands investigations indicate future expense or the need to modify his plans for the property.

One last point is worth mentioning. Those buyers who are considering eliminating wetlands or cutting old-growth forest in the process of building a trophy home, run a risk, albeit small, of being targeted by arsonists, some of whom claim to be associated with the Earth Liberation Front (ELF). Homes in subdivisions that drained wetlands near Seattle were targeted in 2004. A high-profile construction project in an environmentally contentious area may be subject to attack. (See http://seattletimes.nwsource.com/html/localnews/2001954671_elf1m.html

2. Floodplains are found where low land lies next to a waterway, lake or ocean (where storm surges cause coastal flooding). Floodplains are usually dry, though they may contain wetlands. We generally associate a floodplain with a low-lying, level area. It is, however, any area that becomes inundated with floodwater. In steeply sided, V-shaped stream valleys, the "floodplain" can extend 30 feet up each leg of the V. In such places, it is not unusual to find houses built on pilings.

As a buyer with dozens of property choices, I would encourage you to avoid those where buildings are in a floodplain. This property will be flooded eventually. Even where no improvements are involved, floodplain properties will sustain damage that you will have to repair. Fences crossing the floodplain and gates will be damaged or destroyed; flood debris will need to be removed, possibly off site; toppled trees will have to be cut up or burned; fill or topsoil may have to be hauled in; septic systems may have to be repaired; roads and culverts will need work, and on and on. Sometimes, federal money will be available to defray some flood costs, but this is not certain and won't cover all your expenses. Federal money has been available on some flooding occasions to restore the bank of our stream to its original shape, but it was not available to remove rock from the channel or build up the bank to keep future floods in place. When you add improvements and personal property—houses, barns, vehicles, storage tanks—to a floodplain, the clean-up costs increase. Despite these warnings, many readers buy floodplain for the obvious reason: it puts them right on the water.

Flooding frequency is expressed in terms of either how often a flood of a particular size occurs or the probability of flooding each year. A 100-year flood can represent either a very large flood or a one percent chance of a flood occurrence. The volume of a 100-year flood will fill a 100-year floodplain. The **Federal Emergency Management Agency (FEMA)** tries to mitigate flood damage proactively, manages post-flooding clean up and provides insurance for floodplain property.

FEMA is charged by the Federal Emergency Management Act with identifying all natural flood areas and developing plans to minimize loss. Accordingly, FEMA's Flood Insurance Administration has developed **flood-hazard maps** for most known floodplains in the United States. The maps show boundary lines of a 100-year flood. The local FEMA office and/or the local or state office that has responsibility for flooding issues can provide these maps for your county where they are available. Even where the map has not been finished, one or more of these offices may be willing to show you the work in progress. The local zoning office or building inspector should also be able to provide both anecdotal flooding histories and additional information. The local U.S. Department of Agriculture office, now called the Natural Resources

Conservation Service, or the state's Soil and Water Conservation District office should have information on the flooding history and any record of publicly funded flood clean-up assistance for individual farms. Finally, ask the seller if he carries flood insurance; if he does, ask about the claims he's filed in the past and the premium costs.

FEMA administers the **National Flood Insurance Program (NFIP)**, which subsidizes insurance to property owners in floodplains. The typical **homeowner or farmowner's insurance policy** does not cover flood loss. Private insurance carriers, however, sell and issue NFIP insurance to individuals for a 31.8 percent commission and a fee of 3.3 percent of any claim amounts. NFIP is the taxpayer's pot of money that pays these claims. With rare exceptions, NFIP will pay insurance losses no matter how many times a floodplain property is damaged. While "repetitive flood-loss properties" account for about two percent of the policy holders, they amount to nearly 40 percent of the NFIP-paid claims. This insurance program encourages development in floodplains, though some construction is discouraged through community land-use controls that are a condition of the insurance. NFIP insurance is necessary to secure a bank mortgage for new construction on land that will predictably flood. FEMA's schizophrenia is the result of the cross-cutting pressures at work: individuals want to build in floodplains; individuals want cheap insurance; insurance companies want big commissions with no risk; politicians find a way to help constituents by spreading the cost.

While FEMA tries both to mitigate loss and compensate property owners as soon as flood loss occurs, more and more communities are restricting, or even banning, floodplain construction through **floodplain district zoning**. Beyond the economic loss argument, proponents of restriction show that the more building there is in a floodplain, the more a flood spreads its area of damage to the extent that buildings occupy space (in the sense of volume) that would have otherwise been partially filled with water. Floodplain zoning ordinances differ. Some prohibit construction of any new structure in designated floodplains; some prohibit residential use of such property; some prohibit damming and filling activities. Opponents argue that such ordinances constitute a government **taking** of value from their property without compensation because the property owner is denied all reasonable uses. The trend appears to be toward more building-and-use restrictions on inland floodplains and in coastal areas.

Floods are frightening events that cause enormous damage. When the waters recede, the landowner is left with a dispiriting and often expensive clean up. I've been through four 100-year floods in the intermittent creek in our back field between 1983 and 2007. I have seen these floods wreck buildings and take lives in my neighborhood. I have spent several thousand dollars cleaning up fences and fields, and building a levee. It never occurred to me to ask the seller of this farm in 1983 about flooding, and even had I asked, the truthful answer was the creek had never flooded before. I don't think I would have walked away from this farm because of flooding, but I would have planted an acre of walnuts on higher ground instead of in the bottom where they've been clobbered repeatedly.

Coastal flooding from hurricanes is a factor that any beach-oriented buyer should consider. Following Katrina, insurers are dropping homeowners' policies from Texas to Rhode Island. Allstate dumped 27,000 customers in New York's coastal counties and 120,000 in Florida in 2006. (Liam Pleven, "Hurricane Losses Prompt Allstate to Pursue New Path," Wall Street Journal, November 24, 2006.) In addition to "hundreds of thousands of policyholders...being dropped by their insurers," a larger number have had to "...swallow double-, even triple-digit increases in premiums and deductibles." Average losses are now running about $17 billion annually. (Karen Breslau, "The Insurance Climate Change," Newsweek, January 29, 2007.) More than half of Americans live within 50 miles of a coast. If climate change increases the number and intensity of coastal storms, prudent buyers will move inland to places where they can obtain insurance. Beaches may become nice to visit, but impossible for residences and second homes.

3. A typical buyer will not be able to "see" **endangered, threatened or sensitive (ETS) plant and/or animal species** unless he knows what to look for and is looking for them. The federal Endangered Species Act protects the habitat of selected flora and fauna whose survival is deemed threatened. More than 1,300 species were protected as of 2005; ten species have been recovered to the point of being delisted. The Act is administered primarily by the U.S. Department of Interior's Fish and Wildlife Service (FWS) and the Department of Commerce's Marine Fisheries Service, depending on the habitat location of the species. ETS species not on the coasts fall under the Endangered Species Office of the Fish and Wildlife Service at http://www.endangered.fws.gov. The EPA's Office of Pesticide Programs (OPP) becomes involved when farmers apply pesticides on their farms that are also ETS habitat or near such habitat. (See http://www.epa.gov/espp/how-to.htm.) Both FWS and OPP can provide maps showing ETS species locations, and OPP can provide a list of pesticides that are limited in such areas. Buyers should be aware that individual states may publish state-specific ETS lists. Properties that have unusual topographic features—high elevations, remote/isolated locales, swamps, marshes, caves, remote running water, unusual trees and atypical ecologies—are the most likely places to find rare species. You can obtain a summary of each state's law, policies and programs related to **biodiversity** at http://ipl.unm.edu/cwl/statbio/.

The presence of an ETS species or its habitat can limit, or even prohibit, a buyer from implementing farming, construction and development plans for newly purchased property. The US Fish and Wildlife Service estimates that about seven million acres of private land is regulated under the 1973 ESA. Woods on the property may not be timbered or a field cleared for agricultural purposes where a highly protected species or a "**critical habitat**" is found. The Service found that "…the cost of critical habitat designation to range from an average $77,000 to protect the San Bernandino Mountains bladderpod, a kind of herb, to $915 million over 20 years for the California coastal gnat-catcher, a tiny bird." (Jenny Johnson, "Fight to save 'species over people' law that infuriates developers," <u>Financial Times</u>, April 21, 2006.) Land and water areas can be assigned a no-disturbance status. Fire-prone brush may not be cleared if it shelters a protected species. Building may be prohibited. Assume, until learning otherwise, that you won't be able to do much of anything with private land that is identified as habitat for a federally listed endangered species. This is too harsh an assumption, but it puts you into the proper state of alert. If a federally listed species is present, you must check with the appropriate federal FWS office for advice on what you can and cannot do with the land you are considering buying. Most states have an **office of natural heritage resources** that has maps showing ETS locations and likely habitats. Some of this mapping is based on field research, but much appears to be based on extrapolating from models that predict the probability of certain species being found in certain conditions.

If you have reason to believe that ETS species may be found on a target property, place a contingency clause in your offer that allows you to back out of the contract without penalty if the results of further study are not satisfactory. Sellers can be expected to balk at accepting such contingency clauses since any finding of ETS species or habitat on their property will generally inhibit their ability to sell it. The market for ETS properties may be limited to individual preservationists and conservation groups. Many buyers will view ETS presence and the limitations imposed as liabilities and a price-discount factor. They will, accordingly, pay less for such properties than what might be otherwise expected.

And to every generalization, the exception must be appended. A waterfront farm can likely fetch a higher price because of the nesting bald eagles in the old snag. If a buyer has no plans to build a house, dock or barn near the snag, the eagles add value. If a house, dock and barn already exist, you may be able to watch the eagles from your front porch. As always, the buyer must take responsibility for sorting this out prior to submitting an offer, to the extent he can. For more information look at The Endangered Species Act of 1973, http://endangered/fws/gov/esa.html.

Property rights advocates see the application of the Act as imposing unreasonable, nonsensical and sometimes dangerous restrictions on landowners. Advocates see the Act as a wise conservation measure whose ultimate benefits are still to be reckoned. A program to compensate landowners for being prohibited from using that portion of their property defined as habitat makes sense to me. I endorse buying habitat to protect species and have been involved in several such purchases.

At the end of 2005, Congress was considering various amendments to the 1973 legislation that would either modify or eliminate some provisions that restrict certain human activities in areas designated as critical habitats. These changes would make permitting for logging and construction shorter and less burdensome. The government would under some proposals be expected to compensate landowners when they suffer economic loss from restrictions on the use of their land arising from the Act. (Eric Bontrager, "In Senate, Endangered Species Act Faces an Overhaul," Wall Street Journal, December 27, 2005.) Land buyers need to review their plans against current laws and regulations as part of their pre-purchase scoping.

4. Polychlorinated biphenyls (PCBs) are a class of up to 209 chlorinated organic compounds that were manufactured by Monsanto in the United States between the 1930s and late 1970s. About two to three billion pounds were made, of which about one percent is estimated to remain as an air and water contaminant. They are odorless oily liquids or solids that are clear to light yellow. They were used as coolants and lubricants in electrical equipment because they don't burn. The major sources of PCB pollution are dump sites where it was manufactured or places where it was handled. Old appliances and old fluorescent lighting may contain them.

On country property, I'd be concerned about PCBs in two distinct areas. If the property is on a river (Hudson) or lake (Great Lakes) that has been identified as a PCB carrier, you need to be careful in using the water or eating fish. PCB-polluted waterways are well-known. The other spot I'd look for is a place behind the barn where used hydraulic oil and other waste liquids were dumped on the ground. Kids, in particular, should stay away. PCB exposure is associated with acne-type rashes in adults and more serious impacts in children. (See www.atsdr.cdc.gov/tfacts17.html and www.epagov/opptintr/pub/.) In 2003, EPA decided that private property contaminated with PCBs could be sold. Known PCB sites will be disclosed as part of the seller's legal obligations. But the "backyard" PCB sites, like the behind-the-barn example, will not be disclosed because the seller does not recognize it to be such.

5. Underground storage tanks (USTs) that hold motor fuels may be found on farms. The federal Resource Conservation and Recovery Act (RCRA) governs USTs, as well as solid and hazardous wastes. Farm-sited underground tanks holding motor fuels and heating oil of 1,100 gallons or less in capacity are exempt from federal regulations. Individual states may, however, impose regulations on such tanks. Federal UST regulations (promulgated in 1988, 40 CFR Parts 280 and 281) also do not apply to: tanks of 110 gallons or less capacity, whether or not sited on farms; tanks storing heating oil used where stored; tanks on or above the floor of underground areas; septic tanks, and storm and wastewater systems. All other USTs larger than 110 gallons are federally regulated if they are not found on farms. You are not likely to find an 1,100-gallon plus UST on a farm, other than the very largest.

USTs of 500 gallons or less, however, were reasonably common, because bulk buying of motor fuel and heating oil saved money. These metal tanks leak, sooner or later, and there will be spills and splashes in the refueling area. Removing a UST requires excavating it and all contaminated soil, then disposing of both properly. New, above-ground tanks employ a concrete containment vessel beneath the tank. Removing an old, leaky tank is expensive when done properly and a potential nightmare when environmental agencies become involved. Trucking contaminated dirt and an old tank to a certified disposal site can be very costly. Most farmers abandon a leaking UST rather than remove it when they become aware of the leak. Federal regulations allow this. For that reason, if no other, the amount of contamination is usually limited to the time between when the leak starts, its discovery and when it's drained. The distance petroleum pollution travels in soil is determined by the amount of the contaminant and the characteristics of the soil and ground where the leak occurs. If the tank site is higher in elevation than a water source that people and livestock use, the water should be tested. The more permeable the soil and the rock beneath it, the more area the contaminant plume will affect. Above-ground bulk fuel tanks offer farmowners convenience and savings, but their containment vessels can deteriorate over time too. Disaster strikes when the metal tank leaks into a cracked containment vessel.

It is possible, though unlikely, that you will find a property with an old UST containing one of RCRA's listed Extremely Hazardous Substances (EHS). Some of these EHSs could have been used in farming operations or on rural property used for various industrial purposes. (For information on hazardous substances, see Code of Federal Regulations, CFR Part 302.4; also Federal Register, Vol. 52, Number 77, April 22, 1987.) The owners of a single tank containing any of EHS is subject to federal regulation. Profiles of these chemicals are available on the Chemical Abstract Service (CAS) Registry, which assigns a number to each substance and provides basic information on its nature, uses, hazards and safe usage. Information on the CAS Registry's 23 million organic and inorganic substances can be accessed at www.cas.org/EO/regsys.html#q9. Databases on scientific information and journals, including agricultural science, are available at www.cas.org/casdb.html. EHSs are more likely to be found in dumps than in USTs whose main farm use was for gasoline, diesel fuel and heating oil, though some may have contained farm chemicals and home-made, wood-preservative brews (dirty motor oil, creosote, insecticides etc.; such brews were an early form of recycling). Regulations on toxic and hazardous materials have been and continue to be far less strict for individual farmers than on other businesses. Creosote, a familiar wood preservative, is still available to farmers for farm applications, though it's been otherwise prohibited. Cattle pens and chutes may show the tell-tale black color, even if the odor has worn off. Working farmers appreciate the regulatory leniency, but working buyers need to avoid acquiring a pollution problem created by barnyard chemistry.

Nearly all of the 714,000 active, federally regulated USTs contain petroleum products, not hazardous substances. It is unlikely that any rural land or farm that you scope will have EHSs in old buried tanks. Still, it's worth asking the seller to disclose his knowledge of any USTs or EHSs (just call them chemicals and hazardous substances in your contract) as part of your purchase offer. An old UST with a lot of old petroleum in it is a situation that should be addressed; it is a "defect" in the property that should be disclosed.

Buyers should have water tested for petroleum products and other chemicals where the seller discloses a UST or where the size of the tract suggests that bulk fuels and chemicals may have been purchased. If a tank is contaminating underground and/or surface water, you, as the new owner, may find yourself with some financial liability for the clean up under state law, even though no federal liability exists. Clean-up costs can be very expensive, and you don't want to buy a clean-up site. Old rural gas stations are especially to be avoided. I know of a remodeled station that a buyer bought to be used to process locally raised organic food products. The buyer found himself with a UST in his front-yard parking area, and the projected cost of removal helped to strangle the project. If you find a leaking tank, get the mess sorted out before you submit a purchase contract. Otherwise, use the appropriate adaptation of a contingency clause like this:

> **Seller warrants to the best of his knowledge and belief that said property contains no underground storage tanks. If such tanks are found subsequently, Seller agrees to bear the full cost of remediation.**
>
> **If Seller knows of or has belief of underground storage tanks on the property, he agrees to identify these tanks and disclose these sites to Buyer. Buyer then has ___ days to study these conditions. If the results of his investigation are not satisfactory, he may void this offer without penalty and have his security deposit returned in full**

and in a timely manner.

Buyer may choose at his expense to determine whether these tanks are polluting surface or groundwater resources, as well as obtain estimates of clean-up costs.

Buyer's offer to Seller is based on the assumption that the property contains no such tanks. Buyer is under no obligation to submit a revised offer in light of the presence of underground tanks and their remediation costs.

6. Waste disposal on site/dumps. Many farm properties I know contain abandoned or active dumps that are principally filled with household garbage, old appliances, farm junk, rolls of rusty wire, unusable buckets, odd pieces of this and that, cans, plastic, scrap wood and a cracked toilet. Waste petroleum products and agricultural chemicals may have been included in past years. In my mountainous area, trash was often thrown into a stream, or dumped down a hill or used as fill in a sinkhole—all environmentally bad practices. Dumping from a public road over the side of a hill was also popular. Whatever contaminants were present when they were dumped have probably leached into the soil and aquifer long ago. Active dumps, of course, can be actively polluting. Farm dumps are of more concern to a buyer if trash has been dumped into flowing water, particularly if containers of hazardous substances are present and still leaking. On the other hand, you should not throw a Greenpeace hissy fit at the sight of a rusted oil can in a creek bed. In that case, the odds are that the contaminants have long done whatever harm they're going to do. When you are worried, have a water sample analyzed.

These common farm trash piles can be left alone, removed, possibly burned or buried. While a farm-variety trash dump is visually repugnant, remember that ordinary rubbish is not a Superfund site. You won't die from it. You might ask the seller to clean it up as part of your purchase offer, but don't hold your breath. The buyer might expect a seller to do a *small* amount of such work, though no one likes to clean up his own mess after being made to feel funny about it. A house should be conveyed to the buyer "broom-clean"; the same standard applied to farm trash is defensible. Where the dump is substantial and you have reason to worry about it, get estimates of clean-up costs from local excavators and disposal companies. If it's just rubbish, it can be machine-loaded and hauled off. If there's asbestos or some other hazardous material, removal becomes more complicated and costly. Burying the mess may make sense with some types of rubbish. In most cases, your best option will probably be to do nothing if the pile presents only visual annoyance. Farm dumps may present an environmental danger where they contain significant quantities of petroleum or hazardous substances. Typical farm garbage is not subject to federal regulation, but local or state laws may prohibit current open dumping. Buyers should not let the presence of a small rubbish dump kill a deal, particularly an old dump that is no longer used. Consider it a trove, awaiting excavation by a future archeologist—perhaps one of your own children. If you get self-righteous and snotty about the seller's dump, you may have the door of your deal slammed in your face.

As part of your scoping, make sure to find out how trash is collected. Certain types of junk—wire fencing, wood, appliances, chemical containers—may have to be hauled to a central facility where you pay a fee. Some counties use open roadside collection dumpsters, and some require proof of local residency for use of their central gathering facilities. Public home-by-home trash collection may be the local practice, or private fee-for-service collectors may operate.

Federal "waste" laws (toxic substances, solid waste, FIFRA and CERCLA/Superfund) rarely bear on the type of farms and other rural land that most readers want to purchase. They can, however, be a factor when hazardous materials in significant amounts have been used or disposed of on the site. Under CERCLA, for example, a current landowner could be held responsible for the cost of cleaning up contamination when there has been a release or a threat of release of a hazardous substance from his newly acquired property. Liability under this law is strict, joint and several, and retroactive—and is determined case by case. Strict liability means the owner is responsible for damages without excuse. Joint and several liability means every owner is personally responsible for damages in whole, with the deepest pocket paying the most. Retroactive liability means former owners can be liable as well. Liability is extended without regard to individual fault. Offsetting this blanket of exposure and liability is SARA's (Superfund Amendments and Reauthorization Act of 1986) provision for **innocent landowner immunity**, which exempts from liability those landowners in the chain of title who were innocent of wrongdoing, where the contamination was caused by another, where the landowner had no knowledge of the hazard, where the landowner came to own the property after the contamination had occurred, where the landowner had used "due care" to determine whether the property he was purchasing contained a hazard, and where the landowner exercised reasonable precautions in exercising his ownership rights. Scoping is one protection for the buyer; the other is a **disclosure clause** in the purchase offer by which the seller warrants that no such waste-disposal sites exist on the property.

I recently sent for information on a 9,000-acre property in West Virginia that featured active coal mining, royalty-producing gas wells and merchantable timber. This type of property can throw off a good bit of cash, and sale of the merchantable timber could do a lot to pay down the mortgage immediately. When I looked at the owner-supplied survey, I noticed the following note in fine print: "3.0-acre +/-soil-covered dump unknown contents." The seller's prospectus contained these statements:

> While the information contained herein is believed to be accurate to the best of Seller's knowledge, the Seller expressly disclaims any and all liabilities for representations or warranties, if any, express or implied, contained in, or omitted from this Offering Memorandum or any other written or oral communication transmitted or made available to you as a prospective bidder. This includes but is not limited to any representations as to possible yields in terms of coal, oil, gas, timber or other mineral products, which are solely estimates.
>
> All properties will be conveyed "AS IS, WHERE IS, WITH ALL FAULTS" regarding any conditions affecting the properties with no representations or warranties whatsoever expressed or implied.

This language is a very big, very red flag. There's no telling what's in the three-acre dump, for example, and whether contaminants are affecting neighboring houses. The seller is clearly trying to exempt himself from all liability, which means he was trying to shift it to the buyer. This seller, I thought, knew or suspected something that he didn't want to disclose. His written warning amounted to a statement: "I ain't tellin' you nothin'. Take it or leave it." I also discovered that the timber volumes were inflated, and the coal was marginal. What I couldn't determine was what was in the dump. Since the tract joined an industrial/chemical area, I assumed the worst. Had the other assets proved up, an offer might have made sense for the tract less the three acres of dump. Or an escrow could have been set up to fund a dump investigation and resolution. As a rule, I advise buyers to stay away from property where the seller is standing in front of it waving a red flag. I told my client to forget this one, which he did.

7. Livestock create waste. Inevitably. Managing manure can range from mucking out a one-horse stall every couple of weeks and giving the stuff to neighbors for their gardens to operating a computer-run, mechanized system to gather and then treat the daily waste of 5,000 hogs. Where livestock grazes on pasture that permits access to running surface water, pollution will appear downstream. You may find algae, aquatic plant growth, suspended solids and higher-than-normal amounts of manure-related substances, including pathogens, nitrogen and phosphorous. The degree of pollution will depend on the amount of "loading" that goes on upstream, the characteristics of the stream itself and your distance from the source. Watersheds (surface waters) would undoubtedly be cleaner were livestock fenced out of running water, but farmers generally oppose doing this owing to its expense (fencing, gates, installation of water tanks), costs (less pasture to graze), maintenance and inconvenience.

Where livestock production is concentrated in factory-like buildings ("houses"), huge amounts of manure are gathered, stored and eventually applied to fields in one or another manner. Manure's potassium, nitrogen and phosphorous substitute for purchased chemical fertilizer. Farmers are expected to manage these nutrients so as to keep them from polluting waterways. The farmer is expected to apply the manure to his fields at a time and rate appropriate to conditions to prevent pollution. The primary problem in this system is its potential to pollute surface waters, though underground waters can also become contaminated. Much depends on how and when the farmer spreads manure. Nutrient-management plans certainly help prevent water pollution, but the continuing presence of polluted waterways suggest that unregulated, "non-point sources" of pollution, such as manured fields, are still a source of pollution.

8. Oil and gas wells involve environmental hazards in getting the resource out of the ground and transporting it away from the well. The typical pattern is for a driller to work on a pad of an acre or less. The drilling occurs in a small area that is circumscribed by an earthen berm high enough to contain spills. Drilling excavates material that can be contaminated with lubricants and other substances. This is generally not a problem, unless severe weather causes a breach in the berm thus allowing the contamination to get into surface waters. An all-weather road needs to be constructed to the drilling site to provide access for heavy service vehicles. Once the drilling is done, a working well has a "Christmas tree" of pipes left in place. Gas is piped from the wellhead to larger lines, usually underground, for transmission. When oil comes up with natural gas, it is separated at the well and collected in large metal tanks. Gas wells and lines, both above-and below-ground, present explosion hazards, though these rarely occur. Where oil pipelines are above ground, they can be a spaghetti of ugliness and may leak. Pumping stations are noisy. Trucks that pick up oil are heavy and often rut up roads and weaken bridges on property where their tanks and lines are located. Property with oil wells are more environmentally burdened than those with gas-only wells. Abandoned oil tanks and pipes may be left on the property to rot. Old leases allow mineral lessees (developers) to do pretty much what they want with the surface, consistent with current state law. A lease you (lessor/owner of minerals) sign with a lessee can include restrictions on surface use.

Coal is mined from Pennsylvania to Alabama, Ohio to the Midwest, Texas and into the Rockies. Abandoned underground (deep) mines can present problems of surface subsidence, fractured water tables and acid (sulfuric) drainage into surface waters, among other things. Underground fires can burn in these old works for years. Old piles of discarded mine wastes are unsightly, can burn and can be unstable when used to impound water. Prior to federal surface-mining regulation in the late 1970s, abandoned surface mines often left high walls winding around a mountain and unstable banks on the down slope where rock and dirt (overburden) had been dumped. Federal law and regulation now require restoring such surface mines to their approximate original contour and controlling water pollution from active mines. Reclamation involves revegetation to control erosion. Flooding has been a major problem in some areas where mountain-top-removal surface mining has occurred.

Active underground and surface mining continue to create contentious environmental situations—flooding, blasting noise, collateral damage, dust, noise, traffic, road damage, water pollution, among others—in areas next to and around the operations. For that reason, I would be very cautious about buying property near an active mine or quarry.

9. Inhalation of air-borne, invisible **asbestos** fibers causes asbestosis (a disease that causes increasing amounts of scar tissue to form in the lungs), mesothelioma (a cancer in the lining of the lungs) and other cancers of the lung, stomach, large intestine, kidneys, larynx and rectum. The more fibers inhaled, the greater the risk of disease. Easily crumpled (friable), disintegrating asbestos is highly dangerous; asbestos that is not friable and disintegrating is not immediately dangerous, because fibers are not being released.

Homes built before 1981 might contain asbestos in the form of pipe or boiler insulation, external shingles, vinyl floor tile, acoustical ceilings ("cottage-cheese" ceilings), plasterboard, cement (glue), fireproofing insulation, roofing insulation (Zonolite is the brand name of the W.R. Grace Company product) or as safety boards shielding walls and floors from woodstoves and fireplaces. Asbestos should be taken seriously. Homeowners are put at risk when asbestos products are disturbed or are disintegrating, thus releasing fibers that are then inhaled. As of 2001, there were between 150,000 and 200,000 lawsuits pending against companies that produced, sold or installed asbestos products, and 300,000 others have been resolved. (Sabrina Jones, "Grace under Pressure," Washington Post, March 19, 2001.) Twenty-six companies have had to seek bankruptcy protection, and claimants were awarded about $20 billion between 1981 and 2001. Six class actions and more than 121,000 claims have been filed against W.R. Grace alone arising from its Zonolite attic insulation. In 2006, class-action lawyers continue to advertise for clients who have suffered asbestos injury. Some of these many asbestos claims are without merit, but many are legitimate.

If the asbestos product is not releasing fibers, you are not in immediate danger. If you suspect disintegrating tile floor, it is probably better to lay a new floor over the old one than to remove the tile, which would release fibers. Similarly, encasing intact asbestos pipe insulation with a sandwich wrap of heavy plastic and duct tape should stabilize the situation and prevent fiber release. If, on the other hand, you find floor tile or pipe insulation actively disintegrating, crumbling, or flaking, then it will have to be removed by a specialist. If you suspect a house has asbestos attic insulation, you may be able to have a specialist contain it in place. You want to avoid any activity—attic fans, human movement, air infiltration—that stirs the insulation, releasing fibers. Any removal work must contain and remove all the fibers released in the removal, a process that involves specialized equipment and training. Both the material and all released (invisible) fibers have to be taken out and disposed of properly. If you suspect asbestos, carefully cut off a small piece of the material (then place it in a plastic bag) and have it tested at a lab. If you find yourself facing a large asbestos-removal problem, get a couple of cost estimates and then determine how to proceed with the contract.

The seller may or may not know he has an asbestos problem. You can certainly ask him to disclose any asbestos as part of your purchase-offer contract. Don't be surprised if he is miffed by your inquiries and sampling. Be especially vigilant on properties being sold as is.

In addition to asbestos in older rural houses, you might look for it in older, insulated farm buildings, shops where asbestos sheets were used as pads for hot metal, around water pipes and furnaces in old poultry houses and trash dumps where you might find a pile of deteriorating house shingles.

10. One country smell that is both pleasant and dangerous is **wood smoke**. Many rural homes, both old and new, burn wood for heat as I do. Fireplaces continue to be a popular feature in new-home construction. The heat from woodstoves and fireplaces is direct, and many individuals, including my wife, prefer it to other forms. The smoke and combustion products from burning wood, however, present health hazards to users, neighbors and communities that shouldn't be ignored. Wood-burning results in smoke that contains over 200 chemicals and chemical-compound groups. These include substances that have been shown to cause various cancers, which occur more often in individuals exposed to wood smoke. The airborne particulate matter in wood smoke ranges from invisible particles that penetrate into the bottom of the human lung where oxygen is exchanged for carbon dioxide to larger particles that can cause respiratory problems in the nose and upper respiratory tract. The dust that you find on your book shelves and television in a house burning wood may be of less concern than the smaller particles. Each time you open the door of a woodstove, a bit of smoke is released into the room, especially if the flue is not drawing well. Old stoves tend to be leaky and not air-tight. If the house you are looking at is tightly caulked, well insulated, with modern windows, you may not have sufficient exchange of outside air for inside air. Smoke particulate will hang around. The dust generated from cleaning out wood ash, flue pipes and chimneys (creosote, tars, etc.) contains concentrations of toxic chemicals; don't mix stove ash into your garden soil. Burning plastics and other household trash exposes the homeowner and his neighbors to additional harmful substances.

Wood smoke can create problems in a neighborhood. Smoke from a neighbor's fireplace, indoor woodstove or outdoor woodstove can infiltrate your non-wood-smoke-burning house, leading to the same kind of harmful exposure. The worst wood smoke generators in my experience are the large **outdoor wood-burning stoves** that are scaled up to supply a house with hot water (for heat and personal use) and operate year round. Unlike an indoor wood stove or fireplace, the tops of their flues are relatively close to the ground. When their smoke is blown around, it can hang low as it visits your house. Outdoor stoves can put out a fair amount of smoke, depending, of course, on the type of wood being burned, intensity of the fire and the design of the stove. Look for a shed with a metal flue near the house; the seller will know whether neighbors use these furnaces.

Local communities in a number of states now regulate the quantity of wood smoke by banning wood-burning devices other than pellet stoves or woodstoves certified by EPA as low-emission and efficient, and requiring gas-burning rather than wood-burning fireplaces. When choosing a heating system, consider that a wood-burning fireplace emits 50 grams/hour of particulate; conventional woodstove, 30 grams/hour; certified woodstove, 7.5 grams/hour; pellet heater, 1 gram/hour; gas fireplace, 0.07 grams/hour. (See "Reducing Wood Smoke Pollution," Bay Area Monitor, March/April 1999; http://bayareamonitor.org/mar99/woodsmok.html.) For all the bad news, go to: Burning Issues/Clean Air Revival, Inc., P.O. Box 1045, Point Arena, California, 95468; 707-882-3601; 707-882-3602 FAX; e-mail: PM10Mary@mcn.org; http://www.burningissues.org.

I have used non-certified woodstoves for years as our primary heat source. As I type these words, my old Vermont Castings Defiant is burning yellow locust in our living room as it has since 1984. Newer stoves are cleaner and more efficient. I think there's enough credible evidence to choose a different, cleaner heating system even though wood is the cheapest heating fuel available to most farms. (Cheapness assumes you already own a pick-up truck, chainsaw, personal equipment and logging stuff.) If you must heat with wood, you can reduce wood-smoke particulate inside your home by using a certified stove; maintaining its seals, gaskets and catalytic converter; burning seasoned high-Btu hardwoods (locust, hickory, sugar maple and oaks, not pine); burning hot fires rather than smoldering, dampered ones; and using a good-quality air-purification unit to remove particulate. The older the stove, the more pollution it will generate for a given quantity of wood.

I think the evidence is that wood-burning as your primary heat source raises your chances of various diseases and respiratory impairments, and adversely impacts your neighbors and community. You will not drop dead from a crackling fire in your fireplace, but the risk-to-benefit calculation is not any different from smoking cigarettes—and some evidence suggests that it's worse. Since wood-burning rural houses are more dispersed, wood smoke health risks from air pollution are greater in more densely populated areas, particularly those that are located in topographical bowls or where there's limited wind. If you're looking for a summer and occasional weekend retreat from the city, you're probably no worse off in front of a country fireplace than you are in your urban apartment breathing diesel fumes from buses and trucks. I write that sentence with regret.

11. Carbon monoxide is an odorless, invisible, tasteless, highly flammable gas that is a combustion product of burning hydrocarbons. Everyone knows not to sit in a closed garage with the car engine running because of the danger of being poisoned by carbon monoxide. The combination of unvented or badly adjusted fuel-burning appliances and tightly insulated and sealed (with caulk) houses can produce illness (dizziness, fainting, nausea, headaches, shortness of breath) or death. About 1,500 Americans die and about 10,000 become ill from CO poisoning annually. Old houses, in the country even those that have had their insulation upgraded, usually exchange air sufficiently to keep CO from building up inside. Be careful, however, in basements and farm shops. If you find yourself with a seller who boasts of the tightness of his recently constructed home, I would be concerned about CO if the house featured fuel-burning space heaters, unvented appliances or woodstoves. If you buy such a place, you should install CO monitors as a precaution and consider changing the heating plan. Combustion of gas, fuel oil, coal and wood creates CO; the less efficient the combustion, the more CO is generated. Wood and coal when burned directly in a stove are the worst of the lot per unit of energy.

12. House buyers often test for **radon,** an invisible, odorless gas that can be both airborne and in the water. Indoor radon is the second-leading cause of lung cancer and high levels are found in nearly one of every 15 U.S. homes. (See www.epa.gov/radon/; National Radon Information Line, 1-800-767-7236; and Radon FIX-IT Program, 1-800-644-6999.) A sampling test kit and analysis can be purchased for $9.95 at 1-800-557-2366. Hardware stores have them as well. Take the sample in the basement where gas is most likely to concentrate.

Radon gas is present in areas where underlying minerals and rock, such as shale, granite and phosphate, contain small amounts of uranium that decay to radium which produces radon. Radon is associated with specific locations around the country—including the eastern divide of the Rocky Mountains, Upper Midwest, Pacific Northwest, eastern Appalachians and most of the East Coast from New Orleans to Maine. The radon risk is higher in air-tight houses. Older houses that are not tight allow an exchange of air, outside for inside. This dilutes and flushes radon-rich inside air. New houses, particularly those with basements that are "wrapped," insulated and caulked, don't leak as much, which is good for heat and bad for radon. If the sample indicates a high concentration, the solution is to ventilate the basement/crawlspace better, either passively through additional vents or mechanically with fans. The buyer can use a high sample result to negotiate a better price with a seller who understands that radon is a real hazard; the buyer is not likely to get much of anywhere with a seller who thinks radon gas is a bunch of foolishness because he's lived in the house for umpteen years and hasn't died of lung cancer, yet. Give the radon results to the seller and tell him that he should disclose them to every buyer who comes after you inasmuch as radon is a latent, material defect in his property.

I once considered buying a very large ante-bellum house. I asked the owner, himself ante-bellum in his attitude toward environmental regulation, to allow me to place two radon samplers in his basement for 24 hours. Since I lived some distance from this property, he reluctantly agreed to send in the samples with the pre-posted containers I provided. He never did. This individual also objected to a home inspection and was offended when his pipe insulation turned out to contain asbestos. I doubted that radon would be a problem, given the limestone geology in the area. The asbestos could have been wrapped and sealed. While I waited for the radon results, he signed another contract. I was miffed that he had not sent in the samples as agreed, but I was thankful in the end that I did not buy a house that cost $2,000 a month to heat in the winter.

In urban and suburban areas, environmental testing and home inspections are routine. They have been less routine in small towns and the countryside, but, I think, they are becoming increasingly so. Many sellers will get fed up with 15 or 20 hazard-related tests; I would too. If a buyer insists on testing for everything, it's likely that a seller will do the sale with the buyer who probes the least and is willing to buy more or less, as is. Each buyer must gauge the level of tolerance a seller has for being inspected and analyzed. If you know from your research that radon is not likely to be found, you can consider not testing for it. The line I'm proposing is finely drawn: test enough to find out what you need to know, but not so much as to kill your own deal.

13. Working farms typically generate a variety of **chemical and hazardous exposures and wastes** in the normal course of raising livestock and crops in conventional ways. The exact substances will vary with the type of farming. Conventional farmers are routinely exposed to a variety of harmful substances from tractor-generated diesel fumes (particulates), dusts and pesticides to disease-carrying livestock and too much sunshine on their skin. Farmers show higher than expected rates of certain cancers and respiratory problems. As a buyer, you will have exposure to various farming-related substances if you do the farm work yourself. Whether you do this work or hire it out, you should read the health and safety literature that comes

with each product regarding handling, application and personal protective gear. You can also obtain the appropriate **Materials Safety Data Sheet (MSDS)** from the U.S. Department of Labor's Office of Safety and Health Administration (OSHA). Individual manufacturers also provide MSDSs on chemicals they make. www.ec.gc.ca/science/sandejean99/current_e.html and www.rtpnc.epa.gov/naaqsfin/pmhealth.html are two comprehensive sites for MSDS information. The sheets spell out the personal and occupational hazards of each chemical.

Most field chemicals that are now sprayed or dusted break down into their constituent elements over time. If a buyer is concerned about possible pollution of this type, he should make a list of the chemicals he believes were used in recent years and investigate the break-down times. A water sample can be analyzed for specific chemicals and substances that might be of concern from chemical use. You should ask the seller where agricultural chemical containers were dumped on the farm and how he got rid of extra chemicals that he didn't need or were somehow contaminated. Farms that are cattle/grazing/hay operations generally have had few chemical inputs, though a crop like corn may have been routinely sprayed. Animal medications and insecticidal waste products are generally tossed into the household trash; that's what I did in any case. Conventionally farmed row crops and orchards always use chemicals to control weeds, pests and disease. The seller should know what chemicals were applied, frequency and method of application, quantity used in a typical application, what was done with containers and where the equipment wash up took place. The most common chemicals and substances involve petroleum products, paints, solvents, wood preservatives, livestock de-licer, pesticides, insecticides, fungicides and fertilizers.

14. Rural air-borne pollution comes in several versions. Dust from mining and quarrying operations is a common problem. Long-range atmospheric transport of pollutants—mainly flowing west to east—produces adverse effects on both human beings and the environment. Coal-fired electric generating plants in the Ohio River Basin, for example, are linked to tree mortality and acidification of lakes and streams in the Mid-Atlantic states and Northeast.

The USEPA announced in December, 2004 that 224 counties in 20 states don't meet clean-air standards for fine particulates, or soot, 2.5 microns or less in diameter. This type of pollution is associated with emissions from power plants, gasoline and diesel engines, wood-burning stoves and the like. Much of Southern California, the New Haven to Washington, D.C. corridor, the Cleveland to Pittsburgh area, cities along the Ohio River and counties around Atlanta, Birmingham, Chicago, Detroit and St. Louis are among those affected. Particles this size penetrate into the lower part of the lung where oxygen and carbon dioxide are exchanged. Premature death, bronchitis and other diseases are associated with particulates. Federal standards are expected to be met in these counties by 2010, but five-year extensions are available. (Associated Press, "EPA says 224 counties fail to meet clean air standards," Staunton News-Leader, December 18, 2004.) While air pollution is concentrated in metropolitan areas, the downwind countryside may also have higher levels than you would assume to be the case. County-level air-pollution data are available from the USEPA.

The Associated Press assembled a map of the United States showing risk intensity from industrial air pollution by Census blocks. (The Associated Press, "Unhealthy air casts shadow on blacks, poor," Staunton News-Leader, December 14, 2005.) Poor and minority neighborhoods tended to have higher risk than white, affluent areas. Map 13-1 shows the AP's findings. What intrigued me was the large number of high-risk neighborhoods—indicated by darker shadings—in rural areas where intuition would not expect them. My guess is that these hot spots are related to the presence of smelters, refineries, paper-making plants, coal- or oil-fired generation plants and the like.

MAP 13-1
U.S. Industrial Air Pollution, 2000

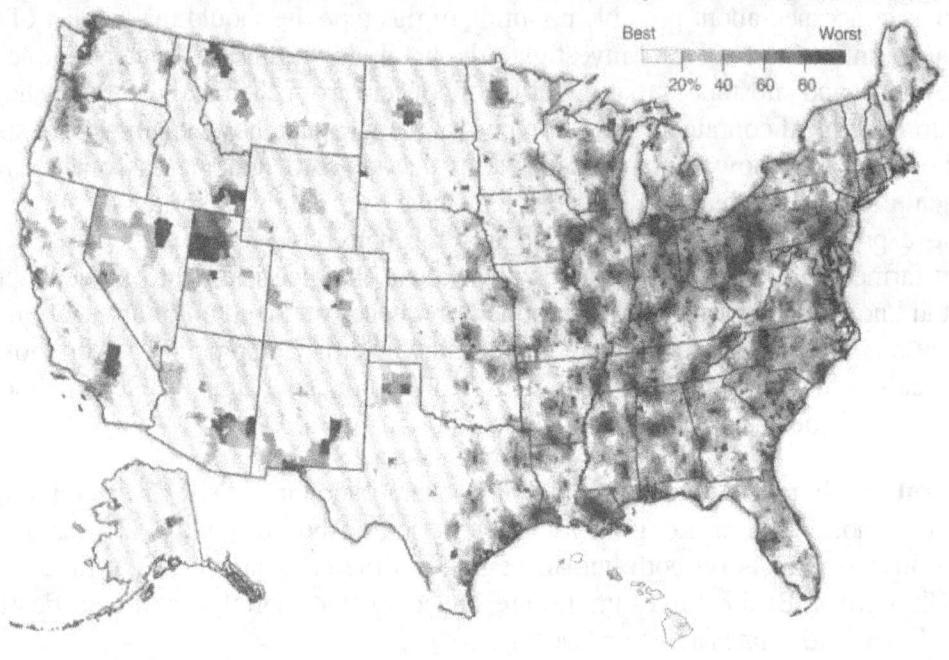

Every country property that I have looked at during the last 15 years has involved at least one of the environmental issues discussed above. The degree of seriousness, however, ranged from obvious deal-killers to ignore and proceed. I no longer assume rural property is environmentally "clean" just because it looks that way. When my initial screening turns up a property that I consider for purchase, I might work up a short environmental history of the property as part of my scoping. I explore the environmental issues I've outlined in this chapter, and then keep my eyes open for other snags. Talk to the seller and the broker to determine what they know, don't know and what they might allow.

You can also include a broad-brush **environmental-disclosure provision** in your purchase contract:

> **Seller warrants that he has disclosed to Buyer in writing all conditions in, on, under, around or otherwise affecting the property of an environmental nature that could adversely impact the Buyer's full use, possession and enjoyment of this Property.**

You can talk through your list of environmental concerns and even hand the seller a yes-no disclosure sheet for him to complete. A provision of this type protects both seller and buyer. The seller protects himself by disclosing what he knows; the buyer is protected to the extent that he is informed. The real-estate agent is also protected. (I am assuming that most states now have an **environmental-disclosure statement** that a seller signs with a listing agent since even Virginia now requires one.) If a seller balks at negotiating a purchase because of this disclosure requirement, I'd find out why. Environmental defects can be dangerous and hugely expensive in the worst case. Their consequences make inquiry worth the effort, even when you feel that you are pushing the seller's envelope of patience.

WATER HAZARDS

Water is usually the venue of most environmental concerns in rural property. Surface water is found in lakes, ponds, streams and wetlands. Underground water is tapped from springs (at or near the surface) and aquifers, which are subterranean water-bearing rock formations. Springs are a common source of rural water for households and livestock alike. They occur where a surface opening allows underground water to escape. Springs and surface water (both ponds and waterways) are readily seen on topographical maps using a 1"=300' scale, where a contour line is drawn at every 40-foot elevation interval. A local surveyor can provide a map of this sort for your target property or you can lift it for free from www.topozone.com. (Less detailed topographical maps are available from the U.S. Geological Service, and are often sold at local sporting goods stores and bookstores.) The topographical map will not show wet-weather springs that only appear in the rainy season. Continuous springs produce anywhere from a couple of hundred gallons per day to thousands. A spring is "good" if it keeps flowing during dry weather, even though the volume is less than normal. Wells, dug or drilled, provide about 80 percent of rural water, usually through the use of pumps.

Chapter 14 discusses water as a resource and the legal framework that has developed to resolve water-related disputes. Water-pollution issues can be governed by state or federal laws, or both. Chapter 14 looks at alternative ways that states govern water and certain pollution issues within their borders.

Rural water—both surface and underground—can be contaminated with many different **pollutants**, both natural and man-made. One of the first "looks" a buyer should cast is at the property "above" the target property, because water flows downhill along the path of least resistance. Do not assume that water flows south; water flowing downhill may be heading north as is the case with the upper reaches of the Potomac River watershed. Property "above you" is land higher in elevation, as well as land that drains upstream of you.

Natural and synthetic chemicals used on upstream farms can contaminate downstream water through storm-water runoff that gets into surface waters. If your uphill/upstream neighbor is applying fertilizer or chemicals in quantities beyond the ability of his land to absorb or break them down, some will end up downhill and downstream. It is harder for chemicals to work their way into underground aquifers than it is for them to contaminate surface waters. Property in intensively worked agricultural areas should have drinking water tested for nitrates and other chemicals associated with natural and chemical fertilizers, pesticides and petroleum compounds. Chemical pollutants can contaminate underground water supplies, particularly in areas underlain by porous rock such as limestone.

In thinking about the purity of the underground water supply in a rural area, the buyer needs to determine what substances are being used on and around the target property that might be a pollution hazard. It will probably be easier to find out what's being used than to figure out if they are being used in safe amounts. Since the agricultural practices of individual farmers are rarely monitored and the water-borne pollution from individual farms is not measured, a buyer in such an area is really looking for a pollutant that turns up at the tap or in some other obvious way.

The buyer might begin by asking the seller and the **county extension agent** what chemical substances have been typically used on the target property and adjoining properties. The extension agent should be able to identify commonly used fertilizers and chemicals in the area of the property, and direct you to publications and resources for more information.

The county extension service is associated in each state with a public university whose faculty is available to residents for advice as part of their appointments. In Virginia, for example, the county extension system is associated with Virginia Polytechnic Institute and State University (Virginia Tech), and each agent is a local Tech representative. The agent will have access to publications and research, much of which is available at little cost through the U.S. Superintendent of Documents or directly from extension-based universities around the country. Extension faculty often post their research on the Internet. Buyers should be aware that many agricultural academics are advocates of conventional, production-oriented agricultural and may deemphasize certain environmental hazards associated with conventional farming operations. Certain faculty may be paid consultants to agricultural-producer groups. I have seen faculty experts on beef cattle and poultry production marginalize environmental problems that might constrain production. Faculty specializing in environmental science may be more helpful on agricultural hazards. State organic agriculture associations will be able to direct a buyer to literature on the hazards of various agricultural chemicals.

If a large-scale agricultural operation drains onto your target property, you must ask questions about the neighbor's farming practices in a tactful, non-accusatory manner. Since both surface and underground water can be polluted by agricultural and non-agricultural activities higher in the **watershed (drainage)** than your target property, the buyer should become knowledgeable about likely sources of pollution upstream. The county sanitarian and/or the local public health official are reliable sources of information about known water-borne pollutants affecting drinking water in the general area, if not on your target property. They will know about nitrate pollution if it has materialized as a health concern. You can also call a couple of local water-treatment companies and ask if they have installed water-purification systems in your property's neighborhood. If they have, ask about the nature of the problem, what pollutants are causing it, what kind of systems have been installed to protect water supplies, and their cost. When you are walking through the house, examine the place where the water-supply line enters. If you see equipment other than a water pump, holding tank and water heater, find out what it is, what it does and why it's needed. If it's on the floor, it's probably a sump pump to drain a chronically wet basement. If it's in line, it could be something as simple as a fiber filter to catch suspended solids, such as dirt and grit. Or it could be a purification unit, which may involve ultra-violet rays, chlorination or other means. Systems designed to control bacteria do nothing to remove or neutralize chemical pollutants.

Nitrate pollution of groundwater is a human-health hazard usually arising in farm areas from the practice of ground disposal of animal manure and poultry-house litter. Nitrate concentrations are related to the amount of urea (ammonia) in the waste. Nitrogen is a beneficial fertilizer, but high concentrations of nitrate (nitrogen/oxygen compound) in the water can hurt adults and cause potentially fatal methelmoglobinemia (blue-baby disease) in infants. A farmer who is regularly applying poultry litter or manure to his fields in the dead of winter (when the land's absorption capacity is lowest) may be applying too much. Excess nitrogen, phosphate and potassium will run into both surface waters and groundwater.

If you find yourself considering property "below" a dairy farm, poultry operation or CAFO, get in touch with the county's **soil conservation officer** who is usually found through the local office of the U.S. Department of Agriculture's Farm Service Agency and the local **water-conservation district official**. Many counties now require such farms and operations to develop and follow a farm-specific **nutrient-management plan** that sets forth when, how and how much waste/litter/manure may be spread on their fields. These individuals may know of water contamination from such operations on or around your target property. The soil conservation official will be able to tell you about the geology and soil types in the area, which will suggest whether underground water sources are likely to be polluted and how far the pollution plume may spread. The water-conservation officer may be the issuer/designer of nutrient management plans; he may also be involved in monitoring runoff and enforcement actions as well. Unless there is some compelling—and I mean *really* compelling—reason to buy a property in the midst of these types of farms, I urge non-farm buyers to avoid them. You will not like the noise, smell and pollution they generate, and you will be able to do little about any of that.

Potable water is safe to drink. Your water supply in the country should be reasonably clear, free of man-made chemicals, free of harmful bacteria, taste good and not smell bad. In the best of circumstances, you will be able to draw water from a spring or well without doing much, if anything, to it. We've drunk spring water for more than 22 years, sometimes using a fabric filter and sometimes not. The bacteria count is probably higher than it should probably be, but neither we nor any guest has become ill from it. You want to avoid circumstances where you have to create your own little municipal water-treatment system at the end of which you end up with chlorinated water, no different than the most urban municipal supply.

The most common farm-based contaminant that affects potability is *e. coliform* **bacteria.** High levels of this bacteria, which is associated with mammalian waste, can cause dysentery and typhoid fever, among other unpleasantries. Sometimes, you can remove the source of pollution by fencing livestock further away from the spring or well. The problem is harder to solve if its source is a neighbor fertilizing his field with manure. In that event, the cheapest way of dealing with the bacteria is to treat the water before it comes out of your tap. You might find that the farmhouse draws from a spring that is being polluted by the farmhouse's own waste system. The solution is to replace or relocate this system, develop a new water source, or treat the incoming water. The first two solutions can range from $2,500 to $20,000; the third is less than $1,000 spent on a purification unit.

If the source is a neighbor spreading manure or litter on his fields just upslope of your spring, it is not likely that he will want to change his practice. Before you say bad things that will instantly create trench warfare between you and your new neighbor, consider that the local judge is not likely to side with your complaint since the practice preceded your ownership. Rise above your anger as you write a check for $1,000 to install a treatment system. If your neighbor agrees to not spread above your spring, consider yourself blessed and show him your appreciation. Offer him the cost of the treatment system in reimbursement and hope that he takes it. Then you're square, which is where you want to be in the country.

E. coliform is the common indicator for contaminated water. Several water-borne diseases are associated with contamination from sewage, human or animal waste. *E. coli* 0157:H7, one strain of Escherichia coli, is found on some cattle farms. When infected cattle are processed, it can be incorporated into hamburger. Live cattle can infect water where you swim or from which you drink. **Giardiasis** is a diarrheal illness that is caused by a one-celled parasite, *Giardia intestinalis*, which lives in the intestines of people and animals and is released in feces. It contaminates surface waters, such as lakes, streams, rivers, pools and springs as well as hot tubs and swimming pools. It can turn up in very remote places. Cryptosporidium is a germ that causes diarrhea and cramps, and Shigellosis is caused by Shigella, a bacteria that produces similar intestinal distress. All of these illnesses can be picked up in country surface waters that are used for drinking, washing utensils and swimming. For more information, see www.cdc.gov/ncidod/dpd/parasites/listing.htm.

Bacteria can be controlled with a home-chorination unit, radiation, ultraviolet rays and other methods. An elevated count can sometimes be cheaply fixed by regular **"shocking"** of the water system. Add a gallon of bleach at the water source, such as a spring box or well. Open the taps in the house and allow the highly treated water to flush through the system: Do NOT drink or use this water! When the tap water no longer smells and tastes of bleach, take another sample. The count should test out at an acceptable level. Most spring systems should be shocked every year or two; it's easy, cheap and effective.

Water-purification systems for the home differ in cost, complexity and objectionable qualities. Where the problem cannot be fixed at the source, the owner has no better choice. Be careful with lakefront properties where the shoreline is heavily developed with homes using septic-tanks and drinking water is pumped directly from the lake.

As a rule, the deeper the water source, the cleaner the water. Deep wells, on the other hand, are expensive to drill and can be a maintenance bother. Water from a drilled well should not be contaminated with bacteria since the earth between surface and aquifer should stop the bacteria from reaching the water. Some dirt and rock are better at filtering pollution than others. Property-owners on limestone karst should be aware that a plume of bacteria can travel a mile or more underground through this porous, cave-riddled rock. Limestone that is less porous provides good drinking water. If you see sinkholes on the surface, ask about karst on and around your property.

A **water sample** and laboratory analysis can usually be performed within two or three weeks. Any result that exceeds federally established levels, which both your lab and local officials (sanitarian and/or public health officer) will know, would be reason for concern. The lab you use will provide the sample kit (s) you will need and sampling instructions. Make sure to sterilize the tap by putting sufficient flame to it, and then fill the sample bottle and send it to the lab. Ask the lab to test for common substances, such as **total hardness, nitrate, iron, chloride, sodium, pH, fluoride, copper, corrosion index, sulfate, manganese, total dissolved solids, total coliform** and *e. coliform* **bacteria.** Testing for these 14 substances costs about $150. Test for **lead i**f you suspect the supply line, and **petroleum products** if you suspect that. Make sure to inform the lab whether the sample is treated (chlorinated, filtered for particulates, etc.) or direct from the source. You should test the water with and without treatment.

Public water systems must monitor for and control contaminants. The Safe Drinking Water Act (SWDA) and the SWDA Amendments set forth the requirements and establish procedures these systems must meet. Rural public systems draw from reservoirs, lakes, rivers, springs and wells. Each water-treatment plant must publish an annual water quality report, explaining the water's sources, what it contains and how it compares to regulatory standards. SWDA requires water-treatment plants to test for **microbial contaminants** (viruses and bacteria) and turbidity that come from sewage, septic systems, livestock and wildlife; **inorganic contaminants** (salts and metals, including fluoride, copper and lead) that can either occur naturally or result from wastewater discharges, oil and gas production, mining, farming and runoff from urban and residential areas; **pesticides and herbicides** that come from agriculture, urban and residential sources; **organic chemical contaminants** (synthetic and volatile organic chemicals) that are by-products of industrial processes, petroleum production, gas stations, septic systems and urban runoff; **radioactive contaminants** that either are naturally occurring or the result of mining and oil and gas production. Certain contaminants, including sodium and sulfate, are unregulated but are often tested anyway. If you are moving to an individual residence or small town in a rural area and are concerned about drinking water, read the water-treatment plant's last three annual reports. If you have concern about a particular chemical or contaminant, talk to the plant manager providing your water, or call the state office that monitors the plant. (You can call the EPA's Safe Drinking Water Hotline, 1-800-426-4791, to obtain more information on contaminants, standards and procedures.)

Very old homes may still rely on **lead pipes** to bring water from a source to the house. The danger of **lead poisoning** from such pipe is especially acute among young children, but lead in drinking water can also harm adults. Some historians pin the decline of the Roman Empire to its leaders poisoning themselves in this fashion. Ask the seller about the age of the water system he uses and what type of pipes are underground. Make sure to have the water lab test for lead whenever an older property relies on its own installed water supply. Lead pipe is now more likely to be found between the water source and the house than inside the house. Old lead pipe often snakes around and may have bulbous joints. Look at the pipe that comes into the basement from the ground. Lead pipe is soft, grey and silvery when you scratch it. Galvanized pipe is silvery, and iron pipe is hard. Lead leaches into water. Houses built before 1930 are most likely to have lead pipes, and those built before 1988 probably used lead-based solder on copper pipe fittings. Brass faucets and fittings made before 1986 are likely to have a lead content higher than eight percent, which is the threshold imposed by the SDWA amendments. Wells can be the source of lead where brass or bronze pumps are used, or lead shot or lead "wool" was used to keep sand out of the water. In-house lead filters are available. See www.propex.com/C_f_env_leadpip.htm and www.checnet.org/healthhouse/education/articles-detail.asp?Main_ID=147. Washington, D.C. decided in 2004 to replace 23,000 lead service lines by 2010 at a cost of $350 million owing to elevated lead levels in household taps.

Rural home-water supplies may also taste of **iron** or **sulfur**, making them unpalatable or unusable. This is a problem in the source of the water and is often difficult to eliminate. Look for iron's tell-tale redness in a toilet bowl and around sink drains. You will smell sulfur-rich water as rotten eggs. Both minerals can be controlled, but the equipment is expensive.

Groundwater can also be **hard** or **soft**, both of which present use problems. Calcium and magnesium cause water hardness which, in sufficient quantities, affects washing and cooking. Soft water is hard to lather and wash with; you never feel rinsed off. Both hard and soft water can be treated.

Spring and well water will also invariably contain bits of one thing or another—"suspended solids," such as particles of dirt, rock and sand. A fabric-type filter cartridge installed in line between the water source and the tap will trap most of this stuff. You will need to change the filter every couple of months; if your water pressure begins to fall at the shower head upstairs, one problem may be a severely dirty filter. Washing machines usually have tiny brass screens in the couplings that connect their flexible hoses to hot and cold taps. These cone-shaped screens keep grit from getting into the wash. Every so often, you should unscrew the couplings and clean the screens. As the crud builds up, the water flow into the washing machine will diminish. This lesson cost me $50 for a Sears house call years ago after I could not figure out why we had good water pressure and flow at our kitchen sink but only a trickle coming into our nearby washing machine. Whatever you find in your washing-machine screen will be in your drinking water as well, unless you have one or more filters.

Harmless water-borne **minerals** also build up in metal pipes and heating radiators. Older farmhouses may still have galvanized steel piping (a metallic grey-silvery color) that, over time, clogs like an artery. Calcium compounds, in particular, drop out of the water chemically and mechanically, and build up inside pipes. I have replaced 3/4-inch galvanized water pipe whose functioning diameter had been reduced to no more than 1/4 inch—thus explaining the lack of water pressure and flow in our second-floor shower. Galvanized pipe should be replaced when it's causing diminished flow and pressure owing to mineral build up. Replacing internal water pipes to and from sinks, toilets, showers and radiators can involve a significant amount of money, particularly where floors, walls and ceilings have to be ripped out and replaced.

Buyers should remember that underground water is an open system, subject to whatever gets into it. Sometimes it defies our best efforts to make assumptions. A neighbor of mine built a new house and drilled a well into a limestone karst formation 15 years ago. The water was plentiful and potable. Ten years later, heavy rains and a large flood recast the underground water flows through much of the valley where we both live. The flow in the aquifer that he tapped was subsequently polluted by the manure of livestock grazing at a higher elevation, a practice that had not affected his water previously. The same flooding reduced the flows to two springs on our farm, which we discovered in subsequent droughts.

A buyer may find a **cistern** for drinking water in dry areas. Cisterns are large, (usually) covered containers that collect rainwater from roofs. They can be as simple as a metal holding tank or an underground, concrete vault. Unfiltered cistern water will be no cleaner than the rain itself, the roof that catches the rain and the container in which it is held. Roofs will also contribute bird droppings, grit, paint flecks, twigs, insects and so on. Sometimes a buyer will find a sand-type filter on the line going into the cistern and other filters on the line coming out of the cistern to the house. Cisterns usually indicate one of two things: a lack of rainfall that forces the property owner to use rainwater or a problem with water in the ground. Virgin Gorda in the British Virgin Islands has a state-of-the-art desalinization plant that uses reverse-osmosis technology, but because the resulting water is then chlorinated some residents prefer to continue drawing drinking water from their cisterns. These cisterns were built to solve the problem of scant rainfall in a near-desert environment, and now solve an unanticipated "taste" problem. Cisterns may also suggest a problem with water quality—iron or sulfur contamination, for instance. In some places, cisterns were used because they were a cheaper way to provide a house with potable water than the alternatives. I've seen cisterns used on ridge tops where the owner could not afford to pump water from a spring down slope, or electricity was not available when the house was built. Properties located in remote areas are more secure for having a large cistern for fire protection. If a cistern supplies drinking water, it must be tested and the system inspected by someone who knows what to look for—cracks/leaks in the container, odors, visible contaminants and colonies of flora and fauna. Crayfish and salamanders are especially fond of these man-made habitats. If you find yourself with the unenviable task of having to clean a cistern, use extreme caution with bleach in closed or limited-air environments. Make sure there is adequate ventilation, and, if there isn't, don't enter without a self-contained, air-supply apparatus. Never clean a closed cistern by yourself.

When you walk through the seller's house, you should test for **water pressure** and **flow volume** by opening four or five taps at the same time. Pressure refers to the force with which water emerges from the tap; flow volume is the amount of water that emerges. They are not the same, though we tend to think of them that way. If you open the tap for ten minutes, you may find a steady volume with weak pressure or weakening pressure over time with concomitant reduction in volume. You want to find steady volume under good, steady pressure. Make sure to check the tap at the end of the line (farthest from the pump) with intermediary taps open. If the last tap still shows good flow and pressure, the system is good. Weakening flow suggests a problem in the pump or supply into the house rather than a clog. Poor pressure and volume can be caused by clogged internal pipes, pump problems, clogged/undersized pipeline from water source to the house, or problems at the source, such as low water levels due to drought or a salamander stuck in the pipe at the spring box. The buyer finding a simple problem—not much pressure at the kitchen tap—may be seeing a symptom of a major illness. In this event, the best thing to do is discuss the problem with the owner, put a plumbing-inspection contingency in the purchase offer and have a local plumber take a look.

Assume that each adult will need at least 50-80 gallons of water per day (gpd) for all household purposes, though it's not that hard to get by with less. If you have seven kids and are buying an old farmhouse from a retired couple who say with quiet confidence that they've always had plenty of water from their spring, make an effort to determine whether their supply as is will meet your much higher demand. And if you plan to water livestock from the same spring the house draws from, figure in 35 gallons per day for each milk cow, 20 gpd for each beef cow, 12 gpd for each horse, four gpd for each hog, two gpd for each sheep and at least one gpd for each dog. The spring system should be designed so that the household is served first, then the livestock. The household pipe at the spring should be lowest in the spring box so that it draws first.

If a buyer determines the need to replace the **water supply line** from the source to the house, its cost will be determined mainly by the excavation requirements—length of the run and depth of the trench. A two-inch-diameter flexible plastic pipe is more than adequate to supply a household and barn; most excavators will recommend one inch to inch-and-a-quarter pipe instead. The extra cost of the larger diameter pipe is small and provides a margin of protection against long-term silt build up. No owner wants to replace this line more than once in a lifetime; actually no owner wants to replace this line ever. Replacing a water line will mean digging a trench from source to house that may cross roads, other buried lines and lawns. The excavation scar will take months to fade. The most complicated part of doing this work is getting the new water line into your basement, which involves exposing the outside basement wall and possibly enlarging the existing entrance hole.

Water lines must be buried below the frost line, which in some northern or high-elevation areas can be as deep as 40 inches underground. The deeper the trench, the more it will cost to excavate. A spring-fed line that contains an open overflow outlet will resist freezing. A plastic water line should not be buried deeper than just below the frost line. A farmer I know who over-engineers all things he builds buried his new plastic line eight feet deep on the theory that if four was recommended eight had to be better. Not so; the extra weight crushed the pipe, which led to every farmer's nightmare—repair the repair you just repaired. Soft dirt, gravel or sand should be hand-shoveled around the new pipe so that when the backhoe refills the trench, sharp, heavy rocks don't puncture the line.

If you're working with a gravity-flow system or one with a pump located at the source, you would do well to install a two-inch-diameter stub line about 50 feet before the line enters the house. Fit the vertical stub with a brass fitting that matches the threads of the local fire department's hoses. This will help a little, but a pumper could easily overload the spring's capacity to supply volume. Still, **a fire stub** is cheap, easy to install and may help a bit. Ponds that are developed for fire protection typically use a four-inch-diameter or larger, L-shaped pipe located about three feet below the water's surface. The vertical section of this pipe appears next to a spot in the road where the fire department can get its pumpers.

If a buyer comes to believe that improving the seller's water system is a necessity, he should gather the proof and present it to the owner as part of the purchase offer. The buyer is not likely to get a seller to replace a functioning, non-hazardous system because it's not functioning to the buyer's higher standard. Buyers must exercise cautious judgment when criticizing a water system the owner has used for years with no apparent problems or ill effects. A seller will interpret nerdy nit-picking as being rooted in the buyer's cultural arrogance or stupidity. A lead problem is not frivolous; a crayfish found in the spring is.

The easiest way to evaluate potential problems is to include a **water contingency** in any purchase offer. It might be worded this way:

The Parties agree that the sale of this property is contingent on Buyer obtaining at his expense water-sample results in the house taps that he deems satisfactory.

Seller agrees to allow Buyer access at a mutually agreeable time to both household tap water and water sources for the purpose of drawing samples. Buyer agrees to take samples within _____ business days of the date on which this Contract between the Parties becomes effective.

Buyer agrees to notify Seller of sample results within __days of their receipt.

The Buyer shall invoke this contingency or remove it within ___ business days of receiving laboratory results.

The Buyer may void this offer without penalty and all deposits shall be returned to him in a timely manner if the results are unsatisfactory and the Parties cannot agree on a mutually satisfactory remedy.

If you suspect one or more water problems may emerge from your contingency, you should give yourself enough time to evaluate the problems and determine the feasibility and cost of appropriate remedies. That could mean a window of as much as six to eight weeks during the contract's escrow period if redeveloping a spring and installing a new pipeline to the house are involved.

Some water-quality problems can be solved with a couple of hundred dollars; others—such as nitrate contamination—may require $1,000 or more in treatment equipment. The buyer should remember that a particular symptom may be caused by one problem or more than one. Low or irregular water flow at the tap can arise from clogged pipes <u>inside</u> the house, a clogged or leaky supply pipe from source to house, or troubles at the source. A high coliform count may suggest contamination of the source, infiltration of polluted water into the supply line, or contamination in the house system, such as bacteria build up in a holding tank. Repair costs will depend on which problem, or combination, is causing the symptom.

Clean water in; dirty water out. The "out" part of a rural water system involves **sewage**—human waste and water dirtied by human activity. The seller's **sewerage system** is largely hidden from the buyer's view even if the old farmhouse is still piping raw sewage directly into a creek behind the barn. I once owned a small farm in West Virginia whose farmhouse had a full set of indoor fixtures—sinks, bath/shower and toilet. An old outhouse was situated below the house, near the corner of a shed. I asked whether the outhouse was still used. The owner laughed and shook her head, no. Only after buying the farm did I discover that a four-inch pipe drained the farmhouse wastewater into the creek, just below the abandoned outhouse. Later, having smartened up a good bit I thought, I asked the owner of another farm whether the house had "an approved septic system" in place. I spoke the words—approved septic system in place—clearly and slowly. She said yes indeed. I later learned that the house used a three-inch metal pipe to drain sewage into a hand-dug hole that was lined with concrete block, with spaces left between each one. This "system"—a cesspool—to my knowledge had worked problem-free for at least 60 years, its waste load mixing with that of the cattle grazing above it. Such "systems" are not approved septic systems. They are still being used in rural areas, as are outhouses. In the right conditions, neither will adversely impact water supplies.

All new septic systems require a permit from the local health department/sanitarian. Buyers can best determine whether a target property has an "**approved septic system**" by asking the county's health department to show you the application and permit. The permit should include a description and schematic of the septic system, its location on the property and its capacity. If you are planning to add a fourth bedroom to a house with a three-bedroom septic permit, your plan will probably require enlarging the septic system if possible and replacing it if not.

A **septic system** is a means for disposing of human waste and household liquids in an environmentally safe manner. The system is composed of a settling (holding) tank—usually a cast-concrete box holding 1,000 gallons or more—that feeds more or less clear liquid into perforated drain lines as the solids settle out. The three or four drain lines are buried in a drainfield. Each line is laid in a trench and embedded in gravel. The design of the drain lines resembles the tines of a pitchfork with the settling tank at the throat where the metal fork is joined to the handle. The liquid disperses through the perforated pipes and seeps into the trenches and then into the underlying earth. The settled solids in the holding tank eventually build up to the point where they have to be removed. (Hire a professional to do this work; it is not something to do with a shovel between halves on a fall Sunday afternoon.) The critical element in septic systems is the type of dirt available in the septic field. Soil types differ in their ability to **percolate** ("perc") liquid, a process that filters and purifies the liquid before it reaches water-bearing rock. Heavy clays won't "perc" because they hold liquid in place, which creates a bacteria-rich marsh with the characteristic odor of septic waste. Other soils perc too quickly, which means that bacteria is not trapped in the ground before it reaches underground water supplies.

A buyer considering an unimproved property will need to think about finding a site for his septic field near his house site. The septic-field dirt must meet the local percolation standard. The county health department will provide an application for a septic system. (The application may also cover a well permit.) The applicant indicates the location and dimensions of the proposed septic field. The field itself will vary in area, i.e., number of square feet, depending on local requirements. Often, the area of the field is pegged to the number of bedrooms or the number of square feet in the house it serves. A 10,000-square-foot drain field—a little less than one-quarter of an acre—is typical.

Testing the drainfield site to see if the soil percs involves either a soils test or a water-percolation test. The object of both tests in most locales is to find a minimum of 36 inches of approvable soil underlying the proposed septic field.

In a **soil test**, the applicant digs three or four holes, each 36 inches deep, usually with a backhoe. The county sanitarian or a private soils consultant (who must be state-certified or state-licensed) will judge the soil's percolation characteristics by the dirt's color, look and feel. Ground that is steep is hard to approve. If lines are pitched too steeply, liquid will "bunch up" at the end of the lines or in the low turn, preventing proper diffusion. On hilly ground, the best chance for a conventional septic field lies with siting it on a reasonably level bench or protruding brow. A common **water-percolation test** uses a power auger at least four inches in diameter to bore four holes, each 36 inches deep. The holes are filled with water. The tester waits for four hours then fills them again and times how long it takes them to drain. A buyer needs to use the specific perc test required by the county's health department. If a private soils consultant is used, you will face a cost of $500 to several thousand dollars for this individual to prepare a permit application. Sanitarians in some counties still do a soils test of some sort for free.

Where a **conventional system**—septic tank and drainfield—cannot be used because the soils won't perc, an **alternative system** must be devised and approved. Alternatives usually involve some form of constructed drainfields, constructed wetlands that filter effluent, aerobic treatment or filtration through an approved medium, such as peat. Where an alternative involves constructing a drainfield over non-percing dirt, the 36-inch depth requirement may be reduced. Buying, hauling and emplacing such dirt or sand can be expensive. A sand-filter system runs between $15,000 and $22,000 to engineer and construct in my low-cost area in 2005. Alternative systems always require retaining a professional engineer to choose the most appropriate option and provide a site-specific design to be submitted for approval. Each state has its own set of approved practices and standards for conventional and alternative systems that counties administer. These practices are posted on the Internet, either through the state's department of health or department of environmental protection (water). Key words to look for are "onsite" and "GMPs," which stands for General Management Practices. The local health official or sanitarian should be able to provide an information booklet on conventional septic systems and the local percolation-test procedures. Information on alternative systems may or may not be available locally.

A great deal of information on conventional and alternative systems is available from the USEPA-established **National Small Flows Clearinghouse** (NSFC), West Virginia University, POB 6064, Morgantown, West Virginia, 26506-6064; 1-800-624-8301; 304-293-4191; 304-293-3161 FAX; www.estd.wvu/nsfc/nsfc. NSFC publishes the "Small Flows Quarterly," which discusses research and septic applications for individual houses and small communities.

If a buyer is so unfortunate as to have his house sited below his drainfield, he will find it necessary to pump waste water uphill into the settling tank. Pumps are expensive and can be cranky; repair is expensive and inconvenient. In this situation, you must be sure that the source of drinking water is located uphill of the septic field with at least 100 feet between them, the more distance the better. Local well and septic standards will guide the buyer as to the minimum separation distance for new homes. Old houses with old systems, however, may not comply with current regulations and persist by virtue of being grandfathered.

Buyers of a country house who seek to upgrade bathrooms, add a bedroom, start a B&B or otherwise find themselves seeking a permit from the county's health department or building administrator, may open themselves to having to install either a new well or new septic system, or both, to serve their projected improvements. Therefore, *before submitting a purchase offer*, the buyer should discuss any such plan with these officials to determine whether the current well and septic systems are county-approved and are capable of handling the increased use anticipated from the buyer's improvements. The other way to handle this is to write a **septic-approval contingency** into your purchase contract:

> **The Parties agree that Buyer's performance on this Contract is contingent on Buyer receiving a satisfactory review of his water and sewerage plans from the appropriate local building and health officials.**
>
> **Buyer may void this Contract without penalty if any such official does not provide a review that Buyer deems acceptable for his purposes.**

If the review suggests you will need to upgrade the well or septic infrastructure, have the official put something to that effect in writing and take it to your seller for negotiation. He is likely to say that any improvements you make for your benefit are on your dime, but if he is a motivated seller, he may help you. Use this time to nail down the cost and time involved in any required well and septic upgrades.

Composting toilets and chemical toilets are alternative systems that may or may not be permitted in a particular county. Do not assume that either type of self-contained toilet will be approved as a substitute for either a conventional septic system or an alternative septic system. Even where non-flush toilets are an acceptable option for handling **black water** (toilet sewage), local rules may still require that the residence have a full-sized functioning septic system for the house's **grey water**—the waste coming from sinks, washing machines and showers. Hunt camps and seasonal residences may not have to meet the same requirements as full-time residences.

Septic-system requirements are getting more stringent rather than less, particularly in populated watersheds with chronically high bacterial pollution. Even the most rural communities and those highest in the watersheds are now tightening their standards, which raises the cost of new residential construction. Buyers who tempt fate by proposing alternatives to conventional septic systems will frequently run into state and local regulations and local officials who will not be sympathetic or flexible. It can be a maddening experience. The rule a buyer should follow is this: learn the regulatory handles before submitting a purchase offer and, at worst, figure the highest cost alternative on top of your purchase price.

Common septic-system problems arise from design, construction and use. Older systems may have been installed on marginal soils, not pitched correctly, or not designed with sufficiently long drainage lines or a sufficiently large absorption area. The perforated pipes may have become clogged with solid material over the years, causing backups. If household water use has increased beyond what the original system was designed to handle, too much wastewater will be flushed into the tank and the drainfield will not be able to disperse fluid fast enough. These conditions can produce a system backup that will be noticed in the house.

Do not drain hot tubs and indoor pools into septic systems because their volume can overload the system and their treated waters—with anti-bacterial agents such as chlorine, sulfur compounds and anti-algae chemicals—will kill the bacteria that help septic systems break down solid waste. Water from gutters should not be directed into the septic system. Inexpensive septic-tank treatments add bacteria to a system; two quarts flushed into a toilet typically treat a 1,000-gallon tank once a year. If the septic drainfield is located in a topographical depression or floodplain, heavy rains or floods will saturate it, fill the drain pipes and settling tank, and prevent waste water from leaving the house. A buyer should look for evidence of water damage and staining on bathroom floors around the bases of toilets located on the ground floor. The seller may disclose a backup problem, or a local plumber looking for future business may flag a backup history for the buyer. Cleaning—"dipping out"—a system's settling tank of accumulated solids may be all that is necessary to make it operational. Cleaning ought to be done prophylactically for obvious reasons. Ask the seller to tell you when his tank was last "dipped" and who did it; check the system's history with this vendor. He should be able to determine whether the seller's tank needs to be dipped and how often you should schedule such work.

CHAPTER 14: RESOURCES—MINERALS AND WATER

DISCRETE ASSETS

Rural land is usually a package of discrete assets that has both a break-up value and an entirety value. It's important for you to know both. The break-up value of a country property should always exceed its entirety value, which, in one sense, is the price you negotiate with the seller.

In their pre-purchase scoping, buyers determine the sale value of each asset that can be leased, rented or sold. The sale of an asset can involve parting with a piece of the surface property or the right to excavate a subsurface mineral. In certain areas, a property will be valuable simply for its access to prized water or land. Air rights may have market value in windy areas. And rights to develop a special property, timber it, mine its minerals and so forth can be sold or donated as easements to conservation organizations.

It's helpful to value all assets in a property whether or not you plan to turn any into cash. Each has future value to you and buyers down the road. When you sell rural property, you will under-price it if you don't value each asset separately and show the proof of these values to potential buyers. Smart land sellers add the separate values of the property's assets—bare land, minerals, timber, water, air rights, aesthetics, improvements, income production, wildlife, crop entitlements, etc.—in justifying asking price. Where a seller can show fair and honest valuations of each asset summed into one asking price, buyers will have a harder time working it down. The flip side, of course is to buy a multi-asset property for a below-market price and then sell one or more of its severable assets for market value. Done shrewdly, the buyer can part out some of the property and pay for much, if not all, of the original acquisition cost. I've done this, and I'm less shrewd than most.

You should look for properties where one or two discrete assets can be readily sold with little degradation of the core assets that attracted you in the first place. Buyers of timberland are always looking for the fully self-financing purchase in which the property is paid for through the quick sale of its merchantable timber.

Buyers and sellers will not always agree on what is an asset and what is a liability. A 20-acre wetlands to a working farmer who is prohibited from draining it and producing crop revenue is a liability; to an environmentalist buyer looking to preserve wetlands for its habitat value, the 20 acres is an asset that may also have a tax-benefit value if it qualifies for a conservation easement. The farmer will value the wetlands low; the environmentalist buyer will value it high…to himself. In negotiating price, the buyer can emphasize the liability aspects of the swamp. On the other hand, the farmer may assign a $20,000 value to a fully-equipped but small and outdated dairy barn, which the vegan environmentalist will consider a demerit of the first rank. The farmer may stick on his $20,000 dairy valuation, because he knows the equipment alone will fetch that.

First-time buyers tend to think of each rural property they visit as a whole, with value determined principally by the size of the tract, condition of the improvements and aesthetics, such as ponds and views. The dirt-smart buyer should also value each asset that can be sold, leased, rented, exchanged, given or swapped. **The three assets that are often misunderstood by inexperienced buyers are minerals, water and timber.**

Typically, a property owner will own both the land's surface and the subsurface, which includes underground solid and liquid resources. The surface owner will also own certain air rights above his property. Air rights can be valuable as a source of solar energy (in which the surface owner wants nothing—like a neighbor's building—to impede direct sunlight) or as the right to air flowing over his property if he wants to lease the surface for wind turbines, which I once saw written as "wind turbans." (Air rights are often modified by zoning ordinances that limit the height of buildings and towers; a surface owner does not have the right to restrict aircraft from flying over.) When the seller owns all resources and the complete bundle of rights in his property, he is said to own the property in **fee simple**, or **in fee**, for short. Dirt-smart buyers always prefer properties that are conveyed in fee simple. Sellers should disclose when they are not selling in fee simple, but this does not always happen. The buyer-paid **title search** should turn up any limitations on fee simple ownership of record. There is, of course, the atypical situation where a property is not being conveyed in fee simple and the severance of some right is not recorded.

Ownership of land can be thought of as owning a layer cake of assets—above, at and below the land's surface—and the right to use, sell, lease, exchange or donate each one. Assets—goods and resources—may have market value. A "good" is often an aesthetic value—the pleasantness of the house site, a partially shaded swimming hole—that has cash value only in context. An asset may also be game habitat that the new owner can lease for hunting, a high spot that's suitable for a communications tower or a trail system that you might want to rent to snowmobilers. Many of the cake's layers can be pulled out legally for sale or rent. Legal separation of one layer from the others is often called, **severance**, or **split estates**.

MINERALS

Subsurface minerals are obvious assets that can be legally separated from the surface. In many areas of the United States, property owners severed some or all of their subsurface minerals—oil, gas, coal, rock, and clay—from surface ownership years ago through sale. Severed subsurface resources do not convey to a buyer of the surface. Subsurface owners have rights to develop and extract them, subject to state and federal laws providing for protection of the surface. Pennsylvania, for example, requires surface owner consent before the owner of the minerals can extract them by mining the surface.

Where a fee-simple owner/seller wants to **retain ownership** of some mineral resource, he is pulling that layer out of his sale to you. Retained ownership is also referred to as a "reservation from the sale." A seller can also retain ownership of a property's timber and water as well as reserve a right to use part of the property you're buying. I would be very cautious about purchasing such properties. The odds are that the seller will do something with the retained resource that you won't like.

Subsurface minerals can be owned by the owner of the surface who lives on the land or an absentee owner 3,000 miles away. Minerals can be produced (extracted) by their owners or by a company who leases the minerals from their owners. With the exception of large minerals-owning corporations, most individual owners of minerals lease them directly to producing companies or to companies who lease them to producing companies. Mineral owners can sell outright, the minerals beneath the surface, in which case, the surface owner has no role in their development. The involvement of the surface when minerals are severed are then subject to lease provisions, if any, and state and federal laws

Mineral rights are commonly severed. Their owners may then sell these rights or lease the minerals to mineral-development companies through agreements of record that typically run for five to ten years and are renewable at the leaseholder's choice. Rights to subsurface minerals are controlled by: 1) mineral deed, where the title to the minerals is sold; 2) reservation, where an owner retains the minerals while selling the surface; 3) lease, where the owner of the minerals sells through a lease agreement the exclusive right to extract the mineral, which he continues to own; and 4) option, where a mineral buyer pays the owner a sum that gives him the right to explore, purchase or lease the minerals for agreed terms by a certain future date. (Frank Gibson, James Karp and Elliot Klayman, <u>Real Estate Law</u>, 3rd ed. [Chicago: Real Estate Education Company, 1992], pp. 29-30.)

With smaller tracts, a surface buyer will often find that the mineral owner has leased the minerals he owns to a company capable of extracting them. A mineral lease allows the leaseholder to explore, develop and extract the last gram of these resources. The lease may set forth restrictions and conditions on his use of the surface, and state and federal law also set forth certain restrictions and reclamation expectations. The empty layer, the hole left by the mineral extraction, stays with the surface owner. Even after a portion of the mineral has been removed, the leaseholder may keep the lease active. New techniques may be developed to access deeper deposits. And natural gas can be stored underground in worked-out gas deposits for sale during the winter. A mineral lease may include all minerals, or only one. The most recent oil and gas (o&g) lease submitted to me amounted to an assignment of these rights in perpetuity with an annual rental of $5 per acre that would never change.

Not a good offer.

The holder of the lease (**lessee**) pays the owner (**lessor**) of the minerals an annual **lease fee (rental)** plus a **royalty** on every unit of production extracted. If the lessee produces nothing, the lessor still gets the annual lease fee but no production royalty. Lease terms are set forth in the **mineral lease** the parties sign. A **lease fee**, or **lease rent,** is usually a modest fixed dollar amount per acre that gives the lessee the right to explore, develop and extract the mineral. The surface acreage is usually the basis of this calculation. An annual lease fee might be $5 to $15 per acre for natural gas and a dollar or two per acre for coal east of the Mississippi River. A **production royalty** is based on an agreed dollar rate per unit of production, which may be a ton (coal, rock), barrel (oil), 1,000 cubic feet (natural gas), gallon, pound, or acre-foot of water. (Natural gas might also use a rate of so many dollars per million Btus produced.) Remember a surface owner who does not own these subsurface resources gets neither lease fee nor production royalty.

Mineral leases are written in small print usually by the **lessee**, the party that is leasing the resource. In the usual landlord-tenant relationship, it is the landlord/owner(**lessor**) who prepares the lease. Landlord-tenant agreements, written by the landlord, not surprisingly favor the landlord. The situation is usually reversed with mineral leases, so a lessor like you (the landlord/owner of the minerals) must do what he can to protect his interests in a "tenant-drafted" agreement. With small o&g leases, the lessor/owner rarely finds himself in a market where two or more potential lessees are bidding for his mineral rights. More often, the owner is approached by the only lease-buyer working his area and is handed a boilerplate contract. Where the mineral owner has a sufficiently large deposit, he may be able to create competitive bidding and negotiate better terms with a lessee. Owners of very large, desirable deposits have bargaining power that owners of a couple hundred of acres and less are denied. You can view a Texas o&g lease at www.landman.org/files/Forms/Texas_Form_659-85.pdf. This site is that of the American Association of Professional Landmen (AAPL) who are mainly involved in the o&g industry. The site provides a contact-information directory for every courthouse in the country along with step-by-step instruction on how to research a deed at https://www.courthousedirect.com/AAPL/Main.asp.

If you are the owner of a small amount of mineral resource, you can still try to wheedle better terms than the boilerplate offered. Unfortunately, most mineral leases in any given locale will be pretty much the same, so shopping around may or may not do any good. If you object to a provision in the lessee's contract, cross it out and write in substitute language. Don't be bashful about doing this. You have nothing to lose. If the lessee objects, a fresh contract will be produced. Before you sign is the only time that you will be in position to bargain over lease terms unless the lease includes a reopener clause, which most don't. Lessees are not likely to budge on the rental fee or royalty payment with small lessors, but you may be able to negotiate important limits and reclamation provisions regarding the surface.

Lessors should pay attention to the specific terms proposed regarding:

- **duration**—how long does the lease run? The lease may say that it runs for a five-year term, but in perpetuity is more likely given the ease of meeting the renewal hurdles.

- **resource definition**—coal leases usually include all seams regardless of depth; a single lease usually covers both oil and gas; a lease could cover all subsurface minerals and non-mineral resources; an area of possible confusion exists regarding whether methane embedded in a coal seam is covered by a coal lease or a gas lease.

- **area covered by lease**—the lease will usually cover every acre underground that you have in surface ownership, i.e., if you own 100 acres of surface, the lease will cover 100 acres directly underneath; some surface areas, however, should be exempt and protected from impacts, such as the acre or more around a house.

- **number and location of o&g wells** and other surface facilities that the lessee may drill and build; the small surface owner's interest generally lies in having as little surface activity and disturbance as possible to protect his property's value. The surface owner benefits most from signing an o&g lease that prohibits wells and other surface facilities on his land.

- **area and siting of mine and excavation**—underground mines involve a relatively small amount of surface in proportion to their size beneath the surface; surface mines, open-pit mines and quarries affect all surface acreage where they operate; locate surface facilities and determine their size in advance.

- **area and siting of any waste products**—how and where does the lessee propose to store or dispose of mine tailings, waste products, drilling muds, etc?

- **renewal**—what does the lessee have to do to be allowed to renew the lease; the answer is usually not much.

- **lease rental**—is the rental fee fixed at a specific dollar figure, regardless of the number of renewals; the lessor benefits from a royalty that increases over time. The lessor can propose that the royalty be adjusted every five years to reflect current market rental rates that the lessee is paying for new leaseholds.

- **royalty**—is the royalty a percentage of gross revenue or gross less expenses and other items, such as taxes, undefined "allowances" and expenses?

- **royalty**—is the royalty figured on gross output produced or net production sold; gross coal output, for example, right out of a mine may be scaled at 100, but after being cleaned and processed, only 85 might be sold.

- **royalty**—how is production measured? How can the lessor confirm the accuracy of the lessee's production data on which the royalty is calculated?

- **royalty**—how is lessee's revenue calculated? What is the definition of sale income for the purpose of calculating royalty? How can the lessor confirm the accuracy of the lessee's sale/income data?

- **payment in production**—does the lease allow lessee to pay lessor the royalty in actual production? (Here is actual language: "Lessee agrees to deliver to the credit of Lessor, free of cost, into the pipeline or storage tanks to which the well may be connected, the actual one-eighth (1/8) part of all produced and saved from the Land, or, from time to time the market price at the wells of such one-eighth (1/8) part of all oil produced and saved from the Land." Since the market price fluctuates, this lessor needs to make sure that he will not be getting product credit primarily during market dips.

- **surface**—what restrictions, if any, does the lessee agree to regarding

    - lessee's structures—type(s), height and location?

    - road location and design.

    - protection of special areas.

    - tanks, size, type, number and location; visual buffers.

    - transportation lines—all buried vs. on-surface pipelines, size and location.

    - frequency of vehicle usage for maintenance.

    - extent of exploration activity—type, location.

    - setbacks from residence—200 feet is typical, but I'd advise 1,000 or more.

    - excluded areas—areas excluded by local, state or federal regulations (e.g., wetlands or endangered species habitat, buffer strips along streams).

    - excluded areas—areas excluded by agreement between lessor and lessee, such as certain fields, woodlands, aesthetically valuable areas, viewsheds.

    - utility lines—size, location.

    - security measures—fences, gates, locks.

- **no surface occupancy (NSO)**—small owners (lessors) may be able to negotiate an NSO provision in their lease in circumstances where the lessee can extract the resource by placing a well on an adjoining property.

- **limited surface occupancy (LSO)**—the owner restricts the lessee to certain areas of the surface, or limits the type of surface structures the lessee is allowed to erect (e.g., no compressors).

- **"nuisance-type" facilities**—things like compressors, towers and storage tanks; they lower the value of surface property; if they're going to be put on your surface, you should negotiate over location and access roads. Ask for vegetative screens.

- **setbacks**—what setbacks in linear feet are included that govern the location of wells and other lessee facilities; setbacks should be applied to waterways, houses, other structures, orchards, roads, other similarly sensitive sites.

- **responsibility**—lessee's plan for spills and other clean-ups.

- **abandonment**—what are the types and level of reclamation that the lessee is expected to do when the lease expires or is released?

- **facilities**—is the lessee expected to dismantle and remove all surface facilities after production ends—he should be, if you can get it.

- **liability**—what liability, if any, does the lessee accept for accidents, environmental damage, damage to surface property, etc.

When leasing solid resources—such as coal, hard-rock minerals, dirt, stone, clay, etc.—make sure that you understand the volumetric base on which your dollar royalty is to be calculated. For example, **run-of-the-mine coal** includes coal plus whatever rock, slate and other impurities are also extracted in the mining process. **Washed coal**, or **"prepped" (prepared) coal**, has been run through a plant that removes the incombustible rock, washes away some impurities and grinds the coal to the size each customer wants. Depending on the intensity of this process and the characteristics of the run-of-the-mine product, prepped coal might be five to 20 percent less in volume than run-of-the-mine. It will make many dollars of difference to the royalty holder whether he is to be paid $1 per run-of-the-mine ton, $1 per washed ton, or $1 per ton washed and prepped. Coal royalties may also take into account the coal's qualities—hence, its market value. A ton of Wyoming's subbituminous coal has about half the heat (Btu) value of eastern coals, but also contains far less pollution-causing sulfur. Eastern coals, themselves, vary by how much sulfur they contain. The best coals for combustion (to make steam to turn a turbine to make electricity) have a high heat value and a low sulfur content. As a result, royalties are sometimes determined not only by volume but also by Btus and/or sulfur content. Royalty on western low-Btu coal will be lower than the higher Btu eastern coal, because the latter sells at a higher price. The royalty owner might also want to know the details of the coal's weighing. It is not unheard of for royalties to not be paid on full production. Another factor to be aware of in estimating the royalty value of underground resources is that each mineral deposit will be extracted at its own **recovery rate**, depending on local conditions and extraction techniques. The recovery rate of natural gas can approach 100 percent, while small, inefficient mines might be satisfied with a recovery rate of 75 percent of the coal in place.

Royalties can amount to very large sums over the years, depending on the quantity produced and the per-unit payment formula. An acre of eastern coal seam that is four-feet thick is usually thought to contain about 4,800 tons of coal; a royalty of $1 per ton over 100 acres of this one seam generates $480,000 in royalty to the owner, assuming 100 percent recovery. It doesn't take much time to mine that acreage, so all of that royalty might come in one or two annual payments. A gas well that produced only 100 million cubic feet over its lifetime at an average price of $4 per 1,000 cubic feet (mcf) would generate $400,000 in gross revenues during its producing life of 15 or 20 years. Gas and oil flows are typically strongest in the first few years and then taper off. The annual revenue from a well is usually split $7/8^{ths}$ to the company producing the gas and $1/8^{th}$ (12.5 percent) to the owner of the mineral rights who has leased the gas to the producing company. The life-time royalty from this gas well would be $50,000, assuming a $1/8^{th}$ royalty payment figured against gross revenues. New gas wells produce much more than this example, and the current well-head price is more than $10 mcf.

It is important to the owner of the mineral rights to understand whether the lease gives you $1/8^{th}$ of the gross revenue realized from the well's production or $1/8^{th}$ of the gross revenue, "less a proportionate part of the costs incurred by Lessee [leaseholder] in delivery or otherwise making such gas or oil merchantable, including a proportionate part of all excise, depletion, privilege and production taxes now or hereafter levied or assessed or charged on oil or gas produced from the land." If you are leasing minerals, you want a $1/8^{th}$ royalty based on gross revenues, not gross less expenses, taxes and undefined items.

States impose different requirements regarding the intensity of o&g development (expressed in number of acres needed per well) and minimum distance between wells. This is often expressed as no more than one oil or gas well on each **drilling unit**. Typically, oil wells will involve a 40-to 80-acre drilling unit while a natural gas unit might be 640 acres (one square mile). If the property contains both oil and natural gas, a new 640-acre gas unit could be developed to have one gas well and as many as 16 oil wells. Surface land may have more than the state's allowable number of wells if they were drilled before current unit rules were enacted. In that case, the existing surface facilities were grandfathered. State rules differ on drilling-unit size, so you need to check locally about how many wells can be drilled on a fixed amount of surface acreage.

Lease rental fees are based on acreage, usually so many dollars per acre per year. O&g royalty income is usually figured against the owner's proportional share in the drilling unit's acreage. In the o&g lease, you will find the developer's right to put together a drilling unit referred to as "**pooling**." If Joe owns 256 of the 640 acres in a gas unit (pool) and Bill owns the rest, Joe will receive 40 percent of the 12.5 percent production royalty taken against gross income and Bill, 60 percent.

If Joe, however, refuses to lease his 256 acres to the company that is organizing Bill's drilling unit, the company may be able to drain Joe's oil and gas without paying him a dime in lease fee or royalty. As long as the drill hole is located on Bill's land and does not slant under Joe, the law has traditionally allowed Joe's oil and gas to be taken without compensating him. In part, this is due to the fact that there's no way to keep the underground oil and gas under Joe from being drawn to Bill's well. The person whose well extracts the oil or gas becomes its operational owner regardless of its origin. This is referred to as **the rule of capture**, and it applies to resources that can migrate underground regardless of which ownership theory of minerals a state follows. (The rule of capture may also apply to underground water resources, allowing one landowner to pump dry the water beneath his surface as well as take water from beneath his neighbors. The rule of capture may or may not be softened by reasonable-use limitations.) If the mineral under Bill was a solid, the mining company under his land could not extract Joe's deposit without his agreement. Joe's refusal to sign an o&g lease will probably cost him his proportional share in the lease fee and royalty from the production of his minerals, but, in turn, he makes sure that no exploration activity, road construction, production or storage facilities mar his surface. While the producing life of a well may be no more than 15 years, surface use and facilities may continue for as long as the leaseholder pays the lease fee and meets the other "use" conditions of the agreement. The rule of capture is well-established law, but some states may be moving toward modifying it as it pertains to oil and gas royalties.

Where Joe highly values protecting his surface, he might either refuse to lease his minerals or lease them subject to surface restrictions. The most rigorous restriction is **No Surface Occupancy (NSO)**, which prohibits a producing company from placing facilities on the surface but permits the extraction of the resource. An NSO would normally include no road construction and no exploration activity as well. Surface-occupancy rules can be written broadly or narrowly, according to the needs of the owner and the producing company. Surface restrictions can exclude certain surface areas from having a well, or confine wells to a particular surface area, or prohibit all transmission facilities, or exclude/limit above-ground tanks and pipelines, or stipulate where access roads may be located and how they're to be constructed and maintained, or limit the types of exploration activities that are permitted. It is unlikely that the owner who severed minerals under the target property sold or leased them with surface restrictions. It's very difficult for the surface owner to persuade a mineral developer to accept surface restrictions beyond what his lease and the law requires.

While mineral developers obviously prefer as few restrictions on their development rights as possible, Joe, the owner of both surface and minerals, may have some leverage regarding surface restrictions on his land when Bill, who has 60 percent of their pooled drilling unit, is willing to give the developer full surface rights. In those circumstances, it's entirely possible that the leaseholder can agree to surface restrictions on Joe, because they may not affect his plans at all. It pays to ask for what you want, and it always helps to have your lawyer in the room when discussions with the mineral developer turn into negotiations.

When dealing with mineral leases and mineral-production companies, it's advisable to keep in mind the words of the late J. Paul Getty, who made his money in oil: The meek may inherit the earth, but not its mineral rights.

Mineral activity can have enormous visual, economic and environmental impacts on the property's surface. Exploration can involve seismic tests whereby dynamite charges are set off just below the surface and their reverberations measured. Less intrusive methods are available. Leases usually give production companies broad rights to explore, construct and maintain roads, drill, lay pipe lines (both above and below the surface), and construct tanks and storage structures. States may impose **set-back requirements** to protect residences, water wells and property lines. The mineral-owning surface owner has an opportunity to negotiate additional restrictions with whomever is buying or leasing his minerals. The fewer surface facilities that mineral developers install, the more protected is the economic value of the surface itself. The exception to this rule is undeveloped land that might benefit from a road network.

Natural gas wells are relatively modest affairs, involving a small "Christmas tree" of pipes and valves, possibly a tank for collecting associated oil, and sometimes a small building and a surface pipeline. The well pad will be serviced by a heavy-duty, all-weather access road that will be wide enough to accommodate well-drilling rigs and trucks. The level well pad is rarely more than one acre, a square approximately 209 feet on a side. Oil well pads are about the same size, but feature a moving pump and possibly several large collection tanks that tanker trucks empty as needed. Both oil wells and gas wells may be hooked directly into their respective pipelines. Pumps and compressors can be intrusively noisy. The possibility of a tank rupture or a gas explosion is always present, but the probabilities are not high. If you, as a surface owner, own the minerals, your lease should specify that all structures, facilities and materials (wells, tanks, pipes, lines, buildings, etc.) associated with mineral production should be removed once production ends or the lease terminates. If the leaseholder intends to use the depleted field for storage, this proposed language is likely to flush out that intention. The life of a well may be a few decades; the life of a storage field is likely to be forever. If surface aesthetics are important to you make sure that you negotiate language prohibiting surface pipe lines to the extent possible. Otherwise, you may find orange plastic or metal pipelines running haywire over your property. I've looked at a number of otherwise pretty properties in West Virginia that are disfigured by this clutter. Gas and oil companies vary with respect to how much cleaning up they're willing to do on both abandoned locations and active ones. The way a buyer determines what a lessee's policy is to ask in writing, either personally or through his lawyer. Your lawyer will also help you determine what level of clean up you might be able to force on a reluctant lessee, given the existing lease terms and state law. This question-asking should take place as part of your pre-purchase scoping, not after you buy the property.

Where the property seller is selling only the surface, you, the surface-only buyer, should expect to pay less for that land for three reasons. First, the seller is selling something less than the full package of land rights and assets. Second, the surface owner may have to put up with all surface activity and uses the mineral lease allows. Third, the surface owner will bear the full loss of discounted property value from the degradation of the surface environment. This can amount to a discount of 50 percent or more from a property's fair market value.

Modern oil-and-gas operations are less offensive than older fields, which, when left in place, can fairly be described in my wife's words as a "big fat mess." The best way to understand how a new mineral lease might affect surface property is to visit a nearby operating field operated by the company that wants to extract your target-property's minerals. Make this visit *before* you buy surface-only property.

A severed coal right presents serious issues to the surface-only buyer. The resource is mined by both underground and surface methods, depending on the seam depths and other geologic factors. It is not uncommon in Appalachia to find a property capable of being mined both ways. Underground mining uses either a vertical shaft excavated down to the seam of coal or a tunnel into a hillside. These mines can involve as few as a half-dozen miners and a couple of surface facilities to several hundred miners and a multi-acre complex of surface facilities, including a washing/preparation plant, settling ponds, refuse heaps, parking lots, bath houses (where miners change clothes), coal piles, loading facilities, power facilities, exhaust fans, equipment sheds and so on. The coal can be taken away from the mine by truck, overland conveyor belt, rail or barge.

Mining companies try to extract as much coal from a seam as is feasible. When deep coal is extracted, the surface can subside as the earth collapses into the open space. **Surface subsidence** can wreck buildings, crack foundations, rechannel underground water and springs, and ruin roads and bridges. Coal companies are now generally held liable for surface damage, but the cost and hassle of getting payment and effecting repairs can be high. Abandoned underground mines can catch fire and smolder for years. These mines can, alternatively, become flooded and leak sulfur-rich water that ruins streams.

Surface mining of coal and other minerals creates obvious impacts on a property's appearance. Surface-mining techniques range from contour stripping that cuts a bench into a mountain slope to access a seam to huge open-pit operations. In Appalachia, **mountain-top-removal mining** is a controversy-generating system that pushes the top of a mountain into the adjacent valley, thereby exposing the mountain's coal seam. This technique is also called **valley fill**, and it used to be called **mountain-top decapitation**. It ends up replacing a ridge-and-valley topography with a plateau amid the ridges and valleys. The 1977 federal Surface Mining Control and Reclamation Act (SMCRA) regulates the various forms of surface-mine operations and their reclamation. The law requires that surface miners regrade mountainside benches to their "approximate original contour." Valley fills are not required to restore ridgelines. There's nothing gentle-on-the-land about surface mining. Post-mining land will not look like the original. With the best reclamation in the world, the surface owner will not have the same piece of land after being surface mined. In some ways, however, it can be better than the original. Reclaimed surface-mined land can have economic value where flat land is rare or where it can grow trees or function as pasture.

I generally recommend against buying surface-only property in coal-mining areas. The surface-impact issues from mining are usually substantial, and your surface property can even be adversely affected by mining on adjoining property. If, however, you are looking for a rough-and-tumble recreation property that lends itself to off-road vehicles and hunting, worked out surface mines and other mining properties can be good buys.

Leases and state laws vary with respect to the rights of surface owners *vis-à-vis* underground and surface mining. The older the lease, the more freedom it grants to the mineral developer. Where coal rights were sold under no-longer-used, anything-goes deeds in eastern mining regions, the surface owner could not even get compensated for damage and loss until the 1960s and, in Kentucky, until the 1990s. These deeds and leases were entered into before surface mining was used. Underground mining—with its more limited surface impacts—was the basic method for extracting coal until after WWII, with the exception of some mines in the Midwest and West. The surface owners could not have anticipated the surface consequences these deeds allowed. A huge amount of "externalized costs" was foisted on surface owners until grass-roots rebellions forced state and then federal legislators to regulate surface mining.

Where minerals have been severed from the surface ownership, the surface buyer must determine whether the state where the property is found has a **surface-owner-consent requirement**, which may force the owner of the minerals to obtain the surface owner's agreement before mining/drilling occurs. Policies differ from state to state, and from mineral to mineral within states. The laws that I've read appear to have a number of "except thats," which restrict surface-owner protection. If you find yourself in this situation, ask your local lawyer to review the state's surface-owner-consent rules (if any) for any mineral that might be beneath the surface you're buying. The rule might be found by looking up "right of entry" if it's not listed under surface-owner consent.

It's interesting to me that I can drive virtually every Interstate mile in West Virginia and see almost no physical evidence of coal mining. These highways largely skirt the coalfields and where they don't, surface mining went on mainly out of sight, behind the ridge. The picture changes on the state's own roads, and the farther back you go, the more you see. A small-plane ride is the only way to understand the size and scope of surface mining. Had surface mining been done in areas more visible to the public, I think it would have been regulated sooner. Today, most surface-mining companies mainly comply with federal reclamation requirements. Erosion should be controlled. The sites will be regraded and seeded. Reclamation has hugely improved the aesthetics of post-mining land. But if you're buying land that is about to be mined, be prepared for a much different topographical look than what you see on the date you take possession.

If the seller cannot or will not convey all mineral rights to the property, you should discover this fact—if, for some reason, your scoping has missed it—when you present your purchase contract to him. You should write that your offer is for **fee-simple ownership**, that is, all surface and all underground rights, including ownership of all minerals and other resources.

You should, of course, get a sense of the degree of his ownership before you ever get to a contract. First, ask the seller and his agent whether the seller owns all rights in the property. Be careful with an answer that goes like this: the seller will convey all the mineral rights he owns. I have found that statement to mean that the owner does not own all the mineral rights, though he will give you title to whatever he has. A related answer is: "I don't know." In mineral country when a seller gives me an "I don't know" about minerals, I assume first, he does know, and second that he doesn't own them. I'm willing to be proved wrong, of course. Second, it's easy enough to look up his deed in the county courthouse and see what he bought and whether he's sold or leased the minerals since then. If you find words in the deed into the seller or an earlier deed in the chain of title like "**excepting minerals**," your seller only owns the surface and that's all he can sell to you. You may then have to track down the **mineral deed** in records that are separate from the land deeds. If the minerals have been leased, that document will also be recorded. The lease may be active or expired. In the latter case, a **release** may or may not have been recorded. When you have the title searched as part of your contract, if not before, make sure that your lawyer determines the degree of mineral ownership that will be conveyed to you and whether there are current leases.

You may also encounter a property where the minerals have been worked in the past, but no mining is currently being done and none appears to be contemplated. The seller of the surface may own the minerals or they may have been severed. If he still owns his minerals, make sure that they are conveyed to you. New mining and drilling technologies become available that allow the extraction of deeper or more difficult deposits that were impractical or uneconomic to work earlier. Some coal deposits now lend themselves to *in situ* gasification or tapping the methane while leaving the coal in place. Higher energy prices make formerly uneconomic resources newly valuable. Minerals can easily have value in the future, though they have none presently. If you don't own the minerals, you may find yourself facing unanticipated and unwanted mineral activity affecting your land at some point in the future. This is unwelcome.

Regardless of who owns the minerals, it's useful to determine whether the property has ever been worked for subsurface minerals for reasons of personal safety and environmental considerations. In the Appalachian coalfields, it was common for small landowners to punch do-it-yourself mines into their hillsides to extract house coal. Now long abandoned, these tunnels are unsafe and may be leaking acidic water. The seller, his neighbors and local surveyors may know the property's mineral history, both official and unofficial.

Some counties may have maps showing the location of worked-out mines. Some topographical maps indicate surface-mined areas and/or known underground mines (using a pickax symbol). You can quickly access such maps at www.topozone.com; use the 1:25,000 scale. You can also check out the **state's geological survey** and/or the state's geology office. Take a look at the **geological map** of the area; it will indicate known mineral resources. These maps are available from the state's geology office. The U.S. Geological Survey (USGS) is another source of mineral/geological maps. The USGS published state surveys in the 1920s and 1930s that contain county-level and sub-county-level information. Local libraries will have them, as will the state geology office and university libraries. Keep in mind that mineral maps show *known* deposits; a future discovery of a new deposit will not appear. Then check with the **state's division of mining** and its **oil and gas division**. Both offices will have maps, records of drilling and exploration, geological information indicating coal seams and o&g formations. In West Virginia, for instance, you can access well-by-well data—including production and ownership—on the state's o&g-division website.

The ground itself may still reveal its early mineral-development history. Look for openings and indentations in hill sides to indicate old coal-mining tunnels; rusting pipes and tanks signal old o&g activity. The Mineral Policy Center estimated in 1993 that the United States had almost 560,000 abandoned hard-rock mines on private, state and federal lands. Hundreds of thousands of abandoned coal mines, both surface and underground, also exist on the estimated 1.1 million acres of abandoned coal lands. Unreclaimed coal shafts, tunnels and high walls left from strip mining claim about 30 lives every year, according to the U.S. Mine Safety and Health Administration. And acid drainage from these old mines has polluted about 9,000 miles of streams, primarily in the eastern United States. Mining companies are no longer allowed to abandon mines without complying with reclamation requirements.

Each mineral has its own system for evaluating the extent of underground deposits. In general terms, a **reserve** is the least proved, most-iffy category; a **resource** is more confirmed. **Inferred resources** are less sure than **demonstrated** which are less sure than **proved**, which have been estimated on the basis of core drillings and/or other tests. Inferring a resource's existence is based on the recovery experience in similar geology and other information. **Economically recoverable resources** should provide a profit at current prices. "Current," however, may not mean contemporary; it may mean the date when the resource was valued. If prices are now higher than before, more resources will be considered economically recoverable. Each mineral has its own nomenclature. USGS and the U.S. Department of Energy classify coal as measured, indicated, demonstrated (measured plus indicated) and inferred. One million tons of a measured economically recoverable coal seam can be readily valued by determining the current market price for coal of that quality in that area. (It can, however, take two years for a mine to be planned and permitted, so the economics of extracting a deposit that is currently feasible may change.) One million tons of inferred coal resource may or may not be there, and if it is, may or may not be worth something. It can be proved up by drilling for samples. As energy prices rise, marginal deposits become economically feasible to develop. Economically recoverable coal is not growing as a result of new discoveries, but by demand-driven price increases.

I've touched on the monetary benefits of mineral development, the risks and costs to surface property and some of the issues that a land buyer needs to consider when minerals are involved. If your pre-offer scoping reveals the presence of minerals, I advise that you hire a local **minerals consultant** to help you evaluate the implications of purchasing this particular property. Your local lawyer is a source of consultant referrals as is the state's office of mines and minerals. This consultant can give you an educated estimated of what's there, its current and potential economic value, the methods that would be most appropriate for its extraction and the likely surface impacts.

It is relatively common in regions with coal and o&g to find surface property being sold without the minerals. These will have been sold, leased or retained by a previous owner. The seller of the surface may be trying to unload his land just prior to a mine being opened on his property. If the mining plan is in its formative stage, you may not be able to discover it. But if it's close, you may be able to learn of these plans by checking with the appropriate state agency that issues **mining permits** for coal, solid minerals and rock, and **drilling permits** for non-solids such as oil, gas and geothermal resources. The mineral developer will have filed a plan with the agency as part of his permit application, which will show the location and extent of the project, descriptive details and, possibly, a proposed reclamation plan. These plans and permits are public documents, and some proposals are subject to public hearings and comments. Ask the agency whether any mining or drilling permit is current or proposed for the property you're scoping. If a permit exists, request a copy of both the plan and the permit. Ask if the property has ever been permitted in the past and get copies of the relevant documents.

The state may have an **environmental agency** that issues permits in addition to the mining agency. These agencies are looking to see how the developer intends to manage the environmental impacts, especially on water resources, of mining or drilling, and how the site will be reclaimed once the mineral has been extracted. Mining generally involves surface waters and the construction of ponds for various purposes. The county's planning office, building administrator and the clerk's office may also know about pending mineral development. Ask these officials if they know of any plans—mining, drilling, development (residential, commercial or industrial), power lines, dams, road construction, public park or other facilities, and the like—that involve or are likely to affect your target property. Finally, call the biggest mining company and biggest drilling company in the area. Ask if they know of any plans that would affect the property you're scoping. Ask enough questions of enough people to make it highly probable that you'll pick up a trail if one exists.

Your right to the seller's full disclosure regarding minerals is not fully established everywhere. Severance of minerals is not what state judges would consider a "material defect" in the seller's property; the law doesn't consider it a defect. Therefore, while many states require the seller to disclose material defects, you can't count on that requirement to give you information on minerals. If the seller is conveying something less than fee-simple ownership, a local court would probably put the burden of this discovery on the buyer and his pre-purchase title search. The seller can, of course, always say that he told you about not owning the minerals, and then it's your word against his. You may face even less disclosure with FSBOs than with brokers, but anything's possible.

A Maryland real-estate agent called me a few years ago to look at a property that was very pretty and had some timber with commercial value. He did not inform me that the property was about to be deep-mined, a fact I subsequently learned from asking around. I also learned that he knew about the impending mining when he called me. Did he have a legal obligation to tell me what he knew: that the minerals had been severed and mining was about to commence? Probably not, given that he was representing the seller. When I asked about mineral ownership, he said he didn't know whether the seller owned the minerals. I took his "don't know" as a signal to go to the courthouse and find out. The deed showed that the seller didn't own the minerals, and a call to a local coal company with mines in the area told me of their plans. I've learned over the years that when a seller or a real-estate agent says, "I don't know," it often means either "I don't want to know" or "I don't want to tell."

Do not count on a seller's real-estate agent to know anything about minerals, though some know a great deal. Do not count on the seller's agent to disclose anything about minerals, unless you ask. If the minerals have been severed, they are not part of the surface property that is for sale, so the agent and the owner may have no legal obligation to alert you to this fact. Some states, such as Colorado, now require that real-estate agents for the seller disclose to potential buyers the ownership of subsurface oil, gas and mineral rights. Colorado contracts now include language that informs the buyer that purchasing land doesn't necessarily mean the buyer is also purchasing underground resources, such as oil and gas, minerals, water and geothermal energy. This provision is buried in five lines in the standard six-page purchase contract. In the event of a future dispute, a mineral developer will point to that very small print as having provided very large notice of possible severance to the buyer who purchased the surface anyway.

Definitive knowledge of a property's mineral ownership will be found in documents recorded in the county courthouse. I have never found a property where the minerals had been severed from the surface without a recorded document, though it's possible that a mineral buyer failed to record for one or another reason. If the buyer did not record his purchase, the mineral seller's recorded deed, or earlier deeds (his chain of title), should show the severance. It's possible that both buyer and seller did not record, in which case you won't find a document showing severance in the courthouse. This is highly improbable. Your backup protection is to have a section in your purchase-offer contract that provides:

Seller warrants that he is conveying the Property in fee-simple ownership with all rights to all resources, both surface and subsurface.

Seller agrees to disclose to Buyer any severance or reservation of interest in the Property's natural resources within five calendar days of this Contract taking effect.

Buyer may void this Contract without penalty if Seller is unable to convey the Property in fee-simple ownership or, alternatively, in a way that is acceptable to the Buyer.

If the seller knows of an unrecorded severance and proceeds with the sale, you will have grounds to be compensated for damages since the seller promised you that he was selling in fee. (You will also need your contract to provide that all seller warranties survive the contract, that is, the escrow period during which the contract exists between buyer and seller.) If the seller does not know of an unrecorded severance and a mining company shows up on your doorstep ready to dig, get a lawyer. Unrecorded mineral deeds are possible, though rare. Some states do not recognize property conveyances unless they are recorded, so your legal situation would be determined by the facts and state law where the property is located. It is unlikely that a mineral developer will try to get a permit without a recorded lease or deed in hand.

With the vast majority of properties, mineral severance will be recorded. But you may not find any mention of either minerals or severance in the seller's deed, which is the most recent one recorded. The seller's deed may be something as vague as "All that property known as the River Place, situated on the east side of Big Bend Road in the Samsom Magisterial District of Blue Ridge County, containing 100 acres as described in earlier conveyances." A deed as poorly drafted as this doesn't tell you whether the seller does or does not own the subsurface minerals. Some deeds will specify that the property does or does not include ownership of subsurface minerals; others won't. Where the seller's deed says something like "all mineral rights included" or "minerals run with the land," you can feel confident that the surface acreage you are buying includes the subsurface rights. Where the seller's deed says nothing about minerals, you or your lawyer need to backtrack the seller's deed to find out whether or not the minerals have been severed.

Mineral leases may be recorded in a set of **grantor/grantee indices and books** that are separate from the grantor/grantee indices and books that reference all other real property. Both types of records will be found in a county office, such as that of the county clerk or land records. A **grantor index** lists alphabetically those persons giving or selling property in one column and to whom the property was given or sold in the next. The index will reveal the date of the transaction and the **deed book (DB) number** and **page number (PN)** where the deed of gift or deed of sale will be found. Remember mineral deeds may not be indexed in the same index as land where mineral ownership has a separate recording system. A **grantee index** provides the same information except that the persons listed alphabetically in the first column are those who acquired ownership through gift or purchase from those in the second column. Mineral deeds and leases are usually indexed and found in their own separate books, but you have to ask the clerk. You may find a twist or two, though the basic system is the same across the country. Ask the clerk for assistance; you will get the hang of deed-researching quickly. Older deeds may or may not be in the county's computer system. Make sure that you check both sets of indices—the first for real property, which can include both surface and subsurface ownership, and the second for minerals alone—so that you don't end up buying surface property without its underlying minerals.

If you are having a lawyer do a **preliminary title search**, which backtracks the chain of title to determine whether the seller is the legal owner of what he is selling (and you are buying), make sure to have him check title for mineral ownership as well even in counties where minerals are not currently being produced. It is worth paying him to find out whether or not you are buying in fee simple. I've known lawyers who do not routinely check for mineral ownership/severance in their title searches. In some places, back-checking should look specifically for severance, leasing and other types of qualifications on the property's water rights as well. The title search will also turn up other *recorded* agreements that affect the property, such as life estates, reservations of interest, conservation easements, leases, rights to water for irrigation and so on.

Once legally severed, subsurface mineral rights can be bought, sold, traded, given away and leased regardless of the surface owner's desires. I've found two common patterns of severance. First, the mineral rights will have been sold to a large corporation that may or may not be a mineral developer. Mineral owners can also be land companies private investors or railroads (which own millions of acres in both the Appalachian coalfields and the West). The other pattern is for the mineral rights to have been severed but retained by a previous fee-simple owner. Where minerals rights have been passed down, several dozen individuals may each own a fraction of the whole. The buyer of surface only will have a next-to-impossible time in acquiring the severed minerals from either type of owner. If all underground resources have been depleted, the mineral rights have been liquidated and revert to the surface owner. But do not assume that because some gas has been tapped and some mining has occurred that the mineral rights are now joined back with the surface. The U.S. Supreme Court ruled in 1982 that mineral rights that were unused for 20 years could revert to the surface owner, but your definition of unused and the definition of use within the lease may not be the same.

When large companies no longer want a mineral lease, they will generally allow it to expire without further communication with the surface owner. Some companies will routinely record a **notice of release** in the courthouse, stating that the owner of the mineral rights of record has abandoned all claim to and interest in the mineral rights on the subject property. A **partial release** would give notice that the mineral owner no longer claims an interest in, say, the property's coal but retains his interest in all other minerals. If a mineral lease has expired and no release has been recorded, you should ask the seller as part of your purchase offer to have the minerals owner record such a notice. The only way that you can be absolutely certain that the last recorded owner of the mineral rights has abandoned his interest is to find a recorded release. The release document itself is boilerplate with the deed particulars filled in. A person representing the leaseholder—usually a local lawyer—records the release by giving it to the clerk, who then notes the time and date and places the document in the appropriate book for mineral deeds and leases.

If the owner of an expired mineral lease is unwilling to respond to a request from you—at the moment, only an interested potential buyer of the surface—a letter to the seller of the target property might produce what you want. This letter to the target property's seller might look like the following:

> As you know, I am considering buying your property. In researching the deed, I discovered that the subsurface minerals were leased to XYZ Corporation some years ago. The lease seems to have expired, but no release was recorded. I have found no record of renewal. It appears that you own the minerals.
>
> I would appreciate a clarification of the minerals situation before I submit an offer.

I am, therefore, asking that you request that XYZ record a minerals release before I submit my offer.

I want to buy your property in fee simple, with all minerals and rights included. I will offer less if XYZ refuses to record a release and may not submit any offer depending on XYZ's plans. The same would be true if you want to retain mineral ownership and sell me surface only.

The release should resemble the following:

XYZ Corporation of _____, ____ (state) which is the last recorded owner of the mineral rights for the following property, _____ acres whose surface is owned by _____, recorded in Deed Book __, Page __, in _____ County, State of _____, under a lease recorded in said county and found in Minerals Book ___, Page__, of same _____ County sets forth that its mineral lease expired as of _____, ____.

XYZ, Inc. claims no reservation of interest or profit of any kind in either the subsurface mineral rights or surface property.

XYZ, Inc. agrees that all mineral rights, in whatever condition, are released and have reverted to _____, the owner of the surface property.

I'd like to talk with you about this situation at your convenience.

XYZ Corporation will know what a release is and does not need to be educated as to its language. The point of the letter is to let the seller understand the nature of a release and put both the release and mineral ownership on the negotiating table.

Where a mineral leaseholder has done nothing under his lease to use the minerals—and "use" is generally construed to mean minimum leaseholder activity—a state may provide that the severed mineral rights revert to the surface owner after the passing of a certain number of non-use years set by statute, typically 20 or 30. A buyer should never assume that mineral rights have reverted to the seller where no drilling or mining has occurred once the statutory time period is met. The mineral owner and/or leaseholder may have met the state's minimum requirements without doing anything that is obvious to you. To find out how the mineral owner and/or the leaseholder feel about mineral rights, you must talk with them, starting with the leaseholder.

The buyer may find himself in a situation where current or past mineral production has left certain environmental and/or legal problems on the land. These may include mine-waste dumps, tailings, unreclaimed surface-mined land, ponds for retaining surface water, ponds for settling out waste (which may include toxic substances), leach fields, miscellaneous dumps of this and that, barrels of waste, etc. Ownership—hence, liability for clean up—varies according to the law and what the problem residue is. (See Chapter 13.)

Certain mineral-related things left are considered **personal property**, rather than real property. Personal property does not convey with the sale of real property, unless specifically included in the contract. A seam of coal is real property, but a heap of mined coal sitting on the ground and a heap of coal-mine waste sitting next to it is the personal property of either the mineral developer or the owner of the mineral rights. Whoever is the owner is likely to take the coal (that is, sell it before or after the property conveys) and is just as likely to leave the waste heap. While real property can be abandoned, it is difficult to do so with certain personal property. On big environmental hazards, federal law governs the ownership and liability questions. On small hazards, the surface buyer may end up with the former mineral leaseholder's personal property, such as a non-hazardous dump. In this situation, the buyer should try to make sure that someone—the surface owner, mineral owner or mineral leaseholder—accepts ownership and responsibility for surface-deposited mineral wastes before submitting a contract offer. Ownership of other minerals-related problems—abandoned tanks and pipes, sources of pollution, wetlands fills and so on—should be similarly flagged and resolved where possible before making an offer. If a small problem is inoffensive, it will stay in place and convey with the land. My understanding of the law is that most courts now hold that the generator/originator of the waste remains liable for any damage that is not covered by applicable federal or state environmental statutes. The buyer will need to determine the extent of any such minerals-related problems, whether they fall under the jurisdiction of a federal or state statute, what potential for damage they present, who is liable for any damage they cause and who will do the clean up.

States differ in how much say a surface owner has over how privately owned subsurface minerals can be extracted and what rights an adjoining landowner has for protecting his property and getting compensated for damage. In the late 1800s, coal companies purchased millions of acres of subsurface mineral rights and billions of tons of coal using deeds that allowed them to use or affect whatever portion of the surface they wanted. Such deeds were upheld for many years even after new techniques—surface mining (using open pits, augers and contour stripping)—appeared which damaged the surface in ways that could not have been foreseen when the contracts were signed. These early deeds and leases allowed coal operators to use the surface without additional permission or compensation for damage. Before such deeds were modified by state laws, hundreds of thousands of acres were left in ruins. In the 1970s, I saw houses, barns and churches damaged when strip mines, operating above them, pushed rock and dirt—called "overburden"—down the hill. I saw stream channels completely filled with this material, to the extent that the water was running over the top of a bridge's planks. Federal regulation forced mining companies into more responsible, protective behavior in the late 1970s. Since **surface-rights** law differs from state to state and mineral to mineral, the buyer must check locally to determine what rights, he, as the surface-only owner, would have with respect to mineral development on his property and around him.

Surface conflicts over mining damage can occur both when the mineral rights are severed and when they are not. Adjoining owners are still impacted by the noise, vibrations, debris, dust, erosion and blasting of surface mines and quarries, though less overall than before the federal legislation was enacted. Mountain-top-removal surface mining has been implicated in flooding, with the loss of 12 lives between 2000 and 2006. When coal is exposed, the heavy metals it contains—mercury, arsenic, lead, barium, beryllium, among others—can get into local water supplies. (See Diana Nelson Jones, "Almost flat, West Virginia," Pittsburgh Post-Gazette, February 26, 2006.)

State and particularly federal agencies, such as the U.S. Forest Service and Bureau of Land Management, own millions of acres of surface and minerals throughout the country. Some federal- and state-owned minerals lie beneath privately held surface. It appears to me that the surface owner enjoys a better set of rights with federal resources under his feet than with privately held minerals. (Opinions differ on this point, I'm sure.) Where the federal government owns land beneath private owners, the energy companies that have leased the federal minerals may be able to drill for oil and gas or mine for coal simply by posting a modest bond. This situation has come to a point in Wyoming where the mineral rights under about 48 percent of private surface is owned by the federal government, often the Bureau of Land Management. Pressure to produce energy on **split estates** has led to conflict between landowners, energy companies and public agencies.

Land buyers in the West may find themselves buying privately held surface only, with the minerals in federal hands or under lease to private interests. The federal government does not mine its own minerals. Large corporations are the principal owners and lessees of federal mineral rights. Federal reservations of mineral rights are called **patents** (deeds) and are recorded in **patents books** in the county courthouse. A moratorium on patenting federal land has been in effect since 1994, which means that the federal government is no longer passing title to a claimant, making the land private. Mining of minerals may still take place on federal land without a mineral patent. Lisa Takeuchi Cullen, "Bittersweet Boom," Time, September 11, 2006.

Federal agencies may agree to a **reconveyance** of the mineral rights if you, the surface owner, can show either that no mineral value exists in the federal mineral rights or that federal ownership interferes with or precludes appropriate development of the surface. The surface owner will have to pay for geological tests to prove no mineral value and may have to pay for the rights themselves. Each reconveyance determination is site-specific, and reconveyance is not a guaranteed outcome. Reuniting surface and minerals, however, adds value to the surface property by removing the possibility of unwanted mineral development from surface ownership and allowing the property to be mortgaged at its full value. Each federal agency has its own procedures, forms and expenses for reconveyance. Agencies will provide pamphlets explaining the process, and you can dig out the procedures by looking at that portion of the Code of Federal Regulations (CFR) that governs the agency. The CFR is available on the Internet and in law libraries. Agencies should provide the relevant documents, and, if all else fails, ask your Congressional representative for help.

The place to begin learning about a target property's minerals is in the county courthouse with the seller's deed and his chain of title. If you find in his chain that the minerals have been severed, look up that deed of sale and any subsequent lease. Limitations, if any, on surface usage will be included in the lease. You will probably find a boilerplate deed of sale and the same type of lease. In that case, check with a local lawyer and state mining/drilling officials to determine statutory and case-law protections that apply to surface ownership. You may end up calling the general counsel's office in the state's mining/drilling agency and talking to a staff lawyer. Ask about restrictions that limit the developer's use of your surface, liability for damages to the surface and its improvements, the surface owner's right to notice, environmental protections that impose setbacks from streams and lakes, and the developer's track record.

The buyer who purchases the surface only cannot void an "active" mineral lease, but the leaseholder (lessee) may be willing to offer some concessions and accommodations for goodwill. It certainly doesn't hurt to establish a personal relationship with the lessee's management as well as any of its crew that appear. In some circumstances, the surface owner may be able to buy back oil and gas rights if the leaseholder can tap the resource from adjoining property or when the leaseholder is persuaded that he's removed all of the resource. My experience is that mineral leaseholders are reluctant to sell their lease rights to surface owners, though it's worth asking.

States tax subsurface minerals differently.

Some apply a **severance tax** that is owed by the owner of the mineral rights as the mineral is produced. (The producer of the minerals may actually be the party that pays the tax, depending on the terms of the lease agreement.) The owner of the surface, whose mineral rights have been severed, owes no severance tax on the minerals produced beneath his land. The severance tax is a state-level tax with some portion usually being repatriated to the county of production. Counties, of course, may impose their own severance tax, sometimes called a **yield tax**, on mineral (or timber) production. Such taxes are either calculated on a measurable production unit, such as a ton of coal or a barrel of crude oil, or levied against the gross sales revenue of the product at its point of origin.

Severance and yield taxes are a marginal factor in deciding whether or not to buy land with mineral resources. I think tax burdens might come into play when the buyer has a choice between mineral properties in different states, one low tax and the other high. In what might be considered high-coal-tax states, such as Wyoming, West Virginia and Kentucky (with its tax on unmined coal and a severance tax), I've seen no backing out of coal ownership or production. Pennsylvania, Virginia, Illinois, Indiana and Texas do not have a coal severance tax.

States change their severance tax rates from time to time; some, like Wyoming, fairly frequently. It makes sense for a buyer of land with minerals to determine what its current tax burden is and keep in mind that politics and public needs will change that burden in the future. On the other hand, I would not worry that a state will tax minerals excessively. States generally try to keep their tax burdens competitive with neighboring states that produce the same mineral so as not to disadvantage their own producers.

A severance tax does not diminish mineral lease rent (fee) paid to the owner of the mineral rights. The lease rent/fee is paid to the mineral owner whether or not production occurs. The amount of rent is not reduced by any tax increases on unmined mineral resources, because that rent payment is established in the lease agreement. The payment of a severance tax should not reduce production royalties as long as the royalty is figured on gross sales or gross production. Royalty would be reduced by state/local taxes if the royalty is figured against after-tax (net) revenue. Mineral owners should not agree to royalty formulas based on production less expenses and taxes.

Unmined minerals may or may not be taxed separately from the **property tax** imposed on the surface. (You might find the local property tax referred to as an *ad valorem* **tax**, that is, a tax based on the market value of the property.)

States, as a rule, do not tax real property, preferring to raise revenue from fees, and taxes on sales and income. Some states, however, do impose a property-type tax on certain unmined minerals, which may also be referred to as a **reserve tax**.

Counties and other sub-state jurisdictions are the principal taxers of property, both real (land, improvements, minerals) and personal (vehicles, boats, equipment). **Real property** is land and the structures attached to it, along with the rights, interests and benefits that come with the ownership of the land. **Personal property** is assets owned by an individual apart from real property. Personal property can be on the land but not attached to it. Planted crops are personal property, standing trees are not.

Counties impose a **property tax** on real property that is calculated on its tax-assessed value multiplied by the local tax rate for the particular type of real property. The tax rate is expressed as so many dollars per $100 of assessed value. You might see a rate shown as, $.85/100, which is eighty-five cents of tax per $100 of assessed value. (A tract of undeveloped land that has been appraised by the county at $100,000 FMV would be taxed at $850 per year.) Tax-assessed values for land (surface) and improvements are based on a county-wide, property-by-property **reassessment** that takes place every few years. Appraisers are hired to do this work.

States use different formulas for valuing unmined minerals. Mineral valuations may or may not be part of the periodic reassessment process that values surface land and improvements. Counties may apply a generic formula, where, for example, it is assumed that so many dollars of mineral value goes with each subsurface acre. Minerals-owning companies are often asked to provide tax authorities with an estimate of the amount of minerals they own, from which their tax payment is calculated.

Each county will have its own way of taxing minerals. In my county, minerals are taxed at the same rate as other real property, but their valuation is no more than token. The county has no practical way of determining how much gas is underground. And the value of that gas, whatever its extent, depends entirely on a field being developed with an associated transportation system. Lacking that investment, the mineral deposit is worth nothing. In counties where minerals are a significant resource, unlike mine, they will be valued separately. You may also find counties where worked out mineral deposits are taxed the same as minerals that are still untouched. Unmined minerals may be taxed at a different rate from surface land, and different tax rates may be applied to different minerals. When all is said and done, minerals are not taxed highly.

Information on local mineral tax rates, assessed valuations and recent tax payments will be found in the property-tax records at the county courthouse in the **Land Book**, or its equivalent. The Land Book is the county's database for all property-tax information. It is generally organized by sub-county jurisdictions, listing owners alphabetically. It shows current tax-assessed values for each parcel of property, divided among land (surface), improvements and minerals. Each parcel of land has a **tax number**, and each parcel is available as a **tax map** in the county's **tax book**. The tax book is a compilation of tax maps showing every tax parcel in the county; the Land Book shows the tax data for every tax parcel. The amount of tax owed is figured against each parcel's tax-assessed values for land, improvements and minerals. Ask the assessor whether the tax-assessed value for land and improvements represents 100 percent of current fair market value (FMV) or some percentage. (Land values in West Virginia, for example, are carried at 60 percent of FMV.) Different types of surface property—farmland, timberland, urban residences, commercial land, etc.—will be taxed at different rates. The Land Book shows the amount of tax owed in each asset category as well as the total. Minerals are unlikely to be carried at 100 percent of FMV. The Land Book gives you the assessed valuation of the target property's minerals for tax purposes alone. This valuation has not much to do with the actual worth of the minerals in place and even less to do with the actual worth of those minerals once invested capital makes them capable of being extracted.

Counties give tax breaks to certain classes of real property. Farmland, for example, may benefit from a **"farm use"** designation, which can cut its property tax by 75 percent or more. Farm use is a tax tool that counties adopt to encourage farming and preserve farmland. It shifts the county's tax burden to non-farm property owners.

Unmined minerals are generally taxed low, whatever the taxing format.

The biggest mineral tax break occurs at the federal level, in the form of the **percentage depletion allowance**. This allows the producers of some 70 minerals to take off a fixed percentage, ranging from ten to 22 percent, of their annual gross revenues against their taxable incomes. The total deduction from the percentage depletion allowance can, and typically does, wind up exceeding the amount of invested capital. Clay, sand and gravel have a ten percent allowance, while lead, sulfur and uranium are at 22 percent.

Minerals in the ground can be valuable or worthless. The presence of a mineral deposit does not necessarily translate into income for its owner. It may not be economically recoverable owing to its size, quality, geological situation, location and a dozen other factors. If it's not economically recoverable, it may be worth something down the road, but it's usually not worth much right now. And it's anyone's guess as to how long the road will be until the deposit acquires value. Dozens of "deals" are around that ask investors to buy into old gold mines, iron-ore deposits, oil-and-gas projects and the like. All of them promise amazing profits. Some involve the purchase of the minerals; others offer participation in the development of a resource. All of these "deals" carry high risk for inexperienced buyers, and I encourage you to stay out of them unless you truly know what you're doing. I'll give one example of the many I could cite.

A group of individuals bought an iron-ore deposit in New York about 30 years ago when its underground mining operation shut down. Depending on which geologist's opinion I wanted to believe, the deposit contained 20 million to as much as 60 million tons of high-grade ore. The mineral rights to whatever was there were priced at $300,000—a steal, given that the royalty on that amount of ore would run into the millions. Two problems, however, became apparent when I scoped it. First, the owner of the minerals owned no surface property. A big, deep mine needs 50 to 100 acres on the surface for its facilities. Perhaps that problem could have been solved. Second, however, was the unfortunate fact that this ore—good as it was—lay deep underground in fractured seams and could only be extracted by expensive, labor-intensive, underground mining methods. No iron-ore company could mine that deposit profitably when surface-mined ore would always be produced at a fraction of the cost. Almost every mineral "deal" that I've looked into has something wrong with it, something big enough to kill it.

Buying land for its minerals and buying mineral rights are not games for amateurs. Investing in minerals is a different book for another author. My concern for an inexperienced buyer of rural land is to make sure that you understand minerals can be a financial asset, a financial zero, a financial loss and an aesthetic/environmental liability. I advise against buying surface only when economically recoverable minerals exist below unless your uses of the land are compatible with the potential surface impacts that mineral development can impose.

WATER AS A FINANCIAL ASSET

Chapter 13 discusses the environmental considerations of **rural water** as they can bear on a buyer. In addition to being a source of life and a vehicle for pollution, water is a natural resource that often has a dollar value. Its flow can be affected by natural and man-made events, which can negatively impact both your land and your pocketbook. As population and development continue to increase, the quantity and quality of rural water is likely to become an ever more prominent issue of law and policy. Drought and global warming affect local water supplies. Metropolitan areas, irrigated agriculture and rural residential developments will lay ever-heavier demands on these supplies. When rural water supply is made into a market, the highest dollar bid will prevail. That fact will change the availability of local supply in rural areas, because the highest money will not be local.

I foresee more reservoirs and pipelines being built from water-supplying rural areas to populated, water-needing areas. I assume that the trend toward **privatization** of municipal water systems will involve the buying of water from distant watersheds. If water is developed like Arabian oil in the 1930s, maybe we "country Saudis" will get rich from this arrangement. But I doubt that will be the way water entrepreneurs will proceed. My guess is that water for export will be "developed" in America's rural areas by water-development companies that lease rights much as domestic oil and gas is now leased. They will store it in large impoundments and ship it to needy areas through a system of pipelines. Counties where water is leased and stored will receive some modest tax benefits. The local property owner might get free water for domestic purposes just as a gas lease usually provides one residence with free gas. It would not surprise me if after the commercially recoverable reserves of Appalachia's coal, oil and gas are mostly gone, the region continues to function as an exporter of natural resources—renewables, such as water, timber and wind-generated electricity.

Whether or not rural water resources are sold and shipped in the future, a land buyer should give thought to a target property's water needs and supply to determine whether they are currently in balance. This is an elementary scoping question both in the arid West and non-arid places where water is valued both on and off site. Water-surplus regions in the future will find both a local and regional market for what can be sold. Even East of the Mississippi River where water supply is generally not the principal factor in a land purchase, I urge readers to think a bit about it. Does the target property have a surplus of water, and, if so, will that continue in the future if you and the neighbors increase your draw? Is there a way to maintain your supply given the water law in the state where the property is located? (See discussion below.) Does the target property's surplus water currently have market value and, if so, what is it? What might be the value of the property's water at various future points?

Surface waters can be thought of in several ways: intermittent or permanent; standing or flowing; navigable or unnavigable. The same stream can share contrary characteristics, depending on the time of year and recent precipitation. These categories have legal and policy implications.

A landowner's rights and obligations to surface water can vary with its category or type. **Intermittent surface water** is linked to precipitation, which recharges underground reserves. Such water can become a legal issue when a landowner does something to capture it or concentrate it, thus affecting the quantity or quality of water flowing onto his neighbors. **Flowing water** (streams, rivers, creeks) is surface water that has value to a landowner for economic purposes, farming (irrigation), livestock, recreation and aesthetics. (Flowing water—even channels that are dry almost all year—is also a potential liability, because it can flood during high-volume precipitations.)

Where precipitation is scarce and surface-water flow uncertain, the right to surface water (both intermittent and permanent) takes on great importance and substantial economic value. Any buyer looking at arid or irrigated land should investigate what legally established rights to water, if any, the seller is also conveying with the land. Do these rights provide a sufficient volume for your purposes? Is the source of irrigated water being reduced upstream by natural factors or man-made reasons? If supply changes gradually from snow pack (stored water) to rain, how will that affect your property? Protracted drought can ruin river-irrigated crops. Ask about the regularity and volume of summer rainfall, especially if you have in mind growing something that hasn't been done successfully before. (Success means crops sold for a profit over a period of time.)

If you are buying irrigated property that depends exclusively on drilled wells or have plans that require drilling a large-volume well, hire a consulting engineer for testing and advice before you purchase. You want his opinion about the feasibility and cost of your plan. You can include a **test-results-acceptable-to-buyer contingency** in your purchase contract. Also, check out the water uses (both actual and potential) above you in the watershed. You may discover a use or planned use above you that will substantially change the amount of surface water available to you. In places where water is always an issue in land sales, discuss things with a local lawyer before you submit a contract. Your ability to use surface waters in the quantity you want may be the single most important factor in selecting among properties.

On certain waterways, you may have to determine whether flowing water on or bordering the target property has been deemed **navigable** or **unnavigable**. Your landowner rights are greater with unnavigable streams; with navigable waters, your water rights are limited to those that do not interfere with public needs and uses. **Navigable** is defined as a waterway that is designated as navigable on a federal survey map that is available from the U.S. Geological Survey. And for regulatory purposes under federal clean-water legislation, navigable has been interpreted to include any waters that have the capability of affecting interstate commerce. Navigable, consequently, includes some watercourses that no one can navigate, including the local ducks. The creek in my backfield is classified as navigable despite being dry at least nine months of the year; a skilled and foolhardy kayacker might paddle a few yards in it about seven days a year. It is "navigable," because it is part of the Potomac River watershed. The current definition of navigable allows federal agencies to control what happens in this non-navigable navigable creek. Court cases are challenging this broad definition, which underlies the extended federal reach. If, for instance, federal water-pollution regulations are amended to require fencing livestock out of waterways, those amendments will be based on the federal government's authority to manage navigable water.

With exceptions, the general rule is that the landowner who borders a navigable stream owns to the low-water line, which allows public use of the water between these lines. The area between the high-water and low-water lines on each side of a waterway is known as **flat land**, with the public holding a right to its use superior to that of the bordering landowner. A fisherman or boater has no right to cross your land to get to a navigable stream, but once there, he may enjoy use of the water even if your enjoyment is reduced. With an **unnavigable** waterway, the bordering landowner owns to its centerline. Both navigable and unnavigable waterways can rework their channels from floods and other natural forces. The boundary lines of bordering owners can change with the gradual, natural shifts of streambeds and the erosion and accretion of land in and around them. Floods, on the other hand, generally do not change boundary lines. Where a deed says something like "the boundary runs with the centerline of the stream channel," the boundary line can change.

Surface-water ownership and usage operate under two legal theories. In most of the eastern United States, states mainly follow the theory of **riparian rights**. **Riparian land** is land over which water flows and land that borders and extends away from a stream. It is land that is owned by a person whose property fronts the flowing water. Not all of a watershed or drainage is considered riparian land, just that which has water frontage. Riparian rights are also used in some non-eastern states, such as Louisiana, Arkansas and Minnesota. Riparian rights run with the land, but they can be severed from its surface through sale, lease or reservation. A large piece of riparian land can be divided in such a way that some parcels continue to border the water and continue to have riparian rights but other parcels lose these rights unless they are specifically reserved in the deed to the buyer. (**Littoral land** borders an ocean, sea, and, in some states, lakes. Littoral rights are like riparian rights, except that littoral owners own to the high-water line, not to the water, with the state owning between that line and the low-water line.)

Riparian theory sets forth that ownership of riparian land establishes an equal right to water use. The riparian owner does not own the water, but he has the same right to use it as every other riparian owner. Each riparian owner loses "control" of the water once it passes his land.

What right does the downstream riparian owner have in the upstream water? There are two doctrines that address this question within riparian theory. Under the **natural flow doctrine**, a downstream owner can limit the upstream owner where the upstream owner interferes with the natural flow of the stream. The doctrine has been modified over time. Maine, New Jersey, Pennsylvania, West Virginia, Georgia, Mississippi, Missouri and South Dakota provide that each riparian owner must do nothing to diminish or impede the natural flow of water downstream.

The second doctrine—**reasonable use**—posits that each riparian owner is allowed to make reasonable use of surface water as it flows by his property. The upstream riparian owner may reduce the flowing water for a reasonable use in a way that does not unreasonably injure down-stream riparian owners. Consider, then, what you, a downstream owner might accept as a reasonable injury? The upstream reasonable use should be for ordinary or domestic purposes (including watering livestock) and is sometimes capped at a specific volume. In the case where an upstream owner is using his water in such a way that it is affecting the quality of the water as it passes the downstream owner, a court would have to decide whether the upstream owner is using the water reasonably and whether the harm suffered by the downstream neighbor is unreasonable in the circumstances. Reasonable use does not guarantee that everyone downstream will have all the water that is wanted or needed; nor does it guarantee the quality that downstream users want or need. An upstream user, however, probably could not get away with making downstream water unusable. An upstream owner would be able to use all the water in a stream or make it unusable where a court determined that his use was reasonable in the circumstances. It depends on how "reasonable" is defined. Riparian-law states apply the reasonable-use doctrine more than the natural-flow doctrine.

The other theory of surface-water rights in the United States is called "**prior appropriation**," which is the basis of water-rights law in the drier states of the West. Some states use both theories. Prior appropriation gives to the person who first uses surface water for an economic or beneficial purpose a superior right to those who follow in time. Colorado rejects riparian rights completely, while California combines the two theories. If the upstream owner was the first to draw water from a Colorado stream for irrigation, his right to take what he wants is stronger than those downstream who established their irrigation uses later. All beneficial uses are not equal; they are usually ranked in a hierarchy of user claims with domestic use at the top. That highest-ranking claimant need not be a riparian landowner. Nine states—California, Kansas, Nebraska, North Dakota, Oklahoma, Oregon, South Dakota, Texas and Washington—follow the California doctrine that gives priority to riparian user-owners over those who are non-adjacent appropriators. The other nine western states—Alaska, Arizona, Colorado, Idaho, Montana, Nevada, New Mexico, Utah and Wyoming—follow prior appropriation doctrine strictly. (See Les and Carol Scher, Finding and Buying Your Place in the Country, 5th Edition [Chicago: Dearborn, 2000.])

I had occasion to scope a ranch southeast of Cody, Wyoming that contained about 9,000 deeded acres and about 45,000 acres under lease from the state and the Bureau of Land Management. Of the deeded acres, almost 1,200 were irrigated hayfields that had first-draw rights from the Greybull River. This ranch had established its first-draw right because it was first in time under the prior-appropriation doctrine. The ranch's irrigated land and its river bottom land were the most valuable acreage in the parcel, both types being valued at between $4,000 to $5,000 per acre. The rest of the property was valued at between $350 and about $600 per acre. Water is money.

The right to use surface and underground waters is crucial to property value in the arid West. A dirt-smart buyer there must also become water-smart. The seller may have rights to surface water by deed, lease, prescription or permit. **Water-appropriation permits** are used in prior-appropriation states (except Montana). They set forth the parameters for the permit holder to take (divert) water, including the location of where the water is to be diverted, amount (cubic feet per day or acre-feet per year), seasonal timing, purpose of the diversion, methods to be used, among other items. A buyer in a prior-appropriation state must check into use patterns on permit waterways through public records and the sophisticated survey-research technique called, "asking around." Permit research may or may not indicate what will happen in the future—or even what actually happened in the past if there was night-time bootlegging. Asking around may prevent the new buyer from finding his stream bone dry when he needs water most.

From a legal perspective, surface water is conceptualized differently than underground water. Surface water is more thought of as a *resource*, particularly lakes and rivers. But it is a resource with a downside.

Snow and rain supply surface waters, mainly through **runoff,** which is also referred to as diffused surface water and storm-water runoff. When surface water appears in a quantity that overwhelms the ability of the land to absorb it, flooding, soil erosion and sediment build-up occur.

Twelve of the 50 states allow a landowner to take any measures to protect himself from runoff and flooding, even those measures that increase the risk and damage to his neighbors. (The 12 are Arizona, Arkansas, Hawaii, Indiana, Missouri, Nebraska, New York, North Dakota, Oklahoma, Virginia, West Virginia and Wisconsin.) All follow the "**common-enemy doctrine**," which allows a landowner any manner of self-defense. This doctrine would allow me to excavate a large drainage ditch in my creek bottom that would channel a flood into my downstream neighbor's backyard. Upstream landowners have, in addition, no obligation to do anything to protect their downstream neighbors. Uphill neighbors may install drainage pipes to capture runoff and direct it onto their adjoining, downhill neighbors. I encountered the reality of the common-enemy doctrine several years ago when I had to install a complicated and expensive drainage system to capture the directed runoff from an uphill neighbor who had installed underground drain tiles that emptied onto my land at our common property line.

In the other 38 states, a landowner may protect his own land from runoff and flooding only if his measures are reasonable and impose minimal harm to adjoining landowners. Eight of the 38—Alabama, California, Georgia, Illinois, Kansas, Kentucky, Pennsylvania and Tennessee—prohibit a landowner from interfering or affecting surface water flow, even where he is harmed by his inaction. These states, following the **natural flow doctrine**, embrace a concept of responsibility that is opposite of the 12 common-enemy states. Either doctrine can directly impact you if you buy property that floods. Look for floodplain, streams, coves, and then evidence of flooding, such as loose rocks on top of bottom land, creek beds filled with rock, vegetation hung on fence lines and household debris festooning creek-side trees.

Underground water resources are classified as either **percolating waters** or **underground streams**. Percolating water is precipitation migrating through the soil, or water from a stream that has seeped out of its bed and is no longer part of the flow. The concept includes veins of water that are not discoverable from the surface, underground lakes and artesian basins. If water is flowing underground, it is an underground stream, not percolating water. The underlying legal rule for percolating waters is that the owner of the land owns them absolutely and may use them without regard to others. This English common law root has been modified by the substitution of the reasonable-use idea, whereby each surface owner has a right to use these waters for his reasonable needs on his land. California rejects both ideas, and says that landowners must share percolating waters in proportion to the surface area each owns. California's theory is called **correlative rights**. Underground streams are difficult to identify from the surface and are, inevitably, connected with percolating water. Where an underground stream is identified, surface water law is usually applied.

In sum, there are four main ideas that make up state water-rights law on ownership and usage: 1) absolute ownership, 2) reasonable use, 3) prior application and 4) correlative rights. While federal environmental laws and regulations control most water-pollution issues, you can find yourself in a situation where the individual state's water doctrine controls the ownership of your property's water, what you and your neighbors can do with it, and how those uses may affect its quantity and quality downstream. Since a state may combine some of these ideas and then have state-specific judicial and legislative interpretations to boot, you will need to consult with a local lawyer who has done water cases to know where you stand on any given question that your scoping identifies.

Water in the East is not generally considered a discrete asset that can be leased or sold independently, though I think that will change as metropolitan demand for water increases. When you buy land in the East, you are usually safe in assuming that you are buying the subsurface (and surface) waters as well, without restrictions. (If constraints other than those imposed by state water law exist, they will appear in the deed or other document of record.) A purchase-offer contract that incorporates the phrase **"fee simple"** or **"in fee"** means that the buyer is making an offer for the property's full bundle of rights and assets. If the seller doesn't own the land's water in fee, he can't convey it to you. Your incorporation of that phrase in your contract forces the seller to disclose any diminution of his rights and ownership. It's fair to assume that the surface owner will have reasonable use rights to the subsurface water beneath the property. "Reasonable use," however, can easily mean reduced water for the next neighbor, which is you in relation to the higher neighbor. Check, therefore, how uphill neighbors use their water. Large farming operations may be tapping into an aquifer to a degree that reduces supply to your target property. Before you submit an offer, consider how any water-using plans you have might affect your neighbors, and vice versa.

It is always possible that you will find a property where a deed has conveyed away a water right that would normally run with the land or otherwise diminished the seller's usage right. This might be a sale that allows a neighbor to draw water from your spring. It might be a right to fish in a pond, or even a life-estate to let a particular family swim there. (A life-estate terminates with the death of the individual holding it.) Any recorded water restriction will bind you as the next owner.

It's not unusual to discover one party using water, such as a spring, located on another's property without any recorded agreement. This is a ticklish situation for both parties. The user may be able to establish a legal right to have his pipe in your spring despite your opposition by invoking some form of **adverse possession** (ownership) or (adverse) **prescription** (right to use) under state law. If he says that the seller gave him permission to put in a pipe, that permission (**license**) expires with the sale of the property or the death of the individual who gave it. If the user has no legal right to use the water from your spring, you then have three choices: put up with his usage, end it, or impose restrictions or conditions. If you put up with his usage despite being against it, he will be able to claim an adverse right after a certain number of years as long as his use meets all the other tests under state law. If you put up with it by giving him permission, then you can revoke permission if and when it suits you. The user acquires no independent and superior right to the spring over time beyond your permission. If you choose to sell the property and know of this spring encroachment, you should reveal it to your buyer before he submits an offer. When all is said and done, the user is taking spring water that did not belong to him when he first started taking it and should not belong to him now, though he may have a valid adverse claim to it. You may need this water, and he may depend on it. This is a problem that needs to be solved, not ignored. Check with your local lawyer as to the user's legal rights and then proceed carefully. This kind of dispute can generate recurring squabbles for many years.

The seller's deed may show that his water originates from a spring on a neighbor's property. This is a **"spring right**," which entitles its holder to draw water from the spring on another. The wording might even specify the diameter of your seller's out-take pipe and its location in the neighbor's spring box. It is not uncommon for a single spring to serve more than one property. We, for example, draw household water by deed from a developed spring on a neighbor's farm located on the other side of a state-maintained road. At another spot, we share a developed water trough that is situated 50-50 in a boundary line fence that is supplied by our spring. (The vernacular way of putting this is, "the spring is on me.") At another place, one neighbor draws water from another neighbor's spring through a pipe laid in a stream that's on me. Only the first of these spring "arrangements" shows up in a title search.

The owner of a spring can sell a permanent right to spring water, rent access to it, or simply grant a use right to a neighbor. The owner cannot, however, void a neighbor's deeded spring right. The owner might be allowed to "reasonably use" his land in such a way that it reduces or even eliminates the spring serving the neighbor. You might ask your local lawyer his opinion were you to drill a well above a shared spring.

The common practice when developing a shared spring is to put the springowner's out-take pipe lowest in the spring box and other users above the owner according to their order of right. In this fashion, the owner reserves to himself the first draw of water in the box. This protects the owner's water supply from the draws of other users, all of whom get water only if the supply in the box comes up to the level of their pipes. Your water supply is at most risk when your out-take pipe in a shared spring is highest in the box and smallest in diameter.

A buyer must check all of the following with developed springs:

- Is the seller's residence served by a spring on the seller's property?
  If not, on whose property is the spring located? Does the seller have
  a deeded right to tap this spring? If not, what is the basis, in law
  and otherwise, for the seller's use of this spring?

- How reliable is the spring during droughts? Measuring flow during
  a rainy period will not give you a reliable answer. You have to
  talk to the seller and his neighbors.

- Is the spring subject to either natural or man-made events that might
  affect its flow? Has the flow been affected by such events—flooding,
  drought, landslide, earthquake, new wells, etc.—in recent memory?

- Has the spring served the seller's property adequately for at least
  the last ten years? If you are going to use significantly more water

than the seller, do you anticipate a shortage? On what do you base your opinion?

- How does water get from the spring to the house? Is the pipe old? Is it corroding? What is it made of? Will it need to be replaced soon?

- How is the water held at the house? Is the tank big enough for your purposes?

- Where does the spring overflow from the house go? If the house takes more, will there be enough supply for these secondary purposes?

- Have you tested the tap in the seller's house for common contaminants? If not, do you need to insert a contingency in your purchase contract for this purpose?

- Is the source of the seller's household water a shared spring? If so, which out-take pipe inside the spring box is the seller's?

- What is the position of the seller's pipe in the spring box with respect to other pipes? What is its internal diameter? Is there a screen over it to keep out dirt and critters? Is the pipe solid and without corrosion? When do you think the pipe will need to be replaced?

- Who is responsible for routine cleaning/maintenance of the spring box, spring house, pump, electricity, underground pipes, etc.?

- How are costs to be divided among the users when the spring has to be repaired or replaced?

- Does the spring box need to be cleaned or repaired?

- Is a neighbor tapping any spring on the seller's property? If so, what is the legal foundation of that neighbor's usage? Does this arrangement negatively affect your plans?

- Does the seller's property have a backup source of household water if the spring were to go dry?

Be very cautious about buying any land whose water and water rights are in any way not being fully conveyed to you as part of the land purchase. You protect yourself in three ways: 1) writing your purchase contract in a way that describes the land that you want to buy and will be conveyed to you as the property in fee (or fee simple), including all waters and water rights; 2) being alert for deeds that reserve a water right for a neighbor, third-party or the seller; and 3) scoping out unrecorded uses. You will need to determine exactly what water rights the owner holds and is conveying, just as you checked the title for mineral rights.

Depending on the particulars of a target property's water situation, you may need to write specific water guarantees into your purchase contract. One objective of doing so is to determine exactly the scope and validity of the seller's ownership of these resources under his signature. If he doesn't own them, you might pay for them but he can't convey them—a situation that you want to avoid. You can only own what the seller owns, even though he may want you to buy what he doesn't own.

Contract writing is discussed in Chapters 29 and 30, but the general requirements are worth summarizing here insofar as they bear on minerals, water, timber and other issues under review.

Your purchase contract should always include language that says your offer is for the seller's property with **a general warranty deed, marketable title and in fee**. The general warranty deed (sometimes referred to as a **"warranty deed"** or **"full-covenant deed"**) conveys the property to the buyer with the maximum amount of seller promises regarding his ownership and clear title. General warranty deeds include five warranties, or seller promises, that are called the **covenants of title.** Among the promises in a warranty deed, is one where the seller promises the buyer that the only encumbrances—debt secured by a lien on the property—on the title are those that are found in the deed. A general warranty deed also means that the seller is offering these promises not only for the time that he's owned the property, but also for the time under previous owners. Other types of deeds may be offered, but they are not as good as a general warranty deed. A **special warranty deed** offers seller promises only for the period under the seller's ownership; it may also be referred to as a **limited warranty deed**. A **bargain-and-sale deed**, which is used in some states, provides fewer promises than a general warranty deed, but should protect the buyer against encumbrances and lack of seller ownership. A **grant deed** provides fewer promises and less protection than a general warranty deed. A **quitclaim deed** provides no promises and no protection, since the owner is selling only his interest in the property, whatever that interest is, which may be none at all.

Any encumbrance, severance or reservation on the owner's water or minerals should be recorded, but you may find something that is off the books. These arrangements may or may not be legal. Consult with your lawyer before submitting a purchase offer.

A **marketable title** is one where no question exists as to who the owner is. When a seller agrees to convey property to a buyer with a marketable title, he is saying that he has good, or clear, title to that which he is conveying. A marketable title should have no defects and should not open the buyer to litigation over ownership. A buyer can reasonably expect that a property conveyed to him with a marketable title can be sold or mortgaged. Buyers want sellers to provide them with marketable title to all land, minerals, water and associated rights where possible. Land can be conveyed without a marketable title if the buyer does not specify marketable title in his purchase contract.

Finally, the buyer wants the seller to convey the property **in fee**, which may also be referred to as fee simple title or fee estate. This level of conveyance gives the buyer complete ownership of all the rights and assets of the land, including minerals and water, with the power to sell, lease, give or encumber them at his discretion, subject to a lender's note or mortgage. To make sure that there is no misunderstanding as to what in fee means, you can provide in your contract that the "**seller agrees to convey to buyer by general warranty deed marketable title to the subject property in fee simple, including all surface and underground minerals, waters and all other resources and rights**." If the seller's ownership is hinky or he owns less than a full set of assets and rights in the property, this language should smoke him out. In the worst case—where the seller signs your contract with this language and you discover after the purchase that his title is flawed or the minerals did not convey—these words in your purchase contract are the foundation of your suit against the seller. He promised you certain things when he signed your contract and could not/did not deliver.

CHAPTER 15: MATCHMAKING

FINDING

How do you find rural property?

The Internet now has several websites that provide such information, including www.landandfarm.com, www.landwatch.com, www.elandusa.com, www.land-fsbo.com, www.land.net, www.fsbo.com, www.landsofamerica.com, www.ebay.com, www.landlister.com, www.forestlandmls.com, www.eaglestar.net, www.unitedcountry.com, RLi@realtors.org, www.owners.com and www.forsalebyowner.com, among others. These sites host sellers looking for buyers, and in some cases, buyers looking for property. Ebay auctions land; the bidding is often on the amount of deposit. Wood-products companies, such as paper manufacturers and sawmills, sell undeveloped land in tracts of all sizes and can generally be accessed through corporate websites. You can find woodland for sale through the websites of timber investment management companies and consulting foresters, such as www.fountainforestry.com and www.landvest.com. Land is also sold by companies whose business is to buy large tracts, divide them and flip them as quickly as possible. These large tracts are bought wholesale and, after division, sold retail. These companies will advertise every week in the Sunday editions of large metropolitan newspapers, usually with toll-free numbers. These parcels are directed toward retail consumers willing to pay full market price for convenience shopping.

The traditional buyer approach is to contact a real-estate broker in the target area and look at properties that are shown to you. The broker in this arrangement is usually working for the seller. Properties on which the broker has the listing will be shown first, because the agency's own listings produce the most money for the broker and his agents when they're sold.

You can take out a **Land-Wanted ad** in the local paper. This strategy is primarily prospecting for a FSBO, though brokers may respond. Ads work best when you are already familiar with the county and have a reasonably clear idea as to what you want and don't want. Make your ad specific in terms of preferred location, acreage, house (or no house) and whatever features you consider necessities. I recommend that you ask sellers to respond to your ad by sending their property information to a local post office box, addressed to "Property Buyer." You might describe yourself and your purpose in the ad, e.g., "family of three looking for old farm property." I would not include a phone number and an address that might lead a seller to infer that you are "rich." Pick up your mail on a Friday afternoon or Saturday morning and look that weekend at the responses with the most promise. The ad should ask the seller to send you a copy of the property's tax map or survey, a road map that locates the property with access marked and a brief description. The seller should also be asked to send his name, mailing address, phone, fax and e-mail address. If you ask for more than this, you will discourage replies. After you've become familiar with your target county, this is sufficient information to allow you to screen a property in or out for further scoping. The cost of local want-ad advertising is small. While an advertising "campaign" may save you time, you should want to spend a certain amount of time "wasted" in looking at properties that don't fit your needs. Each rejected property will teach you a bit more about fitting your search to what's available and what your dollar buys. Looking at properties you don't want is a necessary part of dragging yourself up the local learning curve; you just don't want to drag yourself up the same curve over and over again.

I would not have the ad state either the per-acre price or overall price you are willing to pay. Let the seller propose a price. If you state an able-and-willing price, you will get FSBOs calling to sell you over-priced properties that meet it. The advertising buyer should expect responses from some owners wanting to sell over-priced properties as well as from sellers of something-wrong-with-them properties.

These are "fishing" replies cast in your direction. Smart fish pass on hooks, particularly baited ones.

The best approach to finding property is to develop a friendship with a local contact or two who will let you know when a property that fits your search criteria is about to come to the market. This allows you to take advantage of local word-of-mouth information. The local contacts will screen properties on your behalf. Make sure to arrange to pay these contacts a consultant's fee for your purchase. Two or three percent of the gross selling price is a fair finder's fee. You, the buyer, should initiate the proposal for this type of consulting service.

Word-of-mouth leads can come to you in other ways as well. As you go through a target county, ask about property that might be for sale. The individuals you might ask are those you're working with (lawyer, surveyor, forester) and folks you run into—the motel owner where you stay, the restaurant owner where you like to eat, the banker you've talked to about a mortgage, county extension agent, state forester, building and excavation contractors, and the local building inspector. Word-of-mouth finds are often very attractive purchases when a buyer approaches a seller at just the right moment with a simple, cash offer. The seller's asking price is more than likely set without an appraisal or a comparables analysis. On the other hand, buyers should be aware that some sellers like to "float their property" in this manner to test a high asking price, and others shop their property this way to screen in certain types of buyers and screen out other types.

Most rural property is sold either by **owners themselves** (**For Sale By Owners,** or **FSBOs**) or through **state-licensed, real-estate brokers** (and their **agents**). Property can also be sold by a bank that repossesses it, at auctions of various types or through an attorney handling an estate.

A variation on the usual broker listing is a property that's for sale through a broker but not advertised. This arrangement allows the broker to select "qualified" buyers and match them with particular properties and owners. It spares the seller the publicity of being a seller. The practice may be officially prohibited, because it lends itself to discrimination. From the buyer's perspective, a listing that has not been publicized (yet) can be either a good deal or a set up. My impression is that "off-the-books" listings are sometimes used to steer certain urban clients (who are perceived to be wealthy) to properties that are priced above market value. This often happens just before a broker officially gets or processes a listing. The farm I bought in Blue Grass in 1983 was not advertised by the broker who had the listing, though the neighbors knew it was for sale. I was willing to pay more than the local buyers, so the tactic worked for the seller.

Private auctions are also used to sell rural property, usually as part of settling an estate or when the owner is pinched by debt and needs to raise cash. Auctions are also used by lenders to dispose of **foreclosure properties**, which is real estate that the lender has taken over because the borrower/owner has fallen delinquent in his debt repayment. I discuss auctions below. Foreclosure auctions are rare in my area, and I don't have any first-hand experience with them. In more densely populated rural areas, foreclosures are more common. Two books that cover this topic are George Achenbach, <u>Goldmining in Foreclosure Properties</u>, 3rd ed. (New York: John Wiley & Sons, Inc., 1994), and Ted Thomas, <u>Big Money in Real Estate Foreclosures</u> (New York: John Wiley & Sons, Inc., 1992).

Another matchmaking technique is the **sale of tax-delinquent property**. It's rare that a non-local buyer is able to find the right property through a tax sale, but it's possible. Investors work these sales to make money, not to find a second-home property. Tax sales are announced in the local paper. They are properties whose owners have either chosen not to pay property taxes because the property isn't worth it to them or lost the ability to pay the tax. The sale's trustee—usually a local lawyer—will not provide much information to buyers about the property, and these properties are sold "as is." Owners have redemption rights in most places, which allow them to get their property back by paying the tax bill plus interest to the buyer holding the delinquency within a certain period of time. There's nothing wrong with buying at a tax sale; just remember that the original owner may reclaim his property in states that provide for redemption. You won't lose money in a redemption state, but you may waste time and opportunity.

Buyers need to know the state's rules for purchasing tax-delinquent property before getting involved. Contact the local agency, often the county sheriff's office, to obtain information; then call the state office for further information. (You can get the state office by asking the local official.) Go to a tax-delinquent sale before you are a bidder yourself. Talk to one or two of the regulars; they may be inclined to be helpful if you say you're only looking at one parcel. Make sure you understand the redemption provision and whether the property is burdened by a mortgage or other type of lien—which will have to be settled in one fashion or another. Tax-delinquent properties may also bear other sorrows—such as a questionable access—which led the owner to stop paying the property tax. You shouldn't buy tax-delinquent properties just because they appear to be cheap: they may be cheap because they're worthless. You need to scope them thoroughly. While it is possible to obtain land for back taxes, it's often more complicated and more costly than that. You can acquire information by searching the Internet under "**tax liens**," by state.

Property finders are generally people who primarily do other things in and around real estate. Depending on their position, they may or may not be able to accept a buyer-paid fee. An excavation contractor who gives you a call with a lead should get a **finder's fee**, a banker with the same tip should not. Finders work in various industries, though they are discouraged from working in real estate by state laws that protect the business interests of licensed brokers. A buyer can always contract with an unlicensed individual, acting as a consultant not a broker, to help him find rural land and pay this person a fee for his successful service. The consultant, of course, cannot provide brokerage services. The fee paid to the consultant would vary with the amount of work he performs for you. One to three percent of your gross purchase price would be fair for providing you with a lead that results in a purchase. Where the buyer wants the consultant to scope a property, it's fair to either pay a higher percentage or a lower percentage plus an hourly rate for billed time. On small-dollar properties of, say, $100,000 or less, you might arrange to pay a flat fee and shift the time-risk to the consultant. Small properties often involve as much time-work as large ones. You can also buy a fixed number of hours at an agreed rate, the last eight of which will be used to prepare a report of the consultant's findings. If you work with a consultant, I would advise that you make sure that he is working exclusively for you. Avoid an arrangement where a finder is getting paid by both buyer and seller, because the finder is then working primarily for his own interest in getting the sale done, whether or not it's good for you. A finder-consultant should reveal to a buyer whether or not he expects payment from any other party in the deal.

States differ in allowing a non-broker to act as a **finder**. Nothing prevents a buyer from hiring a consultant-finder to identify and scope a likely property for him. Some states regulate "finding" when it also entails introducing a buyer to a seller. My sense of this is that a finder who does nothing but find (identify) and scope does not run afoul of state laws, but the finder who acts as a **middleman** may, depending on the state. A middleman, unlike a finder, introduces buyer to seller and may facilitate the negotiation and purchase in various ways. That's what a broker does, and that's what states prohibit unlicensed individuals from doing. Some states allow anyone to serve as a middleman, charging one or both parties a fee for the service; other states allow none but licensed real-estate brokers to charge an introduction fee. Brokers in some states are also prohibited from sharing real-estate commissions with unlicensed finders. States that prohibit non-brokers from introducing a buyer to a seller may allow a lawyer in the course of his legal work to perform this function and charge a fee.

Land consultants, who are not licensed brokers, are rare. You probably won't find one in the phone book. Consultants I've met on timberland deals don't advertise and are not interested in working on small purchases. It is not a profession in the sense of having entrance requirements and licenses. A buyer's best chance of finding a knowledgeable local contact who can provide this service is to ask his local lawyer, forester and surveyor. The buyer wants to find an individual who knows local real estate and can bring analytical skills to property evaluation. A land consultant who is a licensed broker and works exclusively for the buyer is a **buyer's broker**.

Even where states do not allow a middleman to charge a fee, a buyer can hire a **land consultant** to bird-dog properties for him and pay for the service. The nature of the consultant's work for each buyer is up to the parties themselves and is subject to state law. Consultants should not be employed to provide legal advice or brokerage services. A consultant can offer an opinion about a boundary encroachment or an access problem, but the buyer needs to keep in mind that the non-lawyer consultant is not offering competent legal advice. In consulting contracts I sign with clients, I always include language where the buyer acknowledges that he understands that he alone is responsible for performing **due diligence**, evaluating any information provided and making the decision to purchase or not. The consultant should be expected to give opinions, framed between his best experience-based judgment and the best interest of his client. Consultants, like stockbrokers and investment advisers, can fail to learn something about an investment or err in calculating benefits. A court would ultimately decide whether the consultant should have reasonably known the fact that led to the buyer's harm. Consultants who deliberately steer clients into bad deals should not be held harmless.

You will get a sense of a consultant's reliability and thoroughness through close examination of any scoping work and written analysis he does on your nickel. If he projects timber values, for instance, he should state clearly the origins and timeliness of the species prices he used in his projections. If you read a consultant's report that is filled with general statements and unsupported assumptions, it's probably a hurry-up job. Property-evaluation reports should be fact-based, logical, transparent and documented. Where assumptions are made, they should be both identified and justified. You want to know how the consultant got to his bottom line, not just what his bottom-line recommendation is. If you get a feeling that the consultant is pushing you toward a buy, back away; he's working for a fee, not his client. Pay attention to what the facts and numbers tell you on their own. Since a land consultant's loyalty and duty are to the buyer (his client), I believe buyers are better served by having a land consultant on their side than by working with a broker who is obliged to represent the seller's interests. Brokers will quarrel with that opinion.

REAL-ESTATE BROKERS: THE SELLER'S AGENT

Buyers typically begin prospecting for rural property by phoning several real-estate **brokers** in their target area. A broker is a private-sector businessperson who has passed several levels of examination and is licensed by the state where he operates. A broker can buy, sell, lease or exchange property for a commission or fee charged to the seller or buyer, or both. He will typically have **agents** (and perhaps other licensed brokers) working for his brokerage **on commission**, that is, for a share of the fees they generate from sales. A commission is usually a percentage of the gross sales price. The typical commission charged by a broker to a seller is five to six percent, though that percentage falls on larger properties. A fee is usually a fixed charge. The terms are often used interchangeably.

The broker and seller sign a contract whereby the broker markets the seller's property for a commission. The seller's property is **listed** with this broker for either a fixed period of time (e.g., six-months, one year) or on an open-ended basis. The seller's contract with the broker is called a **listing agreement**, and it spells out the property to be sold, duration of the listing, commission owed to the broker and other contract terms. Such a broker is the **listing broker**. If another broker finds a buyer for the listing-broker, he is a **cooperating broker**. A real-estate agent who works for the listing broker and who brought the listing to the brokerage is the **listing agent**. An agent from another brokerage who brings a buyer to a listed property is a **cooperating agent**. **All of these individuals represent the seller and his interests, not the buyer and his interests.** The seller's broker/agent (s) has a **fiduciary** responsibility to, and relationship with, the seller, arising from the listing agreement. The broker/agent owes the seller the duties of care, obedience, accounting, loyalty and disclosure (of information or material facts that the agent knows or should have reasonably been expected to know). As a group, I'll refer to the seller's side—his agents and brokers—as the **seller's agent** or the **seller's side**.

The seller's side gets paid its commission when the seller sells the property to a buyer that the seller's side has produced. The commission is paid from the seller's funds at closing by the escrow agent. The commission appears on the **settlement statement** as a debit to the seller's proceeds. Commissions for all real estate averaged a bit over five percent of the gross sales price in recent years, though property in my rural area often bears a ten percent commission.

The seller-paid commission is split among whichever brokers and agents were involved on the seller's side, a number that typically ranges between one and four. A real-estate broker makes the most money on a sale when he is both the listing agent and the individual who sells the property; in that case, he gets 100 percent of the commission. A listing broker will split a commission with a cooperating broker, and each in turn will split his share with any agent who was involved in the sale. This commission structure explains why agents who drive you around take you to their personal listings and the listings of their broker first. If nothing interests you, they will show you listings from other brokers with whom they will become cooperating agents in the event of a sale.

When a buyer is driven around looking at properties with a seller's agent, he is in the company of an individual who is legally obliged to represent only the seller's interest in the sale. No matter how friendly you become, no matter how many cups of coffee you share, *this agent is not working for you.* This should not mean that the seller's agent will lie to you, though this happens. It often means that the agent does not share certain information with you that would put a sale—and the agent's commission—at risk. This behavior can harm a buyer who does not know the right questions to ask with the right words. Agents usually know some of their brokerage's listings better than others. An agent may give a buyer false or misleading information for lack of familiarity, or from being informed erroneously, or from not wanting to know a particular fact, or from making an assumption that turns out to be false. Even where an agent tells a buyer the truth as he genuinely believes it to be, the buyer can be misled if the agent is mistaken.

A seller's agent should not give a buyer information that advantages the buyer at the expense of his client—the seller. This can be a tricky act of judgment for an agent when he is in the vortex of conflicting interests. His client's interest—that is, the seller's—lies in getting his property sold at an acceptable price, as quickly and cleanly as possible, with no post-sale complications. The buyer's interest lies in purchasing some property—if not this seller's, then another's—that fits his goals, at an acceptable price, and free of post-sale surprises or complications. The seller's agent's interest lies in getting a deal done with the least amount of time, work and money invested in the process of matching seller and buyer. The longer a listing stays unsold, the more likely it is that the price will be cut, which in turn lowers his percentage commission. Stale listings may also produce a seller's request that the listing broker lower his commission to allow the seller to lower his asking price. When the listing expires, the disgruntled seller can move the listing to another broker or try to sell it himself. If the agent's listing does not produce a sale, the agent and his brokerage receive nothing for their marketing efforts and expenses. Thus, an ethical line exists between a seller's agent working both seller and buyer toward a mutually acceptable deal and this agent working both seller and buyer toward a deal that's not quite right for either party. You—the buyer—can assume that the seller's agent cares little whether the deal is good for you; remember his fiduciary duty is to the seller. When the seller's agent crosses the line by working for the sale despite his client's best interests, these deals can have **snakes at both ends** in the sense that the seller or the buyer, or both, find themselves bitten after the purchase. Agents must police themselves against pushing a deal that's more for their own benefit than for the seller's. It's fair for a seller's agent to work toward a deal, but it's a red flag for the buyer when he senses that the seller's agent is nudging both sides toward a purchase that the seller's not quite committed to. If an agent is prepared to push his client, the seller, over the edge, consider what he's willing to do to the buyer

I was recently mailed a promotional flyer from a broker in the Southeast who markets mountain property of 20 to 1,000 acres. This seller's agent advises buyers whom he's trying to attract to show his sellers that they "mean business." How does this seller's agent suggest that you show his sellers that you're serious. First, the buyer should put his offer in writing. Absolutely; any other offer is worthless. Second, he advises that the buyer should make his offer as "clean" as possible. What's that mean? Offer the highest price you are willing to pay with no contingencies, he writes. Omit language that gives you, the buyer, a way out. Third, the buyer should offer more earnest money deposit than might normally be expected. Finally, offer to close the deal in a short period of time. Well, well. This behavior will certainly help his clients. Admittedly, occasions exist when a prudent buyer can take one or more of these steps as long as he has scoped sufficiently. But buyers can open themselves to great harm if they follow this path in most circumstances.

I have found sellers' agents to range widely in their knowledge and honesty. I have been shown timberland by agents who could not distinguish one tree species from another and who had no idea about how to value timber on the stump. This did not stop them from advertising tracts as "containing valuable timber" when the tracts didn't or as advertising themselves as "specialists in timber tracts and farms" when they weren't. I have seen brokers advertise woodland property as containing "standing timber," which, I'm sure, is better than the alternative. "Standing timber" is a meaningless phrase in terms of whether or not the trees have commercial value. Very large trees can be absolutely worthless, standing or not. I have also seen agents advertise woodland properties as "pre-cut," as if a buyer receives some benefit from having the kindly seller remove the merchantable timber before selling it. I have had sellers' agents lie to my face, distract me from a defect, mislead me, plead lack of knowledge when they knew what I wanted to know, offer opinions about zoning and regulatory matters that were dead wrong, suggest that I do things that would harm me, advise me to make a full-price offer in order to get a full-price offer with no contingencies from another buyer, and provide false information about the seller. I have seen some agents routinely violate their legal responsibilities to their own clients to get a sale. There are two stereotypical real-estate agents—the ditzy, middle-aged woman and the sleazy guy. I've met them both—and so will you if you're persistent. But I've also had dealings with honest, hard-working, decent sellers' agents who played fair with buyers and their own clients. You have to determine where on the spectrum the seller's agent falls as part of your approach to any property. And remember that you can run into an agent who is both ditzy and sleazy.

Several times a seller's agent has told me that the seller would accept an offer below the listing price, or asking price. What to make of that? If the statement is made without the seller's consent, it strikes me that it's an ethical breach. It may be a ploy to get me to offer the agent-recommended price that is below the asking price when that price is actually higher than what the seller would really accept. Then it's a tactic to get me to pay more, which is fine with both the seller and his agent. Sometimes, however, it is an honest effort to get to a consensus price, sparing each side discordant bargaining that might produce nothing more than deadlock. Your price should be the price you're willing to pay after scoping the property's values and liabilities. If your price is below the seller's bottom, don't go up just because he's come down.

Buyers must be alert to the possibility that one or more of dozens of traps can be waiting for those who do not scope and get accurate answers. An agent once showed me a pretty tract of woods and pasture, but failed to tell me that he knew an underground coal mine was about to start operations beneath the entire acreage. I knew that Garrett County in western Maryland had mining—both surface and underground—in its southern half. And I also knew that an underground mine was active on the other side of a hill—out of sight and sound of the target property—a couple of miles away. Since the seller was only selling the surface rights, I checked into both the ownership of the subsurface minerals and whether plans were afoot to mine them. I did not want to buy the surface and then discover that I was facing subsidence or water problems. A call to the local office of the Maryland Department of Mines found an underground-mining plan on file that projected moving up to the property line. And, finally, a call to the mining company confirmed that it had leased the coal rights and was about to file a plan revision and start mining under my target property within the next couple of months. When I asked this agent—a "land specialist"—whether he had known of the mining plans, he shrugged and said that he thought I was interested in the timber and the pasture—both statements being true. Did he know the possible consequences of luring a buyer into this situation? Undoubtedly, he did. Sleazy.

Another broker once discouraged me from contacting the local electric-utility company to get an estimate of the costs involved in running a new line from the closest existing power pole onto a target property with no electricity. Several thousand feet of new line appeared to be needed. I knew that each power company has its own formula for determining the cost of new lines and spreading them over a period of years. He said, he thought it might come to a "couple of thousand," based on what he had seen on other properties with this utility. The important thing, he said, was for me "to get this 300 acres bought before that rich doctor from Washington buys it out from under you." (Rich doctors, I have found, are always about to buy the places I'm looking at, according to the agents. In my local area, the rich doctor is either from Richmond or Washington, D.C. When I looked for property in Wyoming, he was a Denver surgeon.) I called the utility. The cost estimate came to more than $80,000. It included a warning that in the utility's opinion the adjoining landowner might refuse to grant a utility easement over his property. In that case, the connection would have to be made at an alternative pole on another neighbor with an even higher cost. It became apparent from talking with the utility representative that he had tried to get an easement from the closest neighbor before—without success. I backed away and hoped that all rich doctors diagnosed this property as I did, the cost of which was the price of a phone call. Was this broker being dishonest with me? Absolutely. But he couched his estimate as being based on what he had seen in other circumstances, not on what he knew first hand. Had I accepted his opinion at face value, I would have bought 300 acres—and soon after that a bunch of candles. If a target property does not have an electric pole on it, don't make an offer until you have a cost estimate in hand.

One broker told me that a target property whose listing he had contained 347 acres, more or less. He advertised it so. He knew, however, that it was short, because he had access to an unrecorded survey done by a mineral company who had leased the minerals years earlier and then let the lease expire. When I proposed as part of my offer that we adjust the per-acre price, up or down, depending on what a survey that I paid for showed, he declined. "It's the same money," he said, "whatever the acreage." My surveyor found that the property lacked 27 acres. In his defense, the broker never said that the property contained 347 acres. He said it contained 347 acres, more or less. It's also true that he never volunteered information about the old survey's findings. I had asked my surveyor to run the deed's calls through his computer program to determine acreage before I made my offer. He did, and then told me it was probably seven acres short. The other 20 acres disappeared, it seems, as a result of "bad calls," which showed 20 acres in the deed, but not on the ground. Or something like that.

I was once shown a perfectly nice house and small acreage along a major two-lane highway on a sunny Saturday morning. At the property's back line was a dense stand of large pine trees. An unpaved public road bordered one side of the property about 75 yards from the house. No vehicle turned from the highway onto this unpaved road during the hour or so I was looking around. The broker never told me that a major sawmill lay behind the pine buffer. Since I didn't know the area, I didn't know enough to ask and wasn't smart enough to look. The broker didn't think it was necessary to volunteer that information. Had I visited on a weekday, the mill's activity would have been obvious. This broker didn't tell me something that he knew and I didn't, and he knew I didn't. When I stumbled by chance on this bit of information a few days later, I should have stopped looking with this broker. From that experience, I learned to look and ask about neighbors as part of my scoping.

Had I purchased the property and then learned of the mill, I would have been a fool to take the broker to court. His defense: "Your honor that sawmill's been there for 50 years. Logging trucks go in and out of there every day of the week. Anyone in the neighborhood could have told him about the mill. It's his responsibility to do his own due diligence. The mill is not a legal nuisance, and, to my knowledge, the people who owned this house before never complained. Ours is a rural community that depends on logging. I don't consider this mill, which employs 20 individuals and is the county's third largest employer, a liability or a defect in the property the buyer purchased. I am not required to disclose the presence of neighbors. This is not analogous to a house with termites, which I am obliged to disclose."

My argument would have been: "This broker was told specifically that I only wanted to buy quiet property. He knew that I would not have considered this house had I known of the sawmill. The omission of relevant information constitutes fraud. While the broker represents the seller in this transaction, surely he has a duty to disclose information that he knows I would consider relevant to a purchase decision. I now have a contract to purchase a house I do not want. But for the broker's failure to inform me of the mill's concealed presence, I would not have signed this contract. Therefore, the contract should be voided."

The judge, I think, would have sided with the broker. It is the buyer's responsibility to investigate what he's buying. While the trees concealed the mill and no road sign indicated its presence, it was my duty to understand the property. Since the mill was not a nuisance and since it could not be construed as a defect in the sale property itself, the contract is valid. The judge would say that the buyer did not take reasonable measures to inform himself about neighboring property and nothing prevented him from so doing. The seller's broker has no obligation to do this work for the buyer.

I encourage a buyer to ditch a seller's agent who deliberately puts a buyer in this position. This broker knew that I would have rejected this property out of hand without looking at it. If a broker is willing to pull something like this on one property, he's likely to pull something else on the next. Lawsuits are a bad way to move into a community. Forfeited deposits and purchasing unwanted property are other entrances to avoid.

Everyone who buys and sells real estate has stories about both getting nicked and surviving the near misses.

On the other hand, I've worked with several sellers' agents who went above and beyond their obligations to help me determine whether a property would work for what I had in mind. One spent a day with me and a soils technician taking soil samples with a hand auger as we looked unsuccessfully for a couple of acceptable percolation spots for septic systems. He even did a market analysis to determine whether a modest subdivision might be feasible, given the bad percolation results and the local ordinance. Another helped me think through financing strategies that involved the current owner and the previous owner, an absentee grand dame, who retained an interest in the property by virtue of a note, secured by the property, that she held with the current owner. Another said, after a long conversation that showed he had a two-decades knowledge of a large tract in up-state New York, that it would not fit my client's interest for second-home development. That saved a trip. The usual pattern, in contrast, is for the seller's agent to encourage buyers to come for a visit regardless of whether the property suits the buyer's search criteria.

If you don't like the seller's agent who shows you a property, find another. Let the seller's side work out the commission split in the event of a purchase. Buyers, however, should not be petty or arbitrary in rejecting agents.

If a buyer finds himself working with an agent he has come to distrust, he could stick with the "devil he knows" instead of starting from scratch. Perhaps, you will not be harmed as long as you scope diligently and validate every statement. Nonetheless, it's hard to imagine working productively with such an agent.

The seller's agent that I recommend bailing on immediately is the one who you come to believe will get in the way of your deal. This agent may be inept, manipulative, too shrewd by half or just intellectually clumsy. Don't make a scene; just stop visiting properties with that agent.

I have observed that buyers tend to connect most easily with sellers and agents with whom they share class, education or cultural backgrounds. Buyers would be silly, however, to refuse to work with an agent unlike themselves. To the extent that buyers and those on the selling side share such demographics, they will have a common vocabulary and shared perspectives whether or not their current political and cultural opinions are compatible. Negotiating is easier when both sides have the same style of bargaining.

When a buyer finds he is working with an agent whose opinions and manners he actively dislikes and with whom he feels awkward, he should look for another. I often see ardent, tofu-eating, urban, liberal environmentalists driving around with a broker who hates them sociologically. It's hard for me to imagine how these buyers will succeed with this broker. I once came across a broker who was forthrightly and routinely anti-Semitic, exercising no self-censorship in advising buyers, including Jews, to "Jew down" his own clients. Older Southerners often use "Jew down" and "Jew boy," without, it appears, pointed, personal malice; younger Southerners don't. Kinky Friedman turned those phrases on their heads. When he ran in 2006, he promised, as the first Jewish governor of Texas, that he would lower the state's speed limit to "54.95." Verbs like "gyp" and "welsh" are rooted in ethnic prejudice, but most people who use them don't mean to invoke historical slurs. Whether "queering (spoiling) a deal" reflects homophobic prejudice probably depends on the individual and the context; "queer" carries definitions unrelated to sexual orientation. I have not heard "colored" or "Nigras" from real-estate agents for a long time, though I've heard "black" used as a slightly scrubbed-up replacement. "White trash," and "hillbilly" used synonymously, speak for themselves. I would avoid agents whose vocabulary I find objectionable. A buyer should feel intellectually and culturally comfortable with the seller's agent with whom he's working. It's more productive to negotiate through an agent who is culturally neutral and professional; it's harder with one who is not, though not impossible.

I prefer full-time sellers' agents who are smart, knowledgeable, rational, hard-working and fair-playing. Differences in class, culture, race and religion don't matter to me, but they come into play sometimes when negotiating. Experienced agents are better able to anticipate potential problems, having stumbled into them before. I try to avoid part-time agents who may be smart but tend to be less knowledgeable. I avoid ditzy agents who seem incapable of ever getting anything straight but their commissions. I am very wary of good-old-boy wheeler-dealers whose way is to screw in all directions. You can't trust these guys when they're on your side (because they are mainly working for their own interest at your expense), and certainly not when they're on the seller's side.

I have found that the seller's agent will treat you according to how he perceives you. If he sees you as a rich, dirt-dumb buyer, you are likely to be plucked. The same is often true of those who are urban arrogant or neurotically compulsive about details. Every country boy likes to get the better of a city fancy pants. Don't come across as too smart about land-buying. I have found agents who don't want to work with smart land investors. Perhaps they think that such investors will approach a property with a sharp eye and a sharper pencil. Investors, however, offer the seller's agent a lot of saved time since they know what they need to find in a property and won't waste the agent's time. If you are a dirt-smart buyer, keep this light under a bushel and don't stare too hard at it.

The buyer cannot expect the seller's agent to do his scoping, but it is fair to expect the agent to provide the data on his **listing sheet** as well as assistance about what additional information may be available from various sources, including the seller. Listing-sheet information ranges from perfunctory to detailed. The listing agent should provide you with the basics: acreage; asking price; percent of land in woods, wetlands, pasture, fields, woods, etc.; type and size of buildings; access; whether or not a survey exists; tax-assessed value; annual property tax; whether the owner is selling in fee; tax map; deed book and page number of the seller's deed; type of deed—general warranty deed being the best; recorded easements; whether the seller is carrying a mortgage secured by the property; when woods were timbered last; who the neighbors are; schools; fire protection; and local contact information. Most, if not every seller's agent I've ever dealt with, does not have this information in his file, or does not choose to provide it, or is too lazy to get it. The rule of thumb appears to be that the less a buyer knows, the better for the seller.

The agent may or may not tell a buyer the seller's purchase price, which the buyer himself can usually gather from the seller's deed. Some will give you a **competitive market analysis (CMA)**, which is the recent selling prices of a group of similar properties in the area of your target property. But such an analysis may be more than a small, independent rural broker can, or is willing to, do. You should expect to have a seller's agent produce a CMA that justifies the seller's asking price. A refusal to provide such an analysis to a buyer may suggest the target property is priced above market. Most agents will be quick to tell you if they think the property is priced below FMV. Don't expect to hear any say that the seller's price is over market. Also don't expect a seller's agent to give you information that is beyond his competence. Don't ask him to produce a timber cruise or a minerals analysis. He will not search the seller's chain of title for you. He will, however, pass on documents—an appraisal, timber cruise, legal opinion—that are favorable to the seller's interests.

One trick that I've seen is for a seller's agent to provide a CMA of a part of the seller's property, the most valuable part. This is not dishonest; it's just misleading. A Wyoming agent had a listing for a large ranch that was about ten percent irrigated bottom land and 90 percent dry range. The agent correctly valued the most valuable acreage using recent sales of properties of similar size and characteristics. He gave this work to me. He didn't provide a similar analysis for the remainder of the property—the 90 percent that was barren scrub. On a per-acre basis, the good land was worth at least ten times the rest. But there wasn't enough of the high-value land to justify the straight-through per-acre price for the entire property. A CMA, or comparables analysis, has to be based on a property in its entirety compared with other entireties that are similar in size, location and features.

Sellers' agents in my experience prefer to keep buyers thinking about property as an experiential whole, not the sum of discrete parts that are subject to analysis. Many provide just enough information to get a buyer to visit. But a few agents believe that buyers are worked more efficiently when they have information to process prior to on-site visits. When a buyer finds himself working with an agent who plays hide the ball on basic, readily obtained information, the buyer can anticipate other problems with this individual. If the agent is not minimally helpful, find another.

ALTERNATIVES: BUYER'S BROKER

One way for an out-of-town or inexperienced buyer to acquire a paid ally is to retain a **buyer's broker**. A buyer's broker, or buyer's agent, works for, and has a fiduciary relationship exclusively with, the buyer. Such an agent is sometimes paid his commission out of the seller's funds that are part of the commission paid to the listing broker. While the buyer broker's money is coming from the seller, he should, under this arrangement, be working for the buyer. A buyer can also arrange to pay a buyer broker from his own funds in which case the buyer's broker forgoes any interest in the listing broker's commission. For his money, the buyer's broker should help find the best property for the buyer and shepherd him through the entire process. The buyer looks at properties with his own broker, not the seller's. A true buyer broker is paid exclusively by the buyer; when a "buyer broker" splits the listing agent's commission, he is subject to dual-loyalty pressures.

In most real-estate purchases, the buyer is out there by himself. I like the idea of a buyer having a knowledgeable advocate in his corner, from beginning to end. The problem that can arise with a buyer's broker is that he has a set of permanent business relationships with those on the seller's side that, taken as a whole, can be more important than any single buyer-paid commission. I would avoid working with a buyer's broker who also works as a listing broker. The buyer may not get what he's paying for. A buyer's broker who works exclusively for buyers is a far better option, but such brokers have not been welcomed in many areas and you may have difficulty finding one.

A broker can draw a commission from both the seller and the buyer as long as he discloses his **dual agency** to each party before each signs a contract and obtains consent from both. I see little advantage to the buyer in using a dual broker, but neither do I necessarily see harm. Mainly, the dual broker makes more money for himself.

DISCLOSURES, PUFFING and FRAUD

Matchmaking succeeds for a buyer when he has acquired as much as information as he needs to make an analysis-based purchase. Analysis depends on quality information. A buyer always needs to evaluate information coming from the seller's side.

Many, if not all, states now require that the seller's broker fully disclose all information of which he knows about a property's condition. If the broker doesn't know something, or chooses not to know, a buyer will probably have a hard time proving that the broker should have reasonably known about it. FSBOs are probably held to a lower standard of disclosure in practice. Compliance with disclosure in my experience is followed more rigorously on houses than on raw land, though certain states require disclosure regarding water and other salient land factors.

More often than not, the law reasons that buyers can see for themselves major defects in land when they're on the property. Sellers have a duty to disclose a **latent defect** in a structure or the land itself that an ordinary inspection would not find. One example might be a grassed-over area covering unstable fill—not a place to build a house. Another might be a lake with elevated mercury levels—not a good place to fish for tonight's supper. A third might be a violation of the local building or zoning ordinance. A fourth could be an encroachment of which the seller is aware that results in harm to the buyer, such as the seller's driveway being located on a neighbor's land and which the seller knows the buyer will have to abandon. (See Fillmore W. Galaty, Wellington J. Allaway and Robert C. Kyle, Modern Real Estate Practice, 13th ed. [Chicago: Real Estate Education Company, 1994], p. 45.)

Legal opinion will divide, of course, as to whether a buyer can reasonably be expected to know a defect when it's in front of his nose. A defect in front of one buyer can be no more than an assumed risk in front of another. If, for example, a buyer purchases ten level acres on both sides of a trout stream with a charming old fishing lodge just a cast away from the coldest hole in three counties, the local judge is not likely to be sympathetic to the new buyer's suit against the seller after he discovers four feet of cold water in his living room the following spring. The seller will argue that the property was obvious floodplain—it could be nothing else. And the long-standing house was built way before restrictions were imposed on floodplain dwellings. The seller concealed nothing and certainly disclosed the juxtaposition of the house to the stream. That was, in fact, why the buyer bought it. This defect, latent or otherwise, is also the property's virtue, which is not the usual foundation of a successful lawsuit. The buyer assumed the risk of flooding to get the benefit of trout fishing from his porch. If the buyer had financed the purchase through a lending institution, he would have probably been expected to obtain and maintain federal flood insurance since the property securing the debt was in a special flood-hazard area. In that case, he couldn't claim that he didn't know about a flood risk when he bought the place.

A buyer might win a suit against this seller if he could prove that the seller knowingly misstated the land's flooding history. The buyer is not likely to win on the basis of the following seller representations: "I've owned the property for 15 years, and I've never seen the creek overflow its banks," or "I don't think you'll have a problem with flooding back there." The first statement is factually accurate, and the second is simply an opinion, not a promise or guarantee of future events. To the extent that flooding history and floodplain knowledge are available, the buyer's case is weakened.

The buyer may find better legal footing in the case where this property has flooded every year for the 15 years of the seller's ownership, and the seller said nothing about that pattern to the buyer. In my lay opinion, the gravity of this latent defect—15 years of flooding—requires disclosure, but contrary opinion would argue that 15 years of flooding has disclosed itself.

The legal recourse the buyer has in these disputes is to sue the seller and his agent (if one is involved) for **misrepresentation**. The highest form of misrepresentation is **fraud**, in which the seller intentionally misrepresents a material fact (the property's flooding history) and that misrepresentation leads the buyer to purchase the seller's land to the buyer's detriment. If the buyer never asked about the flooding history, the seller did not intentionally misrepresent anything unless that history was so notorious that the seller had an obvious duty to disclose it. The seller can defend by arguing that the flooding "defect" was open, obvious, knowable, and neither latent nor concealed. The seller loses if he lied, saying that the property did not flood when it regularly did. If the seller says nothing about flooding and the buyer asks nothing, my guess is the seller wins.

Actual fraud (misrepresentation) is intentional deception, and usually involves misstating, lying about or concealing a material fact. (**Constructive fraud** occurs when one party violates the trust or confidence of another party, as when a lawyer breaches a fiduciary duty to a client.) A long history of repeated, severe flooding would be a material fact; a history of one flood 20 years ago would probably not be. A buyer does not want to contribute to his own harm by failing to make reasonable inquiries. I would not expect a local judge to be very sympathetic to a buyer arguing that he should be made whole for a lack of reasonable effort on his own behalf. My back field has flooded four times since we bought it in 1983, though no one recalls this creek flooding before 1985. Were I to sell this farm, I would disclose that history to a buyer, because I think it's a material defect in the property. I've excavated a very large diked channel as a flood-control measure, but I do not assume that an inexperienced buyer would understand its function without explanation. The mortgage holder does not require flood insurance, however, since no improvements are threatened.

When the buyer can prove he was deceived and harmed by misrepresentation, courts will generally provide a remedy to cover the actual damages the buyer experienced. Part of any compensation award will depend on whether the court finds intentional misrepresentation. Intent to deceive is called, **scienter**, which takes place when the seller knowingly makes a misrepresentation (e.g., false statement) or even asserts that something is true or false without actual knowledge of truth or falsehood. **Innocent misrepresentation** would be the unintentional misrepresentation of the flooding history, leading to the buyer's purchase of the property. When an error is unintentional, it is a **mistake,** or an honest misrepresentation. An aggrieved buyer can rescind a contract made on the basis of a mistake of fact supplied to him by the seller's side. Where parties find themselves in a contract that was made under a mistaken belief of a material fact shared by both, either party can rescind the agreement. The better the buyer's proof that the seller knowingly and intentionally tricked him into buying a lemon, the greater are his chances that the court will find in his favor. Intent can be hard to prove, and sellers usually defend by invoking innocent mistake.

Puffing is not considered fraud. Puffing is the expression of an opinion, usually an exaggeration of the property's virtues. Here is an example: "You [the buyer] have nothing to worry about. The seller built this house, and it's probably the best-built house in town. And that timber on the back of the place. I bet it's worth $700 or $800 an acre if it's worth a nickel." Puffing is not fraud, and it's legal. Sellers and sellers' agents do it all the time. As long as the statement is expressed as an opinion rather than a fact, the law finds no fraud insofar as the person offering the opinion is not trying to deceive the buyer. A buyer trying to prove that the opinions above were expressed to deceive him will have a very hard time, despite the obvious truth that the agent is puffing to lure the buyer into a purchase.

The line between puffing—expressed opinion—and misstatement of fact is not always as obvious as a buyer might assume. A FSBO's statement about his drilled well, which would be protected as puffing, might be: "It's a fine well. The water runs good. It's the best well around here; I know that for a fact." The first two statements are opinions, but a pseudo-fact is embedded: the well "runs good." Since neither the seller nor the buyer clarified what "runs good" means, the seller is protected against fraud even if the well runs good only in comparison with other wells that always run bad. I doubt that a court would find either a fact statement in "runs good" or an intent to deceive. The third sentence could be factually true, but it's highly unlikely that every well in the county has been flow tested and even more unlikely that pollution data are available on every well and the seller has reviewed them. This statement is presented to the buyer as fact, and to the extent that it is false, it is fraudulent. But a judge might rule that "I know that for a fact" is nothing more than a vernacular expression and should not construed as establishing a verifiable fact. The seller would probably protect himself against fraud if he had said: "My well has the greatest flow and lowest *e. coli* count of all the wells I know." Since the seller knows of only one well's flow and count—his own—puffing has probably covered him. A fraudulent statement would be: "My well has the greatest flow and lowest *e. coli* count of any in the county," unless, of course, the seller has reviewed flow data and *e.coli* counts on every well in the county, both of which support his assertion.

Consider this five-part FSBO statement to a buyer: "It's a good well [though it's just an average well compared with others]; I've never known it to run dry [a factually correct statement that does not disclose the well always runs weakly in August and September]; you shouldn't have any problem with it [more of an opinion than a prediction]; the water's sweet [sounds good, may taste good too, but what does it mean exactly]; and we've never gotten sick from it [chronic diarrhea, however, seems to run in the seller's family]." These statements individually and collectively are puffing, not fraud. If the buyer is forced to drill a new well, I doubt that a court would make the seller pay for it based on these words. After all, a judge will reason the seller made do with the well during his years of ownership. The seller's words, therefore, were his opinion based on the well's performance judged against his standards, whatever they might be. Accordingly, the buyer's new well, which he had drilled during his first August, is more of a discretionary purchase than a necessity resulting from misrepresentation in the opinion of this court.

Seller-commissioned timber cruises are often given to a buyer, and these cruises can inflate the true merchantable value of the timber by 50 percent or more. Chapter 22 discusses all the ways that cruises can be puffed. Here's a quick example. A seller says to you: "The cruise I commissioned estimates two million board feet of sawtimber stumpage on my 5,000 acres. That volume of timber at current local prices projects to a value of $400,000." Sounds good! You didn't think the scrubby pine and hardwood were worth much of anything. It's a windfall! The seller is being truthful. He did commission a cruise, and it did project two million board feet of sawtimber, which his forester valued at $400,000. Both the seller's statements and the cruise are factually correct in a sense, and are, therefore, not fraudulent—despite being big, fat lies. The seller's cruise does indeed estimate two million board feet of sawtimber on the tract and does in fact project a value of $400,000 at current local prices. But none of this projected sawtimber value is realizable in the real world. How can this be? What is lacking from the seller's statement is the fact that 750,000 board feet of the two million are found on 80-degree slopes that are too steep for timber operations. That's why it's never been cut. Another 250,000 board feet are so far back on the property and the trees are of such poor quality that no logger will pay to cut them. The other one million board feet are in trees so widely scattered that loggers would find it uneconomical to build the skid roads to get to them. While 2,000,000 board feet of sawtimber exist, none are economical or feasible to cut and for that reason the new owner won't realize $400,000 in a timber sale. But the seller's statement is not fraud, though it is certainly misleading.

Courts have increasingly considered the context of statements, narrowing the puffing defense a bit. In specific circumstances, oral and written statements have been found fraudulent, along with actions, failure to act, failure to disclose, concealment and silence. Cases involving seller silence are the hardest for a buyer to win. As a rule, contract law does not require a seller to disclose a fact that is detrimental to the agreement, except when his silence may physically harm a person using the property, or limit the buyer's planned use of the property which is known to the seller, among other exceptions. Half-truths that induce a buy and which then harm the buyer can be the basis for fraud. In fraud cases, the buyer, in addition, must show reliance (that is, he bought the seller's property because he relied on the misrepresentation) and the materiality of the misrepresentation (that is, the fact that was misrepresented must be important and critical to the sale). If reliance was based on puffing, the buyer loses, because puffing is allowed. The remedies to a buyer successful in proving fraud can be upholding his refusal to perform on the purchase, rescinding of the contract, or collection of damages where monetary loss is proved. Punitive damages can be awarded in fraud cases where the buyer proves that he suffered actual monetary loss and that the fraudulent act was gross, oppressive and committed with ill will. If a buyer discovers fraud and does nothing about it, he waives his right to remedy. A seller and his agent do not shield themselves from a misrepresentation suit when a purchase contract contains the boilerplate language that the buyer has not relied on any representations made to him by either the seller or his agent. (See Gibson *et al.*, <u>Real Estate Law</u>, 3rd ed., Chapter 14.)

Lawsuits are aggravating, draining and time-consuming—even when you win. A newcomer does not want to announce joining a rural community by suing an established member, the seller. It will not matter much that the former owner is universally regarded by his former neighbors as a crook. The suit will be interpreted as a shot across the community's bow. Fellowship will not follow from your pursuit of what you see as your stand on the high moral ground. The other factor to keep in mind is that the routine puffing and fraud sellers commit may only involve small amounts of money. It is often wiser to take a small hit and move along than to sue and win, which can be the first successful battle in a losing war. Your own diligent scoping will prevent you from being taken in by either fraud or puffing.

Property involved with estates—especially estates with a number of heirs—is often sold to generate cash. The executor will arrange the sale with the help of a broker, or do it himself, or work through the estate's lawyer. Consequently, local lawyers are sources of early information on estate property. Local papers will eventually carry announcements of estate auctions involving land and personal property. Where heirs cannot agree on the disposition of their shared inheritance, one or more may file a **partition suit**, which forces the sale of the property at auction. These, too, are announced and advertised in the local paper. Such properties often produce above-market prices when family members are bidding against each other.

I phoned a lawyer early in 2006 who was advertising an auction for "approximately 400 acres" that included timber and minerals. I suspected that it was a partition suit since the majority owner was a land company and the minority owner was a set of heirs. I asked the lawyer about the merchantable timber value. "About $200,000," he said. I then asked him a set of forestry-related questions to determine how the number was calculated. In exasperation, he gave me the phone of the forester who had been hired. The forester was honest. He told me that he had done a walk-through and figured a landowner could count on getting $100,000 in a timber sale. Of course, someone might value the timber at $200,000. The 400 acres turned out to be 361.5, which is "approximately" 400. Puffing is a part of real-estate sales. I know of no other profession where puffing is a legitimate sales tactic.

AUCTION BUYING

Rural property is frequently **sold at auction**. One of the virtues of an auction from the seller's viewpoint is that the property is sold quickly, without the protracted wait that often accompanies listing with a broker. Auctions solve the major investment drawback of real estate—lack of liquidity. If the seller finds himself in debt with monthly payments eating him alive—a situation I've been in and did not like—the auction will produce a chunk of money that will pay down, if not retire, the debt. By assembling a crowd of motivated buyers, auctions can generate a price higher than what a seller might net either through listing or selling on his own. The risk to the seller, however, is that the sale is limited to whomever shows up and bids on that one day. Auction sellers can be an individual; public agency (the county selling tax-delinquent land; the IRS selling seized land); U.S. Bankruptcy Court which authorizes the sale to raise cash to pay debt; lending institutions such as a bank; estates; and business entities such as partnerships, non-profits, corporations and limited liability companies.

Auctions are conducted as either **absolute** or **with reserve**. An absolute auction is one where the seller and auctioneer promise the buyers that the property will be sold that day for the highest bid, no matter how low. An **absolute auction above minimum opening bid**, a variation of the absolute auction, becomes absolute as soon as the advertised minimum opening price is met. The seller cannot withdraw his property from the auction process once the minimum opening bid is met, and he cannot bid himself or through a proxy. Absolute auctions encourage buyers to come because they know the property will be sold even if it brings a sum far below fair market value. Sellers who are extremely confident in their knowledge of the value of the property or sellers who are desperate to raise cash use the absolute auction. Buyers are guaranteed that the property will be sold, but the seller has no guarantee as to what he will receive from the sale. Auctioneers prefer absolute auctions, because they will make a sale and get their commission plus expenses. An absolute auction is also known as an **auction without reserve.**

An **auction with reserve** is a contingent sale, subject either to a minimum selling price the seller has set with the auctioneer in advance or a minimum price that a lender imposes on the seller before it will release the property from its note. Also known as an **auction subject to confirmation**, these auctions allow the seller to accept or reject all bids, or withdraw the property from the sale before the auction is completed, depending on how the reserve is structured. Usually, a reserve price is set, and the seller is guaranteed either a minimum amount of gross sale revenue or no sale at all. Buyers are guaranteed nothing. The seller whose property is not bid up to the reserve price must still cover the auctioneer's expenses and fees. When an auction with reserve does not meet the reserve, the seller may choose to let the property go for the high bid anyway or declare the auction sale null and void. A **seller-set reserve price** is one between the seller and the auctioneer; a **bank-set reserve price** is imposed on both auctioneer and seller

Where there is bank debt on a property, the buyer at an auction with reserve may find himself being asked to raise his offer after the auction ends if the **hammer price** at the auction's close is less than the lender's pre-auction imposed reserve. The hammer price is the final high bid, signaled by the auctioneer striking his hammer and announcing, "Sold to Bidder X." When a buyer finds himself with the final bid below the reserve price, the bank will ask him to put more money into the purchase or else lose the property. If the bank fails to release the property, the seller retains the property and continues to owe the bank the amount of the debt. The seller, however, is now poorer by the amount he's paid to the auctioneer. The bank does not want to take possession of the property, so the high bidder has some bargaining leverage. The bidder can wash his hands entirely of the purchase without penalty or come up with more money to meet the lender's reserve. If the seller has personally guaranteed the note to the bank (which is rarely the case on mortgage debt), the bank may sell to the bidder and leave the shortfall on the seller's indebtedness. Buyers in this situation should keep in mind that the bank does not really want to take possession of the property, which will have to go through another sale. This creates good conditions for negotiation, particularly if the buyer is willing to finance the purchase through the bank. For the buyer to gain from this negotiation with the lender, he must be willing to walk away from the property. The bank will call a bluff. The buyer might as part of a negotiation go up one tick and then stop for good. This will either work or not. If the bank senses that you have the resources and motivation to go higher, rest assured that you will be escorted there. I've seen a bank shake out another 33 percent from a motivated high bidder before releasing a property auctioned with a reserve price.

Where the property at auction is only part of the collateral securing the seller's note with a bank, the buyer will want the bank to **release the property** from the seller's note for his bid price, whether or not the reserve was met. This is referred to as a **partial release**. The seller's remaining collateral continues to secure the residual debt. The buyer gets title to that portion of the seller's property he's purchased that has been released from the seller's note.

An auction with reserve provides more certainty for the seller about revenue (because the sale is contingent on the reserve being met), but less certainty about whether or not a sale will take place. Reserves are set to get at least a minimally acceptable price, which is usually below market. A seller-set reserve price provides him with protection against a catastrophically bad auction where the best bid is ridiculously low. Where the best bid approaches the reserve, the seller, in attendance, can signal the auctioneer to accept it. With a bank-set reserve, the bank cannot unilaterally lower its reserve price without agreement from the seller; if the seller does not agree, the sale does not go through.

Auctioneers recommend that the reserve price not be revealed to bidders; they think concealment encourages attendance and bidding action. A buyer who learns the reserve price is advantaged because he knows the price at which the lock is taken off the sale. That is the point where the auction with reserve converts automatically to an absolute auction even when this change is not announced to the auction bidders. The reserve price gives the buyer a good sense of FMV since the lender will set the reserve close to, but usually under, FMV.

Lacking inside information, a buyer can piece together an estimate of a reserve price within a likely range. The bottom of the range would be the 100 percent fair market value that is used for tax-assessment purposes. The top of the range would be the property's FMV as determined by a comparables analysis. This bottom is likely to be too low and this top too high. Therefore, you may have to narrow the range by adding to the bottom number and subtracting from the top. A real-estate agent can give you a quick idea of how much to add and subtract. Professional appraisers and real-estate brokers can provide comparables analysis to establish FMV, for which you should expect too pay. In fact, that may be the method by which the bank sets its reserve price. A bank reserve price, in addition, can be set to cover the seller's debt and costs of collection. If you can find out from the mortgage documents in the courthouse records the amount of the mortgage and its terms, you can estimate the remaining principal owed using an amortization table. Figure in that the bank will be owed some delinquent interest as well. The bank's mortgage paper is usually recorded immediately after the deed and follows it in the deed book. A bank reserve will usually be the amount of principal remaining on the seller's note and the auctioneer's expenses. Depending on local markets, the bank may try to get some portion of its delinquent interest too. Banks, generally, do not make money on the sale of foreclosed property.

Auctioneers believe that a reserve-price format discourages bidding, but I've been unable to find evidence other than their opinions to support that belief. It may be impossible to substantiate it empirically since a property auction on a given day can only be run once either absolute or with reserve. It's impossible to run the same auction on the same day in front of the same bidders in both formats. If auctioneers are right in believing that absolute auctions achieve a higher price, the buyer should expect to pay more for a property auctioned absolute than bid with a reserve. But, an absolute auction always holds out the prospect to a buyer of buying property at a steep discount, even pennies on a dollar of fair value.

When you see an auction ad in the newspaper, it will have the word "absolute" prominently featured if it is such a sale. In Virginia, at least, all auctions by law are with reserve unless specifically advertised and conducted as an absolute sale. If the ad does not say "absolute," buyers here should know it is with a reserve even where it does not say reserve. At the sale itself, the auctioneer will announce the auction's format, absolute or with reserve, in a way that will be plain and unambiguous. Auctions are now videotaped in case a dispute arises.

Auctioneers will usually mail out a **bidder's packet** before the sale. Information provided at the sale just prior to the bidding supersedes all earlier information, both oral and written. Listen carefully to the **auctioneer's announcements** before the bidding begins for changes in what is being sold and how.

The bidder's packet is a set of documents and information pertaining to the property and the auction's rules. Each auctioneer approaches a packet in his own way, some include more property information, others, the minimum. The packet can include copies of some, or all, of the following:

- recorded deed the seller holds and will convey
- easements that run with the land both for and against the benefit of the owner of the sale property
- reservations from the sale (such as the owner excluding—"reserving"—his interest in the current lease; severance of minerals)
- survey or plat (shows the location and boundary dimensions of the property)
- professional appraisal or comparables analysis
- valuations of specific property assets, such as timber, house, equipment
- documents regarding farm income, rent, subsidy payments, royalties, etc.
- property tax data—assessed value, amount of current tax
- other tax information—e.g., rates on personal property, trash tax, surcharges and fees for various purposes
- tax map (showing property location and boundaries) if no survey exists
- permits and letters from regulatory agencies if relevant
- zoning and division ordinances (zoning classification determines what can be done on the property; setbacks for buildings; types of construction permitted, etc.)
- school district and school information
- information related to the property's sewerage and water systems, and other utilities
- percolation-test results (make sure the test was taken near the spot on which you want to build) if relevant
- water-sample results from existing house
- well-drilling information/costs
- utility rates and new-line costs
- road-building cost estimates
- liens filed or pending against the property

- proximity of police and fire-protection services
- location of health-care facilities
- termite inspection if required
- **terms-of-the-sale sheet**

This packet should be in your possession before the auction as part of your own scoping effort. Most of this material will be publicly available. Unrecorded easements and seller reservations will not be public record.

Read carefully the **terms-of-the-sale sheet**, which sets forth the rules and requirements by which the auctioneer will conduct the auction, subject to his announcements prior to the bidding. The sheet will state whether the auction is absolute or reserve. It may include language that allows the auctioneer to bid on behalf of the seller. The terms will tell you how much you are expected to deposit as the winning bidder and in what form. Some auctioneers insist on certified checks or cash. The terms will state your liability in the event that you back out of a winning bid. The sheet will state when closing is scheduled, usually within 30 days of the auction day.

Pre-auction advertising and the terms-of-the-sale information will include what you need to know about becoming a **qualified bidder** if the auctioneer requires that bidders qualify financially at registration. An auctioneer will require personal identification at a minimum. When large amounts of money are involved, expect to present evidence that you are good for the sum you bid. If you do not qualify, you cannot bid. The auctioneer will tell you in advance what materials you need to bring to the auction—or provide beforehand—to establish your credentials. The auctioneer qualifies bidders because he does not want to wind up with a high bidder who can't pay his bid price.

Auctioneers generally charge the seller a ten percent commission on the gross selling price, plus reimbursement for advertising and promotion work. Lower commission rates may be applied to high-dollar properties. Some auctioneers charge as seller-reimbursed expenses all of the costs of conducting the auction, including charges for auctioneering personnel and overhead. The cost to the seller is almost always higher selling through an auctioneer than paying a straight five-to-ten percent commission to a broker if the auctioneer does not sell with a **buyer's premium**, explained below. Auctioneers should spend a lot of (the seller's) money on advertising and promotion to generate interest and bidding for what is a one-day, make-or-break sale. Auctioneers differ in their marketing skills, and these differences can substantially affect the results. Some auctioneers will buy mailing lists, others won't. Some have good in-house mailing lists that can be targeted to likely buyers.

Many auctioneers approach the seller as a goose to be plucked. This is particularly true with sellers in desperate circumstances who are forced into an auction as a way to produce cash quickly. Such auctioneers may refuse to take a seller unless he agrees to an absolute format. They are also likely to insist that the seller do certain things at the seller's expense to improve the value of the property prior to auction, such as obtain septic permits and install gravel roads on undeveloped land, provide a new survey or fix the house. The auctioneer is trying to make the property as cosmetically appealing as possible, to make buying easy and get the highest bid price. Buyers need to look beneath any recently applied make up.

A **buyer's premium** is a percentage fee the high bidder pays in addition to the amount of his winning bid. The premium helps the seller pay for the cost of the auction. Some auctioneers believe a buyer's premium discourages bidding and produces lower net results than an auction free of a buyer's premium. Again, empirical evidence for this belief is hard to find. I don't think a buyer's premium of five percent or less has any depressive effect on bid prices. Most buyers will have adjusted their bidding to take any premium into account. I believe that most buyers will discount their bid by the amount of a premium so that the net bid price is likely to be the same with or without the premium. Buyers should set a cap on their highest bid price before the auctioneer starts his call. That cap should incorporate the buyer's premium and any other associated costs. The cap should also reflect your scoping as to what the property is worth to you.

An auctioneer with whom I worked charged me a ten percent commission on the gross selling price, which was, the winning bid price plus the ten percent buyer's premium. With a bid price of $100,000, the buyer's premium would add $10,000, making a gross selling price of $110,000, on which I paid the auctioneer a ten percent commission, or $11,000, of which $10,000—91 percent—came from the buyer. This format is sometimes referred to as the "**ten-ten system**," a plan whereby the auctioneer is paid 11 percent of the sale price rather than the nominal ten percent. A buyer's premium helps a cash-desperate seller if it doesn't depress bidding. Careless buyers who don't calculate the effect of the buyer's premium can be caught paying more than they planned.

Country people are comfortable with buying and selling through auctions. Livestock is typically sold this way, and farm-dispersal auctions are common. If you are an inexperienced country-auction buyer, you need to get your feet wet before you chance getting soaked. Attend a land auction held by the auctioneer who's scheduled to sell the property you've targeted. You can learn his schedule by logging on to his website or calling his office. Learn his rules. Listen to his calls so that you can understand his numbers. Observe how he closes the bidding: some close quickly, others will suspend everything for 30 minutes and then close it out. Strike up conversations with non-bidders. Try to learn as much as you can about how auctions are managed in your target area.

Auctioneers are licensed by the state in which the auction is being held. Call the state's auction-licensing board to confirm that the auctioneer is licensed and inquire about complaints or board sanctions (disciplines). Auctioneer licenses are usually handled by the state's real-estate office or the board that issues professional licenses. Complaints may or may not tell you something useful about an auctioneer. They can be nothing more than sour grapes from an unsuccessful or unsophisticated bidder. You should ask the auctioneer whether the sale will follow a particular code of professional ethics, and, if so, which one. The **National Auctioneers Association** (NAA, 8880 Ballantine, Overland Park, KS, 66214; 913-541-8084; FAX, 913-894-5281; www.auctioneers.org) has developed the "Standards of Practice of the Certified Auctioneers Institute" and the "Code of Professional Ethics, Certified Auctioneers Institute" that set forth rules for members in dealing with both clients (sellers) and buyers. Not all auctioneers are NAA members. These documents are also found in Stephen J. Martin and Thomas E. Battle, III, Sold! The Professional's Guide to Real Estate Auctions (Chicago: Real Estate Education Company, 1991).

And then there was the "auctioneer" who wasn't. He—a land company—had an office, stationery, business cards and secretary. He appears to have been a real-estate broker who advertised that he performed "auction services." I became suspicious, because he did not include his Virginia auction-license number on his sale notices or business cards. This fellow, it turned out, did everything that an auctioneer did, save call the sale. He hired a licensed auctioneer to perform that task. When I asked him if he had an auctioneer's license, he ducked. When I pressed, he admitted that he did not and explained his way of doing auction services using a hired auctioneer. As long as he was a broker, he could do the sale, and I never pursued why he didn't have an auctioneer's license. I didn't see anything wrong with his auction-services approach, but I would have been more comfortable with it had he been forthright. This quirk was the first of many. The guy always left me with a headache. After weeks of negotiating, it became clear that he would do my auction only as an absolute sale, which I had told him at each of our meetings I did not want. To sellers: if an auctioneer gives you either a headache or the willies, find one who doesn't.

The buyer needs to learn the auctioneer's **bidding system**. The system may or may not be described in the bidder's packet. Auctioneers may vary their system from sale to sale, depending on which format they feel will yield the most money. The simplest system is bidding dollars for the whole property, that is, the buyer's bid represents his price for the **entirety.** In this system, a buyer bidding $100,000 is offering that sum for all of the property's acreage and improvements. The auctioneer will probably call out, "100," to represent $100,000. The most common alternative to entirety bidding is the **dollars-per-acre format**, where the bid price is expressed as dollars for just one acre. The number "100" in this format represents $100 per acre multiplied by the number of acres in the entirety.

To keep your wits about you during the heat of the auction, you need to prepare a **crib sheet** beforehand so that you will know instantaneously what any per-acre bid means multiplied out with the buyer's premium added. The crib sheet below shows a tract of 153 acres and a seven percent buyer's premium.

Dirt-Smart Buyer's Land-Auction Crib Sheet

$ Bid Per Acre	Total Bid Price	Total Price to be Paid with 7% Buyer's Premium
500	$76,500	$81,855
525	80,325	85,948
550	84,150	90,041

I've included three dollar-per-acre bid prices for illustration. Your actual crib sheet will include a wider range, from just below the lowest price you think is possible to just above what you think is possible. In this example, my actual crib sheet might range from $350 per acre (p/A) to $700. Do not scrimp on cribbing! I would also stop my cribbing at my **cap price**, which is the dollar point where I stop bidding. You can fine-tune prices within your projected range by using smaller dollar increments, say $10 per-acre jumps instead of $25. From your crib sheet, you can also calculate that each dollar bid per acre will cost you $163.71 when you write your check to the auctioneer for the entire 153-acre tract. Acreage (153) x $1 = $153 + $10.71 (buyer's premium: .07 x $153 = $10.71); total is $163.71 per dollar bid.

CIRCLE IN RED INK your cap-price, dollar-per-acre bid, which you've dutifully underlined. Now underline it again in RED INK. DO NOT GO ABOVE THAT PRICE. That cap price is the result of your analytical research into the property being sold and reflects your cold-eyed financial assessment. Going above your red-line price moves you backward, from being smart to being impulsive. The auction is designed to pull you into a competitive fray where your emotions rule your head. Resist. Don't be stampeded into a higher price.

I recommend bringing a **helper** along to a land auction, preferably someone who is observant and calm. Both you and the helper should get to the auction site early to look at the pass-out materials from the auctioneer and mingle with the crowd, picking up what you can. Talk to neighbors of the property. Ask the auctioneer's associates who they think will be the likely bidders and why. Look at the auctioneer's registration list for clues as to the types of buyers at the sale. Once the auction begins, the helper should watch the bidders and get a read for who they are and the intensity of their interest. Do not assume that the city person who pulls up in a Hummer wearing his brand-new Orvis outfit has a deeper pocket for this property than the guy in the back spitting tobacco juice into a styrofoam cup. The helper should try to sense when each bidder is reaching his upper limit and give this information to his buyer. The helper should work the calculator for the buyer and warn him when the bidding approaches the buyer's top price, even though both can see that it is circled and underlined in red ink on their crib sheets.

Readers may ask: "Why in the world would the helper need to warn his friend that the red-circle price is close?" That's an excellent question posed by a person who is sitting calmly in the quiet of his own home reading a book. Auctions are designed to be intense, emotional and fast. They want to overload the buyers' sensory systems. They're loud and a little confusing on purpose. Your helper must be a rock in this storm, preferably a rock whose head stays above the chop. I have seen otherwise rational human beings forget their red-circle price in the heat of the moment; I've done it myself.

The bidder should concentrate on listening to the calls and maintaining eye contact with either the auctioneer or one of his ringmen who will acknowledge and confirm each buyer's bid with a whooped "Yup!" or "Yeah!" When your bid is on the floor, you need to know that. I've seen bidders try to up their own bids. I've also seen bidders fail, because they thought the final high bid was theirs when it wasn't. When in doubt, ask the auctioneer to confirm that your bid is high. Better to look like a fool than to be one.

Auctioneers will often do a **combination bidding system** when a property involves sub-parcels. Each sub-parcel is bid separately, on either a dollars-per-acre basis or as a sub-entirety. When all sub-parcels have been bid out to a price, the prices are chalked on the auction board. Then the auctioneer begins auctioning sub-parcels combined in different ways. The combining of sub-parcels may be initiated by individual bidders or proposed by the auctioneer. The auctioneer may impose a $1,000 premium to combine a group of sub-parcels, that is, the bid for the group has to be $1,000 more to start than the chalk-board price of the sub-parcels taken together. The auctioneer's object with combination bidding is to boost the total price the auction achieves. The theory is the more times bidders are run at the entirety from different angles, the higher the ultimate selling price.

A variation on combination bidding is a system that involves a lot of on-the-spot deal-making among buyers who may have to form coalitions with other buyers to buy and defend what they want to buy. The bidding is dollars per acre, with the winner of each round granted his choice of sub-parcel (s), any or all, at that price. The first round winner could take all sub-parcels. In that event, the auctioneer would place the entirety for bid with a premium to start it off. The entirety premium might be $10,000. If no bidder or coalition of bidders come in, the first round winner takes the entirety at his bid price with no premium.

If you wanted three parcels of a ten-parcel entirety, and you were successful in being the first-round high bidder on two of the three you wanted, you can in the second round propose a three-parcel combination by paying the premium. The first-round winner of the third parcel will have to defend. He can bid against you for the three parcels; he can let you have your three and then pull out one or two parcels as his own combination; he can form a rival coalition; he can package his parcel with a fourth, forcing you to bid on a four-parcel group if you want three. You might then resell the parcel you didn't want. When this system works, you find yourself in a three-dimensional chess game. My experience with combination bidding is that its complexity discourages participation. At some point in this maze, some bidders stop playing because of the maze, not the money. I've seen this too-clever-by-half system fail miserably three times.

A buyer can't change the auctioneer's bidding system. The buyer's protection against these sophisticated hustles is the red-circled number on his crib sheet. Never bid above the number in the red circle.

If you find yourself at an auction where the auctioneer is jumping the bidding in large increments, say $5,000 to $10,000, bid a half increment by indicating to him that you want to raise the high bid the auctioneer has (from someone else) by half the increment he's asking for. You do this by sliding your hand horizontally from left to right, or up to down in a chopping motion. If the auctioneer acknowledges that you are the high bid but at the increment he wanted rather than what you indicated, you will have to call out the bid price you wanted to make sure that he understands your number. Do not be shy. It is your money that he's trying to spend.

Most land is auctioned, "AS IS, WHERE IS," which means with all faults included, whether or not any are stated explicitly, which they should be. "AS IS" should be interpreted to refer to the condition of what you can see. It also should mean there's no reservation on the timber or pending sale of a part of the tract. It means that the seller is unwilling to spend any time or money to fix up anything. "WHERE IS" may or may not be of importance. If, for example, the seller's description of his property is actually short 25 acres and you discover—later—that the deedwork really gives you a claim to 25 acres that a neighbor has fenced in as his, you will probably find yourself stuck with the original acreage since you bought what it was, where its observable boundaries were. You can feel confident in the boundaries and acreage when the auctioneer is working from a reasonably current plat or survey. Auctioneers prefer that sellers have surveys to avoid post-auction bidder backouts over disputed acreage. A survey lends credibility to other less-substantiated features of a property.

When the auctioneer announces that the property will be sold "AS IS, WHERE IS," you are within your rights as a bidder to ask him a **general-disclosure-and-endorsement question**: whether either he or the seller knows of any defect, easement or condition in the chain of title, boundaries, physical environment, subsurface and property itself that would negatively affect a bidder's possession, use or enjoyment of the property. If you feel uncomfortable asking this question in public, write it out and hand it to the auctioneer before he starts. Bidders may or may not have a legal right to be given all such information, but how the auctioneer handles your question—forthright answer, no answer, refusal to answer, non-answer answer, weasel answer, hostility at being questioned, wrong answer, misleading answer—will provide you with more information than you had before. If you know of some defect that you can live with or overcome, asking an open-ended question like this is a tactic you can use to scare off marginal bidders. Auctioneers videotape their auctions to have an incontrovertible record of the auction's rules, announcements and conduct in the event of a dispute. False or misleading answers can get them into trouble with the state-licensing board if a bidder goes to the trouble of pursuing a complaint.

A variation on the general-disclosure-and-endorsement question is one about a specific fact whose answer you already know. This tactic can be used to alert other bidders that there's a problem whose repair cost is high or which presents a great deal of uncertainty. For example, a bidder might ask: Can you give me an estimate of how much it will cost to repair the seller's fences? Am I correct in my belief that the deed's calls do not close, and that this property is likely to be about 10 acres short of the 90 advertised? Does the owner have a clear, marketable title to all that he's selling? If a buyer is simply trying to "game" the auction, to knock down the price with his questions, the other bidders will figure this out in a country minute, which is faster than any in New York. Such questions, however, are more than fair when a buyer wants to pin down the auctioneer and seller on critical information before getting into the bidding. If you can't get an answer in your pre-auction scoping, then ask it at the auction, either privately or publicly. It's fair to insist on getting straight answers; it's not fair to deliberately squirrel up a sale.

It is not uncommon for an auctioneer to have a **bogus bidder**, or **shill,** in the crowd who gets the bidding going when starting is hard. Whether or not this practice is legal depends on the auction's groundrules and the shill's intentions and financial capabilities. In an auction with reserve, the bogus bidder is trying to get the sale price up to the reserve price so that the auction can be completed. The shill will bid in and drop out soon, since his job is to get the ball rolling and not to buy the property. The shill will almost always drop out just before the reserve price. If the shill inadvertently "wins" a parcel, the auctioneer will be on the phone the day after the auction trying to sell it to a genuine buyer, starting with the other successful bidders. In an absolute auction, however, an auctioneer's shill is acting illegally, because the seller and the auctioneer have announced that they will sell the property for the highest bid with no reserve or minimum price. A shill's bid effects a minimum price in an absolute auction and would be grounds to contest the sale. But shilling is hard to prove beyond a reasonable doubt. The auctioneer's uncle may be a shill, but he may be nothing more than a bidder.

If you think the auctioneer has a shill, ask him when he is finished with his announcements whether he or anyone associated with him or the seller will be bidding. Anticipate that the auctioneer and the seller will be miffed, because you are asking a question that clouds the auction. Land auctioneers want sunny skies, both meteorologically and metaphysically. The auctioneer's proper response should be to thank you for your question and tell you the truth. At an absolute auction, shilling should not occur. At a reserve auction, the bogus bidder must drop out at the reserve price. At that point, some auctioneers announce that the reserve has been met, and the auction is being converted to an absolute sale. If you ask these questions prior to the auction in private and are not satisfied with the answers, you have no choice but to ask them in public. It's a difficult role to be the dog in the manger, but it's your money at stake. I advise against asking questions, these or any others, for the simple purpose of depressing bidding by raising doubts among the bidders. Besmirching an auction for your own benefit is tawdry and reflects badly on a newcomer. Self-protection is another matter.

Auction results are not predictable from either the seller or the buyers' points of view. If the crowd sits on its hands, the auctioneer will scramble to get a bid on the board. If the crowd is motivated, things can get wild. Suspicion and uncertainty always attend an event where money is in play. Bidders should avoid trying to control an auction by engaging in **collusion**, which is the practice of agreeing amongst themselves to depress competition or otherwise fix prices. Such bidders are known as a "**ring**." The most common form is for the ring members to agree not to bid against each other, letting one of their number win, and then dividing the property according to a pre-bidding deal. This practice is either illegal or pretty close. If the auctioneer or seller gets wind of it, a suit is likely to follow. On the other side, bidders may not know when an auctioneer or the seller is using a shill to run up the price or even calling a **phantom bid** from a phantom bidder. Phantom bidding, also called **trotting**, is illegal. For all of the ways to rig an auction, my impression is that they are at least as clean as conventional buying and selling through a real-estate broker, which speaks for both.

Buyers can get great deals at land auctions that are busts for the seller. They can also find themselves in a frenzied bidding war that produces nonsensically high prices. I have found myself in situations where the auctioneer sweats to get even a below-market price for a wonderful property. I've also seen price jumps in $5,000 increments as fast as bidders can tug their ears for a property that fetched twice its real value. Often, one or two bidders are personally interested in a property owing to a family connection or because they share its boundary. These highly motivated bidders can run up an auction price. Do not assume that because some fool is willing to pay the price he just bid that he must know what he's doing, and therefore you can go him one better and still be in the FMV ballpark. If he's a bidder with an emotional interest in the property, he will bid above where reason and self-interest tell him to stop. So find out before the auction whether family and neighbors will be bidding. Know these people and do not be dragged into a bidding war with them unless you, too, are willing pay whatever you need to pay to win the property. It's best to approach auctions as an investor, not a second-home buyer. Be unemotional and rational. Let your scoping determine your red-circle price, not your heart. Do not exceed what your calculator and brain have decided for you the night before. Don't be swept into the auction's rhythm and momentum. Bid with confident strength, as if you are the deepest pocket in the house. (Of course, if you are the deepest pocket, don't act like it.)

You may run into a bidder who starts the bidding at a price that is equal to or even above where the auctioneer begins. This is a tactic to drive off every other bidder before the bidding starts. If the bid price is below your red-circle number, take him up one notch. The odds are you will win, because that bidder is afraid of an auction and has only one price to play, win or lose.

I've had two bizarre things happen to me at rural auctions, neither of which involved land. When we first bought our farm, the owners auctioned many personal items. I was bidding for an old bureau against a non-local fellow (I later learned he was a Richmond stockbroker), and the price was going up quickly. Suddenly, a casually well-dressed woman yanked my arm as I was bidding, pulling me in her direction and behind a tree in the front yard. She began firing questions at me about the farm and my background. I had been totally buried in the bidding, and then was abruptly disinterred. I tried to answer her out of residual politeness and also get my hand back into the bidding. Her husband, by then, had won the piece. I've never seen this trick pulled again, but it certainly worked on me. It turned out that the broker and his wife had a second home about a mile from me, and I would see them on the weekends when I jogged by. She always disappeared into the house, and he exchanged pleasantries with obvious discomfort. I used to make protracted conversation just to see him squirm.

I was at a house auction with my five-year-old daughter when her eye landed on a tourist trinket box from Niagara Falls. She needed that box, she said. I bid 50 cents, about three times what it was worth. I was the only bidder. The auctioneer's ringman then upped me a quarter, and we were off. I ended up paying $4.50 and was burning mad. The ringman came over and said he was bidding so that the little girl could have it. It is difficult for me to believe that he didn't know I was the little girl's father inasmuch as she's a dead ringer and was sitting on my shoulders at the time.

Auction rules vary from state to state. Auctioneers, their associates and ringmen, are usually allowed to bid if they are genuine buyers, which often they are, or theoretically could be. I have seen the owner of a sale barn bid for livestock at his own auction where he was holding buy orders from individuals who were not in attendance—the effect of which was to run up the price for whomever "won." Bidding ringmen and auctioneer confederates can be bogus bidders whose only goal is to run up the price. In a reserve auction (in Virginia, at least) this is acceptable as long as the bogus bidder drops out at the reserve price. In an absolute auction, bogus bidding is illegal—and I've never seen it happen.

At auction's end, the high bidder will sign an **auctioneer's sales contract—your purchase contract**—with the auctioneer who is representing the seller. The buyer gives the auctioneer a deposit, which is usually ten percent of the gross selling price. The auctioneer prefers that deposits take the form of cash or certified checks, though the seller may authorize personal checks from individuals he knows. I've seen buyers bid without getting qualified regardless of pre-auction instructions and then offer a non-local check. It's better to play by the rules. Land auctions do not require full payment on auction day, though auctions for personal property, machinery and livestock do. Determine how much deposit money and in what form the auctioneer requires, and make sure that you have exactly what is needed. Closing is usually scheduled for 15 to 30 calendar—not business—days after the auction date. Bring your appointment book to the auction and schedule the closing date and place with the auctioneer when you sign the contract.

Auctioneer sales contracts are not standard, boilerplate agreements that you can get from any real-estate agent or local brokers' association. They are shorter, simpler and even less protective of the buyer. They do not, as a rule, include the common state-required inspections and warranties that broker contracts use. They are almost always drawn up by the auctioneer and his lawyer. They are designed to make sure the buyer performs, the auctioneer gets his commission and the auctioneer is protected from liability to the seller in the event of bidder non-performance. In auctions, it is up to the buyer to do all due diligence prior to bidding. Unlike a purchase contract, the buyer at auction is not submitting an offer to the buyer for his consideration; he is buying the property for the price he bid, subject only to satisfying any reserve price imposed by the seller or his lender. If you refuse to sign the auctioneer's sales contract after being high bidder, you should assume the auctioneer and the seller will sue to compel you to buy the property at your bid price. If you sign the sales contract and then decide that you do not want to go through with it, you should anticipate losing your auction-day deposit at the very least.

Once the auction concludes, the high bidder will be expected to sign the auctioneer's sales contract. To avoid surprises, you should secure a sample contract from the auctioneer before the auction. You can review its terms and conditions with your lawyer. High bidders sign previously unread auction contracts all the time. Since the buyer has bought "AS IS, WHERE IS" at auction, post-auction inspections do the buyer no good, except to identify problems. The auctioneer will not allow you to add contingencies to his contract. Buyer failure to find financing or an acceptable septic-system site will not void an auction contract. Where a buyer quickly learns of a dreadful, costly defect in the property, a lawsuit might get the buyer off the hook if the seller and the auctioneer concealed it in some fashion. As a rule, however, the "AS IS, WHERE IS" format of the auction will likely trump most buyer claims. But the cost of defending and the negative publicity may persuade a seller to negotiate with the buyer to avoid a trial. To put the matter as simply as I can: when you buy "AS IS" at an auction, you buy the property's assets and liabilities more or less without any recourse. The exception involves a buyer's ability to prove that 1) either the auctioneer or seller, or both, committed fraud whereby the buyer was intentionally misled, and 2) actual harm resulted from the deception. These points are hard to prove.

The only bit of leverage the winning buyer has in this process occurs between the time the hammer falls and the moment he signs the auctioneer's contract. You will get nowhere by demanding the seller repair an "AS IS" property. But you might be able to resolve an uncertainty, such as writing into the contract that the seller record the survey as it was publicized on auction day without change; or that the seller agree to convey good title to the property (free, for example, of the rumored life estate of his sainted great aunt). You can also ask the seller to help you with non-money details, such as showing you which sections of fence run with the property (but you should have learned this before bidding); or asking the seller to put the word out that you are a hunter and do not want to find other hunters on your new place during hunting season.

If you have not read the contract before the auction, take your time and read it carefully before signing. The auctioneer and seller will be standing there, hovering, wanting a quick signature. TAKE YOUR TIME. READ EVERY SENTENCE. Scratch your ear. Get up and stretch. Ask to consult in private with your spouse. Ask questions and write down the auctioneer's answer. It does not hurt to negotiate then and there on secondary points, but do not expect to get big concessions, such as a financing contingency. PUT EVERYTHING IN WRITING.

Two buyer protections should be included in these contracts, and you are within your rights to insist on both. First, where a house or improvements are involved, the contract should provide that the seller maintain **insurance** until closing for **full-replacement value**. If the contract does not say this explicitly, you may have trouble convincing a judge that full-replacement value was implied in the event of fire. If you are buying woodland with substantial merchantable timber value, you should ask the seller to obtain an insurance binder to cover the timber's value for the 30 days between the auction and closing. If the seller refuses, ask that you be allowed to void the contract if the timber value is substantially damaged, stolen or otherwise diminished. You can probably arrange to insure the timber value on your own, but it will be expensive.

The other language that you should have in an auction contract is a **48-hour, walk-around inspection**, which gives you the right to inspect the property within 48 hours of closing. This should be linked to the seller's agreement that the property will be **conveyed in the same condition** as existed on the date of the auction. "AS IS" should protect the buyer from intentional seller rip offs, such as a last-minute timber cut before closing or the removal of all farm gates. But language that you add to the sales contract makes the point sharper: you expect to have the seller convey exactly what was on the property on auction day. Take photos of the property on auction day and again on walk-around day as a way of making your point, if the need arises.

If tenants are involved in an auction property, the contract should state how their lease (or tenancy without a lease) will be managed. Tenants have the right to stay in the property to the end of their lease, unless otherwise provided. Auction sales typically provide that the sale is subject to the terms of any lease—occupancy, hunting, mineral rights, etc. Landlord-tenant law is community-specific. Even where an occupancy lease has expired, it will take time for an owner to evict a tenant who refuses to move. The seller may dump the eviction process into the buyer's lap despite his responsibilities. Whenever a lease is involved in a property sale, learn its terms before submitting a contract or buying at auction. Certain leases—such as for minerals—are usually recorded; occupancy and hunting leases usually are not and must be supplied by the seller. The pattern common in my area is to **prorate income** from all leases. The seller gets rent up to closing; the buyer, thereafter. Property tax is also prorated.

Property that has been foreclosed—**foreclosures**—is usually sold at auction, which are called **trustee sales** or **trust-deed auctions**. Foreclosures are properties that banks and other lenders have acquired after the owner has defaulted on his mortgage payment or deed of trust. Lenders have no interest in, or capability of, managing property so they use auctions to get rid of foreclosed properties quickly. Large lenders may have a department that does nothing but handle such properties, often referred to as **real estate owned**, or **REOs**. Lenders are willing to sell REOs before incurring carrying and auction costs. Rural lenders do not like the spotlight that finds them when they must foreclose on a customer's land. A quiet, back-door sale can be the preferred alternative. Everyone—lender, owner and even the buyer—gets roughed up in a foreclosure.

In response to a young buyer's question about the pros and cons of buying foreclosures, Robert J. Bruss, the real-estate columnist, provided succinct advice:

> Buying homes that are in the foreclosure process usually isn't a good idea for beginners because of possible complications. There are three foreclosure acquisition opportunities: (1) buy from the defaulting homeowner and cure the default to reinstate the mortgage; (2) purchase at the foreclosure auction for cash; or (3) if there were no auction bidders, buy after the sale from the foreclosing lender that took title to the home.
>
> Foreclosure buyers purchase 'subject to' senior liens, such as unpaid property taxes. If you buy direct from the defaulting borrower before the auction, you also must pay any junior liens, such as a second mortgage. The foreclosure cash sale wipes out junior liens, but not senior liens.
>
> Buying from the foreclosing lender after the auction, if there were no foreclosure sale bidders, often results in easy financing.
>
> However, most lenders usually mark the price up to full market value. (Washington Post, August 28, 2004.)

Lenders will usually set a reserve price in a foreclosure auction, based on what is owed and what the market price is thought to be. The local banker may even openly bid for the property. Remember: the lender does not want to win the bidding. The bank will drop out below the FMV, because its loan was probably for no more than 70 to 90 percent of the property's value at the time the loan was made. The lender, in other words, does not need to get full FMV for its debt to be repaid. Most property is only collateralized by itself, but sometimes the owner's personal guarantee of the debt is involved. In that situation, the bank may not put a reserve on the property since the seller remains personally liable for all residual debt. Buyers may get such a property at a steep discount.

BEEN-HERES AND COME-HERES

Making the match is the first step to making a marriage between you and the right property. The marriage is a longer process than the matchmaking, and its success depends, in part, on how you came into the matchmaking.

When out-of-towners buy rural land and enter a new place the sale affects the local community on many different levels. You, the newcomer, are the new, unknown factor, the disturbance in the neighborhood's equilibrium. How you enter—your manner, interests, your behavior with the seller—will be observed and judged. There is no anonymity in the country.

Behind your purchase and entrance are market factors that have led many others just like you to buy their own country place. This process is shifting the demographic, sociological and economic balance in rural communities. To a greater or lesser extent, the process transforms a place from one of long-established been-heres to a mix of been-heres and come-heres like you. The phenomena of "outsiders moving in" is familiar across the United States—in rural New England, the pretty parts of Appalachia, upstate New York, coastal communities, farmland around college towns, small towns that cater to retirees and recreational destinations such as Jackson, Wyoming. About 445,000 second homes were sold in 2003, according to the National Association of Realtors, and 125,000 are expected to be added to the stock each year during the next decade. (Kristen Gerencher, "A vacation home: to buy or not to buy," Richmond Times-Dispatch, Knight Ridder, August 8, 2004.) These data do not count undeveloped land or sales by FSBOs. The majority of these sales involve newcomers to a community.

Your new rural community will, consequently, have experience with "outsiders" moving in whether or not you have any experience as an outsider moving in. The rural been-heres who are your seller and new neighbors have a right to be angry at the market process that prices them out of buying that which becomes available. Since it is much harder for individuals to pile up cash in rural areas than in urban areas, been-heres sell their principal asset—their land—for a price above what their neighbors can pay. They then find themselves down-sized in the housing market. Rural kids often leave, because jobs and opportunities are in other places. Those who stay may find themselves servicing the come-heres and priced out of property ownership. Resentment is generalized and can be focused against a particular newcomer through no fault of his own. Each newcomer is often seen as representing all newcomers, though each newcomer sees himself only as an individual.

While newcomers enjoy the basic civic rights of all citizens, you will do well to think of yourself at times as a guest resident in another's home—a guest with rights to be there. Admittedly, this is complicated and often maddening. Some will see you in this light, fair or not. Newcomers may be subjected to certain testing behaviors from a few been-heres who are insecure enough to act rudely, boorishly, hostilely or stupidly toward you, but this is not the prevailing attitude in my experience If you roughed up the seller during your purchase, you will be tested. You will be judged locally by your test responses, fair or not. Your scores will get around, far in advance of your meeting those who hear them. Some will look for faults, but most will judge you on how you relate to them as individuals.

Buyers, therefore, should come into the marriage lightly. Buy softly: don't act like a jerk. Don't gloat over a seller's misfortune. Don't boast about how cheaply you bought the seller's family farm. The ordinary work-day personality you use at the corporate office may be too brusque, too business-like for your new neighbors. Be prepared to pass the time at the expense of getting some chore crossed off your list. Passing time glues a lot together in the country. I'm not advising you to become a faux native, which will be seen as phony and condescending. I am suggesting you consider a slow, low-profile, quiet entrance. You are a small piece of a very large demographic and economic change that is rearranging your new community. It's important to remember that the pebble you drop in this pond ripples out and also ripples back.

CHAPTER 16: NEGOTIATING

COMMUNICATION CHANNELS

Dozens of books are available on negotiating, many advocating a particular approach and system. Here are some that I've found to be helpful: Max H. Bazerman and Margaret A. Neale, <u>Negotiating Rationally</u> (New York: The Free Press, 1992); Michael C. Donaldson and Mimi Donaldson, <u>Negotiating for Dummies</u> (Foster City, CA: IDG Books, 1996); Roger Fisher and William Ury, <u>Getting to Yes, Negotiating Agreement Without Giving In</u> (New York: Penguin, 1985); George Fuller, <u>The Negotiator's Handbook</u> (Englewood Cliffs, NJ: Prentice Hall, 1991); Robert Irwin, <u>Tips & Traps When Negotiating Real Estate</u> (New York: McGraw-Hill, 1995); Gary Karrass, <u>Negotiate To Close: How to Make More Successful Deals</u> (New York: Simon & Schuster, 1985); John McDonald, <u>Strategy in Poker Business & War</u> (New York: Norton, 1989); Peter G. Miller and Douglas M. Bregman, <u>Successful Real Estate Negotiation: How Buyers, Sellers and Brokers Can Get Their Share—and More—at the Bargaining Table</u>, rev. ed., (New York: HarperPerennial, 1987); Peter B. Stark, <u>It's Negotiable: The How-To Handbook of Win/Win Tactics</u> (Amsterdam: Pfeiffer, 1994); William Ury, <u>Getting Past No: Negotiating Your Way From Confrontation to Cooperation</u> (New York: Bantam, 1993); and George F. Donohue, <u>Real Estate Dealmaking: A Property Investor's Guide to Negotiating</u> (Chicago: Dearborn Trade Publishing, 2005).

My guess is that some systems work some of the time, none work all of the time and all work every now and then.

Property negotiations work best when at least one of the parties, and preferably both, are operating under pressure to do a deal. The pressure may not be to do your deal, but, rather, to do *a* deal sooner rather than later. The greater the pressure, the harder that party will work to reach a deal. You will benefit from narrowing the seller's generalized pressure to do *some* deal into a focus on doing *your* deal by negotiating reasonably and doing what you can to help him get to where you want him to be.

Buyers should not buy country property under pressure, internal or external. Internal pressure can be the love-at-first-glimpse type that leads to impulse buying. External pressure is a relocation requirement or a deadline. When a buyer feels more pressure to buy than the seller feels to sell, the seller will sense it and the buyer is negotiating at a disadvantage. If you are an externally pressured buyer, conceal it. If you are putting yourself under pressure, stop it.

The first rule of real-estate negotiations is to learn as much about the seller as you can. Does he feel pressure to sell this particular piece of property? If so, what's the nature of that pressure? Is there a clock ticking? Is he in a cash crunch? Is his lender hounding him for missed mortgage payments? What are the consequences of not selling? What are his consequences of not selling to you? Does he need to get a certain price to pay off a mortgage or other debt? If he does not need to sell, why, then, is he selling? Can you estimate his adjusted basis in the property? (If you can estimate his adjusted basis, you can project his after-tax profit at any selling price.) How will his taxable income from the sale be treated for tax purposes—taxed as regular income (a high rate) or capital gains (a low rate)? (You and the seller will have more room to bargain if he will be paying the lower capital-gains rate that kicks in after a year of ownership.) Is there some particular aspect of the property that the seller might want to retain, such as a hunting right or use of a barn? (Such concessions can sweeten your offer and save you money.)

Each seller is part of a socio-economic group. Ethnicity, race, religion, culture, age, gender, education, regional identity, style, vocabulary, manners—all contribute to defining sellers and buyers as individuals. Individuals bargain as individuals, but their style and way of sending messages can be shaped by these characteristics. If you don't understand the bargaining culture of the seller, you can easily submit an inappropriate first offer in the wrong way and then get your counter-offer signals crossed up. I once witnessed a very shrewd mergers-and-acquisitions guy kill his own property purchase by telling the seller that his offer was, "Take it or leave it." In the wheeling-dealing world of the buyer, take-it-or-leave-it meant "we're getting close"; in the wheeling-dealing world of the seller, take-it-or-leave-it was an ultimatum that was to be rejected on principle. It's important for a buyer to understand who the seller is in sociological terms, because those factors shape how he sees you and how he bargains.

A buyer has to develop a **negotiating channel** that works sociologically with the seller, as he is and where he is. A negotiating channel is an approach, a style, that is understood by the seller and accepted as common ground. Part of finding a negotiating channel is to first find those characteristics of the seller that you can relate to outside of negotiating. It could be anything shared. Perhaps you're both fathers of high school basketball players; or vets; or divorced and single; or Methodists; or barbeque lovers, or NASCAR fans; or stock-market victims; or daughters of policemen.

I have found it helpful on occasion to make a channel into a party by bringing in on my side a friend/business colleague who has more connections to that party than I have. When I was trying to bring a client's summer-camp property to the attention of the Mennonite church, I partnered with a Mennonite friend who made the contact.

Another part of finding a negotiating channel is to determine how the seller uses words in relation to how you use words. Some people—by habit or profession—are very precise with what they say and how they say it. Others talk in generalities, often attributing one fact or another to an undefined "they." These channels don't match up well, often leading to messes styled as "miscommunication." The buyer should assume responsibility for learning how best to communicate with the seller and then choose the best negotiating channel.

If the buyer can't find this channel with a seller, he will have to rely on a middleman—a seller's broker if the property's listed; a buyer's broker if the buyer is using one; or a local lawyer who can communicate with the seller—to present the buyer's case. If you choose to bargain through the seller's agent, you must be circumspect in what you reveal. The seller's agent is working for the seller's best interest, not the buyer's. The seller's agent may or may not urge his seller to make a deal with you, depending on what other offers he thinks are in the works. He will also give the seller a frank assessment of the intensity of your interest as well as your financial ability to make a full-price offer. Anything you tell a seller's agent will be used for the seller's benefit.

A more buyer-friendly alternative is to use a local lawyer to bargain on your behalf. This is a less risky way for a newcomer to negotiate the purchase of rural land if he lacks confidence, experience and the ability to develop his own channel. This approach will cost you a very small amount in legal time. All you need to do is tell your lawyer the amount you want to pay and the top amount you will pay.

A second rule is for the buyer to establish negotiating objectives that reflect his own needs and capabilities. A buyer wants to buy for a certain price because that's what his scoping has established is what the property is worth to him. Whether that price is high or low in the local market, whether that price is what the seller is asking or far below it, is immaterial. A buyer's best price should be based only on what it's worth to him.

A buyer's capability to pay for a purchase changes over time. Unanticipated events—death, long unemployment, divorce, illness, job changes—will affect a buyer's capability, but it's hard to anticipate these events and their magnitude at the time you're buying. Since second homes and rural property are almost always discretionary purchases, their cost should never stretch a buyer's current budget or his foreseeable cash flow. Much of life is subject to events individuals cannot control, so every big buy takes place within some lamentable degree of uncertainty. A buyer's margin of financial safety might be defined as something like the ability to carry payments on the rural property for at least 12 months in the absence of all earned income. That year will give you time to sell the property if it becomes necessary. The worth of a property to a buyer should also take into consideration how **liquid** the property is if circumstances change and the buyer needs to sell. A property that can be sold quickly at FMV should be worth more to a buyer than properties that have problems or appeal to a narrow segment of the buyers' market.

In negotiating price with the seller, you can at some point reveal that the offering price now on the table is your "best money," given your financial capabilities. Once you say that, don't budge an inch. This is not a take-it-or-leave-it proposition in tone; it's a this-is-all-I-can-do fact of life. You've now shifted away from negotiating on price to asking the seller whether he wants to sell at your best money. You should not bring more money to the table once you've told the seller that you have no more. That destroys your credibility and creates a hurdle for the seller that he may not want to jump. You can, of course, negotiate on non-price issues to help the seller accept your best money.

A third rule is that buyers must understand that they rarely *need* a particular property. You will like it, even love it, but there will be other properties that you can and will like, even love. Buyers who recognize this about themselves gain bargaining power. Buyers who understand that a want is not a need gain bargaining leverage. Once a seller senses that a buyer's emotions are invested in acquiring his property, the buyer is at a disadvantage. Buyers need to approach any negotiation with the notion that if the target property cannot be purchased for the available money, there are other properties with equivalent virtues that can.

What, then, does a buyer do when he finds himself needing a particular property? First, don't say that you're smitten. Second, don't show it. Third, compliment the seller on individual features of his property, to show interest in and appreciation of the property's most obvious virtues. Fourth, raise some yellow-light issues that you know the seller can address. Finally, don't play around; make a reasonable offer that will be easy for the seller to accept.

The trick, I think, to negotiating astutely for real estate is to use only those tactics that reflect well on you. If the seller asks you a direct question, I would give him a direct answer if you can. If you don't want to reveal an answer, the best thing to do is say that you don't feel comfortable answering that question at this time. That's far better than the alternatives: lying, providing a half-truthful answer and ducking. The straighter the buyer is with the seller, the straighter the buyer should expect the seller to be with him. Straightness should start with the seller, but often doesn't. A seller may not know a fact or two that your scoping has turned up, but a seller should know his property's many features better than you do. And while the seller has a duty to disclose a material defect, not-so-material defects may or may not be disclosed. Property negotiations also have a way of highlighting recent positions that are inconsistent with earlier statements. Owing to that, consistency rewards itself. You can change the terms of an offer, from one to the next, without being inconsistent as long as you explain the reasons for the change. And you can alter the terms of an offer in response to a seller's counter proposal. But you want to avoid promising one thing and then backing away from the promise when it becomes inconvenient. Changing the terms of an offer is part of negotiating; backing off your word spoils the trust that you need to make negotiations work.

If you want to get as much information as possible out of a seller, start by giving him a straight story about yourself and your intentions (if asked). It is, of course, possible that your intentions violate the seller's wishes. He may, for example, object to your plan to tear down his family's crumbling 200-year-old home or carve 20-acre lots out of the back 100 acres. If you lie and conceal your intentions, you will enter your new community with that hanging over your head. Certain intentions cannot be concealed from sellers, because the buyer will have to make his purchase contingent on obtaining a permit from the local zoning agency. If you know the seller is likely to object to a particular idea, I think it's better to talk out with him why you want to do it and let his interest in getting the property sold help you. This doesn't work with sellers who don't need to sell their properties. A seller who can hold indefinitely and pick the buyer that he "likes" won't negotiate in the traditional way because he feels no pressure to make a deal. Try to get this type of seller to like you first and then lead him to negotiate.

NON-PRICE ISSUES

A useful way to approach price with a seller is to back into it as you "front in" all the other issues you want to discuss with him. The most common types of **non-price issues** are:

- important things that you want the seller to do to the property prior to, and as a condition of, your purchase;
- things the buyer introduces into the negotiations that are not important to the buyer and, therefore, are intended to function as buyer concessions;
- things that the buyer can do to help the seller make the deal;
- things that are property liabilities or questions that only the seller can clear up;
- liabilities that can be approached in such a way that both buyer and seller fix a portion of the problem;
- issues that the buyer can, and is willing to, resolve in return for the seller doing other things to facilitate the deal; and
- uncertainties of three kinds: genuine, marginal and tactical (the last of these is one that the buyer knows is less uncertain than the seller believes to be the case).

Non-price issues often involve dickering over money, but not over the selling price of the property.

No single correct way exists to put non-price issues onto the negotiating table. I've found that raising these issues conversationally with the seller (or his agent) prior to submitting an offer and then including language in the offer that addresses the significant ones often works. The buyer does not want to surprise the seller with the terms of his written offer. A buyer should prepare the seller for his offer through whatever preliminary communication channels are open—face-to-face meetings, letters asking for information, letters raising issues of buyer concern, information the buyer has discovered and copies of buyer-paid consultant reports on the property (e.g., unfavorable radon results with an estimate of the cost of remediation or the consultant's report indicating the failure to find soils suitable for a septic system). Preliminary communication flags buyer concerns and begins adding **non-price complexity** to price-only negotiations. The idea behind complexity is not to complicate negotiations or introduce deal-killer issues that can't be resolved. Rather, it is to raise valid (mainly) issues and give the parties opportunities to solve them. The more issues the parties resolve, the more negotiating foundation they will have jointly built. The habit of solving problems will be developed. It is then easier to negotiate price as the last step in a march through a lot of successful negotiating on other matters.

Many non-price issues involve a dollar cost to resolve. If the seller wants the buyer to absorb all these costs, the buyer needs to point out that the property will cost much more than the seller's asking price. In certain circumstances, a buyer can offer to pay the seller full-price *if* the seller fixes the list of buyer-identified problems at the seller's expense. The buyer helps to develop a negotiating rhythm and record of success by conceding the "throw-away" non-price issues he introduced for that purpose and by good-faith bargaining on the genuine ones.

The buyer will get a feel for how the seller negotiates money when they are trying to settle an issue involving cost. The seller may prefer to resolve money issues in one of several ways: split costs 50-50; let's split the difference between your (last) number and my (last) number; buyer puts the money in while seller contributes labor and/or machine time; I'll meet you half way between your (objective, third-party) cost estimate and my (objective, third-party) cost estimate; among others. If a buyer can "read" a seller's preferred way of settling money differences, he can frame the subsequent property price negotiations in advantageous terms. If, for example, a buyer is dealing with a seller who likes to split the difference between the last numbers on the table, the buyer must negotiate up with the same dollar increment as the seller negotiates down—and then split the difference. If the buyer concedes more than the seller, a split the difference proposal ends up with the buyer having given up more than the seller. I think a buyer who offers to meet the seller half way between the asking price and the buyer's offer claims the high ground. If, of course, the buyer has submitted an obvious low-ball price, any offer to meet half way will be a self-evident trick that is likely to anger the seller rather than get him to compromise

I've found it to be easier to engage in give-and-take bargaining orally than in writing. I think this is especially true in buying rural land where the country seller's cultural bargaining style is far more oral than written. But I am a better bargainer on paper than in person. So I try to convert the bargaining to writing as soon as I can. Be forewarned: written bargainers are usually at a disadvantage negotiating orally with oral bargainers. I find this to be true, because written bargainers tend to be more careful with words and draw distinctions between them while oral bargainers are less careful with their words, but not in what they believe these words were intended to mean. It's in the buyer's interest to have his written offer reflect precisely the oral meeting of the minds that's been reached during pre-offer negotiations.

If all issues save price have been settled, then offer your price, clean of contingencies and other issues if you can, packaged with a letter to the seller explaining exactly why you believe this price is both fair to him and reflects the property's FMV considering everything. To the extent the buyer can arrange it, the subsequent price negotiation should revolve around objective valuation of price fairness. Your scoping results establish your talking points. If you inadvertently back the seller into a corner: "This is my price whether or not you [the seller] think it's fair," you have not been negotiating; you've been arguing. Winning an argument with a seller rarely results in purchasing his property at a favorable price. Successful negotiators help the other side get to where they want them to go with facts, logic, third-party opinions, concessions, donations of something new or unexpected, patience, reciprocity and talk. A buyer never wants to push a seller into a take-it-or-leave-it position. When a buyer's head hits a stone wall, the best tactic is to stop hurting himself. Take a time-out for a couple of days. The seller may be so totally fed up with the buyer's persistence that he refuses any additional bargaining. But if your preliminary foundation is in place, the time-out can allow each side to reevaluate its position and then give bargaining one last, best shot.

Sellers want all-cash, full-price contracts with no contingencies or complications. The buyer's job is to build a case for any offer less than that. The best way to build such a case is to insert non-price complexity into the negotiations and use bargaining to resolve each non-price issue as a foundation-building exercise in preparation for price. The non-price issues, of course, are mainly genuine concerns. If preliminary negotiations cannot resolve them, the buyer needs to incorporate them into his written contract offer as contingencies or items requiring additional investigation.

The buyer must strike the right balance between raising issues of property liabilities and overwhelming the seller with complications to the point where he terminates negotiations. If you've introduced throw-away, non-price issues, you can negotiate with yourself and eliminate them. That is, raise the issue and at some subsequent point concede that you will handle it at your expense. You may in some cases be able to get a seller concession for giving up on a throw-away issue. This leaves only the genuine matters of concern for the parties to negotiate. It has also indicated your willingness to compromise for the sake of the deal.

In most situations, the buyer gets one bite—sometimes, a bite and a half—at getting a seller to concede something in return for the buyer accepting a jointly recognized liability. Sellers who refuse to work with a buyer on a jointly recognized liability are betting that the buyer is highly motivated. The buyer has been too enthusiastic, too forthcoming. When a seller replaces give-and-take bargaining with take-and-take, it is time for the buyer to cool the negotiations. The buyer might mention other properties that have fewer liabilities, different virtues and are below the seller's price. A deal is possible, the buyer says, but the buyer says he needs the seller to help him solve their shared problem. Don't burn your bridge to this seller, but remind him that you have alternatives if he doesn't do his share in helping you get across his. If you don't think you have alternatives, you will have them as soon as you begin looking again.

Non-price issues that emerge during a buyer's scoping can include anything, from boundary disputes and unrecorded easements to snakes under the back porch and an old chimney that you suspect needs to be rebuilt. Addressing rural property problems requires time, patience, skill, experience and money in different combinations. Often, it is the time-and-hassle factor of repairs rather than their cost that is the real incentive for a buyer to have a seller get the work done as part of the sale. In this regard, buyers should be extremely cautious about accepting the burden of a particular task, chore or repair without knowing what's really involved.

For example. The seller's farm has livestock fence all around its border. Ownership is either divided between adjoining neighbors section by section or shared jointly. (There are exceptions, e.g., where one side has livestock and the other has none and does not care if the neighbor's livestock visits at will. In that case, for instance, all fence may be owned by the livestock side.) Whatever the case, the owner of this farm will eventually have to "make fence" or hire out the job. If you acquire the seller's farm with seller-owned "bad" fence, the responsibility falls on you. "Making a section of fence" sounds simple enough, but around my place it involves a big tractor or dozer with a hydraulic post-driving attachment; some form of front-end loader to lift and move old wire and posts; dump truck to haul away the refuse; specialized fencing tools, dozens to hundreds of stakes, posts and braces; wire and fence staples; gates and hinge pins; cable for constructing water gaps; and labor that is both skilled and stout. Making fence is expensive and miserable work. No first-time farmer should attempt it on his own. If the buyer can get the seller to repair or replace those sections of the fence that are needy, his first decade of farmownership will be free of the inevitable phone call at 9:30 p.m. on Sunday night: "Is this you? Your cows are out."

The fence example also illustrates the need for a buyer to be very specific with a seller who agrees to fix a non-price item as part of the sale. Your definition of repair or "make fence" and his can be substantially different. With fencing, you need to specify in writing the type of fence (rolled wire comes in different gauges, hole size and width [that is, height]; high-tensile wire is put up with or without electrification and the number of strands must be agreed to, because a five-strand high-tensile fence is far less effective than a nine-strand fence; type of stakes and posts [material, length, width]; placement distance between each stake [every ten feet is stouter than every 16 feet]; bracing standards [location, type, number]; placement and size of gates [material, type of hinges]; depth to which stakes should be driven [at least 30 inches]; style and construction of water gaps [where the fence crosses a stream]; and disposal plan for the old fence [no plan means the old wire will be left in your field]). Many states specify in their Codes what constitutes a **"lawful fence,"** which means any fence built to a lesser standard is not lawful. Such a fence may open a landowner to liability in the event straying livestock cause damage to a neighbor's crops or a road accident. If you are totally ignorant of fences, talk with the county extension agent about which type is best for your purposes. One way of handling the need to repair/rebuild a seller's fence is for the buyer to provide or pay for the materials and the seller to provide the labor and necessary machine time.

If you think I am being a paranoid about fences, I offer the following real-life experiences. I once purchased 200 sharpened locust stakes from a fellow advertising in the local paper. I was careful to make sure they would be delivered sharpened. They were. Each was seven feet long, a foot shorter than the local standard. Each was as thin as the vendor could contrive. About 25 were so lacking in stoutness that I cut them into kindling. My fault: I didn't specify eight feet and stout. Another time, a fence builder drove hillside stakes only 12 inches into the ground because his tractor couldn't maneuver on the steep slope and he didn't want to spend time driving them deeper by hand, even though I was paying him by the hour. He didn't tell me about this adjustment when I paid him. My fault again: I paid in full before inspecting the job. I had to hire another fence contractor the next year and have a second row of new stakes driven in the same fence line between the wobbly ones. The 12-inch fence builder also failed to construct a water gap behind a dense, roadside thicket, which allowed our cattle to liberate themselves onto a public highway. I had quickly inspected this section from both sides before paying, but the thicket concealed the absence of the water gap. I discovered the problem after the third jail break. I've also had to repair two long sections of fence made by a seller who failed to hammer enough staples on each stake. This high-tensile wire should have one staple emplaced wherever it crosses a stake, otherwise livestock wiggle through it. This fence had one staple per wire every three or four stakes. This little trick saved the seller time and money, but forced me to redo part of his job. I've also replaced seller-built fence that was inadequately braced at the corners and turns, facts that became apparent when the tension in the high-tensile wire winched the end posts out of the ground.

If fence repair or rebuilding is part of your negotiations, make sure that your offer refers to "lawful fence" and sets out the details.

PRICE

Some sellers set their asking price unreasonably beyond what they believe is an approximation of fair market value. They may do this in anticipation of giving the buyer steep price cuts in negotiation that end with a price at, or just above, market value. Or they may have no urgent need to sell and will wait for their price. In both cases, the buyer must show the seller evidence of what fair market value is for his property. This can involve comparables research and even an appraisal. The first type of over-priced seller can be brought down to FMV and even, occasionally, below. The second seller may be unmovable, although I've seen simple, all-cash offers work.

Most sellers in a competitive market set their asking price about 20 percent higher than what they hope to net, expecting to concede ten percent in negotiations and spend the rest for commission and expenses. This is not a rule of real-estate sales, but it is often more or less true. Buyers can get a sense for those sellers who are asking about 20 percent more than FMV and those asking much more than that by looking at recent sales of similar properties and the prices of currently listed comparables. Market-priced properties sell within six months in normal markets; over-priced properties can linger for years. Buyers should avoid over-priced properties, because you will have better alternatives, if not immediately, then in time.

Buyers should look for motivated sellers who for reason of cash shortage, emergency, divorce, relocation, lender pressure, college expenses, family squabbles or ill-health, among other reasons, must sell their property quickly. If these sellers need to get a certain price to meet their obligations, they will be willing to help a buyer with non-price issues, particularly those that require labor and not cash. When distressed sellers need to get money out of their property, they may sell for less than market value to a buyer with a simple cash offer. When the seller is a number of heirs who no longer have an emotional interest in the family's property, offer a number that divides out to a round number—$50,000, $100,000—per heir.

When a buyer finds a property priced ten percent or more below what he has determined to be its approximate FMV, it's usually a sign of one of three conditions: 1) the property has a big, easily discovered liability that can't be readily resolved; 2) the seller is in distress and needs to raise cash immediately; or 3) the seller has underestimated the true value of his property, which can happen with FSBOs. The first of these conditions is a yellow light bordering on red; the second and third are high-intensity green lights for buyers. Listed real estate is priced below market either when the owner insists that he needs a quick sale or, more rarely, when the true value of the property has not been ascertained. With under-priced property, the buyer should negotiate quickly. Driving a bargain harder than necessary may be a buyer's style when dealing with a wounded seller, but I advise against it. Piling on is never admired, and it's a bad way to move into a new place. I've seen greedy buyers lose under-priced property when they forgot that a speedy deal was their goal, not squeezing the last nickel out of a bleeding seller.

Fair market value should be the axis around which the buyer wants negotiations to spin. Whether FMV is established as a single dollar figure or a range, it has a hardness and concreteness that gives the buyer an objective platform of fact and analysis from which to negotiate. With sellers who are having trouble budging from their asking price, the buyer's FMV analysis may draw down the seller if reduction is in the cards. An FMV approach won't win the day in and of itself, but it has the effect of setting a reasonable, market-based cap **for the buyer**. To the extent that a seller insists on demanding an above-market price, he is not being market-based, hence he's being "unreasonable." The more the buyer can orient negotiations around establishing an FMV through comparables, appraisals, tax-assessed valuations and so on, the more he can shift negotiating to a rational comparison of numbers and number-based conclusions.

The persuasive power of a buyer-supplied FMV in negotiations depends on its market integrity. Any buyer who deliberately deflates a target property's FMV by selective use of comparable properties, or small arithmetic mistakes or paying for a low-ball appraisal is no better than the seller who misrepresents his property to a good-faith buyer. If a seller figures out that a buyer is peddling false information, the seller should terminate additional talks.

An FMV looks hard and sounds hard, but it can be a spongy number on rural properties, particularly those that are out of the ordinary, remote or feature an idiosyncratic structure. (FMV analysis is far more accurate in a city where the seller is marketing a three-bedroom apartment in a building that contains 50 identical units, five of which have sold within the last six months.) FMV depends on looking backward and assuming forward. FMV for most real estate is determined by finding the selling prices of recently sold similar properties in the general area of the target property. Once that is done, it is then assumed that the same market will exist in the near future. That assumption gets progressively weaker as time passes from the date when the FMV of a property is calculated and the physical distance increases between the target property and its comparables. **Comparables analysis** adjusts prices to account for differences in similar properties, given that no set of properties are likely to be identical in size, attributes and improvements. Buyers should remember that an FMV analysis gives an approximate value based on sales of other properties, not based on the target property itself. Don't get trapped into insisting on paying no more than the FMV based on comparables analysis. In real life, your target property's estimated FMV may be less than its real value if it has special features that are hard to compare with recent sales or the available comparables are not really comparable. Comparable analysis for undeveloped woodland has limited utility when the commercial value of the timber is not fairly evaluated for all properties in the set. If woodland is selling for $1,000 an acre, regardless of timber value, FMV is $1,000 an acre, regardless of the fact that your target property contains $2,000 an acre in merchantable timber value.

A buyer can readily compare the **tax-assessed values of similar properties** in relation to their recent sales prices to establish FMV for the target property. If, for instance, seven comparable properties have sold for 125-135 percent of their tax-assessed values, it's reasonable to project that the FMV of your target property is about 130 percent of its tax-assessed value as long as general market conditions have not changed. The buyer can also check to see whether the pre-sale tax-assessed values of the seven properties were roughly the same as the target property's value on a per-acre basis. They should be: that's one of the guidelines a buyer can use to establish comparability. Remember, however, that tax-assessed values can have little direct relationship to actual land value when dealing with timberland, because appraisers for the county do not determine timber value when assigning value to woodland. It is, therefore, possible to find a property with a lot of timber value that is under-priced in relation to its comparables using tax-assessed values. Similarly, crop land will differ in fertility and wetness, while pasture will differ in the amount of forage it produces owing to aspect, weeds, wetness, grass-type and elevation. A buyer can judge when per-acre comparables help his side of the negotiations. More often than not, taxed-assessed valuations of country property are lower—often substantially lower—than current FMV.

Professional appraisers are paid to determine fair market value for buyers, sellers and institutional lenders. Both buyers and sellers can commission an appraisal to frame negotiations and offer an objective, third-party opinion about a property's value. An appraiser's FMV should be more accurate than the tax-assessed property values that necessarily use some generic values and, in any case, are less current. Sellers want high appraisals from appraisers they hire; buyers want low numbers (until, of course, they become owners).

Buyers are often required to pay for an appraisal once they sign a contract to purchase with the seller. This appraisal is submitted to the institutional lender who will then lend 80 to 90 percent of either the purchase price or the appraised value, *whichever is less.* If, for instance, a buyer agrees with a seller to pay $200,000 for unimproved land, he is usually hoping that the appraisal will come in at more than $200,000. Were the appraisal's FMV to be $150,000, the bank would lend this buyer 80 percent of the appraised value, that is, only $120,000. This buyer is left with the job of coming up with $80,000 to make the purchase. In contrast a selling-price appraisal of $200,000 would require him to find only $40,000, which is, 20 percent of both the purchase price and the appraised value. The buyer, faced with a low-end appraisal, should reconsider buying the property at the price he negotiated. He can back out of the contract for this reason only if he put a contingency in his purchase contract that allows him to void the offer if the lender's appraisal comes in at less than the agreed price. If the buyer wants to complete the purchase in spite of a low appraisal, he can increase his cash investment or ask the seller to "take back" a second mortgage for $30,000, or more.

Buyers can protect themselves against low appraisals by inserting a contingency such as the following:

> **Buyer reserves the right to void this purchase contract without penalty if the appraisal required for lender financing does not meet or exceed at least 100 percent of the agreed purchase price.** (You can insert a number less than or more than 100 percent if the circumstances warrant it.)

An appraisal contingency can shape your negotiations. It tends to deflate over-priced sellers, and it's worth something to the seller to have a buyer agree to not include it. If the buyer has already procured an appraisal, he can bargain away this contingency without risking anything. The buyer and seller can also agree that in the event of a below-purchase-price appraisal, the seller will finance some or all of the additional cash needed by the buyer at terms written into the contract offer.

Since most institutional lenders require a buyer-paid appraisal as part of their lending process, I recommend buyers get one done *before* offering a purchase contract on any property that is under serious consideration. Buyers should not commission appraisals frivolously since they cost several hundred dollars each. If the buyer-commissioned appraisal comes in below the seller's asking price, the appraisal figure is FMV and should be the buyer's target price in negotiations. If the appraisal comes in at the seller's asking price, the buyer should not introduce the appraisal into negotiations, because it will not help him. He can still provide it to his lender as part of his mortgage application. If the appraisal is higher than the asking price, the buyer should keep that to himself. Buyers have no obligation to inform competent sellers of their property's appraisal value.

A buyer should not dismiss a property that he cannot buy for his appraiser's FMV or below. I would consider buying at as much as ten percent above FMV if the cash difference wasn't that important to me, and I liked the property.

Most sellers do not commission appraisals as part of marketing their property, at least in my experience. The reason for this is unknowable, but it would not surprise me to learn that these sellers believe that a professional appraisal would not confirm their asking price. During negotiations, either buyer or seller can propose that the final purchase price be determined by a neutral appraisal, the cost of which is to be shared equally between the parties. If a buyer has an appraisal in hand, he might propose this with a high-degree of confidence in the outcome. The same is true for a seller holding an appraisal. Where a buyer and seller agree on a jointly sponsored appraisal, they should also agree to direct the appraiser to use the **"market approach"** for finding FMV. This is the typical methodology for land and most non-commercial real estate. It looks at the prices of three recently sold comparable properties, adjusts for differences in acreage and other factors, and then sets the FMV for the subject property in relation to the comps. The appraiser uses his judgment to adjust the selling price of each comparable in direct comparison with his subjective evaluation of the subject property. Once the three comparables prices are tweaked as the appraiser feels it necessary, the three can be averaged to come up with the FMV for the target property. Two other appraisal techniques—**"replacement cost"** and **"income"**—are generally not appropriate for most rural land, with the exception of the income approach for a full-time farm business.

A not uncommon technique for investment partners, heirs or spouses trying to divide jointly held property is to commission three appraisals, the deal price to be the average of the three. The appraisers should be told explicitly that the cost of the appraisal will be divided equally and the appraisal is for both sides. If one appraisal comes in significantly higher or lower than the other two, the parties should talk with the appraisers to determine the reason. Using the same appraisal approach, appraisers should arrive at three FMVs that are within at least ten, if not five, percent of each other in the majority of situations.

When using appraisals to set an FMV on rural woodland, it is important to keep in mind that real-estate appraisers do *not* appraise the tract's timber value. Appraisers using the "market approach" will simply find other recently sold wooded tracts. They are comparing wooded land but not the value of the merchantable timber on each tract, which can obviously drive real value up or down. Therefore, when a buyer wants to obtain complete information about a wooded property's value, he needs to purchase both an appraisal and a timber evaluation. Other consultant opinions may be necessary if minerals, water and farm income are involved.

Appraisers work in gross, not net. What I mean by that is that they compare properties by their large dimensions—such as number of acres and square feet in a house—rather than looking at the quality of the component assets. Two houses can each contain 3,000 square feet, four bedrooms, two baths, two-car garage and have been built in the same year. Yet one might be fairly valued at $150 per square foot, and the other at $100. Similarly, two 100-acre parcels of open land may differ markedly in their soil and water quality, which directly affects their agricultural value. Appraisals may not value rural land for their soil qualities, fencing and topography although each contributes or detracts from value. The appraiser will mainly compare on the basis of size, location and general type, e.g., open land to open land, same size house to same size house, especially in low-population areas where he needs to scrape the barrel's bottom to come up with three recent sales that are even remotely similar. Appraisals should take into consideration water supply and quality where they are important factors.

Appraisers may or may not include the value of subsurface minerals in their appraisals. If a "market approach" is used, the appraiser may not increase the value of a subject property whose owner has, for example, leased its oil and gas rights for $500 a year and has received an average of $1,000 royalty annually for the last five years. A conscientious appraiser will include a note about the mineral lease and royalties when he knows about them. Known minerals can multiply the value of an unimproved tract many times over. Appraisers, in my experience, may not do a title search as part of their appraisal, so buyers cannot count on the appraiser to flag land that does not convey with its subsurface. Another possible asset that may be of interest is a tract's potential for siting a wind-turbine farm. Such enterprises are increasingly proposed and becoming more common along Appalachian ridgelines, parts of the West and along coasts.

Buyers should remember that every FMV is an estimate based on both "hard" numbers (actual selling prices) and the appraiser's judgment. The buyer should see the appraiser's FMV number as the middle of a range of defensible market values. Buyers can use a single FMV number in their negotiations, but they will help themselves by thinking of FMV as a range on either side of that amount. Buyers will be harming themselves if they refuse to pay a penny over the appraised FMV, because "it is above market."

Appraisals are used by sellers to justify a higher asking price and by sellers to justify a lower offering price. If the seller has an appraisal, a buyer should get his own appraisal; otherwise, the buyer is entering the bargaining arena unarmed. If the seller does not have an appraisal, the buyer should seriously consider getting his own as a means of reorienting the seller's expectations around the buyer's FMV number. When a seller has an appraisal that the buyer hasn't seen and he says that he will sell the property for its "appraisal price," the buyer is being suckered into paying a price that in all probability is higher than the property's objective FMV. Beware a seller's appraisal.

Critical to the buyer's success in negotiations is "helping" the seller move negotiations toward "What's a defensible and fair price based on recent comparable sales?" and away from "This is what I want; take it or leave it." Conversely, the buyer is rarely advantaged by making a single offer that he will not change. Both sides in negotiation feel psychologically better about an agreement when there's been some give-and-take bargaining. Deals are often made on the basis of a buyer's final offer that is still subject to some last-minute changes. By inserting the concept of fair market value into the negotiations, the buyer is structuring the negotiations around real numbers—actual selling prices of properties the seller is likely to know. FMV negotiations edge into a give and take that compares the assets and liabilities of recent sales relative to the seller's property rather than a personalized buyer-seller tug of war that is experienced as winning and losing. The buyer should become familiar enough with the properties used for comparison as is necessary to have this conversation.

A buyer starts searching for a fair and reasonable purchase price for a particular property by working two sides of the same street.

First, the buyer does what he can to determine analytically the objective value of the target property using an appraisal, tax-assessed valuations, selling prices of comparable properties, asking prices of currently listed comparable properties (available in the local real-estate guide), timber cruises and other information in whatever combination he thinks is appropriate for the target property. The purpose of the buyer's effort is to come at the yet unknown FMV from various known points. This is the buyer's FMV—his most accurate and honest evaluation of the target property's current market value. It may be a number the buyer keeps to himself or shares with the seller.

Second, the buyer begins testing the seller's perception of fair market value by feeling for the bottom of the seller's range of acceptable selling prices. One way to do this is to find out what prices the seller has recently rejected. If the asking price is $350,000 and the seller rejected a contract for $300,000 two months ago, the buyer knows the seller's bottom was between the two at that time. But the buyer should remember that the same price can net different amounts to a seller. A $300,000 offer that was replete with a seller-financing contingency and a demand that the seller fix the roof is not as high as a no-contingency, all-cash offer of $300,000. If $300,000 is the FMV that the buyer has established, the buyer can offer it with a clean contract after laying the proper foundation with the seller. If the seller rejects a clean-contract, all-cash offer of $300,000, then his bottom is higher than your FMV at this time. (Six months later, he may have reduced his bottom number to $300,000.)

The buyer might look for the seller's bottom with a first offer that is five to ten percent or more below what the buyer's FMV is. This tactic is intended to end up with a deal price around the buyer's FMV number. Some sellers set an asking price (above what they think FMV is) and then tell the buyer what they'll accept. That number is often a false bottom, but it will take work to loosen the seller's grip on it. I've also run into sellers who set an asking price, then the price they'll take, and allow me to work them off this false-bottom price—and their real bottom is still above the objective FMV.

Sellers usually have their own objective FMV in mind. That number may come from their listing broker's competitive market analysis used to set the asking price, which is likely to be 15 to 20 percent higher to allow for costs and negotiation. Or it may come from nothing more than a seller's intuitive sense of what his property is worth in the market based on what he knows and has heard. In both cases, circumstances may force a seller to accept a price below his FMV and, in rare cases, below his bottom price. Negotiations will lead a buyer to that seller hell hole, but the seller gets there because of pressure unrelated to your skill as a negotiator. It behooves a buyer to know the difference between his bargaining talents and serendipitous good fortune. Where a buyer has not determined his own objective FMV, he can offer 30 to 35 percent below the seller's asking price in hope of discounting it by 20 percent.

I have in front of me two properties that are over-priced. One is 220 acres of woods on a mountain top in western Maryland. It's surface only, and there are strip mines on two sides. It is not accessible year-round. The FSBO owners—Mom and her five kids—are asking $1.2 million, or about $5,450 per acre. The other is about 310 acres in a not-very-desirable spot in a West Virginia county that borders Virginia. This one has a 1960s ranch house, some river-bottom land (that floods) and steep woodland. It's priced at about $2,990 per acre. In both counties, there are properties of this size that have sold for such prices, but neither of these merit their prices. The Maryland property is worth about $1,500 per acre. The West Virginia tract is in the $1,600-to-$2,000-per-acre range. With the Maryland FSBO, I would offer $1,200 per acre and move up to $1,500. The sellers know their asking price is crazy, so if a realistic offer doesn't work, I'd just skip it. On the West Virginia parcel, I would be interested in buying the wooded part, leaving the floodplain and the house for another buyer. I might offer $600 to $800 per acre for the woods, depending on the timber value. That's a huge discount, but I think it's justified in so far as the 250 acres I want are steep and not easily accessed. I'm leaving the prime assets in the seller's hand. If there's no timber value, I won't make an offer. Even as little as $20,000 in immediate timber-sale income would be enough to pay the interest for a year, giving me that amount of time to resell the property as a capital gain. In both examples, the sellers will make a huge profit on their sales even at my price since the tracts were bought in the late 1940s for a few thousand each and have no mortgage. This is windfall money, and the sellers know it. Both properties would be bought for investment, and I need neither one. My feelings won't be hurt if the sellers reject my offers. In both cases, I would make all-cash, no-contingency offers to show that my offer is real even though it's far below what the seller has asked. A buyer loses nothing in making a low offer for over-priced property.

Any offer that lowers the asking price significantly should be accompanied by a letter or personal buyer-to-seller conversation that lays out the buyer's factual basis for what otherwise will be considered an insulting and not serious **low-ball offer**. No seller will be inclined to accept a low-ball offer, but some sellers will end up agreeing to about the same money if the buyer can show that figure represents an honest FMV. I don't suggest offering a low-ball price as a bargaining tactic, but I would always offer a low price that is based on objective FMV analysis. The buyer should do what he can to lift a low-ball offer out of that category in the seller's mind. No seller wants to give up genuine fair value for his property. (Giving up an inflated asking price is to be expected.) A seller maintains his self-respect if he sells for FMV as long as he can resist thinking that he's giving it away to a low-ball buyer. The buyer can sweeten a low-money offer by doing other things for the seller, such as allowing him to retain hunting rights for a certain number of years or granting him a life-time estate over a small piece of the property. A buyer helps his cause when he can show that his FMV offer reflects a fair price in the current market and his low offer is not simply a bargaining tactic. The easiest way to communicate this to the seller is for the buyer to say to the seller, "I know my offer is a lot lower than your asking price, but it's exactly what I've determined to be objective fair market value at this time—and here's the evidence that I've used."

A common low ball is to offer the **tax-assessed value** of the property, assuming, of course, that the tax value is substantially lower than the objective FMV. Farms and other rural land are commonly appraised and assessed for tax purposes at less than their FMV. Cash-pinched rural landowners are helped by below-market tax valuations and the resulting low property taxes. The current tax-assessed value of county property can be several years out of date, which usually puts it below market. Nonetheless, the tax-assessed value of a property—updated where need be—arguably represents 100 percent of an objective FMV. A buyer starting at 100 percent of tax-assessed value has grabbed a reasonable bargaining position. The seller is forced to show why and how the county's tax-assessed value differs from FMV when they're supposed to be the same. Where comps support the tax-assessed FMV, show them to the seller.

A low-ball offer, as a tactic, works occasionally for those who are discretionary buyers, such as investors who are only looking for property as a vehicle for making money. These individuals know that a purchase below market value strips much of the risk out of trying to make a profit.

If you are considering using a low-ball tactic, you must think through your next step after the seller rejects it—and perhaps rejects you too—if you are interested in the property as anything other than a take-it-or-leave-it deal. A buyer can "allow himself" to be persuaded by the seller's objections and arguments on behalf of his property to raise his low-ball offer. This disingenuousness grants both sides enough face-saving to go forward. The seller may feel some psychological edge in having worked a buyer up from a ridiculously low starting point, just as a buyer may feel the same sense of victory after working a seller down from a ridiculous high. The low-ball buyer, however, should be willing to come up a bit (which places him well below FMV). The question for this buyer is whether to come up to his final number in one jump or be stepped up in a series of concessions. I think the step-up approach is more psychologically rewarding to the seller and improves the climate of the deal.

If you are more interested in a property than just looking for a steal, I advise starting with a below-market offer that you justify to the seller as best you can. That starting price should not be insultingly low, but it can be 20 percent or more below FMV and, in some cases, even 30 to 40 percent below an over-priced asking price.

I bought a wooded tract of 116 acres some years ago from a college-educated professional who I thought would be persuaded by numbers. He had priced the property at $100,000, a number too round to have any credibility with me. A professional forester did a timber cruise and placed the current value of the merchantable timber at just under $80,000. That meant we had good reason to believe that we could sell the timber to a sawmill within a month or so of buying the land for about 80 percent of the seller's asking price. I went to the courthouse to dig a bit. I discovered that the seller had bought the property for $55,000 a few years before and had about $45,000 remaining on his note. Since I knew that tax-assessed valuations never value the timber on woodlands, I found a representative sample of about a dozen nearby woodland properties of similar size and noted their tax-assessed values. I converted these property values to dollar-per-acre numbers, which averaged $560. I then wrote the seller a letter outlining the method by which I had derived an estimate of FMV for his tract. I included all the information I found, identifying each parcel by Deed Book and Page number, owner, location, acreage and tax-assessed value. I ended this analysis by multiplying his acreage (116 acres) by the average tax-assessed per-acre value of comparable woodlands ($560), to come up with an FMV-based offer of $64,960. I included a purchase contract for that amount with the letter. I made the contract as simple as I could—no contingencies of any kind, all cash and a 30-day closing. The seller figured that he would pay off his note and have $10,000 in his pocket before paying capital-gains tax. He accepted the offer after his over-priced, fancy lawyer in Washington asked for a few unimportant language changes that I made without complaint. The seller informed me that he knew the timber had no value, an opinion I acknowledged hearing without agreeing. The timber was sold two years later for $128,000 when stumpage prices were at the top of their fairly predictable cycle. I did not, of course, share the cruise results with the seller, and he never thought it necessary to spend $500 to have a cruise done before he put his property up for sale.

My offer was 35 percent below the seller's asking price but was deeply and impeccably grounded in hard, verifiable numbers. Indeed, $560/acre *was* a fair market value for all wooded land in this area at that time. And it was $85/acre more than the seller paid for it a few years earlier. The seller didn't argue against the numbers and knew that $100,000 had no local foundation. I don't think the seller saw my $64,960 offer as a low ball, because he knew that he had set his asking price unreasonably high in relation to comparables. In this fashion, a buyer can sometimes work a seller's own over-pricing tactic against him. It helped, of course, that the seller had on his own acquired the opinion that his timber had no value.

I draw a distinction between a low-ball offer and what I did on this timber tract. I was a highly motivated buyer since I knew the value of the timber and the seller did not. But I was motivated only up to $80,000, the value of the merchantable timber. The seller stalled for a couple of weeks, looking for other buyers, but never made a counter proposal. I told him that I would withdraw the offer if he wasn't prepared to respond. Second, I was not making an offer that would produce a loss to this seller, only less profit than he would get at a higher price. This distinction is very important in negotiations. Often, the difference between a real loss and less profit is only a few thousand dollars, and there's no sensible reason for a buyer to insist on forcing a loss. Third, I knew that the seller had paid more for the property than he should have based on comparables sold at the time, and I figured that he knew that too. I assumed that he would reason something like this: "If I had been smart and paid $44,000 rather than $54,000, I would make $20,000 on Seltzer's offer, instead of $10,000. It's my own fault. His offer is not that low; it's just that I paid too much." Fourth, this seller was a FSBO who was figuring that he would keep the ten percent broker's commission in his pocket. Fifth, I detected that the seller's emotional investment in the property had waned. He had planned to build a second home on a 4,000-foot ridge, a plan that proved to be impractical. Finally, I think he was persuaded by the transparency of the numbers and reasoning I used. The analytical framework and the vocabulary were familiar to him as they would be to any high-income professional. I also made the deal as simple and easy for him as I could, so that he wouldn't have to take time from his lucrative practice. I supplied the purchase contract, which saved him some legal fees. This approach can work with busy college-educated, absentee owners whose profit from the sale is not central to their financial well-being. It does not work with individuals who "want their price" and are willing to hold a property until they get it.

The buyer may find little budge in a seller's price. The buyer needs to determine whether the seller's rigidity is a matter of choice or lack of choice. Where a seller is forced into a sale to raise cash to meet debt or unanticipated expenses, he may be both desperate to sell and unable to move off his price. A buyer should try to work this type of seller on non-price concessions. The buyer can also shift the negotiations from talking about price to talking about the terms of the purchase, including seller financing, seller sweetening the pot by throwing in farm equipment or building new fence, and seller agreeing to pay transaction costs, such as a tax or lender points. If a seller takes the negotiating position of always saying no and refusing to move on any issue, including price, the buyer faces a take-it-or-leave-it situation. If the seller's price is fair and you can live with the non-price issues, take it. If, as is usually the case, such a seller has also priced his property above market, walk away while offering to talk things over again at the seller's convenience. If you haven't heard from the seller in a couple of weeks, find another property. If you submit to a stick up, you may never feel quite right about the place. If money is no object and you can afford to be robbed, put up your hands.

How the seller feels about a negotiation can play a role in price bargaining. A client was aiming at a large tract that was mainly water, woods and a very large white elephant of a recording studio. The seller had built a custom structure and then lost interest. He probably had $10 or $11 million in the property as a whole. That, at least, was the appraisal value based on replacement cost. The seller listed at $6.25 million. My client did not want to pay over $5.25. Price was the only issue between them. I thought $5.25 was the seller's bottom. My client started with a bit over $5 million, which I thought was the right place for credibility. The seller eventually came down to $5.35 million. My client came up, but not to $5.25 million. Then they stalled. The seller in my opinion did not need the money from this sale, but he did need to extract some psychological positive out of a situation where he knew he was losing a lot of money. I advised my client to couch his last offer in terms of "That's all folks—the seller has gotten my last available nickel. I am stretched to the limit." This allowed the seller to shift his thinking away from the enormity of his loss (which he really didn't care that much about) to the idea that he was squeezing every last penny out of the buyer—and therefore winning. The deal got done at $5.2 million when the seller could feel that he was at least not losing the negotiations with the buyer regardless of the fact that the buyer was winning the deal over the property. Each side got what it wanted.

HORSE-TRADING

The fact-and-numbers approach I used with the absentee owner above is not the way most rural sellers are accustomed to bargaining. A lot of price bargaining occurs in rural areas between individuals, and its style is usually described as old-fashioned **horse-trading**.

Horse-trading is not something I learned at my father's knee. In fact, I never saw either parent negotiate anything of a commercial nature, though I'm sure they did so in the course of operating a small business. I never learned anything remotely relevant to negotiating in college or graduate school, though I studied negotiated settlements in international politics and the deal-making of domestic politics. Growing up in a suburban Pittsburgh neighborhood, I had no experience in thinking about commodities, let alone pricing and trading them. People who grow up in rural areas and, particularly, on farms, learn to understand their immediate world in terms of commodities that are valued and sold as cents per pound, dollars per pound of gain, dollars per acre and dollars per thousand board feet. Any farmer who buys stocker cattle in the spring at the livestock auction must calculate the present cost and the future projected values of different grades of cattle priced in pennies per pound multiplied by thousands of projected pounds where weight gain can vary by 25 percent depending on an animal's genetics, health and the weather. Buying and selling rural commodities involves on-the-spot, face-to-face negotiations where give and take is expected. It's worked for farm animals, crops, trees and land for centuries. The idea of trading seems to be known in all cultures.

Horse-trading in its most elementary form is swapping one thing for a like thing, this horse for that one. It requires that each party understand the value of what he has and the virtues and liabilities of what he wants from the other. Horse-trading in this form involves no cash, though it might involve "**boot**," which is something extra—possibly cash—to even the swap. The essence of swapping is equivalence, that is, both sides benefit when the outcome is, as kids say, "even-steven." Each trader is trying to better his position, and neither would turn down the chance to get the better of the swap. Swapping generates risk when one side fails to know a defect in the other's horse—and horses are the perfect example of goods with hidden defects. Sellers are not expected to disclose defects in their horses; it's strictly, "protect yourself at all times."

Horse-trading has come to mean a negotiating technique rather than the process of swapping one like thing for another. As a technique I have seen it used during several decades of residing in a farming community. It refers to a mutually agreed process of bid and counter bid in search of a price and terms that both sides can live with. The buyer wants the seller to set the asking price. The seller expects the buyer's first bid to be too low, and the buyer knows that he will have to come up. These negotiations often take place over the hood of a pick-up truck parked under a shade tree. The more formal sessions take place around the seller's kitchen table. Nothing is put in writing until there is agreement on price and terms. Participants are expected to hold to their word. Oral contracts are enforceable in court, *except those* involving real estate. Still, a lot of rural real estate seems to bargained orally as a first step and then put in writing. A party who starts to "crawdaddy" away, backing off from his oral commitment, is not playing by the rules. Writing up an oral agreement is sometimes referred to where I live as "doing up a paper." The written agreement should not contain surprises or zingers. I have seen horse-trading work well among people who share the same values, background and vocabulary. I've also seen a university professor and his wife walk away from an oral agreement when a better offer came along.

Face-to-face horse-trading has the potential to work badly, or not at all, between individuals from different community cultures, typically a rural seller experienced with oral horse-trading in that place and an urban buyer who is more comfortable with words on paper and a different style of oral negotiations. Typically, the choice of negotiating frameworks is the buyer's since he must make an offer. Where a real-estate broker is involved, the bargaining should always be paper-based.

An urban/suburban buyer may find himself in an awkward situation where a rural seller, especially a FSBO, is unfamiliar with his negotiating framework. Sellers of this type fear being tricked by a city slicker's paper, while buyers fear they will be skunked by a crafty seller in overalls. I have seen very smart buyers—high SATs in verbal and math—negotiate very badly with honest rural people when they are not comfortable with face-to-face negotiating and don't like the give and take the seller assumes is normal. If you don't feel comfortable horse-trading with a FSBO, ask your local lawyer to do it for you, subject to your confirmation. If you try it yourself, raise your offer slowly, always getting something equivalent in return and don't exceed your scoping-based top offering price. Take your time; digress when you don't have a response; and never say, "Take it or leave it." If horse-trading doesn't lead to a deal, walk away on friendly terms. Horse-traded deals have a way of working out. Horse-trading is a skill that most people get better at with practice. Horse-trading survives on the pennant-draped lots of auto dealers and in the tourist markets of the Caribbean. And if you're a friend of Rick, the seller always has a special price.

There are two other pitfalls I will point out in horse-trading across class cultures. People who work with words—writers, lawyers, economists, scientists and the like—use hedge verbs, conditionals and qualifiers as a matter of routine. Such a person is comfortable with this sentence: "I would not think it impossible to consider $125,000 were we to agree on everything today." The vernacular seller does not hear in the subjunctive: he hears $125,000 hard and the conditional context soft. It's easy to see how the seller will feel the buyer is sliding around if one or more of the buyer's conditions—included in "everything"—isn't met. The buyer should not be obscure, and he should hold the seller to the same standard of clarity. Rural sellers may speak in generalities that are clear to them, but not to you. In that situation, you need to get it straight with the seller when he says something when he says it, not later.

The second pitfall involves the fine print in the purchase offer contract. All real-estate contracts contain fine print, some of which can be monumentally important. Phrases like: Time is of the essence;

Warranties do or do not survive the Contract; Buyer's purchase is subject to the Seller's mortgage; Property to convey As Is as of the day when this Contract takes effect or As Is on the day of Closing—can make or break deals and result in one side or the other bearing unexpected expenses. If you and your lawyer are preparing a contract for the seller to sign, make sure that you explain each and every sentence of significant fine print that you want to include at the end of your oral negotiations. You do not want the written contract to surprise the seller. I have advised sellers to have their lawyer look over a contract before they sign so as to avoid future fine-print misunderstandings. If the seller's lawyer fails to explain the meaning of the contract's words to the seller, he is to blame, not you.

If you're horse-trading, you must make sure that you understand the seller's vocabulary and intent, and he yours. A constant source of amusement are conversations between an owner and an "outside" buyer that run like this:

Buyer: Where's the back property line?

Seller: Oh you go up there to where the big sugar is. Then you follow it out. You can't miss the pin. Then you head out on up the ridge. Just go along the chops. Then come back around. (These "directions" will make perfect sense once the buyer is on the ground and is oriented, but they are worthless for the purpose of helping an urban buyer who has no idea what is meant by a "big sugar" or a "chop.")

A similar conversation can occur over the conveyance of farm equipment in the property sale:

Seller: We're planning an auction to clear out the place before you move in.

Buyer: Good.

Seller: Sure. We'll get rid of all that junk out in the barn for you.

Buyer: I thought I bought all that under "farm equipment."

Seller: Now son, you did buy the "farm equipment." That means the *mechanical* equipment—the tractor, bushhog, grain elevator—things that have moving parts and do some machine work. Hell, I'll even throw in a hay wagon. (The buyer assumed he had already purchased all four of the seller's hay wagons, worth about $1,000 each.)

Buyer: What about the five new farm gates, the four rolls of fence wire and the board fencing stacked out back?

Seller: Those are supplies, not equipment. You're free to buy all of that stuff at the auction.

Buyer: But the gates and wire were in the barn when you took me around.

Seller: "Equipment" doesn't mean hay in the barn, or tools, or any of that other stuff you want 'cause you're going to need it. There's no free lunch on a farm.

The only defense against oral misunderstanding is for the buyer to take responsibility for being unambiguous and specific, and insist that the seller explain what his words mean. Spoken words mean what they mean, and then they also mean something more or something less, and sometimes, something different. If you're going to horse-trade land with a horse-trader, you better know exactly what he means when he says something such as "all one money." Your definition of "all" should match his definition of "all," item for item.

Horse-trading over land has its own peculiarities. While horse-trading always revolves around price, terms of the purchase are not usually on the table at the same time. But terms in real-estate sales can be equally critical, as expressed in the old saw: "I'll pay your price [$1,000,000], if you agree to my terms [$1.00 per year for one million years]." Horse-trading tends to disadvantage a buyer because it skews the bargaining toward price first. If a seller insists on talking price first, the buyer must immediately raise all the other issues and leave them hovering with the warning that price can't be concluded apart from all the other issues. If a buyer does not do this at the outset, the seller will be righteously indignant when the buyer starts backing away from a price. Horse-trading tends to neglect discussion about contingencies that protect the buyer. Buyers, therefore, must set out terms and contingencies along with price so that the seller has a complete view of the buyer's agenda. Inexperienced horse-traders should be careful not to get caught agreeing to a thing in isolation from other things that are related. If you feel that horse-trading has thrown you before you've ever started, submit a written offer; don't start what you don't think you can finish.

Being specific and detailed in horse-trading also avoids the problem of a seller feeling he has a certain residual claim to stuff left on the property after closing. I have seen bad feelings generated when a seller takes lumber left in the barn that he felt was his "personal property" and just hadn't had a chance to haul it off. The buyer rightly assumed anything left on the property after closing was his unless prior arrangement was made. A new owner does not want to bring a court case against the seller since all of his new neighbors will think him to be grabby and litigious. The new owner swallows his sense of violation but doesn't forget.

A variation on this post-closing last bite occurs when a neighbor informs the new owner of an obligation made by the seller that he feels "runs with the land." The neighbor built a section of fence for the seller 15 years ago, but was never paid. The neighbor informs the new owner of this fact along with the additional information that the former owner gave him the right to cut 20 sawtimber trees in lieu of payment. The seller, of course, never informed the buyer of any claim. The new owner has no legal obligation to live up to a claim of this sort even if it's genuine. The new owner needs to navigate this strait with care since he has to live with the neighbor, not the seller. The best defense is to ask the seller during negotiations whether he has knowledge of any such claims. And if the buyer is still suspicious, he can insert a clause in his purchase offer:

> **Seller warrants that to the best of his knowledge, neither he nor any of his neighbors have outstanding claims against each other that would adversely affect the Buyer's title, ownership, use and enjoyment of the subject property, its rights, assets and goods as conveyed and/or found on the property at closing.**

The biggest problem with the horse-trading style of negotiation for land is that it is entirely oral. **Oral agreements to buy and sell real estate do not bind the parties and are not enforceable until they are put into writing and signed by all parties.** (The Statute of Frauds requires that a real-estate contract must be supported by a written document that is signed by the party against whom the other party is seeking enforcement. But a memo or a letter of understanding can take the place of a formal contract; and several documents can constitute a contract. Moreover, if one party partially performs on a real-estate contract, a court may find that a valid contract exists even if it's oral. Partial performance to establish a contract might be found in possession by the buyer, payment and possession, or possession and improvement of the property.) If you start a real-estate purchase by horse-trading, you need to convert it to writing to avoid legal wrangles.

Horse-trading tends to focus on the big items—price, closing date, possibly seller financing, contingencies. A dozen smaller-but-still-important items are likely never to be discussed. If they are talked about, some may never be nailed flush. Certain "small" items can be deal-killers. If, for instance, the buyer is assuming that the seller is conveying title in fee simple with a General Warranty Deed and it then turns out when the purchase offer contract is written that the seller can do neither, the buyer has no obligation to go through with what amounted to an oral agreement on some things and not on others. A seller of real estate, similarly, has no obligation to go through with an oral agreement on some or even all terms until he has signed a contract and accepted the buyer's earnest money.

If a buyer finds himself horse-trading with a horse-trader, he should bring to their face-to-face oral negotiation a written draft purchase-offer contract that the parties complete in writing as each item is negotiated orally. The written contract provides structure to the final oral negotiations, and the buyer is assured at each step on the way that he and the seller are in an agreement that binds them both. A buyer and seller leave much too much to chance if they don't use their last face-to-face meeting to convert their oral understandings to writing. Once the terms of the contract are roughed in, both sides should initial and date the draft contract with a copy to each. The final, clean copy can then be produced by either side. The buyer submits his deposit money to an escrow agent when he signs the finished contract and hands it to the seller. The buyer should not give his deposit to the seller. If you are inexperienced in buying rural land, make sure to have your lawyer with you when you are negotiating and filling in a contract.

Buyers who prefer paper-based bargaining must be careful not to fall victim to their own preferences. While paper-based, back-and-forth bargaining may be the buyer's preference, standard real-estate contracts used by broker/agents are written to favor the seller (who is the listing broker's client). Such contracts are almost always filled in with the "help" of the real-estate broker/agent representing the seller, leaving the buyer on his own. They are rarely reviewed prior to submission to the seller by a lawyer representing the buyer. The burden of thinking up legal language to protect the buyer's interests falls totally on the buyer in a pressured situation orchestrated by a broker/agent representing the seller. Even experienced buyers are likely to forget to think of inserting both a **survival** clause in the offer, which obligates the seller to stand by the promises he makes in the purchase contract after the purchase is completed, and a **liquidated-damages** clause, which limits the buyer's financial exposure to his deposit in the event he won't or can't perform on the contract after the contingencies are removed.

Paper-based negotiation should always be the format when a seller lists his property with a real-estate broker. All offers and counter-offers are made in writing and channeled through the broker/agent. The broker/agent in this case can involve any one, or a combination, of the following individuals: listing broker, listing agent, cooperating broker and cooperating agent. The commission the seller pays can go to one person (listing broker who shows the property to buyer), two individuals (listing broker and listing agent, associated with his brokerage, who shows property to buyer), three individuals (listing broker, listing agent and cooperating broker who shows property) or four (listing broker, listing agent, cooperating broker and cooperating agent who shows property). The more individuals working the deal on the seller's side, the more opportunities are created for miscommunication in interpreting the paper. Buyers should pick a single negotiating channel to the seller, using the most reliable and precise person representing the seller. I am no longer shy about asking the seller's side to let me work through the one of their number who I feel is my best communication channel. I have seen agents who are intellectually sloppy screw up communications and the deal itself. Never let one of the seller's side professionals negotiate on your behalf.

Direct negotiation between buyer and seller generally does not occur when broker/agents are involved, except possibly in the final stages when details or a small price difference needs to be resolved. Broker/agents discourage buyers from direct contact with sellers in part because they want to manage the negotiations and in part because they want to limit the opportunities for volatile personality conflicts to mess up the deal. I usually try to talk directly with the seller, because I find it helpful to hear him answer questions; get a sense of his needs, resources, opinions; and how he weighs the various assets of the property. Most important, the seller knows the property better than anyone else. I always find it better to talk directly with a seller when my wife is present. She is a dirt lawyer and is, therefore, familiar with real-estate contracts. But more valuable for negotiations, she has a softer, friendlier way about her. (If your spouse thinks he is Donald Trump or comes across as a banshee on speed, better dicker with the seller on your own.) A buyer should expect brokers and agents to resist allowing him direct access to the seller—

and sometimes for good reason. A buyer can do himself more harm than good if he is clumsy in his approach. Sellers may balk at dealing with buyers; after all, part of their rationale for paying the broker/agent a commission is to have him do all of the property's marketing, including the "management" of individual buyers and their inquiring ways. The buyer should push for direct contact *only when* he thinks it will help make the deal.

Inept real-estate agents can foul up a buyer's purchase and, thereby, work their perverse magic against their client, the seller. Property is listed in such a way that it can be co-brokered, which means that a cooperating agent who never met the seller is writing the buyer's purchase contract. Though these agents are working for the seller, they don't know his financial needs and which elements of a sale are most important to him. This leaves a buyer flying into an offer on the wings of a blind bird, apart from the question of whether this particular bird starts his flight ten feathers short a wing. Some cooperating agents have never been on the property itself. Contract offers in these circumstances are necessarily generic. They serve neither the seller nor the buyer very well. They make it difficult for the buyer's offer to be credible and predispose the seller toward rejection.

I once lost a buyer who offered me a very good price that I would have taken, but he took a cooperating agent's advice and packaged it in such a way that acceptance was next to impossible. Had the agent touched based with me or my listing agents, a possibility existed—considering the agent, I think it was at best a small possibility—that my objections could have been anticipated or even worked out prior to submitting the contract. Instead, the agent advised the buyer to put me under the gun. The buyer then became invested in one-sided terms that were deal-killers, terms that were marginal to him but important to me. One was a 48-hour response time. The offer was dropped off at my wife's law office about noon on the first of my two days. I didn't see it until late that night. We didn't have a chance to think about it because of previous commitments. I could have requested an extension, but I was not inclined to negotiate through an agent who could not help getting in his own way. He believed in bullying sellers when he could. This agent—who was legally representing me! as a cooperating listing agent—told the buyer that we were distressed sellers and would, therefore, accept a "hardball" offer. In distress I was, but I had a backup plan and did not need to accept the buyer's too-clever-by-half offer.

If you—as either buyer or seller—feel pressure to make the deal, resist unless your next best alternative is worse. A large part of successful real-estate investing and negotiation is the ability of one party to generate an acceptable alternative to his one best and preferred outcome.

I find it useful in negotiations to have the seller know to whom he is selling, but I have also seen that knowledge work against me. It depends on the seller's attitudes toward buyers like (or unlike) himself and the various uses to which the sold property might be put. Without direct contact, the seller will have only the broker/agent's thumbnail profile of you, such as "He's a rich doctor and drives a Mercedes" or "They're tree-huggers from the city." If a buyer believes his personality and ability to connect will help his offer, push for direct contact through the broker.

Buyers need to be aware of how they come across in negotiations. Even after living for the better part of 30 years in rural West Virginia and even more rural Virginia, I still look like a college professor and talk like a Yankee, despite blue jeans, boots, pick-up truck and the ability to mumble passably about cattle. Sometimes my Yankee speech and odd ways work against me. I don't try to disguise that I'm "not from around here." Generally, but not always, I can get beyond such handicaps by emphasizing shared interests in working a sale. It helps to have a wife from the South who talks like it. (The fact that she brought home a Yankee husband is one of her character deficiencies that her family has accepted but don't talk about too much when I'm around.) A buyer who feels that he might find himself similarly misaligned with a seller needs to do a quick cost-benefit analysis regarding whether he will help or hurt his chances with the seller through a personal meeting. When the buyer is absolutely convinced that the real-estate professionals on the seller's side are clunking things up, he should initiate contact with the seller. Getting a good deal done is more important to a buyer than following protocol—and a personal visit in no way diminishes the commission due the seller's agent.

As a seller, I prefer face-to-face contact with a buyer brought to my property by a real-estate broker/agent. I don't insist on doing this, but I believe I am the best source of information and, therefore, more persuasive than an agent who knows my property superficially. The same risks of personality and style are present when I am the seller. I've had buyers appear who are angry that I've priced a property higher than they want to pay and blame it on who I am or how I look; that I'm "not from around here"; and that I've written covenants to run with divided land. Since each of us can not change, or even disguise very well, who we are, I advise both sellers and buyers to be friendly, straight-forward, helpful and flexible. That is, I think, the best way to encourage reciprocal behavior. If you have firm opinions about politics, religion, ethnic and racial groups, no need exists for you to share them in negotiations over land. If you are in the habit of using expressions like "Jew down," "gyp," "nigger-rigged," "welsh on a deal," "Indian giver" and the like, adopt a new habit for negotiating, if not permanently. It's interesting to note how many of these expressions relate to the trans-cultural process of bargaining over goods and money. Sellers, in addition, may make themselves vulnerable to suit if they discriminate against a buyer from a legally protected minority. Words and expressed opinions will be evidence in such a suit.

Buyer-initiated contact with the seller works best when the buyer has no interest in altering the seller's property. A different dynamic can occur when a buyer wants to divide the property or recast it as something else, especially where a seller is emotionally involved in the property. Here, a buyer needs to make a choice between being open about his possibly alienating intentions and not. Where a buyer needs rezoning or other permitting before dividing or using land for a different purpose, he will have to make his offer contingent on acquiring all necessary approvals and permits—hence, you can't conceal plans of this type from a seller. If a buyer does not make his purchase contingent on obtaining these "papers," he will have to go through with the deal and then hope that his plans are approved. This is a chancy perch on which a buyer should not rest.

Sellers who truly want to preserve their property following its sale, will write deed covenants to that effect or impose conservation easements—and accept a price discount. Sellers often want full FMV for their property *and* some lingering control over the use of "their" land after sale to the buyer. When a buyer finds himself about to be whipsawed like this, I suggest he say to the seller: "You've listed the property at this price without restrictive covenants or easements. That means you are retaining no interest in or control over the property after you sell it to me. I will base my offer to you on the property's value as it is for sale today. If you want to curtail what I do with the property after I buy it, I will lower my offer proportionately or move on to the next property. And remember every future use that you restrict means the property is worth less on today's market, to me and every other buyer." Most sellers doused with this dose of reality will opt for the money. But where a seller feels no pressure to sell a property he's put up for sale, he's likely to be financially indifferent about burdening the property with restrictions. This is a take-it-or-leave-it seller who is better left.

In negotiating over land, cash rules. Some sellers—those who are facing a huge tax hit—may prefer a structured schedule of payments, spread over a period of years. But most sellers want an all-cash, right-now deal, even though some would net more in the end if they considered how to soften their tax hit. Cash, in the form of fresh $100 bills, is also the best way of negotiating land-related side bars, such as an access easement. Cash (folding) works in kitchen-table negotiations. The obverse rule is this: when a buyer spreads new bills on your table, make sure you are absolutely certain of the value of what you're selling *to this buyer* before you grab them.

A paper-oriented buyer may look for ways to use written language to his advantage when a listing forces a conversation-oriented rural seller to negotiate through the exchange of written offers. In this case, I advise a seller to hire a lawyer to help with deciphering the legal implications of the buyer's proposals. Agents/brokers are rarely lawyers and should not be relied on for legal advice. The buyer in this situation, however, should avoid being too smart for his own good. It's easy to slide language traps into contracts, shift liability and make the contract too one-sided. The contract offer is an opportunity to promote and protect the buyer's interests but it also should be straight and transparent. Buyer efforts to design a contract with curves banked to slide a seller into a ditch is sleazy and counter-productive. Don't buy rural land through word tricks.

Occasions, however, may arise where the seller and his agent may not understand the legal implications of something a buyer has proposed even when the buyer has stated it clearly and simply. At such a point, the buyer needs to ask himself: Is it fair and reasonable to expect *this* seller to understand the offer and its implications? Sellers differ in their analytical capacities as well as in their ability to hire expert help. An 85-year-old widow with an eighth-grade education who's never traveled farther than 20 miles from her 200 acres has a far lower level of capacity and ability than a seller who, for example, is an experienced accountant. Savvy buyers should not take advantage of aged, impaired or unsophisticated sellers who are susceptible to cash and lawyerly legerdemain. I know professional land buyers who prey on such individuals. I know a couple of scoundrels who comb the rural obituaries looking for recent widows with farms. With an able seller, however, I don't believe a buyer has any responsibility to protect him from his own failure to be informed about his own property.

A buyer will occasionally stumble into a situation where a seller is desperate to sell and cash-strapped to boot. A buyer who forces this individual into swallowing a ridiculously low price is playing too hard for my taste. The last dollars of concession are not worth wringing out, because they will cost the buyer a lot in terms of self-image, reputation and future dealings. I'm sure some readers think that statement is hilariously wimpy or economically inefficient, or both. So be it. I've heard buyers boast of deals where they "gave him the boots." I would caution the prosperous non-rural buyer in particular to not stomp the distressed rural seller into the dirt unless he cares little for the consequences of being a thug.

MUSHY BOTTOMS AND HARD FRAMEWORKS

A buyer should try to identify the seller's **acceptable price range**. That range will have no top, but it may not have a hard bottom either. Sellers usually start out with a rock-bottom price in mind, but my experience is that a rock-bottom price often softens over time and also gains elasticity when the buyer offers seller-friendly terms. Where the seller's price is unmovable, the buyer may consider offering that price packaged with adverse terms that substantially ease the buyer's burden. A buyer gets a sense of the seller's acceptable price range through suggesting different hypothetical price-and-terms offers with the seller.

Buyers are looking to find a terms-flexible seller with a mushy bottom. A mushy bottom price is one on which the seller is willing to negotiate if the buyer offers him favorable terms, the best of which include all cash at closing, no contingencies and a short escrow period. Sellers should value the absence of requests for seller financing and seller-provided repairs. Sellers understand that there is a **time cost** in holding mortgaged property, which includes monthly principal and interest, property taxes, other maintenance charges (insurance, upkeep) and risk of loss. This time cost increases the longer the seller holds his property beyond when he could have sold it to you. Time has a money value, and where time piles up without a proportional financial gain, it becomes an **opportunity cost**—lost money—to the seller. The time-cost factor stops working on behalf of your offer where the seller has a backup buyer in the wings who is able and willing to step in at or above your price or where the seller's carrying costs are minimal (no mortgage, low property taxes, no maintenance needed).

A buyer can also point out to the seller that an immediate sale has a **time value** to the seller. He can use the sale income to earn money, and every day that the buyer's money is not used by the seller is a day of lost opportunity to put that money to work. If the seller ends up selling his property eight months after he rejects your offer for the same money, he has lost that time value of his net from the forgone sale to you, and it has cost money to carry it for the extra months. Time cost and time value are two sides of the same coin. If property values are appreciating at a high rate, then time usually works against the buyer's argument about time value. In a slow market, however, time cost can be persuasive.

Buyers may find a FSBO who advertises a property without an asking price. "Make me an offer," this seller will say. I've read real-estate gurus who counsel buyers not to do this since they believe "he who puts a number on the table first, loses the negotiation." This is nonsense. Where a seller insists that *his* only negotiating format is for the buyer to move first, the buyer can either walk or start the game. With such a FSBO, the buyer must be up to speed on comparables and know, after scoping, both the property's FMV as well as what it's worth to him. Start with an offer that's at least 50 percent lower than your absolute best money. Peg it, if you can, to the property's tax-assessed value, which is often lower than FMV. This type of seller may either be scared that he will under-price his property or hope that Santa Claus will drop down his chimney with a buyer's bag of cash. Simple, all-cash offers packaged with an evidence-based discount price can work with these sellers. The buyer should remember that the Make-Me-An-Offer crowd feels at home in the give and take of oral horse-trading.

Some sellers try to signal their bottom price by including "**firm**" in their advertisements. "Firm" should mean that the stated price is the only price the seller will accept. This may or may not be the case. With land, "firm" can mean hard bargaining ahead. It can mean a seller under no pressure. It can mean a high starting point. It can mean nothing more than a bluff. It can mean a seller who's scared to death of negotiating; it's a preemptive defense against give and take. It is also a way for a seller to ascertain the financial capabilities of the buyer by forcing a buyer to reveal that he can pay the "firm" price. A buyer need only test how firm "firm" is by making a hypothetical reasonable offer just slightly below the firm price the buyer would pay. "What would you do if I were to offer you $x less than your price?" Don't be surprised if firm in theory means mushy in practice.

A buyer's first offering price is important insofar as it establishes his minimum bid, at which, or above which, negotiations will occur. The buyer's first offer is his direct response to the seller's asking price. It reflects all of the buyer's scoping efforts to determine the value of the seller's property to him. It also establishes the range of prices in which the negotiation occurs. The seller now knows that this buyer can afford at least his first offer and probably more. No rule of thumb exists that says a buyer's first offer should be x percent of the seller's asking price. I have bought properties with my first offer at the full asking price as well as less than 65 percent of it, and at points in between. Each first offer depends on where the seller's asking price is in relation to the value of the property in the market and to the buyer. Where a seller has under-priced his property, I would advise the buyer to not fool around with low offers: put a clean and simple purchase contract in front of the seller as soon as possible and reasonably close to the undervalued asking price. The only argument for not making such a first offer to an under-priced seller is one where the buyer does not want to create a case of price remorse in the seller. Where the seller has set his asking price at more than you can afford, offer close to your top money and inform the seller that you can do a little better, but not much, if he can help you on one or two items. Where the seller sets his asking price at an objective FMV, the buyer must decide whether or not FMV equals the value of the property to him. If the value to the buyer is less than FMV/asking price, offer less; otherwise make the deal. Buyers need to keep in mind that a FSBO can stick with his asking price, reduce it or even raise it in response to a buyer's offer. I've seen FSBOs set low asking prices and then raise them in response to an offer. A buyer with a *listed* property may stick with or reduce his asking price; if he rejects a clean, full-price offer he may find himself having to pay a commission without a sale. If he rejects and raises his asking price, the same commission obligation may kick in unless he is the lucky beneficiary of offers above his asking price. A seller is not legally obliged to accept a full-price offer with contingencies on a listed property.

A buyer must never submit a first offer without first testing the seller to see if he will reveal the low end of his price range, what other issues might be important to him and what amount of negotiating he will accept. You can feel around for the seller's low end—and maybe even find his rock-bottom price—by asking him how he went about setting his asking price. Was it based on an appraisal? Was it based on a comparables analysis he did himself or a competitive market analysis (CMA, similar idea) done by the listing agent? Which comparables did he use and how did he adjust his property's price in relation to them? How much of the asking price does he need right away? The buyer says, "I can come up with __ dollars [70 to 90 percent of the asking price] in cash at closing, but because of the work I need to do on the place, I can't do much better than that. And I can't borrow any more, given my cash flow." The last statement, of course, is the one that may get the seller to begin to show his low end; the others are useful but essentially diversions. The percentage figure that you use to calculate the dollar figure in that question will depend on your assessment of the seller's circumstances (pressure to sell; ability to carry) and his asking price in relation to FMV and your determination of what the property is worth to you.

If the seller replies, "I know what land is bringing around here and my asking price is just what it's worth," the buyer has the opportunity to move his own numbers into the seller's field of vision. The buyer will eventually discern the degree of attachment the seller has to his asking price during pre-offer discussions and negotiations. The seller may tell the buyer that he just came up with an asking price and later in the negotiations begin introducing comparables and other facts that suggest the price is based on the same type of research the buyer's done. This doesn't happen very often. Sellers tend to be impatient in getting to a deal so buyers usually learn what the seller wants to reveal toward the front end of the negotiations.

The buyer with hard, research-based numbers should time their introduction to get the maximum impact. I once monkeyed around for months with an individual who could be either a seller of his interests in a property or a buyer of mine. Nine months passed without a serious discussion of price, because he refused to meet with me. Instead, he had his big-shot lawyer—a blow-hard who brought absolute ignorance of the property in question to his work—spend a lot of his money on baseless challenges. Finally, his lawyer called and asked me for a price on my interests. I said the number. He exploded. I replied, "Do you know what the property is worth?" My client, he declaimed, knows every square inch of it. [In fact, his client hadn't been on the property for 30 years, which is why his client didn't know its value.] "Let me fax you some information," I said, "and then we can talk again." I then faxed an honest timber cruise done by a reputable forester whom his client trusted. The cruise placed the value of the timber at several hundred thousand dollars above the other party's most optimistic guess. I sold my interest to him in a couple of days. It appeared to me that he needed to go through a bunch of bullying and legal huffing and puffing to get to the point where reality would fall on receptive ears.

If negotiations can be moved toward more of a **hard framework**—where tax-assessed value, appraisals, consultant reports, comparables analysis and recent asking prices increasingly supplant "I WANT THIS PRICE BECAUSE."—the bargaining advantage should swing to the party who is better researched and more reality-based. It may not work that way in every negotiation, but if you take this approach you are doing what you can to help yourself. The buyer's insertion of a harder framework into the bargaining should be done gently. Don't dismiss the seller's price as arbitrary rubbish or pie in the sky. Put facts on the table in the spirit of sharing (publicly) available information. Don't quarrel with the seller or make it personal. Just keep introducing one little fact after another to support your position. Let the facts accumulate their own weight on the other side. The buyer must be careful to distinguish between a seller rejecting his hard framework of negotiation and a seller rejecting negotiations. A seller who knows that he will be disadvantaged by facts will dismiss a fact framework out of hand. Just keep working them in patiently and without a triumphant gloat.

Framing negotiations is a process intended to get the seller to come around to his best price and terms for you. That may take five minutes or five months. It may produce a split-the-difference deal. The buyer needs to have his finger on the pulse of the process. There comes a **tipping point in land negotiations** where the seller feels the momentum of his position shift toward making the deal with you rather than holding on to the property in hope of a better deal. When you sense the seller has tipped, both sides can anticipate flexibility and accommodations. A firm price may become less firm if you can help the seller on something else. Introducing a hard, researched-based framework is intended to get the seller to his tipping point in an agreeable frame of mind. The facts are hard, but the approach is soft. Buyers should use hard evidence to erode a seller's asking price—never, to diminish the seller personally. Facts should be offered with tact, diplomacy, friendliness and in the spirit of mutual problem-solving.

The buyer's first offer seeks negotiation, not necessarily acceptance—though acceptance might happen. Rejection is fine as long as it's accompanied with a seller counter. A counter signals that the seller is willing to negotiate. If your first offer is a low ball, it should be a **soft low ball**, that is, packaged with other things that the seller will like. A **hard low ball** amounts to a take-it-or-leave-it proposal, which is the opposite of the negotiations that usually benefit buyers. A deal is killed on the first offer when a seller rejects the buyer's offer to negotiate. A hard low ball may insult a desperate-but-proud seller or convince a seller than any alternative is likely to be better than bargaining with you.

The price and terms of your first offer reflects your reading of the seller's position and his alternatives to negotiating a deal with you. Part of a buyer's pre-offer scoping is to determine the nature of his competition. Where a property has been on the market for more than six months, a buyer may assume the seller is antsy, perhaps desperate. But you also need to be alert for another buyer showing up at the same time you do—at which point the seller will start a three-way negotiation that works against both buyers. Every seller wants to be in the middle of a bidding war. Savvy sellers often tell a buyer that he is in a competitive situation. I now anticipate a certain type of rural seller or agent informing me as a matter of course that a highly motivated buyer—usually a rich doctor from Washington—just left the property or is expected to arrive as soon as I leave. I now joke about it with the seller: "That guy has been following me around for years." If it's true—which it can be—the buyer must bring his negotiations to a head quickly. Some buyers may have to bail out of a truly competitive situation, especially when a "**big money buyer**" is on the scene. Big money almost always wins competitive contests, because chips don't mean as much to him, and he has more in his pile than the other players. Sometimes, you can out-think Big Money by raising doubts about the property based on your research, but you can't outbid him.

Some buyers try to scope a seller's low end by using a tactic where they ask the seller who has set an asking price, "**Well, what'll you take for it?**" In effect, the buyer is asking the seller to bargain with himself, to lower his asking price without the buyer offering anything at all in any form. This buyer is asking the seller to name his bottom price in the form of a first offer to himself on the buyer's behalf. A smart seller will *never* bite at this invitation to lower his price on his own initiative; never. I am insulted when the tactic is used against me, and tend to dismiss such buyers as tire-kickers. The seller must make a judgment as to the buyer's *bona fides* after asking the seller to reduce his price to get things started. If the seller believes the buyer is genuine, the seller might repeat his asking price in a friendly fashion and remind the buyer that only written offers with signatures are binding in the sale of real estate. Alternatively, the seller can say, "I'll take my asking price, or something reasonably close if there are terms that help me. Why don't you put an offer in writing?" Undoubtedly, the what-would-you-take tactic works with some sellers. Where a seller has blatantly over-priced his property and you are a genuine buyer, I suppose it's worth a try.

How does a buyer know how much a seller has padded his asking price above where he is willing to settle? There's no rule that sellers are advised to follow. And sellers may have in mind a price at which they want to settle and then end up settling at a lower price, the one they're willing to take. A buyer should begin with the assumption that all sellers are willing to reduce their asking price by at least by five to ten percent as anticipated bargaining concessions. Some others can and will cut their asking price more deeply. For a buyer to gauge the seller's bargaining margins, he has to research the seller's financial circumstances, motives for selling, other commitments that will pressure the seller toward a deal (such as a purchase of his own contingent on selling this land) and time pressures, such as moving to a new job by a certain date. If you think you've determined his padding, offer five percent or more below that and see what happens.

A buyer can test a padding factor with sellers who have sold other properties by learning about these transactions. Ask the buyers of these properties how much the seller came off the asking price to make the deal. You can also search the records. Take, for example, a seller who has sold five tracts during the last seven years. The buyer can find out the selling price for each of these tracts from the recorded deeds. He can then go back in local newspaper files to dig out the advertised asking price for each property. The spreads between asking price and selling price may indicate a pattern. If the newspaper records are not available, the buyer can ask the agent with whom he's working to do some asking around. I would also ask the local lawyer you're working with to give you a sense of how the seller is likely to bargain.

It is always beneficial for a buyer to design his offer to help a seller with federal income taxes. Where a seller is selling his principal residence and his profit is less than the current exemption—now $500,000 for a jointly filing married couple and $250,000 for an individual—all profit up to those caps is tax free. A tax-smart offer won't help a buyer with a seller whose profit is fully sheltered by these caps. But many sellers of rural land—and, of course, all rural property not used as the taxpayer's principal residence, such as pasture, farmland and woods—will not be able to take advantage of this break. Sellers who should be most approachable with a tax-smart offer are: 1) those who have owned the property for less than a year and are thus obliged to pay tax on the sale at their ordinary rate (i.e., probably in the 30 percent plus range), 2) those who have a low basis in the property, hence a large taxable gain on which they will probably owe 15 percent capital-gains tax and 3) those whose profit from the sale will bump them into a higher tax bracket in the sale year.

The buyer can help a seller's tax situation in several ways. First, payment can be structured so that a relatively small sum is paid at closing and the balance paid after a year has passed, which allows the seller who's doing a flip to treat the big balance of his profit as a capital gain (lower rate) rather than as current income (higher rate). Second, payment can be structured over a period of years, which spreads the seller's profit. This can help a seller stay out of a higher tax bracket in the sale year. Third, there may be some ways that the seller can increase his basis in the property prior to the sale. Finally, the seller may want to consider a 1031 like-kind exchange that allows him to defer all profit on investment property until such time as he sells and cashes out (which may be never). It's worth the effort for a buyer to think of ways that his offer can be structured to maximize the seller's **after-tax net income**, which is his real bottom line.

Every seller has only so much **give** in his asking price, whether the give is set by circumstances or the seller's arbitrary bottom line. The amount of give available to the typical seller is the difference between his asking price and what he needs to net after taxes. A seller may wind up giving all of his give, none of it or some of it. The give in a seller's price is directly related to his circumstances and degree of motivation. If the buyer can roughly determine what the seller needs to net immediately, he can structure his offer accordingly. It's worth getting help from a tax accountant to prepare a tax-friendly offer.

Certain sellers are not highly motivated to get their property sold. Such sellers may be rich by way of effort or inheritance, and the property that interests the buyer is on the market to simplify the seller's life or generate some cash for no particular current purpose. The unmotivated seller may have a heaping plate of negotiating give—and not part with a morsel. Such sellers can set a price and wait without worry. This seller presents a buyer with a take-it-or-leave-it deal. If a buyer finds himself in the dreadful position of needing this property, he takes it. But few buyers of rural property are ever objectively in this position, and buyers should not brainwash themselves into thinking that they must have a particular property. It is the rare parcel that is both absolutely perfect for the buyer of a rural second home, hunting camp or timber investment—and priced right. Next-best alternative properties will work for most buyers.

The worst example of a seller being uninterested in selling involved about 14,000 acres in New York's Adirondack Park owned by a wealthy individual in his early 80s. He had been rich his entire life, from a fortune made 150 years earlier. When approached with a more-than-fair $6 million offer, he asked, "What am I going to do with another $6 million?"

One way of edging a reluctant seller into negotiating is to agree to his price, packaged with buyer-friendly terms. Nothing guarantees that you will succeed, but you lose nothing in the attempt. If, for example, your seller can wait for his price, he can wait for his money. It may be in his interest to spread the purchase price over several years for tax reasons, and he may be willing to give you that time cheaply—after all you did meet his price. A common buyer technique used in this situation—and others—is to ask the seller to finance a portion of the purchase price at a below-market interest rate, say one half the local bank's 30-year, fixed mortgage rate or one half the bank's prime rate. Or you might borrow from the seller with interest paid at the end of a multi-year period rather than yearly. You're not trying to trick the seller with this type of financing; you're simply trying to get him to bargain with you on terms if not on price. Of course, you want to keep in mind that one little agreement can lead to another. The buyer has to figure both his yearly costs and his total costs for each possible financing arrangement to determine how his own benefits and obligations would be affected. The buyer is looking for a win-win arrangement, one that benefits both sides.

A seller getting his full asking price may be surprisingly flexible about agreeing to below-market rates for seller-financing. You can always start by proposing that you pay the current passbook interest rate—the interest rate the seller would receive from a bank were he to put the sum being financed into a savings account. Then, if necessary, move up to one half of the bank's 30-year, fixed mortgage rate or one half prime. Your individual situation may also benefit tax-wise from having the interest be paid in different ways, such as paying the loan's entire interest in one lump sum at a particular time or paying a lower rate on the first couple of payments and a higher rate on the declining balance. Seller financing also saves the buyer money that would otherwise go to lender's points, fees and other transaction costs—which can add five percent or more to a loan's face value.

If the full asking price is $100,000, the buyer can propose paying $55,000 on closing and the next $45,000 over three years. If the buyer were to borrow that $45,000 at closing from a bank for three years at ten percent, each of his 36 principal-and-interest payments would be $1,452.03. The buyer would end up paying $7,273.08 in interest on top of the $45,000 in principal. Assume the bank charges two percent of the loan principal for points and fees, the buyer eventually pays $9,273.08 in interest and lender charges, which is 20.6 percent of the $45,000 borrowed. The buyer ultimately pays the bank $54,273.08 for the use of $45,000 over three years. Instead, borrowing the same $45,000 from the seller at four percent passbook rate paid in two 18-month installments would look like this:

    Day 0 to Day 540   Due on 540th day
       4 % interest due on $45,000 $1,800
       Principal due   22,500

    Day 541 to Day 1,080

        4 % interest due on $22,500   900
           Principal due   22,500
                                                 $47,700

    With the break in interest, no upfront points and a two-payment schedule, the buyer has saved himself $6,573.08 and still paid the seller's full price. The cost to the seller of working with the buyer in this fashion is that he has probably received a lower return on his $45,000 than he would have from an alternative investment during the debt's term. If the seller compares the buyer's offer with what $45,000 might bring in the stock market, the rate of return becomes entirely hypothetical given the market's short-term volatility and the vagaries of picking stocks. The buyer should not quarrel with a seller's assertion that over a long period the Dow Jones Industrial Average or any broad basket of stocks like an index fund appreciates more than many investments. The buyer need only point out that three years is not the time period when this "rule" has held true historically. Inherent in any stock purchase is the possibility the investor will either earn a return lower than the passbook rate or even lose principal. Every stock investor knows that dogs bite. I have teeth marks to prove it.

    A variation on seller financing is a **land contract** or **installment sale**, which allows the seller to retain title (deed) to the property until all scheduled payments are made. Seller financing and a land contract allow the seller to be taxed only on the proportional amount of gain (profit and interest) he receives each year from the sale. The seller is allowed to report a certain percentage of each payment (after subtracting interest) as installment sale income. This is called gross profit percentage, and it is calculated by dividing the seller's gross profit from the sale by the contract price. If the seller's contract price is $5,000 and his gross profit is $2,500, his gross profit percentage is 50 percent. After subtracting interest, the seller reports 50 percent of each payment, including the down payment, as installment sale income from the sale for the tax year in which he receives it. The balance of each payment is tax-free inasmuch as it represents the seller's proportional share of his adjusted basis in the property. (See http://www.irs.gov/publication/p537/ar02.html#d0e455.) A land contract is a risky proposition to both seller and buyer. It can, on the other hand, give the seller a full asking price and tax benefits as well as providing the buyer with a 100-percent-financed purchase. DO NOT PROPOSE A LAND CONTRACT WITHOUT FULLY UNDERSTANDING THE LEGAL AND TAX IMPLICATIONS FOR BOTH YOU AND THE SELLER.

    The ultimate sweeteners a buyer offers the seller in return for financing are that the debt is secured by the seller's own property and the seller usually gets a big chunk of cash upfront that he keeps if the buyer defaults. (Some buyers try to substitute other collateral, a gimmick that is often intended to put sellers at risk.) If the buyer in the $100,000 sale example above fails to make either of the two scheduled 18-month payments, the seller can declare the note in default, keep the $55,000 and remove the buyer's claim against his property. The buyer generally loses the $55,000 in such a default, but it may take some lawyer time to make it stick depending on the note's language. It is essential for the parties to have a written note that spells out in unambiguous terms the degree of exposure the buyer faces in the event of default, how the default will be determined (default occurs when payment is ____calendar/business days past due; seller must provide written notice of default) and who pays the cost of collection. If the buyer doubts his ability to make the payments, he should not propose seller financing. But a seller who doubts the buyer's ability may sniff an opportunity for a double profit.

    Be flexible and creative with a seller who won't budge. Take him to supper. Send him a book that he'll like. Find common ground beyond your interest in his property.

    The buyer can also try shifting from participating in the first-person to **negotiating from a third-person perspective**. Third-person allows the buyer to participate as a kind of facilitating consultant to both parties where the outcome is no longer a matter of self-interest. The third-person-negotiator persona the buyer adopts on his own behalf is designed to get the seller thinking and acting as if he were negotiating. The buyer's objective is to get the seller to budge—on anything. It is the budging, not the "anything," that is important. The first budge is emotionally and intellectually the hardest for a seller fixed on his asking price. Once this seller takes a first step—no matter how tiny—he's taken *his* largest step. Take a slightly larger one back toward him. Don't look at your feet. Smile at your partner. You're dancing!

Off-angle ideas can stimulate discussion, with a chance of carrying you to a deal. You might suggest that you're really just interested in a piece of his property instead of the whole—the house and ten acres, or just the woods, or the back pasture with an access easement. Propose different combinations of his property's components to get him moving. Throw in stuff. Offer some service the seller values. Buy him ten hours of financial advice from the planner of his choice. Or provide a paint job for his new house. Or underwrite a Christmas vacation to the Caribbean. Or tutor his grandchild on how to take SATs.

A buyer who has completed his scoping and is faced with a set-in-concrete seller might pose an offer orally and hypothetically: "If I can arrange to offer you an all-cash deal at _____ dollars [start with 10 percent less than the asking price] with no more than two contingencies—financing and a 30-day study period with results acceptable to the buyer, can we work a deal?" The buyer in this case has communicated that he's willing to *try* to pay 90 percent of the asking price, but he's not promising that he can arrange it. Note, however, that this oral and hypothetical "offer" obligates the buyer to buy nothing at all were the seller to respond, "It's a deal." Real-estate "deals" made orally are not deals until they are written and signed. Hypothetical offers are not genuine offers. A smart seller will tell such a buyer to put his offer in writing and stop playing games.

The buyer might stick with his tactic and offer 95 percent of the asking price in this form: "Would you take $1,000 per acre?" The buyer has moved no closer to making a genuine offer, but he appears to be making both a concession and a firmer proposal. The buyer is not offering $1,000 per acre when he asks, "Would you take...?" He is just testing the seller and trying to get him to negotiate. Smart sellers **never** bargain with themselves. The seller's best response is simple: "I only consider written offers."

I don't recommend these two buyer ploys, because they can end up with no deal and a lot of hard feelings. But I have seen them work. When a seller does respond, the buyer needs to convert the oral discussion to paper as soon as possible.

A classic seller trick is to agree over the phone to one price only to increase it when the buyer appears in person able and willing to sign at that price. It is especially suited to a buyer defined as "wealthy" by the seller, and who has to travel some distance to get to the property's location. The first time this was pulled on me, I fell for it. The seller had agreed to sell the night before over the phone at a certain price. When I arrived at the property the next day after a five-hour drive, the seller insisted that the agreed price was $5,000 above the phone figure. (Remember: an oral agreement on real estate binds no one.) Maybe, I had misheard the seller's statement, I thought. Maybe, the seller was hard of hearing. Maybe, my mind was playing a trick on me. Actually, the seller had "read me" perfectly. I was highly motivated to get the deal done. We settled between the phone figure and the higher one. This seller, I later learned, was not unfamiliar with this type of bargaining.

Faced with a "misunderstanding" ploy, a highly motivated buyer should not challenge the seller's integrity. The buyer should announce that he is able and willing to buy at the phone/oral price, but not higher. The buyer can then hand a signed purchase contract to the seller at that price, with a 24-hour signing window—and leave on friendly terms. The odds are that a bad-faith seller will either sign or continue to negotiate. The second time I faced this trick I was at least smart enough to recognize it. The seller—a woman of self-proclaimed sophistication and wealth—jumped the price by $100,000 over what her son, a lawyer, quoted over the Internet. I didn't much like her property after I saw it, and had no inclination to negotiate with her. A month later, the son tried to get the deal going again. The third time I saw this used was when I was accompanying a client who thought he was looking at 45,000 acres of timberland and a sawmill. The acreage turned out to be 12,000 and the price of the mill jumped $4 million when we walked into the mill's office. If a buyer is highly motivated to make a deal with such a seller, he can respond by ignoring the changed price and remembering several items of his own that the seller should keep in mind, such as, the buyer needs 100 percent seller financing at one percent interest over 40 years, for starters. When a seller wants to reopen price, the buyer wants to reopen everything else. This tactic can reorient the bargaining or collapse it altogether.

When a buyer finds himself bargaining with a seller who is richer than he is, the buyer may go into the negotiations thinking that he is at a disadvantage. The buyer has a tendency to come up more than he should. Very rich people have gotten very rich by selling something. They may have more ability to hang on to a property until their price arrives, but they want to get rid of the property quickly—and don't want to go through negotiating pressure. You can get good deals just as often from a rich seller as a poor one.

In buying real estate, a buyer has no way to force a seller to come down on his price and offer favorable terms. A buyer can approach a seller as if negotiation is expected and do what he can to stimulate that process. Most sellers expect to negotiate as do most buyers, though either side can adopt a take-it-or-leave-it position. If you are faced with a a seller who insists on a price that is higher than you can afford or one that exceeds what the property is worth to you, keep looking.

Sellers tend to think that buyers have the advantage in negotiations, and buyers think the opposite. I think it's important for a buyer to show confidence in his scoping-based facts and information, but I think it's counter-productive to feel that you thereby have the seller at a disadvantage. The seller will pick up the buyer's attitude and run the other way. The attitude that I think does help the buyer is one of **patient problem-solving and professed reluctance about doing the deal**. The more the buyer comes toward—not at—the seller with this approach, the more the seller is encouraged to embrace it himself.

Negotiating is not about getting the better of the other side. It's about getting a deal that works for you.

CHAPTER 17: PROPERTY LOCATION—SURVEYS AND SUCH

Every land buyer must ask and answer at least three "physical" questions about every property he's scoping for purchase:

1. Where is the acreage located?

2. How much acreage will be conveyed by the seller to the buyer?

3. Are the boundaries, as marked on the ground, legally accurate and free of dispute?

I am constantly surprised by how often buyers do not ask these questions and, when asked, fail to obtain accurate answers.

You want a property about which you can say: "It contains X.00 acreage. I know this because I had the boundaries in the deed checked against the boundaries on the ground. I know where it is located in relation to adjoining properties. The property is being conveyed to me in fee, with all rights, free of boundary disputes, claims, unrecorded easements and encumbrances of various sorts that would diminish its value to me."

The knowledge on which each of these statements is based is not a matter of intuition, gut-feelings or faith. It is, rather, based on facts you gather before you submit a purchase offer by scoping the target property. This chapter discusses how to think about these questions and gather these facts.

LOCATION

Land involves two types of location: 1) legal location, as described in deed and/or drawn in a survey, and 2) physical location, that is, on the ground, in relation to the legal and physical location of adjoining properties. Your scoping task is to make sure, first, that the legal location is correct, and, second, that it matches the property's boundaries on the ground.

We use three principal systems of legally describing real-estate boundaries and establishing acreage: 1) rectangular (or, government) survey, 2) subdivision and lot and 3) metes and bounds. The last of these is the system that is used with rural property in most of the East. I occasionally run into large-lot, rural subdivisions that have been developed to one degree or another. Metes and bounds is the oldest of the three, and from my experience, it's the system most likely to contain acreage and boundary errors.

The **rectangular-survey system**, or **government system,** covers most of the United States, excepting the original 13 colonies (and Kentucky, Tennessee, Vermont, parts of Maine and West Virginia), Texas and a piece of Ohio. This system began in 1785 when land ceded to the new United States by Britain was surveyed into a grid using **north-south meridian** lines and **east-west baselines**. This grid allows property to be divided into smaller and smaller squares, starting with a **township** (six miles on each side, 36 square miles), **section** (one mile on each side, 640 acres) and then descending fractions of sections. A township contains 36 sections.

Townships north and south of a given baseline are laid out in **tiers**, such that township-one-south (T1S) would lie in the first tier of townships south of the baseline with the township's north boundary being the baseline. Township-two-south (T2S) would be directly below T1S. Several dozen township tiers can be laid out both north and south of a baseline. T20S, for instance, would be the twentieth township tier south of a baseline.

Principal meridians, running north-south, intersect with baselines and are used to locate townships east-west of themselves. Six miles east and west of every principal meridian is a **range line**, which forms the east or west boundary of the township. Townships are laid out in rows, east to west, and tiers, north to south.

Thus, a township will be described both in its north-south location, say T1S, and along its east-west dimension, say R1E (range-one-east). This township lies immediately southeast of the intersection of the baseline and the principal meridian; it is the township closest to that intersection in the southeast quarter that intersection forms.

Once the township is described, property within it is described as a particular fraction of a particular 640-acre section of that township. The township's 36 sections are numbered, 1-36. Sections are laid out in a 36-cell grid in each township with Section 1 situated in the northeast corner of the township. Figure 17-1 shows the conventional numbering system for Township X.

FIGURE 17-1

Township X

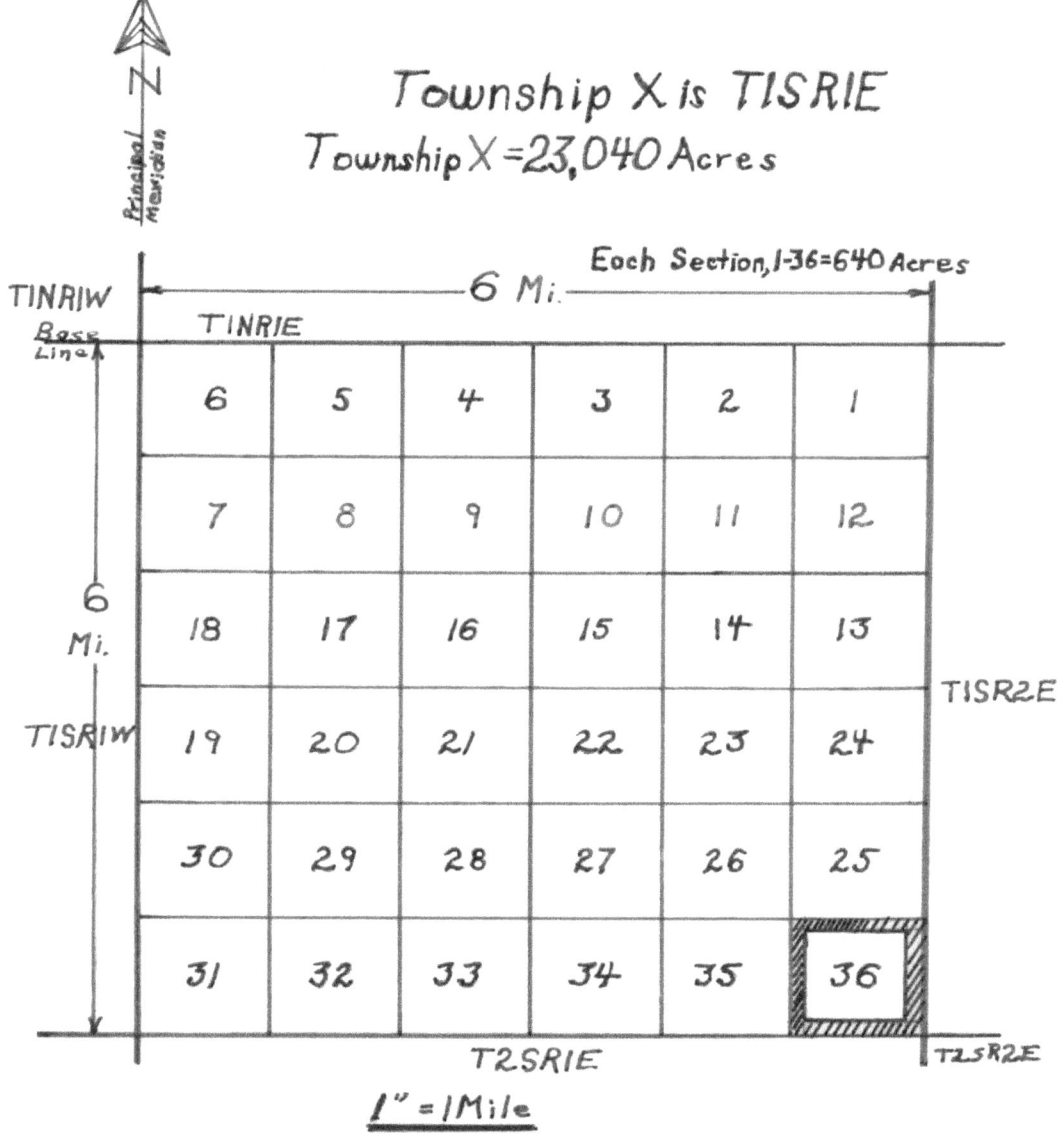

A deed description might read: SW 1/4 NE 1/4 NE 1/4 N 1/2 of Section 36 T1S R1E. This is code for ten acres in Section 36 of the Township that lies in the first tier south of the baseline (T1S) and one row east (R1E) of the principal meridian. The ten acres lies in the 320 acres of the northern half of Section 36 (N1/2), in the 160 acres representing the northeast quarter (NE 1/4) of that one half section. In the northeast quarter (NE 1/4) of that northeast quarter lies 40 acres. This ten acres is the southwest one quarter (SW 1/4) of the northeast one quarter (NE 1/4) of the northeast one quarter (NE 1/4) of the north half (N1/2) of Section 36. You have to work backward in the description, from the township to the section to the half section to the quarter section to the fraction of the quarter section. The decoding process is akin to narrowing your frame of vision and then focusing so that only the land in question appears in your mind's eye.

A 100-foot by 50-foot lot within this ten acres can be fixed by continuing the same process, then locating the given point of beginning in feet and inches on a north-south or east-west line of the smallest referenced section fraction. Figure 17-2, the shaded area, shows the location of this ten-acre property in Section 36 of Township X.

FIGURE 17-2

Township X, Section 36

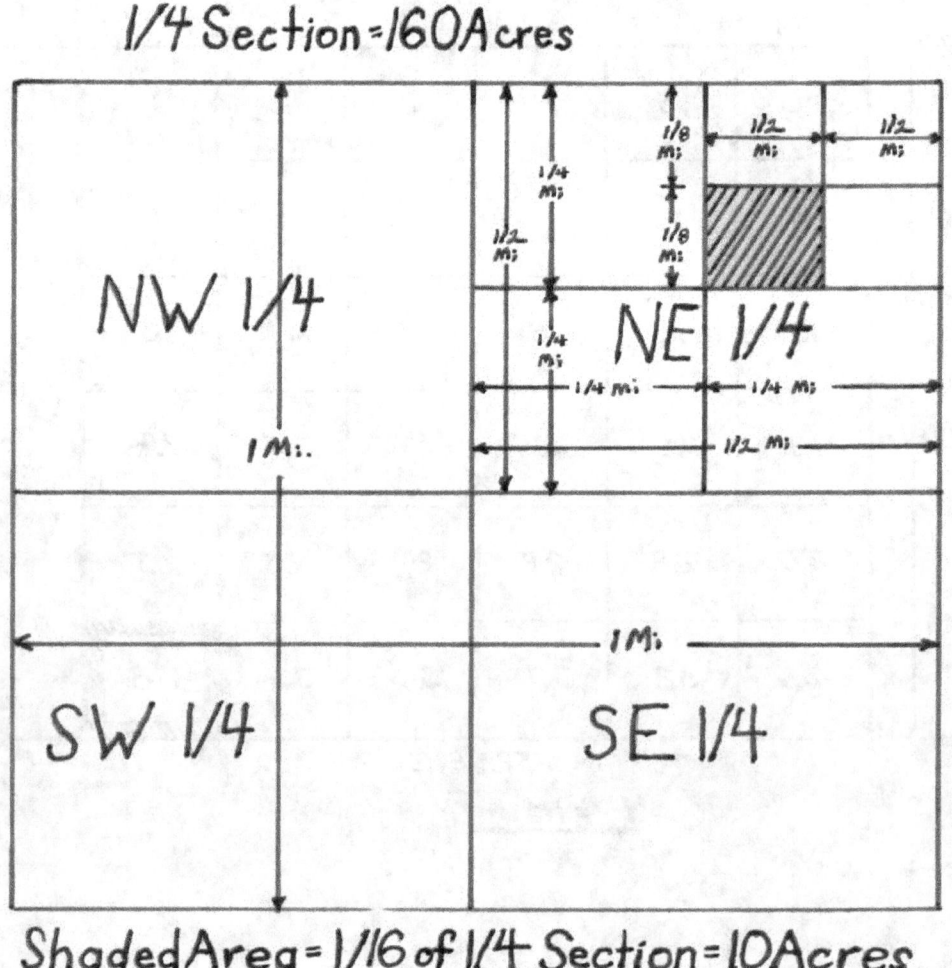

324

These simplified examples illustrate the basic concepts underlying the rectangular survey system. It is complicated in practice by various corrections and adjustments. You may run into an acreage uncertainty where townships join or where original surveys, done by different teams, connect. If you find yourself bewildered in a courthouse that uses this system, don't panic. Look pitiful and politely ask the clerk to help you. Tell the clerk you have a Ph.D. in nuclear physics to get especially patient treatment.

Subdivision and lot is based on a surveyed **plat**, or **plat map,** which shows the precise, surveyed dimensions of each lot within the subdivision. The plat will also show the location and dimensions of roads, utility easements, common areas and other subdivision features. The location of the subdivision as a whole will be shown on the plat in terms of known streets, roads, intersections, waterways and the relevant jurisdiction. Where a field-surveyed plat of an entire subdivision exists and has been recorded, you should feel confident that the lot you are buying contains the indicated acreage and no boundary uncertainties exist. **You should be wary of subdivision drawings that either are not based on field work and/or have not been approved by local zoning authorities**. A plat that has not gone through the zoning process is not binding on anyone. It is no more than a seller's "concept drawing." A buyer can feel safe with a subdivision plat when the zoning office says that the plat in his hand has been approved.

I should note a special case. Auctions are sometimes used to sell land that's been projected into lots. Five hundred acres might be drawn conceptually as five 100-acre lots. This proposed division can be done by computer and then flagged on the ground. The division may or may not be recorded prior to the auction. Presumably, the unrecorded concept division has been done in accord with local zoning rules. A buyer should determine whether the concept division has been given preliminary approval by the appropriate zoning official. If the auction produces separate buyers for each lot, the seller records the plat prior to closing with these individuals. If one individual buys all five lots, it is then his choice as to whether he wants the 500 acres recorded as five 100-acre lots or left as is. No harm arises from this **hypothetical division**, except where it would not comply with the local division regulations. I've seen hypothetical divisions of this sort work with no complications for buyers.

While neither a surveyed plat nor recordation of a survey establishes clear title, a developer whose lot titles will be searched for each sale is likely to have made sure he has good title to the entire tract and each of its lots. If the seller has good title, he will convey good title to the buyer. Aside from the special case of an auction, do not buy a lot in a division whose plat with your lot shown is not approved by the appropriate local authority and recorded. You're likely to find title problems in a lot that lacks these two building blocks of good title. Don't buy a "concept" lot from a developer; make him produce a **recorded, marked-on-the-ground survey**.

Subdivision and lot is no longer confined to suburbs; I increasingly find **large-lot subdivisions** in rural areas where each lot can be hundreds of acres, though 20 acres is more common. They are often described in marketing materials as hunting or recreational lots. Corporate land dividers are often behind this type of development. They scout for properties that have second-home and recreational appeal, survey for division, obtain approval, do the required infrastructure work and market the lots in nearby metropolitan areas. They may do a limited high-grade, timber cut—called a **"residential cut"**—before selling lots. This approach removes a relatively small number of the highest-value trees. Corporate subdividers now know enough to play by the zoning rules.

Since some counties still do not manage land division through zoning and approval by a public board (zoning/planning commission), you cannot assume that all rural division plats you are shown have been legally established, based solely on the drawing in front of you. Look for some notice of official approval, usually signed and dated, on the plat. In non-zoning counties, division rules may be non-existent or insufficiently protective of the lot-buyer's interests. In the latter instance, a lot buyer may find that he has purchased a lot with an access problem, ambiguous water right or impracticalities owing to the absence of infrastructure. If the county has a subdivision ordinance and the plat the buyer holds has gone through the approval process, a buyer can be confident in each lot's location, boundary lines and acreage. A phone call to the zoning office will determine whether the developer's plat is approved.

In **planned unit developments (PUDs)**, land is divided and developed intensively. Multi-unit residences, such as townhouses, and high-density projects are often involved. PUDs commonly use a condominium form of organization. The approved PUD plat may even show where house **footprints** will be located. You may run into a rural PUD, though the land unit for sale is likely to be small. A 1,000-acre PUD, might be marketing 100 one-acre lots, townhouses on 150 acres, with 750 acres held as common land that is available to all owners. PUDs devoted to recreation, such as skiing or lake sports, and second homes in rural communities are in increasing evidence. I would have confidence in a PUD's unit acreage; its plat will have been prepared by a licensed surveyor and have gone through zoning approval prior to marketing.

Subdivisions are designed to comply with local zoning ordinances that establish rules and specifications regarding lot size, roads, density and other features. In jurisdictions with zoning, a subdivision must go through a process of design, review by appropriate local officials, public hearing and approval. The developer will submit a detailed surveyor-drawn plat, along with engineering plans for water, sewerage, storm-water drainage, roads and utilities. The larger the rural subdivision, the more expensive its homes and the closer it is to a town, the more paper—drawings, impact studies, reports—and infrastructure are likely to be required. Local officials will review preliminary plans and both suggest and require changes if necessary. In such divisions, it's safe to assume the acreage contained in each lot is accurate and so are its boundaries, both in the deed and on the ground.

Every division and lot survey should carry the **surveyor's state seal and license number**, as well as a date. If you don't see these items on the developer's drawings, ask for an explanation and listen with a skeptical ear. You can hire a surveyor to verify boundary lines and acreage on the ground and in the deed, but I would be very suspicious of a lot in a division where that double-checking precaution is necessary.

Recordation of a document—survey, plat, deed, lease, or note—provides public (constructive) notice that the document exists and, where appropriate, is in place between its parties. An unrecorded document—deed or note—has no legal authority, except between the parties who made it. An unrecorded plat or survey may be no more than a "representational drawing," preliminary sketch, concept or marketing idea.

If you find yourself interested in purchasing a lot whose *bona fides* don't quite smell right, you need to have a surveyor and, perhaps a lawyer, check the legal location on the ground and in the deed's chain of title. If you decide to purchase this lot, make sure to include your own survey and/or verified legal description as part of your purchase offer. Submitting a purchase contract for "Lot A in Mr. Developer's Muddied Waters project" won't protect you.

If you can't verify location and acreage during your scoping, you can insert a **survey contingency** in your purchase contract. The contingency can take one of two forms. First, you can insist that the seller provide a survey acceptable to you as a condition of purchase. This survey, of course, should be prepared by a licensed surveyor. Second, you can make the purchase contingent on having a surveyor of your choice and at your expense prepare a survey whose results must be acceptable to you. A proper, accurate survey is a cost that a buyer should expect a land divider or developer to bear.

Many jurisdictions now require that most divisions of land involving multiple lots meet local subdivision standards. Exceptions may be made for off-conveyances to family members or for no more than one or two sales. Some rural counties, like mine, continue to draw a distinction in their zoning ordinance between a subdivision, which must meet all requirements, and a **non-subdivision division** that does not. Location, lot size, density (number of houses per acre) and road access distinguish one from the other. A non-subdivision division has to meet less rigorous standards. A non-subdivision division can be perfectly trustworthy in terms of lot boundaries and acreage. I've sold both non-subdivision land and subdivision land using the same licensed land surveyor and his same standards of precision in each case. Nonetheless, a buyer should approach a non-subdivision division cautiously. Zoning codes also provide for **variances** and **conditional uses**, which allow subdivisions to go forward even when they don't meet the established standards. In these cases, a lot buyer should determine the nature of the exception and figure out how it might affect him before making an offer.

Metes and bounds is the oldest system of deed description and the one I've found to be susceptible to acreage discrepancies and boundary peculiarities. **Metes** refer to linear measures of distance, the most common being feet and inches, links (7.92 inches each), rods (16.5 feet each), pole or perch (one rod or 25 links), chains (one Gunter chain is 66 feet or 100 links) and miles. You may also find metes in metrics, though I haven't. Regional metes can include the *vara* (33 inches, a measure you might find in California and the Southwest) and the Texas *vara* (33.5 inches, beginning in 1919). While the acre is the most common area unit of rural land, you may also run across the rood, which is .25 acre (10,890 square feet) and the arpent (approximately .85 acre, which was used in grants from the French King). **Bounds** are the compass directions (headings) and landmarks that, with the metes, establish a property's boundaries. Landmarks include natural features, such as waterways and trees, and man-made reference points, such as roads and iron pins. Document 17-1 is excerpts from the first two pages of my farm deed, which uses a metes (poles)-and-bounds description of the boundary lines.

DOCUMENT 17-1

Metes and Bounds Deed

That for an in consideration of the sum of TEN ($10.00) DOLLARS, cash in hand paid to the parties of the first part, and for other good and valuable considerations, the receipt of which is hereby acknowledged, the said parties of the first part do hereby grant, bargain, sell and convey, with GENERAL WARRANTY of Title, unto the said Curtis I. Seltzer, all those four certain adjoining tracts or parcels of land, with all buildings and improvements thereon and all appurtenances thereto belonging, situate about one and one-half miles north of Blue Grass, Blue Grass Magisterial District, Highland County, Virginia, adjacent to and on the west side of Route 640, adjoining the lands of William C. Will and others, containing 33 acres, 23.562 acres, 16.812 acres and .154 acre for a total of 73.528 acres, more or less, this, however, being a sale in gross and not by the acre and intended to include all the land that Russell T. Andrews and his wife acquired from W. Lurty Arbogast and wife and all the land which the said Russell T. Andrews and Eva Ruth Andrews, his wife, owned in Highland County, Virginia. The 33 acre tract is bounded and described as follows:

BEGINNING at a set stone on the west edge of the right of way of the said highway, a common corner with the 21.186 acre tract, this being the new division corner, and with the new division line of the 21.186 acre tract, N. 38 degrees W. 34.48 poles to a set stone; thence N. 54 degrees W. 67.20 poles to a set stone on the old line, and with the same N. 20 degrees E. 49 1/2 poles to a locust; thence S. 61 1/2 degrees E. 95 poles to a rock near a chestnut stump; thence S. 15 1/2 degrees W. 36 poles to a rock between the barn and the shed; thence S 61 1/2 degrees E. 2.64 poles to the said

highway, and with the same, S. 29 degrees W. 29.44 poles to the beginning, containing 33 acres, more or less.

Metes and bounds, which are also referred to as the **deed's calls**, start at the surveyor's **point of beginning (POB)**. The tract's boundary line follows the distance and direction calls from the POB and ends there as well. The distance north should equal the distance south, and the distance west should equal the distance east. Surveyors refer to this balancing from the POB as "mathematical closure." When all boundary sides balance, as they should, the **calls are said to close** (at the POB). When a property's calls don't close, you may find the reason in an error in the deed's description (e.g., a typo), or an error the surveyor made in his survey, or several types of error in combination. When calls do close, the acreage said to be contained within them should be accurate. Anyone with a surveyor's computer program can check both closure and acreage. The process of **"plotting the calls"** involves typing in the metes and bounds from a deed or survey, and then directing the program to draw them to scale and calculate the acreage contained.

When calls do not close, the acreage may still be reasonably accurate if the explanation for the failure is something minor and acceptable. Old surveys, which relied on relatively unsophisticated transits and steel tapes, often contain small errors that prevent perfect closure. In such cases, the "more or less" that follows the deeded acreage is a useful and legitimate fix. On the other hand, I've seen calls that don't close because of a 100-acre screw up on a 300-acre tract.

Metes and bounds were a clear improvement over a description like "that pasture lying east of John's meadow," but many opportunities exist for errors. Old metes-and-bounds descriptions are only as good as the equipment the surveyor used, his linear units (the smallest unit being presumptively more accurate than the largest), his competence and the meticulousness of those who copied the original calls each time the property was sold.

SURVEYS 101

"**Survey**," as a verb, is the process by which a surveyor determines the location of property boundaries on the ground, from which its area and location on the earth can be fixed. "Survey" can also refer to either this process or the finished drawing the surveyor makes from his ground measurements. Surveyors can also determine and map out the height and contours of the ground's surface in relation to some known, fixed height, usually sea level. **Elevations** refer to distances above or below a fixed point. House construction on slopes or tricky road excavations require a surveyor to "shoot" elevations so that foundations and road beds are dug to the correct depths, thus allowing the finished construction to top out at the right height.

"**Plotting**," or **deed mapping**, refers to the process and finished product of drawing a deed's calls—distances and bearings—on paper. Plotting is now done by readily available computer programs, though it can still be done by hand using graph paper, ruler and compass. The surveyor enters the calls, and the program draws the boundary lines in two dimensions and calculates the acreage contained within them. Calls can be drawn on plain paper or imposed on **a topographical map** (**topo**), discussed below. A **plot** of this sort is not a field-tested survey. It is only as good as the calls inputted. It may or may not line up with how boundary lines are marked on the ground.

Plotting is the method by which you begin to verify the seller's boundaries and acreage. The advantage of hiring a surveyor to draw boundaries on a topo for you is that he can check the deed's calls for closure and acreage. A survey's calls used for plotting should be more reliable than those from a deed, though the deed's can be, and should be, accurate.

If a seller gives you a topo with boundaries, it may or may not be accurate. Ask the seller to tell you who drew the boundaries and from what data. Sellers have handed me topos with boundaries drawn by a surveyor, their real-estate agent, their auctioneer, their friend "who's good with a pencil" and themselves. In one case, a seller drew boundaries on a topo that included a 400-acre parcel he didn't own. In another case, a helpful real-estate agent, relying on what he later described as "artistic license," drew boundaries with a 15-acre mistake in a 50-acre property. His defense was: "I drew it the way the seller said his Granddaddy always said it lay." Granddaddy was wrong, to the seller's benefit.

Buyers should understand that a plot is as accurate as the inputted calls. If something is wrong with the calls, the lines won't close. A plot may close, but its acreage can still be wrong in the sense that it includes more or less land than the owner is entitled to. At that point, the surveyor will have to go into the field and/or the courthouse to dig out the error. A buyer has no guarantee that a survey will be 100 percent accurate, and a survey does not guarantee legal ownership of all land shown within the boundaries.

Some Americans in the East and mid-South still own the land that was conveyed to their ancestors from an English King, or a land company with a royal charter or as a grant for war service. The first land documents emerging from these origins were based on approximate surveys of huge tracts, such as those George Washington did in the 1750s. They incorporated easily found topographic features, such as ridgelines and waterways. These surveys might refer to all the land between this ridge and the branch of that river. The first generation or two of surveys could be almost as rough. Early deeds might use descriptions such as "being the land of Jones" or "the Dry Fork bottom of Bates, joining Smith on the North, Brown on the South, the run of Dry Fork on the East and Grayson on the West."

The following excerpt is a 1685 survey description of land that is now part of Washington, D.C., but then known as Port Royal in the Maryland colony: "Land called port Royall lying in Charles County in the freshes of the potomoke River near the head of a Creek called Broad Creek [Tiber Creek] beginning at a marked white oak within half a mile of the head of said Creek and running east by north for the length of 500 p. to a bounded hickory then for the length of 160 p. to marked red oak then west by south for the length of 500 p. to a marked white oak then with a straight line to the first bounded tree." (Michael Farquhar, "The Past is Present," <u>Washington Post Magazine</u>, March 23, 2003.) Such descriptions were good enough for frontier legal work when all concerned understood and agreed with how these descriptions fit ground-level reality, but they were not good enough when disputes arose, land changed hands and time passed.

While descriptions gained specificity as land was divided and surveying improved, landowners, as taxpayers, had a financial incentive to undercount the acreage in their holdings. I've found land with old calls that contained an **acreage undercount** in the deed on which property tax assessments were based. (The periodic property-tax reassessments that update valuations of each parcel of land in the country do not check acreage as carried in the county's records.) Old-fashioned tax avoidance may explain why these properties have more land in the field than on paper. You might find an **acreage overcount**—where the deed shows more land than what exists on the ground. An acreage overcount in the deedwork means the buyer will pay for more than he's actually getting. An overcount can arise from unrecorded off-conveyances; gifts to family members; errors by clerks, lawyers, owner-dividers or surveyors; long-ago chicanery; unrecorded resolutions of disputes; and simple self-interest, where, for example, an owner knows that his acreage is undercounted in his deed but the cost of correction was greater than the tax savings. Acreage overcounts benefit sellers who appear to be selling more than they really are. Acreage undercounts benefit buyers because you get more land than you're paying for.

As land moved out of the families with the original deeds, the ground-level knowledge on which those deed descriptions were made faded. Trees used as points of deed reference, or **corners**, disappeared. In working with one 110-year-old survey, I found some corner trees still standing (though in bad shape) and others gone without a trace. As time air-brushed communal memory and removed points of reference, oral versions of reality could acquire validity in the minds of their speakers. I know of several examples where a seller sold land that had been in his family for generations after walking the boundaries—as he believed them to be—with the buyer. The seller would say words to the effect, "This is how the deeded acres lay." The buyer would assume the seller knew the boundaries and never bothered to verify the deed's calls and acreage. Later, the buyer—now owner—learned that the seller's idea of the boundaries was wrong.

As the original large tracts in the East were divided and sold repeatedly, deed descriptions and acreage numbers got better. Nonetheless, it is common to buy land in rural areas using deeds that rely on calls that are more than 100 years old, have never been verified and have been hand-copied as the parcel changed hands. Sellers, in my experience, rarely make the effort to clean up a deed's calls and verify acreage prior to putting their property up for sale. The burden of verification falls on the buyer. Since land can be sold without a survey, the buyer has to nail down boundaries and acreage on any tract lacking a survey, with an old survey, and where he finds a discrepancy between acreage on the tax map and the deeded acreage. Occasionally, you might find a property that is being sold without an acreage figure in the deed. In that event, you will have to be extra careful in determining the acreage contained in the legal description and then make sure that boundaries are not in dispute.

Owing to the messy origins of both deed descriptions and title, a land buyer is required to go back 60 or so years in his **title search** in determining whether the seller's title is sound. Each state sets how far back the title search must be taken to **certify good title**. It is often a good practice, however, for a title search on rural property to be taken back more years than any statutory requirement if the property has not been sold for a long time or the deedwork reveals a problem in acreage or ownership. A title search determines whether the owner can sell a piece of land by confirming his **ownership through a chain of title**.

A title search does not guarantee that what is being sold actually contains the acreage or boundaries claimed. Title searches verify ownership of a parcel, but not necessarily its acreage. In other words, your lawyer can back-track the 100 acres that you want to buy for 100 years through a half-dozen sales, and you can still end up with acreage being short of 100 acres legally and on the ground because of an error made 125 years ago. In each subsequent sale, the land was referred to in the deed as 100 acres; no one bothered to check whether it was true legally and on the ground. Acreage on the ground may have been changed from acreage in the deed by adverse possession, force, mutual consent, theft or trickery. **Title insurance**, which protects against certain defects in title, may not make up the difference if the policy excludes acreage discrepancies that an accurate survey would disclose. If you can prove an acreage shortage is the result of fraud, forgery, lack of legal competence, incapacity or impersonation, then title insurance should make you whole.

Discrepancies between deeded acreage and on-the-ground acreage are caught when someone does the work necessary to verify acreage. This can involve one of more of the following techniques: 1) survey; 2) computer mapping of the deed's calls which are then field checked; and 3) researching the deed's antecedents, including, if necessary, the deeds of adjoining neighbors, to resolve an acreage discrepancy.

A quick way for a buyer to alert himself to a possible significant acreage discrepancy is to apply a **planogrid** to a scaled topographical map with the property's boundaries drawn. The transparent planogrid provides a rough approximation of acreage. (See discussion below.)

Various problems can arise with the acreage and location of country property. Before you submit a purchase offer, you want to ask and answer the following questions:

1. **What are the physical dimensions of the property in linear distance and compass bearings, as described in the deed?**

   The three common formats of property description—rectangular/government survey, subdivision and lot, and metes and bounds—provide these dimensions in narrative and drawings. (I'll use "calls" to refer to the linear measurements and compass bearings in all three systems.)

2. **Can the deed's reference points—corners, rock piles, iron pipes and trees—be found on the ground?**

   The POB, corners and significant angles are the most important points. They should match up exactly with the calls in the deed and/or survey. For exact checking, you'll need to have a surveyor shoot the lines; for acceptable checking, a surveyor or forester can walk the boundaries. With a compass and a set of calls, you should be able to walk the boundaries and find the most important corners.

   If you acquire a property that is missing crucial ground points, you will need a surveyor to reset them if you plan to divide it or a boundary line is in dispute.

3. **Are the boundary lines on the ground identical with those in the deed and/or survey?**

   Do not be surprised to find that the deed calls say one thing and you find something else in the field. A familiar example is a boundary fence being "off" from where the calls fix the boundary. Fence lines have a way of being adjusted, with and without mutual agreement, over time. Roads also have a way of taking the easiest path, whether or not a recorded access easement exists.

4. **Do the calls close?**

   Sometimes, this is called "closure of the land" or the "balance" of the calls. Whatever the terminology, the buyer wants the calls in the deed to produce a closed boundary line. When the calls close, it should mean that the calls are accurate and correct. However, exceptions to that generalization may exist. A frustrated surveyor 150 years ago might have jiggered the calls to get them to close when those taken from his field notes would not. Rather than go back and find the error, he "adjusted" his numbers.

   If the calls do not close, how big is the problem? Some "failure-to-close" problems are the result of nothing more than a transcribing error where, for example, a "3" was written or typed as an "8," a "1" became a "7" or a bearing "N 45 degrees W" was copied as "W 45 degrees N." If easy explanations can't be found, a surveyor will have to go into the field and figure it out.

5. **When the calls close, you then need to ask three other questions.**

   First, does the acreage contained within the checked calls match the acreage stated in the deed and/or survey? It should. A discrepancy between the acreage figured by running the calls through a computer program and the acreage in the deed needs to be resolved before submitting a purchase offer.

   Second, does the acreage in the deed's checked calls and/or survey match the acreage contained within the boundaries on the ground? It should. You won't need a full-fledged survey to determine whether they match; a walk-around will do.

Third, is the acreage located where it's supposed to be? It's possible that the calls close and the acreage is right, but the entire tract is actually a number of feet to one side or another of where the deed places it. A property boundary may be found in the field on the west side of a creek (thus enclosing the creek) rather than on the east side (thus excluding it) where the deed puts it. "Misplacements" of this sort can work for or against a buyer. In either case, you want to know about one before you submit a purchase offer.

The discussion that follows shows how you can answer these questions and what to do when you find different answers to the same question.

SURVEYS 102

Old surveys are often unreliable; and the older the survey, the more this is likely to be true. Old surveyor instruments were far less accurate than those used today. This affected linear measurements, angles and compass bearings. Modern instruments are adjusted for barometric pressure and ambient temperature; the older ones were not. The still-used basic instruments are a **transit**, which can measure horizontal and vertical angles and show compass readings in magnetic degrees, and a **steel tape** for linear measurements. In addition to **transits**, surveyors now use a **theodolite**, which is a souped-up transit, or a **total station**, one model of which employs laser-pulse technology to determine distance and can measure electronically up to 4,000 meters to within 5 mm +/-. Old transits could be fussy to adjust and were not as precise as a total station. Distance measured horizontally with a steel tape was subject to error from sag. If this were not enough, an error can creep into calculations from survey to survey as magnetic north itself shifts. Field surveying done even with the most modern devices is not perfectly exact. Normally, rural land surveying can get by with an **error of closure** of one foot in every 5,000 feet. Boundaries that close within the error of closure are fine.

Where an original survey from the 17th or 18th Century was vague, it may have been easier for later surveyors to either avoid or finesse ambiguities than fix them. Repeated for a long enough time, small fictions can become large facts. Unreliability can also result from human error in the field, conditions on the ground (ranging from weather to the disappearance of reference points (**corners**), human error in writing and copying deeds and drawings, misinterpretation, illegibility and a dozen other factors.

Where an old survey established a boundary line in a waterway, it's likely that you will find a note that the line "**runs with the meander**" of the stream. This language can appear in either a deed or on a survey drawing, or both. Absent further information, such a line could run down the centerline of the stream or along either bank. It can also mean: 1) no calls were taken for the meander; or 2) calls were taken, or 3) the surveyor "straightened" the meander by imposing an arbitrary line. Confirming the line of a meander may also involve the inconvenient fact that the channel of the creek has changed since the survey's date as floods cut new channels. Don't count on the functioning fence line to reflect the true boundary line in a meander mess. Locating a true boundary in a meander can be extremely important where, for instance, the stream is the only source of livestock water and your neighbor's fence is on your bank thus fencing you out, or where the stream's channel has changed leaving you with bottom land less rich than was intended in the initial division. One way to resolve the first type of dispute is for the neighbors to agree to run the fence line on one bank for a stretch and then the other, giving livestock of both parties adequate water access. A section of fence, called a **watergap**, must be constructed across the water at a right angle to its flow to keep livestock properly separated. The flap-like watergap is hung from a stout cable, allowing surging water to push the gap up and then close when the water resides. Watergaps are not hard to build, but they are a nuisance to maintain, particularly when high water is common.

Where a deed or survey says the boundary line **runs with the channel of a waterway**, I would take that to mean the waterway's centerline. Remember that waterways change their channels, which means the centerline/boundary line will change too unless the original channel centerline was surveyed and incorporated into the deed. When a waterway works *gradual* changes in the land—giving some to one landowner, taking from another—the parties are expected to accept the **accretion** of land or its **dereliction**. Changes of a catastrophic nature, such as those from a flood or earthquake, do not change settled boundaries

Surveyors, themselves, have become better trained and more skilled over the years. Many states did not impose licensing standards until the 20th Century; some states did not require **land surveyors** to be licensed until the 1950s. Even today's best surveyor can make a mistake or fail to note something that is relevant. There are, in addition, occasions where two equally competent surveyors will look at the same facts and reach different conclusions. And there is always a chance that another party has a legal claim to own or use land belonging to your seller even though the boundary line is perfectly accurate. In such cases, a survey does not establish ownership. Adverse possession and related ideas are discussed in Chapter 26.

You may find a parcel of land that is **orphaned** in terms of a survey, or a chain of title, or on the ground. Either no one claims the orphan parcel, or no one's claim is definitive. Sometimes a parcel is orphaned because surveyors made a mistake. The Monongahela National Forest in West Virginia includes a small orphan tract of genuine virgin timber whose existence is due to just such an error. Orphan tracts are uncommon. If your seller claims that he owns an orphan tract, your scoping will have to determine the basis and strength of his claim in light of other claimants. As a rule, I would avoid tracts whose legal ownership the seller can't persuasively establish. If the orphan is a survey problem, a surveyor may be able to fix it; if it's a chain of title issue, both a surveyor and a lawyer may be needed.

Other acreage errors arise from the messy origins of land distribution in the original colonies and their westward claims. Various systems of granting land succeeded each other—royal, colonial, state and federal—and each were burdened by exceptions, overlaps, conflicting claims and, of course, squatters. Early deeded **grants** (also called **patents**) went to individuals and companies following a survey. (See www.ultranet.com/~deeds/landref.htm for a discussion of the origins of landownership east of the Mississippi River.) The surveys on which these grants were based were subject to all of the problems noted above. Later surveys should have resolved uncertainties, but you cannot assume this to be the case. My own rule for buyers is to plot the calls of every target property, no matter how recent the survey. If the computer plotting shows something amiss or a field inspection turns up a mismatch, then you have a problem in need of solution.

You cannot protect yourself with 100 percent certainty against errors in a survey, though there are steps you can take to reduce your exposure. When hiring a surveyor to double-check the seller's survey, I think it's good practice to find a local individual who's done considerable work in the county—even the area of the county—where your target property is. Such an individual will have acquired a feel for those surveyors who've worked this land before. He may even have access to some of their archives. An out-of-town surveyor will not have this sense for ancestral habits and quirks, such as how one individual in the mid-1800s printed his "1s" and "4s" to look like "7s" when they came in the middle of a number.

A second qualification that I recommend is that the surveyor you choose be "good in the courthouse." He should be both skilled and dogged in digging out land history. Some surveyors are competent at shooting boundary lines, but not at solving problems, particularly those involving words and law. You'll need to plumb local opinion as to which surveyors are good both in the field and with the books. Local lawyers are probably the best reference.

Third, you generally want to avoid a surveyor who is doing, or will be doing, business with the seller. You want exclusive loyalty. You may not be able to avoid hiring an individual who's worked for the seller in the past. This is not cause for alarm in and of itself. Ask those whom you interview whether or not they can work for you free and clear of any ties to the seller. In sparsely populated areas you will always find that a lot of professionals live with open conflicts of interests, arising from the inherent problem of a small number of individuals having to wear many local hats. It is not uncommon for a surveyor to work for both a seller and a buyer; the same is true for lawyers and real-estate brokers in small communities. I've seen these situations managed ethically and without harm to either party; I've also seen the opposite. As a newcomer, you should anticipate that local professionals may have history with your seller. When that history has been good, you can assume that they have a default protectiveness for the seller's interests. The seller may also have family who employs the professional from time to time. You must, therefore, screen a surveyor—and other professionals—for dual allegiances. You have a right to expect fairness, impartiality and loyalty, even from those who are friends of the seller. As a first-time buyer in a community, I would avoid arrangements where one professional works for both seller and buyer. I would also avoid using any local professional who is related by blood or marriage to the seller, a member of the same fraternal order or church, or a close friend.

Finally, I'd ask each surveyor you're thinking of hiring to show you a couple of recent surveys he's done on similarly sized properties. If you feel awkward about doing this, go into the land records office in the county courthouse and work backward through the deed books. Surveys are often recorded with deeds, usually immediately following. I have, however, also found surveys kept in a separate book. Compare the work of different surveyors. Some include more detail than others; I've always found detail handy in the field, particularly the location of prominent features, such as roads, 4WD "roads," utility easements and watercourses. You may also find notes of boundary uncertainties, possible overlaps, acreage discrepancies and potential claims both for and against the current property owner. Don't be a minimalist when it comes to surveys: more information is better.

A survey refers to both a drawing and a physical marking of boundaries in the field. It is obviously essential that the measurements on the ground match those on the drawing, both of which match those found in the deed. A three-layer coincidence is what a buyer wants. And even with such a match, an error could be embedded or an adverse claim not noted.

A survey (drawing) is a two-dimensional picture of a property's boundaries, expressed in units of length and compass bearings. Every point where the line changes bearing (direction), no matter how slight, is usually referred to as a **corner** in deed descriptions. Major corners, such as the four in a rectangle, will be well-marked on the ground by an iron rod, paint, ribbons, a chevron of slashes in a corner tree, rock piles or, on occasion, an implanted car axle. Boundary lines are projected on a plane, both in the field and on flat paper; a drawn survey is an exercise in **planimetry**. Illustration 17-1 is a typical field survey, expressed in metes and bounds.

ILLUSTRATION 17-1
Survey

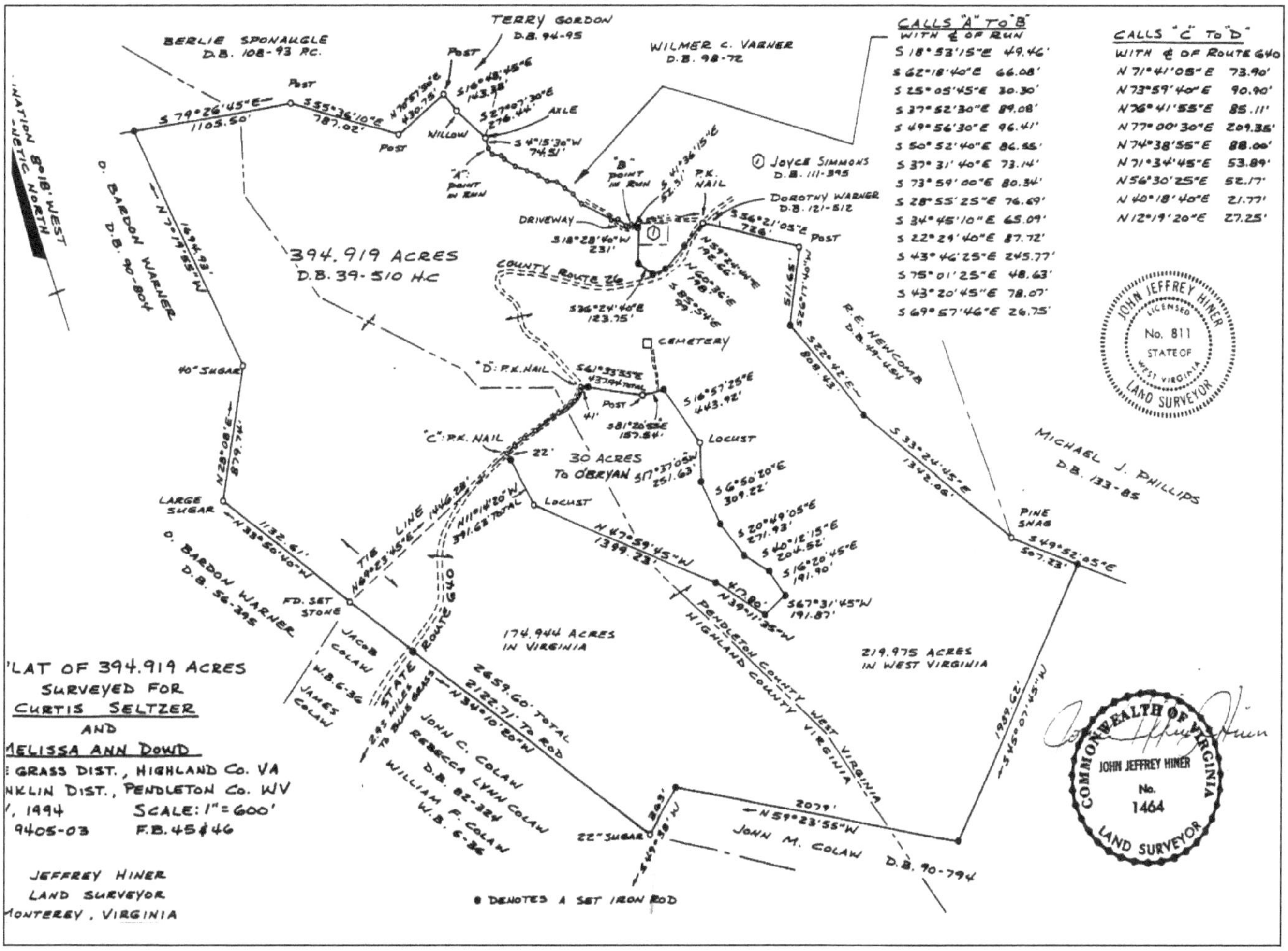

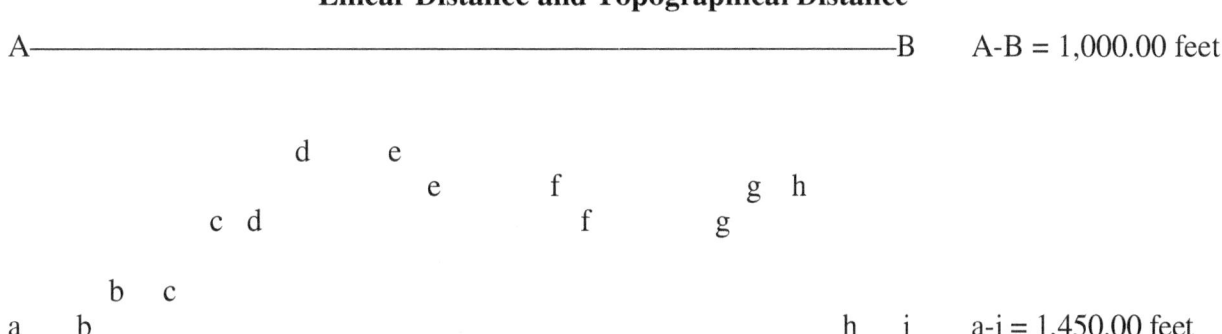

Remember that land boundaries drawn on a plane are measured horizontally on the ground and do not run with the land's topography. A 1,000-foot surveyed boundary line between points A and B on paper is a straight horizontal line of exactly 1,000 feet in length in the field. In Illustration 17-2 you can see the difference between a surveyor's 1,000 feet of boundary line, A-B, and the actual linear distance of that boundary, 1,450 feet, as it runs on a parcel of land with its own topography, a-i.

ILLUSTRATION 17-2

Linear Distance and Topographical Distance

A————————————————————————————————B   A-B = 1,000.00 feet

```
                    d    e
                         e    f    g  h
               c  d                f    g
          b  c
      a  b                                    h  i    a-i = 1,450.00 feet
```

Non-flat land always contains more acreage on the ground than the calculated acreage a survey

335

shows as enclosed within its boundaries. The more irregular the land's surface, the more acreage above the surveyed amount there will be. If you were to flatten mountains, like smoothing out a rumpled bedspread, 100 surveyed acres (contained within the horizontally measured boundaries) would increase as you pulled the corners and sides to their limits. In contrast, 100 surveyed acres of Iowa cornfield that is as level as a championship billiard table will contain 100 acres.

A surveyor should always **mark his lines on the ground** when he's doing a survey for a landowner. Make sure that you and the surveyor are agreed on ground marking; he may charge more for it.

A surveyor can draw an accurate, field-based survey without ever actually walking—or marking—*all* the boundary lines. This is done through basic geometry. The transit is set up within the property's boundaries where the surveyor can "shoot" two points (corners) in a boundary line. He will know the three angles and the length of two legs of the triangle that vee-out from his transit. From that information, he can then calculate the length of the third leg without ever having walked between its two points. This technique is called **triangulation**. There's nothing wrong in using triangulation in certain circumstances. A buyer, however, will want his new boundary lines well-marked on the ground. Some surveyors triangulate when they don't want to negotiate a laurel thicket, briar patch or swamp through which a boundary line runs. It's fair for a surveyor to use triangulation when the land is impassable, but not when the surveyor is just lazy. I've seen a new owner have to hire a surveyor to mark lines that the seller's surveyor had triangulated just a few weeks earlier prior to the sale.

When you are handed a seller's survey, routinely ask whether *all* the boundaries are marked on the ground. If you run into a triangulated seller survey, you might ask the seller as part of your offer to have his surveyor mark the lines. Lay off as much surveying cost on the seller as you can. When you are hiring a surveyor to "do a survey" for your own property, make sure his quoted linear-foot price includes ground marking. If you plan to sell the timber from your property, the boundary line should be clearly marked with bright ribbon, paint and/or slashes at the time your forester sends out his timber-sale packet so that the buyers know where your property and timber end.

When walking a boundary line through woods, do not confuse a **blaze**, which is a removal of bark two or three inches wide by four-to six-inches long and often painted, with a surveyor's **slash marks**, or **chops**, which are two or three machete hacks into the bark, parallel to the ground, a couple of inches apart. A painted blaze is used to show a boundary line; the U.S. Forest Service and certain paper companies do so. Hiking trails are often marked with painted blazes. Surveyors I know who are marking a line for an individual landowner use slashes. A double chop is a surveyor's mark for a boundary line, and a triple chop represents an important corner in the line. A tree marked by a surveyor is called a **"line tree."** It is owned jointly by the adjoining landowners. Do not cut down a line tree.

As your surveyor marks your boundaries, any place where the surveyed boundary line and the functional boundary line, such as a fence, are non-congruent will be immediately obvious. Ask your forester or surveyor to tell you about any such areas; if you don't give the surveyor this instruction, you may not be told. Boundary misalignments can be minor or significant, so you should determine their cause and importance as part of your due diligence during scoping. I have found misalignments involving a few acres to several hundred. I've discovered a 75-acre error on a tract advertised as 300.

Boundary lines can be drawn on a **topographic** map, which shows land in a third dimension—elevation. **Topos** portray the lay of the land's surface features. They do this by using elevation lines—or, **contour lines**—to indicate height in relation to sea level and each other. Each elevation line might, for example, represent a 40-foot change in height, up or down from the next closest line. Lines closer together show steepness; further apart, flatness. With a little practice, you'll be able to recognize valleys, knobs, ridges, cliffs and benches. Woods are colored green or shaded; open land is white. You can read a topo in the field to determine your approximate location by fixing yourself in relation to surface land features that you can see.

Boundary lines found on topographic maps are measured horizontally. A 1,000-foot-long line drawn on a topo by a computer program is 1,000 feet long on an imaginary level plane though it may be 1,400 feet long walking over the ups and downs of the ground itself. When boundaries from a survey are imposed on a topographic map, they are drawn to the map's scale. Be careful to check the scale of any topographical map you use. Some now express height in meters rather than feet: the conversion is one meter equals 3.3 feet.

When a forester or surveyor draws boundaries on a topo, the calls are usually left off. You can judge distance in the field using the topo's scale and a small ruler (which is often built into a plastic compass that you should be carrying). Bearings can be taken off the drawn lines using the same see-through plastic compass laid atop the topo. With a bit of practice, you will get a feel for how a given distance, say 500 feet, walks out in various field conditions. If you want to step up the preciseness of your own measurements, you will need to use a compass and a 100-foot-long tape (fiberglass or steel). You can temporarily mark lines and corners with plastic "flagging" ribbon. Help in using a compass can be found at www.learn-orienteering.org.

So far, you have two or three documents in your effort to confirm boundaries and acreage: 1) the calls from the deed, 2) survey, if available, and 3) topo with plotted boundary lines produced by a surveyor or forester using the calls. You may also have acquired a fourth document—the property's **tax map showing boundaries**. Tax-map boundary lines and acreage figures may not be accurate, and they are not legally binding. Use a tax map in the field if you have nothing else to suggest boundaries. Tax maps are discussed below.

Boundaries drawn on a topo also give you several ways to estimate acreage quickly and cheaply.

The first method involves a **planimeter**—an expensive, pencil-like, digital instrument that physically rolls along a map's boundary line and calculates acreage according to the topo's scale. Most land surveyors and US Forest Service district offices have planimeters and can estimate your acreage in a few minutes. You need to bring a topo with the property's calls drawn to scale. Planimeters are accurate to about one acre in 100, depending on the steadiness of your hand as you roll it over your topo.

A second method is to use a **surveyor's transparency**, which is a see-through grid divided into ten-acre squares each of which is divided into $1/10^{th}$-acre squares. You have to match the scale of the transparency to the scale of the topo. By counting squares, you can closely approximate acreage contained within boundary lines.

A third approach is to use a **planogrid**, a transparency with dots that you lay over the topo. Each dot represents a certain number of acres. The planogrid will have dot-acreage formulas for ten or so common scales. By counting dots within the boundary lines, you can approximate acreage. A planogrid is inexpensive and good enough to get started.

None of these substitute for determining acreage through computer plotting, using a program such as DeedPlotter Plus, available from Z-Law Software, Inc., POB 40602, Providence, RI, 02940-0602; 1-800-526-5588; e-mail: info@z-law.com. There's no reason for a land buyer to invest in a plotting program, however. A surveyor or forester can do this work for you for a nominal sum.

Topographical maps are usually available in each county at a retail outlet—surveyor's office, sporting goods store or stationery supply. You can order the U.S. Geological Survey's (USGS) 7.5 Minute Topographic Quadrangle Series, commonly called a "topo quad" or just a "quad," from the U.S. Department of the Interior, U.S. Geological Survey, Reston, Virginia 22092; map sales at 1-800-435-7627; map information at 1-888-275-8747; www.usgs.gov (click on "topographic maps"). Their scale is 1:24,000 (1 inch equals 2,000 feet; 2.6 inches roughly equals 1 mile; 1 square inch equals roughly 90 acres) with 20-foot contour-interval lines. While other map scales are available, quads cover a good bit of area and are convenient to use for broadly understanding a general area's topography. A topo with boundaries for a target property should be drawn with a smaller scale than the quad's. For a 100-acre parcel, a topo scaled 1 inch = 200 feet is easily read, and 1:400 is readily used. Quads are updated periodically using aerial photography to show physical changes such as new buildings and surface mines.

USGS also supplies digital topographic maps, and maps of areas prone to earthquakes and landslides. Individual states may also supply topographic maps. (Bureau of Land Management [BLM] shows topography as well as federal, state and private ownership.) You can download your own topographic maps of a target property for free from www.topozone.com at different scales. The www.topozone.com maps average about 20 years old. The scales are consistent among themselves, but the printed copy is affected by the size of your computer monitor. The USGS maps are scanned at 250 dots per inch (one inch = 24,000 inches = 2,000 feet = 250 pixels). Owing to the translation problem, the printed map you hold may not replicate the scaled topo map you've downloaded. Other GIS and geospatial maps are available from www.maptech.com and www.data.geocomm.com/catalog/US; some are free, others carry a fee. www.googleearth.com is available for those with high-speed Internet access. National Forest maps are available from www.edcdaac.usgs.gov/ dataproducts.html.

Map 17-1 shows a topo at 1:50,000 scale (one inch = 50,000 inches in the original) with boundary lines drawn for 95 acres my wife and I own on the border of Virginia (South and West) and West Virginia. Green represents forest; white, open land—in this case, pasture. Blue represents water. Small black squares are houses or agricultural structures. The bolder contour lines are spaced every 200 feet in elevation, with the lighter lines drawn at 40-foot intervals. Flat areas are found where contour lines are widely set; the closer together the lines, the steeper the land.

Map 17-2 shows the same property in 1:25,000 scale. This scale is readily used for walking boundaries, though even a 1:50,000 can be used in a pinch.

Map 17-3 is a topo with boundaries drawn for us by a local surveyor. I have added additional detail, including the location of roads and a sugar house built in the mid-1990s.

MAP 17-1

Topographical Map with Boundary Lines, 1:50,000

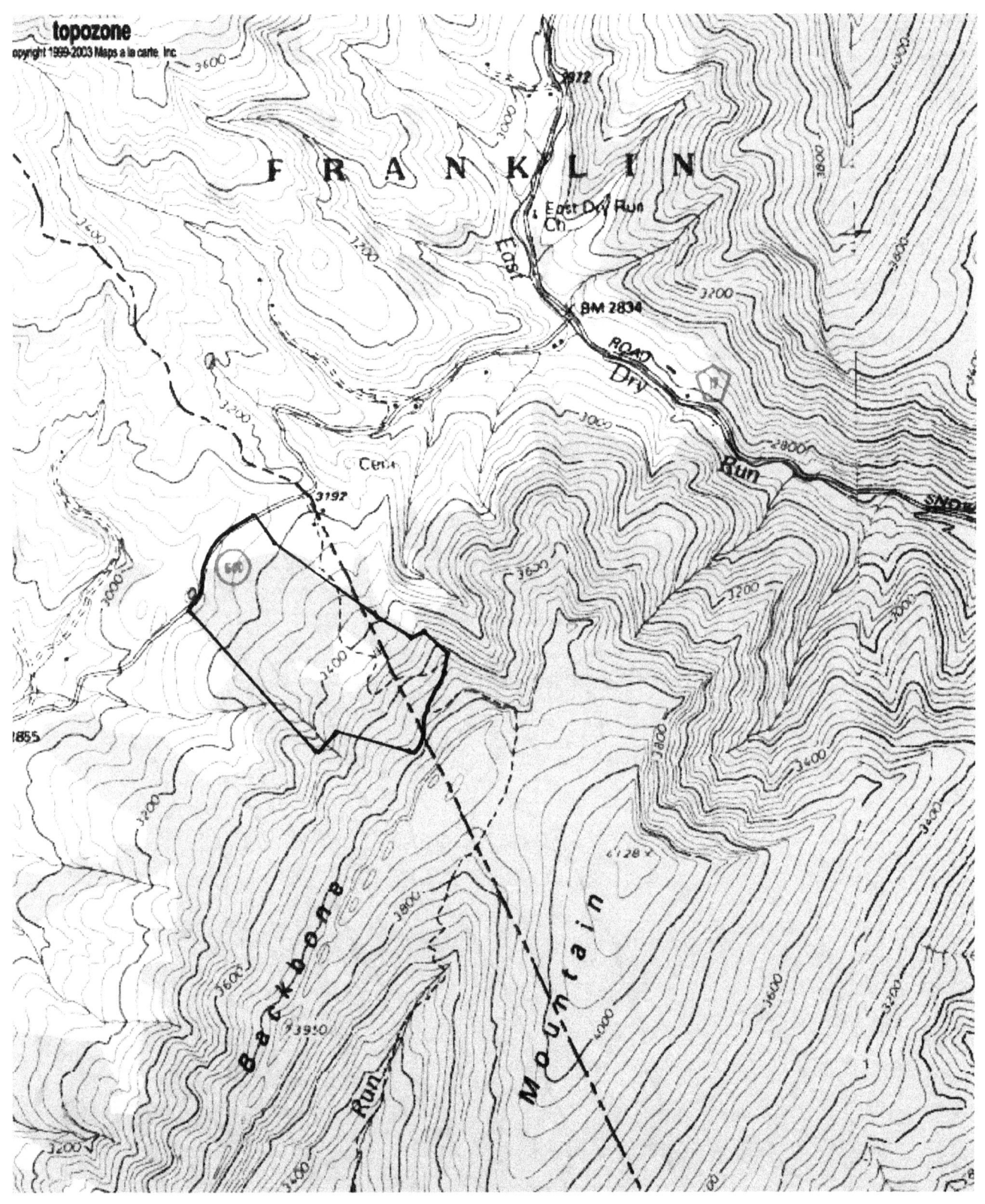

Source: www.topozone.com

MAP 17-2

Topographical Map with Boundary Lines, 1:25,000

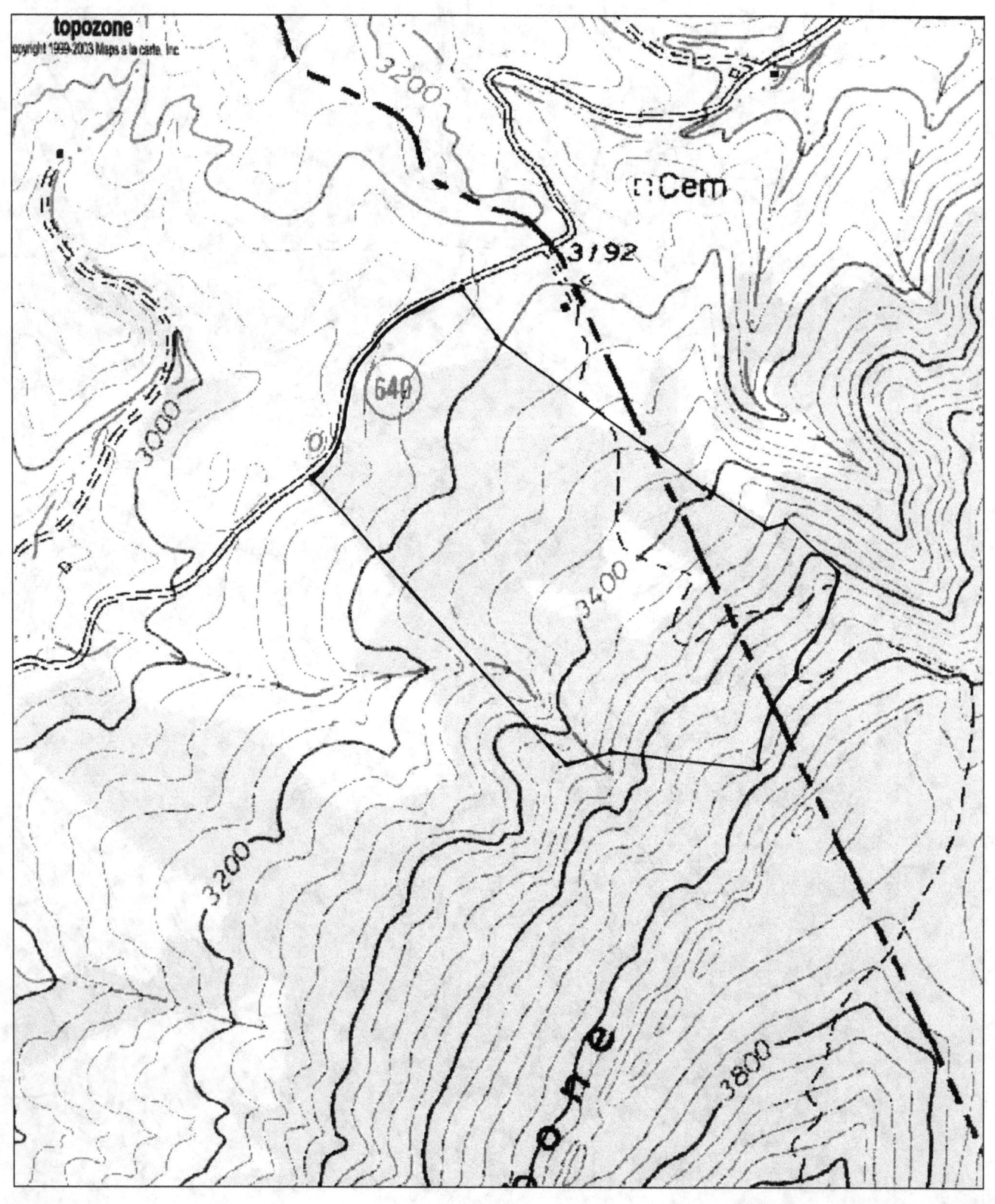

Source: www.topozone.com

MAP 17-3

Topographical Map, with Surveyor-drawn Boundaries

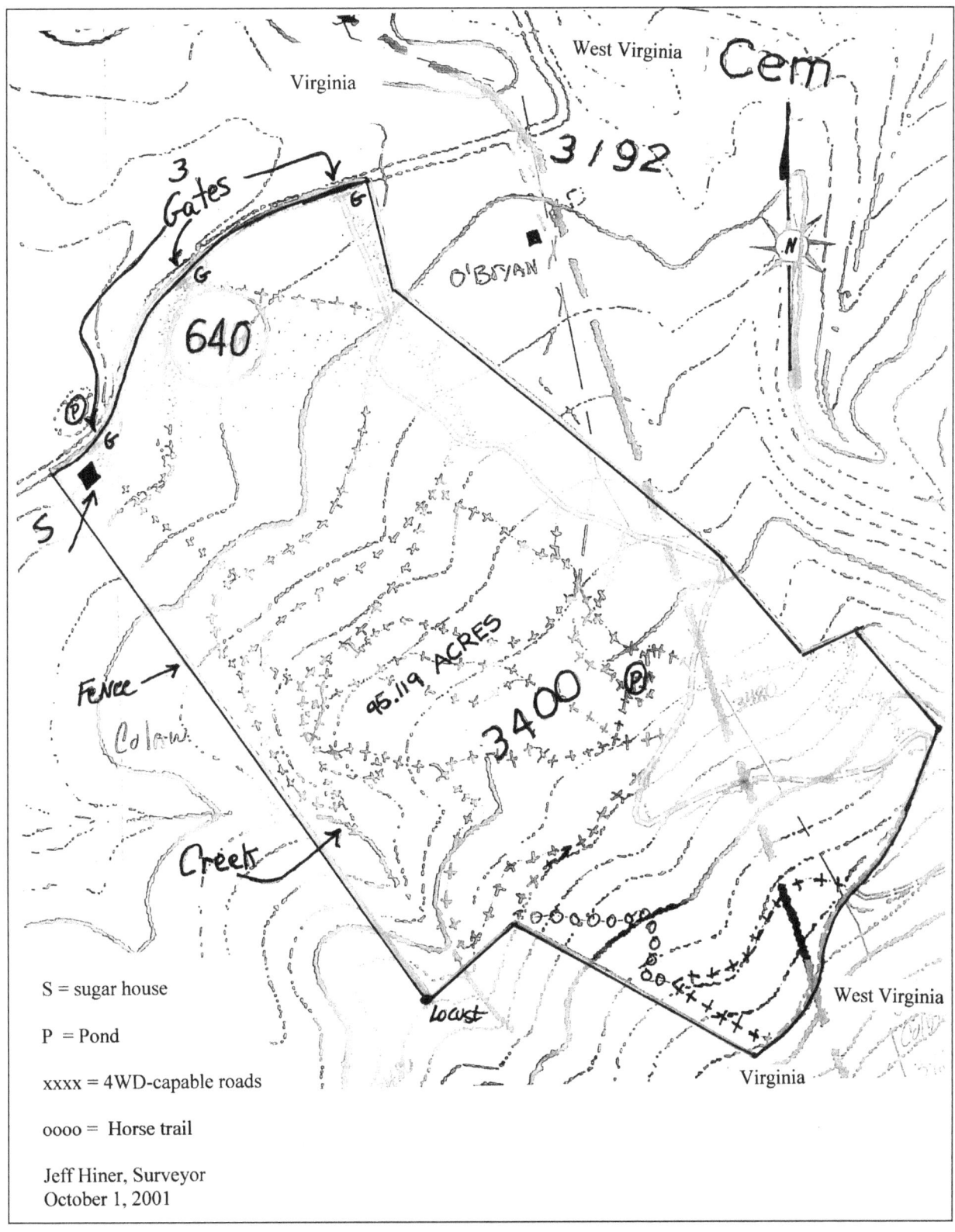

A buyer can use a topo like Map 17-2 or Map 17-3 to understand the lay of a target property before setting foot on its dirt. Such maps show you likely road locations, existing watercourses and potential building sites—relatively flat spots that might perc. They give a buyer a sense of how topographic features exist spatially in relation to each other and in relation to compass points.

DeLorme Atlas & Gazetteers are available for the 50 states for $19.95 each, excepting Texas at $24.95. The DeLorme topos are scaled 1:150,000, which are usable, but are not sufficiently detailed for boundary walking. I use DeLorme Atlas and Gazetteers to get a first-cut sense of a property's features and its location relative to nearby "goods and bads," such as public land, surface water, mines and buildings. DeLormes are available in book stores and at www.delorme.com; 207-846-7000.

While on the subject of maps, I'll mention several other orientation tools that are often useful in buying land.

Aerial photographs are available through the county's USDA's Farm Service Agency, which will provide the map number for the target property. That photographic map can be ordered from: USDA-FSA, Aerial Photography Field Office, 2222 West 2300 South, Salt Lake City, Utah, 84119-2020 or POB 30010, Salt Lake City, Utah, 84130-0010; 801-975-3500. Aerial maps are easy to understand and show functional boundaries, but they're not good for calculating acreage. The ones I've used were done in the 1960s. When the photos are shot in the winter, it's easy to distinguish between conifers (evergreens) and deciduous trees. Remember large crowns do **not** necessarily indicate timber value. A hardwood tract that's been repeatedly high-graded will show largely worthless trees with very broad crowns. Big, old, wide-crown trees standing by themselves in open fields rarely have much timber value owing to internal flaws, rot and poor formation. Aerial photos help a land buyer visualize the property's topography, land uses and the spatial relationships between various land features.

A number of Internet sites offer aerial photographs for a fee. www.topozone.com offers a simple version of these photographs for free. You can also check out http://kh.google.com; www.globexplorer.com; http://edc.usgs.gov/products/aerial/napp.html; www.MYTopo.com; and www.terrafly.com.

Another useful map, available from federal agencies, shows land in and around **national forests, wildlife refuges, national parks and the Bureau of Land Management**. These maps can be purchased from facilities in the field and through the agency. I've used national forest maps a lot since I often look at land that is near two national forests, the Monongahela (primarily in West Virginia) and Virginia's George Washington-Jefferson. The scale on the Monongahela's map is one inch equals two miles, which is easy to use. It shows all the National Forest's (NF) holdings in dark green and privately owned land in white. Privately owned land within a national forest is called an "**in-holding**." These parcels can carry a price premium for private buyers and, when appropriations allow, may be sold to the federal forest after an FMV appraisal. Many rural land buyers, particularly hunters, like to "border national forest," because it gives them private access to public land. I've found NF maps to be detailed and accurate. Individual states may also issue maps. New York, for example, provides maps of the Adirondack Park that show private and public holdings, which is helpful to a land buyer.

Do not be surprised if a seller hands you a **tax map**, rather than a survey or a topo with boundaries. Each county has a set of tax maps that, together, show all of its taxed land represented as **tax parcels**. A tax map is a two-dimensional drawing that looks like a survey but displays no bearings or measurements. Each map shows the division of a certain portion of the county into coded tax-map parcels. A tax-map parcel is land that is known for tax purposes. Privately owned property is taxed, parcel by parcel; non-profit and public property are not taxed. Your target property may consist of one tax-map parcel or a dozen. You will find a **tax-parcel number** for each parcel owned, which is used for administering county tax records. (The tax map may also show an acreage number.) The tax-parcel number is not the same as the **tax-map number**. The tax-map number (s) of the seller's property will be the number referenced in the tax-maps index. Map 17-4 shows the Highland County (Virginia) Tax Map 10-A, with the four parcels—tax-map numbers 10-A-42, 10-A-47, 10-A-48 and 10-A-50—of our farm residence outlined.

MAP 17-4

Tax Map, Section 10-A

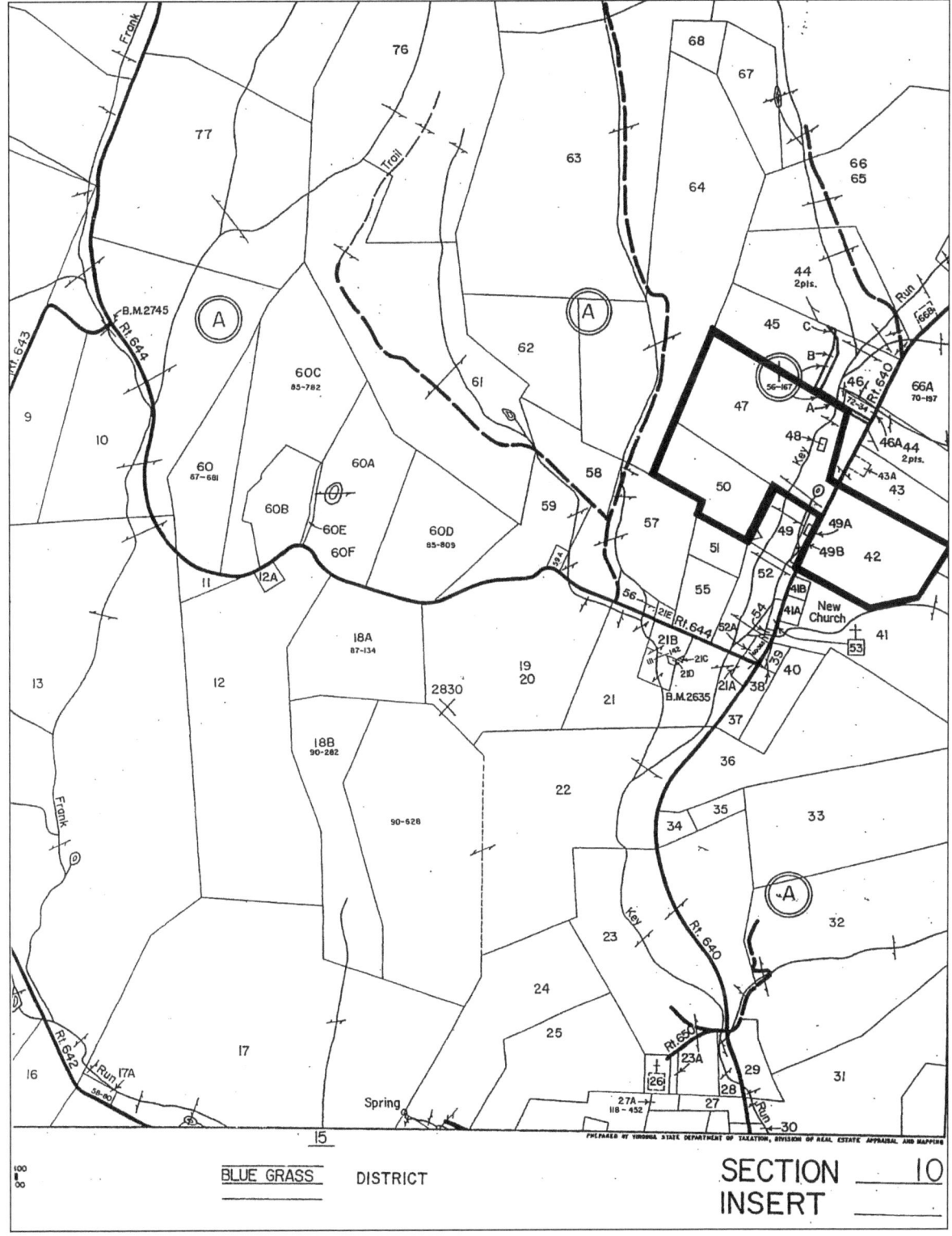

The set of tax maps and its index is usually found in the office of the county tax assessor. The index provides a tax-map number for each land parcel on each map, along with acreage and ownership information. This acreage number is the one used for taxing the parcel; it may or may not be accurate in terms of what the seller owns and will convey to a buyer. The tax map will also show the *approximate* boundary lines and some physical features such as roads, cemeteries and waterways. Document 17-2 is the tax map legend for real property in Highland County, Virginia.

DOCUMENT 17-2
Tax Map Legend

REAL PROPERTY IDENTIFICATION MAP OF HIGHLAND COUNTY VIRGINIA

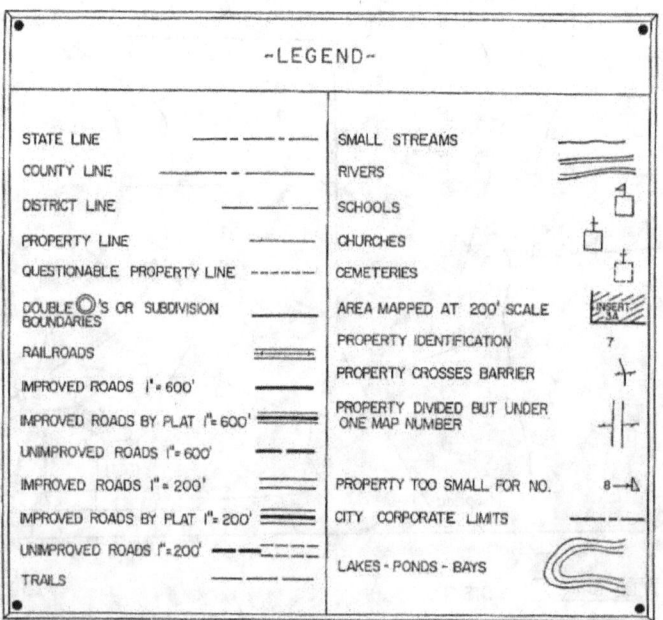

You can back your way into the tax maps by starting with the county's **Land Book**, copies of which will be, at minimum, in the offices where deeds are recorded and taxes are handled. The Land Books I've used are organized by sub-county areas; in my area these are magisterial districts. Once you're in the right sub-county district, look up the seller's name. The Land Book lists owners alphabetically. The seller may go by his first initials, or a business entity or hold the property jointly with his wife. The Land Book will provide the tax-map number of each parcel, along with the owner's address; deedbook and page number where the owner's deed is recorded; acreage, as established for tax purposes; jurisdiction; assessed valuations for improvements, land and minerals; tax rate information by land type (class); whether the land is in "land use" if a county has adopted it; and finally, the amount of current property tax levied. Document 17-3 is an excerpt from the 2004 Highland County Land for two parcels my wife and I own:

DOCUMENT 17-3

Land Book

```
                    VALUE OF TRACTS OF LAND, LOTS IN THE COUNTY STANDING TIMBER, TREES, BUILDINGS                PAGE  337
                    AND IMPROVEMENTS AND COUNTY LEVIES ASSESSED THEREON FOR THE TAX YEAR 2004
                    IN THE COUNTY OF HIGHLAND BY Bobbie J. Griffin COMMISSIONER OF THE REVENUE
                            Tax Rate on Every $100 = 0.67 ALL DISTRICTS AND TOWNS COMBINED
 MAP NUMBER/                                          --------ASSESSED VALUES--------
 NAME AND ADDRESS                   DESCRIPTION         LAND      IMPS      TOTAL   CLASS    TOTAL TAX


 11(A)6
 SELTZER, CURTIS & MELISSA ANN
 DOWD                               DB117-671          51,800    2,400     54,200              363.14
 HCR-02, BOX 20                     83.978 ACRES
 BLUE GRASS, VA  24413                                                              5
                                                       51,800    2,400     54,200              363.14     BLUE GRASS DISTRICT
 10(A)42
 SELTZER, CURTIS I.  ETUX                                                                        
 HCR-02, BOX 20                     DB73-523           18,900      100     19,000              127.30
 BLUE GRASS, VA  24413              23.562 ACRES
                                                                                    5
                                                       18,900      100     19,000              127.30     BLUE GRASS DISTRICT
 ------------------------------------------------------------------------------------------------------------------------------
 PAGE TOTALS                                          443,000   63,500    506,500             3,393.55
                                                      443,000   63,500    506,500             3,393.55

    CLASS-1      CLASS-2     CLASS-3    CLASS-4    CLASS-5     CLASS-6    CLASS-7    CLASS-8    CLASS-9

                 64,300                            129,200     313,000                                     1
```

Once you have tax-parcel numbers from the Land Book, you can go to the assessor's office and look up the appropriate tax map in the index. Then go to the set of tax maps to find the target property. Make a photocopy for your property file.

Using the Land Book and the tax maps is easy enough once you've done it. If you need help getting started, ask the clerk to walk you through the system. Once you've made a photocopy of the seller's tax-map parcel, highlight the seller's boundaries. This can be tricky, so don't hesitate to ask the clerk for assistance. You can then compare the shape of the seller's property as shown on the tax map with the shape drawn from the deed calls that are mapped on a topo. They should be identical, but are often not, usually owing to tax-map errors. Tax maps are useful to a buyer, because they provide a general idea of where the seller's property is located, its relation to adjoining properties and acreage. But they are unreliable on all three counts, and you should never assume they carry the authority of a survey.

Newer tax maps are based on high-quality aerial photographs that may or may not be verified through other sources. Older tax maps, which you often find in small rural counties, may be based on out-of-date aerial photos. Boundary lines may have been located from the functional boundary lines visible from the air. These may or may not have been checked against other records. Corrections may or may not have been made as surveys were done in later years. **Boundary lines and acreage figures from tax maps are not legally binding on anyone**. You should use a tax map for preliminary scoping and getting oriented, but it is no substitute for a survey or a surveyor-drawn boundary line on a topographical map.

Never pick a fight with a seller or his neighbors based solely on a tax map.

As I write, hand-held **Global Positioning Systems (GPS)** are available for $200 to $400 that will help you navigate into and out of unfamiliar terrain. The Garmin models, for example, allow you to load topographic data from a three-CD ROM set onto a PC and then to the compatible GPS receiver. If you like gadgetry, you can rig yourself out, but a GPS capability is an unnecessary expense for a land buyer. Most properties that a typical buyer will scope are neither so big nor so remote that they require GPS technology for safety in the field. A see-through compass and a topographical map are good enough for most properties. Such compasses can be purchased for between $10 and $20. If you can't get the hang of a compass and a map, you will find a GPS outfit even more bewildering.

You can find all of these items—planimeter, planogrid, compass and GPS—at The Forestry Suppliers Catalog, PO Box 8397, Jackson, MS, 39284-8397; 1-800-647-5368; 1-800-543-4203 FAX; www.forestry-suppliers.com.

As you walk the property with topo in hand, make sure its boundary lines coincide with where you find boundaries marked on the ground.

Keep in mind that boundaries on the ground can be of two kinds: **marked and functional**. A marked line is one that carries a surveyor's marks. The functional boundary line—a fence, waterway, road, etc.—is the one that divides landowners in practice. The best case, of course, is to find a boundary line that is consistent with the deed's calls and which is both marked and functional. That combination gives you, the buyer, the best hope for a boundary line that is free of disputes.

All the paper boundary lines—deed calls, survey and surveyor-drawn boundary lines on a topo—should line up with each other, and all the paper lines should line up with both the marked and functional boundary lines in the field. If you find a functional boundary in a place other than on the boundary line as set forth in the deed or survey, something ain't right.

A marked line shows physical signs of having been deliberately designated a boundary. Markings typically include plastic ribbon on trees, paint on trees, surveyor slashes (chops) into trees, iron rods (rebar), old pipes, car axles, wood stakes in the ground, fence lines with ribbons, marked corner trees, piles of rock, a set stone and the like. When looking for a boundary line in the field, you hope to find markings that are unambiguous, recent, frequent and aligned with the deed calls, survey and/or lines drawn on a topo. Be skeptical: don't trick yourself into thinking that a crack in a tree's bark is a surveyor's chop. Surveyors almost always use two parallel slashes about breast height to mark a boundary line and three on an important corner; a single slash is not a surveyor's boundary mark. If you find what you think is a boundary mark by itself and obviously off the marked lined you've been following, chances are that it is not a line mark.

The coincidence of marked and functional lines signals, at the very least, that the boundary lines are where the seller and his neighbors think they are supposed to be. To be certain that the seller's lines are dispute free, you must question both the seller and every neighbor. The absence of pending litigation does not mean that everyone agrees on everything. If a long-standing boundary grievance exists, the buyer may inherit it. At the very least, you should be on record with the neighbors that you asked the seller to fix such disputes as part of your negotiations. You do not want to inherit the seller's position in a grudge and then be expected by your new neighbors to solve it at your expense, though this is often the case.

www.ingramcontent.com/pod-product-compliance
Lightning Source LLC
Chambersburg PA
CBHW081104170526
45165CB00008B/2326